بِسْمِ اللهِ الرَّحْمٰنِ الرَّحِيْمِ

تُحْفَةُ الْجُمُعَةِ

GIFT *of* JUMUʿAH

VOLUME TWO

A COLLECTION OF FORTY FRIDAY
SERMONS TO ENHANCE OUR FAITH

MOHAMMED BADAT

Gift *of* Jumuʿah – Volume Two

Edited by Arifa Hudda

Book and Cover design by Islamic Publishing House – www.iph.ca

ISBN: 978-0-9950787-3-4
10 9 8 7 6 5 4 3 2 1

Dedicated to my parents

Table of Contents

Acknowledgments ix

Sincerity and Good Intentions in Deeds Both Public and Private xi

FOREWORD: Impressions and Testimonials of a Muslim Foreigner Visiting Canada xvii

On the Study Desk - Urdu xxii

On the Study Desk – English xxvi

KHUṬBAH 41: Knowing Allāh (ﷻ) 37

KHUṬBAH 42: Blessings of Having a Heart Connected with Allāh (ﷻ) 53

KHUṬBAH 43: Remember Allāh Much that You may be Successful 69

KHUṬBAH 44: Pay Attention to Ṣalāt! Pay Attention to Ṣalāt! 85

KHUṬBAH 45: Ḥayā': The Distinct Moral Standard of Islām 103

KHUṬBAH 46: The Ways of Doing Good 119

KHUṬBAH 47: Insight versus Eyesight! 129

KHUṬBAH 48: Watch Your Words 143

KHUṬBAH 49: Al-ʿĀfiyah [Well-Being]: The Key to All Goodness 155

KHUṬBAH 50: Taking Heed from the Unceasing Passing of Days, Nights, and Seasons 171

KHUṬBAH 51: Elimination of Racial Discrimination 185

KHUṬBAH 52: The Need for Preserving Unity in the Midst of Diversity 195

KHUṬBAH 53: Getting Right What You Have Done Wrong 207

KHUṬBAH 54: Stop. Think. Vote. 223

KHUṬBAH 55: Being in Debt is a Serious Matter Indeed! 232

KHUṬBAH 56: Shayṭān through the Lens of Qur'ānic and Prophetic Narratives 249

KHUṬBAH 57: On the Arrival of the Month of Ramaḍān 273

KHUṬBAH 58: Saving Money: The Islāmic Outlook 283

KHUṬBAH 59: Keys to a Lasting Marriage 297

KHUṬBAH 60: Behold Your Elders: The Forgotten Ones 313

KHUṬBAH 61: Be Thankful in All Things 327

KHUṬBAH 62: The Hazards of Haste 343

KHUṬBAH 63: The Qur'ānic Narrative of Prophet Yūnus (ﷺ) 359

KHUṬBAH 64: On the Road to Righteousness of One's Words and Inner Thoughts 377

KHUṬBAH 65: Understanding Ikhtilāf in Islāmic Scholastic Traditions 391

KHUṬBAH 66: When Opportunity Knocks 405

KHUṬBAH 67: Recounting the Prophet's (ﷺ) Children 419

KHUṬBAH 68: The Prophet (ﷺ) was Faithful in All Ways 437

KHUṬBAH 69: He is Al-Fattāḥ, the All-Knowing 460

KHUṬBAH 70: Water in the Qur'ān 471

KHUṬBAH 71: Indeed, the Religion of Allāh is of Ease 489

KHUṬBAH 72: The Gift of Wealth 505

KHUṬBAH 73: Divorce: The Most Hated of Permissible Things 523

KHUṬBAH 74: Visiting Others: Manners and Etiquettes 537

KHUṬBAH 75: So, For This Let the Competitors Compete 555

KHUṬBAH 76: Magnanimity and Generosity during the Month of Ramaḍān 571

KHUṬBAH 77: Not Losing One's Good Deeds in the Month of Ramaḍān 585

KHUṬBAH 78: Finding Inner Strength in the Month of Ramaḍān 599

KHUṬBAH 79: Angels: Allāh's Heavenly Messengers 612

KHUṬBAH 80: Your Grave: Either a Garden or a Pit. 643

GLOSSARY OF ARABIC TERMS 644

Acknowledgments

The completion of this undertaking could not have been possible without the participation and assistance of so many people whose names may not all be enumerated. Their contributions are sincerely appreciated and gratefully acknowledged.

Above all, I am extremely grateful to Allāh (ﷻ) for giving me the strength and opportunity to complete this noble project.

May Allāh (ﷻ) accept from all of us our good deeds.

Āmīn

Mohammed ibn Salim Badat
Ottawa, Canada
August 6th, 2020 – 17th Dhū al-Ḥijjah, 1441
Thursday after ʿIshā - During the Global Coronavirus [COVID-19] pandemic

Sincerity and Good Intentions in Deeds Both Public and Private

Allāh (ﷻ) says in the Qur'ān:

﴿وَمَآ أُمِرُوٓاْ إِلَّا لِيَعۡبُدُواْ ٱللَّهَ مُخۡلِصِينَ لَهُ ٱلدِّينَ حُنَفَآءَ ۝٥﴾ [البيّنة الآية ٥]

"And they were not commanded but to worship Allāh, making their submission exclusive for Him with no deviation." (Bayyinah 98:5)

Allāh (ﷻ) also says:

﴿لَن يَنَالَ ٱللَّهَ لُحُومُهَا وَلَا دِمَآؤُهَا وَلَٰكِن يَنَالُهُ ٱلتَّقۡوَىٰ مِنكُمۡۚ ۝٣٧﴾ [الحج الآية ٣٧]

"It is neither their meat that will reach Allāh, nor their blood, but what reaches Him is piety from you." (Ḥajj 22:37)

[1] Our Shaykh al-Muftī Raḍā al-Ḥaq (may Allāh preserve him) informed us that al-Shaykh Amīn Gul informed us that al-Shaykh Nūr al-Ḥasan informed us that al-Shaykh al-Qārī ʿAbd al-Raḥmān al-Fānī Fatī informed us that al-Shaykh Muḥammad Isḥāq al-Dihlawī informed us that al-Shaykh al-Shāh ʿAbd al-ʿAzīz al-Dihlawī informed us that al-Shaykh al-Shāh Walī Allāh Aḥmad ibn ʿAbd al-Raḥīm al-Dihlawī informed us that al-Shaykh Abū Ṭāhir Muḥammad ibn Ibrāhīm al-Kurdī al-Madanī informed us that al-Shaykh Ibrāhīm al-Kurdī al-Madanī informed us that al-Shaykh Aḥmad al-Kushāshī informed us that al-Shaykh Aḥmad ibn ʿAbd al-Quddūs Abū al-Mawāhib al-Shinnāwī informed us that al-Shaykh Shams al-Dīn Muḥammad ibn Aḥmad ibn Ḥamzah al-Ramalī informed us that al-Shaykh Zayn al-Dīn Zakarīyyāh ibn Muḥammad Abū Yaḥyā al-Anṣārī informed us that al-Shaykh al-Ḥāfiẓ Abū al-Faḍl Shihāb al-Dīn Aḥmad ibn ʿAlī ibn Ḥajar al-ʿAsqalānī informed us that al-Shaykh Ibrāhīm ibn Aḥmad al-Tanūkhī informed us that al-Shaykh Abū al-ʿAbbās Aḥmad ibn Abī Ṭālib al-Ḥajjār

---

[1] This is the author's complete *isnād* (transmission chain) of this first *ḥadīth* from Ṣaḥīḥ al-Bukhārī to the Prophet (ﷺ).

informed us that al-Shaykh al-Sirāj al-Ḥusayn ibn al-Mubārak al-Zubaydī informed us that al-Shaykh Abū al-Waqt ʿAbd al-Awwal ibn ʿĪsā ibn Shuʿayb al-Sijzī al-Harawī informed us that al-Shaykh Abū al-Ḥasan ʿAbd al-Raḥmān ibn Muẓaffar al-Dāwūdī informed us that al-Shaykh Abū Muḥammad ʿAbdullāh ibn Aḥmad al-Sarakhsī informed us that al-Shaykh Abū ʿAbdullāh Muḥammad ibn Yūsuf ibn Maṭar ibn Ṣāliḥ al-Firābrī informed us that al-Imām Abū ʿAbdullāh Muḥammad ibn Ismāʿīl ibn Ibrāhīm al-Bukhārī informed us that ʿAbdullāh ibn al-Zubayr ibn ʿĪsā al-Ḥumaydī narrated to us that Sufyān ibn ʿUyaynah narrated to us that Yaḥyā ibn Saʿīd al-Anṣārī narrated to us that Muḥammad ibn Ibrāhīm ibn al-Ḥārith al-Taymī narrated to us that ʿAlqamah ibn Waqqās al-Laythī narrated to us that ʿUmar ibn al-Khaṭṭāb said on the *mimbar* (pulpit) the following:

سَمِعْتُ رَسُولَ اللَّهِ ﷺ يَقُولُ: «إِنَّمَا الأَعْمَالُ بِالنِّيَّاتِ، وَإِنَّمَا لِكُلِّ امْرِئٍ مَا نَوَى، فَمَنْ كَانَتْ هِجْرَتُهُ إِلَى دُنْيَا يُصِيبُهَا، أَوْ إِلَى امْرَأَةٍ يَنْكِحُهَا، فَهِجْرَتُهُ إِلَى مَا هَاجَرَ إِلَيْهِ».

(رواه البخاري)

> "I heard the Messenger of Allāh (ﷺ) saying: 'Deeds are judged according to their intentions, and every man shall receive what he intended. Therefore, whoever migrates for the world in order to obtain it, or to a woman in order to marry her, then his migration will be for that which he migrated for.'" (Bukhārī)

This is one of those ḥadīth which make up the foundation of Islām.

Not only is it authentic, but there is also agreement amongst the scholars in regards to its authenticity and the scholars are also unanimous as to the great status and importance of this saying.

The early scholars and those who followed them liked to begin their writings with this ḥadīth, to make the readers aware of the merit of always having a good intention, encouraging the believers to attach importance to their intention in every aspect of life.

I ask Allāh the Generous for ability, repentance, assistance, guidance and protection. I ask Him to make all the good that I intend easy for me, and to grant me persistence in all noble deeds which I embark upon as ultimately, it is solely Allāh who is the One Who grants success.

My trust is in Him, my dependence and reliance are on Him, and to Him are all concerns entrusted.

اَصْلِحُوْا الْخَلَلَ وَاَخْلِصُوْا النِّيَّةَ

وَقَوِّمُوْا الزَّلَلَ فَإِنَّكُمْ مَسْؤُوْلُوْنَ غَدًا عَنِ الْقَوْلِ وَالْعَمَلْ

فَأَمَّا مَنْ ثَقُلَتْ مَوَازِيْنُهُ فَهُوَ فِيْ عِيشَةٍ رَاضِيَةٍ

وَأَمَّا مَنْ خَفَّتْ مَوَازِيْنُهُ فَأُمُّهُ هَاوِيَةٌ

Rectify errors and purify intentions,
Repair wrongdoings for the reason that tomorrow you will be questioned about your words and deeds,
So he whose scales of deeds in the balance will be heavy, He will be in luxury and delight,
But as for him whose scales of deeds in the balance will be light, His abode will be Hāwīyah (a pit in Hell)!

FOREWORD

Impressions and Testimonials of a Muslim Foreigner Visiting Canada

As a Muslim and citizen of the Republic of Mali, and a retired official from the Ministry of Foreign Affairs of Mali - I have been in Ottawa, since Wednesday, June 25, 2019, at the invitation of my beloved son, Mr. Ibrāhīma ʿOūmar Traore, and his wife Maīmouna Camara.

As soon as I arrived in Ottawa at 6:00 pm from Montreal, I headed directly to Masjid Bilāl, where according to Prophet Muḥammad's (ﷺ) *Sunnah*, I did two units of prayer to thank Allāh (ﷻ), and make *du'ā* of blessings for my beloved son Ibrāhīma ʿOūmar Traore who led me to this *masjid.* These blessings are also addressed to his wife Maīmouna Camara and their children.

Since June 25, 2019 until today, almost every day, I pray in the Masjid Bilāl. It is the incredible sympathy and warm welcome of Imām Mohammed ibn Salim Badat especially who encouraged me to regularly attend this *masjid* that I like very much as if it is my own home. When Imām Mohammed ibn Salim Badat first saw me, on entering the *masjid*'s main prayer area, he greeted me by saying: "My friend."

It was his first words which he expressed by greeting me fraternally; and since then he has not ceased to sympathize and fraternize with me, to such extents that I have considered him from that time as a very good friend, because he put me at ease. I requested and obtained an interview with him in his office accompanied by an interpreter. I asked him many questions to be better informed about the state of Islām - especially when interacting with a great Imām, a great intellectual, researcher and a great writer.

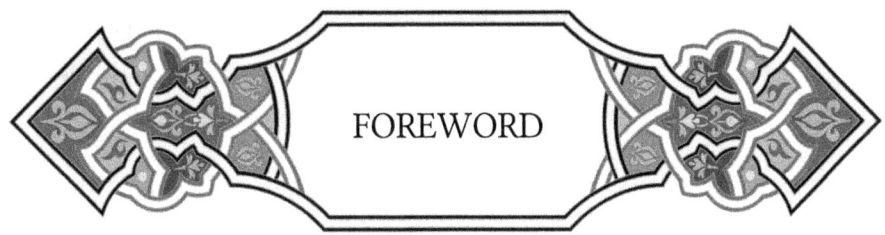

For me, it is as if I am at school facing my teacher who dictates the lesson. I learned a lot from him. He dedicated his book titled: *"Astounding Manifestation from the Pride of the Universe Muḥammad* (ﷺ)" to me. He gifted me the Holy Qur'ān and invited me to the knowledge and love of Allāh (ﷻ). He gifted me a coat and a hat. He gifted me two books, and pens: and he invited me twice to the basement of the *masjid* to have a meal. He also gave me bread and marmalade for my family. To remember him, I took pictures in his company near the *mimbar* of the *masjid.* It was at my request and he accepted.

For me, Imām Mohammed ibn Salim Badat is an extraordinary Imām. Today I am a senior, 73 years old; and during these 73 years, I have never seen an Imām like Mohammed ibn Salim Badat. This man has excellent interpersonal communication skills dealing with the faithful Muslims who attend the *masjid.* He is humble and simple. He does not put himself above others with a haughty air. He talks to everyone. He sits in the main prayer room to talk to people before the prayer times.

He holds to the discipline, the order of the people, and to the cleanliness of the *masjid* - we see him picking up small specks of dirt with a cloth, wiping the cupboards and putting things in their place. This man is well-educated, very open-minded and tolerant. The proof of this is that during an interview I had with him in his office, he advised me to adopt tolerance and moderation by saying that the practice of Islām varies according to the four major schools of *fiqh* namely: *Ḥanafī, Shāfiʿī, Mālikī, and Ḥanbalī.* He emphasized that it is crucial to be very tolerant in accepting the practice of others. He advocates tolerance and moderation and he emphasized that it is justified to accept the practice of others. He advocates tolerance and moderation.

Imām Mohammed ibn Salim Badat is a great religious leader, and a great manager who has mastered the principles of interpersonal communication and interaction. Due to his simplicity, modesty, and good manners, he has encouraged and attracted people to frequent Masjid Bilāl.

It is not uncommon to see this Imām attend to the upkeep of the *masjid*. The faithful Muslims consult him in many places in the *masjid* such as: at his office, in the main prayer hall, on the stairs, etc. He responds to solicitations with pleasure and does not get angry with other faithful Muslims. I have seen many Imāms in my country, Mali, and I saw many Imāms in France and I want to say once again, that I am 73 years old - but I never saw an Imām like Mohammed ibn Salim Badat. He has impressed me a lot! As an Imām and author, he makes substantial efforts through his writings, his lectures and his preachings, and by his simple and exemplary behaviour to make Islām respected and valued.

The Muslim community that attends Masjid Bilal must be very proud of their Imām. They no doubt feel indebted to him for his valuable contribution to Islām, through his books, lectures and exemplary behaviour.

All Muslims who pray at Masjid Bilāl must recognize Imām Mohammed ibn Salim Badat and encourage him to continue to pursue his noble and exalting mission in the service of Islām, *Allāhu Akbar!*

I also noticed with great pleasure that the Muslims who pray in Masjid Bilāl are of several nationalities: Pakistanis, Palestinians, Indians, Indonesians, Somalis, Djiboutian, Senegaleses, Burkinabes, Mauritanians, Algerians, Moroccans, Lebanese, Afghanis, etc. I am very happy to see this, because as we know Prophet Muḥammad (ﷺ) was sent to all of humanity, to all nationalities, and not to just one person. I noticed that all of the nationalities who pray in Masjid Bilāl rub shoulders in a warm and fraternal atmosphere. This also encouraged me to attend this *masjid* regularly.

It must be said that Masjid Bilāl is a reflection of three important things for me:

1. It is a place of worship, where I pray, behind a great Imām, researcher, and excellent writer;
2. It is a school in which I consult, to improve my Islāmic practices;
3. It is a meeting place, where I make new acquaintances and friends.

For me, Masjid Bilāl of Ottawa is a place of worship that has many benefits and privileges Alḥamdulillāh.

Call to Islām ... Call to Islām

I believe that the Muslims who are here on planet Earth must first worship Allāh (ﷻ). It is even the duty of every creature! It is also the first mission of creation!

The second mission which is holy, noble and exhilarating, is to treasure and value Islām as much as possible.

In Western societies everyone knows that today Islām is wrongfully confused with terrorism because of an unacceptable behaviour of some of us - unfortunately! It is therefore up to the Western Muslims to fulfill your sacred duty, and holy mission to restore the good image of Islām, and to make it well respected and well appreciated here through your behaviour daily in society, and by a large-scale through the dissemination of its values and principles, as advocated by our beloved Prophet Muḥammad (ﷺ).

Here in the Western society, the Muslims live happily in law and democracy, so the conditions are conducive to freely express our beliefs and religious conceptions without fear, but only if they fall within the confines of the law and values of this great country.

In this beautiful context, it is up to the Muslims of the West to take Islām out of the *masjid* where they are confined in and make it known to the public by organizing open houses for neighbours, through social media (radio, television, newspapers and internet), and by writing books, and distributing free literature, etc. In a nutshell, the Ottawa's Masjid Bilāl, our *masjid*, must think and organize itself to make Islām respected and appreciated by others within the limits of the laws of the land. May Allāh guide our thoughts and actions in the best way! *Āmīn! Āmīn! Āmīn!*

Dear brothers, and dear sisters in Islām, may Allāh (ﷻ) bless us all with mercy, generosity, and blessings - in this world and beyond, and

Inshā-Allāh in the eternal and vast Paradise *Jannat al-Firdaus*, our eternal home, *Āmīn, Āmīn, Āmīn!*

Your brother in Islām, a Muslim foreigner visiting Canada.

Dr. ʿOūmar Aba Traore, Ph. D.
Doctor of Political Science Diploma from the University of Laval, Quebec
Foreign Affairs Advisor
Citizen of the Republic of Mali and a child from Korientze, Mali

On the Study Desk - Urdu

Shaykh ʿAbbās Ibn Ādam Sarīgat - Dārul ʿUlūm Zakarīyā
South Africa

مطالعے کی میز پر

بسم اللہ الرحمن الرحیم

الحمد لله وحده والصلاة والسلام على من لا نبي بعده

آج بروز اتوار ۱۳ محرم الحرام ۱۴۴۰ مطابق ۲۳ ستمبر ۲۰۱۸ عزیزم مولوی محمد بدات زید مجدہ وسلّمہ کی تصنیف لطیف بنام «تُحْفَةُ الْجُمُعَةِ» نظر نواز ہوئی۔ کتاب موصول ہوتے ہی ورق گردانی شروع کی۔ اللہ کے خاص فضل سے ۶۷۸ صفحات پر ایک طائرانہ نظر دالی گئی۔ الحمد للہ پوری کتاب پر از معلومات، حوالات، عربی نصوص، متقدمین علماء فقہاء ادباء محدثین مفسرین کے اقوال سے مزین ہیں۔

حقیقت یے ہیکہ موصوف مکرم نے دوران مطالعہ سینکروں صفحات سے علمی افادات، قرآنی وحدثیں، علوم ومعارف اور علمی جواہر کو محفوظ کر کے اب انہیں ایک لڑی میں پرو کر ائمۂ مساجد اور علماء کرام کی خدمت میں بصورت تحفہ پیش کیا ہے۔ جی چاہتا ہیکہ قارئین کو بھی شریک مطالعہ کیا جائے تا کہ جزء سے کل پر استدلال کرنا آسان ہو جائے

[۱] خطبہ نمبر دو میں علامہ ابن قیمؒ (م ۷۵۱ھ) کی عبارت پڑھیے:

وقد جعل الله تعالى لكل مطلوب مفتاحا يفتح به فجعل مفتاح الصلاة الطهور كما قال: «مفتاح الصلاة الطهارة ومفتاح الحج الإحرام ومفتاح البر الصدق ومفتاح الجنة التوحيد».

[۲] دلوں کو جلاء بخشنے والے یہ اشعار بھی پڑھیے (ص ۷۰):

نقر بأن الله جلّ جلاله ❁ سميع لأقوال العباد بصير
ونؤمن أن العرش من فوق سبعة ❁ تطوف به أملاكه وتدور
عليه حجاب النور والنور حوله ❁ وأنهار نور حوله تتوقد
هو الله ربي في السماء محجب ❁ لعزته تعنو الوجوه وتسجد
إليه تعالى طيب القول صاعد ❁ وينزل منه بالقضاء أمور

[۳] ص ۱۷۷ سے ۱۹۰ تک حضرت علیؓ اور حضرت ابن عباس رضی اللہ عنہما سے دریافت کردہ سوالات اور ان کے حکیمانہ جوابات جس سے دونوں کی بصارت وبصیرت، علمی گہرائی اور گیرائی کا اندازہ ہوتا ہے۔

[۴] آج امت کا ایک بڑا طبقہ نماز کی اہمیت سے بے خبر ہے، نماز پڑھنے والوں کی تعداد کالملح فی الطعام۔ آیئے اس ماحول میں حضرت عمرؓ کا واقعہ پڑھیے جو تازیانہ عبرت سے کم نہیں ہے (ص ۹۴):

حَدَّثَنِي يَحْيَى عَنْ مَالِكٍ عَنْ هِشَامِ بْنِ عُرْوَةَ عَنْ أَبِيهِ أَنَّ الْمِسْوَرَ بْنَ مَخْرَمَةَ أَخْبَرَهُ أَنَّهُ دَخَلَ عَلَى عُمَرَ بْنِ الْخَطَّابِ مِنَ اللَّيْلَةِ الَّتِي طُعِنَ فِيهَا، فَأَيْقَظَ عُمَرَ لِصَلَاةِ الصُّبْحِ، فَقَالَ عُمَرُ: "نَعَمْ، وَلَا حَظَّ فِي الْإِسْلَامِ لِمَنْ تَرَكَ الصَّلَاةَ"، فَصَلَّى عُمَرُ وَجُرْحُهُ يَثْعَبُ دَمًا.

٥ قیام اللیل کی اہمیت کے متعلق ابن عمر رضی اللہ عنہما کا حکیمانہ مقولہ پڑھئے محظوظ ہوئیے اور عمل کی نیت کیجئے (ص١٥٥):

قال ابن عمر: "أولُ ما ينقُصُ من العبادة التهجُّد بالليل"

٦ دنیا کی بے ثباتی آخرت کے مقابل اسکی بے حیثیت اب نثر سے نظم کی طرف آئے (ص١٢٧):

أيا مَنْ عاش في الدنيا طويلًا ❁ وأفنى العُمْرَ في قيلٍ وقالِ
وأتعب نفسَهُ فيما سيفنى ❁ وجمَّع من حرامٍ أو حلالِ
هَبِ الدُّنيا تُقادُ إليك عفواً ❁ أليس مصيرُ ذلك للزوالِ

٧ علامہ ابن عبد البر المالکیؒ (م ٤٦٣ھ) کی عبارت فتح الباری کے حوالہ سے غیر اختیاری نیند کی وجہ سے نماز اگر وقت پر نہ ادا ہو سکی پھر بھی کیسی تسلی کی بات بیان فرمارہے ہیں (ص١٣٧):

وَقَالَ ابْنُ عَبْدِ الْبَرِّ: "هَذَا الذَّمُّ يَخْتَصُّ بِمَنْ لَمْ يَقُمْ إِلَى صَلَاتِهِ وَضَيَّعَهَا، أَمَّا مَنْ كَانَتْ عَادَتُهُ الْقِيَامَ إِلَى الصَّلَاةِ الْمَكْتُوبَةِ أَوْ إِلَى النَّافِلَةِ بِاللَّيْلِ فَغَلَبَتْهُ عَيْنُهُ فَقَدْ ثَبَتَ أَنَّ اللهَ يَكْتُبُ لَهُ أَجْرَ صَلَاتِهِ وَنَوْمُهُ عَلَيْهِ صَدَقَةٌ"

٨ ص١٣٧ سورۂ نحل آیت نمبر ٣٢ ﴿الَّذِينَ تَتَوَفّٰهُمُ الْمَلٰٓئِكَةُ طَيِّبِينَ﴾، طَيِّبِينَ کی تعریف امام المفسرین قرطبیؒ کی عبارت پڑھئے:

طيبين: طاهرين من الشِرك، صالحين زاكيةً أفعالُهم وأقوالُهم، وتكون وفاتُهم طيبةً سهلةً، لا صعوبة فيها، ولا عسر، ولا ألَم، مُعافين من الكَربِ وعذابِ الموتِ، تقول لهم الملائكةُ: "سلامٌ عليكم" طمأنينةً لقلوبهم وترحيباً بقدومهم، "ادخُلُوا الجنَّةَ بما كُنتُم تعملون" تعجيلاً لهم بالبشرى.

٩ ﴿إِنَّ أَكْرَمَكُمْ عِندَ اللهِ أَتْقٰكُمْ﴾ کی تفسیری وضاحت کے لئے یہ اشعار پڑھئے (ص١٥١):

لَعَمْرُكَ ما الإنسانُ إلّا بدينِهِ ❁ فلا تَتْرُكِ التقوى اتِّكالاً على النَّسَبْ
فقد رفَعَ الإسلامُ سلمانَ فارِسٍ ❁ وقد وضعَ الشِركُ النَّسِيبَ أبا لَهَبْ

١٠ مردود وملعون شیطان کن کن راہوں سے گمراہ کرتا ہے (ص١٦٠):

حدّثني سُرَيجُ بن يونس، حدّثنا عليّ بن ثابتٍ، عن خطّابِ بن القاسم، عن أبي عثمان قال: كان عيسى عليه الصلاة والسلام يصلي على رأسِ جبلٍ، فأتاه إبليسُ
فقال: "أنت الذي تزعُم أنّ كل شيء بقضاءٍ وقدرٍ؟"

قال: "نعم"

قال: "أَلْقِ نفسَكَ من الجبلِ وقُلْ قُدِّرَ عَلَيَّ"

قال: "يا لَعينُ، الله يختَبِر العبادَ، وليس لِلعبادِ أن يختبروا الله عزّ وجلّ"

١١ صبر کے اسوۂ عظیم کے لئے عمران بن حصینؓ کا واقعہ ضرور پڑھنا چاہئے (ص ٢٢٠):

وكان به استسقاءٌ فطال به سنين كثيرة، وهو صابر عليه، وشُقَّ بطنُه، وأُخذ منه شحم، وثقب له سرير فبقي عليه ثلاثين سنة.

١٢ امام قرطبیؒ کا اور ایک حکیمانہ ارشاد (ص ٢٤١):

من كثُرت ذنوبُه فعليه بسَقْيِ الماء، وقد غفر اللهُ ذنوبَ الّذي سَقَى الكلبَ، فكيف بمن سقى رجلاً مؤمناً موَحِّداً وأحياهُ.

١٣ حضرت امام شافعیؒ صحبت صالح اور قیام اللیل کے متعلق کیا فرماتے ہیں؟ (ص ٢٧٩):

يقول الإمام الشافعي: "لولا القيام بالأسحار وصحبة الأخيار ما اخترت البقاء في هذه الدار"

١٤ ﴿كُلُّ حِزْبٍ بِمَا لَدَيْهِمْ فَرِحُونَ﴾ "وللناس فيما يعشقون مذاهب" ﴿وَلِكُلٍّ وِجْهَةٌ هُوَ مُوَلِّيهَا﴾

حضرت بن الخطابؓ کی عجیب و غریب تمنا (ص ٢٨٤):

عن عمر الخطّاب أنه قال لأصحابه: "تمنَّوا" فقال رجل: "أتمنَّى لو أنّ لي هذه الدارَ مملوءة ذهباً أنفقُه في سبيل الله" ثم قال: "تمنَّوا" فقال رجل: "أتمنَّى لو أنّها مملوءة وزبرجداً وجوهراً أنفقُه في سبيل الله وأتصدّق" ثم قال: "تمنَّوا" فقالوا: "ما ندري يا أميرَ المؤمنين" فقال عمرُ: "أتمنَّى لو أنّ هذه الدار مملوءة رجالاً مثلَ أبي عبيدةَ بن الجرّاح ومعاذ بن جبلٍ وسالمٍ مولى أبي حذيفة وحذيفة بن اليمان".

١٥ نبی کریم ﷺ کی ایک جامع دعاء میں آپ بھی شریک ہو جاؤ (ص ٣٣٥):

عن ابن عمر رضي الله عنهما قال: كان من دعاء رسول الله ﷺ اللَّهُمَّ إِنِّي أَعُوذُ بِكَ مِنْ زَوَالِ نِعْمَتِكَ وَتَحَوُّلِ عَافِيَتِكَ وَفُجَاءَةِ نِقْمَتِكَ وَجَمِيعِ سَخَطِكَ.

١٦ حدیث کے ابواب میں مکثرین فی الحدیث کے اسماء مبارکہ بصورت شعر یاد کر لیجئے اور برکت حاصل کیجئے (ص ٣٤١):

سبع من الصحب فوق الألف قد نقلوا ❁ من الحديث عن المختار خير المضر
أبو هريرة، سعد، جابر، أنس ❁ صديقة، وابن عباس، كذا ابن عمر

١٧ حضرت عمر بن عبد العزیزؒ کا حکیمانہ کلام ذکر کی اہمیت کے متعلق (ص ٦٠٩):

وقال عمر بن عبد العزيز: "الكلام بذكرِ اللهِ عزّ وجلّ حَسَنٌ والفِكرةُ في نِعَمِ اللهِ أفضلُ العبادةِ".

۱۸ انہی کا دوسرا ارشاد جو واعظین اور خطباء کے لئے مشعلِ راہ ہے (ص ۶۷۵):

قال عمر بن عبد العزيز: "لا ينفَع القلبَ إلّا ما خرجَ من القلبِ".

اختتام

یہ تقریباً ۶۷۸ صفحات پر ایک طائرانہ نظر دال کر ڈھیر میں سے بطور نمونہ چند لعل و جواہر کو پیش کرنے کی ناتمام سعی کی گئی ہے۔ قارئین کی اکتاہت کا اندیشہ دامنگیری نہ ہوتا تو اور بھی موتی چنے جاتے۔ للعاقل تكفيه الإشارة جزء سے کل پر استدلال کرنے کے لئے امید ہیکہ یہ کافی اور وافی ہونگا نیز قارئین کی تشویق اور ترغیب کا باعث اور وہ خود انشاءاللہ پوری کتاب سے ضرور استفادہ کرینگے۔

عزیز موصوف کتاب کی ترتیب پر مبارکباد کے لائق ہے نیز وہ بجاطور پر رُبّ مبلّغ أوعى من سامع کے بھی مصداق ہے۔ حق جل شانہ موصوف کی تصنیف لطیف کو قبول فرمائے اور عوام اور خواص کو استفادہ کی توفیق عطاء فرمائے آمین۔

ملاحظة: الحمد للہ موصوف کی یہ کتاب انگریزی زبان میں ہے اس لئے انگریزی داں ائمہ مساجد خطباء واعظین مقررین کے لئے گراں قدر تحفہ ہے۔ انشاءاللہ کتاب سے ضرور استفادہ کیا جائے گا وما ذلك على الله بعزيز.

عباس بن آدم سریگت،

دار العلوم زکریا،

جنوب افریقہ

۱۳ محرم الحرام ۱۴۴۰ مطابق ۲۳ ستمبر ۲۰۱۸

On the Study Desk – English

Shaykh ʿAbbās Ibn Ādam Sarīgat - Dārul ʿUlūm Zakarīyā
South Africa

In the Name of Allāh, the Most Merciful, the Most Compassionate

All praise belongs to Allāh alone. Peace and blessings be upon that Prophet after whom there is no other prophet.

Today, Saturday, the 13th of Muḥarram 1440 H coinciding with the 23rd of September 2018, I had the opportunity to glance over the valuable book entitled: *'Gift of Jumuʾah – Volume One'*, authored by my dear student Shaykh Mohammad Badat (may he be honoured and protected). Upon receiving the book, I immediately started to read various parts of it. With the special favour of Allāh (ﷻ), I was able to glance over the 678 pages. All praise belongs to the Almighty, the entire book is embellished with information, insightful facts, occurrences, stories, references, Arabic texts, and statements of classical scholars, jurists, professors of Qurʾānic exegesis, and Prophetic traditions.

The reality is that the respected author has studied thousands of pages of knowledge, beneficial information, verses, Prophetic reports, scientific facts, and insights. He has captured these pearls of knowledge and aligned them together in this compilation. He has prepared and presented it in the form of a gift, in the service of imāms of different masājid and honourable scholars. My heart desires that readers get an idea of what this incorporates. I hereby highlight some parts of the book, which will in turn, give a strong indication towards the entirety of the book, since parts can often elucidate the whole.

1. In sermon number 2, Shaykh Ibn Qayyim's (d. 751 AH) text reads:

»وَقَدْ جَعَلَ اللهُ سُبْحَانَهُ لِكُلِّ مَطْلُوبٍ مِفْتَاحًا يُفْتَحُ بِهِ فَجَعَلَ مِفْتَاحَ الصَّلَاةِ: الطُّهُورُ، وَمِفْتَاحُ: الْحَجِّ الْإِحْرَامُ، وَمِفْتَاحُ الْبِرِّ: الصِّدْقُ، وَمِفْتَاحُ الْجَنَّةِ: التَّوْحِيدُ«.

(سنن ابن ماجه)

"Allāh, the Glorified, has made a key to open every goal that one wants to achieve. Cleanliness is the key to prayer. Thus, it is has been reported that: "The key to prayer is ablution; the key to pilgrimage is *iḥrām* (being in a ritual state); the key to righteousness is truthfulness; and the key to Paradise is the belief in the One and only Allāh." (Sunan Ibn Mājah)

2. Read the following couplets which pierce into the hearts (page 70):

نُقِرُّ بِأَنَّ اللَّهَ جَلَّ جَلَالُهُ ۞ سَمِيعٌ لِأَقْوَالِ الْعِبَادِ بَصِيرُ

وَنُؤْمِنُ أَنَّ الْعَرْشَ مِنْ فَوْقِ سَبْعَةٍ ۞ تَطُوفُ بِهِ أَمْلَاكُهُ وَتَدُورُ

عَلَيْهِ حِجَابُ النُّورِ وَالنُّورُ حَوْلَهُ ۞ وَأَنْهَارُ نُورٍ حَوْلَهُ تَتَوَقَّدُ

هُوَ اللَّهُ رَبِّي فِي السَّمَاءِ مُحَجَّبٌ ۞ لِعِزَّتِهِ تَعْنُو الْوُجُوهُ وَتَسْجُدُ

إِلَيْهِ تَعَالَى طَيِّبُ الْقَوْلِ صَاعِدٌ ۞ وَيَنْزِلُ مِنْهُ بِالْقَضَاءِ أُمُورُ

We testify that Allāh is the All-Hearing, the All-Seeing.
We believe that the angels circumambulate the Throne,
Above the seven heavens,
The curtains of divine light surrounding Him are perpetually radiant.
He is my Lord, the Almighty and the Elevated.,
In His honour do faces prostate and submit.
To Him reach our good words and supplications,
And from Him descends the decisions of all matters.

3. Pages 177 to 190 cover the questions posed to both ʿAlī (ﷺ) and Ibn ʿAbbās (ﷺ), and their wisdom-filled responses. Such replies give us an idea about the great depth of knowledge and insight that both of these individuals possessed.

4. In the present era, a large contingent of the community is unaware about the importance related to prayer. The number of those punctual with prayers is like salt in food. Read the

occurrence of ʿUmar ibn al-Khaṭṭāb (ﷺ) in a crucial time which bears a powerful lesson.

عَنْ هِشَامِ بْنِ عُرْوَةَ عَنْ أَبِيهِ، أَنَّ الْمِسْوَرَ بْنَ مَخْرَمَةَ أَخْبَرَهُ، أَنَّهُ دَخَلَ عَلَى عُمَرَ بْنِ الْخَطَّابِ مِنَ اللَّيْلَةِ الَّتِي طُعِنَ فِيهَا، فَأَيْقَظَ عُمَرَ لِصَلَاةِ الصُّبْحِ، فَقَالَ: عُمَرُ: «نَعَمْ. وَلَا حَظَّ فِي الْإِسْلَامِ لِمَنْ تَرَكَ الصَّلَاةَ»، فَصَلَّى عُمَرُ، وَجُرْحُهُ يَثْعَبُ دَمًا.

(موطأ مالك)

"Maswarah ibn Makhramah entered upon ʿUmar ibn al-Khaṭṭāb after the night he was stabbed. He awakened him for morning prayers, and ʿUmar ibn al-Khaṭṭāb said: "Yes [I must get up and pray], there is no place in Islām for one who abandons the prayer." (Muwaṭṭaʾ of Mālik)

ʿUmar ibn al-Khaṭṭāb (ﷺ) then prayed while there was blood dripping from his wounds.

5. Regarding the importance of vigil prayers, Ibn ʿUmar's (ﷺ) wisdom-filled quote should be read with an intention to act upon it.

«أَوَّلُ مَا يَنْقُصُ مِنَ الْعِبَادَةِ التَّهَجُّدُ بِاللَّيْلِ».

(رهبان الليل)

"The first downfall of worship [from people] is abandoning the night vigil prayer." (Ruhbān al-Layl)

6. The instability of the world in comparison to the hereafter, and its insignificance can be seen in these words (page 127):

أَيَا مَنْ عَاشَ فِي الدُّنيا طَوِيلًا ۞ وَأَفْنَى الْعُمْرَ فِي قِيلٍ وَقَالِ
وَأَتْعَبَ نَفْسَهُ فِيمَا سَيَفْنَى ۞ وَجَمَّعَ مِنْ حَرَامٍ أَوْ حَلَالِ
هَبِ الدُّنْيَا تُقَادُ إِلَيْكَ عَفْوًا ۞ أَلَيْسَ مَصِيرُ ذَلِكَ لِلزَّوَالِ؟

O the one who lives in this world for a numbered amount of days,
And diminishes one's life in senseless gossip,
You tire yourself in fleeting pursuits,
You hoard the permissible and the impermissible,
Know well that the perishing world is definitely a sign of termination and end.

7. The text of this great scholar, Ibn ʿAbd al-Barr al-Mālikī (d. 463 AH), with reference to *Fatḥ al-Bārī*, gives comfort and hope in the matter of performing prayers after the fixed time due to involuntary sleep (page 137). He says:

«هَذَا الذَّمُّ يَخْتَصُّ بِمَنْ لَمْ يَقُمْ إِلَى صَلَاتِهِ وَضَيَّعَهَا، أَمَّا مَنْ كَانَتْ عَادَتُهُ الْقِيَامُ إِلَى الصَّلَاةِ الْمَكْتُوبَةِ أَوِ النَّافِلَةِ بِاللَّيْلِ فَغَلَبَتْهُ عَيْنُهُ فَقَدْ ثَبَتَ أَنَّ اللَّهَ يَكْتُبُ لَهُ أَجْرَ صَلَاتِهِ، وَنَوْمُهُ عَلَيْهِ صَدَقَةٌ».

(فتح الباري)

"The disgrace [and punishment] is specifically for one who does not establish the prayer and deliberately discards it. As for the one who is generally punctual in their mandatory prayers or optional prayers during the night, but sleep overcomes them, then it is reported that Allāh will write for them the rewards of the [missed] prayer and also the sleep, as a reward of charity." (Fatḥ al-Bārī)

8. Page 137 highlights Sūrah al-Naḥl, verse 32 where Allāh says:

﴿ٱلَّذِينَ تَتَوَفَّىٰهُمُ ٱلْمَلَٰٓئِكَةُ طَيِّبِينَ ﴿٣٢﴾﴾ [النّحل الآية ٣٢]

"The ones whom the angels take in death, [being] good and pure." [Naḥl 16:32]

The Imām of commentators, Al-Qurṭubī's (ﷺ) definition of 'good and pure' [mentioned in the verse], can be read as follows:

«طيبين: طاهرين مِن الشِّرك، صالِحين زاكيةً أفعالُهم وأقوالُهم، وتكون وفاتُهم طيبةً سهلةً، لا صعوبةَ فيها، ولا عُسرَ، ولا ألَمَ، مُعافَين مِن الكَربِ وعذابِ المَوتِ، تقولُ لهم الملائكةُ: سَلامٌ عليكم؛ طمأنةً لقُلوبِهم، وترحيبًا بقُدومِهم، ﴿ٱدۡخُلُواْ ٱلۡجَنَّةَ بِمَا كُنتُمۡ تَعۡمَلُونَ ۝٣٢﴾ [النَّحل الآية ٣٢] تعجيلًا لهم بالبُشرى».

(تفسير القرطبي)

"The pure refers to those who are pure from associating partners with Allāh, righteous in their words and actions - their death will be easy and pleasant. There will be no difficulty, challenge, or pain; and they will be saved from the difficulties and punishments during death. The angels will say to them: 'Peace be with you.' This will bring peace to their hearts and also serve as a form of welcome on their arrival, and it will be said to them: 'Enter Paradise as a result of the good actions that you used to do' – this will be an advance glad tiding for them." (Tafsīr al-Qurṭubī)

9. For an explanation and commentary of verse 13 of Sūrah al-Ḥujurāt:

﴿إِنَّ أَكۡرَمَكُمۡ عِندَ ٱللَّهِ أَتۡقَىٰكُمۡۚ ۝١٣﴾ [الحُجُرَات الآية ١٣]

"Surely, the most noble of you with Allāh is the one who is the most mindful (of Allāh)." [Ḥujurāt 49:13]

Read the following couplets (from page 151):

لَعَمْرُكَ مَا الْإِنْسَانُ إِلَّا بِدِينِهِ ۞ فَلَا تَتْرُكِ التَّقْوَى اتِّكَالًا عَلَى النَّسَبِ

لَقَدْ رَفَعَ الْإِسْلَامُ سَلْمَانَ فَارِسٍ ۞ وَقَدْ وَضَعَ الشِّرْكُ الشَّقِيَّ أَبَا لَهَبِ

By your life, humans are only judged [by Allāh] through their religion [and character],
Therefore, never abandon 'mindfulness of Allāh' in reliance on your linage.

For indeed, Islām raised Salmān al-Fārsī
And shirk [associating partners with Allāh] debased the famous Abū Lahab.

10. The methods of the accursed devil to misguide people (are mentioned on page 160):

عَنْ أَبِي عُثْمَانَ، قَالَ: كَانَ عِيسَى، عَلَيْهِ السَّلَامُ، يُصَلِّي عَلَى رَأْسِ جَبَلٍ فَأَتَاهُ إِبْلِيسُ فَقَالَ: «أَنْتَ الَّذِي تَزْعُمُ أَنَّ كُلَّ شَيْءٍ بِقَضَاءٍ وَقَدَرٍ؟». قَالَ: «نَعَمْ». قَالَ: «أَلْقِ نَفْسَكَ مِنْ هَذَا الْجَبَلِ وَقُلْ: قَدَرٌ عَلَيَّ». فَقَالَ: «يَا لَعِينُ، اللَّهُ يَخْتَبِرُ الْعِبَادَ، وَلَيْسَ الْعِبَادُ يَخْتَبِرُونَ اللَّهَ، عَزَّ وَجَلَّ».

(فتح الباري)

It has been narrated from Abī ʿUthmān that he said: "Jesus, peace be upon him, was praying on a hilltop when the devil came to him and said: 'You are the one who claims that everything is decreed?' Jesus replied: 'Yes.' He (the devil) said: 'Then throw yourself from the mountain top and say: 'This was decreed!' Jesus responded: 'O the doomed one, Allāh is the One who tests His slaves, it is not for the slaves to test the Almighty.'" (Fatḥ al-Bārī)

11. For a great example of patience, one should definitely read the incident of ʿImrān ibn Ḥuṣayn (which can be found on page 220):

«وكان به استسقاءٌ فطال به سنين كثيرة، وهو صابر عليه، وشُقَّ بطنه، وأُخذ منه شحم، وثقب له سرير فَبَقِي عليه ثلاثين سنةً».

(أسد الغابة في معرفة الصحابة)

"He was inflicted with the dropsy disease and remained patient during it. His stomach was torn open, and his flesh decayed. He spent thirty years in this situation on his bed, due to this circumstance - yet he did not complain!" (Usd al-Ghābah fī Maʿrifat al-Ṣaḥābah)

12. Another statement which is full of wisdom is that of Imām al-Qurṭubī (ﷺ) where he says:

«مَنْ كَثُرَتْ ذُنُوبُهُ فَعَلَيْهِ بِسَقْيِ الْمَاءِ. وَقَدْ غَفَرَ اللَّهُ ذُنُوبَ الَّذِي سَقَى الْكَلْبَ، فَكَيْفَ بِمَنْ سَقَى رَجُلًا مُؤْمِنًا مُوَحِّدًا وَأَحْيَاهُ».

(تفسير القرطبي)

"The one whose sins are plenty should try to facilitate water for others. If Allāh forgave the person who quenched the thirst of a dog, then for sure Allāh will forgive a believer and revive him [of his sins]." (Tafsīr al-Qurṭubī)

13. See what Imām al-Shāfiʿī (ﷺ) states regarding good companionship and vigil prayers (on page 279):

قَالَ الإِمَامُ الشَّافعي رَحِمَهُ اللهُ: «لَوْلا القِيَامُ بالأسحار، وَصُحْبَةُ الأخيار، ما اخْتَرْتُ البَقَاءَ فِي هَذِهِ الدَّارِ».

(موسوعة الدين النصيحة)

Imām al-Shāfiʿī (may Allāh have mercy upon him) has said: "If there was no standing in the prayer at dawn time, or no companionship of the pious, then I would not desire to remain in this world." (Mawsūʿah al-Dīn al-Naṣīḥah)

As it is said:

﴿كُلُّ حِزْبٍ بِمَا لَدَيْهِمْ فَرِحُونَ ۝٣٢﴾ [الرّوم الآية ٣٢]

"Every group is pleased with what they have." (Rūm 30:32)

«وَلِلنَّاسِ فِيمَا يَعْشَقُونَ مَذَاهِبُ».

(كتاب العناية شرح الهداية)

"People have their ways in everything they love" (Kitāb al-ʿInāyah Sharḥ al-Hidāyah)

﴿وَلِكُلٍّ وِجْهَةٌ هُوَ مُوَلِّيهَا ۖ ﴿١٤٨﴾﴾ [البَقَرَة الآية ١٤٨]

"For everyone, there is a direction they have adopted." (Baqarah 2:148)

ʿUmar ibn Khaṭṭāb's (ﷺ) amazing wish is recorded (on page 284):

عَنْ عُمَرَ رَضِيَ اللَّهُ عَنْهُ أَنَّهُ قَالَ لِأَصْحَابِهِ: «تَمَنَّوْا» ، فَقَالَ بَعْضُهُمْ: أَتَمَنَّى لَوْ أَنَّ هَذِهِ الدَّارَ مَمْلُوءَةٌ ذَهَبًا أُنْفِقُهُ فِي سَبِيلِ اللَّهِ وَأَتَصَدَّقُ، وَقَالَ رَجُلٌ: أَتَمَنَّى لَوْ أَنَّهَا مَمْلُوءَةٌ زَبَرْجَدًا وَجَوْهَرًا فَأُنْفِقُهُ فِي سَبِيلِ اللَّهِ وَأَتَصَدَّقُ، ثُمَّ قَالَ عُمَرُ: «تَمَنَّوْا» فَقَالُوا: مَا نَدْرِي يَا أَمِيرَ الْمُؤْمِنِينَ، فَقَالَ عُمَرُ: «أَتَمَنَّى لَوْ أَنَّهَا مَمْلُوءَةٌ رِجَالًا مِثْلَ أَبِي عُبَيْدَةَ بْنِ الْجَرَّاحِ، وَمُعَاذِ بْنِ جَبَلٍ، وَسَالِمٍ مَوْلَى أَبِي حُذَيْفَةَ، وَحُذَيْفَةَ بْنِ الْيَمَانِ».

(حلية الأولياء وطبقات الأصفياء)

"ʿUmar (ﷺ) asked his companions to express what they wish for." One of them said: "I wish I had this entire room filled with gold so that I may spend it in God's path." Another one said: "I wish this hall was filled with jewels and pearls that I may spend it in charity." He (ʿUmar) then said: "What else do you want?" They replied: "We do not know of anything else, O our leader." Thereafter, ʿUmar ibn Khaṭṭāb said: "I wish this room was filled with men, the likes of Abū ʿObaidah ibn al-Jarrāḥ, Muʿādh ibn Jabal, and Ḥudhayfah ibn Yamān." (Ḥilyat al-Awliyāʾ wa Ṭabaqāt al-Aṣfiyāʾ)

14. You can also be part of the Prophet's (ﷺ) comprehensive supplication where he asks the Almighty (as explained on page 335):

«اللَّهُمَّ إِنِّي أَعُوذُ بِكَ مِنْ زَوَالِ نِعْمَتِكَ، وَتَحَوُّلِ عَافِيَتِكَ، وَفُجَاءَةِ نِقْمَتِكَ، وَجَمِيعِ سَخَطِكَ».

(رواه مسلم)

"O Allāh I seek refuge in You from the depletion of Your blessings, I seek refuge in You against the declining of Your favours, passing of safety, the suddenness of Your punishment, and all of that which displeases You." (Muslim)

15. In the field of Prophetic statements, the blessed names of those who have narrated the most Prophetic reports can be memorized in the form of the following poem, thus attaining blessings (as seen on page 341):

سَبْعٌ مِن الصَّحبِ فَوقَ الأَلفِ قد نَقَلُوا ۞ مِن الحَدِيثِ عن المُختَارِ خَيرِ مُضَر

أَبُو هُرَيرَةَ سَعْدٌ جَابِرٌ أَنَسٌ ۞ صِدِّيقَةٌ وابْنُ عَبَّاسٍ كَذَا ابنُ عُمَر

Seven from the companions who have narrated over 1000 aḥādīth,

From the chosen one who is the best of the Muḍar clan;

Abū Hurairah, Saʿad, Jābir, Anas,

Ṣiddīqah (ʿĀʾishah), Ibn ʿAbbās, and likewise Ibn ʿUmar.

16. The speech of ʿUmar ibn ʿAbd al-ʿAzīz (ﷺ) which is full of wisdom, on the importance of *dhikr* (page 609):

«الْكَلَامُ بِذِكْرِ اللَّهِ عَزَّ وَجَلَّ حَسَنٌ، وَالْفِكْرَةُ فِي نِعَمِ اللَّهِ أَفْضَلُ الْعِبَادَةِ».

(تفسير ابن كثير)

"The speech of the remembrance of Allāh (ﷻ) *(dhikr)* is the best talk. To ponder upon the blessings of Allāh is the best worship."

17. Another statement of ʿUmar ibn ʿAbd al-ʿAzīz (ﷺ) which is a light on the path for lecturers and orators is: (found on page 675):

«لَا يَنْفَعُ الْقَلْبَ إِلَّا مَا خَرَجَ مِنَ الْقَلْبِ».

(البيان والتبيين)

"The hearts will only benefit with that which comes from the heart." (Al-Bayān wa al-Tabyīn)

CONCLUSION

The above is a display of a few of the pearls and gems as examples from approximately 678 pages [from volume one], just as a glance from the heap of many. If it was not for the weariness of the readers, I would have chosen many more gems.

«لِلْعَاقِلِ تَكْفِيْهِ الْإِشَارَةُ».

"For the intelligent, even an indication is enough."

I hope this partial amount which is an indication to the whole is adequate. Allāh (ﷻ) willing, the readers will have a craving and desire to read the complete book and benefit from it greatly.

The dear author is worthy of praise and congratulations for putting this work together. He is also entitled to be amongst those who fall into the category of:

«رُبَّ مُبَلَّغٍ أَوْعَى مِنْ سَامِعٍ».

"At times a listener retains more than the conveyor."

May the Almighty accept this lovely compilation. May it be a means of benefit for both - the leaders, as well as the common folk. *Āmīn.*

NOTE: All praise belongs to Allāh (ﷻ), the author's book is in the English language. This will serve as a valuable gift for English orators, lecturers, the imāms of *masājid*, and teachers. God willing, they will certainly derive benefit from this book.

﴿وَمَا ذَٰلِكَ عَلَى ٱللَّهِ بِعَزِيزٍ ۝٢٠﴾ [إبراهيم الآية ٢٠]

"And that is not difficult for Allāh." (Ibrāhīm 14:20)

ʿAbbās ibn Ādam Sarīgat
Dārul ʿUlūm Zakarīyyā - South Africa
13th of Muḥarram, 1440 AH – 23rd of September, 2018

KHUṬBAH 41

Knowing Allāh (ﷻ)

Among the things which a believer (*mū'min*) strives to attain is beneficial knowledge.

Our Prophet (ﷺ) used to supplicate to Allāh (ﷻ) in the following way:

«اللَّهُمَّ إِنِّي أَسْأَلُكَ عِلْمًا نَافِعًا وَرِزْقًا طَيِّبًا وَعَمَلا مُتَقَبَّلا».

(سنن ابن ماجه)

> "O Allāh, I ask You for beneficial knowledge, goodly provision and acceptable deeds." (Sunan Ibn Mājah)

The Prophet (ﷺ) would also supplicate:

«اللَّهُمَّ انْفَعْنِي بِمَا عَلَّمْتَنِي وَعَلِّمْنِي مَا يَنْفَعُنِي وَزِدْنِي عِلْمًا».

(سنن ابن ماجه)

> "O Allāh, I implore you to enable me to benefit from the knowledge that You have granted me, bestow upon me knowledge that benefits me, and increase me in knowledge." (Sunan Ibn Mājah)

We can understand from these two *aḥadīth* that the Prophet (ﷺ) only asked for that knowledge which was beneficial, and he strove to teach his *ummah* that they must also ask Allāh (ﷻ) to grant them that knowledge which will benefit them.

In fact, direct encouragement to do so can be found in the statement of the Prophet (ﷺ):

«سَلُوا اللَّهَ عِلْمًا نَافِعًا وَتَعَوَّذُوا بِاللَّهِ مِنْ عِلْمٍ لاَ يَنْفَعُ».

(سنن ابن ماجه)

"You must ask Allāh for beneficial knowledge and seek refuge with Allāh from knowledge that is of no benefit." (Sunan Ibn Mājah)

However, a true servant of Allāh (ﷻ) should not only request that Allāh (ﷻ) grant him beneficial knowledge, but he should seek an increase of it from Him as well. Allāh (ﷻ) instructed the Prophet (ﷺ):

﴿وَقُل رَّبِّ زِدْنِي عِلْمًا ١١٤﴾ [طه الآية ١١٤]

"And (supplicate) say: 'O My Lord, increase me in knowledge.'" (Ṭāhā 20:114)

In other words, "My Lord, grant me knowledge in addition to the knowledge which You have already granted me." Therefore, Allāh (ﷻ) instructed His Prophet (ﷺ) to request that he be granted benefits from knowledge which he had not already been granted.

In fact, Allāh (ﷻ) did not instruct His Prophet (ﷺ) to seek an increase in anything except for knowledge. This clearly shows the virtue of knowledge and the fact that its acquisition is the most virtuous of deeds. The Prophet (ﷺ) continued to increase and advance in knowledge all of his life until Allāh (ﷻ) took him back to Him. The most important type of knowledge to have is knowledge about Allāh (ﷻ).

Ibn Rajab (رحمه الله) writes:

«أفضلُ العلمِ العلمُ بالله، وهو العلمُ بأسمائه وصفاته وأفعاله التي تُوجِبُ لصاحبها معرفةَ الله وخشيتَه ومحبتَه وهَيْبَتَه، وإجلالَه وعظمتَه، والتبتُّل إليه والتوكُّل عليه، والرضا عنه، والانشغال به دون خَلْقه».

(مجموع رسائل ابن رجب الحنبلي)

“The most virtuous of knowledge is knowing Allāh. That entails knowing His names, attributes, and actions. Knowing about these allows a person to be aware of who Allāh is, and to have reverential fear of Him, have love for Him, revere Him, exalt Him, remain devoted to Him, place full trust in Him, be pleased with Him, and give Him priority - rather than be preoccupied with others among His creation.” (Majmūʿ al-Rasā’il of Ibn Rajab al-Ḥanbalī)

Scholars mention the following:

«وَأَمَّا الْعِلْمُ فَيُرَادُ بِهِ فِي الْأَصْلِ نَوْعَانِ: أَحَدُهُمَا: الْعِلْمُ بِهِ نَفْسِهِ؛ وَبِمَا هُوَ مُتَّصِفٌ بِهِ مِنْ نُعُوتِ الْجَلَالِ وَالْإِكْرَامِ وَمَا دَلَّتْ عَلَيْهِ أَسْمَاؤُهُ الْحُسْنَى. وَهَذَا الْعِلْمُ إذَا رَسَخَ فِي الْقَلْبِ أَوْجَبَ خَشْيَةَ اللَّهِ لَا مَحَالَةَ فَإِنَّهُ لَا بُدَّ أَنْ يَعْلَمَ أَنَّ اللَّهَ يُثِيبُ عَلَى طَاعَتِهِ؛ وَيُعَاقِبُ عَلَى مَعْصِيَتِهِ؛. وَالنَّوْعُ الثَّانِي يُرَادُ بِالْعِلْمِ بِاَللَّهِ: الْعِلْمُ بِالْأَحْكَامِ الشَّرْعِيَّةِ مِنْ الْأَوَامِرِ وَالنَّوَاهِي وَالْحَلَالِ وَالْحَرَامِ».

(مجموع الفتاوى)

“Knowing Allāh basically entails two things. The first thing is knowing Allāh Himself. This refers to knowing His majestic attributes, and what His magnificent names mean. When that knowledge takes root in one’s heart, it will inevitably bring out proper reverential fear of Allāh, since it will undoubtedly apprise a person that Allāh grants rewards for obeying Him, and He also imposes punishments for disobeying Him. The second thing is knowing the commands and prohibitions that Allāh prescribed as the directives of Islām, and the things that He permitted and prohibited.” (Majmūʿ al-Fatāwā)

Imām Ibn al-Qayyim (ﷺ) states:

«فالعلمُ بالله أصلُ كلِّ علمٍ، وهو أصلُ علمِ العبدِ بسعادته، وكماله ومصالح دنياه وآخرته، والجهلُ به مستلزِم للجهل بنفسه ومصالحها وكمالها، وما تزكو به وتُفلِح، فالعلمُ به سعادةُ العبدِ، والجهلُ به أصلُ شقاوته».

(مفتاح دار السعادة)

"Knowledge about Allāh is the basis of all knowledge. It is the basis for a person to know how to achieve happiness, how to attain excellence, and recognize everything that is best for him in this world and the hereafter. Being ignorant about Allāh will lead to a person being ignorant about his own soul and what benefits it, how to bring it to perfection, purify it, and enable it to attain success. True happiness for a person comes from knowing Allāh, whereas the root of misery for a person lies in being ignorant about Allāh." (Miftāḥ Dār al-Saʿādah)

He (ﷺ) further adds:

«ولا سعادةَ للعباد ولا صلاحَ لهم، ولا نعيمَ إلَّا بأن يعرفوا ربَّهم، ويكون وحدَه غايةَ مطلوبهم، والتعرُّف إليه قُرَّةَ عيونهم، ومتى فَقَدُوا ذلك كانوا أسوأَ حالًا من الأنعام، وكانت الأنعامُ أطيبَ عيشًا منهم في العاجل، وأسلَمَ عاقبةً في الآجِل».

(مفتاح دار السعادة)

"People will not attain genuine happiness, have matters set right for themselves, or experience true enjoyment unless they know their Lord, make Him alone their primary objective, and find delight in making themselves known to Him by obeying Him. When people lose that, they will end up in a worse state than the animals that Allāh created. The animals will have a life more wholesome than such people, and a better ending than them as well." (Miftāḥ Dār al-Saʿādah)

A person's faith (*īmān*) is in proportion to how well he knows Allāh (ﷻ). The more a person increases in knowing Allāh (ﷻ), the more his *īmān* will increase. A similar relationship holds true for decrease as well.

The Prophet (ﷺ) said:

«إِنَّ أَتْقَاكُمْ وَأَعْلَمَكُمْ بِاللَّهِ أَنَا».

(رواه البخاري)

> "I am the most conscious of Allāh and know Allāh better than all of you do." (Bukhārī)

It can be understood from this that the stronger a person's knowledge about Allāh (ﷻ) is, the stronger that person's adherence to Allāh's (ﷻ) religion will be.

Having full knowledge about Allāh (ﷻ) dictates having proper reverential fear of Him. Allāh (ﷻ) says:

﴿إِنَّمَا يَخْشَى ٱللَّهَ مِنْ عِبَادِهِ ٱلْعُلَمَٰٓؤُا۟ ۝٢٨﴾ [فاطر الآية ٢٨]

> "From Allāh's bondsmen (servants) it is only the learned ones who fear Him." (Fāṭir 35:28)

Shaykh Aḥmad al-Anṭākī (رحمه الله) states:

«مَنْ كَانَ بِاللَّهِ أَعْرَفَ كَانَ مِنَ اللَّهِ أَخْوَفَ».

(لطائف المعارف)

> "The more a person knows Allāh, the more reverential fear he will have for Allāh." (Laṭā'if al-Maʿārif)

Therefore, the more knowledge a person acquires about Allāh's names, attributes, actions, and directives, the greater that person's observance of *taqwā* and reverence for Allāh (ﷻ) will be. This is why the Prophet (ﷺ) stated:

«لِلَّهِ تِسْعَةٌ وَتِسْعُونَ اسْمًا مَنْ حَفِظَهَا دَخَلَ الْجَنَّةَ».

(رواه مسلم)

"Allāh has ninety-nine names, and whoever preserves them (commits them to memory) will enter Paradise." (Muslim)

Imām al-Nawawī (ﷺ) commenting on this narration writes:

«مَنْ حَفِظَهَا وَقِيلَ أَحْصَاهَا عَدَّهَا فِي الدُّعَاءِ بِهَا وَقِيلَ أَطَاقَهَا أَيْ أَحْسَنَ الْمُرَاعَاةَ لَهَا وَالْمُحَافَظَةَ عَلَى مَا تَقْتَضِيهِ وَصَدَّقَ بِمَعَانِيهَا وَقِيلَ مَعْنَاهُ الْعَمَلُ بِهَا وَالطَّاعَةُ بِكُلِّ اسْمِهَا».

(شرح النووي على مسلم)

"To preserve them is said to mean to enumerate and count them in one's supplication. It is said it means to persevere in them, respect them in the best manner, guard what they require, and affirm their meanings. It is also said that the meaning is to act by them, and obey Allāh according to the implications of every name." (Imām al-Nawawī's commentary of Muslim)

In contrast, a person's *taqwā* and reverence will lack in proportion to the knowledge about Allāh (ﷻ) that one lacks. Knowing Allāh (ﷻ) and worshipping Him are two inseparable matters. Neither one can remain without the other. Both of them are objectives in and of themselves, but neither one can take the place of the other.

This can be understood from the statement of Allāh (ﷻ):

﴿فَٱعْلَمْ أَنَّهُۥ لَآ إِلَٰهَ إِلَّا ٱللَّهُ وَٱسْتَغْفِرْ لِذَنۢبِكَ ﴿١٩﴾﴾ [محمد الآية ١٩]

"Know well that none is worthy of worship but Allāh and seek forgiveness for your shortcomings." (Muḥammad 47:19)

"Know well" is a command related to knowing something, and "seek forgiveness" is a command related to doing something. In reality, acquiring knowledge about Allāh's (ﷻ) directives and His rulings which comprises what He has permitted and prohibited emanates from knowing Allāh (ﷻ). After knowing Allāh (ﷻ), a true servant of His will want to please Him, obey Him, and comply with all of His directives. As a result, the individual will embark upon acquiring knowledge of Allāh's (ﷻ) directives in order to do what Allāh (ﷻ) has commanded, and avoid that which will incur His wrath. When that takes place, the knowledge that a person will have acquired about Allāh's (ﷻ) directives will lead him to knowledge about Allāh (ﷻ) Himself.

However, when a person seeks knowledge about the directives of Allāh (ﷻ) for a motive other than Allāh (ﷻ), then there is no doubt that such knowledge will end up being to the disadvantage of that person.

The Messenger of Allāh (ﷺ) has said:

«مَنْ تَعَلَّمَ عِلْمًا مِمَّا يُبْتَغَى بِهِ وَجْهُ اللّٰهِ عَزَّ وَجَلَّ لَا يَتَعَلَّمُهُ إِلَّا لِيُصِيبَ بِهِ عَرَضًا مِنَ الدُّنْيَا لَمْ يَجِدْ عَرْفَ الْجَنَّةِ يَوْمَ الْقِيَامَةِ».

(رواه أبو داود)

"A person who acquires (religious) knowledge, which is (normally) acquired to gain the Pleasure of Allāh, (for the sole reason) to secure worldly gains will not even smell the fragrance of *Jannah* (Paradise) on the Day of Resurrection (i.e. will not enter Paradise)." (Abū Dāwūd)

Imām al-Awzāʿī (رحمه الله) stated:

«سَأَلَ رَجُلٌ ابْنَ مَسْعُودٍ أَيُّ الْأَعْمَالِ أَفْضَلُ قَالَ: الْعِلْمُ، فَكَرَّرَ عَلَيْهِ ثَلَاثًا كُلُّ ذَلِكَ يَقُولُ الْعِلْمُ، ثُمَّ قَالَ وَيْحَكَ إِنَّ مَعَ الْعِلْمِ بِاللّٰهِ يَنْفَعُكَ قَلِيلُ الْعِلْمِ وَكَثِيرُهُ، وَمَعَ الْجَهْلِ بِاللّٰهِ لَا يَنْفَعُكَ قَلِيلُ الْعِلْمِ وَلَا كَثِيرُهُ».

(شرح صحيح البخارى لابن بطال)

"A man once asked ʿAbdullāh ibn Masʿūd (رضي الله عنه) which deed is most virtuous. He replied: 'Knowledge.' The man repeated his

> question three times. ʿAbdullāh ibn Masʿūd (ﷺ) gave the same response each time and then said: 'May Allāh have mercy upon you! When you have knowledge about Allāh, both small and large amounts of deeds would benefit you. However, when you are ignorant about Allāh, neither small nor large amounts of deeds will bring you any benefit.'" (Commentary of Bukhārī by Ibn Baṭṭāl)

Just as knowledge about Allāh (ﷻ) is the knowledge which produces the greatest benefits for a person in this world and the hereafter, ignorance about Allāh (ﷻ) is the worst form of ignorance and it produces the gravest of harms.

When someone neglects using one's mind to know Allāh (ﷻ), that person is in fact among the ignorant. Such is the case even if one is outstanding in the knowledge of this world. This is the reason behind Allāh (ﷻ) praising knowledge and its people, and dispraising ignorance and its people.

Allāh (ﷻ) has informed us that these two groups of people can never be considered equal.

He instructed the Messenger (ﷺ) by saying:

﴿قُلْ هَلْ يَسْتَوِى ٱلَّذِينَ يَعْلَمُونَ وَٱلَّذِينَ لَا يَعْلَمُونَ ۗ إِنَّمَا يَتَذَكَّرُ أُو۟لُوا۟ ٱلْأَلْبَٰبِ ﴿٩﴾﴾

[الزُّمَر الآية ٩]

> "Say, 'Can those with (spiritual) knowledge be equal to those who do not have knowledge? Only those with (spiritual) intelligence (wisdom) will heed (good advice).'" (Zumar 39:9)

When a person knows Allāh (ﷻ), what is there that one is really ignorant about; and when a person is ignorant about Allāh (ﷻ), then what is there that one really knows?

Imām Ibn al-Qayyim (ﷺ) states:

«فَأَيُّ شَيْءٍ عَرَفَ مَنْ لَمْ يَعْرِفِ اللَّهَ وَرُسُلَهُ؟ وَأَيُّ حَقِيقَةٍ أَدْرَكَ مَنْ فَاتَتْهُ هَذِهِ الْحَقِيقَةُ؟ وَأَيُّ عِلْمٍ أَوْ عَمَلٍ حَصَلَ لِمَنْ فَاتَهُ الْعِلْمُ بِاللَّهِ وَالْعَمَلُ بِمَرْضَاتِهِ وَمَعْرِفَةُ الطَّرِيقِ الْمُوَصِّلَةِ إِلَيْهِ وَمَا لَهُ بَعْدَ الْوُصُولِ إِلَيْهِ».

(هداية الحيارى)

"What does a person know if he does not know Allāh and His Messengers? What reality does a person grasp if he does not grasp that reality? What knowledge or action does a person have to his credit if he lacks knowledge about Allāh, lacks actions that please Allāh, and lacks understanding about the path to Allāh, and what lies ahead after reaching Him?" (Hidāyah al-Ḥayārā)

CONCLUSION

- If the hearts of people are not moved by knowing Allāh (ﷻ) and revering Him, then those hearts will become stagnated and covered by darkness.
- What does a heart want if it does not know Allāh (ﷻ)? When a person immerses oneself in a life of materialism and remains far from anything that reminds the heart about the knowledge of Allāh (ﷻ), then that will undoubtedly produce distress, sorrow, a lack of guidance, and – on top of that even - a lack of enjoying life.
- What enjoyment is there in the life of a person who does not know Allāh (ﷻ), or is perhaps even heedless of how to know Allāh (ﷻ) to begin with?
- If we genuinely understand how vital it is for us to know Allāh (ﷻ), as well as the fruits which that knowledge bears for a person, then the obvious question which will come to our minds and occupy our thinking should be: how do we go about knowing Allāh (ﷻ)?

- In short, the answer to this is: by contemplating on the Qur'ān, which is the speech of Allāh (ﷻ) Who is perfect in every way; by making it part of our lives to know Allāh's (ﷻ) magnificent names and exalted attributes through learning them, as well as understanding their meanings and significance; by performing sincere acts of worship, especially that of contemplation; and by seeking to draw nearness to Allāh (ﷻ), in all our acts of worship.
- We must realize that both knowing and worshipping Allāh (ﷻ) comprises the purpose for which the Kaʿbah – the Sacred House of Allāh (ﷻ) – was built in Makkah for mankind.

Allāh (ﷻ) says:

﴿جَعَلَ ٱللَّهُ ٱلْكَعْبَةَ ٱلْبَيْتَ ٱلْحَرَامَ قِيَٰمًا لِّلنَّاسِ وَٱلشَّهْرَ ٱلْحَرَامَ وَٱلْهَدْىَ وَٱلْقَلَٰٓئِدَ ۚ ذَٰلِكَ لِتَعْلَمُوٓا۟ أَنَّ ٱللَّهَ يَعْلَمُ مَا فِى ٱلسَّمَٰوَٰتِ وَمَا فِى ٱلْأَرْضِ وَأَنَّ ٱللَّهَ بِكُلِّ شَىْءٍ عَلِيمٌ ﴿٩٧﴾﴾ [المائدة الآية ٩٧]

"Allāh has made the Kaʿbah, the sacred house, as well as the sacred months, the sacrificial animal and the garlands (placed around the necks of such animals to signify that they are to be slaughtered) a means by which (the physical and spiritual safety and well-being of) mankind is maintained. This is so that you may know that to Allāh belongs what is in the heavens and what is in the earth and that verily Allāh has knowledge of all things." (Mā'idah 5:97)

NOTE: In Arabic the word Kaʿbah is the name of a place which is square.[2] After mentioning the Kaʿbah, Allāh (ﷻ) describes it as being "the sacred house." Circumambulation (*Ṭawāf*) will be made around it until eternity because Allāh (ﷻ) declared the sanctity of it.

---

[2] The Arabic text of this is as follows:

عن مجاهد قال: إنما سميت الكعبة لأنها مربعة

Due to the sanctity of the Kaʿbah, the entire area around it (called the *Ḥaram*) has also been sanctified, and the animals therein cannot be hunted or harmed, nor can the vegetation be cut. Any kind of hostilities have been prohibited there for the same reason, and this was even understood during the period of ignorance.

Imām al-Suyūṭī (ﷺ) in his work, *Al-Durr al-Manthūr* reports that in the period of ignorance criminals would seek amnesty in the *Ḥaram* and could not be killed therein.[3]

Allāh (ﷻ) mentions in the above verse that He made the Kaʿbah a means for mankind to remain in existence, and a place of peace and security for them. It also enables many people to earn their living (Tafsīr Abī al-Saʿūd).[4] The people of Makkah receive revenue from the multitudes of people who flock to Makkah every year for *ḥajj* and *ʿumrah.* The effect of this spreads throughout the world and it is as a result of this that Allāh (ﷻ) allows commerce to flourish internationally.

Consequently, it is because of the Kaʿbah that thousands of ships, trucks and other vehicles transport millions of tons of merchandise throughout the world.

Everything in the world is thus allowed to remain in existence because of the Kaʿbah.

Allāh (ﷻ) says:

﴿أَوَلَمْ نُمَكِّن لَّهُمْ حَرَمًا ءَامِنًا يُجْبَىٰٓ إِلَيْهِ ثَمَرَٰتُ كُلِّ شَىْءٍ رِّزْقًا مِّن لَّدُنَّا وَلَٰكِنَّ أَكْثَرَهُمْ لَا يَعْلَمُونَ ۝٥٧﴾ [القصص الآية ٥٧]

"Have We not granted them a peaceful *Ḥaram* (sanctuary), to which the fruit of everything is attracted as a provision from Us? However, most of them have no knowledge." (Qaṣaṣ 28:57)

---

3 The Arabic text of this is as follows:

حواجز أبقاها الله في الجاهلية بين الناس، فكان الرجل لو جر كل جريرة ثم لجأ الحرم لم يتناول ولم يقرب

4 The Arabic text of this is as follows:

ومعنى كونه قياماً لهم أنه مدارٌ لقيام دينهم ودنياهم إذ هو سببٌ لانتعاشهم في أمور معاشِهم ومَعادِهم، يلوذ به الخائفُ، ويأمَن فيه الضعيف، ويربح فيه التجار، ويتوجه إليه الحجاج والعُمّار

Ḥajj is a momentous act of worship instituted for the remembrance (*dhikr*) of Allāh (ﷻ), and it is this very remembrance of Allāh (ﷻ) that is the life and soul of this world. In this way also, the Kaʿbah becomes the means whereby mankind remains in existence.

The Prophet (ﷺ) has mentioned:

«لَا تَقُومُ السَّاعَةُ حَتَّى لَا يُقَالَ فِي الأَرْضِ اللّٰهُ اللّٰهُ».

(رواه مسلم)

> "The Hour will not be established until 'Allāh, Allāh' is not said on the Earth." (Muslim)

The respected master of *Tafsīr,* ʿAṭā' (رحمه الله) has mentioned this very subject in the following words:

«لَوْ تَرَكُوهَا عَامًا وَاحِدًا لَمْ يُنْظَرُوا وَلَمْ يُؤَخَّرُوا».

(تفسير البحر المحيط)

> "As long as people keep turning towards it (the Kaʿbah) and *ḥajj* keeps being performed, the world will remain." (Tafsīr al-Baḥr al-Muḥīṭ)

Allāh (ﷻ) also says in the Qur'ān:

﴿ٱللَّهُ ٱلَّذِى خَلَقَ سَبْعَ سَمَٰوَٰتٍ وَمِنَ ٱلْأَرْضِ مِثْلَهُنَّ يَتَنَزَّلُ ٱلْأَمْرُ بَيْنَهُنَّ لِتَعْلَمُوٓا۟ أَنَّ ٱللَّهَ عَلَىٰ كُلِّ شَىْءٍ قَدِيرٌ وَأَنَّ ٱللَّهَ قَدْ أَحَاطَ بِكُلِّ شَىْءٍ عِلْمًۢا ﴿١٢﴾﴾ [الطَّلَاق الآية ١٢]

> "It is Allāh Who created the seven heavens and the earth in a like manner (in seven layers). He sends commands between them (between the heavens and the earths) so that you may know that Allāh has power over all things, and that Allāh's knowledge encompasses everything." (Ṭalāq 65:12)

This verse establishes that knowing Allāh (ﷻ), knowing His attributes, and worshipping Him alone are the objectives of Allāh's (ﷻ) creation and command.

When a person knows Allāh (ﷻ) and gives Allāh (ﷻ) His due right, then that person will revere Allāh (ﷻ) Himself, as well as everything that Allāh (ﷻ) has given reverence to. Allāh (ﷻ) says in the Qur'ān:

﴿ذَٰلِكَۖ وَمَن يُعَظِّمۡ شَعَٰٓئِرَ ٱللَّهِ فَإِنَّهَا مِن تَقۡوَى ٱلۡقُلُوبِ ٣٢﴾ [الحج الآية ٣٢]

"So, it is (such is Allāh's command). Whoever honours (sincerely) the landmarks (distinctive signs) of the *dīn* (religion) of Allāh (which are unique to Islām and that are designated by Allāh as rites through which He is Worshipped), then this (respect) is because of the *taqwā* of the hearts (respect for these landmarks denotes *taqwā* in a person's heart)." (Ḥajj 22:32)

Therefore, having reverence for what Allāh (ﷻ) has given reverence is a proof of *taqwā* and soundness of *īmān* because reverence for all such things comes from having reverence for Allāh (ﷻ).

Among the things which Allāh (ﷻ) has granted reverence and special virtue to are the inviolable months. Allāh (ﷻ) says in the Qur'ān:

﴿إِنَّ عِدَّةَ ٱلشُّهُورِ عِندَ ٱللَّهِ ٱثۡنَا عَشَرَ شَهۡرٗا فِي كِتَٰبِ ٱللَّهِ يَوۡمَ خَلَقَ ٱلسَّمَٰوَٰتِ وَٱلۡأَرۡضَ مِنۡهَآ أَرۡبَعَةٌ حُرُمٞۚ ذَٰلِكَ ٱلدِّينُ ٱلۡقَيِّمُۚ فَلَا تَظۡلِمُواْ فِيهِنَّ أَنفُسَكُمۡ ٣٦﴾

[التوبة الآية ٣٦]

"Indeed, the number of months (in a year) according to Allāh are twelve months (as specified) in the Book of Allāh (the *Lawḥ al-Maḥfūẓ*), (on) the day He created the heavens and the earth. Among these, four are sacred (Dhū al-Qaʿdah, Dhū al-Ḥijjah, Muḥarram, and Rajab are sacred because no fighting should take place during these months). This is the upright and correct religion, so do not oppress (or wrong) yourselves in these months (by committing sins)." (Tawbah 9:36)

The four inviolable months are:

1. Dhū al-Qaʿdah
2. Dhū al-Ḥijjah
3. Muḥarram
4. Rajab

ʿAbdullāh ibn ʿAbbās (ﷺ) commenting on this verse states:

عَنْ اِبْنِ عَبَّاس فِي قَوْله:﴿فَلَا تَظْلِمُواْ فِيهِنَّ أَنفُسَكُمْ ۚ ٣٦﴾ [التَّوْبَة الآية ٣٦] :«فِي كُلّهنَّ ثُمَّ اِخْتَصَّ مِنْ ذَلِكَ أَرْبَعَة أَشْهُر فَجَعَلَهُنَّ حَرَامًا وَعَظَّمَ حُرُمَاتهنَّ وَجَعَلَ الذَّنْب فِيهِنَّ أَعْظَم وَالْعَمَل الصَّالِح وَالْأَجْر أَعْظَم».

(تفسير ابن كثير)

> "'You must not wrong yourselves during those months' refers to all of them, but then Allāh specified four months with certain qualities: He made them inviolable, He emphasized their sanctity, He made sins committed during those months worse than ones at other times, and He made righteous deeds performed during them greater in reward than those (performed) at other times." (Tafsīr Ibn Kathīr)

In conclusion, if someone knows Allāh (ﷻ), then that person should revere what Allāh (ﷻ) has given reverence to, sense the sanctity of time and location, not transgress the limits of Allāh (ﷻ), and not do anything which He has prohibited.

وَاجِبٌ عَلَى النَّاسِ أَنْ يَتُوبُوا ۞ لَكِنَّ تَرْكَ الذُّنُوبِ أَوْجَبُ
وَ الدَّهرُ فِيْ صَرْفِهِ عَجِيبٌ ۞ وَغفلَةُ النَّاسِ فِيْهِ أَعْجَبُ
وَالصَّبْرُ فِيْ النَّائِبَاتِ صَعْبٌ ۞ لَكِنَّ فَوْتَ الثَّوَابِ أَصْعَبُ
وَكُلٌّ ما يُرْتَجَى قَرِيْبٌ ۞ وَالْمَوْتُ مِنْ كُلِّ ذَاكَ أَقْرَبُ

It is the duty of the people to repent, however to abandon sins is even more necessary.

Time in its passage is strange, however heedlessness of people is even stranger.
Patience in adversity is difficult, however losing the reward [of patience] is even harder.
Everything you desire for is near, however in comparison, death is even closer.

KHUṬBAH 42

Blessings of Having a Heart Connected with Allāh (ﷻ)

Allāh (ﷻ) has created human beings in such a manner that no matter what circumstances we find ourselves in, we will always remain dependent upon Allāh (ﷻ). Allāh (ﷻ) is the One who provides us with everything. He is the One whom we must rely on, and the One to whom we must resort to at all times.

It is for this very reason that the Prophet (ﷺ) used to remember Allāh (ﷻ) in all of his affairs.

ʿĀ'ishah (رضي الله عنها) narrates that:

«كَانَ رَسُولُ اللَّهِ ﷺ يَذْكُرُ اللَّهَ عَلَى كُلِّ أَحْيَانِهِ».

(رواه الترمذي)

"The Messenger of Allāh (ﷺ) used to remember Allāh in all circumstances." (Tirmidhī)

In another narration it is mentioned that the Prophet (ﷺ) has said:

«كُلُّ كَلَامٍ، أَوْ أَمْرٍ ذِي بَالٍ لَا يُفْتَحُ بِذِكْرِ اللهِ، عَزَّ وَجَلَّ، فَهُوَ أَبْتَرُ، أَوْ قَالَ: أَقْطَعُ».

(مسند احمد)

"Every important word or matter that does not begin with the remembrance of Allāh is incomplete." (Musnad Aḥmad)

A true servant is the one who remains humble towards Allāh (ﷻ) and is sincerely devoted to Him.

When a servant of Allāh (ﷻ) is consistently obedient to Allāh (ﷻ) and maintains a strong connection with Him, then that servant will be granted thorough guidance, a firm resolve, direction to the right path, and strength to adhere to the directives of Allāh (ﷻ).

Prophet Hūd (عليه السلام) told his people:

﴿وَيَٰقَوۡمِ ٱسۡتَغۡفِرُواْ رَبَّكُمۡ ثُمَّ تُوبُوٓاْ إِلَيۡهِ يُرۡسِلِ ٱلسَّمَآءَ عَلَيۡكُم مِّدۡرَارٗا وَيَزِدۡكُمۡ قُوَّةً إِلَىٰ قُوَّتِكُمۡ وَلَا تَتَوَلَّوۡاْ مُجۡرِمِينَ ۝٥٢﴾ [هود الآية ٥٢]

> "And O my people! Seek forgiveness from your Lord, then turn to Him in repentance (by fulfilling His commands). He will then send abundant rains to you and add strength to your strength; and do not turn (constantly) away as wrongdoers (persisting in your transgression)." (Hūd 11:52)

It is noteworthy to mention that Prophet Hūd (عليه السلام) told his people in this same verse that:

﴿وَيَزِدۡكُمۡ قُوَّةً إِلَىٰ قُوَّتِكُمۡ ۝٥٢﴾ [هود الآية ٥٢]

> "He (Allāh) will make you stronger than you already are" (Hūd 11:52)

Although his people were among the strongest of people.

Allāh (ﷻ) mentions in the Qur'ān that they had boastfully said about themselves:

﴿فَأَمَّا عَادٞ فَٱسۡتَكۡبَرُواْ فِي ٱلۡأَرۡضِ بِغَيۡرِ ٱلۡحَقِّ وَقَالُواْ مَنۡ أَشَدُّ مِنَّا قُوَّةًۖ ۝١٥﴾ [فصّلت الآية ١٥]

> "As for (the people of) 'Ād, they were arrogant (proud) on the earth without reason, and said, 'Who can be more powerful than us?'" (Fuṣṣilat 41:15)

Prophet Hūd (عليه السلام) assured them that if they had sound beliefs and carried out righteous deeds, then Allāh (ﷻ) would grant them additional strength.

It can be understood from the aforementioned Qur'ānic verse that when the forgiveness of Allāh (ﷻ) is pursued and sins are abandoned, then it will be a means to attaining provision, prosperity, and increased strength.

Ḥāfiẓ ibn Kathīr (رحمه الله) comments and says:

«وَمَنِ اتَّصَفَ بِهَذِهِ الصِّفَةِ يَسَّرَ اللَّهُ عَلَيْهِ رِزْقَهُ، وَسَهَّلَ عَلَيْهِ أَمْرَهُ وَحَفِظَ شَأْنَهُ».

(تفسير ابن كثير)

> "When someone consistently seeks Allāh's forgiveness, then Allāh will enable him to attain provision with ease, facilitate matters for him, protect him, and preserve him (i.e. his strength)." (Tafsīr Ibn Kathīr)

On the occasion when Fāṭimah (رضي الله عنها) requested the Prophet (ﷺ) for a servant to assist in the household work to ease the physical strain, he expressed to her, as well as her husband ʿAlī (رضي الله عنه):

«أَلَا أَدُلُّكُمَا عَلَى خَيْرٍ مِمَّا سَأَلْتُمَا؟ إِذَا أَخَذْتُمَا مَضَاجِعَكُمَا - أَوْ أَوَيْتُمَا إِلَى فِرَاشِكُمَا - فَسَبِّحَا ثَلَاثًا وَثَلَاثِينَ، وَاحْمَدَا ثَلَاثًا وَثَلَاثِينَ، وَكَبِّرَا أَرْبَعًا وَثَلَاثِينَ، فَهُوَ خَيْرٌ لَكُمَا مِنْ خَادِمٍ».

(رواه البخاري)

> "Should I not direct the two of you to something even better than what you have requested? When you go to bed, recite '*Subḥān Allāh*' thirty-three times, '*Alḥamdulillāh*' thirty-three times, and '*Allāhu Akbar*' thirty-four times. That will be better for both of you than a servant.'" (Bukhārī)

Therefore, the Prophet (ﷺ) directed his daughter, Fāṭimah (رضي الله عنها) to those phrases of *dhikr* which would provide her with sufficient physical strength which would in turn enable her to do even more than a servant would be able to.

Ḥāfiẓ ibn Ḥajr (ﷺ) commenting on the statement of the Prophet (ﷺ):

«أَلاَ أَدُلُّكُمَا عَلَى خَيْرٍ مِمَّا سَأَلْتُمَا؟»

"Should I not direct the two of you to something even better than what you have requested?"

Says that:

«أَنَّ الَّذِي يُلاَزِمُ ذِكْرَ اللهِ يُعْطَى قُوَّةً أَعْظَمَ مِنَ الْقُوَّةِ الَّتِي يَعْمَلُهَا لَهُ الْخَادِمُ أَوْ تَسْهُلُ الْأُمُورُ عَلَيْهِ بِحَيْثُ يَكُونُ تَعَاطِيهِ أُمُورَهُ أَسْهَلَ مِنْ تَعَاطِي الْخَادِمِ لَهَا».

(فتح الباري)

"When someone is consistent in making the *dhikr* of Allāh, that person will be granted even greater strength than what could be obtained from a servant working for them; or matters will be made easier for him to take care of by himself than they would be for a servant." (Fatḥ al-Bārī)

Allāh's (ﷻ) true and dutiful servants are mindful and confident of the fact that the *dhikr* of Allāh (ﷻ) is a source of nourishment for them, and that the need which their souls have for this nourishment is even greater than the need of nourishment for their bodies.

In fact, when the souls are nourished, then the bodies attain strength as well. Therefore, the hearts remain attached to Allāh (ﷻ) and the tongues constantly mention Him.

In a *ḥadīth* narrated by Jābir ibn Samurah (رضي الله عنه) it is mentioned:

«أَنَّ النَّبِيَّ ﷺ كَانَ إِذَا صَلَّى الْفَجْرَ جَلَسَ فِي مُصَلَّاهُ حَتَّى تَطْلُعَ الشَّمْسُ حَسَنًا».

(رواه مسلم)

"When the Prophet (ﷺ) finished praying *fajr*, he would sit (and do *dhikr*) until the sun had risen quite a bit (until the sun shone brightly)." (Muslim)

The renowned commentator on *Ṣaḥīḥ al-Muslim*, Ḥāfiẓ Abū al-ʿAbbās al-Qurṭubī (رحمه الله) elucidates and says:

«هذا الفِعلُ مِنه - ﷺ - يدُلُّ على استِحبابِ موضِعِ صلاةِ الصُّبحِ للذِّكر والدُّعاء إلى طُلوع الشمسِ؛ لأنَّ ذلك الوقت وقتٌ لا يُصلَّى فيه، وهو بعد صلاةٍ مشهُودة، وأشغالُ اليوم بعدُ لم تأتِ، فيقعُ الذِّكرُ والدُّعاءُ على فراغِ قلبٍ، وحُضورِ فهمٍ، فيُرتجَى فيه قبُولُ الدُّعاء، وسماعُ الأذكار».

(المفهم لما أشكل من تلخيص كتاب مسلم)

"That what was done by the Prophet (ﷺ) shows that it is *mustaḥab* (meaning an optional, yet encouraged righteous deed) for a person to remain in his place of prayer after completing the *fajr* (prayer) in order to engage in *dhikr* and *duʿā* until sunrise. That interval is a time during which prayers are not to be performed. It is an interval that comes after a prayer that was witnessed, and before the activities of the day begin. Therefore, *dhikr* and *duʿā* at that time can take place while one has a clear heart, an attentive mind, and comprehension of what one is saying. Those are factors due to which a person can hope that one's *duʿā* will be accepted, and the words of dhikr will be heard." (Al-Mufhim)

Walīd ibn Muslim (رحمه الله) recounts the practice of Imām al-Awzāʿī (رحمه الله) and says:

«رَأَيتُ الأَوْزَاعِيَّ يَثْبُتُ فِي مُصَلاَّهُ، يَذْكُرُ اللهَ، حَتَّى تَطلُعَ الشَّمْسُ، وَيُخْبِرُنَا عَنِ السَّلَفِ: أَنَّ ذَلِكَ كَانَ هَدْيَهُم، فَإِذَا طَلَعَتِ الشَّمْسُ، قَامَ بَعْضُهُم إِلَى بَعْضٍ، فَأَفَاضُوا فِي ذِكْرِ اللهِ، وَالتَّفَقُّهِ فِي دِيْنِه».

(سير أعلام النبلاء)

"I saw Imām al-Awzāʿī (※) remain in his place of prayer engaged in the *dhikr* of Allāh until sunrise. He would narrate to us that this was the practice of the *Salaf* and that once the sun had risen, they would interact with each other and engage in even more *dhikr* of Allāh by learning about His *dīn*." (Siyar ʿAlām al-Nublā')

Imām Ibn al-Qayyim (※) relates an encounter which he had with his teacher, Imām Ibn Taymīyyah (※).

Imām Ibn al-Qayyim (※) states:

«وحضَرتُه مرَّةً صلَّى الفجرَ، ثم جلَسَ يذكُرُ اللهَ تعالى إلى قريبٍ مِن انتِصافِ النَّهارِ، ثم التفَتَ إليَّ وقال: هذه غَدوَتي، ولو لم أتغَدَّ الغداءَ سقَطَت قُوَّتي، أو كلامًا قريبًا من هذا»

(الوابل الصيب من الكلم الطيب)

"I was once present with Shaykh al-Islām Ibn Taymīyyah (※) when he offered his *fajr* and then sat engaged in the *dhikr* of Allāh until near the middle of the day. He then turned to me and said, 'This is my morning meal. If I do not have this morning meal, I will lose my strength!' Or a statement to that effect." (Al-Wābil al-Ṣayyib)

When a person accustoms oneself to this amazing action and begins one's day devoted to Allāh (※) with the words of *dhikr*, humbling oneself before Allāh (※) and eager of His reward, what do you think the rest of that person's day would be like, what state would he be in, and how much energy would he have?

It is an established fact that *dhikr* strengthens the heart, as well as the body in general. So, imagine what would be the result when '*dhikr* by way of words' is combined with '*dhikr* by way of deeds?' Consider the *tahajjud* prayer, for instance. It combines both of these forms of *dhikr*. In fact, it combines many forms of *dhikr* like reciting the Qur'ān, making *duʿā*, glorifying Allāh (ﷻ), and so on.

There is no doubt that all of these increases the strength of a person's body and soul. The Prophet (ﷺ) was extremely keen on performing *tahajjud* prayers.

ʿĀ'ishah (رضي الله عنها) narrates:

«أَنَّ نَبِيَّ اللَّهِ ﷺ كَانَ يَقُومُ مِنَ اللَّيْلِ حَتَّى تَتَفَطَّرَ قَدَمَاهُ، فَقَالَتْ عَائِشَةُ: لِمَ تَصْنَعُ هَذَا يَا رَسُولَ اللَّهِ، وَقَدْ غَفَرَ اللَّهُ لَكَ مَا تَقَدَّمَ مِنْ ذَنْبِكَ وَمَا تَأَخَّرَ؟» قَالَ: «أَفَلاَ أُحِبُّ أَنْ أَكُونَ عَبْدًا شَكُورًا».

(رواه البخاري)

> "The Prophet (ﷺ) used to offer prayers at night (for such a long time) that his feet used to crack. I asked him, 'Why do you do this, while you have been forgiven your former and latter sins?' He replied, 'Should I not be a grateful slave of Allāh?'" (Bukhārī)

This particular act of worship nourishes and strengthens the soul, and it also trains a person to have a strong resolve.

Therefore, it is no surprise to find the remarkable level of perseverance which the Prophet (ﷺ) had in dealing with the difficulties that he encountered in Allāh's (ﷻ) path, confronting turmoil and harm, and facing the schemes of the adversaries.

Allāh (ﷻ) directed the Prophet (ﷺ) by saying:

﴿وَلَقَدْ نَعْلَمُ أَنَّكَ يَضِيقُ صَدْرُكَ بِمَا يَقُولُونَ ۝٩٧ فَسَبِّحْ بِحَمْدِ رَبِّكَ وَكُن مِّنَ ٱلسَّـٰجِدِينَ ۝٩٨﴾ [الحجر من الآية ٩٧ الى الآية ٩٨]

> "And We know very well that your bosom (your heart) is tightened (distressed, hurt) by what they say (their taunts and ridicule). So (to combat the effects of this distress and hurt, you should) glorify the praises of your Lord, and be among those who prostrate (those who perform *ṣalāt*)." (Ḥijr 15:97-98)

As a result, whenever any matter distressed the Messenger of Allāh (ﷺ) he would pray to the Almighty.

Prayers offer a person the most effective comfort in remaining resolute and steadfast.

Allāh (ﷻ) also directed the Prophet (ﷺ) by saying:

﴿ٱتْلُ مَآ أُوحِىَ إِلَيْكَ مِنَ ٱلْكِتَٰبِ وَأَقِمِ ٱلصَّلَوٰةَ ۖ إِنَّ ٱلصَّلَوٰةَ تَنْهَىٰ عَنِ ٱلْفَحْشَآءِ وَٱلْمُنكَرِ ۗ وَلَذِكْرُ ٱللَّهِ أَكْبَرُ ۗ ﴿٤٥﴾﴾ [العنكبوت الآية ٤٥]

"Recite the Book (the Qur'ān) which has been revealed to you and establish the *ṣalāt.* Verily the *ṣalāt* (performed with all of its conditions and etiquette) prevents (the person performing the *ṣalāt* from) immoral (indecent) behaviour and evil. Without a doubt, the *dhikr* of Allāh is the greatest (greater than other forms of worship which are devoid of Allāh's remembrance)." (ʿAnkabūt 29:45)

In addition, Allāh (ﷻ) consoled the Prophet (ﷺ) by informing him about the example set by another righteous servant and chosen Prophet of Allāh (ﷻ).

It was the example of strength and vigor in worship that was demonstrated by Prophet Dāwūd (ؑ). Allāh (ﷻ) told the final Prophet (ﷺ):

﴿ٱصْبِرْ عَلَىٰ مَا يَقُولُونَ وَٱذْكُرْ عَبْدَنَا دَاوُۥدَ ذَا ٱلْأَيْدِ ۖ إِنَّهُۥٓ أَوَّابٌ ﴿١٧﴾﴾ [ص الآية ١٧]

"Be patient with all they say and remember Our slave Dāwūd (ؑ) the strong (willed). He was certainly penitent (constantly turning to Allāh)." (Ṣād 38:17)

ʿAbd al-Raḥmān ibn Nāṣir al-Sāʿdī in his commentary on the Qur'ān, *Tafsīr al-Sāʿdī* mentions about this verse:

«مِن الفوائِدِ والحِكَمِ في قصة داود: أنَّ الله تعالى يمدَحُ ويُحبُّ القُوَّة في طاعته: قُوَّة القلبِ والبدَن، فإنَّه يحصُلُ مِنها مِن آثار الطاعة وحُسنِها وكثرتِها ما لا يحصُلُ مع الوَهن وعدم القُوَّة،

وإنَّ العبدَ ينبغي له تعاطِي أسبابِها، وعدم الرُّكُون إلى الكَسَل والبَطالَة المُخِلَّة بالقُوَى، المُضعِفة للنَّفس».

(تفسير السعدي)

"The lessons and wisdom from the narrative about Prophet Dāwūd (ﷺ) include the fact that Allāh commends and loves for His servants to obey Him with strength - both spiritual and physical strength. That strength allows for performing acts of obedience properly and abundantly, as well as having the effects of those actions to come to fruition. This cannot happen while in a state of weakness and lack of strength. Additionally, a servant of Allāh has to pursue the necessary means to (reach) his objective. He must not be complacent or lazy since those diminish one's strength and weaken the soul." (Tafsīr al-Sāʿdī)

Our Prophet (ﷺ) did not restrict himself to only one method of strengthening his connection with Allāh (ﷻ). Rather, he used various different methods.

In *Ṣaḥīḥ al-Bukhārī*, there is a *ḥadīth* narrated by Abū Hurairah (رضي الله عنه) in which he narrates:

«نَهَى رَسُولُ اللَّهِ ﷺ عَنِ الوِصَالِ» فَقَالَ لَهُ رِجَالٌ مِنَ المُسْلِمِينَ: فَإِنَّكَ يَا رَسُولَ اللَّهِ تُوَاصِلُ، فَقَالَ رَسُولُ اللَّهِ ﷺ: «أَيُّكُمْ مِثْلِي، إِنِّي أَبِيتُ يُطْعِمُنِي رَبِّي وَيَسْقِينِ».

(رواه البخاري)

"The Messenger of Allāh (ﷺ) forbade *al-Wiṣāl* (fasting continuously for more than one day without taking any meals). As a result, one of the men among the Muslims remarked, 'But you do *al-Wiṣāl*, O Messenger of Allāh (ﷺ)!' So, the Prophet (ﷺ) replied, 'Who among you is like me? Throughout the night, my Lord provides me with food and drink.'" (Bukhārī)

Shaykh 'Abd al-Raḥīm Mubārakpūrī (؏) in his commentary on Tirmidhī, *Tuḥfat al-Aḥwadhī* elucidates:

»وَيُحْتَمَلُ أَنْ يَكُونَ الْمُرَادُ بِقَوْلِهِ يُطْعِمُنِي وَيَسْقِينِي أَيْ يَشْغَلُنِي بِالتَّفَكُّرِ فِي عَظَمَتِهِ وَالتَّمَلِّي بِمُشَاهَدَتِهِ وَالتَّغَذِّي بِمَعَارِفِهِ وَقُرَّةِ الْعَيْنِ بِمَحَبَّتِهِ وَالِاسْتِغْرَاقِ فِي مُنَاجَاتِهِ وَالْإِقْبَالِ عَلَيْهِ عَنِ الطَّعَامِ وَالشَّرَابِ«.

(تحفة الأحوذي)

"This means that the Prophet (؏) remained occupied in contemplating the magnificence of his Lord, and was nourished by the knowledge, recognition, solace, and devotion which emanated from that - rather than from food and drink." (Tuḥfat al-Aḥwadhī)

He further writes and quotes Imām Ibn al-Qayyim (؏) saying:

»قَدْ يَكُونُ هَذَا الْغِذَاءُ أَعْظَمَ مِنْ غِذَاءِ الْأَجْسَادِ وَمَنْ لَهُ أَدْنَى ذَوْقٍ وَتَجْرِبَةٍ يَعْلَمُ اسْتِغْنَاءَ الْجِسْمِ بِغِذَاءِ الْقَلْبِ وَالرُّوحِ عَنْ كَثِيرٍ مِنَ الْغِذَاءِ الْجُسْمَانِيِّ وَلَا سِيَّمَا الْفَرِحُ الْمَسْرُورُ بِمَطْلُوبِهِ الَّذِي قَرَّتْ عَيْنُهُ بِمَحْبُوبِهِ«.

(تحفة الأحوذي)

"This form of nourishment can be far greater than physical nourishment of the body. If a person is genuine in his love for Allāh and has experienced this type of nourishment, then this person will know that the nourishment given to the heart and soul can very well suffice a person from needing many other forms of physical nourishment, especially in the case of someone who is elated by achieving his utmost objective which is drawing closer to Allāh whom he loves more than anyone else." (Tuḥfat al-Aḥwadhī)

Dhikr is the foundation for all acts of worship, and it is the easiest and simplest form of worship that a person of faith can engage in. Accordingly, it will only be correct for a servant to fulfill Allāh's (ﷻ) command in which He says:

﴿يَـٰٓأَيُّهَا ٱلَّذِينَ ءَامَنُوا۟ ٱذْكُرُوا۟ ٱللَّهَ ذِكْرًا كَثِيرًا ﴿٤١﴾﴾ [الأحزاب الآية ٤١]

> "O, you who have faith (*īmān*)! Remember Allāh in abundance (at all times by engaging in plentiful *dhikr* of Allāh)." (Aḥzāb 33:41)

Commenting on this verse Imām al-Qurṭubī (رحمه الله) states:

«أَمَرَ اللَّهُ تَعَالَى عِبَادَهُ بِأَنْ يَذْكُرُوهُ وَيَشْكُرُوهُ، وَيُكْثِرُوا مِنْ ذَلِكَ عَلَى مَا أَنْعَمَ بِهِ عَلَيْهِمْ. وَجَعَلَ تَعَالَى ذَلِكَ دُونَ حَدٍّ لِسُهُولَتِهِ عَلَى الْعَبْدِ. وَلِعِظَمِ الْأَجْرِ فِيهِ».

(تفسير القرطبي)

> "Allāh has commanded His servants to remember Him and express gratitude to Him, and to do it in abundance for the favours which He has conferred upon them. Allāh did not place any limit on it because of how easy it is for His servants to perform, as well as how immense of a reward it carries." (Tafsīr al-Qurṭubī)

It is for this very reason that Abū Saʿīd (رضي الله عنه) has reported the following from the Prophet (ﷺ):

«أَكْثِرُوا ذِكْرَ اللهِ حَتَّى يَقُولُوا: مَجْنُونٌ».

(مسند أحمد)

> "Remember Allāh so much that people start saying, 'He has gone insane.'" (Musnad Aḥmad)

The heart has certain nourishments that it requires in order for it to remain strong. That nourishment takes the form of having correct beliefs about Allāh (ﷻ) and performing righteous actions. The more of that which a person has, the stronger his heart will be and the more steadfast he will be in adhering to the truth.

True life is life of the heart. However, the heart's life cannot come to completion without doing those actions which please Allāh (ﷻ). This is why the Prophet (ﷺ) said:

«مَثَلُ الَّذِي يَذْكُرُ رَبَّهُ وَالَّذِي لا يَذْكُرُ رَبَّهُ مَثَلُ الْحَيِّ وَالْمَيِّتِ».

(رواه البخاري)

"The likeness of someone who engages in the *dhikr* of his Lord versus someone who does not is like that of the living and the dead." (Bukhārī)

CONCLUSION

- When the heart has a connection with Allāh (ﷻ) and constantly returns to Him, then it will attain unimaginable nourishment and delight. However, when a person is heedless of his Lord and is diverted from obeying Him, then that person's heart will die. Therefore, without obedience to Allāh (ﷻ), a person's heart will not find rest and his mind will not find peace.
- By Allāh's (ﷻ) permission, the acts of worship that a servant of Allāh (ﷻ) carries out are a means of providing him peace, perseverance, and steadfastness; ridding him of distress, frustration, and sorrow; and rescuing him from whatever suffering he may feel due to the hardships of this world.
- The greatest fruits of faith are a strong connection with Allāh (ﷻ), recognizing one's constant need for Him alone, remaining devoted to the Almighty, finding solace with Him, and being a worshipping servant to the Creator whether times are difficult or easy.

- A strong connection with Allāh (ﷻ) will allow a person to obey Him unwaveringly and comply with all of His directives. When a person does that, then he will be rewarded with the fine life that Allāh (ﷻ) has promised the people of faith. Allāh (ﷻ) says in the Qur'ān:

﴿مَنْ عَمِلَ صَٰلِحًا مِّن ذَكَرٍ أَوْ أُنثَىٰ وَهُوَ مُؤْمِنٌ فَلَنُحْيِيَنَّهُۥ حَيَوٰةً طَيِّبَةً ۖ وَلَنَجْزِيَنَّهُمْ أَجْرَهُم بِأَحْسَنِ مَا كَانُوا۟ يَعْمَلُونَ ﴿٩٧﴾﴾ [النحل الآية ٩٧]

"If anyone, whether man or woman performs righteous deeds while having sound beliefs (*īmān*), We will certainly grant them a good (fine, peaceful and contented) life (in this world) and most surely reward them (in the hereafter as well) for the good that they do." (Naḥl 16:97)

Remaining attached to Allāh (ﷻ) and maintaining a strong connection with Him nurtures a person such that he carries out righteous deeds, holds himself accountable for whatever he does - no matter how big or small it might seem, and bears in mind that Allāh (ﷻ) always sees him, giving that precedence over what anyone else may think of him.

When a person protects his limbs from doing what Allāh (ﷻ) has prohibited, Allāh (ﷻ) will increase him in strength and allow him to continue benefitting from his limbs. This is something any person of faith hopes for.

Part of a *duʿā* that the Prophet (ﷺ) used to make frequently was:

«وَمَتِّعْنَا بِأَسْمَاعِنَا وَأَبْصَارِنَا وَقُوَّتِنَا مَا أَحْيَيْتَنَا، وَاجْعَلْهُ الْوَارِثَ مِنَّا».

(رواه الترمذي)

"Bless us to benefit from our hearing, sight, and strength throughout the life that You have granted us, and allow that blessing to remain all the way until we leave this world." (Tirmidhī)

In this supplication, we are asking Allāh (ﷻ) to enable us to benefit from our hearing, sight, and all of the other senses and faculties, whether inward or outward. This means that we are asking Allāh (ﷻ) to enable us to use them to obey Him throughout our entire lives.

When a person fulfills one's duties towards Allāh (ﷻ) while young and strong, then Allāh (ﷻ) will protect that person when he grows old and weak, and Allāh (ﷻ) will bless him to benefit from his hearing, sight, senses, limbs, strength, and mind *Inshā' Allāh.*

Change My Heart

A Plea to Allāh for Tawfīq and Forgiveness

Wash away all of the filth and change my dead heart,
Make me alive again, give me a fresh start.
Wash away all of the filth and change my dead heart,
So change my heart please and wash away the filth.
Do not leave me drowning here alone and astray,
I spent my life running away from You,
But now I have nowhere to turn except towards You.
I turn to You and beg to be saved,
And change me into an obedient slave.
Wash away all of the filth and change my dead heart,
Make me alive again, give me a fresh start.
All of my life I have been doing what I craved,
Shayṭān and Nafs have always held me enslaved.
I am ashamed that I have broken Your rules,
Worshipped my Nafs and a few ignorant fools.
But now I know the path leading me to You,
I bow to You and ask You to help me.
Wash away all of the filth and change my dead heart,
Make me alive again, give me a fresh start.
I wish Your name to be engraved in my heart,
I will be grateful to You, please change this dead heart.

I wish your name to be engraved in my heart,
I will be grateful to You, please change this dead heart.
My heart is dark and so my eyes remain dry,
Hypocrisy and pride will not let me cry.
I am at your door begging You to let me in,
Don't push me back to my hopeless life of sin.
I am at Your door begging You to let me in,
Don't push me back to my hopeless life of sin.
So change my heart and forgive my sins this day,
Don't leave me drowning here alone and astray.
Wash away all of the filth and change my dead heart,
Make me alive again, give me a fresh start.
Wash away all of the filth and change my dead heart,
Make me alive again, give me a fresh start!

(Mū'min Kā Hatyār, Shaykh Muḥammad Yūnus Pālanpūrī)

KHUṬBAH 43

Remember Allāh Much that You may be Successful

Days elapse ever so quickly, and the passing of hours and years is indeed swift. Not too long ago, we were looking forward to one of the most magnificent acts of worship and most majestic of deeds which draw people closer to Allāh (ﷻ). We were looking forward to the most glorious days in this world – the Day of *ʿArafah* – as well as the Day of *Īd al-Aḍḥā* and *Ayyām al-Naḥr* - 'the Days of Sacrifice.'

The Pilgrims (*Ḥujjāj*) who went to Allāh's (ﷻ) Sacred House have returned rejoicing over the grace and mercy that the Almighty granted them. They are individuals whom Allāh (ﷻ) blessed to perform *ḥajj* at His House, favoured over others among His creation, and boasted about them to His angels.

They were present in *Minā* and *ʿArafah*, spent a night in *Muzdalifah*, performed *Ṭawāf* at the Kaʿbah, proclaimed the *Talbīyah* with everyone else who did so, and strove to seize the opportunity to attain Allāh's (ﷻ) mercy.

They called upon the Most Generous Lord. When He gives, it enriches the one who asks. When He bestows blessings, He is the most generous. No sin is too big for Him to forgive, and no favour is too much for Him to grant.

These past days and nights were ones of unparalleled virtue. In the Qur'ān it says:

﴿قُلْ بِفَضْلِ ٱللَّهِ وَبِرَحْمَتِهِۦ فَبِذَٰلِكَ فَلْيَفْرَحُوا۟ هُوَ خَيْرٌ مِّمَّا يَجْمَعُونَ ﴿٥٨﴾﴾ [يونس الآية ٥٨]

> "Say, in the bounty of Allāh and in His mercy - in that let them rejoice; it is better than anything of this world that they can amass for themselves." (Yūnus 10:58)

Among the greatest aims of performing the *ḥajj* is *dhikr* - making mention of Allāh (ﷻ). *Dhikr* is an immensely virtuous act of worship. In fact, nothing draws a person nearer to Allāh (ﷻ) like *dhikr* does, and all acts of worship were prescribed with *dhikr* as their purpose.

Ṭawāf at the Kaʿbah, *Saʿī* between *al-Ṣafā* and *al-Marwah*, and stoning the *Jamarāt* were only prescribed in order for people to make mention of Allāh (ﷻ).

When the *Ḥujjāj* complete the rites of *ḥajj*, *dhikr* is to be the conclusion and completion of their deeds. Allāh (ﷻ) says:

﴿فَإِذَا قَضَيْتُم مَّنَـٰسِكَكُمْ فَٱذْكُرُوا۟ ٱللَّهَ كَذِكْرِكُمْ ءَابَآءَكُمْ أَوْ أَشَدَّ ذِكْرًا ۗ ٢٠٠﴾

[البقرة الآية ٢٠٠]

> "Once you have completed your Ḥajj rites (duties), remember Allāh as you remember your forefathers, or (rather with) an even greater remembrance." (Baqarah 2:200)

Imām al-Qurṭubī (رحمه الله) writes:

«كَانَتْ عَادَةُ الْعَرَبِ إِذَا قَضَتْ حَجَّهَا تَقِفُ عِنْدَ الْجَمْرَةِ، فَتُفَاخِرُ بِالْآبَاءِ، وَتَذْكُرُ أَيَّامَ أَسْلَافِهَا مِنْ بَسَالَةٍ وَكَرَمٍ، وَغَيْرِ ذَلِكَ، فَنَزَلَتِ الْآيَةُ لِيَلْزَمُوا أَنْفُسَهُمْ ذِكْرَ اللهِ أَكْثَرَ مِنَ الْتِزَامِهِمْ ذِكْرَ آبَائِهِمْ أَيَّامَ الْجَاهِلِيَّةِ».

(تفسير القرطبي)

> "The custom of the Arabs was that when they completed the *ḥajj*, they would stand at the *Jamrah* and boast about their forefathers and mention the glorious feats of their ancestors, so this verse was revealed commanding them to remember Allāh more than they used to remember their forefathers in the time

of the *Jāhilīyyah* (the era of ignorance prior to Islām).” (Tafsīr al-Qurṭubī)

ʿAbdullāh ibn ʿAbbās (ﷺ) said:

«مَعْنَى الْآيَةِ وَاذْكُرُوا اللَّهَ كَذِكْرِ الْأَطْفَالِ آبَاءَهُمْ وَأُمَّهَاتِهِمْ: أَبَهْ أُمَّهْ، أَيْ فَاسْتَغِيثُوا بِهِ وَالْجَئُوا إِلَيْهِ كَمَا كُنْتُمْ تَفْعَلُونَ فِي حَالِ صِغَرِكُمْ بِآبَائِكُمْ».

(تفسير القرطبي)

“The meaning of the verse is: ‘Remember Allāh as children remember their fathers and mothers. Seek help from Him and seek refuge with Him as you did with your parents when you were a child.’” (Tafsīr al-Qurṭubī)

Another group of commentators of the Qur’ān mention that the verse means:

«مَعْنَى الْآيَةِ اذْكُرُوا اللَّهَ وَعَظِّمُوهُ وَذُبُّوا عَنْ حَرَمِهِ، وَادْفَعُوا مَنْ أَرَادَ الشِّرْكَ فِي دِينِهِ وَمَشَاعِرِهِ، كَمَا تَذْكُرُونَ آبَاءَكُمْ بِالْخَيْرِ إِذَا غَضَّ أَحَدٌ مِنْهُمْ، وَتَحْمُونَ جَوَانِبَهُمْ وَتَذُبُّونَ عَنْهُمْ».

(تفسير القرطبي)

“Remember Allāh and esteem Him, defend His sanctity and repel those who desire to introduce shirk into His *dīn* and rites, just like you would speak well of your parents when someone criticized them, and protect and defend them.” (Tafsīr al-Qurṭubī)

ʿAbdullāh ibn ʿAbbās (ﷺ) narrates:

«كَانَ أَهْلُ الْجَاهِلِيَّةِ يَقِفُونَ فِي الْمَوْسِمِ فَيَقُولُ الرَّجُلُ مِنْهُمْ: كَانَ أَبِي يُطْعِمُ وَيَحْمِلُ الْحَمَالَاتِ، وَيَحْمِلُ الدِّيَاتِ، لَيْسَ لَهُمْ ذِكْرٌ غَيْرُ فِعَالِ آبَائِهِمْ، فَأَنْزَلَ اللَّهُ عَلَى مُحَمَّدٍ ﷺ ﴿فَاذْكُرُوا اللَّهَ كَذِكْرِكُمْ آبَاءَكُمْ أَوْ أَشَدَّ ذِكْرًا ۝٢٠٠﴾ [البَقَرَة الآية ٢٠٠] »

(تفسير ابن كثير)

"The people of *Jāhilīyyah* would stand during the days of *ḥajj* and one of them would say things like: 'My father used to feed people, fight courageously, and pay off any financial compensation that was to be given to the heirs of anyone who had been murdered, or killed by accident.' All that they would mention was the exploits of their forefathers, so Allāh revealed to Prophet Muḥammad (ﷺ) the verse saying: 'Once you have completed your *ḥajj* rites (duties), remember Allāh as you remember your forefathers, or (rather with) an even greater remembrance.'" (Baqarah 2:200) (Tafsīr Ibn Kathīr)

Dhikr should be prominent during *ḥajj* and after it as well. All acts of worship have been prescribed with the aim of *dhikr* - remembering Allāh (ﷻ).

Dhikr itself is the easiest and most virtuous act of worship. In fact, it is greater than everything else. Allāh (ﷻ) says:

﴿وَلَذِكْرُ ٱللَّهِ أَكْبَرُۗ وَٱللَّهُ يَعْلَمُ مَا تَصْنَعُونَ ۝٤٥﴾ [العنكبوت الآية ٤٥]

"*Dhikr* of Allāh is greater (than everything else), and Allāh has complete knowledge of everything that you do." ('Ankabūt 29:45)

Furthermore, Allāh (ﷻ) rewards those who mention Him by making mention of them. He says:

﴿فَٱذْكُرُونِىٓ أَذْكُرْكُمْ وَٱشْكُرُوا۟ لِى وَلَا تَكْفُرُونِ ۝١٥٢﴾ [البقرة الآية ١٥٢]

"Therefore, you must make mention of Me. (If you do so) I will make mention of you. Continue being grateful to Me, and do not deny Me." (Baqarah 2:152)

Allāh (ﷻ) also commends the people of faith who mention Him. He says:

﴿إِنَّ فِي خَلْقِ ٱلسَّمَٰوَٰتِ وَٱلْأَرْضِ وَٱخْتِلَٰفِ ٱلَّيْلِ وَٱلنَّهَارِ لَءَايَٰتٍ لِّأُو۟لِى ٱلْأَلْبَٰبِ ﴿١٩٠﴾ ٱلَّذِينَ يَذْكُرُونَ ٱللَّهَ قِيَٰمًا وَقُعُودًا وَعَلَىٰ جُنُوبِهِمْ وَيَتَفَكَّرُونَ فِي خَلْقِ ٱلسَّمَٰوَٰتِ وَٱلْأَرْضِ رَبَّنَا مَا خَلَقْتَ هَٰذَا بَٰطِلًا سُبْحَٰنَكَ فَقِنَا عَذَابَ ٱلنَّارِ ﴿١٩١﴾﴾ [آل عمران من الآية ١٩٠ الى الآية ١٩١]

"Indeed, the creation of the heavens and the earth, and the alternation of night and day, contain signs for people of understanding. Those are individuals who mention Allāh whether they are standing, sitting, or lying on their sides. They contemplate the creation of the heavens and the earth, and they say, 'Our Lord, You have not brought this into existence aimlessly. You are perfect, and above doing such a thing. Thus, protect us from the torment of the hellfire.'" (Āle ʿImrān 3:190-191)

Dhikr - the mention and remembrance of Allāh (ﷻ) - makes up the seeds of Paradise, and the residents of Paradise will be inspired to engage in *dhikr* just as they are inspired to breathe.

A *ḥadīth* in the *Sunan of Imām al-Tirmidhī* (رحمه الله) states that the Messenger of Allāh (ﷺ) said:

«لَقِيتُ إِبْرَاهِيمَ لَيْلَةَ أُسْرِيَ بِي فقَالَ: يَا مُحَمَّدُ، أَقْرِئْ أُمَّتَكَ مِنِّي السَّلَامَ وَأَخْبِرْهُمْ أَنَّ الجَنَّةَ طَيِّبَةُ التُّرْبَةِ عَذْبَةُ المَاءِ، وَأَنَّهَا قِيعَانٌ، وَأَنَّ غِرَاسَهَا سُبْحَانَ اللَّهِ وَالحَمْدُ لِلَّهِ وَلَا إِلَهَ إِلَّا اللَّهُ وَاللَّهُ أَكْبَرُ».

(رواه الترمذي)

"The night that I was taken up through the heavens, I met Prophet Ibrāhīm who said, 'Muḥammad, convey my *Salām* to your *ummah* and tell them that the soil of *Jannah* is pure, its water is sweet, it is a flat treeless plain, and its seeds are the phrases *Subḥān Allāh* (Allāh is perfect in every way),

> *Alḥamdulillāh* (All praise is due to Allāh), *Lā ilāha illā Allāh* (none has the right to be worshipped except Allāh), and *Allāhu Akbar* (Allāh is the Greatest).'" (Tirmidhī)

The Messenger of Allāh (ﷺ) also instructed his companions (رضي الله عنهم) to remain engaged in *dhikr* at all times.

A *ḥadīth* in the *Sunan of Imām al-Tirmidhī* (رحمه الله) mentions that a man once asked:

«أَنَّ رَجُلًا قَالَ: يَا رَسُولَ اللَّهِ إِنَّ شَرَائِعَ الإِسْلَامِ قَدْ كَثُرَتْ عَلَيَّ، فَأَخْبِرْنِي بِشَيْءٍ أَتَشَبَّثُ بِهِ، قَالَ: لَا يَزَالُ لِسَانُكَ رَطْبًا مِنْ ذِكْرِ اللَّهِ».

(رواه الترمذي)

> "O Messenger of Allāh, the directives of Islām have become many for me. I would like you to inform me about something to which I can constantly adhere." He replied, "Ensure that your tongue remains moist with remembrance of Allāh." (Tirmidhī)

The Prophet (ﷺ) also once took the hand of Muʿādh ibn Jabal (رضي الله عنه) and said to him:

«يَا مُعَاذُ، وَاللَّهِ إِنِّي لَأُحِبُّكَ، وَاللَّهِ إِنِّي لَأُحِبُّكَ. أُوصِيكَ يَا مُعَاذُ لَا تَدَعَنَّ فِي دُبُرِ كُلِّ صَلَاةٍ تَقُولُ: اللَّهُمَّ أَعِنِّي عَلَى ذِكْرِكَ، وَشُكْرِكَ، وَحُسْنِ عِبَادَتِكَ».

(رواه أبو داود)

> "O Muʿādh, I swear by Allāh that the love I have for you is very great. Therefore, Muʿādh, I advise you to not neglect to say at the end of each prayer, 'O Allāh, I implore You to assist me in making mention of You, being grateful to You, and worshipping You in the best way.'"(Abū Dāwūd)

When we examine the texts of the Qur'ān and *Sunnah*, we find that all goodness comes from the *dhikr* of Allāh (ﷻ). By it, people have distress and sorrow removed, they acquire provision, they attain happiness, and they are endowed with honour and radiance.

Remembering Allāh (ﷻ) through *dhikr* brings great benefits, such as spiritual well-being, tranquility and softening of the heart. Allāh (ﷻ) says:

﴿ٱلَّذِينَ ءَامَنُوا۟ وَتَطْمَئِنُّ قُلُوبُهُم بِذِكْرِ ٱللَّهِ ۗ أَلَا بِذِكْرِ ٱللَّهِ تَطْمَئِنُّ ٱلْقُلُوبُ ﴿٢٨﴾﴾

[الرَّعد الآية ٢٨]

> "(The guided ones are): Those who believe, and whose hearts find rest in the remembrance of Allāh, Verily, in the remembrance of Allāh do hearts find rest." (Raʿd 13:28)

The *dhikr* of Allāh (ﷻ) is one of the best forms of devotion, among the greatest of worships, and one of the most elevated of ways in drawing close to Allāh (ﷻ).

A *ḥadīth* in the *Sunan of Imām al-Tirmidhī* (رحمه الله) mentions that the Prophet (ﷺ) once asked his companions (رضي الله عنهم):

«أَلَا أُنَبِّئُكُمْ بِخَيْرِ أَعْمَالِكُمْ، وَأَزْكَاهَا عِنْدَ مَلِيكِكُمْ، وَأَرْفَعِهَا فِي دَرَجَاتِكُمْ»؟ قَالُوا: بَلَى. قَالَ: «ذِكْرُ اللَّهِ تَعَالَى».

(رواه الترمذي)

> "Should I not inform you about the best of your deeds, and the purest of them with your Lord, and the greatest in raising your ranks? They said: 'Of course, O Messenger of Allāh.' He (ﷺ) replied: 'It is the remembrance of Allāh (ﷻ).'" (Tirmidhī)

Muʿādh ibn Jabal (رضي الله عنه) states:

«مَا شَيْءٌ أَنْجَى مِنْ عَذَابِ اللَّهِ مِنْ ذِكْرِ اللَّهِ».

(رواه الترمذي)

"There is nothing that brings more salvation from the punishment of Allāh than the remembrance of Allāh." (Tirmidhī)

After the Qur'ān, the most virtuous words of *dhikr* are: *Subḥān Allāh* (Allāh is perfect in every way), *Alḥamdulillāh* (All praise is due to Allāh), *Lā ilāha illā Allāh* (none has the right to be worshipped except Allāh), *Allāhu Akbar* (Allāh is the Greatest) and *Lā ḥawla wa lā quwwata illā billāh* (there is no power or strength except by Allāh). These are righteous deeds whose rewards remain forever.

The Prophet (ﷺ) has said:

«الْبَاقِيَاتِ الصَّالِحَاتِ: إِنَّهَا قَوْلُ الْعَبْدِ: اللَّهُ أَكْبَرُ، وَسُبْحَانَ اللهِ، وَالْحَمْدُ لِلَّهِ، وَلاَ إِلَهَ إِلاَّ اللَّهُ، وَلاَ حَوْلَ وَلاَ قُوَّةَ إِلاَّ بِاللَّهِ».

(موطأ مالك)

"The lasting good deeds are: (the saying of) *Subḥān Allāh* (Allāh is perfect in every way), *Alḥamdulillāh* (all praise is due to Allāh), *Lā ilāha illā Allāh* (none has the right to be worshipped except Allāh), *Allāhu Akbar* (Allāh is the greatest), and *Lā ḥawla wa lā quwwata illā billāh* (there is no power and no strength except by Allāh). (Muwaṭṭā' Mālik)

If someone recites the following one hundred times: *'Subḥān Allāhi wa bi Ḥamdihī'* (I proclaim the perfection of Allāh and I praise Him), then that person's sins will be pardoned even if they are as much as the foam on the sea.

The Prophet (ﷺ) states:

«مَنْ قَالَ سُبْحَانَ اللَّهِ وَبِحَمْدِهِ فِي يَوْمٍ مِائَةَ مَرَّةٍ: حُطَّتْ خَطَايَاهُ، وَإِنْ كَانَتْ مِثْلَ زَبَدِ الْبَحْرِ».

(موطأ مالك)

"Whoever recites one hundred times during the day: '*Subḥān Allāhi wa bi Ḥamdihī*' (I proclaim the perfection of Allāh is and

I praise Him) - his sins will be forgiven even though they may be as much as the foam on the sea." (Muwaṭṭā' Mālik)

The phrase *Lā ḥawla wa lā qūwwata illā billāh* (there is no power or strength except by Allāh) is one of the treasures of Paradise.

Abū Mūsā al-Ashʿarī (ﷺ) narrates:

«أَلَا أَدُلُّكَ عَلَى كَلِمَةٍ مِنْ كُنُوزِ الْجَنَّةِ - أَوْ قَالَ: عَلَى كَنْزٍ مِنْ كُنُوزِ الْجَنَّةِ -؟ فَقُلْتُ: بَلَى، فَقَالَ: لَا حَوْلَ وَلَا قُوَّةَ إِلَّا بِاللهِ».

(رواه مسلم)

"The Messenger of Allāh (ﷺ) said to me, 'Shall I not guide you to a treasure from the treasures of *Jannah*?' I said, 'Yes, O Messenger of Allāh!' Thereupon he (ﷺ) said, '(Recite) *Lā ḥawla wa lā qūwwata illā billāh* (there is no power or strength except by Allāh).'" (Muslim)

In addition, a *ḥadīth* in *Ṣaḥīḥ al-Bukhārī* mentions that there are two statements which are light on the tongue, but heavy in the scale, and beloved to Allāh (ﷻ).

«كَلِمَتَانِ حَبِيبَتَانِ إِلَى الرَّحْمَنِ، خَفِيفَتَانِ عَلَى اللِّسَانِ، ثَقِيلَتَانِ فِي الْمِيزَانِ سُبْحَانَ اللَّهِ وَبِحَمْدِهِ، سُبْحَانَ اللَّهِ الْعَظِيمِ» .

(رواه البخاري)

"Two words are beloved to the Most Merciful. They are light on the tongue, but heavy on the scale (and they are): *Subḥān Allāhi wa bi-Ḥamdihī* (I proclaim the perfection of Allāh and I praise Him) and *Subḥān Allāhil ʿAẓīm* (I proclaim the perfection of Allāh, the Most Magnificent)." (Bukhārī)

Furthermore, glad tidings of Paradise are promised for those who recite the *tahlīl* and *takbīr*.

The Prophet (ﷺ) states:

«مَا أَهَلَّ مُهِلٌّ قَطُّ إِلَّا بُشِّرَ، وَلَا كَبَّرَ مُكَبِّرٌ قَطُّ إِلَّا بُشِّرَ» قِيلَ: يَا رَسُولَ اللَّهِ، بِالْجَنَّةِ؟ قَالَ: «نَعَمْ».

(المعجم الأوسط للطبراني)

"No person ever proclaims the *tahlīl* (saying *Lā ilāha illā Allāh*) except that he is given glad tidings; and no person ever proclaims the *takbīr* (saying *Allāhu Akbar*) except he is given glad tidings." The companions asked the Prophet, "O Messenger of Allāh, is this [glad tidings] of Paradise?" He responded, "Yes." (Al-Muʿjam al-Awsaṭ of al-Ṭabarānī)

If someone turns away from the *dhikr* of Allāh (ﷻ), then Allāh (ﷻ) will turn away from that person. How distant a person is from the Almighty One is in direct proportion to how much the person turns away from mentioning Allāh (ﷻ). When a person is heedless about Allāh (ﷻ), then there will remain distance between him and Allāh (ﷻ), and nothing can remedy that besides *dhikr*. Allāh (ﷻ) says:

﴿يَـٰٓأَيُّهَا ٱلَّذِينَ ءَامَنُوا۟ لَا تُلْهِكُمْ أَمْوَٰلُكُمْ وَلَآ أَوْلَـٰدُكُمْ عَن ذِكْرِ ٱللَّهِ ۚ وَمَن يَفْعَلْ ذَٰلِكَ فَأُو۟لَـٰٓئِكَ هُمُ ٱلْخَـٰسِرُونَ ۝٩﴾ [المُنَافِقُون الآية ٩]

"O believers, do not let your wealth and children divert you from remembering Allāh. Whoever is diverted will suffer a great loss." (Munāfiqūn 63:9)

Ḥāfiẓ ibn Kathīr (رحمه الله) writes:

«يَقُولُ تَعَالَى آمِرًا لِعِبَادِهِ الْمُؤْمِنِينَ بِكَثْرَةِ ذِكْرِهِ، وَنَاهِيًا لَهُمْ عَنْ أَنْ تَشْغَلَهُمُ الْأَمْوَالُ وَالْأَوْلَادُ عَنْ ذَلِكَ، وَمُخْبِرًا لَهُمْ بِأَنَّهُ مَنِ الْتَهَى بِمَتَاعِ الْحَيَاةِ الدُّنْيَا وَزِينَتِهَا عَمَّا خُلِقَ لَهُ مِنْ طَاعَةِ رَبِّهِ وَذِكْرِهِ، فَإِنَّهُ مِنَ الْخَاسِرِينَ الَّذِينَ يَخْسَرُونَ أَنْفُسَهُمْ وَأَهْلِيهِمْ يَوْمَ الْقِيَامَةِ».

(تفسير ابن كثير)

> "Allāh orders His faithful servants to remember Him frequently and to refrain from being distracted from His remembrance by indulging in their properties and children excessively. Allāh informs them that those who engage in this life, its delights and attributes and were busied from the obedience and remembrance of Allāh for which they were created, will be among the losers. They will lose themselves and their families on the Day of Resurrection." (Tafsīr Ibn Kathīr)

We also have to realize that the *jawārih* (limbs) are inroads to the heart. What we do on the outside affects the state of our heart and its receptivity to *dhikr*. We have to stop those actions which are hurting and killing our hearts. Along with that, we have to try and cure and revive our hearts with remembrance of Allāh (ﷻ).

The Prophet (ﷺ) states:

«إِنَّ لِكُلِّ شَيْءٍ جِلَاءً، وَإِنَّ جِلَاءَ الْقُلُوبِ ذِكْرُ اللهِ عَزَّ وَجَلَّ».

(شعب الإيمان)

> "For everything there is a cleansing agent, and the cleansing agent of the heart is the *dhikr* of Allāh, the Most-High." (Shuʿab al-Īmān)

CONCLUSION

- *Dhikr* is an all-embracing term, which in addition to including the ritual acts of worship, covers an array of activities of the tongue and heart.
- *Dhikr* involves thinking of and making mention of Allāh (ﷻ) at all times and in every area of our lives.
- *Dhikr* is a worship that has no special time, but it should be performed constantly so that it permanently links up a person's life with Allāh (ﷻ) and His obedience.

- The importance of constant *dhikr* cannot be emphasized enough, particularly if we desire to be on the receiving end of Allāh's (ﷻ) attention, grace and mercy.

The Prophet (ﷺ) has said:

«إِنَّ اللَّهَ عَزَّ وَجَلَّ يَقُولُ: أَنَا مَعَ عَبْدِي إِذَا هُوَ ذَكَرَنِي وَتَحَرَّكَتْ بِي شَفَتَاهُ».

(سنن ابن ماجه)

"Surely Allāh, the Grand and Majestic said: 'I am with My servant when he remembers Me, and his lips move in My remembrance.'" (Sunan Ibn Mājah)

The purpose of *dhikr* is to develop the quality of being mindful of Allāh (ﷻ) so that we can live a life of awareness, and not a life of being neglectful towards Allāh (ﷻ). In addition to our ritual acts of worship which we perform, such as the most regular one namely *ṣalāt*, there are many other ways of remembering Allāh (ﷻ). Among these, reading and reciting the Qur'ān is foremost.

Allāh (ﷻ) refers to the Qur'ān as *'Al-Dhikr'* which means: 'The Remembrance' or 'The Reminder' in as many as 55 places in the Qur'ān. In Sūrah Ṣād, Allāh (ﷻ) tells us:

﴿صٓ ۚ وَٱلْقُرْءَانِ ذِى ٱلذِّكْرِ ۝١﴾ [ص الآية ١]

"By the Qur'ān, full of reminder *(dhikr).*" (Ṣād 38:1)

﴿هَٰذَا ذِكْرٌ ۚ ۝٤٩﴾ [ص الآية ٤٩]

"This (the Qur'ān) is (no less than) a reminder (*dhikr*)." (Ṣād 38:49)

- Reading, understanding, reflecting and pondering on Allāh's (ﷻ) words is the most effective way of remembering Him.

- *Dhikr* also includes remembering Allāh (ﷻ) when one gets up in the morning, prior to starting anything, before eating, upon leaving the house, and before carrying out any other activities.
- Our Prophet (ﷺ) has taught us specific supplications for every occasion, and if we can recite these with understanding, then all of our activities will *Inshā' Allāh*, amount to His remembrance and worship.
- If for any reason one cannot remember the appropriate supplication for a specific occasion, then even saying *Bismillāh* (I begin in the Name of Allāh), and being conscious of Allāh (ﷻ) will amount to *dhikr* and will be a source of *barakah* – blessing in everything we do.
- It is vital for our salvation that we always remember Allāh (ﷻ), both in private and when amongst people.

The men and women who remember Allāh (ﷻ) have been specially mentioned in the Qur'ān among the categories of people who are very dear to Him. Allāh (ﷻ) says:

﴿وَٱلذَّٰكِرِينَ ٱللَّهَ كَثِيرًا وَٱلذَّٰكِرَٰتِ أَعَدَّ ٱللَّهُ لَهُم مَّغْفِرَةً وَأَجْرًا عَظِيمًا ۝٣٥﴾

[الأَحْزَاب الآية ٣٥]

"And for the men who engage much in Allāh's remembrance, and the women who remember - for them has Allāh prepared forgiveness and a great reward." (Aḥzāb 33:35)

We must also keep in mind that no matter how much a person strives to remain steadfast, he is still prone to errors and shortcomings. This is why Allāh (ﷻ) has said:

﴿فَٱسْتَقِيمُوٓاْ إِلَيْهِ وَٱسْتَغْفِرُوهُ ۗ وَوَيْلٌ لِّلْمُشْرِكِينَ ۝٦﴾ [فُصِّلَت الآية ٦]

"So, remain devoted to Him and seek forgiveness from Him." (Fuṣṣilat 41:6)

Any time a servant of Allāh (ﷻ) errs, he should repent, return to Him, strive to do what is correct, and consistently continue performing righteous deeds - even if they may seem small. That is what a person must do all of the way until one meets the Lord, and is admitted to Paradise out of Allāh's (ﷻ) mercy.

A *ḥadīth* documented by both Imām al-Bukhārī and Imām Muslim (رحمهما الله) mentions that the Messenger of Allāh (ﷺ) said:

«سَدِّدُوا وَقَارِبُوا، وَأَبْشِرُوا، فَإِنَّهُ لَنْ يُدْخِلَ الْجَنَّةَ أَحَدًا عَمَلُهُ» قَالُوا: وَلَا أَنْتَ؟ يَا رَسُولَ اللّٰهِ قَالَ: «وَلَا أَنَا، إِلَّا أَنْ يَتَغَمَّدَنِيَ اللّٰهُ مِنْهُ بِرَحْمَةٍ، وَاعْلَمُوا أَنَّ أَحَبَّ الْعَمَلِ إِلَى اللّٰهِ أَدْوَمُهُ وَإِنْ قَلَّ».

(رواه مسلم)

> "Strive to do all that is correct, strive to come as close as possible to what is best, and receive glad tidings. Furthermore, realize that no individual among you will be admitted to Paradise only because of his deeds." The companions asked, "O Messenger of Allāh, not even you?" He replied, "Not even me, unless Allāh encompasses me with mercy from Himself. You must also realize that among the most beloved deeds to Allāh are the ones performed consistently, even if they may seem small." (Muslim)

It is appropriate for every Muslim, man or woman, to be keen to remember Allāh (ﷻ), and keep their tongue moist with *dhikr* and fill the record of their deeds therewith.

May Allāh (ﷻ) make us among those who remember Him often with a heart-felt remembrance, those who are thankful to Him, and who worship him in the best and most beautiful of ways. *Āmīn.*

طَاعَةُ اللَّهِ خَيْرُ مَا لَزِمَ الْعَبْدُ ۞ فَكُنْ طَائِعًا وَلَا تَعْصِيَنْهُ

مَا هَلَاكُ النُّفُوسِ إِلَّا الْمَعَاصِي ۞ فَتَوَقَّ الْهَلَاكَ لَا تَقْرَبَنْه

إِنَّ شَيْئًا هَلَاكُ نَفْسِكَ فِيهِ ۞ يَنْبَغِي أَنْ تَصُونَ نَفْسَكَ عَنْه

The obedience of Allāh is the best thing which a person can earn.
You should therefore be obedient to Allāh and never disobey him.
It is sins which destroy people.
So, abstain from whatever you have been prohibited from, and never approach it.
If anything entails your destruction, it is your duty to safeguard yourself against it.

KHUṬBAH 44

Pay Attention to Ṣalāt! Pay Attention to Ṣalāt!

In the Noble Qur'ān, Allāh (ﷻ) has clarified to human beings the objectives of His religion. He has also explained to them the laws of His *dīn*.

Allāh (ﷻ) has obligated upon His servants to safeguard, protect, maintain, preserve, uphold and be consistent with the five daily obligatory prayers every single night and day. Allāh (ﷻ) commands us in the Qur'ān:

﴿حَٰفِظُواْ عَلَى ٱلصَّلَوَٰتِ وَٱلصَّلَوٰةِ ٱلْوُسْطَىٰ وَقُومُواْ لِلَّهِ قَٰنِتِينَ ﴿٢٣٨﴾﴾ [البَقَرَة الآية ٢٣٨]

"Strictly guard (maintain with care) your prayers (perform them at their correct times), especially the middle one (the *ʿaṣr ṣalāt*) and stand humbly (obediently and devoutly) before Allāh." (Baqarah 2:238)

Whoever intentionally forsakes the prayers, refuses to offer them on time, and forsakes reciting them or establishing them altogether - they have no share in Islām.

Jābir ibn ʿAbdullāh (رضي الله عنه) quotes the Prophet (ﷺ) as having said:

«إِنَّ بَيْنَ الرَّجُلِ وَبَيْنَ الشِّرْكِ والكُفْرِ، تَرْكَ الصَّلَاةِ».

(رواه مسلم)

"Between a man and associating partners with Allāh and disbelief, there stands his abandonment of the prayers." (Muslim)

It is also narrated from ʿUmar ibn al-Khaṭṭāb (ﷺ) that he said:

«لَا حَظَّ فِي الْإِسْلَامِ لِمَنْ تَرَكَ الصَّلَاةَ».

(السنن الكبرى للبيهقي)

"There is no share in Islām for a person who abandons the prayers." (Sunan al-Kubra al-Bayhaqī)

Abū al-Dardā' (ﷺ) states that my close friend, the Prophet (ﷺ) advised me:

«لَا تُشْرِكْ بِاللَّهِ شَيْئًا، وَإِنْ قُطِّعْتَ وَحُرِّقْتَ ، وَلَا تَتْرُكْ صَلَاةً مَكْتُوبَةً مُتَعَمِّدًا ، فَمَنْ تَرَكَهَا مُتَعَمِّدًا ، فَقَدْ بَرِئَتْ مِنْهُ الذِّمَّةُ ، وَلَا تَشْرَبِ الْخَمْرَ ، فَإِنَّهَا مِفْتَاحُ كُلِّ شَرٍّ » .

(رواه ابن ماجة)

"Do not associate anything with Allāh, even if you are cut and burned. Do not neglect any prescribed prayer deliberately; for whoever neglects it deliberately no longer has the protection of Allāh; and do not drink wine, for it is the key to all evil." (Ibn Mājah)

The scholars are unanimous on the fact that the daily prayers have known and specific times. Each prayer has a beginning time and an end time; and that it is not permissible for a Muslim to pray an obligatory prayer before its due time or to delay it after its time. Allāh (ﷻ) says:

﴿إِنَّ ٱلصَّلَوٰةَ كَانَتْ عَلَى ٱلْمُؤْمِنِينَ كِتَٰبًا مَّوْقُوتًا ﴿١٠٣﴾﴾ [النِّسَاء الآية ١٠٣]

"Indeed, the prayer has been made obligatory for the believers at fixed hours (and can therefore not be brought forward, nor delayed)." (Nisā' 4:103)

ʿAbdullāh ibn Masʿūd (ﷺ) states:

«إِنَّ لِلصَّلَاةِ وَقْتًا كَوَقْتِ الْحَجِّ».

(المعجم الكبير للطبراني)

> "Indeed, the prayer has a set time just like *ḥajj* does." (Al-Muʿjam al-Kabīr of al-Ṭabarānī)

Therefore, just like one cannot perform the *ḥajj* in other than the month of Dhū al-Ḥijjah, nor can one make *'wuqūf'* (standing) in the plains of ʿArafah before or after its time, nor can one make the Friday prayer on a Saturday, similarly one cannot be relaxed regarding the time of the obligatory prayers.

Allāh (ﷻ) has severely warned those who pray but delay the obligatory prayers past its due time and they do not offer it until the time expires. He says in the Qur'ān:

﴿فَوَيْلٌ لِّلْمُصَلِّينَ ۝٤ ٱلَّذِينَ هُمْ عَن صَلَاتِهِمْ سَاهُونَ ۝٥﴾ [الماعون من الآية ٤ الى الآية ٥]

> "So, Woe to those performers of *ṣalāh*, who are neglectful of their *ṣalāh* (who delay their prayers from their stated fixed times)." (Māʿūn 107:4-5)

This is the case of hypocritical Muslims and those with weak faith who pray the day prayers at night, or the night prayers in the day.

They pray based on their desires and not based on the condition for the validity of their acts of worship. They do so out of carelessness, sinfulness, and belittlement of the prayer's rights.

Nawfal ibn Muʿāwiyah (رضي الله عنه) reports the Prophet (ﷺ) as having said:

«مَنْ فَاتَتْهُ الصَّلَاةُ فَكَأَنَّمَا وُتِرَ أَهْلَهُ وَمَالَهُ».

(صحيح ابن حبان)

> "A person who misses the prayer it is as if he has been deprived (robbed) of his family and his wealth." (Sahih Ibn Ḥibbān)

The deprived one mentioned in this *ḥadīth* is a person who has lost a loved one or who had a loved one killed, or all of his wealth was taken, and he could not regain his right nor seek a settlement.

The similarity between the two is that: a person who misses the prayer is afflicted with two agonies - the agony of sin and the agony of losing a great reward; and a deprived person is afflicted with the anguish of confiscation of his wealth and the anguish of seeking a settlement.

Missing prayers as mentioned in the *ḥadīth* means that an individual delays it passed its allowed time without a valid excuse.

Shaykh Ibn Taymīyyah (ﷺ) was asked about a person who deliberately left a single prayer with the intention of making it up after its time - are his actions counted as one of the major sins? He replied:

«نَعَمْ تَأْخِيرُ الصَّلَاةِ عَنْ غَيْرِ وَقْتِهَا الَّذِي يَجِبُ فِعْلُهَا فِيهِ عَمْدًا مِنَ الْكَبَائِرِ».

(مجموع الفتاوى)

"Yes, intentionally delaying the prayer past its obligatory time is from among the major sins." (Majmūʿ al-Fatāwā)

He also said:

«بَلْ قَدْ قَالَ عُمَرُ بْنُ الْخَطَّابِ - رَضِيَ اللَّهُ عَنْهُ - الْجَمْعُ بَيْنَ الصَّلَاتَيْنِ مِنْ غَيْرِ عُذْرٍ مِنَ الْكَبَائِرِ».

(مجموع الفتاوى)

"In fact, ʿUmar ibn al-Khaṭṭāb (رضي الله عنه) said: 'Combining two prayers without a valid excuse is from among the major sins.'" (Majmūʿ al-Fatāwā)

He also adds:

«فَمَنْ فَوَّتَ صَلَاةً وَاحِدَةً عَمْدًا فَقَدْ أَتَى كَبِيرَةً عَظِيمَةً، فَلْيَسْتَدْرِكْ بِمَا أَمْكَنَ مِنْ تَوْبَةٍ وَأَعْمَالٍ صَالِحَةٍ. وَلَوْ قَضَاهَا لَمْ يَكُنْ مُجَرَّدُ الْقَضَاءِ رَافِعًا إِثْمَ مَا فَعَلَ بِإِجْمَاعِ الْمُسْلِمِينَ».

(منهاج السنة النبوية)

> "Whoever intentionally misses a single prayer has committed a major sin. He must make up for that with whatever he can with repentance and good deeds. Even if he was to make it up, merely making it up will not remove the sin of what he did by consensus of the Muslims." (Minhāj al-Sunnah al-Nabawiyya)

Therefore, whoever misses a prayer due to forgetfulness or oversleeping, they must make it up.

A person who was sleeping must make it up when one wakes up, and a person who forgot about reciting a prayer must make it up when one remembers.

The Prophet (ﷺ) said:

«مَنْ نَسِيَ صَلاَةً، أَوْ نَامَ عَنْهَا، فَكَفَّارَتُهُ أَنْ يُصَلِّيَهَا إِذَا ذَكَرَهَا، لاَ كَفَّارَةَ لَهَا إِلاَّ ذَلِكَ».

(متفق عليه)

> "Whoever forgets a prayer or oversleeps, then its expiation is to pray it when one remembers it - there is no other expiation for it." (Agreed Upon)

Among the indications of carelessness is to remain asleep even after the prayer time enters, or to continue sleeping until the time of the prayer expires. If a person is certain that someone will wake them up or one is self-confident that they will wake up to an alarm, then there is no harm.

In addition, a person cannot delay the *ʿaṣr* prayer without a valid excuse to such an extent that the sun begins to turn orange in colour. If one does this then it is a sin according to the strongest opinion. This is because the Prophet (ﷺ) said:

«وَوَقْتُ الْعَصْرِ مَا لَمْ تَصْفَرَّ الشَّمْسُ».

(رواه مسلم)

> "The time for *ʿaṣr* prayer (continues) as long as the sun has not turned yellow (darker yellow and thus becomes pale in colour)." (Muslim)

Concerning the delaying of *ʿaṣr* prayers, Anas ibn Mālik (ﷺ) quotes the Prophet (ﷺ) as having said:

«تِلْكَ صَلَاةُ الْمُنَافِقِينَ، تِلْكَ صَلَاةُ الْمُنَافِقِينَ، تِلْكَ صَلَاةُ الْمُنَافِقِينَ يَجْلِسُ أَحَدُهُمْ حَتَّى إِذَا اصْفَرَّتِ الشَّمْسُ فَكَانَتْ بَيْنَ قَرْنَيْ شَيْطَانٍ، أَوْ عَلَى قَرْنَيِ الشَّيْطَانِ قَامَ فَنَقَرَ أَرْبَعًا لَا يَذْكُرُ اللَّهَ فِيهَا إِلَّا قَلِيلًا».

(سنن أبي داود)

> "This is the prayer of the hypocrites, this is the prayer of the hypocrites, this is the prayer of the hypocrites! One of them sits (delays the ʿAṣr prayers) until the sun becomes orange, and is in between the devil's horns or upon the devil's horns, and then gets up and quickly offers four *rakʿah* (he stands and pecks out four units of prayer) barely remembering Allāh in them except for a little." (Sunan Abū Dāwūd)

If it was permitted to delay the *ʿaṣr* prayer past the point when the sun turns orange, then the Prophet (ﷺ) would not have dispraised this act or considered it a sign of hypocrisy!

The *ʿishā'* prayer should not be delayed past the middle of the night because the Prophet (ﷺ) said:

«وَوَقْتُ الْعِشَاءِ إِلَى نِصْفِ اللَّيْلِ» .

(رواه مسلم)

> "The time for *ʿishā'* is until the middle of the night (the midpoint between sunset and *fajr*." (Muslim)

In addition, whoever recites one complete *rakʿah* with its *rukūʿ* and *sujūd* within the stipulated time before it expires, he has caught the prayer. The Prophet (ﷺ) said:

«مَنْ أَدْرَكَ رَكْعَةً مِنَ الصَّلَاةِ فَقَدْ أَدْرَكَ الصَّلَاةَ».

(متفق عليه)

"Whoever catches one *rakʿah* of a prayer, (in its proper time) he has caught the prayer." (Agreed Upon)

Islām has emphasized performing the *farḍ ṣalāt* (obligatory prayer) at its prescribed time. Therefore, whoever deliberately sets one's alarm past sunrise and is accustomed to not caring to offer the *fajr ṣalāt* on time, or does not adopt the means to wake up on time, for instance, does not sleep early or does not instruct anyone to wake them up, then as a result, they will be sinful due to their negligence; and could be considered like one who purposely abandons the prayer.

As for those whose sleep is heavy, yet they are keen on waking up on time and strive to do so by adopting the means for waking up, then there is no fault upon them if they oversleep because they were not negligent.

Abū Qatādah relates that once he and a group of companions came to the Prophet (ﷺ) and told him they had slept in and missed the prayer. Upon this, the Prophet (ﷺ) said:

ذَكَرُوا لِلنَّبِيِّ ﷺ نَوْمَهُمْ عَنِ الصَّلَاةِ، فَقَالَ: «إِنَّهُ لَيْسَ فِي النَّوْمِ تَفْرِيطٌ، إِنَّمَا التَّفْرِيطُ فِي الْيَقَظَةِ، فَإِذَا نَسِيَ أَحَدُكُمْ صَلَاةً، أَوْ نَامَ عَنْهَا، فَلْيُصَلِّهَا إِذَا ذَكَرَهَا».

(سنن الترمذي)

"There is no deliberate negligence (on the part of an individual) in case he is asleep (and misses the prayer). Negligence occurs when one abandons the prayer (while one is) awake. Therefore, if anyone among you forgets the prayer or sleeps through the time, then he should offer it upon remembering." (Sunan Tirmidhī)

The above shows that the Prophet (ﷺ) explained that a prayer missed due to some compelling situation due to sleep or any other legitimate reason can be offered immediately upon remembering it, and one should try and gain control over the hindrance.

It is for this reason that the Prophet (ﷺ) disliked engaging in useless and futile activities after the *'ishā'* prayers.

Abū Barzah (رضي الله عنه) reports:

«أَنَّ رَسُولَ اللَّهِ ﷺ كَانَ يَكْرَهُ النَّوْمَ قَبْلَ الْعِشَاءِ وَالْحَدِيثَ بَعْدَهَا».

(رواه البخاري)

> "The Prophet (ﷺ) disliked sleeping before *'ishā'* and talking after it." (Bukhārī)

Likewise, it is essential to wake up those who are sleeping so that they can pray on time because this is 'aiding one other in piety and righteousness;' plus this hindrance of sleep can be removed just like a person who is forgetful can be reminded.

A person should wake up one's family with enough time to perform the ritual purification (*wuḍū*) and offer the complete prayer before the sun begins to rise.

Anas ibn Mālik (رضي الله عنه) narrates:

«أَنَّ رَسُولَ اللَّهِ ﷺ كَانَ يَمُرُّ بِبَابِ فَاطِمَةَ سِتَّةَ أَشْهُرٍ إِذَا خَرَجَ إِلَى صَلَاةِ الْفَجْرِ يَقُولُ: الصَّلَاةَ يَا أَهْلَ الْبَيْتِ ﴿إِنَّمَا يُرِيدُ ٱللَّهُ لِيُذْهِبَ عَنكُمُ ٱلرِّجْسَ أَهْلَ ٱلْبَيْتِ وَيُطَهِّرَكُمْ تَطْهِيرًا ﴿٣٣﴾﴾ [الأحزاب الآية ٣٣] ».

(سنن الترمذي)

> "For six months, the Messenger of Allāh (ﷺ) would pass by the door of Fāṭimah when going to the *fajr* prayer and say: '*Al-Ṣalāt*, O household of the Prophet! Allāh only wishes to rid you of (spiritual) filth (such as sin), O members of the household (of the Prophet), and to purify you thoroughly (from all evil). (Aḥzāb 33:33)'" (Sunan Tirmidhī)

Abū Bakrah (ﷺ) relates:

«خَرَجْتُ مَعَ النَّبِيِّ ﷺ لِصَلَاةِ الصُّبْحِ، فَكَانَ لَا يَمُرُّ بِرَجُلٍ إِلَّا نَادَاهُ بِالصَّلَاةِ، أَوْ حَرَّكَهُ بِرِجْلِهِ».

(سنن أبي داود)

"I went out with the Prophet (ﷺ) to pray the *fajr* prayer. Whenever he passed by a sleeping man, he would call him for prayer or nudge him with his foot." (Sunan Abū Dāwūd)

It is mentioned about Ṣalāh al-Dīn al-Ayyubī (ﷺ) that:

وكان صلاح الدين الأيوبي يمر على جنوده فينظر: إن رآهم في قيام الليل وقراءة القرآن وذكر الله قال: « من هنا يأتي النصر »، وإن مر عليهم فوجدهم يمرحون ويلعبون قال: « من هنا تأتي الهزيمة ».

(شرح أصول اعتقاد أهل السنة للالكائي)

Whenever Ṣalāh al-Dīn al-Ayyubī would pass by his troops and find them busy in *ṣalāt*, recitation of the Qur'ān and the remembrance of Allāh, he would say: "Triumph (success) will come from here." But if he passed by his troops and found them busy in amusement and fun he would say: "Failure (defeat) will come from here." (Sharḥ Uṣūl al-Iʿtiqād Ahl as-Sunnah of al-Lālikā'ī)

Imām al-Nawawī (ﷺ) comments and says:

«يُسْتَحَبُّ إِيقَاظُ النَّائِمِ لِلصَّلَاةِ لاسيما إِنْ ضَاقَ وَقْتُهَا لِقَوْلِهِ تَعَالَى: ﴿وَتَعَاوَنُوا۟ عَلَى ٱلْبِرِّ وَٱلتَّقْوَىٰ﴾ [المَائِـدَة الآية ٢] ».

(كتاب المجموع شرح المهذب)

"It is recommended to wake up a sleeping person for the prayer, especially if its time is short (i.e. its time will expire soon), as Allāh says: 'And encourage (one another) in righteousness and piety.' (Mā'idah 5:2)'"

Ḥāfiẓ ibn al-Ḥajr (ﷺ) states:

«فِيهِ اسْتِحْبَابُ إِيقَاظِ النَّائِمِ لِإِدْرَاكِ الصَّلَاةِ، وَلَا يَخْتَصُّ ذَلِكَ بِالْمَفْرُوضَةِ، وَلَا بِخَشْيَةِ خُرُوجِ الْوَقْتِ؛ بَلْ يُشْرَعُ ذَلِكَ لِإِدْرَاكِ الْجَمَاعَةِ، وَإِدْرَاكِ أَوَّلِ الْوَقْتِ وَغَيْرِ ذَلِكَ مِنَ الْمَنْدُوبَاتِ. وقَالَ الْقُرْطُبِيُّ رحمه اللهٰ: وَلَا يَبْعُدُ أَنْ يُقَالَ إِنَّهُ وَاجِبٌ فِي الْوَاجِبِ، مَنْدُوبٌ فِي الْمَنْدُوبِ؛ لِأَنَّ النَّائِمَ وَإِنْ لَمْ يَكُنْ مُكَلَّفًا، لَكِنْ مَانِعُهُ سَرِيعُ الزَّوَالِ، فَهُوَ كَالْغَافِلِ، وَتَنْبِيهُ الْغَافِلِ وَاجِبٌ».

(فتح الباري)

"There is a recommendation for waking up a sleeping person to perform the prayers; and this is not limited to the *farḍ* prayers only,[5] or due to the fear of the time ending. Rather this is prescribed in order to recite the congregational prayers and catch the beginning time, as well as for other recommended acts. Imām Qurṭubī (ﷺ) says: 'It could be said that waking up a sleeping person would be mandatory for a mandatory act, and recommended for a recommended act. Even though a sleeping person is not religiously accountable. However, the cause of impediment is quickly removable, therefore the sleeping person is like an oblivious person and cautioning (alerting) an oblivious person is compulsory.'" (Fatḥ al-Bārī)

[5] The Arabic text of this is as follows:

«كَانَ النَّبِيُّ ﷺ يُصَلِّي صَلَاتَهُ مِنَ اللَّيْلِ كُلَّهَا وَأَنَا مُعْتَرِضَةٌ بَيْنَهُ وَبَيْنَ الْقِبْلَةِ، فَإِذَا أَرَادَ أَنْ يُوتِرَ أَيْقَظَنِي فَأَوْتَرْتُ».

(رواه مسلم)

Young children must also be encouraged to pray even if it is not compulsory upon them so that they get accustomed to it. Allāh (ﷻ) says in the Qur'ān:

﴿وَأۡمُرۡ أَهۡلَكَ بِٱلصَّلَوٰةِ وَٱصۡطَبِرۡ عَلَيۡهَاۖ ١٣٢﴾ [طه الآية ١٣٢]

> "Instruct (encourage) your family to perform *ṣalāt* and (you) yourself (must) remain steadfast on it." (Ṭāhā 20:132)

The Prophet (ﷺ) states:

« مُرُوا أَوْلادَكُمْ بِالصَّلاةِ وَهُمْ أَبْنَاءُ سَبْعِ سِنِينَ ، وَاضْرِبُوهُمْ عَلَيْهَا وَهُمْ أَبْنَاءُ عَشْرٍ ، وَفَرِّقُوا بَيْنَهُمْ فِي الْمَضَاجِعِ ».

(سنن أبي داود)

> "Command your children to perform *ṣalāt* (prayer) when they are seven years old and admonish them for (not offering) it when they are ten, and do not let (boys and girls) sleep together." (Abū Dāwūd)

Additionally, mature children who are engaged in play and amusement whether at home or outside, and as a result typically neglect to offer the prayers or are thoughtless about the importance of prayers causing them to disregard this great act of worship and incur a great sin.

Therefore, it is essential for their guardians to take care of this and it is obligatory upon them to advise them and remind them about this great responsibility.

Imām al-Qurṭubī (رحمه الله) writes that Muqātil (رحمه الله) said:

وَقَالَ مُقَاتِلٌ: «ذَلِكَ حَقٌّ عَلَيْهِ فِي نَفْسِهِ وَوَلَدِهِ وَأَهْلِهِ وَعَبِيدِهِ وَإِمَائِهِ. قَالَ الْكِيَا: فَعَلَيْنَا تَعْلِيمُ أَوْلَادِنَا وَأَهْلِينَا الدِّينَ وَالْخَيْرَ، وَمَا لَا يُسْتَغْنَى عَنْهُ مِنَ الْأَدَبِ. وَهُوَ قَوْلُهُ تَعَالَى: ﴿وَأۡمُرۡ أَهۡلَكَ بِٱلصَّلَوٰةِ وَٱصۡطَبِرۡ عَلَيۡهَاۖ ١٣٢﴾ [طه الآية ١٣٢]. وَنَحْوَ قَوْلِهِ تَعَالَى لِلنَّبِيِّ ﷺ: ﴿وَأَنذِرۡ

عَشِيرَتَكَ ٱلۡأَقۡرَبِينَ ۝﴾ [الشُّعَرَاء الآية ٢١٤]. وَفِي الحَدِيثِ: مُرُوهُمْ بِالصَّلَاةِ وَهُمْ أَبْنَاءُ سَبْعٍ».

(تفسير القرطبي)

"This is a duty that he owes to himself, his children, his family, and his male and female dependents." Alkiyā (🕒) said, "We must teach our children and families religious commitments and goodness, and good manners. This is what Allāh says: 'Instruct (encourage) your family to perform ṣalāt and (you) yourself (must) remain steadfast on it.' (Ṭāhā 20:132)" Allāh also instructed the Prophet (🕒): "Warn your closest relatives." It is mentioned in a ḥadīth: "Command them (children) to pray when they are seven years old." (Tafsīr al-Qurṭubī)

Ibn al-Qayyim (🕒) writes:

«أنه كان ملك كثير المال وكانت له ابنة لم يكن له ولد غيرها، وكان يحبها حباً شديداً. وكان يلهيها بصنوف اللهو. فمكث كذلك زماناً، وكان إلى جانب الملك عابد، فبينا هو ليلة يقرأ إذ رفع صوته وهو يقول:﴿يَٰٓأَيُّهَا ٱلَّذِينَ ءَامَنُواْ قُوٓاْ أَنفُسَكُمۡ وَأَهۡلِيكُمۡ نَارٗا وَقُودُهَا ٱلنَّاسُ وَٱلۡحِجَارَةُ﴾ [التَّحۡرِيم الآية ٦]: فسمعت الجارية قراءته فقالت لجواريها: كفوا. فلم يكفوا وجعل العابد يردد الآية والجارية تقول لهم: كفوا. فلم يكفوا. فوضعت يدها في جيبها فشقت ثيابها فانطلقوا إلى أبيها فأخبروه بالقصة. فأقبل إليها فقال: يا حبيبتي ما حالك منذ الليلة؟ ما يبكيك؟ وضمها إليه. فقالت: أسألك بالله يا أبه، لله عَزَّوَجَلَّ دار فيها نار وقودها الناس والحجارة؟ قال: نعم. قالت: وما يمنعك يا أبه أن تخبرني؟ والله لا أكلت طيباً ولا نمت على لين حتى أعلم أين منزلي في الجنة أو النار؟».

(صفة الصفوة)

> There was a king who had a lot of wealth, and he had a daughter, but no other children. He loved her very much, and he used to let her enjoy all kinds of leisure. This went on for a long time. Beside the king there lived a devoted worshipper, and when he was reciting (the Qur'ān) one night, he raised his voice when he said: "O you who believe! Save yourselves and your families from the Fire (of hell), the fuel of which is people and stones. (Taḥrīm 66:6)" The girl heard his recitation and said to her servants: "Stop!" But they did not stop. The worshipper started to repeat the verse, and the girl kept telling them to stop, but they did not stop. She put her hands to her collar and tore her garment, and the servants went to her father and told him what transpired. He went to her and said: "My dear, what happened to you tonight? What made you weep?" He hugged her. She said: "I ask you by Allāh, O my father, to tell me, does Allāh have a Fire the fuel of which is men and stones?" He replied: "Yes." She asked him: "Why did you not tell me? By Allāh I will not eat any good food or sleep on any soft bed until I know whether my abode is in Paradise or Hell!" (Ṣifat al-Ṣafwah)

Furthermore, if a person missed some prayers, they must make them up in order - especially if they are *Ṣāḥib al-Tartīb.*

A *Ṣāḥib al-Tartīb* is a person who has missed less than six *ṣalāt.* In principle, if a person is *Ṣāḥib al-Tartīb* and he missed a *ṣalāt*, then he must make up the *qaḍā'* of that *ṣalāt* before he performs the next *ṣalāt.* We should all endeavour to become *Ṣāḥib al-Tartīb* in regard to our *ṣalāt.*

The reason a sequential order is required is due to the statement of the Prophet (ﷺ) wherein he said:

«مَنْ نَامَ عَنْ صَلَاةٍ أَوْ نَسِيَهَا، فَلَمْ يَذْكُرْهَا إِلَّا وَهُوَ مَعَ الْإِمَامِ، فَلْيُصَلِّ الَّتِي هُوَ فِيهَا، ثُمَّ لِيُصَلِّ الَّتِي ذَكَرَهَا، ثُمَّ لِيُعِدْ الَّتِي صَلَّى مَعَ الْإِمَامِ».

(نصب الراية)

"Whoever missed a prayer due to sleep or forgetfulness and did not remember it until he was praying with the Imām, he must complete the one he is praying, and then pray the one that he missed, and thereafter repeat the one which he prayed with the Imām!" (Naṣb al-Rāyah)

From this *ḥadīth* the *fuqahā* have concluded that:

«الترتيب بين الفائتة والوقتية وبين الفوائت مستحق، ويسقط بأحد ثلاثة أشياء: ضيق الوقت المستحب في الأصح، والنسيان، وإذا صارت الفوائت ستا غير الوتر فإنه لا يعد مسقطا وإن لزم ترتيبه».

(نور الإيضاح)

To maintain a sequential order between a missed prayer and the current one is necessary. The sequential order is also required between the missed prayers. This order is excused with one of three things:

1) When the desirable part of the prayer time is insufficient, and this the most correct view;
2) Forgetting is an exception to the order, because a person cannot offer something that he cannot remember;
3) The third is when the missed prayers become six not including the *witr*. Verily, the *witr* is not a reason to excuse the order even though one must still perform it in order after the *'ishā'* prayer. (Nūr al-Īḍāḥ)

NOTE: The reason the order is excused when a person misses six prayers is that if one had to repeat them in order, it would burden him, and Islām is opposed to this.

Allāh (ﷻ) states in the Qur'ān:

﴿هُوَ ٱجۡتَبَىٰكُمۡ وَمَا جَعَلَ عَلَيۡكُمۡ فِي ٱلدِّينِ مِنۡ حَرَجٖۚ ٧٨﴾ [الحج الآية ٧٨]

"He has chosen you (to be Muslims in the nation of the best Prophet (ﷺ) and has not placed any hardship (difficulty) upon you in religion (*dīn*)." (Ḥajj 22:78)

Therefore, if a person who is *Ṣāḥib al-Tartīb* prays the current prayer forgetting that he has to make up a prayer, then he should continue his current prayer and he does not have to repeat it in order. If the time for the current prayer becomes too tight then the obligation of maintaining the order in regards to the missed prayers is removed, as he must pray the current prayer on time and then make up his missed prayer afterwards.

It is also of great importance that we not should let our wealth, children, businesses, marketplaces, and houses, etc. distract us from attending the congregational prayers.

We should be keen and enthusiastic for praying on time and taking care of this great trust Allāh (ﷻ) that has given us, especially in the places which have been designated specifically for it such as the *masājid*.

ʿAbdullāh ibn Masʿūd (رضي الله عنه) states:

«مَن سَرَّهُ أَنْ يَلْقَى اللَّهَ غَدًا مُسْلِمًا، فَلْيُحَافِظْ عَلَى هَؤُلَاءِ الصَّلَوَاتِ حَيْثُ يُنَادَى بِهِنَّ، فإِنَّ اللَّهَ شَرَعَ لِنَبِيِّكُمْ ﷺ سُنَنَ الهُدَى، وإِنَّهُنَّ مِن سُنَنَ الهُدَى، وَلَوْ أَنَّكُمْ صَلَّيْتُمْ فِي بُيُوتِكُمْ كما يُصَلِّي هذا المُتَخَلِّفُ فِي بَيْتِهِ، لَتَرَكْتُمْ سُنَّةَ نَبِيِّكُمْ، وَلَوْ تَرَكْتُمْ سُنَّةَ نَبِيِّكُمْ لَضَلَلْتُمْ، وَلَقَدْ رَأَيْتُنَا وَما يَتَخَلَّفُ عَنْهَا إِلَّا مُنَافِقٌ مَعْلُومُ النِّفَاقِ، وَلَقَدْ كانَ الرَّجُلُ يُؤْتَى به يُهَادَى بيْنَ الرَّجُلَيْنِ حتَّى يُقَامَ فِي الصَّفِّ».

(رواه مسلم)

"If anyone would like to meet Allāh tomorrow as a Muslim, then he should persevere in observing the five prayers (in congregation) whenever the call for them is made, for Allāh has chosen for your Prophet (ﷺ) practices of guidance; and the [five prayers in congregation] are part of these practices of guidance. If you were to pray them in your houses, as the one

> who stays behind in his house, then you would be leaving a *Sunnah* of your Prophet (ﷺ). If you leave the *Sunnah* of your Prophet (ﷺ), then you will go astray. Verily, I have seen a time when no one abandoned them [the congregational prayers] except for the hypocrites who were well known for their hypocrisy. A man would be brought, supported by two people [due to his weakness or illness] until he was placed in a row (in the congregation)." (Muslim)

What voice is sweeter and more beautiful than the voice of a *mu'adhin* calling to prayer and making the *adhān*?

فَأَسْمِعِ القلوبَ يا مؤذنُ ۞ فالقلبُ بالصلاة سوف يسكن

وأيقِظِ النُّوَّمَ بالأذان ۞ يا داعي الناس إلى الرحمن

"O mu'adhin let the hearts hear,
For the heart will find peace with the prayer.
Wake up those sleeping O mu'adhin,
O he who calls the people to the Most Merciful."

أُخَيَّ أُخَيَّ، يا من يسمع الأذان ولا يجيب ۞ يا من يتراخى ويتوانى ويتقاعس

يا من يتثاقل ويتشاغل ويتساهل ۞ هذه الأجور تُقَسَّم

وأنتَ في لهوك تغرم وتأثم ۞ هذه مَواطِنُ الزلفى والتكريم والأجور

وأنت في مواطن الشرور والغرور

"My brother, my brother,
O he who hears the adhān and does not answer,
O he who delays and is neglectful,
O he who is too busy and too relaxed,
All these rewards are being distributed,
While you are entertaining yourself gaining debts and sins.
These are the places where one gets close to Allāh and gets honoured and rewarded,
While you are far away in the places of evil and deception."

Let us seriously think for a moment! The one who goes to the *masjid* in the morning or evening - who is he visiting? Whose guest is he? Who is he approaching?

He is in the hospitality of Allāh (ﷻ), the Most Generous, acquiring His benevolence, blessings, and favours.

Abū Hurairah (رضي الله عنه) states:

«مَنْ غَدَا إِلَى الْمَسْجِدِ، أَوْ رَاحَ، أَعَدَّ اللهُ لَهُ فِي الْجَنَّةِ نُزُلًا، كُلَّمَا غَدَا، أَوْ رَاحَ».

(متفق عليه)

"Whoever goes to the *masjid* in the morning or in the evening, Allāh prepares for him a good hospitality in Paradise as often as he goes to the *masjid*, morning or evening." (Agreed Upon)

Just look at what kind of hospitality, honors, blessings and welcome Allāh (ﷻ) prepares for His guests! What a great reward this is! What a great privilege this is!

No one would give up going to the *masjid* after knowing this great reward except for the one who is truly deprived and unlucky.

Let us not be from among those whom the Messenger of Allāh (ﷺ) described in the following *ḥadīth*:

«لاَ يَزَالُ قَوْمٌ يَتَأَخَّرُونَ حَتَّى يُؤَخِّرَهُمُ اللَّهُ عَزَّ وَجَلَّ».

(رواه مسلم)

"If people continue to fall (lag) behind (in acquiring virtues), then Allāh will put them behind." (Muslim)

We ask Allāh (ﷻ) to correct our situations, and protect us all from the deviations of trials and temptations.

May Allāh (ﷻ) keep us steadfast on the true *dīn*, and keep our hearts fully dedicated to Him alone.

KHUṬBAH 45

Ḥayā': The Distinct Moral Standard of Islām

Inviting to high moral standards was one of the most important goals of the mission of the final Prophet (ﷺ).

Imām Aḥmad (ﷺ) in his *Musnad* has recorded a Prophetic narration wherein the Prophet (ﷺ) said:

«إِنَّمَا بُعِثْتُ لِأُتَمِّمَ صَالِحَ الْأَخْلَاقِ».

(مسند أحمد)

> "Indeed, I was sent to complete high moral standards." (Musnad Aḥmad)

High moral standards and belief go hand in hand.

Abū Hurairah (ﷺ) narrates that the Prophet (ﷺ) said:

«أَكْمَلُ الْمُؤْمِنِينَ إِيمَانًا أَحْسَنُهُمْ خُلُقًا».

(رواه أبو داود)

> "The most perfect believer in terms of faith is the one who is the best of them in manners." (Abū Dāwūd)

Īmān gets greater and more perfect with noble high moral standards. Moreover, high moral standards will tip the balance in the hereafter and elevate one's belief to perfection.

Among the high moral standards that are associated with faith is *ḥayā'* (modesty). The less *ḥayā'* one has, the less faith one will have.

Imām al-Ḥākim (ﷺ) in his Mustadrak has reported on the authority of Ibn ʿUmar (ﷺ) that the Prophet (ﷺ) said:

«إِنَّ الْحَيَاءَ وَالْإِيمَانَ قُرِنَا جَمِيعًا، فَإِذَا رُفِعَ أَحَدُهُمَا رُفِعَ الْآخَرُ».

(المستدرك على الصحيحين للحاكم)

"*Ḥayā'* and faith are firmly intertwined. Should one be gone, the other will go as well." (Mustadrak ʿalā al-Ṣaḥīḥḥayn of Imām al-Ḥākim)

Explaining that *ḥayā'* has superiority over all other moral standards, the Prophet (ﷺ) said:

«إِنَّ لِكُلِّ دِينٍ خُلُقًا، وَخُلُقُ الْإِسْلَامِ الْحَيَاءُ».

(سنن ابن ماجه)

"Every religion has a distinct moral standard, and the distinct moral standard of Islām is *ḥayā*." (Sunan Ibn Mājah)

Sālim (ﷺ) narrates from his father (ﷺ) that once the Prophet (ﷺ) heard a man urging his brother to have *ḥayā'* so he said:

«سَمِعَ النَّبِيُّ ﷺ رَجُلًا يَعِظُ أَخَاهُ فِي الْحَيَاءِ، فَقَالَ: إِنَّ الْحَيَاءَ شُعْبَةٌ مِنَ الْإِيمَانِ».

(سنن ابن ماجه)

"Indeed, *ḥayā'* is a branch of faith." (Sunan Ibn Mājah)

The presence of *ḥayā'* will beautify everything, but the absence of it will make everything unpleasant.

The scholars of Islām mention:

«الحياءُ أصلٌ لكلِّ خيرٍ، وهو أفضلُ وأجلُّ الأخلاق، وأعظمُها قدرًا، وأكثرُها نفعًا، ولولا هذا الخُلُق لم يُوفَ بالوعدِ، ولم تُؤدَّ الأمانة، ولم تُقضَ لأحدٍ حاجة، ولا تحرَّى الرجُلُ الجميلَ فآثَره، والقبيحَ فتجنَّبه، ولا ستَرَ له عورَة، ولا امتنعَ عن فاحِشة. وكثيرٌ مِن الناسِ لولا الحياءُ

الذي فيه لم يُؤدِّ شيئًا مِن الأمور المُفترَضَة عليه، ولم يَرعَ لمخلوقٍ حقًّا، ولم يصِل له رَحِمًا، ولا
بَرَّ له والِدًا».

(مفتاح دار السعادة)

> "*Ḥayā'* is the origin of all good - it is the best, the most sublime, the most valuable and the most beneficial of all moral standards. Had it not been for this particular moral standard, no promise would have been kept, no trust would have been rendered, no hand would have been lent in the time of need, no good deed would have been observed, and no bad deed would have avoided. Without it, no faults would have been concealed and no major sins would have been shunned. Were it not for *ḥayā'*, many people would not have carried out any of their responsibilities, and would have hesitated to give others their rights; they would not have maintained their connections with their relatives or showed obedience to their parents." (Miftāḥ Dār al-Saʿādah)

Ḥayā' is derived from the word *ḥayāt* (life). Consequently, *ḥayā'* is an innate characteristic which keeps one ethically and spiritually alive. Just like a body gets its value from being alive, the spirit, soul, character, and person gets their value from having *ḥayā'*. The reality of *ḥayā'* is that it is that trait which motivates a person to do what is good. This same trait discourages an individual from doing anything shameful and immoral. It is the one quality that makes a Muslim distinct from others.

Other words that encompass aspects of *ḥayā'* are:

- bashfulness
- coyness
- diffidence
- modesty
- shame
- shyness
- timidity

There are 2 types of *ḥayā'*:

1. Innate, natural *ḥayā'* that we are all born with due to *fiṭrah* (natural disposition). This type of *ḥayā'* comes from Allāh (ﷻ);
2. Acquired *ḥayā'* from our beliefs, environment, surroundings, etc. This is our code of ethics and comes primarily from our values and environment. If a person cultivates it, then it will make one the best person possible; but if a person's natural *ḥayā'* is destroyed, then it will be difficult for one to acquire this type of *ḥayā'*.

Ḥayā' was the moral standard of all of the Prophets, Messengers, companions, repenters (*tābiʿīn*), and the pious predecessors who followed in their path.

Describing the *ḥayā'* of Prophet Mūsā (ﷺ), the final Prophet (ﷺ) said:

«إِنَّ مُوسَى كَانَ رَجُلاً حَيِيًّا سِتِّيرًا، لاَ يُرَى مِنْ جِلْدِهِ شَيْءٌ اسْتِحْيَاءً مِنْهُ».

(رواه البخاري)

> "Verily Mūsā (ﷺ) was a shy and modest man, who never showed anything of his skin out of extensive shyness." (Bukhārī)

As for our Prophet (ﷺ), he occupied the loftiest ranks of *ḥayā'*.

Describing the *ḥayā'* of the Prophet (ﷺ), Abū Saʿīd al-Khudrī (رضي الله عنه) says:

«كَانَ النَّبِيُّ ﷺ أَشَدَّ حَيَاءً مِنَ العَذْرَاءِ فِي خِدْرِهَا، فَإِذَا رَأَى شَيْئًا يَكْرَهُهُ عَرَفْنَاهُ فِي وَجْهِهِ».

(رواه البخاري)

> "The Prophet (ﷺ) was more bashful than a veiled virgin girl. When he did not like something, we knew it from his face." (Bukhārī)

This means that when he did not like something, he would not talk about it out of *ḥayā'*. Rather, his face would change, and his companions (ﷺ) would understand his aversion to the issue at hand.

Another narration describes the *ḥayā'* of the Prophet (ﷺ) as:

«لَمْ يَكُنِ النَّبِيُّ ﷺ فَاحِشًا وَلاَ مُتَفَحِّشًا».

(رواه البخاري)

"The Prophet (ﷺ) was neither *fāḥish* (a person who uses obscene language to make people laugh), nor *mutafaḥḥish* (a person who habitually uses bad language)." (Bukhārī)

ʿĀ'ishah (ﷺ) narrates that once:

«سَأَلَتِ امْرَأَةٌ النَّبِيَّ ﷺ كَيْفَ تَغْتَسِلُ مِنْ حَيْضَتِهَا؟ قَالَ: فَذَكَرَتْ أَنَّهُ عَلَّمَهَا كَيْفَ تَغْتَسِلُ. ثُمَّ تَأْخُذُ فِرْصَةً مِنْ مِسْكٍ فَتَطَهَّرُ بِهَا. قَالَتْ: كَيْفَ أَتَطَهَّرُ بِهَا؟ قَالَ: تَطَهَّرِي بِهَا سُبْحَانَ اللهِ! وَاسْتَتَرَ - وَأَشَارَ لَنَا سُفْيَانُ بْنُ عُيَيْنَةَ بِيَدِهِ عَلَى وَجْهِهِ - قَالَ: قَالَتْ عَائِشَةُ: وَاجْتَذَبْتُهَا إِلَيَّ وَعَرَفْتُ مَا أَرَادَ النَّبِيُّ ﷺ».

(رواه مسلم)

"A woman asked the Prophet (ﷺ) about how to bathe herself after her menses were over. The Prophet (ﷺ) told her how to do that and added: 'Then, clean yourself with a piece of cloth scented with musk.' The woman asked: 'How shall I clean myself with it?' The Prophet feeling diffident, covered his face, turned away and replied: 'Clean yourself with it, *Subḥān Allāh* (Glory be to Allāh)!'" Sufyān ibn ʿUyaynah gave a demonstration by covering his face as the Prophet (ﷺ) had done. ʿĀ'ishah (ﷺ) says, "I pulled her aside and told her what the Prophet (ﷺ) meant to say." (Muslim)

Once the Prophet (ﷺ) felt shy (for fear that his guest may be offended) to let his guests know that they had overstayed, and had remained busy in conversation among themselves for a long time in his house. So Allāh (ﷻ) revealed the following verse:

﴿فَإِذَا طَعِمْتُمْ فَٱنتَشِرُوا۟ وَلَا مُسْتَـْٔنِسِينَ لِحَدِيثٍ ۚ إِنَّ ذَٰلِكُمْ كَانَ يُؤْذِى ٱلنَّبِىَّ فَيَسْتَحْىِۦ مِنكُمْ ۖ وَٱللَّهُ لَا يَسْتَحْىِۦ مِنَ ٱلْحَقِّ ۚ ﴿٥٣﴾﴾ [الأحزاب الآية ٥٣]

"And disperse (depart) once you have eaten without (remaining behind and) engaging in a (lengthy) conversation. Indeed this (arriving too early and remaining behind afterward) hurts the Prophet (ﷺ), but he is shy of you (out of modesty he does not tell you such that you feel offended). (However), Allāh does not shy away from (avoid) the truth (and makes it clear to everyone without exception)." (Aḥzāb 33:53)

It has been mentioned that on one occasion:

«مَرَّ النَّبِيُّ ﷺ عَلَى رَجُلٍ، وَهُوَ يُعَاتِبُ أَخَاهُ فِي الحَيَاءِ، يَقُولُ: إِنَّكَ لَتَسْتَحْيِي، حَتَّى كَأَنَّهُ يَقُولُ: قَدْ أَضَرَّ بِكَ، فَقَالَ رَسُولُ اللَّهِ ﷺ: دَعْهُ، فَإِنَّ الحَيَاءَ مِنَ الإِيمَانِ».

(رواه البخاري)

The Prophet (ﷺ) passed by a man who was admonishing his brother regarding *ḥayā'* saying: "You are too shy, and I am afraid that might harm you." Upon hearing that, the Prophet (ﷺ) said: "Leave him, for *ḥayā'* is (a part) of faith." (Bukhārī)

It is for this very reason that the Prophet's (ﷺ) companions (رضي الله عنهم) used to instill in their children the noble character of *ḥayā'* and bring them up on it like the Prophet (ﷺ) did with them.

ʿAbdullāh ibn ʿUmar (رضي الله عنهما) was a young boy who used to attend the assemblies of the Messenger of Allāh (ﷺ).

He narrates that once the Prophet (ﷺ) asked:

«إِنَّ مِنَ الشَّجَرِ شَجَرَةً لاَ يَسْقُطُ وَرَقُهَا وَهِيَ مَثَلُ الْمُؤْمِنِ حَدِّثُونِي مَا هِيَ؟ قَالَ عَبْدُ اللهِ: فَوَقَعَ النَّاسُ فِي شَجَرِ الْبَوَادِي وَوَقَعَ فِي نَفْسِي أَنَّهَا النَّخْلَةُ. فَقَالَ النَّبِيُّ ﷺ: هِيَ النَّخْلَةُ فَاسْتَحْيَيْتُ أَنْ أَقُولَ قَالَ عَبْدُ اللهِ: فَحَدَّثْتُ عُمَرَ، بِالَّذِي وَقَعَ فِي نَفْسِي. فَقَالَ: لأَنْ تَكُونَ قُلْتَهَا أَحَبَّ إِلَيَّ مِنْ أَنْ يَكُونَ لِي كَذَا وَكَذَا».

(رواه الترمذي)

"Indeed, there is a tree that does not shed its foliage, and it is similar to the believer. Can any of you tell me what it is?" ʿAbdullāh relates: "The people started thinking about the trees of the desert; and it occurred to me that it could be the date-palm." Then the Prophet (ﷺ) said: "It is the date-palm." But I was shy - meaning to say anything. ʿAbdullāh further adds, "So I informed ʿUmar (رضي الله عنه) about what I had thought about and he said, 'If you had said it, that would have been more beloved to me than this or that.'" (Tirmidhī)

Ḥayā' is also an attribute of Allāh (ﷻ) and one of His names (حَيِيٌّ). The *ḥayā'* of Allāh (ﷻ) is an attribute characterizing the generosity, kindness, benevolence, and sublimity of Allāh (ﷻ). Allāh (ﷻ) is so modest and generous to His servants that if they raise their hands in supplication, He will not turn them away empty-handed. He is too modest to punish those who grow old in Islām.

Once the Prophet (ﷺ) saw a man washing in a public place without a lower garment. So he climbed the pulpit, praised and extolled Allāh (ﷻ) and then said:

«أَنَّ رَسُولَ اللهِ ﷺ رَأَى رَجُلاً يَغْتَسِلُ بِالْبَرَازِ بِلاَ إِزَارٍ، فَصَعِدَ الْمِنْبَرَ، فَحَمِدَ اللهَ وَأَثْنَى عَلَيْهِ، ثُمَّ قَالَ ﷺ: إِنَّ اللهَ عَزَّ وَجَلَّ حَيِيٌّ سِتِّيرٌ يُحِبُّ الْحَيَاءَ وَالسَّتْرَ، فَإِذَا اغْتَسَلَ أَحَدُكُمْ فَلْيَسْتَتِرْ».

(رواه أبو داود)

> "Surely Allāh, the Grand and Magnificent is (*Ḥayīyun*) characterized by modesty and concealment, and He loves modesty and concealment. So, when any of you washes, he should conceal himself." (Abū Dāwūd)

The Prophet (ﷺ) also stated:

«إِنَّ اللَّهَ حَيِيٌّ كَرِيمٌ يَسْتَحِي إِذَا رَفَعَ الرَّجُلُ إِلَيْهِ يَدَيْهِ أَنْ يَرُدَّهُمَا صِفْرًا خَائِبَتَيْنِ».

(رواه الترمذي)

> "Indeed, Allāh is *Ḥayīyun* and Generous, He feels ashamed when someone raises his two hands in *duʿā*, to turn him away empty-handed and frustrated." (Tirmidhī)

Anas (رضي الله عنه) reports that the Prophet (ﷺ) said:

«يَقُولُ اللَّهُ تَبَارَكَ وَتَعَالَى: إِنِّي لَأَسْتَحْيِي مِنْ عَبْدِي وَأَمَتِي يَشِيبَانِ فِي الْإِسْلَامِ، فَتَشِيبُ لِحْيَةُ عَبْدِي وَرَأْسُ أَمَتِي فِي الْإِسْلَامِ أُعَذِّبُهُمَا فِي النَّارِ بَعْدَ ذَلِكَ».

(مسند أبي يعلى الموصلي)

> "Allāh says: 'I feel shy of my male and female servants who have aged in the religion of Islām about punishing them with the hellfire after the fact that my male servant's beard and female servant's hair have turned grey in the religion of Islām.'" (Musnad Abū Yaʿlā al-Mawṣilī)

It has been reported in an *Athar*[6] that Allāh (ﷻ), the Almighty says:

«مَا أَنْصَفَنِي عَبْدِي. يَدْعُونِي فَأَسْتَحْيِي أَنْ أَرُدَّهُ. وَيَعْصِينِي وَلَا يَسْتَحْيِي مِنِّي» .

---

[6] An aṭhar is that which comes from other than the Prophet (ﷺ) such as the Ṣaḥābah, or from the Tābiʿīn, or other than them.

(مدارج السالكين)

> "My servant is not fair to Me. He invokes Me and I am too considerate not to answer his invocation, yet he disobeys Me shamelessly." (Madārij al-Sālkīn)

A true Muslim will be too embarrassed when he feels that the Creator is looking at him and should not hesitate to obey Him, nor forget to thank Him for His graces.

One will avoid being seen where Allāh (ﷻ) has forbidden him to be, and will not be absent from where Allāh (ﷻ) has ordered him to be.

Allāh (ﷻ) deserves to be shown consideration more than anyone else.

It is narrated in the *Makārim al-Akhlāq* of Imām Abū Bakr ibn Abī al-Dunyā (رحمه الله) that a man asked the Prophet (ﷺ):

«إِنَّ رَجُلًا قَالَ: يَا رَسُولَ اللَّهِ، أَوْصِنِي. قَالَ: أُوصِيكَ أَنْ تَسْتَحْيِيَ مِنَ اللَّهِ عَزَّ وَجَلَّ، كَمَا تَسْتَحْيِي رَجُلًا صَالِحًا مِنْ قَوْمِكَ».

(مكارم الأخلاق لابن أبي الدنيا)

> "Give me advice!" The Prophet (ﷺ) replied: "I advise you to show Allāh *ḥayā'* as you do a righteous man of your people." (Makārim al-Akhlāq of Ibn Abī al-Dunyā)

ʿAbdullāh ibn Masʿūd (رضي الله عنه) narrates that the Prophet (ﷺ) said:

«اسْتَحْيُوا مِنَ اللَّهِ حَقَّ الْحَيَاءِ ، قَالَ : قُلْنَا : يَا رَسُولَ اللَّهِ , إِنَّا لَنَسْتَحْيِي وَالْحَمْدُ لِلَّهِ ، قَالَ : لَيْسَ ذَاكَ وَلَكِنَّ الِاسْتِحْيَاءَ مِنَ اللَّهِ حَقَّ الْحَيَاءِ أَنْ تَحْفَظَ الرَّأْسَ وَمَا وَعَى ، وَتَحْفَظَ الْبَطْنَ وَمَا حَوَى ، وَتَتَذَكَّرَ الْمَوْتَ وَالْبِلَى ، وَمَنْ أَرَادَ الْآخِرَةَ تَرَكَ زِينَةَ الدُّنْيَا ، فَمَنْ فَعَلَ ذَلِكَ فَقَدِ اسْتَحْيَا مِنَ اللَّهِ حَقَّ الْحَيَاءِ».

(رواه الترمذي)

> "Have *ḥayā'* for Allāh as is His due." Upon this, the companions (رضي الله عنهم) said: "O Messenger of Allāh! We have *ḥayā'* *Alḥamdulillāh*." The Prophet (ﷺ) replied: "That is not what I mean. Showing Allāh true *ḥayā'* means - to protect the head and what it contains, the stomach and what goes into it, and to remember death and decay. Whoever intends the hereafter abandons the adornments of this worldly life. He who does this will have shown Allāh true *ḥayā'*." (Tirmidhī)

In this comprehensive *ḥadīth*, the Prophet (ﷺ) has highlighted four matters that encompass all forms of good.

To protect the head and what it contains means that one does not prostrate themselves to anyone except to Allāh (ﷻ), nor does a person raise their head in pride regarding Allāh (ﷻ). This also includes protecting one's ears, eyes, and tongue from whatever Allāh (ﷻ) has forbidden.

Allāh (ﷻ) says in the Qur'ān:

﴿وَلَا تَقۡفُ مَا لَيۡسَ لَكَ بِهِۦ عِلۡمٌۚ إِنَّ ٱلسَّمۡعَ وَٱلۡبَصَرَ وَٱلۡفُؤَادَ كُلُّ أُوْلَٰٓئِكَ كَانَ عَنۡهُ مَسۡـُٔولٗا ٣٦﴾ [الإسراء الآية ٣٦]

> "And do not pursue what you have no knowledge about (do not comment on subjects you have no knowledge about or speak about something that has not been verified). Indeed questioning (on the Day of Judgement) shall take place with regards to (what) the ears (heard), (what) the eyes (saw), and (what thoughts and wrong beliefs) the hearts (harboured)." (Isrā' 17:36)

To protect the stomach against the consumption of prohibited foods, and to safeguard the body parts that are related to it, such as the heart, the hands, the private parts, and the feet from committing what is prohibited.

The Prophet (ﷺ) states:

«مَنْ يَضْمَنْ لِي مَا بَيْنَ لَحْيَيْهِ وَمَا بَيْنَ رِجْلَيْهِ أَضْمَنْ لَهُ الْجَنَّةَ».

(رواه البخاري)

> "Whoever gives me a guarantee to safeguard (the chastity of) what is between his legs (i.e. his private parts), and what is between his jaws (i.e. his tongue), I shall guarantee him Paradise." (Bukhārī)

Then, the Prophet (ﷺ) highlighted an additional two significant matters. The Prophet (ﷺ) said:

«وَتَذَكَّرِ الْمَوْتَ وَالْبِلَى ، وَمَنْ أَرَادَ الْآخِرَةَ تَرَكَ زِينَةَ الدُّنْيَا».

(رواه الترمذي)

> "Remember death and decay. Whoever intends the hereafter abandons the adornments of this worldly life." (Tirmidhī)

Undeniably, whoever remembers that one will die and decompose, and will stand before Allāh (ﷻ), and that Allāh (ﷻ) will bring him to account on the Day of Judgement for what he has done in this worldly life, will truly feel ashamed that perhaps he might meet Allāh (ﷻ) on the Day of Judgement with shameful and disgraceful actions.

On one occasion when one of the *tābiʿīn*, Aswad ibn Yazīd (رحمه الله) was on his deathbed, he began weeping excessively. When he was rebuked for doing so, he said:

« وَاللهِ لَوْ أُتِيتُ بِالمَغْفِرَةِ مِنَ اللهِ، لأَهَمَّنِي الحَيَاءُ مِنْهُ مِمَّا قَدْ صَنَعْتُ، إِنَّ الرَّجُلَ لَيَكُوْنُ بَيْنَهُ وَبَيْنَ آخَرَ الذَّنْبُ الصَّغِيْرُ فَيَعْفُو عَنْهُ، فَلاَ يَزَالُ مُسْتَحِياً مِنْهُ».

(سير أعلام النبلاء)

> "I swear by Allāh that even if I was granted forgiveness from Allāh I would be anxious to feel ashamed in front of Him for what I have done. By analogy, a person may forgive another

person’s small offense, but still, the latter continues to feel embarrassed from him.” (Siyar al-ʿAlām al-Nublā)

Having *ḥayā’* is a sign of sublime moral character and a pure mind. It is a rule of conduct with people, a path for good and righteousness, it is happiness and success in this worldly life and the hereafter.

Ḥayā’ was the motto of the pious and the dictate of the righteous ones. However, if a servant of Allāh (ﷻ) insists on sinning and wrongdoing and does not seek repentance, then he will be stripped of *ḥayā’*. As a consequence, whoever is deprived of *ḥayā’* will soon perish, because he will go very far in pursuing his desires, and as a result, his blemishes will surface and good qualities will be buried, and he will become insignificant in the sight of Allāh (ﷻ).

The great scholar of Islām, Abū ʿAbdullāh ibn Abī Bakr (رحمه الله) writes:

«وَالْحَيَاءُ مُشْتَقٌّ مِنَ الْحَيَاةِ، فَمَنْ لَا حَيَاءَ فِيهِ فَهُوَ مَيِّتٌ فِي الدُّنْيَا شَقِيٌّ فِي الْآخِرَةِ، وَبَيْنَ الذُّنُوبِ وَبَيْنَ قِلَّةِ الْحَيَاءِ وَعَدَمِ الْغَيْرَةِ تَلَازُمٌ مِنَ الطَّرَفَيْنِ، وَكُلٌّ مِنْهُمَا يَسْتَدْعِي الْآخَرَ وَيَطْلُبُهُ حَثِيثًا، وَمَنِ اسْتَحَى مِنَ اللَّهِ عِنْدَ مَعْصِيَتِهِ، اسْتَحَى اللَّهُ مِنْ عُقُوبَتِهِ يَوْمَ يَلْقَاهُ، وَمَنْ لَمْ يَسْتَحِ مِنْ مَعْصِيَتِهِ لَمْ يَسْتَحِ اللَّهُ مِنْ عُقُوبَتِهِ».

(الجواب الكافي)

“*Ḥayā’* is derived from *ḥayāt* (life). Therefore, a person who has no *ḥayā* is dead in this worldly life and wretched in the hereafter. For there is no separation between sins, shamelessness, and lack of jealousy - each of which calls for the other. Indeed, whoever feels shy regarding Allāh upon disobeying Him, Allāh will feel shy about punishing him on the Day of Judgement; and whoever does not feel shy regarding Allāh, and disobeys Him, then Allāh will not feel shy about punishing him.” (Al-Jawāb al-Kāfī)

Among the manifestations of shamelessness are the prevalence of obscene words, disgraceful forms of behaviour, immorality, vulgarity, lying, deception, and disrespect for other people's feelings.

Such manifestations are common especially on social media platforms, the internet, etc. which all contribute to creating a pervasive atmosphere of permissiveness.

Another major manifestation of shamelessness is to commit sins and wrongdoings openly and then to brag about them. This is a cause for the lack of spiritual well-being in this life and the hereafter.

The Prophet (ﷺ) states:

«كُلُّ أُمَّتِي مُعَافًى إِلاَّ الْمُجَاهِرِينَ، وَإِنَّ مِنَ الْمَجَانَةِ أَنْ يَعْمَلَ الرَّجُلُ بِاللَّيْلِ عَمَلاً، ثُمَّ يُصْبِحَ وَقَدْ سَتَرَهُ اللَّهُ، فَيَقُولَ يَا فُلاَنُ عَمِلْتُ الْبَارِحَةَ كَذَا وَكَذَا، وَقَدْ بَاتَ يَسْتُرُهُ رَبُّهُ وَيُصْبِحُ يَكْشِفُ سِتْرَ اللَّهِ عَنْهُ».

(رواه البخاري)

"All of the sins of my followers will be forgiven except those of the *Mujāhirīn* (those who commit a sin openly or disclose their sins to people). An example of such disclosure is that a person commits a sin at night and though Allāh screens it from the public, he says in the morning: 'O so-and-so, I did such-and-such (evil) deed yesterday,' though he spent his night screened by his Lord (none knowing about his sin) - in the morning he removes Allāh's screen from himself." (Bukhārī)

There are three things which develop *ḥayā'* in a man's heart regarding Allāh (ﷻ) which are:

1. Glorifying Allāh (ﷻ);
2. Knowing Him;
3. Being conscious that He sees and knows everything.

Accordingly, when a man's heart glorifies Allāh (ﷻ), knows Him and is aware that He knows and sees everything, the heart will then be moved towards *ḥayā'* concerning Allāh (ﷻ).

When *ḥayā'* prevails in a society, then it is the people's morals and ethics which will be elevated to sublimity and nobility. It will spread amongst them good traits, and commendable virtues; and it will bring them only good as the Prophet (ﷺ) has stated:

«الْحَيَاءُ كُلُّهُ خَيْرٌ، وَالْحَيَاءُ لَا يَأْتِي إِلَّا بِخَيْرٍ».

(رواه مسلم)

> "*Ḥayā'* is good altogether, and *ḥayā* does not bring anything except good." (Muslim)

Bushayr ibn Kaʿab (رحمه الله) says:

«مَكْتُوبٌ فِي الْحِكْمَةِ: إِنَّ مِنَ الْحَيَاءِ وَقَارًا، وَإِنَّ مِنَ الْحَيَاءِ سَكِينَةً».

(رواه مسلم)

> "It is written in the books of wisdom that *ḥayā* leads to seriousness (quality of being serious and dignified), and *ḥayā* leads to tranquility (peace of mind)." (Muslim)

يَعِيشُ المَرْءُ ما استحيَى بِخَيرٍ ۞ ويبقى العودُ ما بقيَ اللحاءُ

فلا واللهِ ما في العيشِ خيرٌ ۞ ولا الدُّنيا إذا ذَهبَ الحَياءُ

إذا لم تخشَ عاقبةَ الليالي ۞ ولمْ تستحِي فافعَلْ ما تَشاءُ

A man will live well as long as he is diffident,
In the same way, a twig continues to be,
As long as it is covered by its bark.
By Allāh, there is no good in living,
Nor is there good in this worldly life if diffidence is gone.
If you do not fear the consequence of the nights,
And if you feel no shame, then do as you wish.

KHUṬBAH 46

The Ways of Doing Good

It is an established fact that the people of faith are required to seize opportunities, prepare their provisions for the hereafter, and perform good deeds as long as they are alive.

Allāh (ﷻ) says:

﴿يَٰٓأَيُّهَا ٱلَّذِينَ ءَامَنُواْ ٱرۡكَعُواْ وَٱسۡجُدُواْ وَٱعۡبُدُواْ رَبَّكُمۡ وَٱفۡعَلُواْ ٱلۡخَيۡرَ لَعَلَّكُمۡ تُفۡلِحُونَ ۩ ٧٧﴾ [الحج الآية ٧٧]

> "O people who believe, bow down to your Lord, prostrate to Him, worship Him, and strive to engage in all forms of goodness so that you may attain success." (Ḥajj 22:77)

Therefore, it is only right for us to make the most of the opportunities which we have been given in this life to acquire Allāh's (ﷻ) mercy, favour, and kindness.

The following are some basic guidelines regarding doing what is good and capitalizing on the chance. We hope that Allāh (ﷻ) enables us to benefit from them.

[1] The first guideline is to ensure that doing what is good constantly remains your primary focus. This comes about by always having the intention and firm resolve to do good things. If Allāh (ﷻ) enables you to carry them out, then you will attain the reward of what you did; and if something prevents you from carrying out what you had intended to do then you will attain the reward of what you had intended to perform.

ʿAbdullāh, the son of Imām Aḥmad (ﷺ), once asked his father to advise him. His father replied:

«أَوْصِنِي يا أَبَتِ، فقال؟ يا بُنَيَّ انْوِ الخَيْرَ؛ فَإِنَّكَ لا تَزالُ بِخَيْرٍ ما نَوَيْتَ الخَيْرَ».

(الآداب الشرعية)

"O my son, always intend to do good things. You will continue to be in a good state as long as you intend to do what is good." (Al-Ādāb al-Sharʿīyah)

This is truly a profound piece of advice. If a person abides by it, then one will be rewarded continuously for as long as one's intention remains intact. Even if a person eventually ends up being unable to perform the deed that was intended, one will still be rewarded if the intention was genuine.

Our Prophet (ﷺ) who spoke the truth and received revelation that was the truth said:

«فَمَنْ هَمَّ بِحَسَنَةٍ فَلَمْ يَعْمَلْهَا، كَتَبَهَا اللَّهُ لَهُ عِنْدَهُ حَسَنَةً كَامِلَةً، فَإِنْ هُوَ هَمَّ بِهَا فَعَمِلَهَا، كَتَبَهَا اللَّهُ لَهُ عِنْدَهُ عَشْرَ حَسَنَاتٍ، إِلَى سَبْعِمِائَةِ ضِعْفٍ، إِلَى أَضْعَافٍ كَثِيرَةٍ».

(رواه البخاري)

"If someone intends to perform a righteous deed but ends up unable to perform it, then Allāh will record with Himself a complete righteous deed for that person. If someone intends to perform a righteous deed and follows through with it, then Allāh will record that with Himself for that person - anywhere from ten righteous deeds up to seven hundred, or many times more than that." (Bukhārī)

Furthermore, constantly thinking about what is good, prompts a person to perform righteous deeds, and prepares the provisions from them which one needs.

It is reported that ʿAbdullāh ibn ʿAbbās (ﷺ) said:

«أَنَّ التَّفَكُّرَ يَدْعُو إِلَى الخَيْرِ وَالعَمَلِ بِهِ، وَالنَّدَمَ عَلَى الشَّرِّ يَدْعُو إِلَى تَرْكِهِ».

(إحياء علوم الدين)

"Thinking about what is good will urge one to perform it, and regretting (having deep sorrow for) what is evil, will urge one to avoid (performing) it." (Iḥyā' ʿUlūm al-Dīn)

Consequently, we should strive to occupy our minds with what is good, the rewards that will be earned for those who do good deeds, and the praiseworthy outcome to which they will lead us to.

In addition, one should strive to feel remorse over the wrong actions which they have committed, and that should provide enough deterrent from performing any further sins.

[2] The second guideline is to remain certain that performing good things is what will give a person the provisions that are stored away for him and will benefit him on the Day of Resurrection. None of it goes to waste no matter how large or little it may seem.

Allāh (ﷻ) says in the Qur'ān:

﴿وَمَا يَفْعَلُوا۟ مِنْ خَيْرٍ فَلَن يُكْفَرُوهُ ۗ ١١٥﴾ [آل عِمْرَان الآية ١١٥]

"No matter what good they do, its reward will not go to waste with Allāh." (Āle ʿImrān 3:115)

﴿وَمَا تُقَدِّمُوا۟ لِأَنفُسِكُم مِّنْ خَيْرٍ تَجِدُوهُ عِندَ ٱللَّهِ هُوَ خَيْرًا وَأَعْظَمَ أَجْرًا ۚ 20﴾

[المُزَّمِّل الآية ٢٠]

"And whatever good you send ahead for yourselves; you will find it with Allāh in a better and more rewarding state." (Muzzammil 73:20)

﴿فَمَن يَعْمَلْ مِثْقَالَ ذَرَّةٍ خَيْرًا يَرَهُۥ ٧ وَمَن يَعْمَلْ مِثْقَالَ ذَرَّةٍ شَرًّا يَرَهُۥ ٨﴾

[الزَّلْزَلَة من الآية ٧ الى الآية ٨]

> "So whoever does any good action (even) to the weight of a particle will see it; and whoever does evil (even) to the weight of a particle will see it." (Zalzalah 99:7-8)

Ibn ʿAbbās (ﷺ) commenting on this verse says:

«لَيْسَ مُؤْمِنٌ وَلَا كَافِرٌ عَمِلَ خَيْرًا وَلَا شَرًّا فِي الدُّنْيَا، إِلَّا أَتَاهُ اللَّهُ إِيَّاهُ. فَأَمَّا الْمُؤْمِنُ فَيُرِيهِ حَسَنَاتِهِ وَسَيِّئَاتِهِ، فَيَغْفِرُ اللَّهُ لَهُ سَيِّئَاتِهِ. وَأَمَّا الْكَافِرُ فَيَرُدُّ حَسَنَاتِهِ، وَيُعَذِّبُهُ بِسَيِّئَاتِهِ».

(تفسير الطبري)

> "There is no believer or unbeliever who does anything good or evil in this world except that Allāh, the Most Exalted, will show it to him. The believer will see the good and evil which he did, but he will be pardoned for the evil, and rewarded for the good. The unbeliever will also see the good and evil which he did, but the good will be rejected, and he will be punished for the evil." (Tafsīr al-Ṭabarī)

[3] The third guideline is to remain around goodness for as long as you are in this world, especially during times of special virtue. Goodness is the best company that a person can keep.

Ḥātim al-Aṣam (ﷺ) once remarked:

«ورَأَيْتُ لِكُلِّ رَجُلٍ صَدِيقاً يُفْشِي إِلَيْهِ سِرَّهُ، وَيَشْكُو إِلَيْهِ، فَصَادَقْتُ الخَيْرَ لِيَكُوْنَ مَعِيَ فِي الحِسَابِ، وَيَجُوْزَ مَعِيَ الصِّرَاطَ».

(سير أعلام النبلاء)

> "I found that every person has a companion to whom he discloses what is confidential and to whom he shares his grievances with. I chose to keep goodness as my companion so that it will be with me when I am held to account (for my deeds), and when I have to cross the bridge over the hellfire." (Siyar Aʿlam al-Nubalā')

فَأَكْثِرْ أَخِي دَوْمَاً مِنْ الخَيرِ إِنَّهُ ۞ هُوَ النُّورُ فِي القَبْرِ لِمَنْ مَاتَ يَحْصُلُ

O my brother continually strive to do all of the good that you can since,
It is the light that a person will have in his grave after he passes away.

[4] The fourth guideline is to be a servant of Allāh (ﷻ) who opens the channels to goodness and closes the channels to evils.

The Prophet (ﷺ) explained that people are of two types in this statement:

«إِنَّ مِنَ النَّاسِ مَفَاتِيحَ لِلْخَيْرِ ، مَغَالِيقَ لِلشَّرِّ ، وَإِنَّ مِنَ النَّاسِ مَفَاتِيحَ لِلشَّرِّ ، مَغَالِيقَ لِلْخَيْرِ ؛ فَطُوبَى لِمَنْ جَعَلَ اللَّهُ مَفَاتِيحَ الْخَيْرِ عَلَى يَدَيْهِ ، وَوَيْلٌ لِمَنْ جَعَلَ اللَّهُ مَفَاتِيحَ الشَّرِّ عَلَى يَدَيْهِ».

(سنن ابن ماجه)

> "Indeed, among mankind, there are those who open channels to goodness and close channels to evils, and there are also those who close channels to goodness and open channels to evils. Immense reward awaits those in whose hands Allāh allows goodness to be opened, while ruin awaits those at whose hands Allāh allows evils to be opened." (Sunan Ibn Mājah)

Among the indicators of Allāh (ﷻ) being pleased with His servant is that He enables the individual to open pathways to goodness. When people see such a person, they remember Allāh (ﷻ) because they see that individual constantly involved in doing what is good, saying what is good, thinking about what is good, and striving to have within oneself all that is good. He opens passages to goodness wherever he may be and this is a cause for others around him to do what is good as well.

In contrast, there is the type of person who is constantly involved in doing what is bad, saying what is bad, thinking about what is bad, and striving to have within oneself all that is bad. Such a person is one who opens routes to evils.

Additionally, you must realize that a person's faith cannot come to completion until one loves goodness for others.

The Prophet (ﷺ) has stated:

«لَا يُؤْمِنُ أَحَدُكُمْ حَتَّى يُحِبَّ لِأَخِيهِ مَا يُحِبُّ لِنَفْسِهِ مِنَ الْخَيْرِ».

(سنن النسائي)

"None of you can have complete faith until he loves for his brother the goodness that he loves for himself." (Sunan al-Nasā'ī)

[5] The fifth guideline is to direct others to goodness because doing this, merits tremendous rewards.

The Prophet (ﷺ) said:

«مَنْ دَلَّ عَلَى خَيْرٍ فَلَهُ مِثْلُ أَجْرِ فَاعِلِهِ».

(رواه مسلم)

"If a person directs others to doing what is good, then that individual will attain a reward similar to those who do that good action." (Muslim)

The Prophet (ﷺ) also said:

«إِنَّ الدَّالَّ عَلَى الْخَيْرِ كَفَاعِلِهِ».

(رواه الترمذي)

"Someone who directs others to doing good deeds is like the person who did the good action himself." (Tirmidhī)

The most beneficial things that a person can present to others are: imparting knowledge, offering sincere advice, directing them to do what is good, encouraging them to make the best use of their time, and urging them to seize opportunities to draw nearer to Allāh (ﷻ).

[6] The sixth guideline is to beseech Allāh (ﷻ) to keep you steadfast in adhering to His religion, implore Him to make you someone who constantly obeys Him and observes taqwā, and seek refuge with Him from causing you to regress such that you stop doing good and then become inclined to bad things and end up doing them instead of the good actions.

Abū Dharr (رضي الله عنه) states:

»وَلَا تَيْأَسْ مِنْ رَجُلٍ أَنْ يَكُونَ عَلَى خَيْرٍ فَيَرْجِعَ إِلَى شَرٍّ فَيَمُوتَ بِشَرٍّ، وَلَا تَيْأَسْ مِنْ رَجُلٍ يَكُونُ عَلَى شَرٍّ فَيَرْجِعُ إِلَى خَيْرٍ فَيَمُوتَ بِخَيْرٍ.«

(تاريخ دمشق لابن عساكر)

"Do not think that if a person does good things, then he is immune to regressing to bad things and dying in that state; and do not think that if a person does bad things, then there is no hope of him returning to good things and dying in that state."
(Tārīkh Dimashq by Ibn ʿAsākir)

It is for this very reason that we must take ourselves to account for our shortcomings towards Allāh (ﷻ), and we must implore our Lord to keep us steadfast in pursuing goodness all of the way until we leave this world.

ʿUmar ibn al-Khaṭṭāb (رضي الله عنه) would say:

»حَاسِبُوا أَنْفُسَكُمْ قَبْلَ أَنْ تُحَاسَبُوا، وَزِنُوا أَنْفُسَكُمْ قَبْلَ أَنْ تُوزَنُوا، فَإِنَّهُ أَخَفُّ عَلَيْكُمْ فِي الْحِسَابِ غَدًا أَنْ تُحَاسِبُوا أَنْفُسَكُمُ الْيَوْمَ، وَتَزَيَّنُوا لِلْعَرْضِ الْأَكْبَرِ: ﴿يَوْمَئِذٍ تُعْرَضُونَ لَا تَخْفَى مِنكُمْ خَافِيَةٌ﴾ [الحاقة الآية ١٨].«

(حلية الأولياء وطبقات الأصفياء)

"Take account of yourselves before you are brought to account for; weigh yourselves before you are weighed, for that will make the Reckoning easier for you tomorrow. If you take balance of yourselves today and prepare yourselves for the great presentation on the Day when you will be brought to

Judgement, then not a secret of yours will be hidden." (Ḥilyat al-Awliyā' wa Ṭabaqāt al-Aṣfiyā')

[7] The seventh guideline comes from contemplating the statement of Allāh (ﷻ).

﴿وَمَا تَفْعَلُوا۟ مِنْ خَيْرٍ يَعْلَمْهُ ٱللَّهُ ﴿١٩٧﴾﴾ [البَقَرَة الآية ١٩٧]

"And no matter what good you do, Allāh has complete knowledge of it." (Baqarah 2:197)

Keeping this in mind puts one's soul to rest and brings tranquility to one's heart.

When someone does good to others and is sincere to Allāh (ﷻ) throughout that action, such a person is not looking for them to show him gratitude or appreciation. Rather, when an individual does what is good and remains certain that the Lord will reward him, then he will not be troubled if there are people who rebuff any kindness which he extends.

He calls to mind what Allāh (ﷻ) has said that His righteous servants say within themselves:

﴿إِنَّمَا نُطْعِمُكُمْ لِوَجْهِ ٱللَّهِ لَا نُرِيدُ مِنكُمْ جَزَآءً وَلَا شُكُورًا ﴿٩﴾﴾ [الإنسان الآية ٩]

"We only extend this kindness to you because we seek Allāh's pleasure. It is not our aim to seek any repayment, praise, or gratitude from you." (Insān 76:9)

CONCLUSION

- The term "goodness" is a comprehensive one and it is not confined to any specific realm. It refers to everything that benefits a person in both the short term and the long term.
- We should ensure that we show Allāh (ﷻ) goodness from ourselves during our time in this world, and do not waste any opportunity.

- A discerning person should not neglect to perform righteous deeds or procrastinate about seizing any chance to draw nearer to Allāh (ﷻ).
- On the contrary, he will remain mindful and make amends for whatever has passed.

وَلَا تُرْجِ فِعْلَ الْخَيْرِ يَوْمًا إِلَى غَدٍ ۞ لَعَلَّ غَدًا يَأْتِي وَأَنْتَ فَقِيدُ

Do not put off doing good today until tomorrow.
It may well be that when tomorrow comes, you will no longer be here.

Muʿāwiyah ibn Abī Sufyān (رضي الله عنه) states:

«عَوِّدُوا أَنْفُسَكُمُ الْخَيْرَ فَإِنِّي سَمِعْتُ رَسُولَ اللَّهِ ﷺ يَقُولُ: الْخَيْرُ عَادَةٌ وَالشَّرُّ لَجَاجَةٌ، وَمَنْ يُرِدِ اللَّهُ بِهِ خَيْرًا يُفَقِّهْهُ فِي الدِّينِ».

(مسند الشاميين للطبراني)

"Make yourselves accustomed to good because I have heard the Prophet (ﷺ) say: 'Goodness is a (natural) habit, while evil is an urging (constant poking from Shayṭān). When Allāh wills good for a person, He gives him an understanding of the *dīn*.'" (Musnad al-Shāmiyyīn al-Tabarānī)

- A Muslim should seek to do as much good as he can so that he keeps doing good things until he meets Allāh (ﷻ).
- A Muslim has an obligation of striving to do good at all times in general, but he should also be even more diligent in making optimal use of the time which he has in this world.
- There is no doubt that the goodness of the hereafter is the greatest and most virtuous thing that brings delight to any person of faith and is precisely what one should seek to attain. That is what Allāh (ﷻ) has instructed us to do.

- He has directed us to do our utmost in attaining the virtues that He offers us during the times and opportunities that He grants us.

KHUṬBAH 47

Insight versus Eyesight!

Something every sensible person of faith knows is that there is a difference between eyesight and insight.

Eyesight sees the apparent appearances of things; while insight sees their inner realities. Eyesight takes place by way of the eyes through which a person sees; however, insight takes place by way of the light that Allāh (ﷻ) puts in a person's heart which provides him with guidance. It is by this light that a person can acquire the correct knowledge of Allāh (ﷻ), can distinguish the truth from falsehood, can learn the correct path that one must tread, and come to know about the final destination where people will end up. This is the true difference between the two kinds of sights.

Eyesight is a blessing which a servant of Allāh (ﷻ) must safeguard and not misuse. The directives of Islām teach us to divert our gaze away from that which is prohibited by Allāh (ﷻ), the One who sees all things and is completely acquainted with everything.

Allāh (ﷻ) says in the Qur'ān:

﴿قُل لِّلْمُؤْمِنِينَ يَغُضُّوا۟ مِنْ أَبْصَٰرِهِمْ وَيَحْفَظُوا۟ فُرُوجَهُمْ ۚ ذَٰلِكَ أَزْكَىٰ لَهُمْ ۗ إِنَّ ٱللَّهَ خَبِيرٌۢ
بِمَا يَصْنَعُونَ ﴿٣٠﴾ وَقُل لِّلْمُؤْمِنَٰتِ يَغْضُضْنَ مِنْ أَبْصَٰرِهِنَّ وَيَحْفَظْنَ فُرُوجَهُنَّ ﴿٣١﴾﴾

[النّور من الآية ٣٠ الى الآية ٣١]

"Instruct the believing men to lower their glances and to preserve their chastity. That is purer for them. Allāh is completely acquainted with everything that they do. And instruct the believing women to lower their glances and to preserve their chastity as well." (Nūr 24:30-31)

Additionally, the Prophet (ﷺ) told ʿAlī ibn Abī Ṭālib (ؓ):

»يَا عَلِيُّ لَا تُتْبِعِ النَّظْرَةَ النَّظْرَةَ فَإِنَّ لَكَ الْأُولَى وَلَيْسَتْ لَكَ الْآخِرَةُ«.

(رواه الترمذي)

"O ʿAlī, do not follow one glance with another. The first was for you [since it was unintentional], but the other is not." (Tirmidhī)

Protecting one's eyesight and diverting it from the impermissible will contribute to a person having insight.

The righteous among the *Salaf* would say:

»مَنْ غَضَّ بَصَرُهُ عَنِ الْمَحَارِمِ وَأَمْسَكَ عَنِ الشَّهَوَاتِ، وَعَمَرَ بَاطِنُهُ بِدَوَامِ الْمُرَاقَبَةِ وَظَاهِرَهُ بِاتِّبَاعِ السُّنَّةِ، وَعَوَّدَ نَفْسَهُ أَكْلَ الْحَلَالِ لَمْ تُخْطِئُ فِرَاسَتُهُ«.

(حلية الأولياء)

"When a person keeps his eyes away from the prohibited, refrains from giving in to disobedient desires, maintains himself on the inside by remembering that Allāh is always watching him, maintains himself on the outside by following the *sunnah*, and makes it his constant practice to eat what is permissible, then that person's insight will not be mistaken." (Ḥilyat al-Awliyā')

»إن الإنسان إذا فُتِنَ بالنظر عَمِيَتْ بصيرةُ القلبِ«.

(مدارج السالكين)

"If an individual has been afflicted with the trial of his eyesight by looking at the impermissible, then the insight of his heart will go blind." (Madārij al-Sālikīn)

When Allāh (ﷻ) mentions the narrative about the people to whom Prophet Lūṭ (ﷺ) was sent, and them being afflicted with the trial of committing certain sins, He says afterwards:

﴿إِنَّ فِي ذَٰلِكَ لَآيَٰتٖ لِّلۡمُتَوَسِّمِينَ ٧٥﴾ [الحجر الآية ٧٥]

"Indeed, in this are (clear) signs for those who have (correct) foresight (by this they can understand the severe consequences of those who disobeyed the Prophets.)." (Ḥijr 15:75)

Scholars of *tazkiyyah* (purification of the soul) have mentioned:

«وَاللَّهُ تَعَالَى يَجْزِي الْعَبْدَ عَلَى عَمَلِهِ بِمَا هُوَ مِنْ جِنْسِ عَمَلِهِ فَغَضُّ بَصَرِهِ عَمَّا حَرُمَ يُعَوِّضُهُ اللَّهُ عَلَيْهِ مِنْ جِنْسِهِ بِمَا هُوَ خَيْرٌ مِنْهُ؛ فَيُطْلِقُ نُورَ بَصِيرَتِهِ وَيَفْتَحُ عَلَيْهِ بَابَ الْعِلْمِ وَالْمَعْرِفَةِ وَالْكُشُوفِ وَنَحْوِ ذَلِكَ مِمَّا يَنَالُ بِبَصِيرَةِ الْقَلْبِ».

(مجموع الفتاوى)

"Allāh recompenses His servants with what is similar in nature to the deeds which they perform. When a person averts his eyes from the prohibited, then Allāh grants him a recompense similar in nature and even better than that deed. As a result, Allāh enlightens that person's insight, and opens for him the gates of righteous deeds, knowledge, understanding, and other similar things which are received through the insight of the heart." (Majmūʿ al-Fatāwā)

There are many people who may have sight in both eyes, but their hearts are dark and blind. The eyesight of such people does not truly benefit them because they lack proper insight.

In contrast, there are many people who may not have sight in their eyes, but their hearts are strong, alert, and possess deep insight. Such people are not harmed by lacking eyesight since Allāh (ﷻ) compensates them by blessing them with an enlightened insightful heart.

'Abdullāh ibn 'Abbās (◉) would say after he became blind during his final years:

»إِنْ يَأْخُذِ اللَّهُ مِنْ عَيْنَيَّ نُورَهُمَا، فَفِي لِسَانِي وَسَمْعِي مِنْهُمَا نُورٌ«.

(البداية والنهاية)

"If Allāh has taken the light from my eyes (it does not matter) because I still have an enlightened and insightful speech and hearing." (Al-Bidāyah wa al-Nihāyah)

There is no doubt that the loss of eyesight is a test from Allāh (◉). However, if a person loses his eyesight and bears that with patience, then he has been promised a tremendous reward from Allāh (◉).

Anas ibn Mālik (◉) narrates:

»سَمِعْتُ النَّبِيَّ ﷺ يَقُولُ: إِنَّ اللَّهَ قَالَ: إِذَا ابْتَلَيْتُ عَبْدِي بِحَبِيبَتَيْهِ فَصَبَرَ، عَوَّضْتُهُ مِنْهُمَا الجَنَّةَ. يُرِيدُ: عَيْنَيْهِ«.

(رواه البخاري)

"I heard the Messenger of Allāh (◉) saying that Allāh has said: 'If I test My servant by taking the two things which are beloved to him and he bears that with perseverance, then I will compensate him with Paradise as a result.' That was said in reference to a person's two eyes." (Bukhārī)

However, the true test does not lie in losing eyesight. Rather, it lies in losing insight.

Allāh (◉) says in the Holy Qur'ān:

﴿فَإِنَّهَا لَا تَعْمَى ٱلْأَبْصَٰرُ وَلَٰكِن تَعْمَى ٱلْقُلُوبُ ٱلَّتِي فِي ٱلصُّدُورِ﴾ [الحج الآية ٤٦]

"It is really not the eyes that become blind (which are affected by blindness that destroys one's life in both worlds), but it is the hearts that lie in their chests which become blind (to the truth, causing people to be destroyed in this world, as well as in the next).” (Ḥajj 22:46)

Allāh (ﷻ) has explained to us in the Qur'ān the various consequences of our insight going blind.

He says:

﴿وَمَنْ أَعْرَضَ عَن ذِكْرِى فَإِنَّ لَهُۥ مَعِيشَةً ضَنكًا وَنَحْشُرُهُۥ يَوْمَ ٱلْقِيَـٰمَةِ أَعْمَىٰ ﴿١٢٤﴾﴾

[طه الآية ١٢٤]

“If someone turns away in aversion from My mention and obedience, then he will have a miserable life and We will raise him blind on the Day of Resurrection.” (Ṭāhā 20:124)

Ikrimah (رحمه الله) comments that “We will raise him blind” means:

«قَالَ عِكْرِمَةُ: عُمِّيَ عَلَيْهِ كُلُّ شَيْءٍ إِلَّا جَهَنَّمَ».

(تفسير ابن كثير)

“He will be made blind to everything except Hell.” (Tafsīr Ibn Kathīr)

Further “He will have a miserable life” means:

«{فَإِنَّ لَهُ مَعِيشَةً ضَنْكًا} أَيْ: فِي الدُّنْيَا، فَلَا طُمَأْنِينَةَ لَهُ، وَلَا انْشِرَاحَ لِصَدْرِهِ، بَلْ صَدْرُهُ [ضَيِّقٌ] حَرَجٌ لِضَلَالِهِ، وَإِنْ تَنَعَّمَ ظَاهِرُهُ، وَلَبِسَ مَا شَاءَ وَأَكَلَ مَا شَاءَ، وَسَكَنَ حَيْثُ شَاءَ، فَإِنَّ قلبه مَا لَمْ يَخْلُصْ إِلَى الْيَقِينِ وَالْهُدَى، فَهُوَ فِي قَلَقٍ وَحَيْرَةٍ وَشَكٍّ، فَلَا يَزَالُ فِي رِيبَةٍ يَتَرَدَّدُ. فَهَذَا مِنْ ضَنْكِ الْمَعِيشَةِ».

(تفسير ابن كثير)

“His life will be hard in this world. He will have no tranquillity and no peace. Rather, his chest will be constrained and in difficulty due to his misguidance. Even if he appears to be in comfort outwardly and he wears whatever he likes, eats whatever he likes and lives wherever he wants, he will not be happy. For verily, his heart will not have pure certainty and guidance. He will be in agitation, bewilderment, and doubt. He will always be in confusion and a state of uncertainty. This is from the hardship of life." (Tafsīr Ibn Kathīr)

Without insight, a person has no true worth.

Allāh (ﷻ) says:

﴿وَلَقَدْ ذَرَأْنَا لِجَهَنَّمَ كَثِيرًا مِّنَ ٱلْجِنِّ وَٱلْإِنسِ ۖ لَهُمْ قُلُوبٌ لَّا يَفْقَهُونَ بِهَا وَلَهُمْ أَعْيُنٌ لَّا يُبْصِرُونَ بِهَا وَلَهُمْ ءَاذَانٌ لَّا يَسْمَعُونَ بِهَآ ۚ ﴿١٧٩﴾﴾ [الأعراف الآية ١٧٩]

"Without a doubt, We have created a large number of *jinn* and mankind for Hell. They have hearts with which they cannot understand (the truth), eyes with which they cannot see (the truth), and ears with which they cannot hear (the truth)." (Aʿrāf 7:179)

Without correct insight, a person lives in this world confused, like a blind individual walking along a path without knowing where he is going or how to find his way.

Allāh (ﷻ) says.

﴿أَفَمَن يَمْشِي مُكِبًّا عَلَىٰ وَجْهِهِۦٓ أَهْدَىٰٓ أَمَّن يَمْشِي سَوِيًّا عَلَىٰ صِرَٰطٍ مُّسْتَقِيمٍ ﴿٢٢﴾﴾

[المُلْك الآية ٢٢]

"Is the one who walks head down on his face more guided or the one who walks upright on the straight path?" (Mulk 67:22)

Insight has three levels:

1. The first is insight concerning Allāh's (ﷻ) names and attributes.
2. The second is insight concerning Allāh's (ﷻ) commands and prohibitions.

3. The third is insight concerning Allāh's (ﷻ) promises and warnings.

[1] Insight concerning Allāh's (ﷻ) names and attributes involves a person having correct knowledge about his Lord by way of His names and attributes. This is what enables a servant of Allāh (ﷻ) to remain upon the straight course that the Almighty has prescribed. His Lord is the One whose words are complete in terms of both truth and justice, whose attributes are beyond any sort of comparison with His creatures, whose essence does not resemble anything else, and whose actions encompass all of the creations with justice, wisdom, mercy, and kindness.

All creations and commands belong to Him alone; all blessings and favours belong to Him only; all dominion and praise belong to Him solely; and all glorification and majesty belong to Him.

He is the first and none is before Him; He is the last and none is after Him; He is the highest and none is above Him: He is the nearest and none is nearer than Him. All of His names are those of praise, exaltation, and glorification; all of His attributes are those of perfection; all of His qualities are ones of majesty; and all of His actions are ones of wisdom, mercy, goodness, and fairness.

Everything throughout His creation is evidence of Him and directs everyone who sees it with insight towards Him.

When the Supreme Lord – the only One who deserves all worship – is known, feared as befits Him, hoped in, worshipped, and glorified, then no created being would be exalted to the level of being thought of as all-seeing like Allāh (ﷻ), or feared more than Allāh (ﷻ). Many of the ailments which affect those who traverse their path to Allāh (ﷻ) happen because people themselves lack proper knowledge about Allāh (ﷻ). As a result, they become bold and deal with Allāh (ﷻ) in an unbefitting manner, all in proportion to knowledge that they lack about their Lord, the Most Exalted.

[2] Insight concerning Allāh's (ﷻ) commands and prohibitions involves knowing what Allāh (ﷻ) wants from His servants, knowing what limits He has set and abiding by those directives. This is what enables a person to be steadfast in following the straight path prescribed by Allāh (ﷻ) and in observing *taqwā*. When a person does that, he actualizes what it means to be a worshipping servant of Allāh (ﷻ). There would not be the slightest bit of opposition in his heart towards Allāh's (ﷻ) commands, prohibitions, directives, or decrees. In that way, a person would submit to Allāh's (ﷻ) decrees pertaining to the directives which He has prescribed, as well as His decrees pertaining to His creations.

[3] Insight concerning Allāh's (ﷻ) promises and warnings involves recognizing that Allāh (ﷻ) will hold every individual accountable for all of the good and bad which he has done, whether short-term or long-term. This is part of Allāh (ﷻ) being the Supreme Lord, the One who deserves all worship, the One who is the Most Just, and the One who is the Most- Wise.

Therefore, when a person stands in prayer before Allāh (ﷻ), he should imagine himself on the bridge over the hellfire, leading towards the garden. He should imagine himself between Paradise and the hellfire. He should think about the abode of the hereafter along with all of its details that Allāh (ﷻ) has informed us about, as though he can actually see them, and he should then act in accordance with that knowledge. Insight based on faith will transform an individual and his life overall.

Allāh (ﷻ) says:

﴿أَفَمَن شَرَحَ ٱللَّهُ صَدۡرَهُۥ لِلۡإِسۡلَٰمِ فَهُوَ عَلَىٰ نُورٖ مِّن رَّبِّهِۦۚ ٢٢﴾ [الزمر الآية ٢٢]

"So is the one whose heart Allāh has opened up for Islām, and consequently he proceeds with a light from his Lord. (Can he be equal to the one whose heart is hardened?)" (Zumar 39:22)

﴿أَوَمَن كَانَ مَيْتًا فَأَحْيَيْنَٰهُ وَجَعَلْنَا لَهُۥ نُورًا يَمْشِى بِهِۦ فِى ٱلنَّاسِ كَمَن مَّثَلُهُۥ فِى ٱلظُّلُمَٰتِ لَيْسَ بِخَارِجٍ مِّنْهَا ۚ ﴿١٢٢﴾﴾ [الأنعام الآية ١٢٢]

"Then the one who was dead (in a state of ignorance and rejection of the truth), and We gave him a life, and we established a light (the light of guidance) for him by which he walks among mankind, (is he) like the one whose example is in layers of darkness from which he will not be coming out?" (Anʿām 6:122)

A person granted insight based on faith lives a life of happiness, has full trust in Allāh (ﷻ), in His help, His mercy, and has confidence in His guidance.

The focus of such a person is fulfilling Allāh's (ﷻ) commands and avoiding His prohibitions. His attention is to remain on the straight path that Allāh (ﷻ) prescribed. In the Qur'ān, Allāh (ﷻ) draws our attention to some of His most virtuous servants who were granted insight and lived their entire lives centered on it.

Allāh (ﷻ) says:

﴿وَٱذْكُرْ عِبَٰدَنَآ إِبْرَٰهِيمَ وَإِسْحَٰقَ وَيَعْقُوبَ أُو۟لِى ٱلْأَيْدِى وَٱلْأَبْصَٰرِ ﴿٤٥﴾﴾ [ص الآية ٤٥]

"Remember (also) Our servants: Ibrāhīm, Isḥāq and Yaʿqūb (ﷺ) who were men of strength (skilled and proficient in worldly matters), and of insight (intelligent and possessing keen judgement in matters of the *dīn*)." (Ṣād 38:45)

This refers to insight about Allāh's (ﷻ) religion, which enables one to recognize what is correct. Allāh (ﷻ) granted these Prophets (ﷺ) the strength to obey and worship Him, and to have insight and deep understanding of religion.

CONCLUSION

- The most virtuous people are those with illuminating insight.
- They recognize what is correct based on their evidence, and they see things as they truly are.
- Such individuals are the ones who remain steadfast when doubtful matters appear and when disobedient inclinations arise.
- They remain firm because of the complete certainty that they have, which is what keeps them from wavering when faced with those things that sweep many people away.
- When a person lacks insight and does not try to attain it, one will live in misguidance and remain like those whom Allāh (ﷻ) has rebuked in the Qur'ān.

Allāh (ﷻ) says:

﴿أَفَلَمْ يَسِيرُوا۟ فِى ٱلْأَرْضِ فَتَكُونَ لَهُمْ قُلُوبٌ يَعْقِلُونَ بِهَآ أَوْ ءَاذَانٌ يَسْمَعُونَ بِهَا ۖ فَإِنَّهَا لَا تَعْمَى ٱلْأَبْصَٰرُ وَلَٰكِن تَعْمَى ٱلْقُلُوبُ ٱلَّتِى فِى ٱلصُّدُورِ ۝٤٦﴾ [الحج الآية ٤٦]

"Have the people who reject Allāh not traveled through the earth so that they could use their intellects to think about the end result of the people who were before them, and use their ears to hear about what happened to those people, in order to take heed? True blindness is not that of the eyes; rather it is the hearts in people's chests that go blind." (Ḥajj 22:46)

People of this type do not follow or comply with the truth even when it is right in front of them. On the contrary, they hasten to follow falsehood, adhere to it, and call others to it. However, this is nothing strange since matters for such people are all mixed and confused. They use their own feelings and inclinations as a point of reference.

Allāh (ﷻ) says:

﴿أَفَرَءَيْتَ مَنِ ٱتَّخَذَ إِلَٰهَهُۥ هَوَىٰهُ وَأَضَلَّهُ ٱللَّهُ عَلَىٰ عِلْمٍ وَخَتَمَ عَلَىٰ سَمْعِهِۦ وَقَلْبِهِۦ وَجَعَلَ عَلَىٰ بَصَرِهِۦ غِشَٰوَةً فَمَن يَهْدِيهِ مِنۢ بَعْدِ ٱللَّهِ ۚ أَفَلَا تَذَكَّرُونَ ﴿٢٣﴾﴾ [الجاثية الآية ٢٣]

"Have you not seen the person who makes his own inclinations his object of worship by obeying everything which they tell him to do? Allāh leaves him to stray after he knew the truth but rejected it; and He places a seal over his hearing, his heart and a cover over his sight. Thus, who can guide him after Allāh (left him astray)? Will you not then take heed?" (Jāthiyah 45:23)

Reminding ourselves about the importance of having insight about Allāh's (ﷻ) religion is a crucial matter, especially at times of strife and turmoil. In such circumstances, many people slip after previously doing what was correct, thus losing their steadfastness; and many people end up following various misconceptions and disobedient inclinations without looking for a way out of those pitfalls.

Therefore, if an individual wants goodness and salvation for himself then it is vital for him to strive and attain whatever fosters insight, and to avoid all that extinguishes it.

One of the most important things that cultivate insight is observing the *taqwā* of Allāh (ﷻ) (being mindful of Him at all times) whether one is in private or public.

Allāh (ﷻ) says:

﴿يَٰٓأَيُّهَا ٱلَّذِينَ ءَامَنُوٓا۟ إِن تَتَّقُوا۟ ٱللَّهَ يَجْعَل لَّكُمْ فُرْقَانًا ﴿٢٩﴾﴾ [الأنفال الآية ٢٩]

"O you who believe, when you observe the *taqwā* of Allāh, then He will grant you a criterion by which you (will be able to) distinguish between right and wrong." (Anfāl 8:29)

Ḥāfiẓ ibn Kathīr (رحمه الله) commenting on this verse writes:

«فَإِنَّ مَنِ اتَّقَى اللَّهَ بِفِعْلِ أَوَامِرِهِ وَتَرْكِ زَوَاجِرِهِ، وُفِّقَ لِمَعْرِفَةِ الْحَقِّ مِنَ الْبَاطِلِ، فَكَانَ ذَلِكَ سَبَبَ نَصْرِهِ وَنَجَاتِهِ وَمَخْرَجِهِ مِنْ أُمُورِ الدُّنْيَا، وَسَعَادَتِهِ يَوْمَ الْقِيَامَةِ، وَتَكْفِيرِ ذُنُوبِهِ -وَهُوَ مَحْوُهَا -وَغَفْرُهَا: سَتْرُهَا عَنِ النَّاسِ -سَبَبًا لِنَيْلِ ثَوَابِ اللَّهِ الْجَزِيلِ».

(تفسير ابن كثير)

"Certainly, those who have the *taqwā* of Allāh by obeying what He ordained and abstaining from what He forbade, will be guided to differentiate between the truth and falsehood. This will be a triumph, safety, and a way out for them from the affairs of this life, all the while acquiring happiness in the hereafter. They will also receive forgiveness, thus having their sins erased; and pardon, thus having their sins covered from other people; as well as being directed to a way to gain Allāh's tremendous rewards." (Tafsīr Ibn Kathīr)

The opposite of *taqwā* entails committing sins, being bold towards Allāh (ﷻ) by disobeying Him, and not feeling any sense of shame towards the Almighty. These comprise some of the most significant ways by which insight is extinguished.

Another factor which fosters insight is constantly being engaged in the *dhikr* (remembrance) of Allāh (ﷻ), and to remain in His obedience because that will give life to the heart. The most virtuous form of this is reading, understanding, and contemplating on the Qur'ān. How enlightened a person's insight will be is in direct proportion to that.

In contrast, insight will be extinguished by heedlessness because this relates to the absence of the remembrance and obedience of Allāh (ﷻ), and this will eventually lead to the severest of results.

Allāh (ﷻ) says:

﴿وَلَا تُطِعْ مَنْ أَغْفَلْنَا قَلْبَهُۥ عَن ذِكْرِنَا وَٱتَّبَعَ هَوَىٰهُ وَكَانَ أَمْرُهُۥ فُرُطًا ۝٢٨﴾ [الكهف الآية ٢٨]

"And do not obey one whose heart We have made heedless of Our remembrance, who pursues his (own) passions, and whose (every) affair entails transgressing (by not living within the laws of Allāh)." (Kahf 18:28)

Something else which fosters insight is being displeased when Allāh's (ﷻ) prohibitions are perpetrated, and when the limits that He has prescribed are violated. When that quality decreases in a person, then his insight will also diminish.

If a person feels no displeasure when Allāh's (ﷻ) rights are not being fulfilled, or His prohibitions are perpetrated, then that person's insight will become blinded.

Even greater than all of the aforementioned factors will come when Allāh (ﷻ) grants His servant guidance, and places the light of truth in his heart. That is a blessing from Allāh (ﷻ) which He grants to whomsoever He wills. No one can mislead a person whom Allāh (ﷻ) guides, and no one can guide a person whom Allāh (ﷻ) leaves to stray.

Therefore, it is imperative to ask Allāh (ﷻ) for insight, guidance, piety, and steadfastness. Praying to Him for these things is among the most effective means of gaining insight, being guided to what is correct, and attaining protection from all that is harmful.

The Prophet (ﷺ) would often supplicate:

«اللَّهُمَّ اجْعَلْ فِي قَلْبِي نُورًا، وَاجْعَلْ فِي لِسَانِي نُورًا، وَاجْعَلْ فِي سَمْعِي نُورًا، وَاجْعَلْ فِي بَصَرِي نُورًا، وَاجْعَلْ خَلْفِي نُورًا، وَأَمَامِي نُورًا، وَاجْعَلْ مِنْ فَوْقِي نُورًا، وَمِنْ تَحْتِي نُورًا، اللَّهُمَّ وَأَعْظِمْ لِي نُورًا».

(سنن أبي داود)

"O Allāh, place light in my heart, light in my tongue, light in my hearing, light in my eyesight, light on my right hand, light on my left hand, light in front of me, light behind me, and light below me. O Allāh, give me abundant light." (Sunan Abū Dāwūd)

May Allāh (ﷻ) guide us all on the straight path and prevent us from straying off of it. May He protect us from misguidance and evil temptation; decrease the number of our sins and increase the number of our good deeds. May He purify for us our intentions, increase our wisdom and knowledge, and grant us the good from His endless bounty - both in this life and in the hereafter. May our remembrance of the One Allāh (ﷻ) be constant and perfect.

KHUṬBAH 48

Watch Your Words

Allāh (ﷻ) has honoured human beings with many blessings and has favoured them over many of His other creations in numerous ways. He has distinguished humans with the means of expression by which they can clarify their intents and achieve their objectives.

Allāh (ﷻ) says in the Qur'ān:

﴿ٱلرَّحْمَٰنُ ۝١ عَلَّمَ ٱلْقُرْءَانَ ۝٢ خَلَقَ ٱلْإِنسَٰنَ ۝٣ عَلَّمَهُ ٱلْبَيَانَ ۝٤﴾ [الرَّحْمَن من الآية ١ الى الآية ٤]

"Ar-Raḥmān (The Most Compassionate - Allāh) taught the Qur'ān (to the Prophet (ﷺ) and to mankind, guiding them with it). He created man (and in addition to this favour, He even) taught humans means of articulation and expression." (Ar-Raḥmān 55:1-4)

The ability of self-expression would not have been possible if Allāh (ﷻ) had not granted humans with a tongue which moves to form letters, as well as two lips which are used for articulation.

Allāh (ﷻ) says:

﴿أَلَمْ نَجْعَل لَّهُۥ عَيْنَيْنِ ۝٨ وَلِسَانًا وَشَفَتَيْنِ ۝٩﴾ [البَلَد من الآية ٨ الى الآية ٩]

"Have We not given (humans) two eyes, a tongue, and two lips (for talking and eating)?" (Balad 90:8-9)

An Arabic proverb states:

«مَا الْإِنْسَانُ لَوْلَا اللِّسَانُ إِلَّا صُورَةٌ مُمَثَّلَةٌ، أَوْ بَهِيمَةٌ مُهْمَلَةٌ».

(كتاب المغني)

"Without a tongue, the human being would be nothing more than a lifeless statue or a wild beast." (Kitāb Al-Mughnī)

Therefore, it is crucial for us to recognize the extent of what our tongues can do.

It is the fleshy organ between a person's two jaws which expresses the words that one composes. The tongue is the heart's spokesperson. By the words that people choose to use, they choose the course which they follow – leading themselves to either safety or destruction.

It is for this very reason that the Prophet (ﷺ) said:

«وَهَلْ يَكُبُّ النَّاسَ فِي النَّارِ عَلَى وُجُوهِهِمْ أَوْ عَلَى مَنَاخِرِهِمْ إِلَّا حَصَائِدُ أَلْسِنَتِهِمْ».

(رواه الترمذي)

"Most people will be thrown into the hellfire, face down because of the transgressions of their tongues." (Tirmidhī)

The tongue is a double-edged sword, meaning that if a person uses it properly, then he will achieve praiseworthy results; but if he misuses it, then he will only attain remorse and loss.

Many problems, disputes, hostilities, and severing of ties, etc. that take place are initiated by nothing more than words and slips of the tongue. Just like fires can be ignited from mere twigs, disputes can be ignited from mere words and the irresponsible use of the tongue.

Allāh (ﷻ) instructed the Prophet (ﷺ) by saying:

﴿وَقُل لِّعِبَادِي يَقُولُوا۟ ٱلَّتِي هِيَ أَحْسَنُ ۚ إِنَّ ٱلشَّيْطَٰنَ يَنزَغُ بَيْنَهُمْ ۚ إِنَّ ٱلشَّيْطَٰنَ كَانَ لِلْإِنسَٰنِ عَدُوًّا مُّبِينًا ﴿٥٣﴾﴾ [الإسراء الآية ٥٣]

"And tell My bondsmen (servants) that they should speak what is good (to Muslim and non-Muslim alike). Undoubtedly Shayṭān will (make every attempt to) create friction (trouble) between them (especially by what they will say to each other).

Indeed, Shayṭān is an open enemy to man (and will spare no effort to lead man to hell by causing them to fight against one another)." (Isrā' 17:53)

There is no doubt in the fact that Shayṭān cannot find any opportunity to sow problems between people unless their tongues deviate from saying good things.

Undeniably, actualizing righteousness and *taqwā* in the heart and limbs will not come about unless the tongue continues to say what is correct.

Allāh (ﷻ) tells us:

﴿يَٰٓأَيُّهَا ٱلَّذِينَ ءَامَنُوا۟ ٱتَّقُوا۟ ٱللَّهَ وَقُولُوا۟ قَوْلًا سَدِيدًا ۝٧٠ يُصْلِحْ لَكُمْ أَعْمَٰلَكُمْ وَيَغْفِرْ لَكُمْ ذُنُوبَكُمْ ۝٧١﴾ [الأحزاب من الآية ٧٠ الى الآية ٧١]

"O you who believe! Fear Allāh and speak what is right. (Speak the truth, speak with justice, speak about matters related to *Dīn*, and speak everything good, especially the *dhikr* of Allāh). (If you do this then) Allāh will correct (guide you to perform) your (righteous and good) deeds and forgive your sins." (Aḥzāb 33:70-71)

When a person's mind and religious practices are sound, then it will lead one to constantly be aware of the crucial role that is played by the tongue, as well as the various consequences of one's words that will be for or against him.

A slip of the tongue is far more dangerous than a slip of the foot; and danger lies in the fact that people perceive the tongue to be small, insignificant and unimportant when compared to the rest of the body parts.

Allāh (ﷻ) reminds us about the consequences of our words by saying:

﴿مَّا يَلْفِظُ مِن قَوْلٍ إِلَّا لَدَيْهِ رَقِيبٌ عَتِيدٌ ۝١٨﴾ [ق الآية ١٨]

"Whenever a word escapes (from a person's mouth), there is a guard ready by him. (Meaning that an angel immediately records the good or bad speech)." (Qāf 50:18)

Consider how often, due to mere words of the tongue, lives have been lost, integrities violated, problems created in the family and community, truth twisted into falsehood, and falsehood twisted into truth.

All of this is due to using the tongue in ways that are impermissible and irresponsible, or restraining it from what is befitting. Not only that, but the tongue's dangers and harms take effect more swiftly than its benefits.

The Prophet (ﷺ) states:

«إِنَّ الرَّجُلَ لَيَتَكَلَّمُ بِالْكَلِمَةِ مِنْ رِضْوَانِ اللَّهِ، مَا كَانَ يَظُنُّ أَنْ تَبْلُغَ مَا بَلَغَتْ، يَكْتُبُ اللَّهُ لَهُ بِهَا رِضْوَانَهُ إِلَى يَوْمِ يَلْقَاهُ، وَإِنَّ الرَّجُلَ لَيَتَكَلَّمُ بِالْكَلِمَةِ مِنْ سَخَطِ اللَّهِ، مَا كَانَ يَظُنُّ أَنْ تَبْلُغَ مَا بَلَغَتْ يَكْتُبُ اللَّهُ لَهُ بِهَا سَخَطَهُ إِلَى يَوْمِ يَلْقَاهُ».

(موطأ الإمام مالك)

"Sometimes a person says something good, but he does not realize how far his words will go. Yet it earns him the pleasure of Allāh until the day he will meet Him. On the other hand, sometimes a person says something bad, but he does not realize how far his words will go. Yet it earns him the wrath of Allāh until the day he will meet Him." (Muwaṭṭā' of Imām al-Mālik)

Another *ḥadīth* highlights the same issue in a different way.

«إِذَا أَصْبَحَ ابْنُ آدَمَ فَإِنَّ الأَعْضَاءَ كُلَّهَا تُكَفِّرُ اللِّسَانَ فَتَقُولُ: اتَّقِ اللَّهَ فِينَا فَإِنَّمَا نَحْنُ بِكَ، فَإِنْ اسْتَقَمْتَ اسْتَقَمْنَا وَإِنْ اعْوَجَجْتَ اعْوَجَجْنَا».

(رواه الترمذي)

"Every morning all of the limbs of a person plead with one's tongue: 'Fear Allāh for our sake, for our fate is tied to yours. If

> you follow the straight path then so shall we, but if you go astray then so shall we.'" (Tirmidhī)

With respect to the tongue, there are three types of people:

1. Wise
2. Reckless
3. Ignorant

The first type of people are the wise ones. They are guided by the presence of their mind and also by their adherence to their religion, which restrains them from doing wrong. They know how the tongue can be used to bring honor or cause disgrace. They know that words can be the key to their success or the reason for their downfall. They know what words will cause them to either regret or rejoice. They know that once a person speaks a word, it controls him; whereas if he has not yet said the word, then he controls it. As a result, they take great care and pay special attention to their tongues.

ʿAlī ibn Abī Ṭālib (﵁) says:

«الْكَلَامُ فِي وَثَاقِكَ مَا لَمْ تَتَكَلَّمْ بِهِ، فَإِذَا تَكَلَّمْتَ بِهِ صِرْتَ فِي وَثَاقِهِ، فَاخْزُنْ لِسَانَكَ كَمَا تَخْزُنُ ذَهَبَكَ وَوَرِقَكَ فَرُبَّ كَلِمَةٍ سَلَبَتْ نِعْمَةً وَجَلَبَتْ نِقْمَةً».

(نهج البلاغة)

> "Words are in your control until you have not uttered them, but when you have spoken them out you are under their control. Therefore, guard your tongue as you guard your gold and silver, for often one expression snatches away a blessing and invites punishment." (Nahj al-Balāghah)

The second type of people are the reckless ones. They allow themselves to be led by carelessness, negligence, arrogance, and constant impatience. Deliberation has no meaning to them and there are no words that they consider off-limits. Rather, they use whatever words they want, and leave their tongue to speak without any restraints whatsoever. They give no consideration to the meanings or consequences of what they say.

Words of insult, praise, unity, and division are all equal to them because they have no standards by which they evaluate them. Their words are controlled by their anger, directed by their recklessness, and provoked by their impatience. They only come to their senses once their words have already spread far and wide, but subsequently, it is too late then to express remorse or regret their actions.

Abū Ayyūb al-Anṣārī (ﷺ) reports:

«جَاءَ رَجُلٌ إِلَى النَّبِيِّ ﷺ فَقَالَ: عِظْنِي وَأَوْجِزْ، فَقَالَ: إِذَا قُمْتَ فِي صَلَاتِكَ فَصَلِّ صَلَاةَ مُوَدِّعٍ، وَلَا تَكَلَّمْ بِكَلَامٍ تَعْتَذِرُ مِنْهُ غَدًا، وَاجْمَعِ الْإِيَاسَ مِمَّا فِي يَدَيِ النَّاسِ».

(سنن ابن ماجه)

> "A man came to the Prophet (ﷺ) and asked him: "O Messenger of Allāh, teach me something, but make it concise." The Prophet (ﷺ) said, "When you stand for your prayer, then pray as if you are saying farewell. **Do not say anything for which you must apologize**, and abandon any desire to acquire what other people have." (Sunan Ibn Mājah)

The third type of people are the ignorant ones. When people are unaware about what their tongues can do, they will be negligent about the words that they use. Consequently, they will not be able to differentiate between what is beneficial and what is harmful.

A person who is ignorant in this manner does not understand when to speak and when to remain silent because they lack the knowledge that would enable them to understand; and because of this ignorance, these types of people cause destruction to themselves.

A well know proverb states:

«لَمْ يَبْلُغِ الْأَعْدَاءُ مِنْ جَاهِلٍ، مَا يَبْلُغُ الْجَاهِلُ مِنْ نَفْسِهِ».

(ميزان الاعتدال)

> "Even enemies cannot inflict as much damage upon a person as what his own ignorance can inflict upon him." (Mīzān al-Iʿtidāl)

We must also bear in mind that having a lot to say is not a sign of knowledge. Although speaking does often reflect knowledge, there are times when knowledge is demonstrated by silence.

In fact, there were scholars among the predecessors whose times of silence were almost the same as their times of speech.

Ṭalḥa ibn ʿUbaidullāh (ﷺ) states:

«وافق ركوبي ركوب أحمد بن حنبل في السفينة من غير تعبية، فكان يطيل السكوت فإذا تكلم قال: اللهم أمتنا على الإسلام والسنة».

(تاريخ دمشق لابن عساكر)

> "I happened to embark upon a ship alongside Imām Aḥmad (ﷺ) and (I noticed) that he had long periods of silence, but when he did speak, he would say: 'Oh Allāh cause me to die upon Islām and the *sunnah*!'" (Tārīkh Dimashq by Ibn ʿAsākir)

Simāk ibn Ḥarb (ﷺ) reports:

«قُلْتُ لِجَابِرِ بْنِ سَمُرَةَ: أَكُنْتَ تُجَالِسُ رَسُولَ اللَّهِ ﷺ؟ قَالَ: نَعَمْ، وَكَانَ طَوِيلَ الصَّمْتِ، قَلِيلَ الضَّحِكِ، وَكَانَ أَصْحَابُهُ يَذْكُرُونَ عِنْدَهُ الشِّعْرَ، وَأَشْيَاءَ مِنْ أُمُورِهِمْ، فَيَضْحَكُونَ، وَرُبَّمَا تَبَسَّمَ».

(رواه أحمد)

> "I said to Jābir ibn Samurah (ﷺ): 'Did you used to sit with the Messenger of Allāh (ﷺ)?' He replied: 'Yes! Indeed, He used to be in long periods of silence and would laugh little. His companions used to mention poetry and would discuss their affairs in his presence, and they would laugh, but he would usually smile.'" (Aḥmad)

There are times when silence speaks far louder than words. Silence does not necessarily mean that someone is ignorant about something. Rather, the first thing it means is that there is nothing which deserves being spoken about.

There is no doubt that if a person knows when to remain quiet, then he will know when to speak. Individuals like this are rare gems which are hard to find in environments filled with words that have no real purpose, or are merely spoken loudly just to be heard. It is also worthwhile to keep in mind that a person unleashing one's tongue to speak about everything is blameworthy.

Among the worst of words are those which emanate from the tongue for the sake of show, outdoing others, or deceiving people in general. A person with a tongue who does such things is among the people most despised to Allāh (ﷻ) and His Messenger (ﷺ).

Jābir (رضي الله عنه) relates that the Prophet (ﷺ) said:

«إِنَّ مِنْ أَحَبِّكُمْ إِلَيَّ وَأَقْرَبِكُمْ مِنِّي مَجْلِسًا يَوْمَ القِيَامَةِ أَحَاسِنَكُمْ أَخْلَاقًا، وَإِنَّ أَبْغَضَكُمْ إِلَيَّ وَأَبْعَدَكُمْ مِنِّي مَجْلِسًا يَوْمَ القِيَامَةِ الثَّرْثَارُونَ وَالمُتَشَدِّقُونَ وَالمُتَفَيْهِقُونَ».[7]

(رواه الترمذي)

> "The most despised among you, and those who will be the farthest away from me on the Day of Resurrection are those who speak excessively, try to show off in the way they speak, or who say many things so as to seem important." (Tirmidhī)

Another point to consider is that when someone speaks outside of their area of expertise, then they become an exposed target which people can readily ridicule. Respecting other people's areas of expertise is common sense, and a person should not try to involve themselves in every

[7] The Arabic text of this is as follows:
الثَّرثارُ هو كثيرُ الكلامِ. والمُتشدِّقُ هو المُتطاوِلُ على الناسِ بكلامِه تفاصُحًا وتعظيمًا لنفسِه. والمُتفيهِقُ هو المُتوسِّعُ في كلامِه غُرورًا، وكِبرًا، وإظهارًا لفضلِه على غيرِه.

matter that arises. Rather, they should confine themselves only to what they are proficient in.

When people speak outside of what they know well, then they bring undesirable consequences upon themselves. The tongue of a scholar is not the same as the tongue of a doctor. The tongue of a politician is not the same as the tongue of a *khaṭīb* (orator/preacher/speaker).

Ḥāfiẓ ibn Ḥajr (ﷺ) made a very precise statement by saying:

«ومَن تكلَّمَ فيه غير فنِّه أتَى بالعجَائِبِ».

(فتح الباري)

> "When a person speaks outside of his area of expertise, then he will say many strange things." (Fatḥ al-Bāri)

The Prophet (ﷺ) has mentioned:

ثُمَّ ذَكَرَ الرَّجُلَ يُطِيلُ السَّفَرَ أَشْعَثَ أَغْبَرَ يَمُدُّ يَدَيْهِ إِلَى السَّمَاءِ يَا رَبِّ يَا رَبِّ وَمَطْعَمُهُ حَرَامٌ وَمَشْرَبُهُ حَرَامٌ وَمَلْبَسُهُ حَرَامٌ وَغُذِيَ بِالْحَرَامِ فَأَنَّى يُسْتَجَابُ لِذَلِكَ.

(رواه مسلم)

> "A man who having journeyed far, is disheveled and dusty, and spreads out his hands to the sky saying: 'O my Lord! O my Lord!' but his food is *ḥarām*, his drink is *ḥarām*, his clothing is *ḥarām*, and he has been nourished with *ḥarām*, then how can his supplication be answered?!" (Muslim)

We must also realize that the true danger of a word does not merely lie in its size, rather it lies in the word's meaning. For instance, consider the Arabic word *'uff'* which expresses irritation. It consists of only two letters, but it is an immensely offensive word when used towards one's parents.

Allāh (ﷻ) says:

﴿فَلَا تَقُل لَّهُمَآ أُفٍّ وَلَا تَنْهَرْهُمَا وَقُل لَّهُمَا قَوْلًا كَرِيمًا ﴿٢٣﴾﴾ [الإسراء الآية ٢٣]

"Do not even tell them 'uff!' (You must not let them hear the slightest word which expresses your irritation or anything else that may cause them hurt) and do not rebuke them (even though they may be at fault). (Always) Speak gently to them. (Never raise your voice when speaking to them, speak with respect and never speak to them harshly.)" (Isrā' 17:23)

An Arabic proverb states:

«اللِّسَانُ جِرْمُهُ صَغِيرٌ وَجُرْمُهُ كَبِيرٌ وَكَثِيرٌ».

(مرقاة المفاتيح)

"Although the tongue is small in size, yet its impact (harm) is paramount (detrimental)." (Mirqāt al-Mafātīḥ)

CONCLUSION

- Truly, from among the greatest blessings of Allāh (ﷻ), the tongue is one of His most sophisticated and unique creations of all of the organs in the body.
- A tongue which exercises restraint properly will lead a person to Paradise, whereas a tongue that is reckless will lead a person to Hell.
- A righteous tongue will provide light for a person, whereas a corrupt tongue will bring about darkness.

The Prophet (ﷺ) would supplicate:

«اللهُمَّ اجْعَلْ لِي فِي قَلْبِي نُورًا، وَفِي لِسَانِي نُورًا، وَفِي سَمْعِي نُورًا، وَفِي بَصَرِي نُورًا».

(رواه مسلم)

"O Allāh, place light in my heart, light on my tongue, light in my hearing, and light in my sight." (Muslim)

- Those who do not control their tongues will fall prey to the Shayṭān's influence.

- Every individual must give careful consideration to the words that come out from their tongues.
- We should endeavour to speak positively rather than negatively because many times our words have an impact on certain outcomes. This can be found in the guidance of the Prophet (ﷺ).

Once the Prophet (ﷺ) visited a Bedouin who was ill and said to him:

«أَنَّ النَّبِيَّ ﷺ دَخَلَ عَلَى أَعْرَابِيٍّ يَعُودُهُ ، قَالَ : وَكَانَ النَّبِيُّ ﷺ إِذَا دَخَلَ عَلَى مَرِيضٍ يَعُودُهُ فَقَالَ لَهُ : لاَ بَأْسَ ، طَهُورٌ إِنْ شَاءَ اللَّهُ قَالَ : قُلْتَ : طَهُورٌ ؟ كَلَّا ، بَلْ هِيَ حُمَّى تَفُورُ ، أَوْ تَثُورُ ، عَلَى شَيْخٍ كَبِيرٍ ، تُزِيرُهُ القُبُورَ ، فَقَالَ النَّبِيُّ ﷺ: فَنَعَمْ إِذًا».

(رواه البخاري)

"May no harm come to you. This illness will be a means of purification if Allāh wills." The Bedouin replied: "Purification you say?! On the contrary, this is an intense fever that is blazing upon an old man and it will take him to his grave." The Prophet (ﷺ) replied: "If that is what you wish for yourself, then it will be so." (Bukhārī)

NOTE: Some narrations mention that the man passed away later the same day or the following day.[8]

- The tongue of a Muslim should be a reflection of his society and the people of his faith.
- Other people should only hear from a person constructive advice, true words, and beneficial reminders.

[8] The Arabic text of this is as follows:

عند الطبراني وغيره، فقال -ﷺ: أما إذا أبيت فهي كما تقول وقضاء الله كائن، فما أمسى الأعرابي من الغد إلا ميتًا، وعند الدولابي، فقال -ﷺ: ما قضى الله فهو كائن، فأصبح الأعرابي ميتًا.

- A person should be far from looking for other people's faults, becoming abusive during disagreements, being selective in a biased manner, and having double-standards.
- Furthermore, a person should not remain quiet when it comes to words that yield advantage, show kindness, or fulfill other people's rights.
- A person should not let one's tongue loose concerning matters that are to remain confidential.
- In today's time when people's words, ideas, and thoughts about each other contain much contention, there is nothing better than remaining safe; and if safety in such circumstances could be divided into ten portions, then nine of them lie in remaining silent.

Imām al-Awzāʿī (ﷺ) states:

«الْعَافِيَةُ عَشَرَةُ أَجْزَاءٍ: تِسْعَةُ أَجْزَاءٍ مِنْهَا صَمْتٌ، وَجُزْءٌ مِنْهَا اعْتِزَالُكَ عَنِ النَّاسِ».

(العزلة والانفراد)

"Safety is in ten parts, nine of them are connected to silence, while the tenth is in seclusion from the people." (Al-ʿUzlat wa al-Infirād)

ʿUqbah ibn ʿĀmir (ﷺ) once asked:

«قُلْتُ يَا رَسولَ اللهِ مَا النَّجاةُ؟ قَال: أَمْسِكْ عَلَيْكَ لِسانَكَ، وَلْيَسَعْكَ بَيْتُكَ، وابْكِ عَلَى خَطِيئَتِكَ».

(رواه الترمذي)

"O Messenger of Allāh, how can salvation be achieved?" He replied: "Control your tongue, keep to your house, and weep over your sins." (Tirmidhī)

أَقْلِلْ كَلامَكَ وَاسْتَعِذْ مِنْ شَرِّهِ ۞ إِنَّ البَلاءَ بِبَعْضِهِ مَقْرُونُ

وَاحْفَظْ لِسَانَكَ وَاحْتَفِظْ مِنْ غَيِّه ۞ حَتَّى يَكُونَ كَأَنَّهُ مَسْجُونُ

وَكِّلْ فُؤادَكَ باللِّسَانِ وَقُلْ لَهُ ۞ إِنَّ الكَلامَ عَلَيْكُمَا مَوْزُونُ

Minimize your words and seek refuge from their evil,
As troubles are linked to some of our statements.
Safeguard your tongue and protect it from its destruction,
And keep it as though it is imprisoned.
Connect your inner heart to the tongue and let it know,
That words will be accounted for.

KHUṬBAH 49

Al-ʿĀfiyah [Well-Being]: The Key to All Goodness

The greatest need which the human soul has is the need for Allāh (عزّ وجلّ). Our souls need Allāh (عزّ وجلّ) more than our bodies need food and drink. All matters ultimately lie with Him, and He is the Bestower who has no needs.

Allāh (عزّ وجلّ) says in the Holy Qur'ān:

﴿ ۞ يَٰٓأَيُّهَا ٱلنَّاسُ أَنتُمُ ٱلْفُقَرَآءُ إِلَى ٱللَّهِ ۖ وَٱللَّهُ هُوَ ٱلْغَنِيُّ ٱلْحَمِيدُ ﴿١٥﴾ ﴾ [فاطِر الآية ١٥]

> "O people! You are all beggars (in need) of Allāh (dependent on Him for everything) and (Only) Allāh is independent (not in need of anyone or anything), Most Worthy of Praise." (Fāṭir 35:15)

Allāh (ﷻ) also said:

«يَا عِبَادِي كُلُّكُمْ ضَالٌّ إِلَّا مَنْ هَدَيْتُهُ فَاسْتَهْدُونِي أَهْدِكُمْ، يَا عِبَادِي كُلُّكُمْ جَائِعٌ إِلَّا مَنْ أَطْعَمْتُهُ فَاسْتَطْعِمُونِي أُطْعِمْكُمْ، يَا عِبَادِي كُلُّكُمْ عَارٍ إِلَّا مَنْ كَسَوْتُهُ فَاسْتَكْسُونِي أَكْسُكُمْ».

(رواه مسلم)

> "O My servants, all of you are astray except those whom I guide, so seek guidance from Me and I shall guide you. O My servants, all of you are hungry except those whom I feed, so seek food from Me and I shall feed you. O My servants, all of you are naked except those whom I clothe, so seek clothing from Me and I shall clothe you." (Muslim)

This is why supplicating to Allāh (ﷻ) is an act of worship. We should also take note of the fact that half of Sūrah al-Fātiḥah comprises of supplicating to Allāh (ﷻ).

Furthermore, Prophet Muḥammad (ﷺ) was the most complete individual that there has ever been on the face of this earth, and the most knowledgeable person in regards to Allāh (ﷻ).

Out of all people, the Prophet (ﷺ) had the most reverential fear of Allāh (ﷻ) and observed *taqwā* the most. He had the most honest and eloquent of words as well.

After the speech of Allāh (ﷻ), his words are the best of words and his guidance is the best of guidance. Out of all people, he was the one who most sincerely wanted what was best for other human beings. He did not leave anything that was advantageous for people, without directing them to it. He had the best knowledge about what people needed to ask from their Lord, and what would put all matters in order for them - whether religious or mundane.

The companions (ﷺ) would learn his supplications just like they would learn a Sūrah from the Qur'ān.

Ḥāfiẓ ibn al-Ḥajar (ﷺ) states in his renowned work *Al-Iṣābah fī Tamīz al-Ṣaḥabah* under the biographical account of ʿAbdullāh ibn Hishām (ﷺ) that:

«كَانَ أَصْحَابُ النَّبِيِّ ﷺ، يَتَعَلَّمُونَ هَذَا الدُّعَاءَ إِذَا دَخَلَتِ السَّنَةُ أَوِ الشَّهْرُ: اللَّهُمَّ أَدْخِلْهُ عَلَيْنَا بِالْأَمْنِ، وَالْإِيمَانِ، وَالسَّلَامَةِ، وَالْإِسْلَامِ، وَرِضْوَانٍ مِنَ الرَّحْمَنِ، وَجَوَازٍ مِنَ الشَّيْطَانِ».

(الإصابة في تمييز الصحابة)

> "The companions of the Prophet (ﷺ) would learn supplications (*duʿā*) as they would learn the Qur'ān. If a new month or year came upon them, they would supplicate: 'O Allāh, bring it (this month/new year) upon us with security, faith, safety, Islām, the pleasure of the Compassionate (Allāh), and protection from Shayṭān.'" (Al-Iṣābah fī Tamīz al-Ṣaḥabah)

His supplications and comprehensive words expressed sincere devotion and the worship of Allāh (ﷻ), glorification of Him, and desire for His reward. They also addressed all matters that a person needs in this world and the hereafter. These factors indicate the necessity of using his supplications and contemplating upon their meanings.

We should bear in mind that using other means to invoke Allāh (ﷻ) will result in a loss for a person who does so; let alone using words and formulas that contravene the *sunnah* and guidance of our Prophet (ﷺ).

One of the most notable and authentic supplications from the Prophet (ﷺ) has been collected by Imām Tirmidhī and others in their respective *ḥadīth* works reported on the authority of ʿAbbās ibn ʿAbd al-Muṭṭalib (ﷺ).

He recounts and says:

«قُلْتُ: يَا رَسُولَ اللهِ عَلِّمْنِي شَيْئًا أَسْأَلُهُ اللَّهَ عَزَّ وَجَلَّ، قَالَ: سَلِ اللَّهَ العَافِيَةَ، فَمَكَثْتُ أَيَّامًا ثُمَّ جِئْتُ فَقُلْتُ: يَا رَسُولَ اللهِ عَلِّمْنِي شَيْئًا أَسْأَلُهُ اللَّهَ، فَقَالَ لِي: يَا عَبَّاسُ يَا عَمَّ رَسُولِ اللهِ، سَلِ اللَّهَ، العَافِيَةَ فِي الدُّنْيَا وَالآخِرَةِ».

(رواه الترمذي)

> "I once said: 'O Messenger of Allāh, teach me something that I may ask Allāh for.' The Messenger (ﷺ) replied: 'Ask Allāh for well-being.' So I waited for a few days and I went to him again and asked: 'O Messenger of Allāh, teach me something that I may ask Allāh for.' He (ﷺ) said to me, 'O ʿAbbās, O uncle of Allāh's Messenger, you should ask Allāh for well-being in this world and the hereafter.'" (Tirmidhī)

This is a truly outstanding supplication which the Prophet (ﷺ) taught his uncle, ʿAbbās (ﷺ). The Prophet (ﷺ) used to treat his uncle as his own father. The fact that he taught him the aforementioned supplication after being asked more than once shows that no other supplication has the same merit, and no other statement can take its place when making *duʿā* to Allāh (ﷻ).

This *ḥadīth* encourages people to make this *duʿā* consistently, and there are approximately fifty narrations which show that the Prophet (ﷺ) would pray for well-being, either in wording or in meaning. This is because if a person has well-being in this world and the hereafter, then he will attain the utmost objective that can be pursued. Having well-being is the key to acquiring a livelihood, blessings, happiness, and all goodness in general. Without well-being one's life will become unpleasant. The blessing of well-being can only be fully valued by someone who has lost it at some point in any matter, whether religious or mundane.

This is why the Prophet (ﷺ) said:

«سَلُوا اللَّهَ الْعَافِيَةَ، فَإِنَّهُ لَمْ يُعْطَ عَبْدٌ شَيْئًا أَفْضَلَ مِنَ الْعَافِيَةِ».

(مسند أحمد)

"Ask Allāh for well-being. A person cannot be granted anything better than well-being." (Musnad Aḥmad)

The greatest form of well-being is protection from sins, and being guided to repentance. This entails Allāh (ﷻ) concealing the wrong doings that a person commits.

Abū Hurairah (رضي الله عنه) states:

«سَمِعْتُ رَسُولَ اللَّهِ ﷺ يَقُولُ: كُلُّ أُمَّتِي مُعَافًى إِلَّا الْمُجَاهِرِينَ».[9]

(رواه البخاري)

"I heard the Prophet (ﷺ) say: 'All of my *ummah* will be granted well-being except for those who are openly sinners.'" (Bukhārī)

Consequently, when people sin openly, they will be deprived of well-being. Deprivation of well-being is among the worst of misfortunes, and the Messenger of Allāh (ﷺ) would seek refuge with Allāh (ﷻ) from that.

The Prophet (ﷺ) would supplicate:

«كَانَ مِنْ دُعَاءِ رَسُولِ اللهِ ﷺ: اللهُمَّ إِنِّي أَعُوذُ بِكَ مِنْ زَوَالِ نِعْمَتِكَ، وَتَحَوُّلِ عَافِيَتِكَ، وَفُجَاءَةِ نِقْمَتِكَ، وَجَمِيعِ سَخَطِكَ».

(رواه مسلم)

[9] The Arabic text of this is as follows:

(معافى) بضم الميم وفتح الفاء مقصورًا اسم مفعول من العافية أي يعفى عن ذنبهم ولا يؤاخذون به (إلا المجاهرون) بكسر الهاء إلا المعلنون بالفسق

"O Allāh, I seek refuge with You from the disappearance of Your blessings, change in the well-being that You have granted me, Your punishment overtaking me suddenly, and from all forms of Your anger." (Muslim)

Allāh (ﷻ) is the One who grants people well-being and hides their faults. However, the unfortunate people are those ones who do not seek to bring about a change within themselves.

Allāh (ﷻ) says in the Qur'ān:

﴿إِنَّ ٱللَّهَ لَا يُغَيِّرُ مَا بِقَوْمٍ حَتَّىٰ يُغَيِّرُواْ مَا بِأَنفُسِهِمْۗ ١١﴾ [الرَّعْد الآية ١١]

"Surely Allāh will not change the condition of a people until they change their own condition." (Raʿd 13:11)

Another form of well-being is that a person does not owe anyone anything, and meets Allāh (ﷻ) without there being any claim against them in relation to the dignity or property of others.

A man once wrote to ʿAbdullāh ibn ʿUmar (رضي الله عنهما) and asked him to write back all of the knowledge that there is. So ʿAbdullāh ibn ʿUmar (رضي الله عنهما) wrote back the following:

«كَتَبَ رَجُلٌ إِلَى ابْنِ عُمَرَ : أَنِ اكْتُبْ إِلَيَّ بِالْعِلْمِ كُلِّهِ ، فَكَتَبَ إِلَيْهِ ابْنُ عُمَرَ : إِنَّ الْعِلْمَ كَثِيرٌ ، وَلَكِنْ إِنِ اسْتَطَعْتَ أَنْ تَلْقَى اللَّهَ خَفِيفَ الظَّهْرِ مِنْ دِمَاءِ النَّاسِ ، خَمِيصَ الْبَطْنِ مِنْ أَمْوَالِهِمْ ، كَافًّا لِسَانَكَ عَنْ أَعْرَاضِهِمْ ، لَازِمًا لِأَمْرِ جَمَاعَتِهِمْ فَافْعَلْ ، وَالسَّلَامُ».

(تاريخ دمشق لابن عساكر)

"Knowledge is a lot. However, if you are able to meet Allāh without shedding the blood of people, without consuming their property, without insulting their integrity, and ensuring that you adhere to their *jamāʿah* (when they agree on a matter then it is incumbent to follow them), then those are the things which you must do. Wassalām." (Tārīkh Dimashq by Ibn ʿAsākir)

With the advancement of modern technology and people's dependence on social media, etc. in our time, we should ask ourselves how often is caution exercised when it comes to the integrity of others?

The only person who can remain safe is the one whom Allāh (ﷻ) safeguards, and there is nothing better than being protected, safe and remaining blameless of any wrongdoings towards the integrity of others.

Allāh (ﷻ) says:

﴿لَّوْلَآ إِذْ سَمِعْتُمُوهُ ظَنَّ ٱلْمُؤْمِنُونَ وَٱلْمُؤْمِنَٰتُ بِأَنفُسِهِمْ خَيْرًا وَقَالُوا۟ هَٰذَآ إِفْكٌ مُّبِينٌ ﴿١٢﴾ [النّور الآية ١٢]

"Why, when you heard it, did not the believing men and the believing women think good of one another and say: 'This is an obvious falsehood!'" (Nūr 24:12)

﴿وَلَوْلَآ إِذْ سَمِعْتُمُوهُ قُلْتُم مَّا يَكُونُ لَنَآ أَن نَّتَكَلَّمَ بِهَٰذَا سُبْحَٰنَكَ هَٰذَا بُهْتَٰنٌ عَظِيمٌ ﴿١٦﴾ [النّور الآية ١٦]

"And why did you not, when you heard it, say: 'It is not right for us to speak of this. Glory be to You (O Allāh) this is a great lie.'" (Nūr 24:16)

Another form of well-being is protection from the effects of *fitnah* (dissension, discord, disharmony), and from being involved in strife by way of even half-a-word after having already been protected by Allāh (ﷻ).

Miqdād ibn al-Aswad (رضي الله عنه) narrates:

«إِنَّ السَّعِيدَ لَمَنْ جُنِّبَ الْفِتَنَ، إِنَّ السَّعِيدَ لَمَنْ جُنِّبَ الْفِتَنِ، إِنَّ السَّعِيدَ لَمَنْ جُنِّبَ الْفِتَنُ، وَلَمَنْ ابْتُلِيَ فَصَبَرَ فَوَاهًا».

(رواه أبو داود)

> "I swear by Allāh that I heard the Messenger of Allāh (ﷺ) say: 'A fortunate person is the one who is kept away (safe) from dissension. A fortunate person is the one who is kept away from dissension. A fortunate person is the one who is kept away from dissension, and it is amazing for someone who is afflicted yet shows endurance.'" (Abū Dāwūd)

Therefore, it would be completely imprudent for anyone to bring about discord after Allāh (ﷻ) protects one from it, or to involve oneself in dissension after the Almighty grants a person well-being, or to play an active role in spreading doubts and defiant inclinations, or to expose oneself or one's society to harm after Allāh (ﷻ) has covered one with well-being.

Allāh (ﷻ) says in the Qur'ān:

﴿وَمَن يُبَدِّلْ نِعْمَةَ ٱللَّهِ مِنۢ بَعْدِ مَا جَآءَتْهُ فَإِنَّ ٱللَّهَ شَدِيدُ ٱلْعِقَابِ ٢١١﴾ [البَقَرَة الآية ٢١١]

> "And whoever changes the favour of Allāh after it has come to him, then surely Allāh is severe in retribution." (Baqarah 2:211)

Another form of well-being pertains to safety, peace, the blessing of freedom and stability of one's country.

The Prophet (ﷺ) states:

«لاَ تَتَمَنَّوْا لِقَاءَ الْعَدُوِّ، وَسَلُوا اللَّهَ الْعَافِيَةَ».

(رواه مسلم)

> "Do not wish for an encounter with the adversary. Rather, ask Allāh for well-being (safety)." (Muslim)

That well-being includes living with fellow citizens in a state of mutual love, friendliness, compassion, understanding, sympathy, adhering to noble values, and righteous principles. It also includes cooperating with one another for the good and betterment of one's country; as well as caring and protecting one's country from evil and harm.

Another form of well-being is for a person to reach the morning with his family and dwelling safe, his health intact, and having provisions for the day. When that happens, it is as if the entire world has been gathered together for him.

This is why the Prophet (ﷺ) said:

«مَنْ أَصْبَحَ مِنْكُمْ آمِنًا فِي سِرْبِهِ، مُعَافًى فِي جَسَدِهِ، عِنْدَهُ قُوتُ يَوْمِهِ، فَكَأَنَّمَا حِيزَتْ لَهُ الدُّنْيَا».

(رواه الترمذي)

> "Whoever among you wakes up in the morning secure in his household, free from physical illness, and having enough food for his day, it is as if he possesses the whole world." (Tirmidhī)

Therefore, every morning we should supplicate to Allāh (ﷻ) for well-being by using the *duʿā* which was narrated by ʿAbdullāh ibn ʿUmar (رضي الله عنهما). He reports that when the Messenger of Allāh (ﷺ) reached the latter part of the day, as well as the beginning of the day, he would not neglect to say:

« اللَّهُمَّ إِنِّي أَسْأَلُكَ الْعَافِيَةَ فِي الدُّنْيَا وَالْآخِرَةِ ، اللَّهُمَّ إِنِّي أَسْأَلُكَ الْعَفْوَ وَالْعَافِيَةَ فِي دِينِي وَدُنْيَايَ وَأَهْلِي وَمَالِي ، اللَّهُمَّ اسْتُرْ عَوْرَتِي ، وَقَالَ عُثْمَانُ : عَوْرَاتِي وَآمِنْ رَوْعَاتِي ، اللَّهُمَّ احْفَظْنِي مِنْ بَيْنِ يَدَيَّ ، وَمِنْ خَلْفِي ، وَعَنْ يَمِينِي ، وَعَنْ شِمَالِي ، وَمِنْ فَوْقِي ، وَأَعُوذُ بِعَظَمَتِكَ أَنْ أُغْتَالَ مِنْ تَحْتِي قَالَ أَبُو دَاوُدَ : قَالَ وَكِيعٌ يَعْنِي الْخَسْفَ».[10]

(رواه أبو داود)

> "O Allāh, I implore You to pardon me and grant me well-being in this world and the hereafter. O Allāh, I implore You to

[10] The Arabic text of this is as follows:
(قَالَ وَكِيعٌ يعني الخسف) أي يريد النبي بِالِاغْتِيَالِ مِنَ الْجِهَةِ التَّحْتَانِيَّةِ الْخَسْفَ قَالَ فِي الْقَامُوسِ خَسَفَ اللَّهُ بِفُلَانٍ الْأَرْضَ غَيَّبَهُ فِيهَا

> pardon me and grant me well-being in my religion, my worldly affairs, my family, and my property. O Allāh, conceal my faults and calm my fears. O Allāh, protect me from the front, from behind, on my right, on my left, and from above, and I seek refuge in Your Greatness from being suddenly afflicted from beneath myself." Abū Dāwūd (رحمه الله) states: "Wakīʿ (رحمه الله) said, that is to say, being swallowed by the earth." (Abū Dāwūd)

We should memorize this supplication and teach it to our families as well.

Once Ziyād ibn Abī Sufyān (رحمه الله) asked his companions:

«مَن أنعَمُ النَّاسِ عَيشًا؟، قالوا: أنت أيها الأميرُ، قال: لا، ولكنَّه رجُلٌ مُسلِمٌ له زَوجةٌ مُسلِمة، لهما كَفافٌ مِن عيشٍ، قد رضِيَت به ورضِيَ بها، لا يعرِفُنا ولا نعرِفُه».

(العقد الفريد)

> "Who has the nicest life?" They replied: "Our leader, you do." He said: "That is not the case. Rather, it is a man who is a Muslim, has a Muslim wife, and the two of them have the minimum that they need to live; plus she is pleased with him, and he is pleased with her; he does not know us, and we do not know him." (Al-ʿAqd al-Farīd)

Another one of the remarkable supplications of the Prophet (ﷺ) has been recorded by Imām Aḥmad (رحمه الله) in his *Musnad.*

Busr ibn Arṭāh (رضي الله عنه) narrates that he heard the Messenger of Allāh (ﷺ) supplicate:

« اللَّهُمَّ أَحْسِنْ عَاقِبَتَنَا فِي الْأُمُورِ كُلِّهَا، وَأَجِرْنَا مِنْ خِزْيِ الدُّنْيَا، وَعَذَابِ الْآخِرَةِ».

(مسند أحمد)

"O Allāh, grant us the best outcome in all matters, and protect us from disgrace in this world and punishment in the hereafter." (Aḥmad)

The words of this supplication show admission of one's own inability, as well as the necessity of delegating matters to Allāh (ﷻ). He is the One who knows all things, whereas we do not. He is the One who is able to do all things, whereas we are not. He has knowledge of all things that are unseen to us.

Throughout the course of each day and night, a person does not know the outcome of things which he embarks upon. He can start something, but he does not know how things will end. This applies to matters that are both religious and mundane. Therefore, we need to ask Allāh (ﷻ) for the best outcome in every single thing.

Something we may have tried to avoid might actually bring us happiness in the end, while something else we may have hoped for might make us feel regret in the end. However, if Allāh (ﷻ) grants us the best outcome, then we will constantly find guidance and success during our life in this world, as well as in the hereafter. Allāh (ﷻ) will save us from disgrace in this world and from the punishment in the hereafter.

We have to ask Allāh (ﷻ) for the best outcome in all matters, and that includes asking for steadfastness in adhering to our religion, as well as asking to be protected from going astray.

We need to constantly supplicate to Allāh (ﷻ) by saying:

﴿رَبَّنَا لَا تُزِغْ قُلُوبَنَا بَعْدَ إِذْ هَدَيْتَنَا وَهَبْ لَنَا مِن لَّدُنكَ رَحْمَةً ۚ إِنَّكَ أَنتَ ٱلْوَهَّابُ ۝٨﴾ [آل عِمْرَان الآية ٨]

"Our Lord, do not cause our hearts to stray after You have guided us. Grant us Your mercy (O turner of hearts, keep my heart steadfast on your *dīn*) for verily You are the Great Giver" (of all things). (Āle ʿImrān 3:8)

Another one of the incredible supplications that was made by the Prophet (ﷺ) has been recorded by Imām Muslim in his *Ṣaḥīḥ*.

Abū Hurairah (رضي الله عنه) narrates that the Messenger of Allāh (ﷺ) used to supplicate by saying:

« اللَّهُمَّ أَصْلِحْ لِي دِينِي الَّذِي هُوَ عِصْمَةُ أَمْرِي، وَأَصْلِحْ لِي دُنْيَايَ الَّتِي فِيهَا مَعَاشِي، وَأَصْلِحْ لِي آخِرَتِي الَّتِي فِيهَا مَعَادِي، وَاجْعَلِ الْحَيَاةَ زِيَادَةً لِي فِي كُلِّ خَيْرٍ، وَاجْعَلِ الْمَوْتَ رَاحَةً لِي مِنْ كُلِّ شَرٍّ ».

(رواه مسلم)

> "O Allāh, rectify my religion for me, which is what I hold onto for protection. Rectify my worldly life for me, which contains my livelihood. Rectify my hereafter for me, which will be my final abode. Make life for me an increase in all good things, and make death for me relief from all evil things." (Muslim)

This splendid supplication contains five points which set all things right for a person, whether religious or mundane, and whether they pertain to this world or the hereafter. When mundane matters are put in order, but religious ones are not, then that state is not one which is soundly rectified. Building upon a foundation in which values have been demolished will not provide any benefit. Life in this world is nothing more than a mechanism for establishing the religion of Allāh (ﷻ).

Similarly, when religious matters are put in order, but mundane ones are not given any importance and the livelihood of people is neglected or lacking, then that state is also not one which is completely correct.

True order, rectification, and well-being come about when Allāh (ﷻ) rectifies a person's religion and worldly life. His religion is what he holds onto for protection, and his worldly life is what contains his livelihood. On top of that, full refinement will come about when Allāh (ﷻ) also rectifies the hereafter for a person, which will be everyone's final abode. This will enable a person to be admitted into Paradise and protect one from the hellfire.

Allāh (ﷻ) says in the Qur'ān:

﴿فَمَن زُحۡزِحَ عَنِ ٱلنَّارِ وَأُدۡخِلَ ٱلۡجَنَّةَ فَقَدۡ فَازَۗ وَمَا ٱلۡحَيَوٰةُ ٱلدُّنۡيَآ إِلَّا مَتَٰعُ ٱلۡغُرُورِ ١٨٥﴾ [آل عِمۡرَان الآية ١٨٥]

"Whoever is saved from the fire (of hell) and entered into Paradise shall truly be successful. The life of this world is merely an enjoyment (of place, wealth, etc) of deception (but after a limited period of enjoyment, it will come to an end)." (Āle ʿImrān 3:185)

From this, it can be understood that it is necessary for us to pursue all of the means which lead to the well-being of our religious and mundane matters, and it is also necessary to eliminate any channels that serve to corrupt them.

Islām's perspective of religion and this world is one of moderation and justice. This is well-defined by the statement of Allāh (ﷻ) which says:

﴿وَكَذَٰلِكَ جَعَلۡنَٰكُمۡ أُمَّةٗ وَسَطٗا ١٤٣﴾ [البَقَرَة الآية ١٤٣]

"And We have made you [the nation of the Prophet (ﷺ)] an *ummah* of moderation." (Baqarah 2:143)

Islām does not advocate monasticism. Rather, it balances between religious and mundane, between the *masjid* and the marketplace, and between the *muṣḥaf* (worship) and livelihood.

Allāh (ﷻ) says in the Qur'ān:

﴿فَٱمۡشُواْ فِي مَنَاكِبِهَا وَكُلُواْ مِن رِّزۡقِهِۦۖ وَإِلَيۡهِ ٱلنُّشُورُ ١٥﴾ [المُلۡك الآية ١٥]

"Therefore, you are free to travel throughout all parts of the earth and eat from the wholesome provisions which Allāh has granted you. To Him alone, you will be resurrected." (Mulk 67:15)

﴿فَإِذَا قُضِيَتِ ٱلصَّلَوٰةُ فَٱنتَشِرُواْ فِى ٱلْأَرْضِ وَٱبْتَغُواْ مِن فَضْلِ ٱللَّهِ وَٱذْكُرُواْ ٱللَّهَ كَثِيرًا لَّعَلَّكُمْ تُفْلِحُونَ ۝﴾ [الجُمُعَة الآية ١٠]

"And when the prayer has been concluded, disperse within the land and seek from the bounty of Allāh, and remember Allāh often that you may succeed." (Jumuʿah 62:10)

Yet another splendid supplication of the Prophet (ﷺ) can be found in a *ḥadīth* that has been recorded by Imām Aḥmad (rahimahullah) in his *Musnad* from Shaddād ibn Aws (radiyallahu 'anhu). He narrates:

«وَاحْفَظُوا مِنِّي مَا أَقُولُ لَكُمْ: سَمِعْتُ رَسُولَ اللهِ ﷺ يَقُولُ: إِذَا كَنَزَ النَّاسُ الذَّهَبَ وَالْفِضَّةَ، فَاكْنِزُوا هَؤُلَاءِ الْكَلِمَاتِ: اللهُمَّ إِنِّي أَسْأَلُكَ الثَّبَاتَ فِي الْأَمْرِ، وَالْعَزِيمَةَ عَلَى الرُّشْدِ، وَأَسْأَلُكَ شُكْرَ نِعْمَتِكَ، وَأَسْأَلُكَ حُسْنَ عِبَادَتِكَ، وَأَسْأَلُكَ قَلْبًا سَلِيمًا، وَأَسْأَلُكَ لِسَانًا صَادِقًا، وَأَسْأَلُكَ مِنْ خَيْرِ مَا تَعْلَمُ، وَأَعُوذُ بِكَ مِنْ شَرِّ مَا تَعْلَمُ، وَأَسْتَغْفِرُكَ لِمَا تَعْلَمُ، إِنَّكَ أَنْتَ عَلَّامُ الْغُيُوبِ».

(مسند أحمد)

"Remember what I am going to say for I have heard the Messenger of Allāh (ﷺ) saying: 'If people store up gold and silver as treasure for themselves, the following words are what you need to store up as treasure for yourself - O Allāh, I earnestly ask You for steadfastness in all matters, and strong resolve with sound direction. I ask You for all of the factors which will allow me to attain Your mercy and Your forgiveness. I ask You to allow me to be grateful for Your blessings and to perfect Your worship. I ask You for a sound heart and a truthful tongue. I ask You for the good of all that You know, and I seek refuge in You from the evil of all that You know, and I ask Your forgiveness for all that You know. Indeed, You have full knowledge of all things unseen.'" (Musnad Aḥmad)

This supplication is an incredible treasure which deserves to be learned and preserved, mainly because it is something which remains and does not deplete.

Allāh (ﷻ) says:

﴿ٱلۡمَالُ وَٱلۡبَنُونَ زِينَةُ ٱلۡحَيَوٰةِ ٱلدُّنۡيَاۖ وَٱلۡبَٰقِيَٰتُ ٱلصَّٰلِحَٰتُ خَيۡرٌ عِندَ رَبِّكَ ثَوَابٗا وَخَيۡرٌ أَمَلٗا ۝٤٦﴾ [الكهف الآية ٤٦]

"Wealth and children are the adornments of the life of this world. But the good righteous deeds (five compulsory prayers, deeds of Allāh's obedience, good and nice talk, remembrance of Allāh with glorification, praises, and thanks, etc.) that will last, are better with your Lord for rewards and better in respect of hope." (Kahf 18:46)

In this supplication, the Prophet (ﷺ) combined a multitude of good things.

He began by asking for steadfastness in his religion, steadfastness throughout life, steadfastness at the time of death, and steadfastness while crossing the bridge of *Ṣirāṭ* - which will be a time when people's feet will slip. A person's steadfastness upon the bridge of *Ṣirāṭ* on the Day of Resurrection will be proportional to his steadfastness upon the straight path in this world.

He then asked Allāh (ﷻ) for strong resolve with sound direction. This entails the desire to do what is right, diligence in following through, and perseverance while doing so.

If a person realizes that many people are diverted from the truth and the desire to do right is weak, then he will realize how great his need is to make this supplication.

May Allāh (ﷻ) grant us the best outcome in all of our matters, and protect us from disgrace in this world, and the punishments in the hereafter. Āmīn.

ما زلَّ من طلبَ السلامةَ إنها ۞ للمرءِ حِصنٌ في الصُّرُوفِ العاتِية

لم يُعطَ إنسانٌ ولا ذو همَّةٍ ۞ بعد اليقين بمثلِ تلك العافية

It is only right to seek well-being,
For it is a fortress in hard times.
No human being, nor any resolute person can get,
After yaqīn, anything better than well-being.

ثَمَانِيَةٌ حَتْمٌ عَلَى سَائِرِ الْوَرَى ۞ فَكُلّ امْرِئٍ لا بُدَّهُ مِنْ ثَمَانِيَهْ

سُرُورٌ وَاجْتِمَاعٌ وَفُرْقَةٌ ۞ وَعُسْرٌ وَيُسْرٌ ثُمَّ سُقْمٌ وَعَافِيَهْ

All mankind experiences 8 things,
With which every person must inevitably meet.
Happiness and sadness,
Union and separation,
Hardship and ease,
And finally, sickness and health.

KHUṬBAH 50

Taking Heed from the Unceasing Passing of Days, Nights, and Seasons

The unceasing passing of days and the changing of seasons – one after the next – contains major lessons for anyone who desires to take heed or be grateful to Allāh (ﷻ). It is essential for an intelligent individual to take heed from such lessons, take account of themselves, and think about what lies ahead. There are many steps we take in life, and a lot of time which we spend on things, but we rarely take heed of the lessons that we need to learn.

Allāh (ﷻ) says in the Qur'ān:

﴿وَهُوَ ٱلَّذِى جَعَلَ ٱلَّيۡلَ وَٱلنَّهَارَ خِلۡفَةٗ لِّمَنۡ أَرَادَ أَن يَذَّكَّرَ أَوۡ أَرَادَ شُكُورٗا ٦٢﴾

[الفُرْقَان الآية ٦٢]

> "He is the One who made the night and the day come in succession, for those who desire to remember, or desire to give gratitude." (Furqān 25:62)

We must continue to keep in mind that time is something whose moments do not return. When this reality is ignored, a person's time passes by and opportunities are lost, one will then have many regrets. When a person realizes all that one has missed out on, everyone will want to turn back the hands of time, but it will be way too late by then.

وَمَا الْمَرْءُ إِلاَّ رَاكِبٌ ظَهْرَ عُمْرِهِ ۞ عَلَى سَفَرٍ يُفْنِيهِ بِالْيَوْمِ وَالشَّهْرِ

يَبِيتُ وَيُضْحِي كُلَّ يَوْمٍ وَلَيْلَةٍ ۞ بَعِيدًا عَنَ الدُّنْيَا قَرِيبًا إِلَى الْقَبْرِ

Every person remains on a constant journey,

That draws closer to its ending with each passing day and month.
Each night a person sleeps and in the day he awakes,
He becomes farther away from this world and closer to his grave.

The days of winter which we are passing through, with record amounts of snowfall, and bitterly cold temperatures, urges us to take heed of many lessons, and serves as a reminder of the bitter cold of the hellfire.

It has been mentioned in a *ḥadīth* which has been documented both by Imām al-Bukhārī and Imām Muslim (ﷺ) that the Prophet (ﷺ) said:

«اشْتَكَتِ النَّارُ إِلَى رَبِّهَا، فَقَالَتْ: يَا رَبِّ أَكَلَ بَعْضِي بَعْضًا، فَأَذِنَ لَهَا بِنَفَسَيْنِ، نَفَسٍ فِي الشِّتَاءِ، وَنَفَسٍ فِي الصَّيْفِ، فَهْوَ أَشَدُّ مَا تَجِدُونَ مِنَ الْحَرِّ، وَأَشَدُّ مَا تَجِدُونَ مِنَ الزَّمْهَرِيرِ».

(متفق عليه)

"Hellfire complained to its Lord saying: 'O my Lord! My different parts have consumed each other.' So Allāh allowed it to take two breaths, one in winter and the other in summer. The most intense heat which you feel is from the extreme heat of the hellfire, and the bitterest cold which you feel is from the extreme cold of the hellfire." (Agreed Upon)

Ḥasan al-Baṣrī (ﷺ) says:

«كلُّ بَرْدٍ أَهْلَكَ شيئًا فهو من نَفَسِ جهنَّمَ، وكلُّ حَرٍّ أَهْلَكَ شيئًا فهو من نَفَسِ جهنَّمَ».

(لطائف المعارف)

"Any cold which causes destruction is from the breath of the hellfire, and any heat which causes destruction is from the breath of the hellfire." (Laṭā'if al-Maʿārif)

Ḥāfiẓ ibn Rajab (ﷺ) states:

«كلُّ ما في الدنيا فهو مُذَكِّر بالآخرة ودليلٌ عليه، فشدة حر الصيف يُذَكِّر بحرِّ جهنمَ، وهو من سمومها، وشدة برد الشتاء يُذَكِّر بزمهرير جهنمَ، وهو من زمهريرها».

(لطائف المعارف)

> "Everything in this world alerts us to matters of the hereafter and draws our attention to them. The extreme heat of summer reminds us about the heat of the hellfire, and in fact, it actually comes from the heat of the hellfire. Similarly, the extreme cold of the winter reminds us about the extreme cold of the hellfire and in fact, it actually comes from the cold of the hellfire." (Laṭā'if al-Maʿārif)

Therefore, one of the most important lessons regarding winter is being provided with a reminder of the extreme cold of the hellfire.
This prompts us to seek refuge with Allāh (ﷻ) from it, and we implore Allāh (ﷻ) to grant all of us His protection *Inshā' Allāh.*

Imām Aḥmad (رحمه الله) has documented a *ḥadīth* in his *Musnad*, as well as Imām al-Bayhaqī (رحمه الله) who writes in his *Sunan al-Kabīr*, on the authority of Abū Saʿīd al-Khudrī (رضي الله عنه) that the Messenger of Allāh (ﷺ) said:

«الشِّتَاءُ رَبِيعُ الْمُؤْمِنِ، قَصُرَ نَهَارُهُ فَصَامَ، وَطَالَ لَيْلُهُ فَقَامَ».

(السنن الكبير للبيهقي)

> "Winter is an enjoyable time for a believer. Its days are short, so he can fast; and its nights are long, so he can stand in prayer." (Sunan al-Kabīr of al-Bayhaqī)

Ḥāfiẓ ibn Rajab (رحمه الله) states:

«إنما كان الشتاء ربيع المؤمن؛ لأنه يرتع فيه في بساتين الطاعة، ويسرح في ميادين العبادات، وينزّه قلبه في رياض الأعمال الميسّرة فيه».

(لطائف المعارف)

> "Winter is an enjoyable time for a believer because he finds enjoyment in obeying Allāh (ﷻ), worshipping Him, and performing righteous deeds which are facilitated during that time of year." (Laṭā'if al-Maʿārif)

> "Winter is a spring for the believer because he grazes in the orchards of obedience and wanders freely in the fields of worship, and his heart seeks pleasure in the gardens of deeds that are easy in winter."

The companions of the Prophet (ﷺ) were happy when the winter would approach due to them finding enjoyment in obeying Allāh (ﷻ) and worshipping Him during that season.

ʿAbdullāh ibn Masʿūd (رضي الله عنه) would say:

«مرحبًا بالشتاء، تُنَزَّل فيه البركةُ، ويطول فيه الليل للقيام، ويقصر فيه النهار للصيام».

(لطائف المعارف)

> "We welcome the winter because during it: blessings descend, the night is long for prayer, and the day is short for fasting." (Laṭā'if al-Maʿārif)

Muʿādh ibn Jabal (رضي الله عنه) wept when his death was imminent and said:

«إنما أبكي على ظمأ الهواجر، وقيام ليل الشتاء، ومزاحمة العلماء».

(لطائف المعارف)

> "I only weep because I will miss no longer feeling thirst in the heat of the day, praying during the nights of winter, and being in the company of the scholars." (Laṭā'if al-Maʿārif)

ʿUbaid ibn ʿUmair (رحمه الله) would say:

«يا أهل القرآن: طالَ ليلُكم لقراءَتكم فاقرؤوا، وقصُرَ النهارُ لصيامِكم فصُوموا».

(لطائف المعارف)

"O people of the Qur'ān! Your night time has stretched so that you can recite the Qur'ān - so carry on with your Qur'ān recital; and your daytime has shortened so that you can fast - thus, carry on with your fasting." (Laṭā'if al-Maʿārif)

كم يكون الشتاءُ ثم المَصِيفُ ۞ وربيعٌ يمضي ويأتي خريفُ

وانتقالٌ من الحَرور إلى الظِّلِّ ۞ وسيفُ الرَّدى عليك مُنيفُ

يا قليلَ البقاءِ في هذه الدا ۞ رِ إلى كم يَغرُّك التسويفُ

Throughout the passage of each winter and summer,
Elapsing of each spring and fall, and change of the heat to cold,
The inevitable reality is that your current life will end one day.
You are in this world for only a short time, so how much longer will you procrastinate?

Some of the pious predecessors would say:

«ينبغي للإنسان أن يعرف شرفَ زمانه، وقدر وقته، فلا يضيع منه لحظة في غير قُرْبَة».

(قيمة الزمن عند العلماء لعبد الفتاح أبو غدة)

"It is necessary for every individual to recognize the status and value of one's time, and a person should not let a moment of it pass in anything besides drawing nearer to Allāh." (Qīmat al-Zaman 'Inda al-ʿUlamā' of ʿAbd al-Fattāḥ Abū Ghudda)

Imām ibn al-Qayyim (ﷺ) in his work titled *Miftāḥ Dār al-Saʿādah* writes:

«لو كان الزمان كله فصلا واحدا لفاتت مصالحُ الفصول الباقية فيه؛ فلو كان صيفًا كله لفاتت مصالح منافع مصالح الشتاء، ولو كان شتاء لفاتت مصالح الصيف، ففي الشتاء تغور الحرارةُ في الأجواف وبطون الأرض والجبال فتتولَّد مواد الثمار وغيرها، وتبرد الظواهر، ويستكثف فيه الهواء فيحصل السحاب والمطر والثلج والبرد الذي به حياة الأرض وأهلها».

(مفتاح دار السعادة)

> "If time existed as only one season, then the advantages which we attain from the other seasons would be lost. If it was always summer, then the advantages of winter would be lost. If it was always winter, then the advantages of summer would be lost. In winter, heat which has penetrated into the earth and the mountainous areas contribute to the formation of the essentials from which fruits and other plants will grow later on. In addition, the atmosphere becomes cooler, the air becomes denser, clouds form, and there is precipitation – rain, snow, and hail – which leads to life for the earth and its inhabitants." (Miftāḥ Dār al-Saʿādah)

Among the many lessons which we can learn from winter and one of the ample opportunities that we should capitalize on is that when we put on our winter coats, jackets, gloves, toques, and winter clothing, we must also remember that we have people in many places of the world who are suffering from the cold and snow, yet they lack winter supplies.

They live in tents, camps, or even out in the open. All they can spread beneath them is the ground, and all they have to cover themselves is the sky. The winter comes upon them with bitterness and its cold bites them.

We have many people in various parts of the world who are refugees and have been displaced or expelled from their homes. Accordingly, one of the virtuous deeds that a person can do in winter to get closer to Allāh (ﷻ) is helping the homeless, poor and destitute. With many of them battling against the bitterness of winter without ample clothing, food, and shelter, each Muslim household should aim to provide for at least one underprivileged family during the cold days and help alleviate their suffering - which Allāh (ﷻ) out of His Mercy, has saved us from.

The Prophet (ﷺ) has stated:

«أَيُّمَا مُؤْمِنٍ أَطْعَمَ مُؤْمِنًا عَلَى جُوعٍ أَطْعَمَهُ اللَّهُ يَوْمَ القِيَامَةِ مِنْ ثِمَارِ الجَنَّةِ، وَأَيُّمَا مُؤْمِنٍ سَقَى مُؤْمِنًا عَلَى ظَمَإٍ سَقَاهُ اللَّهُ يَوْمَ القِيَامَةِ مِنَ الرَّحِيقِ المَخْتُومِ، وَأَيُّمَا مُؤْمِنٍ كَسَا مُؤْمِنًا عَلَى عُرْيٍ كَسَاهُ اللَّهُ مِنْ خُضْرِ الجَنَّةِ».

(رواه الترمذي)

> "Whoever feeds a hungry believer, Allāh will feed him with the fruits of Paradise; and whoever gives a drink to a thirsty believer, Allāh will quench his thirst (on the Day of Judgement) with an exquisite 'sealed nectar' drink of Paradise; and whoever clothes a believer, Allāh will clothe him from the green garments of Paradise." (Tirmidhī)

As Muslims, it is our duty to be concerned about the welfare of other people, and not just be concerned about ourselves. We should inquire about our relatives, elderly neighbours, or anyone who is more vulnerable during the cold, and ensure that they have what they need to stay warm and safe. If we can save an elderly person the trouble of going out in the cold and do their shopping for them, or run other errands for them, then we should do so, as we will earn immense rewards from Allāh (ﷻ) *Inshā' Allāh.*

Sulaym ibn ʿĀmir (رضي الله عنه) narrates that when winter would arrive, ʿUmar ibn al-Khaṭṭāb (رضي الله عنه) would be extra mindful and write to the companions (رضي الله عنهم) and advise them as follows:

«كان عمر بن الخطاب رَضِيَ اللَّهُ عَنْهُ إذا حضر الشتاء تعاهدهم، وكتب لهم بالوصية: إن الشّتاءَ قد حضَرَ وهو عدوٌّ لكم، فتأهَّبُوا له أُهبتَه من الصُّوفِ والخِفافِ والجوارِب، واتَّخِذوا الصُّوفَ شِعارًا ودِثارًا ، فإنَّ البردَ عدوٌّ سريعٌ دخولُه، بعيدٌ خروجُه».[11]

[11] The Arabic text of this is as follows:

شِعارًا أي: ما يلي الأجساد، ودِثارًا أي: فوق الملابس

(لطائف المعارف)

"Winter, which is an enemy (challenging), has arrived, so prepare for it with woolen clothes, shoes, and socks. Wear woolen underwear and heavy garments, because the cold is an enemy which enters quickly - but leaves slowly." (Laṭā'if al-Ma'ārif)

Ḥāfiẓ ibn Rajab (رحمه الله) comments:

«وإنما كان يكتب عمر إلى أهل الشام لما فتحت في زمنه فكان يخشى على من بها من الصحابة وغيرهم ممن لم يكن له عهد بالبرد أن يتأذى ببرد الشام، وذلك من تمام نصيحته وحسن نظره وشفقته وحياطته لرعيته رضي الله عنه.»

(لطائف المعارف)

"'Umar (رضي الله عنه) would write this advice to the people of Shām when it was conquered in his era, as he was worried that the companions of the Prophet (ﷺ) and others who had not previously experienced such cold would be harmed by the cold of Shām. This was out of his complete well-wishing, graceful vigilance, compassion, and safeguarding of his subjects. May Allāh be pleased with him." (Laṭā'if al-Ma'ārif)

From the many virtuous deeds, one can do in these wintery days is to thank Allāh (ﷻ) for the winter provisions which He has provided us with such as: heated homes, boots, winter coats, jackets, gloves, toques, and other things.

Allāh (ﷻ) reminds us about these abundant favours in the Qur'ān, such as winter gear, etc. to keep ourselves warm.

﴿وَٱلْأَنْعَٰمَ خَلَقَهَا لَكُمْ فِيهَا دِفْءٌ وَمَنَٰفِعُ وَمِنْهَا تَأْكُلُونَ﴾ [النَّحْل الآية ٥]

"And He (Allāh) also created livestock. In them is warmth for you (when you use their skins for clothing), and many other benefits (such as transport and labour), and you even eat (some of them). (Naḥl 16:5)

NOTE: Notice how Allāh (ﷻ) has mentioned warmth exclusively in the verse above, although it is one of the many benefits.

Allāh (ﷻ) also says:

﴿وَٱللَّهُ جَعَلَ لَكُم مِّنۢ بُيُوتِكُمْ سَكَنًا وَجَعَلَ لَكُم مِّن جُلُودِ ٱلْأَنْعَٰمِ بُيُوتًا تَسْتَخِفُّونَهَا يَوْمَ ظَعْنِكُمْ وَيَوْمَ إِقَامَتِكُمْ وَمِنْ أَصْوَافِهَا وَأَوْبَارِهَا وَأَشْعَارِهَآ أَثَٰثًا وَمَتَٰعًا إِلَىٰ حِينٍ ﴿٨٠﴾﴾ [النّحل الآية ٨٠]

"And Allāh has granted you an abode (a place to rest and to live) in your homes and made homes (tents) for you from the hides of animals, which you find light (to carry) when you travel and when you pitch camp (on a journey). There are household articles (such as mats, blankets, water bags) and other things of benefit (derived) from their wool, fur and hair (which are of use to you) for a period (as long as you live or as long as they last)." (Naḥl 16:80)

Qatādah (رحمه الله) says:

«علِمَ الله أن شدَّة الحرِّ تُؤذِي، وشدَّة البردِ تُؤذِي، فوقاهُم الله أذاهُما جميعًا».

(لطائف المعارف)

"Allāh knew that extreme heat and cold are harmful, so He put in place measures to protect them (His servants) against their harm." (Laṭā'if al-Maʿārif)

All of this urges us to think about matters carefully, learn the necessary lessons from the remarkable things which Allāh (ﷻ) has put in this world, and take heed of the admonitions which come from the passing of the days, nights, and seasons.

One of the focal points of contemplation and reflection on the lessons to be learned from winter is that a person should remember and ponder about the days that have gone by.

How many winters have we been through in our life? How many days and years have passed by us? With each day that finishes, our life is fading away. Therefore, it is upon us to be prudent, to remember the hereafter, and prepare for it by increasing in good deeds, repenting to Allāh (ﷻ), and seek forgiveness from Him.

We must keep in mind that our lives in this world are passing by very quickly and will not last forever, therefore we must prepare the necessary provisions for ourselves.

Allāh (ﷻ) says:

﴿وَٱتَّقُواْ يَوۡمٗا تُرۡجَعُونَ فِيهِ إِلَى ٱللَّهِۖ ثُمَّ تُوَفَّىٰ كُلُّ نَفۡسٖ مَّا كَسَبَتۡ وَهُمۡ لَا يُظۡلَمُونَ ٢٨١﴾ [البَقَرَة الآية ٢٨١]

"And fear the day (of Qiyāmah) when you (all) shall be returned to Allāh (for reckoning), then every soul will be repaid (each one should worry about one's own actions) in full and they shall not be oppressed (neither will a person be deprived of any reward that one deserves, nor punished for any sin that one did not commit)." (Baqarah 2:281)

In a Prophetic narration it is mentioned that the Messenger of Allāh (ﷺ) has stated:

«مَا مِنْكُمْ مِنْ أَحَدٍ إِلاَّ سَيُكَلِّمُهُ رَبُّهُ لَيْسَ بَيْنَهُ وَبَيْنَهُ تَرْجُمَانٌ، فَيَنْظُرُ أَيْمَنَ مِنْهُ فَلاَ يَرَى إِلاَّ مَا قَدَّمَ، وَيَنْظُرُ أَشْأَمَ مِنْهُ فَلاَ يَرَى إِلاَّ مَا قَدَّمَ، وَيَنْظُرُ بَيْنَ يَدَيْهِ فَلاَ يَرَى إِلاَّ النَّارَ تِلْقَاءَ وَجْهِهِ، فَاتَّقُوا النَّارَ وَلَوْ بِشِقِّ تَمْرَةٍ، فَمَنْ لَمْ يَجِدْ فَبِكَلِمَةٍ طَيِّبَةٍ».

(رواه البخاري)

"There is not anyone of you but that his Lord will speak directly to him, without any interpreter between them. Then he will look to his right, and he will not see anything except what he had sent ahead from his deeds; and he will look to his left, and he will not see anything except what he had sent ahead. He will look in front of him, and he will not see anything except the fire in front of his face. So, protect yourselves from the fire even if it should be by half a date, and if he does not have it, then with a kind word." (Bukhārī)

NOTE: If half a date can save a slave from the punishments of the fire, then we should try and free ourselves from the fire of hell - even if it is with something very small!

The nights, days, seasons, and years all belong to Allāh (ﷻ) and succeed in accordance with His perfect laws. As a result, when winter passes, spring comes with all of its beauties and life is restored once again. The advent of spring is welcomed as the return of earth to fertility. It is the season of new growth and hope. Green shoots spring from the soil and leaf buds unfurl into the air.

Allāh (ﷻ) says in the Qur'ān:

﴿وَمِنْ ءَايَٰتِهِۦٓ أَنَّكَ تَرَى ٱلْأَرْضَ خَٰشِعَةً فَإِذَآ أَنزَلْنَا عَلَيْهَا ٱلْمَآءَ ٱهْتَزَّتْ وَرَبَتْ ۚ إِنَّ ٱلَّذِىٓ أَحْيَاهَا لَمُحْىِ ٱلْمَوْتَىٰٓ ۚ إِنَّهُۥ عَلَىٰ كُلِّ شَىْءٍ قَدِيرٌ ﴿٣٩﴾﴾ [فُصِّلَت الآية ٣٩]

"And from His signs (demonstrating His great powers) is that you see the earth bare (dead). Then, when We send rain upon it, it begins to stir (with life) and flourish (with vegetation). Verily, the One Who gives life to it (the dead earth) is the One Who gives life to the dead (Who will resurrect people on the Day of Judgement). Indeed, He has power over all things (can do anything)." (Fuṣṣilat 41:39)

أَتَاكَ الرَّبِيعُ الطَّلْقُ يَخْتَالُ ضَاحِكاً ۞ مِنَ الْحُسْنِ حَتَّى كَادَ أَنْ يَتَكَلَّمَا

أَحَلَّ فَأَبْدَى لِلْعُيونِ بَشَاشَةً ۞ عَلَيْهِ كَمَا نَشَّرْتَ وَشْياً مُنَمْنَمَا

When winter passes, spring comes along happily with all of its beauty,
Smiling so broadly that it practically speaks.

It eventually sets in and shows people all of the fine things it brings,
Just like they can see the beauty of a fine garment that anyone wears.

Ḥāfiẓ ibn Rajab (ﷺ) mentions:

«كان بعض السلف -رحمهم الله- يخرج في أيام الرياحين والفواكه إلى السوق فيقف وينظر ويعتبر ويسأل اللهَ الجنةَ».

(لطائف المعارف)

"Some of the pious predecessors (ﷺ) would go to the market place during days when flowers and fruits had bloomed. They would look at those things, take heed of the lessons which they contained, and ask Allāh to admit them to Paradise." (Laṭā'if al-Maʿārif)

In spring, the effects of the rain appear, trees become green, the earth is beautified for everyone, and the environment overall becomes lush.

Allāh (ﷻ) says:

﴿فَٱنظُرْ إِلَىٰٓ ءَاثَـٰرِ رَحْمَتِ ٱللَّهِ كَيْفَ يُحْيِ ٱلْأَرْضَ بَعْدَ مَوْتِهَآ ۚ إِنَّ ذَٰلِكَ لَمُحْيِ ٱلْمَوْتَىٰ ۖ وَهُوَ عَلَىٰ كُلِّ شَىْءٍ قَدِيرٌ ۝٥٠﴾ [الرّوم الآية ٥٠]

"So, look at (and appreciate) the evidence (signs) of Allāh's mercy and how He revives the earth after its death. Undoubtedly, (only) He gives life to the dead and He has power over all things (one should therefore never lose hope in Him)." (Rūm 30:50)

Imām Ibn al-Qayyim (ﷺ) in his renowned work *Zād al-Maʿād* writes:

«وأصحُّ الفصول فصل الربيع؛ فيه تقلُّ الأمراضُ، وتصحُّ الأبدانُ والأرواحُ».

(زاد المعاد)

> "The healthiest of seasons is spring. During it, illnesses are reduced, and well-being of the bodies and souls is increased." (Zād al-Maʿād)

ما الدَّهرُ إلا الرَّبيعُ المُستَنيرُ إذا ۞ جاء الرَّبيعُ أتاك النَّوْرُ والنُّورُ

The prime of the year is none besides the spring,
As it brings with it blossoms and brightness.

Consequently, we must continue to strive and give Allāh (ﷻ) due gratitude for His blessings and favours.

By way of gratitude, blessings will remain. Do not let heedlessness find its way into our hearts during any of the seasons. Rather, each one of them is a time in which we must take heed from the many lessons which they can provide. Doing this will enable us to please our Guardian, the Almighty, the Continuously Forgiving One.

KHUṬBAH 51

Elimination of Racial Discrimination

Allāh (ﷻ) advised His Select Messenger, Prophet Muḥammad (ﷺ) to adopt the conduct of his predecessors, meaning the Prophets and Messengers (ﷺ) and take them as exemplary models, because Allāh (ﷻ) bestowed on them divine guidance and unequivocal signs of revelation. Allāh (ﷻ) says in the Qur'ān:

﴿أُوْلَٰٓئِكَ ٱلَّذِينَ هَدَى ٱللَّهُۖ فَبِهُدَىٰهُمُ ٱقۡتَدِهۡۗ ۝٩٠﴾ [الأنعام الآية ٩٠]

"They are those whom Allāh had guided. So, follow their guidance." (Anʿām 6:90)

Among their most venerable qualities are: total commitment to following the path of righteousness, abstaining from offending others, exercising restraint in offensive drives, and distancing themselves from committing any sort of harmful acts against any individuals - men, women, and even children.

Their source of motivation was the highly refined ethics, and the sublime moral standards which Allāh (ﷻ), the Supreme Lord imparted to them when He educated them. He taught them that the principle bond to be established among human beings is love, empathy, compassion, and kindness.

ʿAbdullāh ibn Masʿūd (رضي الله عنه) reports that the Prophet (ﷺ) said:

«لَيْسَ الْمُؤْمِنُ بِالطَّعَّانِ، وَلَا اللَّعَّانِ، وَلَا الْفَاحِشِ، وَلَا الْبَذِيءِ».

(رواه الترمذي)

"A believer is neither a defamer, an insulter, a curser, an utterer of obscenity, nor an offender." (Tirmidhī)

It is for this reason that Islām is against all forms of discrimination, racism, prejudice, bias, and bigotry, on the basis of both religion and reason.

Discrimination is defined as the belief that one ethnicity is superior to another, or one colour of skin is superior to another, or that the people of one country are superior to another. It is a type of prejudice to pre-judge some demographic of people based on their origin and arbitrary physical characteristics.

The dictionary meaning of discrimination is:

- Discrimination is the practice of treating one person or group of people less fair or lower than other people or groups.
- Treating a person or group of people differently, especially in a worse way from the way in which you treat other people, because of their skin color, gender, sexuality, etc.
- Prejudice or prejudicial outlook, action, or treatment.
- The unjust or prejudicial treatment of different categories of people, especially on the grounds of race, age, or gender.
- Treatment or consideration of, or making a distinction in favor of or against a person or thing based on the group, class, or category to which that person or thing belongs to, rather than on individual merit: racial and religious intolerance and discrimination.

In human social affairs, discrimination is the treatment or consideration of, or making a distinction in favour of or against a person based on the group, class, or category to which a person is perceived to belong rather than on individual attributes. This includes treatment of an individual or group, based on their actual or perceived membership in a certain group or social category, in a way that is worse than the manner in which people are usually treated.

Such vile beliefs are the traits of *al-Jāhilīyyah* (pre-Islāmic ignorance).

In Islām, we believe that all people are born equal in the sight of Allāh (ﷻ) and the only characteristic that makes a person superior to someone else is righteousness *taqwā* (piety).

Allāh (ﷻ) has dignified the children of Ādam (عليه السلام), meaning all human beings in the world, with blessed provisions such as reason, intelligence, and empathy.

Allāh (ﷻ) says in the Qur'ān:

﴿وَلَقَدۡ كَرَّمۡنَا بَنِيٓ ءَادَمَ وَحَمَلۡنَٰهُمۡ فِي ٱلۡبَرِّ وَٱلۡبَحۡرِ وَرَزَقۡنَٰهُم مِّنَ ٱلطَّيِّبَٰتِ وَفَضَّلۡنَٰهُمۡ عَلَىٰ كَثِيرٖ مِّمَّنۡ خَلَقۡنَا تَفۡضِيلٗا ٧٠﴾ [الإسراء الآية ٧٠]

> "And We have certainly honored the children of Ādam and carried them on the land and the sea, and provided good things for them, and We favored them over much of what We created, with decisive preference." (Isrā' 17:70)

Allāh (ﷻ) created different races and tribes so that people can recognize each other and learn from one another, not so that the races would fight or look down upon others.

Ethnic diversity is part of the Divine plan, and a means of enrichment. Allāh (ﷻ) says:

﴿يَٰٓأَيُّهَا ٱلنَّاسُ إِنَّا خَلَقۡنَٰكُم مِّن ذَكَرٖ وَأُنثَىٰ وَجَعَلۡنَٰكُمۡ شُعُوبٗا وَقَبَآئِلَ لِتَعَارَفُوٓاْۚ إِنَّ أَكۡرَمَكُمۡ عِندَ ٱللَّهِ أَتۡقَىٰكُمۡۚ إِنَّ ٱللَّهَ عَلِيمٌ خَبِيرٞ ١٣﴾ [الحجرات الآية ١٣]

> "O people, indeed We have created you from male and female, and made you into nations and tribes that you may know one another. Verily, the noblest of you to Allāh is the most righteous among you. Verily, Allāh is Knowing and Aware." (Ḥujurāt 49:13)

In fact, Allāh (ﷻ) created different skin colours and languages as a sign of His creative power.

Just like flowers come in many different colours, as different Divine signs in Allāh's (ﷻ) creation, so do human beings come in different colours.

Allāh (ﷻ) says:

﴿وَمِنْ ءَايَـٰتِهِۦ خَلْقُ ٱلسَّمَـٰوَٰتِ وَٱلْأَرْضِ وَٱخْتِلَـٰفُ أَلْسِنَتِكُمْ وَأَلْوَٰنِكُمْ ۚ إِنَّ فِى ذَٰلِكَ لَـَٔايَـٰتٍ لِّلْعَـٰلِمِينَ ﴿٢٢﴾﴾ [الرّوم الآية ٢٢]

"And among His signs is the creation of the heavens and the earth, and the diversity of your languages and your colours. Verily, in that are signs for people of knowledge." (Rūm 30:22)

Abū Mūsā al-Ashʿarī (ؓ) narrates that the Prophet (ﷺ) stated:

«إِنَّ اللَّهَ تَعَالَى خَلَقَ آدَمَ مِنْ قَبْضَةٍ قَبَضَهَا مِنْ جَمِيعِ الأَرْضِ، فَجَاءَ بَنُو آدَمَ عَلَى قَدْرِ الأَرْضِ، فَجَاءَ مِنْهُمُ الأَحْمَرُ وَالأَبْيَضُ وَالأَسْوَدُ وَبَيْنَ ذَلِكَ، وَالسَّهْلُ وَالحَزْنُ وَالخَبِيثُ وَالطَّيِّبُ».

(رواه الترمذي)

"Verily, Allāh created Ādam (ؑ) from a handful which He took from the earth, so the children of Ādam (ؑ) come in accordance with the earth. Some come with red skin, white skin, or black skin, and whatever is in between: easy going, rough, bad, and good." (Tirmidhī)

Righteousness is the only quality that makes someone virtuous in the sight of Allāh (ﷻ), not race, not skin colour, not lineage, not social status, nor country of origin.

This message against racism, discrimination and tribalism was delivered by the Prophet (ﷺ) during his farewell sermon, demonstrating to us how important it is in Islām.

Abū Naḍrah (ؓ) narrates that the Prophet (ﷺ) in the final days of his pilgrimage said:

«يَا أَيُّهَا النَّاسُ، أَلَا إِنَّ رَبَّكُمْ وَاحِدٌ، وَإِنَّ أَبَاكُمْ وَاحِدٌ، أَلَا لَا فَضْلَ لِعَرَبِيٍّ عَلَى عَجَمِيٍّ، وَلَا لِعَجَمِيٍّ عَلَى عَرَبِيٍّ، وَلَا أَحْمَرَ عَلَى أَسْوَدَ، وَلَا أَسْوَدَ عَلَى أَحْمَرَ، إِلَّا بِالتَّقْوَى أَبَلَّغْتُ».

(مسند أحمد)

> "O people, your Lord is one and your father Ādam is one. There is no favour of an Arab over a non-Arab, nor a non-Arab over an Arab, and neither white skin over black skin, nor black skin over white skin, except by righteousness. Have I not delivered the message?" (Musnad Aḥmad)

Imām al-Bayhaqī (رحمه الله) in his renowned work *Al-Jāmʿi Shuʿab al-Īmān* has recorded a narration wherein it is reported that ʿUqbah ibn Āmir (رضي الله عنه) narrates from the Messenger of Allāh (ﷺ) that he said:

«لَيْسَ لِأَحَدٍ عَلَى أَحَدٍ فَضْلٌ إِلَّا بِالدِّينِ أَوْ عَمَلٍ صَالِحٍ، حَسْبُ الرَّجُلِ أَنْ يَكُونَ فَاحِشًا بَذِيًّا بَخِيلًا جَبَانًا».

(شعب الإيمان)

> "No one is better than anyone else except by virtue of faith (*dīn*) or good deeds. It is enough evil for a man to be profane, vulgar, greedy, or cowardly." (Shuʿab al-Imān)

Another *ḥadīth* mentions that the Prophet (ﷺ) said to Abū Dharr (رضي الله عنه):

«انْظُرْ، فَإِنَّكَ لَيْسَ بِخَيْرٍ مِنْ أَحْمَرَ وَلَا أَسْوَدَ إِلَّا أَنْ تَفْضُلَهُ بِتَقْوَى».

(مسند أحمد)

> "Behold! Verily, you have no virtue over one with white skin or black skin, except by favour of righteousness." (Musnad Aḥmad)

ʿAbdullāh ibn ʿAbbās (رضي الله عنهما) states:

«لاَ أَرَى أَحَدًا يَعْمَلُ بِهَذِهِ الْآيَةِ: ﴿يَـٰٓأَيُّهَا ٱلنَّاسُ إِنَّا خَلَقْنَـٰكُم مِّن ذَكَرٍ وَأُنثَىٰ وَجَعَلْنَـٰكُمْ شُعُوبًا وَقَبَآئِلَ لِتَعَارَفُوٓا۟ ۚ إِنَّ أَكْرَمَكُمْ عِندَ ٱللَّهِ أَتْقَىٰكُمْ ﴿١٣﴾﴾ [الحُجُرَات الآية ١٣] ، فَيَقُولُ الرَّجُلُ لِلرَّجُلِ: أَنَا أَكْرَمُ مِنْكَ، فَلَيْسَ أَحَدٌ أَكْرَمَ مِنْ أَحَدٍ إِلا بِتَقْوَى اللهِ».

(الأدب المفرد)

"I do not know anyone who acts by this verse: 'O people, verily We have created you from male and female and made you into nations and tribes that you may know one another. Verily, the noblest among you to Allāh is the most righteous of you.' (Ḥujurāt 49:13) A man might say to another man, 'I am more noble than you,' but no one is more noble except by the mindfulness of Allāh." (Al-Adab al-Mufrad)

The Prophet (ﷺ) would rebuke his companions (رضي الله عنهم) if they ever belittled people because of their race, lineage, or status.

In a well-known incident, the Prophet (ﷺ) sternly criticized his companion Abū Dharr (رضي الله عنه) for disrespecting Bilāl (رضي الله عنه) because he was from an African descent and had dark skin colour.

Abū Umāmah (رضي الله عنه) narrates that once Abū Dharr (رضي الله عنه) reproached Bilāl (رضي الله عنه) about his mother saying:

«عَيَّرَ أَبُو ذَرٍّ بِلاَلاً بِأُمِّهِ، فَقَالَ: يَا ابْنَ السَّوْدَاءِ، وَإِنَّ بِلاَلاً أَتَى رَسُولَ اللهِ ﷺ، فَأَخْبَرَهُ فَغَضِبَ، فَجَاءَ أَبُو ذَرٍّ وَلَمْ يَشْعُرْ، فَأَعْرَضَ عَنْهُ النَّبِيُّ ﷺ، فَقَالَ: مَا أَعْرَضَكَ عَنِّي إِلَّا شَيْءٌ بَلَغَكَ يَا رَسُولَ اللهِ، قَالَ: أَنْتَ الَّذِي تُعَيِّرُ بِلاَلاً بِأُمِّهِ؟ قَالَ النَّبِيُّ ﷺ: وَالَّذِي أَنْزَلَ الْكِتَابَ عَلَى مُحَمَّدٍ - أَوْ مَا شَاءَ اللهُ أَنْ يَحْلِفَ - مَا لِأَحَدٍ عَلَيَّ فَضْلٌ إِلَّا بِعَمَلٍ، إِنْ أَنْتُمْ إِلَّا كَطَفِّ الصَّاعِ».

(شعب الإيمان)

> "O son of a black woman!" Bilāl (رضي الله عنه) went to the Messenger of Allāh (ﷺ) and told him what was said to him. The Prophet (ﷺ) became angry and when Abu Dharr (رضي الله عنه) came to him, although he was unaware that Bilāl (رضي الله عنه) had already told him, the Prophet (ﷺ) turned away from him. So Abu Dharr (رضي الله عنه) asked: "O Messenger of Allāh (ﷺ), have you turned away because of something you have been told?" The Prophet (ﷺ) replied: "Have you reproached Bilal (رضي الله عنه) about his mother? By the One who revealed the Book to Muḥammad, none is more virtuous over another except by righteous deeds. You have none but an insignificant amount." (Shuʿab al-Imān)

Boasting about lineage and ancestors is forbidden in Islām since all people descended from Ādam (عليه السلام) and his wife.

No one is better than anyone else because of the family they were born into or the status that they inherited. The only criterion of superiority for one person over another is faith and righteous deeds.

Abū Hurairah (رضي الله عنه) narrates that the Prophet (ﷺ) said:

«إِنَّ اللَّهَ أَذْهَبَ عَنْكُمْ عُبِّيَّةَ الجَاهِلِيَّةِ وَفَخْرَهَا بِالآبَاءِ، إِنَّمَا هُوَ مُؤْمِنٌ تَقِيٌّ وَفَاجِرٌ شَقِيٌّ، النَّاسُ كُلُّهُمْ بَنُو آدَمَ وَآدَمُ خُلِقَ مِنْ تُرَابٍ».

(رواه الترمذي)

> "Verily, Allāh has removed from you the pride of the time of ignorance with its boasting of ancestors. Verily, one is only a righteous believer or a miserable sinner. All of the people are the children of Ādam, and Ādam was created from dust." (Tirmidhī)

In another narration, the Prophet (ﷺ) states:

«أَنَّ رَسُولَ اللَّهِ ﷺ خطَبَ النَّاسَ يَوْمَ فَتْحِ مَكَّةَ، فَقَالَ: يَا أَيُّهَا النَّاسُ، إِنَّ اللَّهَ قَدْ أَذْهَبَ عَنْكُمْ عُبِّيَّةَ الجَاهِلِيَّةِ وَتَعَاظُمَهَا بِآبَائِهَا، فَالنَّاسُ رَجُلَانِ: بَرٌّ تَقِيٌّ كَرِيمٌ عَلَى اللَّهِ، وَفَاجِرٌ شَقِيٌّ

هَيِّنٌ عَلَى اللَّهِ، وَالنَّاسُ بَنُو آدَمَ، وَخَلَقَ اللَّهُ آدَمَ مِنْ تُرَابٍ، قَالَ اللَّهُ: ﴿يَٰٓأَيُّهَا ٱلنَّاسُ إِنَّا خَلَقْنَٰكُم مِّن ذَكَرٍ وَأُنثَىٰ وَجَعَلْنَٰكُمْ شُعُوبًا وَقَبَآئِلَ لِتَعَارَفُوٓاْ إِنَّ أَكْرَمَكُمْ عِندَ ٱللَّهِ أَتْقَىٰكُمْ ﴿١٣﴾﴾ [الحُجُرَات الآية ١٣] ».

(رواه الترمذي)

"O people, Allāh has removed the slogans of ignorance from you and the exaltation of its forefathers. People are only of two kinds - either righteous, God-fearing believers dignified to Allāh; or wicked, miserable sinners insignificant to Allāh. People are all the children of Ādam, and Ādam was created from dust. Allāh has said: 'O people, We have created you from male and female and made you into nations and tribes that you may know one another. Verily, the most noble of you to Allāh is the most righteous of you. (Ḥujurāt 49:13).'" (Tirmidhī)

Another narration says:

«مَنْ بَطَّأَ بِهِ عَمَلُهُ لَمْ يُسْرِعْ بِهِ نَسَبُهُ».

(رواه مسلم)

"Whoever is slow to good deeds will not be hastened by his lineage." (Muslim)

Likewise, *al-ʿaṣabīyah* or 'tribalism' is a horrendous sin, which is defined in Islām as loyalty to one's tribe or family over the principles of justice.

The Prophet (ﷺ) disavowed himself and Islām from anyone who acts according to the various ideological and cultural manifestations of tribalism.

Jubayr ibn Muṭʿim reports that the Prophet (ﷺ) said:

«لَيْسَ مِنَّا مَنْ دَعَا إِلَى عَصَبِيَّةٍ، وَلَيْسَ مِنَّا مَنْ قَاتَلَ عَلَى عَصَبِيَّةٍ، وَلَيْسَ مِنَّا مَنْ مَاتَ عَلَى عَصَبِيَّةٍ».

(سنن أبي داود)

> "He is not one of us who calls to tribalism. He is not one of us who fights for the sake of tribalism. He is not one of us who dies following the way of tribalism." (Sunan Abū Dāwūd)

Malcolm X, who was known by his Muslim name Al-Ḥajj Mālik al-Shabāzz (ﷺ), was a famous African-American activist who struggled against institutional racism and discrimination in the mid-20th century America.

At first, he embraced a path of extremism in his confrontation with white supremacy, but his heart changed when he performed his *ḥajj.'* In Makkah, Malcolm X saw all kinds of people of different races and ethnicities united by the pilgrimage as one brotherhood. He wrote the following to his friends back in Harlem, USA:

> "America needs to understand Islām because this is the one religion that erases from its society the race problem. Throughout my travels in the Muslim world, I have met, talked to, and even eaten with people who in America would have been considered white, but the white attitude was removed from their minds by the religion of Islām. I have never before seen sincere and true brotherhood practiced by all colors together, irrespective of their color.
>
> During the past eleven days here in the Muslim world, I have eaten from the same plate, drunk from the same glass, and slept on the same rug, while praying to the same God, with fellow Muslims, whose eyes were the bluest of blue, whose hair was the blondest of blond, and whose skin was the whitest of white. And in the words and in the deeds of the white Muslims, I felt the same sincerity that I felt among the black African Muslims of Nigeria, Sudan, and Ghana.

We were truly all the same because their belief in one God had removed the white from their minds, the white from their behavior, and the white from their attitude. I could see from this, that perhaps if white Americans could accept the Oneness of God, then perhaps, too, they could accept in reality the Oneness of Man, and cease to measure and hinder and harm others in terms of their differences in color." (Malcolm X's Letters from Makkah)

CONCLUSION

- Muslims must implement and also share this message of Islām to humanity and to those who still hold on to the disease of racism, discrimination, and tribalism.
- Even among some Muslims, the plague of racism and discrimination exists and persists, despite the Prophet's (ﷺ) clear guidance.
- The only way to completely eradicate discrimination, racism, prejudice, bias, and bigotry in all of its forms is to embrace the authentic understanding of the Oneness of Allāh (ﷻ) - *'Tawhīd'* and the true teachings of the religion, and then to arrive at its common-sense conclusion, the oneness of humanity.

لَعَمْرُكَ مَا الْإِنْسَانُ إِلَّا بِدِينِهِ ۞ فَلَا تَتْرُكِ التَّقْوَى اتِّكَالًا عَلَى النَّسَبِ

لَقَدْ رَفَعَ الْإِسْلَامُ سَلْمَانَ فَارِسٍ ۞ وَقَدْ وَضَعَ الشِّرْكُ الشَّقِيَّ أَبَا لَهَبِ

By your life, man will be judged only by his religion,
Therefore, do not abandon piety or rely on your descent.
For Islām did honour Salmān (رضي الله عنه), the Persian,
While shirk dishonoured the highborn Abū Lahab.

KHUṬBAH 52

The Need for Preserving Unity in the Midst of Diversity

One of the primary reasons for Allāh (ﷻ) sending Prophets (ﷺ) was to establish His religion, promote harmony and unity, and to eradicate divisions and differences.

Allāh (ﷻ) says in the Qur'ān.

﴿ ۞ شَرَعَ لَكُم مِّنَ ٱلدِّينِ مَا وَصَّىٰ بِهِۦ نُوحًا وَٱلَّذِىٓ أَوْحَيْنَآ إِلَيْكَ وَمَا وَصَّيْنَا بِهِۦٓ
إِبْرَٰهِيمَ وَمُوسَىٰ وَعِيسَىٰٓ ۖ أَنْ أَقِيمُوا۟ ٱلدِّينَ وَلَا تَتَفَرَّقُوا۟ فِيهِ ۚ ﴿١٣﴾ ﴾ [الشُّورَى الآية ١٣]

"He has ordained (determined) for you the same religion that He ordained for Nūḥ (ﷺ), as well as what He ordained (prescribed) for Ibrāhīm, Mūsā and ʿĪsā (ﷺ). (We commanded these Prophets and their followers, saying:) 'Establish the religion and do not be divided.'" (Shūrā 42:13)

Therefore, when the Prophet (ﷺ) first set foot in Madīnah, a top priority of his mission was to build a *masjid* and establish fraternity among the *Muhājirīn* (those who migrated from Makkah) and the *Anṣār* (the helpers who were in Madīnah). People consequently shifted from the hostility of the pre-Islāmic state of *Jāhilīyyah* (ignorance) to the bond and friendship of Islām. As a result, strangers became brothers, and these strangers even began sharing with their 'new brothers' their homes and wealth.

Allāh (ﷻ) says about them in the Qur'ān:

﴿وَٱلَّذِينَ تَبَوَّءُو ٱلدَّارَ وَٱلْإِيمَٰنَ مِن قَبْلِهِمْ يُحِبُّونَ مَنْ هَاجَرَ إِلَيْهِمْ وَلَا يَجِدُونَ فِى صُدُورِهِمْ حَاجَةً مِّمَّآ أُوتُوا۟ وَيُؤْثِرُونَ عَلَىٰٓ أَنفُسِهِمْ وَلَوْ كَانَ بِهِمْ خَصَاصَةٌ ۚ وَمَن يُوقَ شُحَّ نَفْسِهِۦ فَأُو۟لَٰٓئِكَ هُمُ ٱلْمُفْلِحُونَ ﴿٩﴾﴾ [الحشر الآية ٩]

"Those (the *Anṣār*) who adopted the place (Madīnah) as their home before them (before the *Muhājirīn* came) and (had adopted) *īmān*. They (the *Anṣār*) loved those who migrate to them (the *Muhājirīn*) and find no want (jealousy or envy) in their hearts for what they (the *Muhājirīn*) are given. They (the *Anṣār*) prefer (others) above themselves (they prefer to give to others) even though they are themselves in need (of the things they give). (Like the *Anṣār*) Those who are saved (protected) from the miserliness (and greed) of the soul are really the successful ones (who will attain salvation)." (Ḥashr 59:9)

The Prophet did not stop at establishing love and fraternity among his companions (رضي الله عنهم), but he was also keen on nourishing these sentiments, so he asked the community to take them to heart and explained their merits out of keenness on the basis of preserving friendship and love.

Imām Muslim in his *Ṣaḥīḥ* reports on the authority of Abū Hurairah (رضي الله عنه) that the Prophet (ﷺ) once mentioned:

«أَنَّ رَجُلًا زَارَ أَخًا لَهُ فِي قَرْيَةٍ أُخْرَى، فَأَرْصَدَ اللهُ لَهُ، عَلَى مَدْرَجَتِهِ، مَلَكًا فَلَمَّا أَتَى عَلَيْهِ، قَالَ: أَيْنَ تُرِيدُ؟ قَالَ: أُرِيدُ أَخًا لِي فِي هَذِهِ الْقَرْيَةِ، قَالَ: هَلْ لَكَ عَلَيْهِ مِنْ نِعْمَةٍ تَرُبُّهَا؟ قَالَ: لَا، غَيْرَ أَنِّي أَحْبَبْتُهُ فِي اللهِ عَزَّ وَجَلَّ، قَالَ: فَإِنِّي رَسُولُ اللهِ إِلَيْكَ، بِأَنَّ اللهَ قَدْ أَحَبَّكَ كَمَا أَحْبَبْتَهُ فِيهِ».

(رواه مسلم)

"A man was on his way to visit a friend of his in another town. Allāh sent him an angel on his way. 'Where are you heading?' the angel asked the man. 'I want to visit a brother of mine in this town,' the man answered. 'Are you hoping to get a certain favour in return for your visit?' the angel questioned. 'No,' the man answered, 'I only love him for Allāh's sake,' and the man continued (on his way). The angel told him: 'I am Allāh's messenger to inform you that Allāh loves you as you love your friend for His sake.'" (Muslim)

The unity of hearts and continuity of bonds cannot be obtained without yearning for it, resilience, humbleness, and condescendence - meaning voluntary descent from one's rank or dignity in dealings with an inferior.

When the Prophet (ﷺ) exhorted Muʿādh and Abū Mūsā al-Ashʿarī (رضي الله عنهما) to Yemen, he told them the following: "Our faith teaches us that such occurrences to which man has no control, occur by the authorization and order of Allāh."

Abū Hurairah (رضي الله عنه) quotes the Prophet (ﷺ) as having said:

«أَنَّ النَّبِيَّ ﷺ بَعَثَهُ وَمُعَاذًا إِلَى الْيَمَنِ، فَقَالَ: يَسِّرَا وَلَا تُعَسِّرَا، وَبَشِّرَا وَلَا تُنَفِّرَا، وَتَطَاوَعَا وَلَا تَخْتَلِفَا».

(رواه مسلم)

> "Show people leniency, do not be hard on them; give them glad tidings of (divine favours in this world and the hereafter), and do not create aversion; work in collaboration with each other and do not be divided." (Muslim)

Unity of opinion demands forsaking personal and worldly gains.

When the Prophet (ﷺ) was distributing the spoils of the expedition after the Battle of Ḥunayn, and favoured those who had recently embraced Islām, the *Anṣār* were displeased. Having sensed their displeasure, the Prophet (ﷺ) reminded them about the blessing of guidance and unity that they were already enjoying.

He told them:

«يَا مَعْشَرَ الأَنْصَارِ أَلَمْ أَجِدْكُمْ ضُلاَّلاً فَهَدَاكُمُ اللَّهُ بِي وَعَالَةً فَأَغْنَاكُمُ اللَّهُ بِي وَمُتَفَرِّقِينَ فَجَمَعَكُمُ اللَّهُ بِي . وَيَقُولُونَ اللَّهُ وَرَسُولُهُ أَمَنُّ فَقَالَ أَمَا تَرْضَوْنَ أَنْ يَذْهَبَ النَّاسُ بِالأَمْوَالِ ، وَتَرْجِعُوا إِلَى رِحَالِكُمْ بِرَسُولِ اللَّهِ ﷺ، فَوَاللَّهِ مَا تَنْقَلِبُونَ بِهِ خَيْرٌ مِمَّا يَنْقَلِبُونَ بِهِ ، قَالُوا : بَلَى يَا رَسُولَ اللَّهِ ، قَدْ رَضِينَا».

(رواه البخاري)

> "O people of *Anṣār*, did I not find you erring and Allāh guided you through me, and (in a state of) being destitute and Allāh made you free from want through me, and in a state of disunity and Allāh united you through me." They all averred that it was the case. He then continued: "Are you not happy to see people go back with material gains and you go back with the Messenger of Allāh? I swear to Allāh that what you return with is much better than what they return with." They answered: "Yes, O Messenger of Allāh, we are satisfied with it." (Bukhārī)

As a preventive measure, and out of being keen on unity, the Prophet (ﷺ) had a practice of settling and defusing disagreements right from the outset.

Jābir ibn ʿAbdullāh (رضي الله عنه) narrates:

«كُنَّا فِي غَزَاةٍ فَكَسَعَ رَجُلٌ مِنَ المُهَاجِرِينَ رَجُلًا مِنَ الأَنْصَارِ، فَقَالَ الأَنْصَارِيُّ: يَا لَلأَنْصَارِ، وَقَالَ المُهَاجِرِيُّ: يَا لَلْمُهَاجِرِينَ، فَسَمَّعَهَا اللَّهُ رَسُولَهُ ﷺ قَالَ: مَا هَذَا؟ فَقَالُوا كَسَعَ رَجُلٌ مِنَ المُهَاجِرِينَ رَجُلًا مِنَ الأَنْصَارِ، فَقَالَ الأَنْصَارِيُّ: يَا لَلأَنْصَارِ، وَقَالَ المُهَاجِرِيُّ: يَا لَلْمُهَاجِرِينَ، فَقَالَ النَّبِيُّ ﷺ: دَعُوهَا فَإِنَّهَا مُنْتِنَةٌ».

(رواه البخاري)

> "We were with the Prophet (ﷺ) on an expedition when a man from the *Muhājirīn* (jokingly) kicked an *Anṣāri* man (on the buttocks with his foot). The man from the *Muhājirīn* said: 'O *Muhājirīn* (help)!' Then the man from the *Anṣār* said: 'O *Anṣār* (help)!' The Prophet (ﷺ) heard this and said: 'What is this? (Slogans of the Days of Ignorance)' They replied: 'A man from the *Muhājirīn* kicked a man from the *Anṣār*.' Upon that, the *Anṣāri* said, 'O *Anṣār* (help)!' and the *Muhājir* said: 'O *Muhājirīn* (help)!' So, the Prophet (ﷺ) said, 'Leave that, for it stinks (it is detestable).'" (Bukhārī)

Compassionate and kind as he was, the Prophet (ﷺ) was harsh on anyone wanting to undermine the unity of the community, or revive the slogans of *Jāhilīyyah* because the Prophet (ﷺ) knew that once the fire of discord, dissent, division, and disunity is ignited, it would be very difficult to put it out.

Abū Dharr (رضي الله عنه) reports:

«إِنَّهُ كَانَ بَيْنِي وَبَيْنَ رَجُلٍ مِنْ إِخْوَانِي كَلَامٌ، وَكَانَتْ أُمُّهُ أَعْجَمِيَّةً، فَعَيَّرْتُهُ بِأُمِّهِ، فَشَكَانِي إِلَى النَّبِيِّ ﷺ، فَلَقِيتُ النَّبِيَّ ﷺ، فَقَالَ: يَا أَبَا ذَرٍّ، إِنَّكَ امْرُؤٌ فِيكَ جَاهِلِيَّةٌ، قُلْتُ: يَا رَسُولَ اللَّهِ، مَنْ سَبَّ الرِّجَالَ سَبُّوا أَبَاهُ وَأُمَّهُ، قَالَ: يَا أَبَا ذَرٍّ، إِنَّكَ امْرُؤٌ فِيكَ جَاهِلِيَّةٌ، هُمْ إِخْوَانُكُمْ، جَعَلَهُمُ اللَّهُ تَحْتَ أَيْدِيكُمْ، فَأَطْعِمُوهُمْ مِمَّا تَأْكُلُونَ، وَأَلْبِسُوهُمْ مِمَّا تَلْبَسُونَ، وَلَا تُكَلِّفُوهُمْ مَا يَغْلِبُهُمْ، فَإِنْ كَلَّفْتُمُوهُمْ فَأَعِينُوهُمْ».

(رواه مسلم)

"I had an argument with a man whose mother was non-Arab. So, I taunted him on account of his mother. The man complained about this to the Prophet (ﷺ), and when I met the Prophet (ﷺ) he said to me: 'O Abā Dharr! You have (remnants of) *Jāhilīyyah* in you!' 'O Messenger of Allāh!' I replied: 'He who swears at men, he (as a consequence) makes them swear at his father and mother.' 'O Abā Dharr! You have (remnants of) *Jāhilīyyah* in you!' the Prophet (ﷺ) once again repeated. They (your servants and slaves) are your brothers. Allāh has put them in your care, so feed them with what you eat, clothe them with what you wear; and do not burden them beyond their capacities, but if you burden them (with an unbearable burden), then help them (by sharing their extra burden)" (Muslim)

The Prophet (ﷺ) prohibited the believers from boasting about their lineage or family descent. All people belong to Ādam, and Ādam was created from clay.

An Arab is not superior to a non-Arab, and a white person is not superior to a black person except by *taqwā*.

Allāh (ﷻ) says in the Qur'ān:

﴿يَٰٓأَيُّهَا ٱلنَّاسُ إِنَّا خَلَقۡنَٰكُم مِّن ذَكَرٖ وَأُنثَىٰ وَجَعَلۡنَٰكُمۡ شُعُوبٗا وَقَبَآئِلَ لِتَعَارَفُوٓاْۚ إِنَّ أَكۡرَمَكُمۡ عِندَ ٱللَّهِ أَتۡقَىٰكُمۡۚ إِنَّ ٱللَّهَ عَلِيمٌ خَبِيرٞ ﴿١٣﴾﴾ [الحجرات الآية ١٣]

"O people, We have created you from male and female and made you into nations and tribes that you may know one another. Verily, the more noble of you to Allāh is the most righteous of you. Verily, Allāh is Knowing and Aware." (Ḥujurāt 49:13)

Further, the Prophet (ﷺ) excluded from faith those who do not wish for others what they wished for themself.

The Prophet (ﷺ) said:

«لَا يُؤْمِنُ أَحَدُكُمْ حَتَّى يُحِبَّ لِأَخِيهِ مَا يُحِبُّ لِنَفْسِهِ».

(رواه مسلم)

"None of you has faith until he loves for his brother what he loves for himself." (Muslim)

The Messenger (ﷺ) also promised pulpits of light on the Day of Judgement for those who love each other for the sake of Allāh (ﷻ), and said that Allāh (ﷻ) will shelter them under His shade when there will be no shade except His.

«إِنَّ اللهَ تَعَالَى يَقُولُ يَوْمَ القِيَامَةِ: أَيْنَ المُتَحَابُّونَ بِجَلَالِي؟ اليَوْمَ أُظِلُّهُمْ فِي ظِلِّي يَوْمَ لَا ظِلَّ إِلَّا ظِلِّي».

(رواه مسلم)

"On the Day of Resurrection, Allāh, the Exalted, will say, 'Where are those who have mutual love for the sake of My Glory? Today I shall shelter them in My shade when there will be no shade except for Mine.'" (Muslim)

«قَالَ اللهُ عَزَّ وَجَلَّ: المُتَحَابُّونَ فِي جَلَالِي لَهُمْ مَنَابِرُ مِنْ نُورٍ يَغْبِطُهُمُ النَّبِيُّونَ وَالشُّهَدَاءُ».

(رواه الترمذي)

"Those who love each other for the sake of My Majesty shall be upon podiums of light, and they will be envied by the Prophets and the martyrs (*shuhadāʾ*)." (Tirmidhī)

Nothing is more detrimental to uniformity and harmony than disunity and division of the hearts. This is why the Prophet (ﷺ) was so keen on preserving the unity of the community, its uniformity, the keeping of its social build-up, and getting together - until his last breath.

Anas ibn Mālik (ﷺ) narrates:

«أَنَّ أَبَا بَكْرٍ كَانَ يُصَلِّي لَهُمْ فِي وَجَعِ النَّبِيِّ ﷺ الَّذِي تُوُفِّيَ فِيهِ، حَتَّى إِذَا كَانَ يَوْمُ الِاثْنَيْنِ وَهُمْ صُفُوفٌ فِي الصَّلَاةِ، فَكَشَفَ النَّبِيُّ ﷺ سِتْرَ الحُجْرَةِ يَنْظُرُ إِلَيْنَا وَهُوَ قَائِمٌ كَأَنَّ وَجْهَهُ وَرَقَةُ مُصْحَفٍ، ثُمَّ تَبَسَّمَ يَضْحَكُ، فَهَمَمْنَا أَنْ نَفْتَتِنَ مِنَ الفَرَحِ بِرُؤْيَةِ النَّبِيِّ ﷺ، فَنَكَصَ أَبُو بَكْرٍ عَلَى عَقِبَيْهِ لِيَصِلَ الصَّفَّ، وَظَنَّ أَنَّ النَّبِيَّ ﷺ خَارِجٌ إِلَى الصَّلَاةِ فَأَشَارَ إِلَيْنَا النَّبِيُّ ﷺ أَنْ أَتِمُّوا صَلَاتَكُمْ وَأَرْخَى السِّتْرَ فَتُوُفِّيَ مِنْ يَوْمِهِ».

(رواه مسلم)

"Abū Bakr (ﷺ) used to lead the people in prayer during the fatal illness of the Prophet (ﷺ) until it was Monday. When the people aligned (in rows) for the prayer, the Prophet (ﷺ) lifted the curtain of his house and started looking at us and was standing at that time. His face was (glittering) like a page of the Qur'ān and he smiled cheerfully. We were about to be enchanted by happiness for seeing the Prophet (ﷺ), and Abū Bakr (ﷺ) retreated to join the rows as he thought that the Prophet (ﷺ) would lead the prayer. The Prophet (ﷺ) beckoned us to complete the prayer and he let the curtain fall. On that same day, he passed away." (Muslim)

Imām al-Nawawī (ﷺ) comments and says:

«سَبَبُ تَبَسُّمِهِ ﷺ فَرَحُهُ بِمَا رَأَى مِنِ اجْتِمَاعِهِمْ عَلَى الصَّلَاةِ وَاتِّبَاعِهِمْ لِإِمَامِهِمْ وَإِقَامَتِهِمْ شَرِيعَتَهُ وَاتِّفَاقِ كَلِمَتِهِمْ وَاجْتِمَاعِ قُلُوبِهِمْ وَلِهَذَا اسْتَنَارَ وَجْهُهُ ﷺ عَلَى عَادَتِهِ إِذَا رَأَى أَوْ سَمِعَ مَا يَسُرُّهُ يَسْتَنِيرُ وَجْهُهُ».

(شرح النووى على مسلم)

"The reason for the Prophet's (ﷺ) smile was his happiness with what he had seen of their gathering for *ṣalāt*, their following of their *imām*, their establishing of his *Sharīʿah*, their unity, and the harmony of their hearts. This is the reason why his face shone, because whenever the Prophet (ﷺ) saw something that pleased him, his face would shine." (Imām al-Nawawī's commentary on Muslim)

Unity and uniformity among Muslims are essential at all times. We are in dire need of it more than ever before. However, if we would really like to be united, then we have to recognize the multiplicity and diversity of opinions, accommodate and tolerate them within the bounds of our blessed *Sharīʿah*.

The Prophets of Allāh (عليهم السلام) were the best of creations. However, they also differed amongst each other at times.

Allāh (ﷻ) mentions the dispute that took place between Prophets Mūsā and Hārūn (عليهما السلام):

﴿قَالَ يَٰهَٰرُونُ مَا مَنَعَكَ إِذْ رَأَيْتَهُمْ ضَلُّوٓا۟ ﴿٩٢﴾ أَلَّا تَتَّبِعَنِ ۖ أَفَعَصَيْتَ أَمْرِى ﴿٩٣﴾ قَالَ
يَبْنَؤُمَّ لَا تَأْخُذْ بِلِحْيَتِى وَلَا بِرَأْسِىٓ ۖ إِنِّى خَشِيتُ أَن تَقُولَ فَرَّقْتَ بَيْنَ بَنِىٓ إِسْرَٰٓءِيلَ
وَلَمْ تَرْقُبْ قَوْلِى ﴿٩٤﴾﴾ [طه من الآية ٩٢ الى الآية ٩٤]

(Mūsā) said: "O Hārūn! When you saw them going astray, what prevented you from following me (to the mountain, thereby disassociating from them so that they could realize that you truly detested their actions)? Did you disobey my instruction?" Hārūn said: "O son of my mother! Do not grab me by my beard or (seize) my head. (I did not disassociate from them because) I feared that you would say: 'You divided the *Banī Isrā'īl* and did not wait for my word (my instructions).'" (Ṭāhā 20:92-94)

A disagreement had taken place between Mūsā and Hārūn (عليهما السلام), but each one of them excused the other. They did not linger and delve into their differences, rather they moved on!

No one has the right to make disagreements a cause for division and hatred. The Prophet (ﷺ) warned us against this.

ʿAbdullāh ibn Masʿūd (رضي الله عنه) says:

«سَمِعتُ رَجُلًا قَرَأَ آيَةً، وَسَمِعتُ النَّبِيَّ ﷺ يَقْرَأُ خِلافَهَا، فَجِئْتُ بِهِ النَّبِيَّ ﷺ فَأَخْبَرْتُهُ، فَعَرَفْتُ فِي وَجْهِهِ الكَرَاهِيَةَ، وَقَالَ: كِلاكُمَا مُحْسِنٌ، وَلَا تَخْتَلِفُوا، فَإِنَّ مَنْ كَانَ قَبْلَكُمُ اخْتَلَفُوا فَهَلَكُوا».

(رواه البخاري)

"I heard a man reciting a verse of the Qur'ān, but I had heard the Prophet (ﷺ) recite it differently. So, I brought the man to the Prophet (ﷺ) and told him about that. Upon looking at his face, I immediately knew that he did not like what I did. Then he said: 'Both of you are correct. However, do not dispute, for those who existed before you disputed and as a consequence, they perished.'" (Bukhārī)

Despite their friendship, mutual compassion, and love for one another, the companions of the Prophet (ﷺ) sometimes disagreed about certain matters. However, their hearts were clean and pure towards one another.

Ḥasan ibn Thābit (رضي الله عنه) was among those who were involved with others in the incident of *Al-Ifk.*

ʿUrwah ibn al-Zubayr (رضي الله عنه) says:

«ذَهَبْتُ أَسُبُّ حَسَّانَ عِنْدَ عَائِشَةَ، فَقَالَتْ: لَا تَسُبَّهُ فَإِنَّهُ كَانَ يُنَافِحُ عَنِ النَّبِيِّ ﷺ».

(رواه البخاري)

"I went to ʿĀ'ishah (رضي الله عنها) and began insulting Ḥasan ibn Thābit in front of her. She said, 'Do not insult him, for he used to defend the Messenger of Allāh (ﷺ).'" (Bukhārī)

ʿAbdullāh ibn ʿAbbās (رضي الله عنهما) would disagree with Zayd ibn Thābit (رضي الله عنه) about certain religious matters; however, despite their disagreements,

ʿAbdullāh ibn ʿAbbās (ﷺ) would hold the halter of the mount of Zayd ibn Thābit (ﷺ) and say:

«تَنَحَّ يَا ابْنَ عَمِّ رَسُولِ اللَّهِ ﷺ، فَقَالَ: هَكَذَا أُمِرْنَا أَنْ نَفْعَلَ بِعُلَمَائِنَا وَكُبَرَائِنَا ، فَقَالَ زَيْدٌ: أَرِنِي يَدَكَ. فَأَخْرَجَ يَدَهُ، فَقَبَّلَهَا فَقَالَ: هَكَذَا أُمِرْنَا أَنْ نَفْعَلَ بِأَهْلِ بَيْتِ نَبِيِّنَا ﷺ».

(حياة الصحابة)

> "This is how we are ordered to deal with our scholars and seniors." On the other hand, Zayd ibn Thābit (ﷺ) would kiss ʿAbdullāh ibn ʿAbbās's (ﷺ) hand and say: "This is how we are ordered to deal with the members of the Family of our Prophet (ﷺ)!" (Ḥayāt al-Ṣaḥābah)

The *tābiʿīn* and those who followed them pursued the same path even when they held different views concerning any matter. By doing this, they preserved the rights of brotherhood, unity, and uniformity.

There were many *fiqh* matters in which Imām Shāfiʿī (ﷺ) differed with Imām Abū Ḥanīfah (ﷺ) but despite this, Imām Shāfiʿī (ﷺ) would say:

«النَّاسُ عِيَالٌ عَلَى أَبِي حَنِيفَةَ فِي الْفِقْهِ».

(كتاب مناقب الإمام أبي حنيفة وصاحبيه)

> "People are the dependents of Abū Ḥanīfah in *fiqh*." (Manāqib al-Imām Abū Ḥanīfah wa Ṣaḥibayh)

Imām Aḥmad (ﷺ) would say regarding his contemporary Imām Isḥāq ibn Rahwayh (ﷺ) with whom he differed on many occasions:

«لَمْ يَعْبُرِ الْجِسْرَ إِلَى خُرَاسَانَ مِثْلُ إِسْحَاقَ، وَإِنْ كَانَ يُخَالِفُنَا فِي أَشْيَاءَ، فَإِنَّ النَّاسَ لَمْ يَزَلْ يُخَالِفُ بَعْضُهُمْ بَعْضاً».

(سير أعلام النبلاء)

> "No one has ever crossed the bridge to Khurāsān (Central Asia) such as Isḥāq even though he differed with us on certain matters; certainly, people are accustomed to differing with one another." (Siyar al-ʿAlām al-Nubalā)

Imām Yūnus al-Ṣadafī (ﷺ) would say regarding Imām Shāfiʿī (ﷺ) with whom he differed on many occasions:

«مَا رَأَيْتُ أَعْقَلَ مِنَ الشَّافِعِيِّ، نَاظَرْتُهُ يَوْماً فِي مَسْأَلَةٍ، ثُمَّ افْتَرَقْنَا، وَلَقِيَنِي، فَأَخَذَ بِيَدِي، ثُمَّ قَالَ: يَا أَبَا مُوسَى، أَلاَ يَسْتَقِيمُ أَنْ نَكُونَ إِخْوَاناً وَإِنْ لَمْ نَتَّفِقْ فِي مَسْأَلَةٍ».

(سير أعلام النبلاء)

> "I have never seen a person more judicious than Al- Shāfiʿī. One day I argued with him about a certain matter and we parted; then he met me, held my hand and said: 'O Abū Mūsā! Can we not be brothers despite our disagreement on a certain (religious) matter?!'" (Siyar al-ʿAlām al-Nubalā)

These brilliant hallmarks from the history of our righteous predecessors are indeed in accordance with the objectives of *Sharīʿah* which require that unity and mutual uniformity prevail among all of the Muslims, and that we abstain from every type of discord and disunity which is the source of every difference, disagreement, and weakness.

Allāh (ﷻ) says in the Qur'ān:

﴿وَأَطِيعُواْ ٱللَّهَ وَرَسُولَهُۥ وَلَا تَنَٰزَعُواْ فَتَفْشَلُواْ وَتَذْهَبَ رِيحُكُمْۖ وَٱصْبِرُوٓاْۚ إِنَّ ٱللَّهَ مَعَ ٱلصَّٰبِرِينَ ﴿٤٦﴾﴾ [الأنفال الآية ٤٦]

> "Obey (the commands of) Allāh and His Prophet and do not fall into dispute (quarrels) with each other, for then you will become cowardly (weak) and your strength will be lost. Exercise patience (tolerance), for verily Allāh is with those who exercise patience (tolerance)." (Anfāl 8:46)

Let us conclude with the saying of Imām Ibn Taymīyyah (﵀) highlighting the importance of maintaining unity and uniformity:

«وَأَمَّا الِاخْتِلَافُ فِي الْأَحْكَامِ فَأَكْثَرُ مِنْ أَنْ يَنْضَبِطَ، وَلَوْ كَانَ كُلَّمَا اخْتَلَفَ مُسْلِمَانِ فِي شَيْءٍ تَهَاجَرَا لَمْ يَبْقَ بَيْنَ الْمُسْلِمِينَ عِصْمَةٌ وَلَا أُخُوَّةٌ، وَلَقَدْ كَانَ أَبُو بَكْرٍ وَعُمَرُ رَضِيَ اللَّهُ عَنْهُمَا سَيِّدَا الْمُسْلِمِينَ يَتَنَازَعَانِ فِي أَشْيَاءَ لَا يَقْصِدَانِ إِلَّا الْخَيْرَ».

(مجموع الفتاوى)

"Difference about jurisprudential rulings is too big to be put under control, and if every two Muslims abandoned each other upon differing on a certain matter, then neither virtuousness, nor brotherhood will remain among the Muslims. The two masters of Muslims - Abū Bakr and ʿUmar (﵄) used do differ about certain matters, while intending only good." (Majmūʿ al-Fatāwā)

KHUṬBAH 53

Getting Right What You Have Done Wrong

Among the features of human beings – and in fact, the indicators of their weakness – is that they change from one condition to another. As a result, they have times of uncertainty, confusion, contradiction, and instability. A person may adopt a certain idea one day, but give it up on another day; or hold a certain opinion one day and go back on it the next day. This is nothing unusual.

Allāh (ﷻ), the One who has full knowledge of everything and complete ability to do all things, explained the psychological, intellectual, and physical make-up of human beings by saying:

﴿وَخُلِقَ ٱلْإِنسَٰنُ ضَعِيفًا ۝٢٨﴾ [النِّسَاء الآية ٢٨]

"And man was created weak." (Nisā' 4:28)

Therefore, human beings have been created weak from all perspectives: in their stature, resolve, willpower, intellect, knowledge, and perseverance.

Yet, despite all of this, there is a feature which distinguishes a person who has faith, shows that his intellect is sound, and demonstrates that he submits to his Lord - and that feature is returning to what is right after realizing that one did something wrong or blameworthy.

A person of faith is not too proud to go back on a statement, action, or opinion when it is found that what is correct is different from what he said, did, or thought. He does not insist on holding on to what is wrong, and he does not give in to those who describe him as inconsistent or unstable.

That is because it is praiseworthy to return to what is right, and doing so is what gives a person true integrity and credibility; contrary to the state of some who are enticed by *Shayṭān* into thinking that integrity, credibility, and honour lie in maintaining one view even if it is wrong.

Allāh (ﷻ) says in the Qur'ān:

﴿إِنَّ ٱلَّذِينَ ٱتَّقَوْا۟ إِذَا مَسَّهُمْ طَٰٓئِفٌ مِّنَ ٱلشَّيْطَٰنِ تَذَكَّرُوا۟ فَإِذَا هُم مُّبْصِرُونَ ۝٢٠١﴾

[الأَعْرَاف الآية ٢٠١]

"Indeed, when the temptation (to do evil) from Shayṭān reaches those who fear Allāh, they remember (Allāh and engage in *dhikr*, thinking about His punishment and recalling the rewards for abstaining from sin), and their (inner) eyes instantly open (they realize Shayṭān's plot and ignore the temptation)." (Aʿrāf 7:201)

Ḥāfiẓ ibn Kathīr (ﷺ) commenting on this verse says that this means:

«وَقَوْلُهُ: {تَذَكَّرُوا} أَيْ عِقَابَ اللَّهِ وَجَزِيلَ ثَوَابِهِ وَوَعْدَهُ وَوَعِيدَهُ، فَتَابُوا وَأَنَابُوا وَاسْتَعَاذُوا بِاللَّهِ وَرَجَعُوا إِلَيْهِ مِنْ قَرِيبٍ».

(تفسير ابن كثير)

"They remember the risk of Allāh's punishment, and the promise of His immense reward. Thus, they repent to Allāh, seek refuge with Him, and return to Him without a delay." (Tafsīr Ibn Kathīr)

Every now and again, we have the chance to review our deeds.

Therefore, whenever an individual makes a mistake, one should hasten to take it back and repent to Allāh (ﷻ). This is because an individual should strive to seek out what is correct, please one's Lord, and comply with His directives. When a person does these things, then one will be included in the description of the best of people, as mentioned in the statement of the Prophet (ﷺ):

«كُلُّ بَنِي آدَمَ خَطَّاءٌ، وَخَيْرُ الْخَطَّائِينَ التَّوَّابُونَ».

(رواه الترمذي)

"Every son of Ādam commits sins, and the best of those who commit sins are those who repent." (Tirmidhī)

The guidance of Islām teaches us how a person must train oneself to return to what is right and be pleased with doing that instead of adhering to the wrong which one has done.

Allāh (ﷻ) says in the Qur'ān:

﴿وَٱلَّذِينَ إِذَا فَعَلُواْ فَٰحِشَةً أَوْ ظَلَمُوٓاْ أَنفُسَهُمْ ذَكَرُواْ ٱللَّهَ فَٱسْتَغْفَرُواْ لِذُنُوبِهِمْ وَمَن يَغْفِرُ ٱلذُّنُوبَ إِلَّا ٱللَّهُ وَلَمْ يُصِرُّواْ عَلَىٰ مَا فَعَلُواْ وَهُمْ يَعْلَمُونَ ﴿١٣٥﴾﴾ [آل عِمرَان الآية ١٣٥]

"And those who, if they carry out an open immoral act or oppress themselves (by committing any other sin), they think of Allāh and repent for their sins. Who can pardon sins except Allāh? And (in addition to repenting) they do not intentionally continue (to repeat) what (wrong) they did while they know." (Āle ʿImrān 3:135)

Therefore, they do not continue perpetrating the sins which they committed. On the contrary, they repent, ask for Allāh's (ﷻ) forgiveness, return to following correct guidance, and do not resemble those about whom the Prophet (ﷺ) described by saying (in the last part of the quote):

«أَنَّهُ قَالَ وَهُوَ عَلَى الْمِنْبَرِ: ارْحَمُوا تُرْحَمُوا، وَاغْفِرُوا يَغْفِرِ اللَّهُ لَكُمْ، وَيْلٌ لِأَقْمَاعِ الْقَوْلِ، وَيْلٌ لِلْمُصِرِّينَ الَّذِينَ يُصِرُّونَ عَلَى مَا فَعَلُوا وَهُمْ يَعْلَمُونَ».[12]

(مسند أحمد)

"Show mercy and you will be shown mercy. Forgive (others) and Allāh will forgive you. Woe to the vessels that catch words (i.e. the ears). Ruin awaits those who persist and consciously

[12] The Arabic text of this is as follows:

وأقماع القول: الذين آذانهم كالقمع يدخل فيه سماع الحق من جانب ويخرج من جانب آخر لا يستقر فيه. وَالْأَقْمَاعُ جَمْعُ قِمْعٍ بِكَسْرِ الْقَافِ وَبِسُكُونِ الْمِيمِ وَفَتْحِهَا كَنِطْعٍ وَنِطَعٍ، وَقِيلَ بِفَتْحِ الْقَافِ وَسُكُونِ الْمِيمِ وَهُوَ الْإِنَاءُ الَّذِي يَنْزِلُ فِي رُءُوسِ الظُّرُوفِ لِتُمْلَأَ بِالْمَائِعَاتِ مِنَ الْأَشْرِبَةِ وَالْأَدْهَانِ. شَبَّهَ أَسْمَاعَ الَّذِينَ يَسْمَعُونَ الْقَوْلَ وَلَا يَعُونَهُ وَيَحْفَظُونَهُ وَيَعْمَلُونَ بِهِ بِالْأَقْمَاعِ الَّتِي لَا تَعِي شَيْئًا مِمَّا يُفَرَّغُ فِيهَا فَكَأَنَّهُ يَمُرُّ عَلَيْهَا مُجْتَازًا كَمَا يَمُرُّ الشَّرَابُ فِي الْأَقْمَاعِ

> continue in doing what (wrong) they are doing." (Musnad Aḥmad)

In this narration, the Prophet (ﷺ) warned those who are informed about what is right, but still refuse to comply with it – those who know what is correct, but they do not pay any mind to that.

Instead, they disregard what is right for reasons such as arrogance, stubbornness, prejudice, extremism, following others in the wrong they do, or thinking the wrong they themselves do is unquestionably right.

Those who are honest with themselves, do not refuse to accept anything which is right, and are not pleased to continue doing something that is wrong. Regardless of how significant their status might be - they are not prevented from returning to Allāh's (ﷻ) directives.

There is a *ḥadīth* that has been documented both by Imām al-Bukhārī and Imām Muslim (رحمهما الله) in which the Prophet (ﷺ) states:

«إِنِّي وَاللَّهِ إِنْ شَاءَ اللَّهُ، لَا أَحْلِفُ عَلَى يَمِينٍ فَأَرَى غَيْرَهَا خَيْرًا مِنْهَا، إِلَّا كَفَّرْتُ عَنْ يَمِينِي، وَأَتَيْتُ الَّذِي هُوَ خَيْرٌ».

(متفق عليه)

> "I swear by Allāh that – if Allāh wills – any time I swear an oath to do or not to do a certain thing, but then find that something else is better, I will give expiation for my oath and do what is better." (Agreed Upon)

It can be understood from this that it is more virtuous for a Muslim to go back on his resolve to do or not to do a certain thing if a person finds that something else will be more advantageous.

Therefore, any time a person swears an oath about a certain thing, but then finds that something else will be more advantageous, then he should give expiation for the oath and do what is the most advantageous thing to perform.

Abū Bakr (﷜) followed precisely that course when a companion, Misṭaḥ, had participated in the slander that was directed at 'Ā'ishah (﷜).

Due to that, Abū Bakr (﷜) said:

»وَاللَّهِ لاَ أُنْفِقُ عَلَى مِسْطَحٍ شَيْئًا أَبَدًا، بَعْدَ الَّذِي قَالَ لِعَائِشَةَ.«

(رواه البخاري)

"I swear by Allāh that I will never again give *misṭaḥ* any sort of financial support after what he said about 'Ā'ishah." (Bukhārī)

Then Allāh (ﷻ) revealed:

﴿وَلَا يَأْتَلِ أُولُو ٱلْفَضْلِ مِنكُمْ وَٱلسَّعَةِ أَن يُؤْتُوٓا۟ أُو۟لِى ٱلْقُرْبَىٰ وَٱلْمَسَٰكِينَ وَٱلْمُهَٰجِرِينَ فِى سَبِيلِ ٱللَّهِ ۖ وَلْيَعْفُوا۟ وَلْيَصْفَحُوٓا۟ ۗ أَلَا تُحِبُّونَ أَن يَغْفِرَ ٱللَّهُ لَكُمْ ۗ وَٱللَّهُ غَفُورٌ رَّحِيمٌ۝﴾ [النُّور الآية ٢٢]

"Those among you blessed with virtue and affluence should not take an oath to stop giving financial support to their relatives, the needy, and those who migrated in Allāh's path. (Instead of bearing a grudge against these people) They should (rather) forgive and pardon. Do you not like Allāh to forgive you? (Just as you would like Allāh to forgive you for your shortcomings, you should also forgive the shortcomings of others. Be like) Allāh (Who) is Most Forgiving, Most Merciful." (Nūr 24:22)

Due to this, Abū Bakr (﷜) said:

»بَلَى وَاللَّهِ إِنِّي لَأُحِبُّ أَنْ يَغْفِرَ اللَّهُ لِي، فَرَجَعَ إِلَى مِسْطَحٍ النَّفَقَةَ الَّتِي كَانَ يُنْفِقُ عَلَيْهِ، وَقَالَ: وَاللَّهِ لاَ أَنْزِعُهَا عَنْهُ أَبَدًا.«

(رواه البخاري)

"Yes, by Allāh I most certainly want Allāh to forgive me." Then he continued to support Misṭaḥ financially. Abū Bakr (ﷺ) also said: "By Allāh I will never withhold this from him (again)." (Bukhārī)

In addition, Abū al-Dardā' (ﷺ) narrates:

«كُنْتُ جَالِسًا عِنْدَ النَّبِيِّ ﷺ، إِذْ أَقْبَلَ أَبُو بَكْرٍ آخِذًا بِطَرَفِ ثَوْبِهِ حَتَّى أَبْدَى عَنْ رُكْبَتِهِ، فَقَالَ النَّبِيُّ ﷺ: أَمَّا صَاحِبُكُمْ فَقَدْ غَامَرَ، فَسَلَّمَ وَقَالَ: إِنِّي كَانَ بَيْنِي وَبَيْنَ ابْنِ الخَطَّابِ شَيْءٌ، فَأَسْرَعْتُ إِلَيْهِ ثُمَّ نَدِمْتُ، فَسَأَلْتُهُ أَنْ يَغْفِرَ لِي فَأَبَى عَلَيَّ، فَأَقْبَلْتُ إِلَيْكَ، فَقَالَ: يَغْفِرُ اللَّهُ لَكَ يَا أَبَا بَكْرٍ ثَلَاثًا، ثُمَّ إِنَّ عُمَرَ نَدِمَ، فَأَتَى مَنْزِلَ أَبِي بَكْرٍ، فَسَأَلَ: أَثَّمَ أَبُو بَكْرٍ؟ فَقَالُوا: لَا، فَأَتَى إِلَى النَّبِيِّ ﷺ فَسَلَّمَ، فَجَعَلَ وَجْهُ النَّبِيِّ ﷺ يَتَمَعَّرُ، حَتَّى أَشْفَقَ أَبُو بَكْرٍ، فَجَثَا عَلَى رُكْبَتَيْهِ، فَقَالَ: يَا رَسُولَ اللَّهِ، وَاللَّهِ أَنَا كُنْتُ أَظْلَمَ، مَرَّتَيْنِ، فَقَالَ النَّبِيُّ ﷺ: إِنَّ اللَّهَ بَعَثَنِي إِلَيْكُمْ فَقُلْتُمْ كَذَبْتَ، وَقَالَ أَبُو بَكْرٍ صَدَقَ، وَوَاسَانِي بِنَفْسِهِ وَمَالِهِ، فَهَلْ أَنْتُمْ تَارِكُوا لِي صَاحِبِي مَرَّتَيْنِ، فَمَا أُوذِيَ بَعْدَهَا».

(رواه البخاري)

"Once he was sitting with the Prophet (ﷺ) when he saw Abū Bakr (ﷺ) approaching from a distance. Abū Bakr (ﷺ) was holding up the edge of his garment and rushing, so much so that his knee became uncovered. The Prophet (ﷺ) said, "Your companion has had an argument." When Abū Bakr (ﷺ) arrived, he extended the *salām* and said: "An exchange took place between me and Ibn al-Khaṭṭāb. I upset him but regretted that. I asked him to forgive me but he refused, so I came to you." The Prophet (ﷺ) repeated three times: "Abū Bakr (ﷺ), may Allāh forgive you." Meanwhile, ʿUmar (ﷺ) also regretted his refusal so he went to Abū Bakr's (ﷺ) home and asked if he was there. They replied in the negative, so ʿUmar (ﷺ) went to the Prophet

> (ﷺ) and extended the *salām* when he arrived. However, anger was clearly visible on the face of the Prophet (ﷺ) and Abū Bakr (رضي الله عنه) feared that something bad might be said to ʿUmar (رضي الله عنه). Thus, Abū Bakr (رضي الله عنه) fell to his knees and said two times: "O Messenger of Allāh, I swear by Allāh that I was more at fault." The Prophet (ﷺ) said, "Indeed, Allāh sent me to you people. You belied me but Abū Bakr (رضي الله عنه) said I was truthful, and he shared his life and wealth with me. Will you not leave my companion alone?" He said that twice. Abū al-Dardā' (رضي الله عنه) also added that Abū Bakr (رضي الله عنه) was never harmed thereafter." (Bukhārī)

We can understand from this that there were instances when even the esteemed companions (رضي الله عنهم) made certain mistakes. They were not infallible; however, they were swift in returning to what was right after having done anything wrong. This is the noteworthy trait that distinguished them.

Imām Aḥmad (رحمه الله) has documented another incident which took place between Abū Bakr (رضي الله عنه) and Rabīʿah al-Aslamī (رضي الله عنه).

Rabīʿah al-Aslamī (رضي الله عنه) narrates:

«إِنَّ رَسُولَ اللهِ ﷺ أَعْطَانِي أَرْضًا، وَأَعْطَى أَبَا بَكْرٍ أَرْضًا، وَجَاءَتِ الدُّنْيَا فَاخْتَلَفْنَا فِي عِذْقِ نَخْلَةٍ فَقُلْتُ: أَنَا هِيَ فِي حَدِّي، وَقَالَ أَبُو بَكْرٍ: هِيَ فِي حَدِّي، فَكَانَ بَيْنِي وَبَيْنَ أَبِي بَكْرٍ كَلَامٌ، فَقَالَ لِي أَبُو بَكْرٍ كَلِمَةً كَرِهَهَا وَنَدِمَ، فَقَالَ لِي: يَا رَبِيعَةُ رُدَّ عَلَيَّ مِثْلَهَا حَتَّى تَكُونَ قِصَاصًا، قَالَ: قُلْتُ: لَا أَفْعَلُ، فَقَالَ أَبُو بَكْرٍ: لَتَقُولَنَّ أَوْ لَأَسْتَعْدِيَنَّ عَلَيْكَ رَسُولَ اللهِ ﷺ فَقُلْتُ: مَا أَنَا بِفَاعِلٍ، قَالَ: وَرَفَضَ الْأَرْضَ وَانْطَلَقَ أَبُو بَكْرٍ رَضِيَ اللهُ عَنْهُ إِلَى النَّبِيِّ ﷺ، وَانْطَلَقْتُ أَتْلُوهُ، فَجَاءَ نَاسٌ مِنْ أَسْلَمَ فَقَالُوا لِي: رَحِمَ اللهُ أَبَا بَكْرٍ، فِي أَيِّ شَيْءٍ يَسْتَعْدِي عَلَيْكَ رَسُولَ اللهِ ﷺ وَهُوَ قَالَ لَكَ مَا قَالَ، فَقُلْتُ: أَتَدْرُونَ مَا هَذَا؟ هَذَا أَبُو بَكْرٍ الصِّدِّيقُ، هَذَا ثَانِيَ اثْنَيْنِ، وَهَذَا ذُو شَيْبَةِ الْمُسْلِمِينَ، إِيَّاكُمْ لَا يَلْتَفِتُ فَيَرَاكُمْ تَنْصُرُونِي عَلَيْهِ فَيَغْضَبَ فَيَأْتِيَ رَسُولَ اللهِ ﷺ

فَيَغْضَبَ لِغَضَبِهِ، فَيَغْضَبَ اللَّهُ عَزَّ وَجَلَّ لِغَضَبِهِمَا فَيُهْلِكَ رَبِيعَةَ، قَالُوا: مَا تَأْمُرُنَا؟ قَالَ: ارْجِعُوا، قَالَ: فَانْطَلَقَ أَبُو بَكْرٍ رَضِيَ اللَّهُ عَنْهُ إِلَى رَسُولِ اللَّهِ ﷺ فَتَبِعْتُهُ وَحْدِي، حَتَّى أَتَى النَّبِيَّ ﷺ فَحَدَّثَهُ الْحَدِيثَ كَمَا كَانَ، فَرَفَعَ إِلَيَّ رَأْسَهُ فَقَالَ: يَا رَبِيعَةُ، مَا لَكَ وَلِلصِّدِّيقِ؟، قُلْتُ: يَا رَسُولَ اللَّهِ، كَانَ كَذَا كَانَ كَذَا، قَالَ لِي كَلِمَةً كَرِهَهَا فَقَالَ لِي: قُلْ كَمَا قُلْتُ حَتَّى يَكُونَ قِصَاصًا فَأَبَيْتُ، فَقَالَ رَسُولُ اللَّهِ ﷺ: أَجَلْ فَلَا تَرُدَّ عَلَيْهِ، وَلَكِنْ قُلْ: غَفَرَ اللَّهُ لَكَ يَا أَبَا بَكْرٍ، فَقُلْتُ: غَفَرَ اللَّهُ لَكَ يَا أَبَا بَكْرٍ، قَالَ الْحَسَنُ: فَوَلَّى أَبُو بَكْرٍ رَضِيَ اللَّهُ عَنْهُ وَهُوَ يَبْكِي».

(مسند أحمد)

"The Prophet (ﷺ) gave me a piece of land near Abū Bakr's. From then on I became concerned with the material things (*dunyā*). I had a dispute with Abū Bakr over a palm tree. 'It is in my land,' I insisted. 'No, it is in my land,' Abū Bakr countered. We started to argue. Abū Bakr cursed me, but as soon as he had uttered the offending word, he felt sorry and said to me: 'Rabīʿah, say the same word to me so that it can be considered as *qiṣāṣ* - just retaliation.' 'No by Allāh, I shall not,' I replied. 'In that case,' replied Abu Bakr, 'I shall go the Messenger of Allāh (ﷺ) and complain to him about your refusal to retaliate against me measure for measure.' He set off and I followed him. My tribe, the Banū Aslam, also set off behind me protesting angrily saying: 'He is the one who cursed you first and then he goes off to the Prophet (ﷺ) before you to complain about you!' I turned to them and said: 'Woe to you! Do you know who this is? This is al-Ṣiddīq, and he is the respected elder of the Muslims. Go back before he turns around, sees you and thinks that you have come to help me against him. He would then be more incensed and go to the Prophet (ﷺ) in anger, and the Prophet (ﷺ) will get angry on his account. Then Allāh will be angry on their account and Rabīʿah would be finished.' So, they turned back. Abū Bakr went to the Prophet and related the incident as it had happened. The Prophet raised his head and said to me: 'O Rabīʿah, what is wrong with you and al-Ṣiddīq?' 'O Messenger of Allāh, he wanted me to say the same words to him as he had said to me and I did not.' The Prophet (ﷺ) replied, 'Yes, do not say the same words to him as he had said to you. Instead say: 'May Allāh forgive you, O Abū Bakr.' With tears in his eyes, Abū Bakr went away." (Musnad Aḥmad)

Ḥāfiẓ ibn al-Ḥajr (رحمه الله) commenting on these incidents says:

«وَفِيهِ ماطبع عَلَيْهِ الْإِنْسَانُ مِنَ الْبَشَرِيَّةِ حَتَّى يَحْمِلُهُ الْغَضَبُ عَلَى ارْتِكَابِ خِلَافِ الْأَوْلَى لَكِنِ الْفَاضِلُ فِي الدِّينِ يُسْرِعُ الرُّجُوعَ إِلَى الْأَوْلَى كَقَوْلِهِ تَعَالَى: ﴿إِنَّ ٱلَّذِينَ ٱتَّقَوْاْ إِذَا مَسَّهُمْ طَٰٓئِفٌ مِّنَ ٱلشَّيْطَٰنِ تَذَكَّرُواْ فَإِذَا هُم مُّبْصِرُونَ ۝٢٠١﴾ [الأَعْرَاف الآية ٢٠١]».

(فتح الباري)

"The foregoing *aḥadīth* shows that human beings by their very nature may be prompted by anger to make choices that are not the best ones to make. However, a truly virtuous individual in terms of his religious practice hastens to return to what is best, as in the statement of Allāh: 'Indeed, when the temptation (to do evil) from Shayṭān reaches those who fear Allāh, they remember (Allāh and engage in *dhikr*, thinking about His punishment and recalling the rewards for abstaining from sin), and their (inner) eyes instantly open (they realize Shayṭān's plot and ignore the temptation).' (Aʿrāf 7:201)" (Fatḥ al-Bārī)

ʿAbdullāh ibn ʿAbbās (رضي الله عنهما) narrates that once ʿUyaynah ibn Ḥiṣn went to ʿUmar ibn al-Khaṭṭāb (رضي الله عنه) and said:

«يَا ابْنَ الخَطَّابِ، وَاللَّهِ مَا تُعْطِينَا الجَزْلَ، وَمَا تَحْكُمُ بَيْنَنَا بِالعَدْلِ، فَغَضِبَ عُمَرُ، حَتَّى هَمَّ بِأَنْ يَقَعَ بِهِ، فَقَالَ الحُرُّ: يَا أَمِيرَ المُؤْمِنِينَ، إِنَّ اللَّهَ تَعَالَى قَالَ لِنَبِيِّهِ ﷺ: ﴿خُذِ ٱلْعَفْوَ وَأْمُرْ

بِالْعُرْفِ وَأَعْرِضْ عَنِ الْجَاهِلِينَ ۝ [الأعراف الآية ١٩٩]، وَإِنَّ هَذَا مِنَ الْجَاهِلِينَ، فَوَاللَّهِ مَا جَاوَزَهَا عُمَرُ حِينَ تَلَاهَا عَلَيْهِ، وَكَانَ وَقَّافًا عِنْدَ كِتَابِ اللَّهِ».

(رواه البخاري)

"O son of al-Khaṭṭāb, I swear by Allāh that you do not give us much and you do not judge between us fairly." That angered 'Umar (؉) to the extent that he considered taking action against 'Uyaynah. However, al-Ḥurr ibn Qays said: "O Amīr al-Mu'minīn, Allāh indeed told His Prophet (؉): 'Keep to forgiveness (O Muḥammad), and enjoin kindness, and turn away from the ignorant.' That individual is certainly one of the ignorant. (A'rāf 7:199)" "By Allāh after hearing that, 'Umar (؉) did not go beyond what he was told. 'Umar (؉) was someone who consistently took heed of what the Book of Allāh said." (Bukhārī)

When 'Umar's (؉) anger was provoked, he was reminded about what Allāh (؉) said, and that caused him to remember that he must obey Allāh (؉). As a result, he regained his composure, immediately returned to what was right, and did not take any punitive measures against the other person.

On one occasion 'Umar (؉) had written a letter to Abū Mūsā (؉) in which he wrote:

«أَمَّا بَعْدُ، لَا يَمْنَعُكَ قَضَاءٌ قَضَيْتَهُ بِالْأَمْسِ رَاجَعْتَ الْحَقَّ، فَإِنَّ الْحَقَّ قَدِيمٌ لَا يُبْطِلُ الْحَقَّ شَيْءٌ، وَمُرَاجَعَةُ الْحَقِّ خَيْرٌ مِنَ التَّمَادِي فِي الْبَاطِلِ».

(السنن الكبرى للبيهقي)

"As to what follows - If you gave a ruling yesterday, but you later questioned yourself about it and were guided to realize that something different was correct, then the ruling which you gave must not prevent you from returning to what is correct. The truth must always remain, and it cannot be annulled by anything. Returning to the truth is better than persistence in adhering to the falsehood." (Sunan al-Kubrā of al-Bayhaqī)

Furthermore, when ʿUbaydullāh ibn al-Ḥasan al-ʿAnbarī (ﷺ) was the chief justice of Baṣrah, he was asked to reconsider an issue that he was mistaken about. He lowered his head for a while, then raised it and said:

«وَقَدْ سُئِلَ مَرَّةً عَنْ مَسْأَلَةٍ، فَأَخْطَأَ فِي الْجَوَابِ، فَقَالَ لَهُ قَائِلٌ: الْحُكْمُ فِيهَا كَذَا وَكَذَا. فَأَطْرَقَ سَاعَةً، ثُمَّ رَفَعَ رَأْسَهُ فَقَالَ: إِذًا أَرْجِعُ، وَأَنَا صَاغِرٌ، لَأَنْ أَكُونَ ذَنَبًا فِي الْحَقِّ أَحَبُّ إِلَيَّ مِنْ أَنْ أَكُونَ رَأْسًا فِي الْبَاطِلِ».

(تاريخ بغداد)

"I take that back as I was mistaken. I take that back as I was mistaken. For me to be in the rear as it relates to what is correct is more beloved to me than being in the lead as it relates to what is wrong." (Tārīkh Baghdād)

This is the way an individual should be. Anytime a fair-minded person is alerted to a slip or an error of his, he should return to what is right.

Imām al-Shāfiʿī (ﷺ) would say:

«كُلُّ مَسْأَلَةٍ تَكَلَّمْتُ فِيهَا صَحَّ الْخَبَرُ فِيهَا عَنِ النَّبِيِّ ﷺ عِنْدَ أَهْلِ النَّقْلِ بِخِلَافِ مَا قُلْتُ فَأَنَا رَاجِعٌ عَنْهَا فِي حَيَاتِي وَبَعْدَ مَوْتِي».

(حلية الأولياء وطبقات الأصفياء)

"In every case that there is an authentic report narrated from Allāh's Messenger (ﷺ) which is at odds with something that I have said, I take back what I said. This applies during my life and even after I pass away." (Ḥilyat al-Awliyā' wa Ṭabaqāt al-Aṣfiyāʾ)

The preceding incidents and statements show the caution, virtue, understanding, and fairness that were present among those esteemed generations. They are the ones whose steps deserve to be followed.

CONCLUSION

- As human beings we make mistakes; and at times we ignore sound judgement; we go against everything we know to be right, and sometimes even make horrible blunders.
- Life is not so much determined by the mistakes which we make, but rather how we handle those mistakes.
- Since we will all make mistakes, we need to be prepared for how we will handle those moments.

Here is what to do right when we have done wrong:

- **Push aside our ego.** We have to remove any pride in order to humble ourselves to genuinely make up the wrong. This shows that we truly value what is right. Even if we do not think that we are in the wrong, we should still apologize and be kind for the sake of Allāh (ﷻ).
- **Admit it.** Living in denial can mask the reality, but it is never beneficial. The first step towards the right path is found by accepting the truth; and admitting a wrong requires humility which is a prerequisite for overcoming a serious blunder.
- **Seek forgiveness.** If another person has been hurt by our actions, then we should seek their forgiveness. Connect with them, explain our mistake, take responsibility, do not blame others (especially them), and ask them to forgive us. Do not just say: "my bad" or "I am sorry." But rather elaborate and say: "I was wrong. I am sorry. Will you forgive me?" While we cannot force others to forgive us, we can do everything in our power to reconcile a relationship. The rest is up to them.
- **Make it right.** We can never undo the past, but many times we can do some tangible actions in an attempt to right a wrong. Attempting to make things right can confirm to us and reveal

to others how much we regret our decision, and desire to do better.

- **Learn from our mistakes.** The most valuable, and often the most overlooked aspect of overcoming a wrong is taking the time to consider why we did something blameworthy. More important than overcoming a wrong action is trying to make sure that we do not repeat it. What value is it to overcome something blameworthy if we are just going to turn back around and commit another wrong? The Prophet (ﷺ) states:

«لاَ يُلْدَغُ الْمُؤْمِنُ مِنْ جُحْرٍ وَاحِدٍ مَرَّتَيْنِ».

(رواه البخاري)

"A believer is not stung twice (by something) from the same hole." (Bukhārī)

A simple process of reflection can help us not to repeat our reprimandable choices.

- **Mistakes happen.** We all have shortcomings and make mistakes. The key is to ensure that we know how to handle them properly, and attempt that we do not repeat them again, *Inshā' Allāh.*

إِلَهي لَئِن جَلَّتْ وَعَظُمَتْ خَطيئَتي ۞ فَعَفوُكَ عَن ذَنبي أَجَلُّ وَأَوسَعُ

إِلَهي لَئِن أَعطَيتَ نَفسي سُؤلُها ۞ فَها أَنا في أَرضِ النَدامَةِ أَرتَعُ

إِلَهي تَرى حالي وَفَقري وَفاقَتي ۞ وَأَنتَ مُناجاتي الخَفيَّةِ تَسمَعُ

إِلَهي فَلا تَقطَع رَجائي وَلا تُزِغ ۞ فُؤادي فَلي في نَهرِ جُودِكَ مَطمَعُ

إِلَهي لِئَن خَيَّبتَني أَو طَرَدتَني ۞ فَمَن ذا الَّذي أَرجو وَمَن لي يَشفَعُ

إِلَهي أَجِرني مِن عَذابِكَ إِنَّني ۞ أَسيرٌ ذَليلٌ خائِفٌ لَكَ أَخضَعُ

إِلَهي لَئِن عَذَّبتَني أَلفَ حَجَّةٍ ۞ فَحَبلُ رَجائي مِنكَ لا يَتَقَطَّعُ

إِلَهي أَذِقني طَعمَ عَفوكَ يَومَ لا ۞ بَنونٌ وَلا مالٌ هُناكَ يَنفَعُ

"O Allāh! Even if my mistakes have become grave and numerous,
Then Your Forgiveness is far greater (than those sins), and limitless.
O Allāh! If I had given my soul all that it desired,
Then there I would be, lost in the land of regret!
O Allāh! You see my position, my poverty and my destitution,
And You hear my softly whispered supplication.
O Allāh! So, sever not my hopes, nor distract my heart (from You),
For I pine for the bounties of Your Generosity.
O Allāh! If You prevent me or chase me away,
Then who can I hope from, and who can I make intercede for me?
O Allāh! Keep me from Your punishment, indeed I am captive,
Abased, fearful, and subservient to You.
O Allāh! Even if You punish me for a thousand years,
My hopes in You will nonetheless never be severed.
O Allāh! Let me savour Your forgiveness on that day,
When neither progeny, nor wealth will be of any avail."

KHUṬBAH 54

Stop. Think. Vote.

For most of us, we have left our birthplaces and native lands in order to brighten and improve our lives and future, and to seek the many wonderful opportunities that this great country has to offer.

In Islāmic terms, this is called *hijrah. Hijrah* can be defined as:

« ترك الوطن إلى بلد غيره للإقامة فيه».

(الموسوعة الفقهية)

> "To leave one's homeland for the sake of seeking residency in another country." (Al-Mawsūʿah al-Fiqhīyah)

Therefore, it is essential that we thank Allāh (ﷻ) for facilitating the means for us to be here and settle in Canada which we now call our home!

It is also important to appreciate this great blessing. However, many a time people do not always recognize the blessings that Allāh (ﷻ) has given them, and this can lead to being unappreciative, complacent, or taking blessings for granted.

Allāh (ﷻ) says in the Qur'ān:

﴿إِنَّ ٱللَّهَ لَذُو فَضۡلٍ عَلَى ٱلنَّاسِ وَلَٰكِنَّ أَكۡثَرَ ٱلنَّاسِ لَا يَشۡكُرُونَ ﴿٦١﴾﴾ [غافر الآية ٦١]

> "Indeed, Allāh is full of bounty to the people, but most of the people are not grateful." (Ghāfir 40:61)

People around the world are ready and willing to place their lives and possessions at risk to be here.

In Canada, we are able to enjoy and witness prosperity, comfort, peace, and safety every day of our lives.

We need to thank Allāh (ﷻ) for everything that Canada has given us. Our careers, jobs, education, healthcare, etc. It is necessary for us to thank Allāh (ﷻ) continuously, throughout all circumstances, to acknowledge His blessings, and be duly grateful to Him.

Imām al-Ṭabarānī (رحمه الله) has recorded a *ḥadīth* from ʿAbdullāh ibn ʿAmr (رضي الله عنه) who narrated that the Messenger of Allāh (ﷺ) once asked a man:

«قَالَ رَسُولُ اللهِ ﷺ لِرَجُلٍ: كَيْفَ أَصْبَحْتَ يَا فُلَانُ؟، قَالَ: أَحْمَدُ اللهَ إِلَيْكَ يَا رَسُولَ اللهِ، فَقَالَ رَسُولُ اللهِ ﷺ: هَذَا الَّذِي أَرَدْتُ مِنْكَ».

(المعجم الأوسط للطبراني)

> "In what state did you reach the morning?" The man replied: "O Messenger of Allāh, I inform you that I offer praise to Allāh." The Prophet (ﷺ) said: "That is what I wanted to hear from you" referring to affirming the praise, gratitude, and glorification of Allāh. (Al-Muʿjam al-Awsaṭ of al-Ṭabarānī)

One of Allāh's (ﷻ) greatest favours upon us is that we enjoy stability in our country of Canada, having been conferred with the blessings of safety, peace, and freedom for us and our families, free to worship Allāh (ﷻ).

This is the reason why the Prophet (ﷺ) stated:

«مَنْ أَصْبَحَ مِنْكُمْ مُعَافًى فِي جَسَدِهِ، آمِنًا فِي سِرْبِهِ، عِنْدَهُ قُوتُ يَوْمِهِ، فَكَأَنَّمَا حِيزَتْ لَهُ الدُّنْيَا».

(رواه الترمذي)

"Whoever among you wakes up in the morning secure in his household, free from physical illness, and having enough food for his day - is as if he possesses the entire world." (Tirmidhī)

Likewise, Allāh (ﷻ) is the One who has created human beings and encouraged them to make beneficial use of the Earth and develop it.

Allāh (ﷻ) says in the Qur'ān:

﴿هُوَ أَنشَأَكُم مِّنَ ٱلْأَرْضِ وَٱسْتَعْمَرَكُمْ فِيهَا ۝٦١﴾ [هود الآية ٦١]

"He is the One who created you from the earth and enabled you to settle (prosper) upon it (and populate it)." (Hūd 11:61)

The populating and prospering referred to in this verse, encompasses all of the necessary things which are beneficial for Allāh's (ﷻ) creations and their lands.

Allāh (ﷻ) gave His servants what they need to develop His earth, He granted them countless apparent and inconspicuous blessings, and He provided them with opportunities to attain success. Thus, an individual who is truly successful is one who is keen to take advantage of these blessings and opportunities in order to benefit himself and develop and uplift his society and community.

The definition of opportunity is:

a) A set of circumstances that makes it possible to do something;
b) A chance for advancement, progress or profit;
c) A situation or condition favourable for attainment of a goal;
d) A good position, chance, or prospect, for advancement or success;
e) A chance to do something, or an occasion when it is easy for you to do something.

Opportunities may come in various forms, such as drawing nearer to Allāh (ﷻ) by performing certain prescribed acts of worship, doing acts of benevolence whose benefit extends to others, participating in developing one's country, or using one's means to benefit a community or society.

A person of high aspirations makes opportunities from what one has been granted. One does not wait for opportunities to come knocking at one's door; rather, that person takes the initiative to seize them, and this applies to whether they are related to this world or the hereafter.

Allāh (ﷻ) praised the Prophets and Messengers (ﷺ) in the Qur'ān by saying:

﴿إِنَّهُمْ كَانُواْ يُسَٰرِعُونَ فِى ٱلْخَيْرَٰتِ وَيَدْعُونَنَا رَغَبًا وَرَهَبًا ۖ وَكَانُواْ لَنَا خَٰشِعِينَ ۝٩٠﴾

[الأنبياء الآية ٩٠]

> "Indeed, they hastened to perform righteous deeds, and they supplicated to Us out of hope and fear, and they were humble to Us." (Anbiyā' 21:90)

This means that they took the initiative to do good things, and they did not neglect any opportunity to pursue whatever virtue they could attain.

Taking the initiative and seizing the opportunity to thank Allāh (ﷻ) for allowing us to be here in Canada where we enjoy the democracy, freedom, and peace of this amazing country - also demands us to cooperate with one another for the good and betterment of this country.

One of the ways we can do that is by "giving back." We can become contributing citizens towards the fabric of society by providing our skills, talents, abilities, time, etc. to make Canada an even better place.

The condition of a believer is such that whenever there is an opportunity to do good either by an action of a deed or a word, they take this golden chance to facilitate the good act to bring about good, voice their opinion to bring about goodness especially when it entails broader goals and perspectives.

This concept of hurrying towards good or taking an initiative, and how a believer never falls back or behind has been mentioned in the Qur'ān by Allāh (ﷻ) where He says:

﴿أُوْلَٰٓئِكَ يُسَٰرِعُونَ فِى ٱلْخَيْرَٰتِ وَهُمْ لَهَا سَٰبِقُونَ ۝٦١﴾ [المؤمنون الآية ٦١]

"It is those people who hasten to perform good acts and are the foremost in it (in the race to do good)." (Mu'minūn 23:61)

Both Imām al-Bukhārī and Imām Muslim (ﷺ) have documented a narration on the authority of ʿĀ'ishah (ﷺ) that once the Prophet (ﷺ) was in his home. The residence of the Prophet (ﷺ) was adjacent to the *masjid*, very close to the place of prayer, and it was a place where the people from the community would come, spend time, and then leave. On one occasion:

«سَمِعَ رَسُولُ اللَّهِ ﷺ صَوْتَ خُصُومٍ بِالْبَابِ عَالِيَةٍ أَصْوَاتُهُمَا، وَإِذَا أَحَدُهُمَا يَسْتَوْضِعُ الآخَرَ، وَيَسْتَرْفِقُهُ فِي شَيْءٍ، وَهُوَ يَقُولُ: وَاللَّهِ لاَ أَفْعَلُ، فَخَرَجَ عَلَيْهِمَا رَسُولُ اللَّهِ ﷺ، فَقَالَ: أَيْنَ الْمُتَأَلِّي عَلَى اللَّهِ، لاَ يَفْعَلُ الْمَعْرُوفَ؟، فَقَالَ: أَنَا يَا رَسُولَ اللَّهِ، وَلَهُ أَيُّ ذَلِكَ أَحَبَّ».

(متفق عليه)

The Messenger of Allāh (ﷺ) heard the voices of an altercation of two disputants at the door - both of whose voices were quite loud. One of them demanded some remission and desired that the other one should show leniency to him, whereupon the (other one) said: "By Allāh I will not do that." So the Messenger of Allāh (ﷺ) came out to them and said: "Who is the one who was swearing by Allāh that he would not do good?" That man replied: "I am that person, O Messenger of Allāh, but now he may do as he wishes." (Agreed Upon)

In this narration, the Prophet (ﷺ) is encouraging us that when there is an opportunity to do good, then we should rush to do it and not procrastinate.

One of the noble things that we can do in order to benefit ourselves and develop and uplift our country, society and community is in regards to the federal elections. Whenever a call is made to every citizen who is eligible to vote to vote then we should educate ourselves, and exercise this right that we have been given to vote and cast our voting ballots on Election Day.

However, there are many questions that may arise in the minds of people, some of which are the following:

1. Should we even bother?
2. Politicians make promises but rarely stand up to their promises!
3. What weight will my vote have?
4. How will my vote make a change?
5. Is voting against the Islāmic rulings?
6. Should we not surrender only to Allāh's (ﷻ) laws? Since Allāh (ﷻ) says in the Qur'ān:

﴿وَمَن لَّمۡ يَحۡكُم بِمَآ أَنزَلَ ٱللَّهُ فَأُوْلَـٰٓئِكَ هُمُ ٱلظَّـٰلِمُونَ ٤٥﴾ [المائدة الآية ٤٥]

"And whoever does not judge by what Allāh has revealed – then it is those who are the wrongdoers." (Mā'idah 5:45)

7. By voting, are we often voting for non-Muslim candidates and non-Islāmic values?

Before we answer these questions, we should ask ourselves: "Am I affected by what goes on in this country?"

By voting or not voting there are people who will be elected to office who will make decisions on our behalf for many things that are related to us. For instance, immigration, housing, education, healthcare, daycare, national security, taxes, rising costs, pensions, human rights, Islāmophobia, etc. All of these are things that affect us in some way or another.

If we do not vote, then decisions could be made that might not be in the greater interest of the over-all public. Muslim jurists have outlined a general ruling of fiqh. They point out that anything which affects us, we need to understand its Islāmic perspective and how to act in regards to that.

A prime example is that of *ṣalāt*. *Ṣalāt* is something which affects us all because it is *farḍ* (an obligation) upon us. Therefore, as Muslims it is obligatory to learn the rulings of *ṣalāt* and all of the matters connected to this act of worship.

The decisions which come about via elected candidates through the political process will certainly affect us in some way or another. We need to be part of the system; and we need to get involved. We are being called to testify to select the most suitable candidate for office.

Allāh (ﷻ) says in the Qur'ān:

﴿وَلَا يَأْبَ ٱلشُّهَدَآءُ إِذَا مَا دُعُوا۟ ۚ ﴿٢٨٢﴾﴾ [البقرة الآية ٢٨٢]

"And let not the witnesses refuse when they are called upon." (Baqarah 2:282)

CONCLUSION

- We live in Canada. This is our country where we pay taxes, work, reside and enjoy the rights of citizenship.
- Our children study here, and this is where they will work and live alongside neighbors of different backgrounds.
- Citizenship bestows on us some rights; and it also imposes duties and responsibilities upon us. Among them is the right to participate in the political process, to exchange views with candidates, to volunteer our services during the process, and to vote.
- This is not only a duty, but it is also in our own interest.
- The government structure and the political process here in Canada are based heavily on its citizen's contribution and involvement.
- Those who are active will reap the rewards by influencing policies, politicians, etc.
- Those who do not invest are not likely to get any returns.
- We should vote as Muslim Canadians, and do so for those candidates and political parties who will serve the best interests of Canada and its citizens - by promoting equality, opportunity, human dignity, freedom, as well as specific policies such as

supporting healthcare, education, research, productivity, families, the ill, seniors, help to immigrants to integrate, environment, better use of taxpayers money, accountability, transparency, etc.

- As Muslims, we should also emphasize that we favour those parties and candidates who treat all communities with respect, and who do not ignore them.
- Politicians should combat racism and discrimination along with ethnic profiling, and those who violate people's rights without due cause in the name of security.
- As Muslims, we should support parties that back the United Nations and human rights universally, instead of supporting gross violations of human rights and international law.
- We should select candidates who promote justice, freedom, security and human rights, and who will try to build a peaceful world so that everyone is able to live in freedom, security, dignity, and hope.
- In addition, (try and select those candidates who will) divert our tax money as much as possible to healthcare, education, job creation, sustainable development, and a better environment, etc.
- It becomes evident that voting is a civic responsibility upon each of us, and not just a right.
- By voting, citizens can send a powerful message to the elected officials.
- A strong voter turnout will show those in office or running for office that citizens are awake, aware and active.
- If you are a registered voter, then you should take the time to cast your ballot on Election Day.
- It does not take that long.
- Even if you are angry, disillusioned and disappointed with politics, still vote anyways. Someone is going to get elected. You are not voting for the perfect candidate, but the candidate who comes closest to representing your interests.

- The fact is that your vote will matter.
- Remember that if your vote did not matter, then there would not be such determined efforts to suppress it by way of anti-candidate campaigns and ads.
- Your vote can make a difference.
- Your vote today will help determine the future for tomorrow.

KHUTBAH 55

Being in Debt is a Serious Matter Indeed!

The Prophet (ﷺ) has informed us that on the Day of Resurrection there will be three records with Allāh (ﷻ):

1. One which contains what He will never forgive, i.e. worshipping others besides Him;
2. Another which contains what He will overlook if He wills, i.e. the sins that are between a person and Himself;
3. The last which contains what He will not overlook until matters are settled between His servants amongst themselves, i.e. rights to be fulfilled, and wrongs that was done to others.

Therefore, on the Day of Judgement, Allāh (ﷻ) will allow all of the people to have their rights claimed.

'Ā'ishah (رضي الله عنها) narrates that the Prophet (ﷺ) said:

«الدَّوَاوِينُ عِنْدَ اللَّهِ عَزَّ وَجَلَّ ثَلَاثَةٌ: دِيوَانٌ لَا يَعْبَأُ اللَّهُ بِهِ شَيْئًا، وَدِيوَانٌ لَا يَتْرُكُ اللَّهُ مِنْهُ شَيْئًا، وَدِيوَانٌ لَا يَغْفِرُهُ اللَّهُ، فَأَمَّا الدِّيوَانُ الَّذِي لَا يَغْفِرُهُ اللَّهُ: فَالشِّرْكُ بِاللَّهِ، قَالَ اللَّهُ عَزَّ وَجَلَّ: ﴿إِنَّهُۥ مَن يُشْرِكْ بِٱللَّهِ فَقَدْ حَرَّمَ ٱللَّهُ عَلَيْهِ ٱلْجَنَّةَ ۝٧٢﴾ [المَائِـدَة الآية ٧٢] وَأَمَّا الدِّيوَانُ الَّذِي لَا يَعْبَأُ اللَّهُ بِهِ شَيْئًا: فَظُلْمُ الْعَبْدِ نَفْسَهُ فِيمَا بَيْنَهُ وَبَيْنَ رَبِّهِ مِنْ صَوْمِ يَوْمٍ تَرَكَهُ، أَوْ صَلَاةٍ تَرَكَهَا، فَإِنَّ اللَّهَ عَزَّ وَجَلَّ يَغْفِرُ ذَلِكَ وَيَتَجَاوَزُ إِنْ شَاءَ، وَأَمَّا الدِّيوَانُ الَّذِي لَا يَتْرُكُ اللَّهُ مِنْهُ شَيْئًا: فَظُلْمُ الْعِبَادِ بَعْضِهِمْ بَعْضًا، الْقِصَاصُ لَا مَحَالَةَ».

(مسند أحمد)

"On the Day of Resurrection, there will be three records with Allāh. One which contains what He will not care about (meaning that He will overlook); another which contains what He will not overlook; and lastly one which contains what He will never forgive. As for the record which He will never forgive - it is worshipping others besides Him. Allāh says: 'Allāh has definitely forbidden Paradise for the one who attributes a partner to Allāh (commits *shirk*).' (Al-Mā'ida, verse 72) As for the record which Allāh will not care about, it is the injustice committed between a servant and Allāh regarding the fasts which he omitted, or the prescribed prayers which he neglected - for verily if Allāh wills he can overlook these and pardon them. As for the record which He will not overlook, it is the wrongs that took place between the servants, for undoubtedly there will be *qiṣāṣ* - just retaliation." (Musnad Aḥmad)

In fact, Allāh (ﷻ) will even allow the animals to have their rights such that a hornless sheep will be given its rights if a horned sheep had injured it.

Abū Hurairah (رضي الله عنه) reports that the Prophet (ﷺ) said:

«لَتُؤَدُّنَّ الْحُقُوقَ إِلَى أَهْلِهَا يَوْمَ الْقِيَامَةِ، حَتَّى يُقَادَ لِلشَّاةِ الْجَلْحَاءِ، مِنَ الشَّاةِ الْقَرْنَاءِ».

(رواه مسلم)

"The claimants will get their claims on the Day of Resurrection, so much so that a hornless sheep will get its claim from the horned sheep." (Muslim)

This reality is one which should make any sincere Muslim exercise extreme caution. A person must ensure that one gives Allāh's (ﷻ) servants the rights to which they are entitled to, so that one can depart from this world without bearing the burden of having wronged others regarding their integrity, property, and any rights in general.

Among the greatest matters included in people's rights – and concerning which much wrongdoing and negligence takes place – is paying off debts that a person owes someone else. This is an issue which has become prevalent in Muslim societies, as well as others.

Among people, we often find those who have either given someone else a loan, or have taken a loan which they must repay. This issue is one that requires examination, and it also requires us to keep certain guidelines in mind.

There are many people who have hastily overdone things with regards to incurring debts, perhaps even at times where there may have been no need to do so. The ease with which loans can be obtained has led many people to incur debts without necessarily planning, and without the required knowledge about Islām's directives concerning the subject. As a result, there are people who were never involved in such matters before, but have now drowned themselves in various debts to be repaid, and rights of others which must be given to them.

It is necessary for any sincere Muslim to ensure that one does not bear these sorts of liabilities because the default when dealing with people's wealth and rights is that they must be given to those who are entitled to them.

Even if someone escapes being held accountable in this world, one cannot escape being held accountable in the hereafter by Allāh (ﷻ), the One who owns absolutely everything and will settle matters with complete justice. He will exact retribution from every individual who was unjust in fulfilling the rights of others.

Anyone who betrays the trusts that one must fulfill will have a banner raised for him on the Day of Resurrection, and a proclamation exposing him will be made saying: "This was the treachery committed by such-and-such person."

It has been narrated on the authority of ʿAbdullāh ibn ʿUmar (رضي الله عنهما) that the Prophet (ﷺ) said:

«إِذَا جَمَعَ اللهُ الْأَوَّلِينَ وَالْآخِرِينَ يَوْمَ الْقِيَامَةِ، يُرْفَعُ لِكُلِّ غَادِرٍ لِوَاءٌ، فَقِيلَ: هَذِهِ غَدْرَةُ فُلَانِ بْنِ فُلَانٍ».

(رواه مسلم)

> "When Allāh will gather together, on the Day of Judgement, all of the earlier and later generations of mankind, a flag will be raised (to mark off) every person guilty of breach of faith, and it will be announced that this is the deceit of so-and-so, son of so-and-so (to attract the attention of other people to his guilt)." (Muslim)

The subject of debts is one that has major gravity with Allāh (ﷻ). The longest *āyah* which He revealed in the Qur'ān, near the end of Sūrah al-Baqarah, is about debts.

Furthermore, it is authentically reported that the Prophet (ﷺ) would often seek refuge with Allāh (ﷻ) from being overpowered by others, from sins in general, and from being burdened by debt.

ʿĀ'ishah (رضي الله عنها) narrates that the Prophet (ﷺ) would supplicate the following during prayers:

«اللَّهُمَّ إِنِّي أَعُوذُ بِكَ مِنْ عَذَابِ القَبْرِ، وَأَعُوذُ بِكَ مِنْ فِتْنَةِ المَسِيحِ الدَّجَّالِ، وَأَعُوذُ بِكَ مِنْ فِتْنَةِ المَحْيَا، وَفِتْنَةِ المَمَاتِ، اللَّهُمَّ إِنِّي أَعُوذُ بِكَ مِنَ المَأْثَمِ وَالمَغْرَمِ، فَقَالَ لَهُ قَائِلٌ: مَا أَكْثَرَ مَا تَسْتَعِيذُ مِنَ المَغْرَمِ، فَقَالَ: إِنَّ الرَّجُلَ إِذَا غَرِمَ، حَدَّثَ فَكَذَبَ، وَوَعَدَ فَأَخْلَفَ».

(رواه البخاري)

> "O Allāh, I seek refuge with You from the punishment of the grave, from the afflictions of the *Masīḥ al-Dajjāl*, (the False Messiah) and from the afflictions of life and death. O Allāh, I seek refuge with You from sins and from debt." Somebody said to him: "Why do you so frequently seek refuge with Allāh from being in debt?" The Prophet (ﷺ) replied: "A person in debt tells lies when he speaks, and breaks promises when he makes (them)." (Bukhārī)

It has also been reported in the *Sunan* of Imām al-Nasā'ī (رحمه الله) on the authority of Muḥammad ibn Jaḥsh (رضي الله عنه) who relates:

«كُنَّا جُلُوسًا عِنْدَ رَسُولِ اللَّهِ ﷺ فَرَفَعَ رَأْسَهُ إِلَى السَّمَاءِ، ثُمَّ وَضَعَ رَاحَتَهُ عَلَى جَبْهَتِهِ، ثُمَّ قَالَ: سُبْحَانَ اللَّهِ، مَاذَا نُزِّلَ مِنَ التَّشْدِيدِ، فَسَكَتْنَا وَفَزِعْنَا، فَلَمَّا كَانَ مِنَ الْغَدِ، سَأَلْتُهُ: يَا رَسُولَ اللَّهِ، مَا هَذَا التَّشْدِيدُ الَّذِي نُزِّلَ؟ فَقَالَ: وَالَّذِي نَفْسِي بِيَدِهِ، لَوْ أَنَّ رَجُلًا قُتِلَ فِي سَبِيلِ اللَّهِ ثُمَّ أُحْيِيَ، ثُمَّ قُتِلَ ثُمَّ أُحْيِيَ، ثُمَّ قُتِلَ وَعَلَيْهِ دَيْنٌ، مَا دَخَلَ الْجَنَّةَ حَتَّى يُقْضَى عَنْهُ دَيْنُهُ».

(سنن النسائي)

> We were sitting with the Messenger of Allāh (ﷺ) when he raised his head towards the sky, then he put his palm on his forehead and said: "*Subḥān Allāh*! What a strict issue has been revealed to me!" We remained silent and were afraid. The following morning, I asked him: "O Messenger of Allāh, what is this strict issue that has been revealed?" He said: "By the One in Whose hand is my soul, if a man was killed in a battle for the sake of Allāh, then brought back to life, then killed and brought back to life again, then killed, and he owed a debt, he will not enter Paradise until any debt that he was responsible for is paid off." (Sunan al-Nasā'ī)

Furthermore, it is mentioned in the *Musnad* of Imām Aḥmad (رحمه الله) that the Prophet (ﷺ) withheld from offering the funeral prayer for a person who had died while he was still owing two dinars (to someone else), until Abū Qatādah (رضي الله عنه) took on the responsibility of settling the debt.

Jābir (رضي الله عنه) relates:

«تُوُفِّيَ رَجُلٌ فَغَسَّلْنَاهُ، وَحَنَّطْنَاهُ، وَكَفَّنَّاهُ، ثُمَّ أَتَيْنَا بِهِ رَسُولَ اللَّهِ ﷺ يُصَلِّي عَلَيْهِ، فَقُلْنَا: تُصَلِّي عَلَيْهِ؟ فَخَطَا خُطًى، ثُمَّ قَالَ: أَعَلَيْهِ دَيْنٌ؟، قُلْنَا: دِينَارَانِ، فَانْصَرَفَ، فَتَحَمَّلَهُمَا أَبُو قَتَادَةَ، فَأَتَيْنَاهُ، فَقَالَ أَبُو قَتَادَةَ: الدِّينَارَانِ عَلَيَّ، فَقَالَ رَسُولُ اللَّهِ ﷺ: حَقُّ الْغَرِيمِ، وَبَرِئَ مِنْهُمَا

الْمَيِّتُ؟، قَالَ: نَعَمْ، فَصَلَّى عَلَيْهِ، ثُمَّ قَالَ بَعْدَ ذَلِكَ بِيَوْمٍ: مَا فَعَلَ الدِّينَارَانِ؟، فَقَالَ: إِنَّمَا مَاتَ أَمْسِ، قَالَ: فَعَادَ إِلَيْهِ مِنَ الْغَدِ، فَقَالَ: لَقَدْ قَضَيْتُهُمَا، فَقَالَ رَسُولُ اللَّهِ ﷺ: الْآنَ بَرَدَتْ عَلَيْهِ جِلْدُهُ».

(مسند أحمد)

> A man died and we washed him, perfumed him, shrouded him, and then brought him to the Messenger of Allāh (ﷺ) and asked him: "Will you offer *janāzah* (funeral) prayers over him?" He (ﷺ) took a few steps and asked: "Is there any debt due upon him?" We replied: "Yes, two *dīnārs*." The Prophet (ﷺ) left. Abū Qatādah then undertook to pay them back. Coming back to the Prophet (ﷺ), Abū Qatādah said: "The two *dīnārs* are my responsibility (on his behalf)." The Messenger of Allāh (ﷺ) asked: "Will the right of creditor be taken care of and the deceased be absolved from them?" Abū Qatādah replied in the affirmative. Thereafter, the Prophet (ﷺ) led them in offering the funeral prayers over him. The following day the Prophet (ﷺ) asked: "Have the two *dīnārs* been repaid?" Abū Qatādah replied: "He only died yesterday!" The next day Abū Qatādah came to the Prophet (ﷺ) and said: "I have repaid them." Upon this, the Messenger of Allāh (ﷺ) said: "It is now that his skin has cooled down." (Musnad Aḥmad)

There was an instance where one of the companions passed away and had a debt to pay off. The Prophet (ﷺ) told that companion's brother: "Your brother has been detained because of his debt, so pay it off for him."

Saʿd ibn Aṭwal (رضي الله عنه) relates:

«مَاتَ أَخِي وَتَرَكَ ثَلَاثَ مِائَةِ دِينَارٍ، وَتَرَكَ وَلَدًا صِغَارًا، فَأَرَدْتُ أَنْ أُنْفِقَ عَلَيْهِمْ، فَقَالَ لِي رَسُولُ اللَّهِ ﷺ: إِنَّ أَخَاكَ مَحْبُوسٌ بِدَيْنِهِ، فَاذْهَبْ، فَاقْضِ عَنْهُ . قَالَ: فَذَهَبْتُ، فَقَضَيْتُ

عَنْهُ، ثُمَّ جِئْتُ، فَقُلْتُ: يَا رَسُولَ اللَّهِ، قَدْ قَضَيْتُ عَنْهُ، وَلَمْ يَبْقَ إِلَّا امْرَأَةٌ تَدَّعِي دِينَارَيْنِ، وَلَيْسَتْ لَهَا بَيِّنَةٌ. قَالَ: أَعْطِهَا، فَإِنَّهَا صَادِقَةٌ».

(مسند أحمد)

His brother died, leaving behind three hundred *dirhams*, and young children. He said: "I wanted to spend it on his children, but the Prophet (ﷺ) said to me: 'Your brother is being detained by his debt, so go and pay off his debts.' So, I went and paid off his debts, then I came back and said: 'O Messenger of Allāh, I have paid them off, except for two *dirhams* which a woman claimed (were owed to her), but she had no proof.' He said: 'Give them to her because that is her due (because she is speaking the truth).'" (Musnad Aḥmad)

Another Prophetic narration mentions:

«وَمَنْ مَاتَ وَعَلَيْهِ دَيْنٌ فَلَيْسَ بِالدِّينَارِ وَالدِّرْهَمِ، وَلَكِنَّهَا الْحَسَنَاتُ وَالسَّيِّئَاتُ».

(السنن الكبير للبيهقي)

"If someone passes away and has a debt to pay off, it will not be settled (in the hereafter) with *dīnārs* or *dirhams*. Rather, it will be done by way of righteous deeds and sins." (Sunan al-Kabīr of al-Bayhaqī)

In addition, someone who is martyred in Allāh's (ﷻ) path will be pardoned for all of their sins, but not for their debts.

ʿAbdullāh ibn ʿAmr ibn al-ʿĀṣ (رضي الله عنهما) narrates that the Prophet (ﷺ) said:

«يُغْفَرُ لِلشَّهِيدِ كُلُّ ذَنْبٍ إِلاَّ الدَّيْنَ».

(رواه مسلم)

"All of the sins of a *shahīd* (martyr) are forgiven except for debt." (Muslim)

Another Prophetic narration mentions:

«نَفْسُ الْمُؤْمِنِ مُعَلَّقَةٌ بِدَيْنِهِ حَتَّى يُقْضَى عَنْهُ».

(رواه الترمذي)

> "The soul of a believer is held hostage by his debt in his grave until it is paid off." (Tirmidhī)

Commenting on this *ḥadīth,* Shaykh ʿAbdur Raḥmān Mubārakpūrī (ﷺ) writes in his commentary of Tirmidhī, *Tuḥfat al-Aḥwadhī*:

«قَوْلُهُ نَفْسُ الْمُؤْمِنِ مُعَلَّقَةٌ قَالَ السُّيُوطِيُّ أَيْ مَحْبُوسَةٌ عَنْ مَقَامِهَا الْكَرِيمِ وَقَالَ الْعِرَاقِيُّ أَيْ أَمْرُهَا مَوْقُوفٌ لَا حُكْمَ لَهَا بِنَجَاةٍ وَلَا هَلَاكٍ حَتَّى يُنْظَرَ هَلْ يُقْضَى مَا عَلَيْهَا مِنَ الدَّيْنِ أَمْ لَا انْتَهَى».

(تحفة الأحوذي)

> Imām al-Suyūṭī said, "It (the soul) is detained and kept from reaching its noble destination. Imām al-ʿIrāqī said, "No judgement will be passed as to whether it will be saved or doomed until it is determined whether his debt will be paid off or not." (Tuḥfat al-Aḥwadhī)

The teachings of Islām treat the subject of debts very seriously in order to protect people's rights, and so that individuals in society do not end up exploiting debts and all of the negative effects that ensue from them.

When someone incurs a debt, he may end up feeling quite unsettled and fearful, especially if he encounters the lender after the loan period is over.

This is the meaning of a *ḥadīth* which has been documented in the *Musnad* of Imām Aḥmad (ﷺ) where the Prophet (ﷺ) states:

«لَا تُخِيفُوا أَنْفُسَكُمْ بِالدَّيْنِ».

(مسند أحمد)

"Do not put yourselves in a state of fear by way of debts." (Musnad Aḥmad)

This means you should try you best not incur debts because that will expose you to various liabilities.

It is for this same reason that once ʿAbdullāh ibn ʿUmar (؟) said to a colleague Ḥumrān (؟) that:

«يَا حُمْرَانُ، اتَّقِ اللَّهَ، وَلَا تَمُتْ وَعَلَيْكَ دَيْنٌ فَيُؤْخَذَ مِنْ حَسَنَاتِكَ لَا دِينَارَ ثَمَّ وَلَا دِرْهَمَ»

(مصنف عبد الرزاق)

"O Ḥumrān, fear Allāh and do not die in debt, otherwise it be taken from your good deeds when there will be no *dīnārs* and no *dirhams*." (Muṣnaf ʿAbd al-Razzāq)

After incurring a debt, a person may even end up lying, breaking promises, deliberately evading the lender, and using deceptive tactics to prove one's inability to pay back the loan.

A narration in *Ṣaḥīḥ al-Bukhārī* states:

«إِنَّ الرَّجُلَ إِذَا غَرِمَ، حَدَّثَ فَكَذَبَ، وَوَعَدَ فَأَخْلَفَ»

(رواه البخاري)

"When a person incurs a debt, he lies when he speaks, and breaks promises when he makes them." (Bukhārī)

In fact, there are times when a big portion of a person's income may go towards paying off debts, and then he may need to take a loan once again. This cycle then repeats such that one continues to be in debt, and a person humiliates oneself in ways that no person of faith should.

There are many people whose debts cause them a lot distress. Some even become ill and lose their health as a result of them. Due to how much their minds are preoccupied with their debts and the lenders who are after them, they may even neglect to perform various acts of worship to Allāh (؟) which would draw them nearer to Him.

Some of the pious predecessors would say:

«مَا دَخَلَ هَمُّ الدَّيْنِ قَلْبًا إِلَّا أَذْهَبَ مِنَ الْعَقْلِ مَا لَا يَعُودُ إِلَيْهِ».

(فتح الباري)

"Any time an issue relating to a debt enters the heart, part of the intellect leaves and will not return." (Fatḥ al-Bārī)

Imām al-Qurṭubī (ﷺ) commenting on the verse:

﴿۞ وَإِن كُنتُمْ عَلَىٰ سَفَرٍ وَلَمْ تَجِدُوا كَاتِبًا فَرِهَانٌ مَّقْبُوضَةٌ ۝٢٨٣﴾ [البقرة الآية ٢٨٣]

"If you are on a journey (and contract a debt) and cannot find a scribe (or any means to record the debt), then something (can be) taken (by the creditor) as security (from the debtor)." (Baqarah 2:283)

Explains that:

«قَالَ عُلَمَاؤُنَا: وَإِنَّمَا كَانَ شَيْنًا وَمَذَلَّةً لِمَا فِيهِ مِنْ شَغْلِ الْقَلْبِ وَالْبَالِ وَالْهَمِّ اللَّازِمِ فِي قَضَائِهِ، وَالتَّذَلُّلِ لِلْغَرِيمِ عِنْدَ لِقَائِهِ، وَتَحَمُّلِ مِنَّتِهِ بِالتَّأْخِيرِ إِلَى حِينِ أَوَانِهِ. وَرُبَّمَا يَعِدُ مِنْ نَفْسِهِ الْقَضَاءَ فَيُخْلِفُ، أَوْ يُحَدِّثُ الْغَرِيمَ بِسَبَبِهِ فَيَكْذِبُ، أَوْ يَحْلِفُ لَهُ فَيَحْنَثُ، إِلَى غَيْرِ ذَلِكَ. وَلِهَذَا كَانَ عَلَيْهِ السَّلَامُ يَتَعَوَّذُ مِنَ الْمَأْثَمِ وَالْمَغْرَمِ، وَهُوَ الدَّيْنُ. فَقِيلَ لَهُ: يَا رَسُولَ اللَّهِ، مَا أَكْثَرَ مَا تَتَعَوَّذُ مِنَ الْمَغْرَمِ؟ فَقَالَ: إِنَّ الرَّجُلَ إِذَا غَرِمَ حَدَّثَ فَكَذَبَ وَوَعَدَ فَأَخْلَفَ. وَأَيْضًا فَرُبَّمَا قَدْ مَاتَ وَلَمْ يَقْضِ الدَّيْنَ فَيُرْتَهَنُ بِهِ، كَمَا قَالَ عَلَيْهِ السَّلَامُ: نَسَمَةُ الْمُؤْمِنِ مُرْتَهَنَةٌ فِي قَبْرِهِ بِدَيْنِهِ حتى يقضى عنه. وَكُلُّ هَذِهِ الْأَسْبَابِ مَشَائِنُ فِي الدِّينِ تُذْهِبُ جَمَالَهُ وَتُنْقِصُ كَمَالَهُ. وَاللَّهُ أَعْلَمُ».

(تفسير القرطبي)

Our scholars have said: "It (a debt) is a disgrace and a humiliation because it preoccupies the mind and makes one worried about paying it off, and makes one feel humiliated before the lender when he meets him, and one feels that he is

> doing a favour when accepting a delay in payment. Perhaps he (the borrower) may promise himself that he will pay it off but then breaks that promise, or speaks to the lender and lies to him, or swears an oath to him but then breaks it, and so on. Moreover, one may die without having paid off the debt thus will be held hostage because of it; as the Prophet (ﷺ) said: 'The soul of a believer is held hostage by one's debt in the grave until it is paid off.' All of that undermines a person's religious commitments." (Tafsīr al-Qurṭubī)

Debts bring distress at night and disgrace during the day. A person in debt ends up thinking about nothing else except for that.

ʿUmar ibn al-Khaṭṭāb (رضي الله عنه) on the severity of debts would say:

«إِيَّاكُمْ وَالدَّيْنَ؛ فَإِنَّ أَوَّلَهُ هَمٌّ، وَآخِرَهُ حَرْبٌ».

(موطأ الإمام مالك)

> "Beware of a debt, for it starts with worry and it ends with war." (Muwaṭṭā' Imām al-Mālik)

Debts become wars in the sense that negligence in paying them off is one of the greatest reasons for people to boycott each other and dispute - even with their own friends and relatives. Matters may even escalate to the level of court cases which result in putting people through major trouble and a lot of stress.

Therefore, it is necessary for Muslims to refrain from the property of others. They should try their best not to enter the realm of debt, since avoiding it will free them from liabilities in this world and the hereafter. They should train themselves and their families to be content, persevere, and be pleased with the provisions which Allāh has apportioned for them in this life.

Additionally, immense goodness results from moderation in spending.

Therefore, Muslims should stay far from wastefulness and extravagance. They should not spend their money on things which have no legitimate purpose just so that they can boast, or keep up with others around them and not be outdone. Falling prey to that wasteful mindset is a major and widespread cause of people putting themselves in debt.

It must also be understood that the directives of Islām do not unrestrictedly prohibit loans or using the wealth of others. Rather, Islām's directives give us various beneficial guidelines about this matter which protect a Muslim from the liabilities and negative consequences of debts.

A Muslim must not incur a debt unless it is for something permitted in Islām and which he is in dire need of. He must not incur a debt for things which are luxuries, objects he does not need, or items which are sinful and prohibited by Allāh.

In addition, a Muslim who takes a loan must have every intention of paying it back. Taking a loan for something permissible in Islām, and having the resolute intention of paying it back is among the most important causes behind Allāh (ﷻ) helping a person in paying off what one owes.

ʿAbdullāh ibn Jaʿfar (رضي الله عنهما) narrates that the Prophet (ﷺ) said:

«إِنَّ اللَّهَ مَعَ الدَّائِنِ حَتَّى يَقْضِيَ دَيْنَهُ، مَا لَمْ يَكُنْ فِيمَا يَكْرَهُ اللَّهُ».

(سنن ابن ماجة)

> "Allāh is certainly with someone who incurs a debt all of the way until he pays it off, so long as his debt was not incurred for something despised by Allāh." (Sunan Ibn Mājah)

Another *ḥadīth* states:

«مَا مِنْ أَحَدٍ يَدَّانُ دَيْنًا، فَعَلِمَ اللهُ أَنَّهُ يُرِيدُ قَضَاءَهُ، إِلَّا أَدَّاهُ اللهُ عَنْهُ فِي الدُّنْيَا».

(سنن النسائي)

"When anyone incurs a debt, and Allāh knows that he intends to pay it back, Allāh will undoubtedly enable him to pay it back." (Sunan al-Nasā'ī)

If a Muslim finds oneself forced to take a loan, it must be done in a manner permitted by Islām. It must not be done in a way that contains doubt, deception, or ploys used to disguise interest. When someone takes a loan that involves impermissible matters, Allāh (ﷻ) would not grant him guidance or assistance. Such a person will be like one trying to use fire in order to protect oneself from heat.

Both sides – the debtor and the lender – should ensure that the loan is recorded and witnessed, as instructed by Allāh (ﷻ) in the *āyah* about debts.

Regardless of how small or large the amount is, neither party should find it troublesome to keep a record of it. That is most just in the court of Allāh (ﷻ) and most conducive to protecting the rights of the parties involved.

The debtor must do one's utmost to pay back the loan as soon as it is due so that one can be freed from any liability as quickly as possible.

There is an authentic Prophetic narration which states:

«إِنَّ خِيَارَ عِبَادِ اللهِ الْمُوَفُّونَ الْمُطَيِّبونَ».

(حلية الأولياء لأبي نعيم الأصبهاني)

"The servants of Allāh whom He considers to be the best are those who are righteous, and give others the full rights to which they are entitled." (Ḥilyat al-Awliyā' of Abū Naʿīm al-Iṣbahānī)

It is not permissible for a person to procrastinate and withhold the rights of others if one has enough money to repay a debt which was incurred. Refraining from paying back a lender is a form of causing one harm. On the contrary, a person deserves to be thanked by giving back what belonged to the other person.

When a person deals with a lender in a lazy or deceptive way, then it shows that the person has quite a low standard of ethics and morals.

That conduct of his constitutes a form of injustice which displeases Allāh (ﷻ).

A *ḥadīth* collected both by Imām al-Bukhārī and Imām Muslim (رحمهما الله) states:

«مَطْلُ الغَنِيِّ ظُلْمٌ».

(رواه البخاري ومسلم)

> "A wealthy person who delays in repaying a debt has done injustice." (Narrated by both al-Bukhārī and Muslim)

In addition, a *ḥadīth* documented in the *Sunan of Ibn Mājah* (رحمه الله) states on the authority of Ismāʿīl ibn Ibrāhīm ibn ʿAbdullāh ibn Abī Rabīʿah who narrates from his father that his grandfather said:

«اسْتَقْرَضَ مِنِّي النَّبِيُّ ﷺ أَرْبَعِينَ أَلْفًا، فَجَاءَهُ مَالٌ فَدَفَعَهُ إِلَيَّ، وَقَالَ: بَارَكَ اللَّهُ لَكَ فِي أَهْلِكَ وَمَالِكَ، إِنَّمَا جَزَاءُ السَّلَفِ الْحَمْدُ وَالْأَدَاءُ».

(سنن ابن ماجة)

> "The Prophet (ﷺ) borrowed 40 000 from me, then some wealth came to him, and he paid me back and said: 'May Allāh bless your family and your wealth for you. The reward for lending is repayment and words of appreciation.'" (Sunan Ibn Mājah)

When a person is forced to incur a debt for something permissible and has the resolute intention of paying it back, then Allāh (ﷻ) will guide and assist him. Allāh (ﷻ) will be with that person until the debt is settled.

The person should also persistently beseech Allāh (ﷻ) to assist him in settling the debt, and make sure to use the remarkable supplication which the Prophet (ﷺ) taught ʿAlī ibn Abī Ṭālib (رضي الله عنه), which is as follows:

«أَلَا أُعَلِّمُكَ كَلِمَاتٍ، لَوْ كَانَ عَلَيْكَ مِثْلُ جَبَلِ صِيرٍ دَيْنًا لَأَدَّاهُ اللَّهُ عَنْكَ؟ قُلِ: اللَّهُمَّ اكْفِنِي بِحَلَالِكَ عَنْ حَرَامِكَ، وَاغْنِنِي بِفَضْلِكَ عَمَّنْ سِوَاكَ».

(مسند أحمد)

> "Shall I not teach you a supplication by which Allāh will enable you to repay a debt that you owe, even if it is as large as the mountain known as Ṣabīr? Say: 'O Allāh, suffice me with what You have made permissible so that I do not resort to anything impermissible, and enrich me from Your bounty so that I would not need anyone besides You.'" (Musnad Aḥmad)

The Messenger of Allāh (ﷺ) also taught us that when we experience any adversity, we must resort to Allāh (ﷻ) for its alleviation and removal since He is the only One Who is able to do all things, and He is not in need of anything or anyone at all.

The Prophet (ﷺ) states:

«مَنْ نَزَلَتْ بِهِ فَاقَةٌ فَأَنْزَلَهَا بِالنَّاسِ لَمْ تُسَدَّ فَاقَتُهُ، وَمَنْ نَزَلَتْ بِهِ فَاقَةٌ فَأَنْزَلَهَا بِاللَّهِ، فَيُوشِكُ اللَّهُ لَهُ بِرِزْقٍ عَاجِلٍ أَوْ آجِلٍ».

(رواه الترمذي)

> "When a person is stricken by poverty and he resorts to people, his need will not be fulfilled. However, when someone is stricken by poverty and he resorts to Allāh, then it will not be long before Allāh grants him provision, either sooner or later." (Tirmidhī)

Anyone who incurs a debt should ensure that one remains moderate in spending, handles the various facets of life with wisdom and sound judgement, and deals with priorities first. This course of action will effectively assist a person in paying off one's debts, and give people the rights to which they are entitled.

Abū Hurairah (رضي الله عنه) reports that the Prophet (ﷺ) said:

«مَنْ أَخَذَ أَمْوَالَ النَّاسِ يُرِيدُ أَدَاءَهَا أَدَّى اللَّهُ عَنْهُ، وَمَنْ أَخَذَ يُرِيدُ إِتْلَافَهَا أَتْلَفَهُ اللَّهُ».

(رواه البخاري)

"If a person takes money from others with the intention of returning it, then Allāh will enable one to pay it back; and if someone takes money from others with the intention of ruining it (or not paying it back), then Allāh will ruin him." (Bukhārī)

Imām al-Qurṭubī (ﷺ) writes commenting on the verse:

﴿وَلَا تَحْسَبَنَّ ٱلَّذِينَ قُتِلُوا۟ فِى سَبِيلِ ٱللَّهِ أَمْوَٰتًۢا ۚ بَلْ أَحْيَآءٌ عِندَ رَبِّهِمْ يُرْزَقُونَ ﴿١٦٩﴾﴾

[آل عِمْرَان الآية ١٦٩]

"And never think of those who have been slain in the cause of Allāh as dead. Rather, they are alive with their Lord, receiving provision." (Āle ʿImrān 3:169)

«الدَّيْنُ الَّذِي يُحْبَسُ بِهِ صَاحِبُهُ عَنِ الْجَنَّةِ وَاللَّهُ أَعْلَمُ هُوَ الَّذِي قَدْ تَرَكَ لَهُ وَفَاءً وَلَمْ يُوصِ بِهِ. أَوْ قَدَرَ عَلَى الْأَدَاءِ فَلَمْ يُؤَدِّهِ، أَوِ ادَّانَهُ فِي سَرَفٍ أَوْ فِي سَفَهٍ وَمَاتَ وَلَمْ يُوَفِّهِ. وَأَمَّا مَنِ ادَّانَ فِي حَقٍّ وَاجِبٍ لِفَاقَةٍ وَعُسْرٍ وَمَاتَ وَلَمْ يَتْرُكْ وَفَاءً فَإِنَّ اللَّهَ لَا يَحْبِسُهُ عَنِ الْجَنَّةِ إِنْ شَاءَ اللَّهُ».

(تفسير القرطبي)

"The debt for which a person will be kept out of Paradise – and Allāh knows best – is that for which he left behind enough to pay it off, but he did not leave instructions to that effect; or he was able to pay it off but did not do so; or he took the loan for some unlawful or extravagant matter and died without having paid it off. As for a person who took a loan for something lawful because he was poor, and he died without leaving behind anything to pay it off, Allāh will not keep him from Paradise because of it, Inshā' Allāh." (Tafsīr al-Qurṭubī)

The directives of our religion teach us all-encompassing ethics to protect the rights of people and their properties.

Islām's directives also provide anyone who incurs a debt with beneficial guidelines which will lead a person to attain a lot of goodness from Allāh (ﷻ) if they comply with what the religion teaches. Therefore, we should never allow ourselves to fall into debt unless it is extremely necessary, and we have the intention and means to pay it back. We should try our best to adjust our lives and cut out all of the extra luxuries if we can, rather than borrow from others.

Those who have fallen into the habit of borrowing may one day become depressed, stressed, disgraced or even suicidal - though they may appear wealthy! If any one of us is in a situation of debt at this moment, then let us try our utmost best to pay off our debts as soon as possible. Strive hard to pay them off, put our trust in Allāh (ﷻ), and pray to Him to make it easy for us *Inshā' Allāh.*

KHUṬBAH 56

Shayṭān through the Lens of Qur'ānic and Prophetic Narratives

The worldly life is an abode of tests and trials, and the worst of trials are those which cut a servant off from his Lord and his religion. A sensible and wise person should pursue to identify who his true friends and foes are. Allāh (ﷻ) has informed us about an open enemy whose trials are the most difficult for mankind because he is the leading and greatest enemy, and the root of everything that harms humankind.

Shayṭān's hatred towards the children of Ādam (ﷺ) is vicious and open. He is undeniably man's most manifest enemy.

Allāh (ﷻ) says in the Qur'ān:

﴿إِنَّ ٱلشَّيۡطَٰنَ لِلۡإِنسَٰنِ عَدُوٌّ مُّبِينٌ ۝٥﴾ [يوسف الآية ٥]

"Undoubtedly Shayṭān is an open enemy to man." (Yūsuf 12:5)

In Arabic, Shayṭān (plural shayāṭīn) comes from:

a) Shaṭaṭa (شَطَطَ): to exceed the limits, to go too far, to transgress, to go into an extreme;

b) Shāṭṭa (شاطَّ): to deviate, stray away from something, to be far away, or to get far away from something;

c) Shāṭa (شاطَ): to burn or to be burned. In Arabic, it is said when someone is extremely angry: "He was burning with anger" (شاطَ بِهِ الغَضَبُ - shāṭa bihi al-ghaḍab);

Consequently, the reason why Shayṭān is called Shayṭān is because he is far away from:

1) The Mercy of Allāh (ﷻ); and
2) Any type of goodness.

Shayṭān exceeded the limits of Allāh (ﷻ) and encourages others to do the same. He deviated from the path of Allāh (ﷻ), and encourages others to diverge and stray awry from the path of Allāh (ﷻ) as well.

Shayṭān is man's constant, ruthless opponent. He swore an oath that he will be the enemy of the children of Ādam (عليه السلام), and that he will try to misguide them all.

Allāh (ﷻ) says in the Qur'ān:

﴿قَالَ فَبِمَآ أَغۡوَيۡتَنِي لَأَقۡعُدَنَّ لَهُمۡ صِرَٰطَكَ ٱلۡمُسۡتَقِيمَ ١٦ ثُمَّ لَأٓتِيَنَّهُم مِّنۢ بَيۡنِ أَيۡدِيهِمۡ
وَمِنۡ خَلۡفِهِمۡ وَعَنۡ أَيۡمَٰنِهِمۡ وَعَن شَمَآئِلِهِمۡۖ وَلَا تَجِدُ أَكۡثَرَهُمۡ شَٰكِرِينَ ١٧﴾

[الأَعْرَاف من الآية ١٦ الى الآية ١٧]

> He (Iblīs) said: "I swear that because You sent me astray, I will definitely waylay (wait in ambush for) them (mankind) on Your straight path (Islām). (I shall do everything to stop them from Islām.) (To mislead them) I will then approach (ambush and confuse) them from their front, and from their backs, and their right, and their left (in every possible manner and method), and You will not find most of them to be grateful (most of them will follow me and not Your religion of Islām)." (Al-Aʿrāf 7:16-17)

The reason for his enmity towards Ādam (عليه السلام) and his offspring is because Allāh (ﷻ) honoured and favoured Ādam (عليه السلام). He created Ādam (عليه السلام) with His Own Hands, made him dwell in Paradise, taught him the names of all things, commanded His angels to prostrate themselves before him, and honoured his offspring after him as well. Shayṭān envied Ādam (عليه السلام) because of these blessings. Driven by arrogance, which is the root of all evil, he refused to prostrate himself to Ādam (عليه السلام) and said:

﴿أَنَا۠ خَيْرٌ مِّنْهُ خَلَقْتَنِى مِن نَّارٍ وَخَلَقْتَهُۥ مِن طِينٍ ۝١٢﴾ [الأعراف الآية ١٢]

"I am better than he (Ādam ﷺ)! You have created me from fire and created him from clay." (While Iblīs argued that fire is better than sand because fire burns upwards and sand falls down, he failed to realize that sand extinguishes fire, and that it is constructive whereas fire is destructive.) (Al-Aʿrāf 7:12)

Following his expulsion from Paradise, he declared his enmity towards man:

﴿قَالَ فَبِعِزَّتِكَ لَأُغْوِيَنَّهُمْ أَجْمَعِينَ ۝٨٢﴾ [ص الآية ٨٢]

He (Iblīs) said, "(I swear) By Your honour! I shall definitely mislead (corrupt) all of them (humankind)..." (Ṣād 38:82)

Shayṭān plotted against Ādam and Ḥawwā (ﷺ) and adorned disobedience to them such that they themselves were also removed from Paradise. He is still scheming against people to harm them physically and morally. He targets their beliefs and acts of worship, their bodies and souls, their wealth and children, and even their food and drink. Shayṭān seeks to harm human beings during their sleep, while they are awake, during their health, in sickness, and in all of their circumstances.

Jābir (ﷺ) narrates that he heard the Prophet (ﷺ) saying:

« إِنَّ الشَّيْطَانَ يَحْضُرُ أَحَدَكُمْ عِنْدَ كُلِّ شَيْءٍ مِنْ شَأْنِهِ».

(رواه مسلم)

"Indeed, Shayṭān is present with every one of you in everything that he does." (Muslim)

His ultimate goal is to spoil a believer's pure faith and beliefs.

Allāh (ﷻ) says:

﴿۞ أَلَمۡ أَعۡهَدۡ إِلَيۡكُمۡ يَٰبَنِيٓ ءَادَمَ أَن لَّا تَعۡبُدُواْ ٱلشَّيۡطَٰنَۖ إِنَّهُۥ لَكُمۡ عَدُوّٞ مُّبِينٞ ٦٠﴾ [يس الآية ٦٠]

(Allāh will remind the people saying,) "O children of Ādam! Did I not emphasize to you that you should not worship (follow the dictates of) Shayṭān (who encouraged you to worship besides Allāh)? He is certainly your open enemy (and will always mislead you)." (Yāsīn 36:60)

The Prophet (ﷺ) states:

«إِذَا أَصْبَحَ إِبْلِيس بَثَّ جُنُودَهُ، فَيَقُولُ: مَنْ أَضَلَّ الْيَوْمَ مُسْلِمًا أَلْبَسْتُهُ التَّاجَ».

(رواه ابن حبّان)

"Every morning, Iblīs (Shayṭān) dispatches his soldiers saying: 'Whoever of you misguides a Muslim, I will make him wear the crown.'" (Ibn Ḥibbān)

Shayṭān pursues to ruin the pure nature of declaring Allāh's (ﷻ) Oneness, which is the most valued thing that a person can possess.

It is mentioned in a *Ḥadīth al-Qudsī* that Allāh (ﷻ) says:

«إِنِّي خَلَقْتُ عِبَادِي حُنَفَاءَ كُلَّهُمْ، وَإِنَّ كُلَّ مَا أَنْحَلْتُ عِبَادِي فَهُوَ لَهُمْ حَلَالٌ، وَإِنَّ الشَّيَاطِينَ أَتَتْهُمْ فَاجْتَالَتْهُمْ عَنْ دِينِهِمْ، وَحَرَّمَتْ عَلَيْهِمُ الَّذِي أَحْلَلْتُ لَهُمْ، وَأَمَرَتْهُمْ أَنْ يُشْرِكُوا بِي مَا لَمْ أُنْزِلْ بِهِ سُلْطَانًا».

(رواه ابن حبّان)

"I created My servants as *ḥunafā'* (having a natural inclination to the worship of Allāh only), but it is Shayṭān who turns them away from the right religion, and makes unlawful what has been declared lawful for them, and commands them to ascribe partnership with Me for which I have not sent down any authority." (Ibn Ḥibbān)

Whoever worships anything other than Allāh (ﷻ) is in fact, invoking and worshipping nothing but Shayṭān.

Allāh (ﷻ) says in the Qur'ān:

﴿إِن يَدْعُونَ مِن دُونِهِۦٓ إِلَّآ إِنَٰثًا وَإِن يَدْعُونَ إِلَّا شَيْطَٰنًا مَّرِيدًا ﴿١١٧﴾﴾ [النِّسَاء الآية ١١٧]

> They worship only females (because the idols of the *mushrikīn* (polytheists) of Arabia had female names such as Lāt, Manāt, and ʿUzzā), and they call upon (worship) the rebellious Shayṭān (by doing whatever he tells them). (Nisā'4:117)

One of the ways in which Shayṭān corrupts people's faith is by teaching them magic so that those who practice it will ultimately become disbelievers in the Oneness of Allāh (ﷻ), just like those who seek their help.

Allāh (ﷻ) says:

﴿وَٱتَّبَعُوا۟ مَا تَتْلُوا۟ ٱلشَّيَٰطِينُ عَلَىٰ مُلْكِ سُلَيْمَٰنَ ۖ وَمَا كَفَرَ سُلَيْمَٰنُ وَلَٰكِنَّ ٱلشَّيَٰطِينَ كَفَرُوا۟ يُعَلِّمُونَ ٱلنَّاسَ ٱلسِّحْرَ ﴿١٠٢﴾﴾ [البَقَرَة الآية ١٠٢]

> And they followed what the Shayāṭīn (devils) gave out (falsely of the magic) in the lifetime of Sulaymān. Sulaymān did not disbelieve, but the Shayāṭīn (devils) disbelieved, teaching men magic.... (Baqarah 2:102)

Muḥammad ibn Isḥāq (رحمه الله) relates:

«وَذَلِكَ أَنَّ رَسُولَ اللَّهِ ﷺ لَمَّا ذَكَرَ سُلَيْمَانَ بْنَ دَاوُدَ فِي الْمُرْسَلِينَ، قَالَ بَعْضُ أَحْبَارِهِمْ: أَلَا تَعْجَبُونَ مِنْ مُحَمَّدٍ، يَزْعُمُ أَنَّ سُلَيْمَانَ بْنَ دَاوُدَ كَانَ نَبِيًّا، وَاللَّهِ مَا كَانَ إِلَّا سَاحِرًا. فَأَنْزَلَ اللَّهُ تَعَالَى فِي ذَلِكَ مِنْ قَوْلِهِمْ: ﴿وَمَا كَفَرَ سُلَيْمَٰنُ وَلَٰكِنَّ ٱلشَّيَٰطِينَ كَفَرُوا۟ ﴿١٠٢﴾﴾ [البَقَرَة الآية ١٠٢] ، أَيْ أَلْقَتْ إِلَى بَنِي آدَمَ أَنَّ مَا فَعَلَهُ سُلَيْمَانُ مِنْ رُكُوبِ الْبَحْرِ وَاسْتِسْخَارِ الطَّيْرِ وَالشَّيَاطِينِ كَانَ سِحْرًا».

(تفسير القرطبي)

> "When the Messenger of Allāh (ﷺ) mentioned Sulaymān (ﷺ) as one of the Messengers, some people remarked by saying: 'Muḥammad claims that the son of Dāwūd was a Prophet! By Allāh, he was nothing but a sorcerer!' Then Allāh revealed: 'Sulaymān did not disbelieve, but in fact the Shayāṭīn (devils) did.' (Baqarah 2:102) This means that the clerics told people that what Sulaymān (ﷺ) did with respect to riding the seas and subjugating the birds and *jinn* was magic." (Tafsīr al-Qurṭubī)

This verse declares the innocence of Prophet Sulaymān (ﷺ). The priests accused him of magic and since magic entails disbelief, they were ascribing disbelief to him. However, Allāh (ﷻ) makes it clear by saying that the disbelief of the Shayāṭīn was established because they were the ones who taught magic to the people.

Towards the end of times, *Dajjāl* will appear and say: "I am your lord." The Prophet (ﷺ) states that:

«وَيَبْعَثُ اللهُ مَعَهُ شَيَاطِينَ تُكَلِّمُ النَّاسَ».

(رواه أحمد)

> "Allāh will send devils with him who will talk to the people." (Narrated by Aḥmad)

The horrifying effects of the Last Hour will come only upon the wickedest of people, whom Shayṭān will command to worship idols.

ʿAbdullah ibn ʿAmr (رضي الله عنه) reports that the Prophet (ﷺ) said:

«يَخْرُجُ الدَّجَّالُ فِي أُمَّتِي فَيَمْكُثُ أَرْبَعِينَ - لَا أَدْرِي: أَرْبَعِينَ يَوْمًا، أَوْ أَرْبَعِينَ شَهْرًا، أَوْ أَرْبَعِينَ عَامًا، فَيَبْعَثُ اللهُ عِيسَى ابْنَ مَرْيَمَ كَأَنَّهُ عُرْوَةُ بْنُ مَسْعُودٍ، فَيَطْلُبُهُ فَيُهْلِكُهُ، ثُمَّ يَمْكُثُ النَّاسُ سَبْعَ سِنِينَ، لَيْسَ بَيْنَ اثْنَيْنِ عَدَاوَةٌ، ثُمَّ يُرْسِلُ اللهُ رِيحًا بَارِدَةً مِنْ قِبَلِ الشَّأْمِ، فَلَا يَبْقَى عَلَى وَجْهِ الْأَرْضِ أَحَدٌ فِي قَلْبِهِ مِثْقَالُ ذَرَّةٍ مِنْ خَيْرٍ أَوْ إِيمَانٍ إِلَّا قَبَضَتْهُ، حَتَّى لَوْ أَنَّ أَحَدَكُمْ دَخَلَ

فِي كَبِدِ جَبَلٍ لَدَخَلَتْهُ عَلَيْهِ، حَتَّى تَقْبِضَهُ، قَالَ: سَمِعْتُهَا مِنْ رَسُولِ اللهِ ﷺ، قَالَ: فَيَبْقَى شِرَارُ النَّاسِ فِي خِفَّةِ الطَّيْرِ وَأَحْلَامِ السِّبَاعِ، لَا يَعْرِفُونَ مَعْرُوفًا وَلَا يُنْكِرُونَ مُنْكَرًا، فَيَتَمَثَّلُ لَهُمُ الشَّيْطَانُ، فَيَقُولُ: أَلَا تَسْتَجِيبُونَ؟ فَيَقُولُونَ: فَمَا تَأْمُرُنَا؟ فَيَأْمُرُهُمْ بِعِبَادَةِ الْأَوْثَانِ».

(رواه مسلم)

"*Dajjāl* will appear in my nation and he will stay (in the world) for forty - I cannot say whether he meant forty days, forty months, or forty years. Allāh will then send ʿĪsā, son of Mariam (ﷺ) who will resemble ʿUrwah ibn Masʿūd. He (ʿĪsā) will chase him and slay him. Then people will live for seven years such that there will be no rancor between two people even. Then Allāh will send a cold wind from the side of Syria such that no one will survive on the earth (even those) having a speck of good in him or faith in him - but he will die, so much so that even if some among you were to enter the innermost part of the mountain, this wind will reach that place also and will cause his death. I heard Allāh's Messenger (ﷺ) saying: 'Only the wicked people will survive and they will be as fast as birds (i.e. to commit evil) and as ferocious towards one another as wild beasts. They will never appreciate good, nor condemn evil.' Then Shayṭān will come to them in the garb of a man and will say: 'Will you not obey me?' They will reply: 'What do you order us to do?' He will command them to worship idols." (Muslim)

As for Shayṭān's plotting against a person's acts of worship, he keeps whispering to the worshipper until one becomes dubious about one's state of purity.

The Prophet (ﷺ) states:

«إِذَا أَتَى أَحَدَكُمُ الشَّيْطَانُ فَقَالَ: إِنَّكَ قَدْ أَحْدَثْتَ، فَلْيَقُلْ: كَذَبْتَ، إِلَّا مَا سَمِعَ صَوْتَهُ بِأُذُنِهِ، أَوْ وَجَدَ رِيحَهُ بِأَنْفِهِ».

(رواه أحمد)

"Indeed, Shayṭān may come to one of you in his prayers and say: 'You have nullified your ablution,' so you should say: 'You are lying! Unless he hears a sound or smells an odor.'" (Aḥmad)

Concentration and devotion in prayer give a worshipper a feeling of spiritual pleasure, as he is in the company of Allāh (ﷻ). However, when a Muslim begins his prayers, Shayṭān prevents him from observing concentration and devotion through his evil whisperings.

The Prophet (ﷺ) has said:

«إِنَّ أَحَدَكُمْ، إِذَا قَامَ يُصَلِّي جَاءَهُ الشَّيْطَانُ فَلَبَسَ عَلَيْهِ، حَتَّى لَا يَدْرِيَ كَمْ صَلَّى».

(متفق عليه)

"When one of you stands up for prayers, Shayṭān comes and fills him with such doubts that he is not sure how many *rakʿahs* he has prayed." (Agreed Upon)

When Shayṭān finds a gap between the rows of the *muṣallīs* (people congregated) while they engage in their prayers, he enters through them.

Abū Umāmah (رضي الله عنه) narrates that the Prophet (ﷺ) stated:

«سَوُّوا صُفُوفَكُمْ، وَسَوُّوا بَيْنَ مَنَاكِبِكُمْ، وَلِينُوا لِأَيْدِي إِخْوَانِكُمْ، وَسَدِّدُوا الْخَلَلَ، فَإِنَّ الشَّيْطَانَ يَدْخُلُ بَيْنَكُمْ مِثْلَ الْحَذَفِ».

(المعجم الكبير للطبراني)

"Straighten your lines, and align your shoulders, and yield your hands to your brothers, and close the gaps, for indeed Shayṭān comes between you through them, just like a small lamb does." (Al-Muʿjam al-Kabīr of al-Ṭabarānī)

Allāh (ﷻ) is in front of a person performing the prayers. Turning one's face (away from the *qiblah*) during prayers is part of the plotting of Shayṭān's plot.

ʿAbdullāh ibn ʿUmar (رضي الله عنهما) narrates that:

«أَنَّ رَسُولَ اللَّهِ ﷺ رَأَى بُصَاقًا فِي جِدَارِ القِبْلَةِ، فَحَكَّهُ، ثُمَّ أَقْبَلَ عَلَى النَّاسِ، فَقَالَ: إِذَا كَانَ أَحَدُكُمْ يُصَلِّي، فَلاَ يَبْصُقْ قِبَلَ وَجْهِهِ، فَإِنَّ اللَّهَ قِبَلَ وَجْهِهِ إِذَا صَلَّى».

(موطأ الإمام مالك)

"The Messenger of Allāh (ﷺ) saw spittle on the wall of the *qiblah* and scraped it off. Then he went up to the people and said: 'Do not spit in front of you when you are praying, because Allāh, the Blessed and Exalted, is in front of you when you pray.'" (Muwaṭṭā of Imām Mālik)

ʿĀ'ishah (رضي الله عنها) reports that:

«سَأَلْتُ رَسُولَ اللَّهِ ﷺ عَنِ الالْتِفَاتِ فِي الصَّلاَةِ؟ فَقَالَ: هُوَ اخْتِلاَسٌ يَخْتَلِسُهُ الشَّيْطَانُ مِنْ صَلاَةِ العَبْدِ».

(رواه البخاري)

"I asked the Messenger of Allāh (ﷺ) about looking around during the prayers. He replied: 'It is the carrying away of a person from his prayers by Shayṭān.'" (Bukhārī)

Shayṭān is extremely keen to interrupt one's prayer as the Prophet (ﷺ) has described:

«إِذَا صَلَّى أَحَدُكُمْ فَلْيُصَلِّ إِلَى سُتْرَةٍ، وَلْيَدْنُ مِنْهَا، لاَ يَقْطَعُ الشَّيْطَانُ عَلَيْهِ صَلاَتَهُ».

(رواه أبو داود)

> "When any one of you prays towards a *sutra* (an object placed as a barrier in front of oneself) then let him draw close to it, so that Shayṭān may not interrupt him in his prayer." (Abū Dāwūd)

The Prophet (ﷺ) also mentioned:

«مَا مِنْ ثَلاثَةٍ فِي قَرْيَةٍ، وَلاَ بَدْوٍ، لاَ تُقَامُ فِيهِمُ الصَّلاَةُ إلاَّ قَد اسْتَحْوَذَ عَلَيْهِم الشَّيْطَانُ».

(رواه أبو داود)

> "If there are three men in a village or in a desert, and they do not perform the prayers in congregation, then Shayṭān will certainly overcome them." (Abū Dāwūd)

Shayṭān's enmity towards human beings is unlimited. He takes part in all of their activities, including food, drink, and even intimate relations.

Allāh (ﷻ) says in the Qur'ān:

﴿وَٱسْتَفْزِزْ مَنِ ٱسْتَطَعْتَ مِنْهُم بِصَوْتِكَ وَأَجْلِبْ عَلَيْهِم بِخَيْلِكَ وَرَجِلِكَ وَشَارِكْهُمْ فِى ٱلْأَمْوَٰلِ وَٱلْأَوْلَـٰدِ وَعِدْهُمْ ۚ وَمَا يَعِدُهُمُ ٱلشَّيْطَـٰنُ إِلَّا غُرُورًا ﴿٦٤﴾﴾ [الإسْرَاء الآية ٦٤]

> "And fool (mislead) as many of them as you can with your voice (with music and everything else that calls them to sin), attack them with your cavalry and infantry (with all of your might), be a partner in their wealth (by causing them to indulge in stealing, interest and other sins of wealth and by causing them to spend for ulterior motives), and (be a partner in their) children (by causing them to have illegitimate children, and by using their children to lead them astray), and promise them (long lives and that there will be no resurrection)." The promises that Shayṭān makes are only deceptive (a delusion to mislead you, so do not fall for them). (Isrā' 17:64)

Consequently, he tries his best to grab food from the children of Ādam (ﷺ). If a person does not mention the name of Allāh (ﷻ) before he starts to eat, then Shayṭān will eat with him. He even eats whatever bits of food fall down while eating.

In this regard, the Prophet (ﷺ) states:

«إِنَّ الشَّيْطَانَ يَحْضُرُ أَحَدَكُمْ عِنْدَ كُلِّ شَيْءٍ مِنْ شَأْنِهِ، حَتَّى يَحْضُرَهُ عِنْدَ طَعَامِهِ، فَإِذَا سَقَطَتْ مِنْ أَحَدِكُمُ اللُّقْمَةُ، فَلْيُمِطْ مَا كَانَ بِهَا مِنْ أَذًى، ثُمَّ لِيَأْكُلْهَا، وَلَا يَدَعْهَا لِلشَّيْطَانِ، فَإِذَا فَرَغَ فَلْيَلْعَقْ أَصَابِعَهُ، فَإِنَّهُ لَا يَدْرِي فِي أَيِّ طَعَامِهِ تَكُونُ الْبَرَكَةُ».

(رواه مسلم)

> "Surely the Shayṭān is present with each one of you in everything that he does: he is present even when he eats food, so if one of you drops a morsel he should remove away anything dirty on it and eat it and not it leave for Shayṭān; and when he finishes (his food) he should lick his fingers, for he does not know in what portion of his food are the blessings." (Muslim)

During intimate relationships between a man and his wife, Shayṭān fears that they may have a righteous child. Therefore, he attempts to make the husband forget to mention Allāh's (ﷻ) name at the beginning of the act.

In this regard, the Prophet (ﷺ) states:

«لَوْ أَنَّ أَحَدَهُمْ إِذَا أَرَادَ أَنْ يَأْتِيَ أَهْلَهُ، قَالَ: بِاسْمِ اللهِ، اللهُمَّ جَنِّبْنَا الشَّيْطَانَ، وَجَنِّبِ الشَّيْطَانَ مَا رَزَقْتَنَا، فَإِنَّهُ إِنْ يُقَدَّرْ بَيْنَهُمَا وَلَدٌ فِي ذَلِكَ، لَمْ يَضُرَّهُ شَيْطَانٌ أَبَدًا».

(رواه مسلم)

> "When one of you intends to have marital relations with his wife, he should say: 'In the Name of Allāh. O Allāh! Protect us from Shayṭān, and also protect what you bestow upon us (i.e. the coming offspring) from Shayṭān,' and if it is destined that

they should have a child then, Shayṭān will never be able to harm that offspring." (Muslim)

Shayṭān also tries his best to enter a person's home if one does not mention the name of Allāh (ﷻ) upon entering it.

The Prophet (ﷺ) states:

«إِذَا دَخَلَ الرَّجُلُ بَيْتَهُ، فَذَكَرَ اللَّهَ عَزَّ وَجَلَّ عِنْدَ دُخُولِهِ، وَعِنْدَ طَعَامِهِ، قَالَ الشَّيْطَانُ: لَا مَبِيتَ لَكُمْ وَلَا عَشَاءَ، وَإِذَا دَخَلَ فَلَمْ يَذْكُرِ اللَّهَ عِنْدَ دُخُولِهِ قَالَ الشَّيْطَانُ: أَدْرَكْتُمُ الْمَبِيتَ، وَإِنْ لَمْ يَذْكُرِ اللَّهَ عِنْدَ طَعَامِهِ قَالَ الشَّيْطَانُ: أَدْرَكْتُمُ الْمَبِيتَ وَالْعَشَاءَ».

(رواه مسلم)

"When a person enters his house and mentions Allāh upon entering it, and before one is about to eat, Shayṭān says (to his mates): 'There is no place here for you to spend the night, and no evening meals.' But when a person enters without mentioning Allāh's name, then at his entering, Shayṭān says (to his mates): 'You have found a place to spend the night.' When he does not mention Allāh's name before eating, then Shayṭān says (to his mates): 'You have found a place to spend the night, and the evening meals.'" (Muslim)

At nightfall, the Shayāṭīn spread out to cause mischief and harm to the people.

The Prophet (ﷺ) states:

«إِذَا كَانَ جُنْحُ اللَّيْلِ - أَوْ أَمْسَيْتُمْ - فَكُفُّوا صِبْيَانَكُمْ، فَإِنَّ الشَّيْطَانَ يَنْتَشِرُ حِينَئِذٍ».

(رواه مسلم)

"When the night falls, or when it is evening, prevent your children from going out, for the Shayāṭīn spread out at that time." (Muslim)

Sleep provides a person with rest to regain energy and vigour. However, Shayṭān also interferes with that.

This why the Prophet (ﷺ) states:

«يَعْقِدُ الشَّيْطَانُ عَلَى قَافِيَةِ رَأْسِ أَحَدِكُمْ، إِذَا هُوَ نَامَ ثَلَاثَ عُقَدٍ، يَضْرِبُ مَكَانَ كُلِّ عُقْدَةٍ عَلَيْكَ لَيْلٌ طَوِيلٌ، فَارْقُدْ، فَإِنِ اسْتَيْقَظَ فَذَكَرَ اللَّهَ انْحَلَّتْ عُقْدَةٌ، فَإِنْ تَوَضَّأَ انْحَلَّتْ عُقْدَةٌ، فَإِنْ صَلَّى انْحَلَّتْ عُقْدَةٌ، فَأَصْبَحَ نَشِيطًا، طَيِّبَ النَّفْسِ، وَإِلَّا أَصْبَحَ خَبِيثَ النَّفْسِ كَسْلَانَ».

(متفق عليه)

"When one of you (goes to) sleep, the devil ties three knots at the back of his neck, sealing each knot with: 'You have a long night, so sleep.' If a person wakes up and mentions Allāh, then one of the knots will be loosened; if he performs ablution, then another knot will be loosened; and if he prays, then the third knot will be loosened; and in the morning he will be active and in good spirits; otherwise he will be in bad spirits and sluggish." (Agreed Upon)

When a servant keeps on sleeping and does not get up for prayers, Shayṭān will urinate in his ears.

Once the Prophet (ﷺ) was informed about a man who had slept throughout the night until the morning and missed his *fajr* prayers. So he said:

«ذَاكَ رَجُلٌ بَالَ الشَّيْطَانُ فِي أُذُنَيْهِ، أَوْ قَالَ: فِي أُذُنِهِ».

(رواه مسلم)

"This is a man in whose ears (or he said "in whose ear") Shayṭān urinated." (Muslim)

Shayṭān spends the night in a person's nose during sleep.

The Prophet (ﷺ) has stated:

«إِذَا اسْتَيْقَظَ أَحَدُكُمْ مِنْ مَنَامِهِ فَتَوَضَّأَ فَلْيَسْتَنْثِرْ ثَلَاثًا، فَإِنَّ الشَّيْطَانَ يَبِيتُ عَلَى خَيْشُومِهِ».

(متفق عليه)

> "When one of you wakes up from his sleep, he must clean his nose (by putting water in it and then blowing it out) three times, for the Shayṭān spends the night inside one's nostrils." (Agreed Upon)

Sleep provides peace and tranquility. However, Shayṭān causes a person to have confused dreams and nightmares during their sleep.

The Prophet (ﷺ) states:

«الرُّؤْيَا مِنَ اللَّهِ، وَالْحُلْمُ مِنَ الشَّيْطَانِ».

(متفق عليه)

> "A good dream is from Allāh, and a bad dream (nightmare) is from Shayṭān." (Agreed Upon)

Affection and harmony are good for individuals and societies, but Shayṭān constantly seeks to cause division among people, and to sow the seeds of discord among them.

The Prophet (ﷺ) has stated:

«إِنَّ الشَّيْطَانَ قَدْ أَيِسَ أَنْ يَعْبُدَهُ الْمُصَلُّونَ فِي جَزِيرَةِ الْعَرَبِ، وَلَكِنْ فِي التَّحْرِيشِ بَيْنَهُمْ».

(رواه مسلم)

> "Indeed, Shayṭān has despaired of being worshipped by those who perform the prayers in the Arabian Peninsula, but he has not lost hope in creating dissension among them." (Muslim)

No human being is spared from the evil effects of Shayṭān. The very moment a child is born, Shayṭān pricks him on both sides of his body.

The Prophet (ﷺ) said:

«مَا مِنْ مَوْلُودٍ يُولَدُ إِلَّا نَخَسَهُ الشَّيْطَانُ، فَيَسْتَهِلُّ صَارِخًا مِنْ نَخْسَةِ الشَّيْطَانِ، إِلَّا ابْنَ مَرْيَمَ وَأُمَّهُ». (متفق عليه)

"No child is born but that he is pricked by Shayṭān, and he begins crying because of the pricking of Shayṭān – except for the son of Maryam and his mother." (Agreed Upon)

Shayṭān follows every course of mischief and even circulates in the human body like blood.

The Prophet (ﷺ) said:

«إِنَّ الشَّيْطَانَ يَجْرِي مِنَ الْإِنْسَانِ مَجْرَى الدَّمِ».

(رواه مسلم)

"Surely Shayṭān flows in the son of Ādam like the circulation of blood." (Muslim)

The Prophet (ﷺ) also stated:

«مَا مِنْكُمْ مِنْ أَحَدٍ، إِلَّا وَقَدْ وُكِّلَ بِهِ قَرِينُهُ مِنَ الْجِنِّ قَالُوا: وَإِيَّاكَ؟ يَا رَسُولَ اللهِ قَالَ: وَإِيَّايَ، إِلَّا أَنَّ اللهَ أَعَانَنِي عَلَيْهِ فَأَسْلَمَ، فَلَا يَأْمُرُنِي إِلَّا بِخَيْرٍ».

(رواه مسلم)

"There is no one among you but that a companion from among the *jinn* has been assigned to him." The companions (رضي الله عنهم) asked him: "Even you, O Messenger of Allāh?" The Prophet (ﷺ) replied, "Even me, but Allāh helped me with him and he became Muslim (or: and I am safe from him), so he only enjoins me to do that which is good." (Muslim)

Shayṭān always attempts to mislead the children of Ādam even when they are in their final moments.

The Prophet (ﷺ) would supplicate with the following words:

«اللَّهُمَّ إِنِّي أَعُوذُ بِكَ مِنَ التَّرَدِّي، وَالْهَدْمِ، وَالْغَرَقِ، وَالْحَرِيقِ، وَأَعُوذُ بِكَ أَنْ يَتَخَبَّطَنِي الشَّيْطَانُ عِنْدَ الْمَوْتِ».

(رواه النسائي)

"O Allāh, I seek refuge with You from being thrown from a high place, or being crushed beneath a falling wall, or drowning, or being burned, and I seek refuge with You from being led astray by the Shayṭān at the time of death." (Al-Nasā'ī)

Shayṭān has many ways to use when plotting against the children of Ādam. He adorns the sin for a sinner and makes it look attractive to the person. This is what he did with Ādam and Ḥawwā (ﷺ).

Allāh (ﷻ) says in the Qur'ān:

﴿فَوَسْوَسَ إِلَيْهِ ٱلشَّيْطَٰنُ قَالَ يَٰٓـَٔادَمُ هَلْ أَدُلُّكَ عَلَىٰ شَجَرَةِ ٱلْخُلْدِ وَمُلْكٍ لَّا يَبْلَىٰ ﴿١٢٠﴾﴾

[طه الآية ١٢٠]

However, (to persuade Ādam to eat from the tree,) Shayṭān whispered to him saying: "O Ādam! Should 1 not show you the tree of eternity and a kingdom in which there is no (decay) weakness?" (He also swore that he is their well-wisher. Not knowing deceit, they believed him and ate from the tree.) (Ṭāhā 20:120)

Another form of his trickery against man is to use what a man loves and desires, pretending to be a sincere adviser and well-wisher to him, just like he did when he said to Ādam and Ḥawwā (ﷺ).

﴿وَقَالَ مَا نَهَىٰكُمَا رَبُّكُمَا عَنْ هَٰذِهِ ٱلشَّجَرَةِ إِلَّآ أَن تَكُونَا مَلَكَيْنِ أَوْ تَكُونَا مِنَ ٱلْخَٰلِدِينَ ﴿٢٠﴾ وَقَاسَمَهُمَآ إِنِّى لَكُمَا لَمِنَ ٱلنَّٰصِحِينَ ﴿٢١﴾﴾ [الأعراف من الآية ٢٠ الى الآية ٢١]

And he said: "(O Ādam and Ḥawwā,) your Lord has not forbidden you (from eating the fruit of) this tree, but (because by eating it) you both will transform into angels (free from human characteristics), or both of you will become (its) permanent residents (i.e., never will you be deprived of this station of proximity)." He took an oath before them saying, "I swear that I am definitely one (sincere friend) who is giving you good advice (a sincere well-wisher)." (Al-Aʿrāf 7:20-21)

Shayṭān makes promises to people and arouses in them false desires, while he is in fact, a real deceiver.

Allāh (ﷻ) says in the Qur'ān:

﴿يَعِدُهُمْ وَيُمَنِّيهِمْ ۖ وَمَا يَعِدُهُمُ ٱلشَّيْطَٰنُ إِلَّا غُرُورًا ﴿١٢٠﴾﴾ [النساء الآية ١٢٠]

"He (Shayṭān) promises them (good results) and creates hopes (vain desires of long life and great wealth) within them. (However) Shayṭān promises them only deception (because none of these promises and hopes will materialize)." (Nisā' 4:120)

Shayṭān deceives people by his false promises.

Allāh (ﷻ) says:

﴿إِنَّ وَعْدَ ٱللَّهِ حَقٌّ ۖ فَلَا تَغُرَّنَّكُمُ ٱلْحَيَوٰةُ ٱلدُّنْيَا ۖ وَلَا يَغُرَّنَّكُم بِٱللَّهِ ٱلْغَرُورُ ﴿٥﴾﴾

[فاطر الآية ٥]

"Indeed the promise of Allāh (about the resurrection) is (most) certainly true, so never let the worldly life deceive you (into thinking that you will never be resurrected), nor should the great deceiver (Shayṭān) deceive you about Allāh (by telling you that you may continue sinning because Allāh will forgive you)." (Fāṭir 35:5)

Shayṭān hinders people from spending wealth for the sake of Allāh (ﷻ) and makes evil suggestions to them that they will become poor if they do so.

Allāh (ﷻ) says:

﴿ٱلشَّيْطَٰنُ يَعِدُكُمُ ٱلْفَقْرَ وَيَأْمُرُكُم بِٱلْفَحْشَآءِ ﴿٢٦٨﴾﴾ [البقرة الآية ٢٦٨]

"Shayṭān promises (threatens) you with poverty (telling you that you will become poor if you spend in charity), and orders you to (do acts of) immodesty." (Baqarah 2:268)

Shayṭān brings grief upon people, and makes them lament past incidents and whispers for instance: "If I had done such-and-such, such-and-such would not have happened."

The Prophet (ﷺ) has said:

«وَإِيَّاكَ وَاللَّوْ، فَإِنَّ اللَّوْ، تَفْتَحُ عَمَلَ الشَّيْطَانِ».

(رواه مسلم)

"And beware of (saying): 'If only,' because 'If only' opens the door to Shayṭān." (Muslim)

Shayṭān also achieves his objective through arousing lustful desires, as the Prophet (ﷺ) has described:

«لَا يَخْلُوَنَّ رَجُلٌ بِامْرَأَةٍ إِلَّا كَانَ ثَالِثَهُمَا الشَّيْطَانُ».

(رواه الترمذي)

"No man stays alone with a (strange) woman but that Shayṭān will be the third one present (with them)." (Tirmidhī)

Shayṭān also instigates men and women to abandon decency and neglect modesty and chastity. When the private parts of people are exposed, divine punishment is sure to take place.

Allāh (ﷻ) says:

﴿فَوَسْوَسَ لَهُمَا ٱلشَّيْطَٰنُ لِيُبْدِىَ لَهُمَا مَا وُۥرِىَ عَنْهُمَا مِن سَوْءَٰتِهِمَا ﴿٢٠﴾﴾ [الأعراف الآية ٢٠]

"So Shayṭān whispered to the two of them to expose (reveal) the private parts of their bodies that were concealed from them." (Al-Aʿrāf 7:20)

Shayṭān also fools people by means of prohibited sounds, such as those of musical apparatuses.

Allāh (ﷻ) says:

﴿وَٱسۡتَفۡزِزۡ مَنِ ٱسۡتَطَعۡتَ مِنۡهُم بِصَوۡتِكَ ۝٦٤﴾ [الإسْرَاء الآية ٦٤]

"And fool (mislead) as many of them as you can with your voice (with music and everything else that calls them to sin)." (Isrā' 17:64)

Shayṭān's footsteps are the greatest trap. He sets traps to lure people in order to achieve his goal, but Allāh (ﷻ) warns us about following in his footsteps:

﴿وَلَا تَتَّبِعُواْ خُطُوَٰتِ ٱلشَّيۡطَٰنِۚ إِنَّهُۥ لَكُمۡ عَدُوّٞ مُّبِينٌ ۝١٦٨﴾ [البَقَرَة الآية ١٦٨]

"And do not follow the footsteps of Shayṭān Indeed, he is your open enemy." (Baqarah 2:168)

In his trickery and animosity towards man, Shayṭān strives hard to achieve evil ends, the worst of which is to mislead people and turn them away from the obedience of Allāh (ﷻ).

﴿قَالَ رَبِّ بِمَآ أَغۡوَيۡتَنِي لَأُزَيِّنَنَّ لَهُمۡ فِي ٱلۡأَرۡضِ وَلَأُغۡوِيَنَّهُمۡ أَجۡمَعِينَ ۝٣٩﴾ [الحِجر الآية ٣٩]

He (Iblīs) said, "My Lord, because You sent me astray, I will certainly beautify things (have them with the attribution of evil) for them (mankind) on earth, and will lead them all astray (using all of the devious means which are at my disposal)." (Ḥijr 15:39)

Shayṭān makes people heedless and causes them to forget the remembrance and consciousness of Allāh (ﷻ).

Allāh (ﷻ) says in the Qur'ān:

﴿ٱسۡتَحۡوَذَ عَلَيۡهِمُ ٱلشَّيۡطَٰنُ فَأَنسَىٰهُمۡ ذِكۡرَ ٱللَّهِۚ ۝١٩﴾ [المُجَادلَة الآية ١٩]

"Shayṭān has overpowered (possessed) them (thereby making them do what he wants) and made them forget to remember Allāh (due to which they disobey Allāh's commands)." (Mujādilah 58:19)

Shayṭān instigates people to every form of vice, and turns them away from every kind of virtue.

Allāh (ﷻ) says:

﴿إِنَّمَا يَأْمُرُكُم بِٱلسُّوٓءِ وَٱلْفَحْشَآءِ وَأَن تَقُولُوا۟ عَلَى ٱللَّهِ مَا لَا تَعْلَمُونَ ١٦٩﴾ [البَقَرَة الآية ١٦٩]

"He (Shayṭān) instructs you to commit evil acts, acts of immodesty, and to attribute to Allāh such things about which you have no knowledge (no knowledge that these matters are or are not from Allāh, such as the things that people declare *ḥarām* by themselves, or when they change the text of what Allāh has revealed)." (Baqarah 2:169)

Shayṭān's ultimate objective is to deprive people from the mercy of Allāh and to cause them to dwell in the hellfire.

﴿يَدْعُوا۟ حِزْبَهُۥ لِيَكُونُوا۟ مِنْ أَصْحَـٰبِ ٱلسَّعِيرِ ٦﴾ [فَاطِر الآية ٦]

"He calls to his party (followers) only so that they become inmates (dwellers) of the Blaze (*Jahannam*)." (Fāṭir 35:6)

Following Shayṭān will lead a person to evil outcomes and dire consequences. Every form of distress in this world and the hereafter is the result of following him. Whoever submits to the whispers of Shayṭān will be in a state of confusion and misguidance. On the Day of Judgement, those who followed him will be gathered together with him.

Allāh (ﷻ) says:

﴿فَوَرَبِّكَ لَنَحْشُرَنَّهُمْ وَٱلشَّيَـٰطِينَ ثُمَّ لَنُحْضِرَنَّهُمْ حَوْلَ جَهَنَّمَ جِثِيًّا ٦٨﴾ [مَرْيَم الآية ٦٨]

"So by your Lord! We will certainly gather them (mankind) and the Shayāṭīn (on the Day of Judgement); then We will present them before Hell (hobbling) on their knees." (Maryam 19:68)

The regret of Shayṭān's followers will intensify when he disowns them on the Day of Judgement by saying to them:

﴿وَقَالَ ٱلشَّيۡطَٰنُ لَمَّا قُضِيَ ٱلۡأَمۡرُ إِنَّ ٱللَّهَ وَعَدَكُمۡ وَعۡدَ ٱلۡحَقِّ وَوَعَدتُّكُمۡ فَأَخۡلَفۡتُكُمۡۖ وَمَا كَانَ لِيَ عَلَيۡكُم مِّن سُلۡطَٰنٍ إِلَّآ أَن دَعَوۡتُكُمۡ فَٱسۡتَجَبۡتُمۡ لِيۖ فَلَا تَلُومُونِي وَلُومُوٓاْ أَنفُسَكُمۖ مَّآ أَنَا۠ بِمُصۡرِخِكُمۡ وَمَآ أَنتُم بِمُصۡرِخِيَّ ٢٢﴾ [إبراهيم الآية ٢٢]

When judgement will take place (and the sinners have entered into the hellfire), "And Shayṭān will say (to those with him in Hell: 'Surely Allāh had made a true promise to you (that you will be resurrected and called to account for your actions). I also made promises to you (that these things will not happen), but I broke them (I failed you). The only control that I exercised over you was that I invited you (but I did not force you to do wrong), and you responded to me. So, do not blame me, but blame yourselves. I cannot be a helper to you (against Allāh's punishment), nor can you be helpers to me." (Ibrāhīm 14:22)

The final abode for both the leader (Shayṭān) and his followers will be the hellfire. What a dreadful destination!

Allāh (ﷻ) said to Shayṭān while expelling him from Paradise:

﴿قَالَ ٱخۡرُجۡ مِنۡهَا مَذۡءُومٗا مَّدۡحُورٗاۖ لَّمَن تَبِعَكَ مِنۡهُمۡ لَأَمۡلَأَنَّ جَهَنَّمَ مِنكُمۡ أَجۡمَعِينَ ١٨﴾ [الأعراف الآية ١٨]

He (Allāh) said (to Iblīs): "Get away from here disgraced (wretched) and banished (rejected). Whoever of them (humankind) will follow you, I will fill hell with all of you." (Al-Aʿrāf 7:18)

Shayṭān is so resolute in his objectives that he even misled some of the children and fathers of Allāh's Prophets (ﷺ), such as the son of Nūḥ (ﷺ), and the father of Ibrāhīm (ﷺ). In fact, he was behind the destruction of some entire nations.

Allāh (ﷻ) says:

﴿وَعَادًا وَثَمُودَاْ وَقَد تَّبَيَّنَ لَكُم مِّن مَّسَٰكِنِهِمْۖ وَزَيَّنَ لَهُمُ ٱلشَّيْطَٰنُ أَعْمَٰلَهُمْ فَصَدَّهُمْ عَنِ ٱلسَّبِيلِ وَكَانُواْ مُسْتَبْصِرِينَ ﴿٣٨﴾﴾ [العَنكَبُوت الآية ٣٨]

"And (We destroyed) 'Ād and Thamūd, whose condition (destruction) is apparent (has become clear) to you by (the ruins that are left of) their dwellings. Shayṭān (secretly) beautified their (evil) actions for them and prevented them from the straight path even though they were people of deep insight. (However, his trickery even fooled them)." ('Ankabūt 29:38)

CONCLUSION

There is no way to protect oneself from Shayṭān's cunning tactics except through piety. The hardest of all people on Shayṭān are Allāh's (ﷻ) faithful, obedient and true servants.

Shayṭān himself admitted this fact when he said:

﴿قَالَ فَبِعِزَّتِكَ لَأُغْوِيَنَّهُمْ أَجْمَعِينَ ﴿٨٢﴾ إِلَّا عِبَادَكَ مِنْهُمُ ٱلْمُخْلَصِينَ ﴿٨٣﴾﴾ [ص من الآية ٨٢ الى الآية ٨٣]

He (Iblīs) said: "(I swear) By Your honour! I will definitely mislead (corrupt) all of them (mankind) except Your chosen slaves (servants) among them (the Anbiyā' and the true believers)." (Ṣād 38:82-83)

Seeking refuge in Allāh (ﷻ) from Shayṭān's evil will provide secure protection; and remembering that Allāh (ﷻ) causes His Mercy to descend can drive Shayṭān away.

Whoever recites *Āyat al-Kursī* when he goes to bed will be protected by a guard from Allāh (ﷻ) all night long, and Shayṭān will not be able to come near him until dawn, as is mentioned in a narration of Bukhārī:

«إِذَا أَوَيْتَ إِلَى فِرَاشِكَ فَاقْرَأْ آيَةَ الْكُرْسِيِّ، لَنْ يَزَالَ عَلَيْكَ مِنَ اللَّهِ حَافِظٌ، وَلاَ يَقْرَبُكَ شَيْطَانٌ حَتَّى تُصْبِحَ».

"Whenever you go to your bed, recite *Āyat al-Kursī* for there will be a guard from Allāh who will protect you all night long, and Shayṭān will not be able to come near you until dawn." (Bukhārī)

In addition, the Prophet (ﷺ) has stated:

«مَنْ قَالَ فِي دُبُرِ صَلاَةِ الْفَجْرِ وَهُوَ ثَانٍ رِجْلَيْهِ قَبْلَ أَنْ يَتَكَلَّمَ: لاَ إِلَهَ إِلاَّ اللَّهُ وَحْدَهُ لاَ شَرِيكَ لَهُ، لَهُ الْمُلْكُ وَلَهُ الْحَمْدُ يُحْيِي وَيُمِيتُ وَهُوَ عَلَى كُلِّ شَيْءٍ قَدِيرٌ عَشْرَ مَرَّاتٍ، كُتِبَتْ لَهُ عَشْرُ حَسَنَاتٍ، وَمُحِيَ عَنْهُ عَشْرُ سَيِّئَاتٍ، وَرُفِعَ لَهُ عَشْرُ دَرَجَاتٍ، وَكَانَ يَوْمَهُ ذَلِكَ كُلَّهُ فِي حِرْزٍ مِنْ كُلِّ مَكْرُوهٍ، وَحُرِسَ مِنَ الشَّيْطَانِ».

(رواه الترمذي)

"Whoever says ten times immediately after finishing the *fajr* prayer, while his feet are still folded, [before moving from his place] or talking to anyone: ' *Lā ilāha illallāh, waḥdahu lā sharīka lahu, lahul-mulku wa lahul ḥamdu, yuḥyī wa yumītu, wa huwa ʿalā kulli shay'in qadīr'*, then ten good deeds will be written for him, ten evil deeds will be wiped away from him, he will be raised up by ten degrees, and it will become a means of protection for him from all types of evil and from the accursed Shayṭān." (Tirmidhī)

The Hand of Allāh (ﷻ) is with the *jamāʿah* (group, community), and the influence of Shayṭān is very far from the one who sticks to that group.

The Prophet (ﷺ) has stated:

«عَلَيْكُمْ بِالجَمَاعَةِ وَإِيَّاكُمْ وَالفُرْقَةَ فَإِنَّ الشَّيْطَانَ مَعَ الوَاحِدِ وَهُوَ مِنَ الاِثْنَيْنِ أَبْعَدُ، مَنْ أَرَادَ بُحْبُوحَةَ الجَنَّةِ فَلْيَلْزَمُ الجَمَاعَةَ».

(رواه الترمذي)

> "Adhere to the *jamāʿah*, beware of separation (isolation, disunity) for indeed Shayṭān is with one, and he is further away from two. Whoever wants the best place in Paradise, should then stick to the *jamāʿah*." (Tirmidhī)

The most beneficial form of protection from Shayṭān is in the abundance of *dhikr* (remembrance) of Allāh (ﷻ). *Dhikr* keeps Shayṭān away from us. Anywhere that the name of Allāh (ﷻ) is mentioned, Shayṭān stays far away from there.

Allāh (ﷻ) says:

﴿إِنَّ ٱلَّذِينَ ٱتَّقَوْاْ إِذَا مَسَّهُمْ طَٰٓئِفٌ مِّنَ ٱلشَّيْطَٰنِ تَذَكَّرُواْ فَإِذَا هُم مُّبْصِرُونَ ﴿٢٠١﴾﴾

[الأَعْرَاف الآية ٢٠١]

> "Indeed, when the temptation (to do evil) from Shayṭān reaches those who fear Allāh, they remember (Allāh and engage in *dhikr*, thinking about His punishment and recalling the rewards for abstaining from sin), and their (inner) eyes instantly open (they realize Shayṭān's plot and ignore his temptation)." (Al-Aʿrāf 7:201)

Defeating Shayṭān is not a one day thing; and his influence is certainly not something that we can assume will never get to us because of how righteous we may think that we are.

Therefore, we should wake up every day with the determination to do our best to keep Shayṭān away from us.

KHUṬBAH 57

On the Arrival of the Month of Ramaḍān

In *ḥadīth* studies, there are narrations which are referred to as the *Isrā'īlīyyāt [narrations from historical sources].*

These are a body of narratives originating from Jewish and Christian traditions; and are found mainly in the works of Qur'ānic commentaries and history compilations.

Muslim scholars generally classify the narratives of the *Isrā'īlīyyāt* into three categories:

1. Those considered to be true because revelation to Prophet Muḥammad (ﷺ) confirms them;
2. Those considered to be false because revelation to Prophet Muḥammad (ﷺ) rejects them;
3. Those not known to be either true or false.

Many religious sources indicate that several individuals who converted to Islām from Judaism among the first generations of Muslims were transmitters of *Isrā'īlīyyāt.*

Among the well-known transmitters of *Isrā'īlīyyāt* traditions is Wahb ibn Munabbih, who lived in the generation after the companions (رضي الله عنهم), and is cited as a trustworthy source for many oral accounts linked to Jewish and Christian traditions.

Another well-known transmitter of *Isrā'īlīyyāt* is Kaʿb al-Aḥbār, a Yemeni Jew who converted to Islām shortly after the death of Prophet Muḥammad (ﷺ). He is credited with many oral and written traditions from the Bible and Jewish sources.

Yet another is ʿAbdullāh ibn Salām, who was described as a rabbi before he converted to Islām.

The Prophet (ﷺ) allowed the companions (رضي الله عنهم) to narrate the *Isrā'īlīyyāt.*

ʿAbdullāh ibn ʿAmr (رضي الله عنه) reports that the Prophet (ﷺ) once said:

«بَلِّغُوا عَنِّي وَلَوْ آيَةً، وَحَدِّثُوا عَنْ بَنِي إِسْرَائِيلَ وَلاَ حَرَجَ، وَمَنْ كَذَبَ عَلَيَّ مُتَعَمِّدًا، فَلْيَتَبَوَّأْ مَقْعَدَهُ مِنَ النَّارِ».

(رواه البخاري)

"Convey from me even a *āyah* of the Qur'ān; relate traditions from Banu Isrā'īl, for there is no harm in it; but he who deliberately forges a lie against me let him have his abode in the hellfire." (Bukhārī)

Regarding this narration, Imām al-Shāfiʿī (رحمه الله) states:

«وَقَالَ الشَّافِعِيُّ مِنَ الْمَعْلُومِ أَنَّ النَّبِيَّ ﷺ لَا يُجِيزُ التَّحَدُّثَ بِالْكَذِبِ فَالْمَعْنَى حَدِّثُوا عَنْ بَنِي إِسْرَائِيلَ بِمَا لَا تَعْلَمُونَ كَذِبَهُ».

(فتح الباري)

"It is known that the Prophet (ﷺ) did not approve of falsehood. Therefore, the meaning was to narrate from the children of Isrā'īl what was known not to be a lie." (Fatḥ al-Bārī)

In another narration ʿAbdullāh ibn ʿAmr (رضي الله عنه) reports that:

«كَانَ نَبِيُّ اللَّهِ ﷺ يُحَدِّثُنَا عَنْ بَنِي إِسْرَائِيلَ حَتَّى يُصْبِحَ، لَا يَقُومُ فِيهَا إِلَّا إِلَى عُظْمِ صَلَاةٍ».

(سنن أبي داوود)

"The Prophet (ﷺ) used to relate to us traditions from the children of Isrā'īl until morning came; he would not get up except for the obligatory prayer." (Sunan Abū Dāwūd)

Due to the above-mentioned narrations of the Prophet (ﷺ), the scholars of *ḥadīth* have deduced the following laws of narrating the *Isrāʾīlīyyāt*:

1. Whatever corroborates the truth or substantiates the teachings of Islām, that narration is permissible to be narrated.
2. Whatever opposes the teachings of Islām or contradicts the truth, those narrations are forbidden to be relayed.
3. Those narrations about which no position is taken, are not of either type, i.e. they are not known to be true or false, and they neither conform to nor contradict with the Islāmic sources, therefore we do not affirm to them, nor do we reject them. Such narrations are permissible to cite in order to derive lessons.

Abū Hurairah (رضي الله عنه) narrates:

«كَانَ أَهْلُ الْكِتَابِ يَقْرَءُونَ التَّوْرَاةَ بِالْعِبْرَانِيَّةِ، وَيُفَسِّرُونَهَا بِالْعَرَبِيَّةِ لِأَهْلِ الْإِسْلَامِ. فَقَالَ رَسُولُ اللَّهِ ﷺ: لَا تُصَدِّقُوا أَهْلَ الْكِتَابِ وَلَا تُكَذِّبُوهُمْ، ﴿وَقُولُوٓاْ ءَامَنَّا بِٱلَّذِىٓ أُنزِلَ إِلَيْنَا وَأُنزِلَ إِلَيْكُمْ وَإِلَٰهُنَا وَإِلَٰهُكُمْ وَٰحِدٌ وَنَحْنُ لَهُۥ مُسْلِمُونَ ﴿٤٦﴾﴾ [العَنكَبُوت الآية ٤٦] ».

(رواه البخاري)

> The people of the Book used to read the Torah in Hebrew and then explain it to the Muslims in Arabic. The Messenger of Allāh (ﷺ) said (to the Muslims). "Do not believe the people of the Book, nor disbelieve them, but say: 'We believe in that which has been revealed to us and revealed to you; our *Ilāh* (God) and your *Ilāh* (God) is One (i.e. Allāh), and to Him we have submitted (as Muslims).'" (Bukhārī)

Imām Mālik (رحمه الله) states:

«الْمُرَادُ جَوَازُ التَّحَدُّثِ عَنْهُمْ بِمَا كَانَ مِنْ أَمْرٍ حَسَنٍ أَمَّا مَا عُلِمَ كَذِبُهُ فَلَا».

(فتح الباري)

> "The permissibility to narrate from them (the Banī Isrā'īl) is regarding the good matters (reliable). As for what is already known about the fabrications, that definitely it forbidden." (Fatḥ al-Bārī)

One such account highlighting a sermon that the Prophet (ﷺ) delivered on the last Friday of Shaʿbān has been attributed to the Prophet (ﷺ) and is documented by Shaykh al-Ṣadūq, a leading Shīʿā jurist and theologian in his work titled *Kitāb al-Amālī* - Book of Dictations.

<u>NOTE</u>: This account has not been documented in any of the major works of *ḥadīth*; however other narrations similar to it in meaning can be found. Therefore, it will be permissible to take lessons from it.

> «عَنْ عَلِيٍّ رَضِيَ اللَّهُ عَنْهُ، قَالَ: إِنَّ رَسُولَ اللَّهِ صَلَّى اللَّهُ عَلَيْهِ وَآلِهِ وَسَلَّمَ خَطَبَنَا ذَاتَ يَوْمٍ فَقَالَ: أَيُّهَا النَّاسُ إِنَّهُ قَدْ أَقْبَلَ إِلَيْكُمْ شَهْرُ اللَّهِ بِالْبَرَكَةِ وَالرَّحْمَةِ وَالْمَغْفِرَةِ، شَهْرٌ هُوَ عِنْدَ اللَّهِ أَفْضَلُ الشُّهُورِ، وَأَيَّامُهُ أَفْضَلُ الْأَيَّامِ، وَلَيَالِيهِ أَفْضَلُ اللَّيَالِي، وَسَاعَاتُهُ أَفْضَلُ السَّاعَاتِ».

> It has been narrated from Ali (﵁) who said that the Prophet, (ﷺ) narrated to us on that day: "O People! The month of Allāh (Ramaḍān) has come with its mercies, blessings, and forgiveness. Allāh has decreed this month the best of all months. The days of this month are the best among the days, and the nights are the best among the nights, and the hours are the best among the hours.

> «هُوَ شَهْرٌ دُعِيتُمْ فِيهِ إِلَى ضِيَافَةِ اللَّهِ، وَجُعِلْتُمْ فِيهِ مِنْ أَهْلِ كَرَامَةِ اللَّهِ، أَنْفَاسُكُمْ فِيهِ تَسْبِيحٌ، وَنَوْمُكُمْ فِيهِ عِبَادَةٌ، وَعَمَلُكُمْ فِيهِ مَقْبُولٌ، وَدُعَاؤُكُمْ فِيهِ مُسْتَجَابٌ».

> This is a month in which you have been invited by Him (to fast and pray). Allāh has honoured you in it. In every breath which you take (there) is a reward from Allāh, your sleep is worship, your good deeds are accepted, and your invocations are answered.

«فَاسْأَلُوا اللَّهَ رَبَّكُمْ بِنِيَّاتٍ صَادِقَةٍ وَقُلُوبٍ طَاهِرَةٍ أَنْ يُوَفِّقَكُمْ لِصِيَامِهِ وَتِلَاوَةِ كِتَابِهِ، فَإِنَّ الشَّقِيَّ مَنْ حُرِمَ غُفْرَانَ اللَّهِ فِي هَذَا الشَّهْرِ الْعَظِيمِ».

Therefore, you must invoke your Lord in all earnestness, with hearts free from sin and evil, and pray that Allāh may help you to keep (the) fast, and recite the Qur'ān. Indeed! Unfortunate is the one who is deprived from the forgiveness of Allāh in this great month.

«وَاذْكُرُوا بِجُوعِكُمْ وَعَطَشِكُمْ فِيهِ جُوعَ يَوْمِ الْقِيَامَةِ وَعَطَشَهُ، وَتَصَدَّقُوا عَلَى فُقَرَائِكُمْ وَمَسَاكِينِكُمْ، وَوَقِّرُوا كِبَارَكُمْ، وَارْحَمُوا صِغَارَكُمْ، وَصِلُوا أَرْحَامَكُمْ، وَاحْفَظُوا أَلْسِنَتَكُمْ، وَغُضُّوا عَمَّا لَا يَحِلُّ النَّظَرُ إِلَيْهِ أَبْصَارَكُمْ، وَعَمَّا لَا يَحِلُّ الِاسْتِمَاعُ إِلَيْهِ أَسْمَاعَكُمْ، وَتَحَنَّنُوا عَلَى أَيْتَامِ النَّاسِ يُتَحَنَّنْ عَلَى أَيْتَامِكُمْ».

While fasting, remember the hunger and thirst of the Day of Judgement. Give alms to the poor and needy. Pay respect to your elders, have sympathy for your youngsters, and be kind towards your relatives and kinsmen. Guard your tongue against unworthy words, and your eyes from scenes that are not worth seeing (forbidden), and your ears from sounds that should not be heard. Be kind to the orphans so that if your children become orphans they will also be treated with kindness.

«وَتُوبُوا إِلَى اللَّهِ مِنْ ذُنُوبِكُمْ، وَارْفَعُوا إِلَيْهِ أَيْدِيَكُمْ بِالدُّعَاءِ فِي أَوْقَاتِ صَلَاتِكُمْ، فَإِنَّهَا أَفْضَلُ السَّاعَاتِ يَنْظُرُ اللَّهُ عَزَّ وَجَلَّ فِيهَا بِالرَّحْمَةِ إِلَى عِبَادِهِ، يُجِيبُهُمْ إِذَا نَاجَوْهُ، وَيُلَبِّيهِمْ إِذَا نَادَوْهُ، وَيُعْطِيهِمْ إِذَا سَأَلُوهُ، وَيَسْتَجِيبُ لَهُمْ إِذَا دَعَوْهُ».

And repent to Allāh for your sins, and supplicate with raised hands at the times of prayer as these are the best times, during which Allāh, Glorified and Exalted is He, looks at His servants with mercy. He answers if they supplicate, responds if they call, grants if He is asked, and accepts if they implore Him.

«أَيُّهَا النَّاسُ: إِنَّ أَنْفُسَكُمْ مَرْهُونَةٌ بِأَعْمَالِكُمْ فَفُكُّوهَا بِاسْتِغْفَارِكُمْ، وَظُهُورَكُمْ ثَقِيلَةٌ مِنْ أَوْزَارِكُمْ فَخَفِّفُوا عَنْهَا بِطُولِ سُجُودِكُمْ، وَاعْلَمُوا أَنَّ اللّٰهَ أَقْسَمَ بِعِزَّتِهِ أَنْ لَا يُعَذِّبَ الْمُصَلِّينَ وَالسَّاجِدِينَ وَ أَنْ لَا يُرَوِّعَهُمْ بِالنَّارِ يَوْمَ يَقُومُ النَّاسُ لِرَبِّ الْعَالَمِينَ».

O people! Your souls are under the yoke of your actions. Make it free by invoking (Allāh) for forgiveness. Your backs may break from the heavy load of your sins, so prostrate yourselves (before Allāh) for long intervals, and make this load lighter. Understand fully that Allāh has promised in His Honour and Majesty that people who perform *ṣalāt* and *sajdah* (prostration) will be guarded against the hellfire on the Day of Judgement.

«أَيُّهَا النَّاسُ: مَنْ فَطَّرَ مِنْكُمْ صَائِماً مُؤْمِناً فِي هَذَا الشَّهْرِ كَانَ لَهُ بِذَلِكَ عِنْدَ اللّٰهِ عِتْقُ نَسَمَةٍ، وَمَغْفِرَةٌ لِمَا مَضَى مِنْ ذُنُوبِهِ، قِيلَ: يَا رَسُولَ اللّٰهِ فَلَيْسَ كُلُّنَا يَقْدِرُ عَلَى ذَلِكَ، فَقَالَ ﷺ: اتَّقُوا النَّارَ وَلَوْ بِشِقِّ تَمْرَةٍ، اتَّقُوا النَّارَ وَلَوْ بِشَرْبَةٍ مِنْ مَاءٍ».

O people! If anyone amongst you arranges for *ifṭār* (meal at sunset) for any believer, then Allāh will reward him as if he has freed a slave, and Allāh will forgive him his sins. A companion said: 'But not all of us have the means to do so,' to which the Prophet (ﷺ) replied: 'Keep yourself away from the hellfire though it may be by means of (only) half a date, or even some water if you have nothing else.'

«أَيُّهَا النَّاسُ: مَنْ حَسَّنَ مِنْكُمْ فِي هَذَا الشَّهْرِ خُلُقَهُ كَانَ لَهُ جَوَازاً عَلَى الصِّرَاطِ يَوْمَ تَزِلُّ فِيهِ الْأَقْدَامُ، وَمَنْ خَفَّفَ فِي هَذَا الشَّهْرِ عَمَّا مَلَكَتْ يَمِينُهُ خَفَّفَ اللّٰهُ عَلَيْهِ حِسَابَهُ، وَمَنْ كَفَّ فِيهِ شَرَّهُ كَفَّ اللّٰهُ عَنْهُ غَضَبَهُ يَوْمَ يَلْقَاهُ، وَمَنْ أَكْرَمَ فِيهِ يَتِيماً أَكْرَمَهُ اللّٰهُ يَوْمَ يَلْقَاهُ، وَمَنْ وَصَلَ فِيهِ رَحِمَهُ وَصَلَهُ اللّٰهُ بِرَحْمَتِهِ يَوْمَ يَلْقَاهُ، وَمَنْ قَطَعَ فِيهِ رَحِمَهُ قَطَعَ اللّٰهُ عَنْهُ رَحْمَتَهُ يَوْمَ يَلْقَاهُ».

O people! Anyone, who during this month cultivates good manners, will walk over the *Ṣirāṭ* (bridge to Paradise) on that day when feet will tend to slip. For anyone who during this month eases the workload of his servants, Allāh will make easy his accounting, and for anyone who does not hurt others during this month, Allāh will safeguard him from His Wrath on the Day of Judgement. Anyone who respects and treats an orphan with kindness during this month, Allāh will look at him with kindness on that Day. Anyone who treats his kinsmen well during this month, Allāh will bestow His Mercy on him on that Day, while anyone who mistreats his kinsmen during this month, Allāh will keep him away from His Mercy.

«وَمَنْ تَطَوَّعَ فِيهِ بِصَلَاةٍ كَتَبَ اللَّهُ لَهُ بَرَاءَةً مِنَ النَّارِ، وَمَنْ أَدَّى فِيهِ فَرْضاً كَانَ لَهُ ثَوَابُ مَنْ أَدَّى سَبْعِينَ فَرِيضَةً فِيمَا سِوَاهُ مِنَ الشُّهُورِ، وَمَنْ أَكْثَرَ فِيهِ مِنَ الصَّلَاةِ عَلَيَّ ثَقَّلَ اللَّهُ مِيزَانَهُ يَوْمَ تَخِفُّ الْمَوَازِينُ».

And whoever offers the recommended prayers during this month, Allāh will save him from the fire, and whoever observes his obligations during this month, his reward will be seventy times the reward during other months. Whoever repeatedly invokes Allāh's blessings on me (meaning the Prophet), Allāh will keep his scale of good deeds heavy, while the scales of others will be light.

«أَيُّهَا النَّاسُ إِنَّ أَبْوَابَ الْجِنَانِ فِي هَذَا الشَّهْرِ مُفَتَّحَةٌ فَاسْأَلُوا رَبَّكُمْ أَنْ لَا يُغَلِّقَهَا عَنْكُمْ، وَ أَبْوَابَ النِّيرَانِ مُغَلَّقَةٌ فَاسْأَلُوا رَبَّكُمْ أَنْ لَا يُفَتِّحَهَا عَلَيْكُمْ، وَالشَّيَاطِينَ مَغْلُولَةٌ فَاسْأَلُوا رَبَّكُمْ أَنْ لَا يُسَلِّطَهَا عَلَيْكُمْ».

O people! The gates of Paradise remain open during this month. Pray to your Lord that they may not be closed for you; while the gates of Hell are closed, pray to your Lord that they never open for you. Shayṭān has been chained, so invoke your Lord not to let him dominate (over) you."

ʿAlī ibn Abī Ṭālib (ﷺ) states:

«فَقُمْتُ فَقُلْتُ: يَا رَسُولَ اللَّهِ مَا أَفْضَلُ الْأَعْمَالِ فِي هَذَا الشَّهْرِ؟ فَقَالَ: يَا أَبَا الْحَسَنِ، أَفْضَلُ الْأَعْمَالِ فِي هَذَا الشَّهْرِ الْوَرَعُ عَنْ مَحَارِمِ اللَّهِ».

"I asked: 'O Messenger of Allāh, what are the best deeds during this month?' He replied: 'O Abāl Ḥasan, the best of deeds during this month is to be far from what Allāh has forbidden.'"

CONCLUSION

- The virtues and greatness of the month of Ramaḍān should never be underestimated.
- We should also realize that good deeds *'ḥasanāt'* and bad deeds *'sayyi'āt'* are the basic currencies that will decide our fate in this life and the hereafter.
- Let us therefore, direct all of our efforts to earn as many rewards as possible this Ramaḍān, and stay away from all sins – no matter how big or small they may be.
- Let us ensure that all of our acts of worship during this holy month are sincere, with our hearts engaged to the fullest.
- It would indeed be a great loss if we only earned hunger, thirst, and sleeplessness from our actions at the end of the month.
- We pray to Allāh (ﷻ) to make us among those who are able to take advantage of the opportunities that are being provided to us in the month of Ramaḍān; and to make us among the people of *taqwā*, to accept our good deeds, to forgive us, to keep us safe and protected from the hellfire, and to make us all enter into Paradise. *Āmīn.*

REASONS WHY RAMAḌĀN IS CALLED RAMAḌĀN

Imām al-Rāghib (رحمه الله) writes:

«شَهْرُ رَمَضانَ هو من الرَّمْضِ، أي: شدّة وقع الشمس، يقال:، أَرْمَضَتْهُ فَرَمِضَ، أي: أحرقته الرَّمْضَاءُ، وهي شدّة حرّ الشمس، وأرض رَمِضَةٌ، يُقال أَيْضاً: رَمِضَت الغَنَمُ، إذا

رَعَتْ فِي شدَّةِ الحَرِّ فقرِحَتْ أَكْبادُهَا، وَسُمِّيَ رَمَضَانَ: لِأَنَّهُ يَرْمَضُ الذُّنُوبَ أَيْ يَحْرِقُهَا وَيُذْهِبُهَا».

(المفردات في غريب القرآن)

"Ramaḍān is taken from the word '*al-ramaḍ*' which means that which is intensely or strongly heated by the sun; and the word '*ramḍā*' means the intense heat of the sun. The Arabs used to say about the sheep that they were 'burned' -'*ramiḍat*' while they were grazing under the scorching heat of the sun to the extent that their livers became damaged by the intense heat of the sun. Ramaḍān was named such because it burns the sins of the believers." (Al-Mufradāt fī Gharīb al-Qurʾān)

Imām al-Qurṭubī (ﷺ) writes:

«يُقَالُ إِنَّهُمْ لَمَّا نَقَلُوا أَسْمَاءَ الشُّهُورِ عَنِ اللُّغَةِ الْقَدِيمَةِ سَمَّوْهَا بِالْأَزْمِنَةِ الَّتِي وَقَعَتْ فِيهَا، فَوَافَقَ هَذَا الشَّهْرُ أَيَّامَ رَمِضَ الحَرُّ فَسُمِّيَ بِذَلِكَ».

(تفسير القرطبي)

"When the Arabs changed the names of the months from the ancient language, they named them according to the seasons in which they fell, and this month fell in the days of intense heat and that is why it was named Ramaḍān." (Tafsīr al-Qurṭubī)

Imām al-Qurṭubī (ﷺ) also writes:

«إِنَّمَا سُمِّيَ رَمَضَانُ لِأَنَّهُ يَرْمِضُ الذُّنُوبَ أَيْ يُحْرِقُهَا بِالْأَعْمَالِ الصَّالِحَةِ».

(تفسير القرطبي)

"This month was named Ramaḍān because it burns the sins of the people with righteous deeds." (Tafsīr al-Qurṭubī)

مَنْ يُرِدْ مُلْكَ الْجِنَانِ ۞ فَلْيَدَعْ عَنْهُ التَّوَانِي

وَلْيُقِمْ فِي ظُلْمَةِ اللَّيْـ ۞ ـلِ إِلَى نُورِ الْقُرْآنِ

وَلْيَصِلْ صَوْمًا بِصَوْمٍ ۞ إِنَّ هَذَا الْعَيْشَ فَانِ

إِنَّمَا الْعَيْشُ جِوَارُ الْـ ۞ ـلَّهِ فِي دَارِ الْأَمَانِ

The one who desires the kingdom of Paradise,
Must give up his laziness.
He must stand up in the darkness of the night,
To the light of the Qur'ān.
He must fast one after the other,
Because this life is fleeting.
The true is in the proximity of Allāh in the abode of peace.

KHUṬBAH 58

Saving Money: The Islāmic Outlook

One of the inborn characteristics of human beings is that many people give a great deal of interest and attention to the growth of their wealth, income, livelihood and provision. It is a fascination that can lead people to become quite distressed, and also greedy or obsessed.

The Prophet (ﷺ) describes this interest and attention which humans have to the growth of their wealth, income, livelihood and provision, where he states:

«لَوْ أَنَّ لِابْنِ آدَمَ وَادِيًا مِنْ مَالٍ لَابْتَغَى إِلَيْهِ ثَانِيًا، وَلَوْ كَانَ لَهُ ثَانِيًا، لَابْتَغَى إِلَيْهِ ثَالِثًا، وَلَا يَمْلَأُ جَوْفَ ابْنِ آدَمَ إِلَّا التُّرَابُ».

(رواه الترمذي)

> "If the son of Ādam had a valley-full of wealth, he would seek a second, and if he had a second, he would seek a third, and nothing fills the belly of the son of Ādam except for dirt, i.e. soil of the grave." (Tirmidhī)

The extent of people's concern about their wealth, income and livelihood can make them either lazy or diligent, greedy or content, negligent or excessive, complacent or reliant upon Allāh (ﷻ) while pursuing the necessary means.

Human beings fail to realize that the blessings in this world will not remain permanently. The circumstances of life fluctuate between difficulty and ease, adversity and prosperity, bitterness and sweet things. It is impossible for things to always remain only one way.

Allāh (ﷻ) says in the Qur'ān:

﴿ ٱللَّهُ ٱلَّذِى خَلَقَكُم مِّن ضَعْفٍ ثُمَّ جَعَلَ مِنۢ بَعْدِ ضَعْفٍ قُوَّةً ثُمَّ جَعَلَ مِنۢ بَعْدِ قُوَّةٍ ضَعْفًا وَشَيْبَةً ﴾ [الرُّوم الآية ٥٤]

> "It is Allāh Who created you in a state of weakness (as a helpless infant), then substituted strength after the weakness (as you grew into an adult) and after the strength, will again give weakness (as you age) and (eventually) old-age." (Rūm 30:54)

With this in mind, we have to remember the fact that Allāh (ﷻ), the One who provides for all of us also instructed us to seek out His provision, earn a living, and pursue the means necessary to bring about a balance in one's livelihoods. Among those means is saving for the future.

The dictionary meaning of saving is:

1. The excess of income over consumption expenditures;
2. The act or an instance of economizing;
3. The activity of keeping money so that you can use it in the future;
4. Something set aside for later use.

In the general context of finance terminology, the term savings refers to that portion of a person's earnings which remains after taking care of all of the expenses.

In Islām having savings is a very important financial principle that ensures the stability of livelihood and finances at both an individual and communal levels. Changes in life are inevitable, and this is a reality which Allāh (ﷻ) has decreed.

Therefore, exercising caution and being prepared are qualities that Islām's teachings encourage in order to protect people from financial difficulties which may drive them to steal or engage in usury – both of which are major sins – or to ask from others, beg, or constantly be in debt.

Having savings comes from a combination of two factors:

1. Believing and being convinced that saving is a requirement.
2. Spending in a manner that fosters saving.

Believing and being convinced that saving is a requirement comes about by correctly understanding the texts of Islām which establish that having savings is prescribed by Islām, is vital for people, and is necessary for an economy to function. The soundness of a person's living depends on how balanced they are in spending on themselves and their dependents.

As for spending in a manner which may foster savings, it comes about from a person who distinguishes between essentials and non-essentials in life, according to the six regulations of religion, and then the person bases one's spending on that.

The six regulations of religion are:

1. الفَرْضُ – *farḍ* (obligatory)
2. الواجِبُ - *wājib* (compulsory)
3. المُحرَّم - *muḥarram* (prohibited)
4. المُستحبُّ - *mustaḥab* (encouraged, but not obligatory)
5. المكرُوه - *makrūh* (detestable or abominable)
6. المُباح - *mubāḥ* (permissible)

When a person bears all of these six regulations in mind and acts in accordance with them, then the financial facets of one's life will be set-in-order based on three significant fundamentals:

1. Careful personal spending;
2. Giving to others appropriately;
3. Saving for the future.

All of these three fundamentals are mentioned in a Qur'ānic verse where Allāh (ﷻ) says:

﴿كُلُوا۟ مِن ثَمَرِهِۦٓ إِذَآ أَثْمَرَ وَءَاتُوا۟ حَقَّهُۥ يَوْمَ حَصَادِهِۦ ۖ وَلَا تُسْرِفُوٓا۟ ۚ إِنَّهُۥ لَا يُحِبُّ ٱلْمُسْرِفِينَ ﴿١٤١﴾﴾ [الأنعام الآية ١٤١]

"Eat from the fruits of the crops when they ripen, and give its due (*zakāh* on produce) on the day of harvesting. Do not waste (do not be wasteful and extravagant), for verily Allāh does not like those who waste." (Anʿām 6:141)

Personal spending can be understood from:

﴿كُلُوا۟ مِن ثَمَرِهِۦٓ إِذَآ أَثْمَرَ﴾

"Eat from the fruits of the crops when they ripen."

Giving to others can be understood from:

﴿وَءَاتُوا۟ حَقَّهُۥ يَوْمَ حَصَادِهِۦ﴾

"And give its due (*zakāh* on produce) on the day of harvesting."

Saving for the future can be understood from:

﴿وَلَا تُسْرِفُوٓا۟﴾

"And do not waste (do not be wasteful and extravagant)."

Spending according to one's own requirements, supporting others who are in need, and saving as a precaution for times of distress are three elements of financial balance for individuals and entire societies.

The Prophet (ﷺ) mentioned all three of these elements together in his statement which has been documented by Imām al-Bukhārī:

«كُلُوا وَأَطْعِمُوا وَادَّخِرُوا».

(رواه البخاري)

"Eat, feed others, and store (save) some." (Bukhārī)

Unbalanced allocation of finances among essentials and non-essentials is undoubtedly a direct cause of amassing debts by people, and those debts will eventually become unbearable. Having a correct concept of savings is an essential foundation in taking precautionary measures related to finances and livelihood since savings provide a means of safeguarding individuals, as well as an entire society.

Those who understand the concept of savings would give importance to retaining a portion of their income as a means of alleviating potential financial burdens that may arise in the event of any unforeseen adversity.

There is no doubt that doing so demonstrates prudence, proficiency in managing finances, and the ability to distinguish between essentials and non-essentials during critical situations that may come knocking on one's door from time to time.

A person's livelihood will remain out of order so long as it fails to balance between spending, giving, and saving. The wisdom of Allāh (ﷻ) is evident in the fact that His directives prescribe giving only a portion of one's wealth.

Allāh (ﷻ) says in the Qur'ān:

﴿أَنفِقُوا۟ مِمَّا رَزَقَكُمُ ٱللَّهُ ۝٤٧﴾ [يس الآية ٤٧]

"Spend (on the poor) from what (wealth) Allāh has provided for you." (Yāsīn 36:47)

This means spend that some of it. Allāh (ﷻ) did not say spend all of what He has provided you with. This clearly brings out the concepts of both spending and saving.

From the standpoints of Islām and common sense, it can be easily understood that when a person spends only a part of his earnings, he will be less likely to find himself in need compared to someone who does otherwise.

ʿUmar (رضي الله عنه) narrates that:

«أَنَّ النَّبِيَّ ﷺ كَانَ يَبِيعُ نَخْلَ بَنِي النَّضِيرِ، وَيَحْبِسُ لِأَهْلِهِ قُوتَ سَنَتِهِمْ».

(رواه البخاري)

"The Prophet (ﷺ) would sell the dates harvested from the orchards of Banī al-Naḍīr, and he would store enough to cover his family's needs for a year." (Bukhārī)

Commenting on this *ḥadīth*, Shams al-Dīn ibn Mufliḥ al-Maqdisī says:

«فِيهِ جَوَازُ ادِّخَارِ قُوتِ سَنَةٍ وَلَا يُقَالُ هَذَا مِنْ طُولِ الْأَمَلِ لِأَنَّ الْإِعْدَادَ لِلْحَاجَةِ مُسْتَحْسَنٌ شَرْعًا وَعَقْلًا».

(الآداب الشرعية والمنح المرعية)

> "This *ḥadīth* shows that it is permissible to save enough for the coming year, and it does not mean that a person is complacently hoping to live for a long time. Preparing oneself for times of need is encouraged by both Islām and common sense." (Al-Ādāb al-Sharʿīyah wa al-Manḥ al-Marʿiyya)

Ḥumayd ibn ʿAbd al-Raḥmān (ﷺ) quotes ʿUmar (ﷺ) as saying:

«الْخُرْقُ فِي الْمَعِيشَةِ أَخْوَفُ عِنْدِي عَلَيْكُمْ مِنَ الْعَوَزِ؛ لِأَنَّهُ لَا يَبْقَى مَعَ الْفَسَادِ شَيْءٌ، وَلَا يَقِلُّ مَعَ الْإِصْلَاحِ شَيْءٌ».

(الزهد لوكيع بن الجراح)

> "I am more fearful for you about clumsiness in (lacking skill in managing) livelihood than poverty, for the reason that there is no shortage when it comes to management. However, nothing remains with carelessness (mismanagement, negligence)." (Al-Zuhd of Wakīʿ ibn al-Jarrāḥ)

Islām is a religion of ease, not difficulty; it does not condemn saving unless it turns into hoarding to satisfy one's greed, causes harm to other people, or withholds the rights due to Allāh (ﷻ) and His servants from the wealth that Allāh (ﷻ) Himself has provided humanity with.

Allāh (ﷻ) says in the Qur'ān:

﴿يَـٰٓأَيُّهَا ٱلَّذِينَ ءَامَنُوٓاْ إِنَّ كَثِيرًا مِّنَ ٱلْأَحْبَارِ وَٱلرُّهْبَانِ لَيَأْكُلُونَ أَمْوَٰلَ ٱلنَّاسِ بِٱلْبَـٰطِلِ وَيَصُدُّونَ عَن سَبِيلِ ٱللَّهِ ۗ وَٱلَّذِينَ يَكْنِزُونَ ٱلذَّهَبَ وَٱلْفِضَّةَ وَلَا يُنفِقُونَهَا فِى سَبِيلِ ٱللَّهِ فَبَشِّرْهُم بِعَذَابٍ أَلِيمٍ ﴿٣٤﴾﴾ [التَّوْبَة الآية ٣٤]

"O you who believe! Verily among the people of prior scriptures, there are many worshippers and learned individuals who falsely (unlawfully) devour (consume) the wealth of people and forbid (others) from the path of Allāh (Islām). Verily those who hoard (amass) gold and silver and do not spend it in the way of (for the pleasure of) Allāh, then give them the good news of a painful punishment (for hankering after worldly desires)." (Tawbah 9:34)

In the Qur'ān, Allāh (ﷻ) informs us about the unique balanced approach that He has prescribed for His servants. This can be found in the narrative of Prophet Yūsuf (※) when he interpreted the dream in which the king saw seven cows.

Prophet Yūsuf (※) said in his interpretation:

﴿قَالَ تَزْرَعُونَ سَبْعَ سِنِينَ دَأَبًا فَمَا حَصَدتُّمْ فَذَرُوهُ فِى سُنبُلِهِۦٓ إِلَّا قَلِيلًا مِّمَّا تَأْكُلُونَ ۝ ثُمَّ يَأْتِى مِنۢ بَعْدِ ذَٰلِكَ سَبْعٌ شِدَادٌ يَأْكُلْنَ مَا قَدَّمْتُمْ لَهُنَّ إِلَّا قَلِيلًا مِّمَّا تُحْصِنُونَ ۝ ثُمَّ يَأْتِى مِنۢ بَعْدِ ذَٰلِكَ عَامٌ فِيهِ يُغَاثُ ٱلنَّاسُ وَفِيهِ يَعْصِرُونَ ۝﴾

[يُوسُف من الآية ٤٧ الى الآية ٤٩]

"He [Yūsuf (※)] replied: 'You will farm for seven consecutive years (symbolized by the seven fat cows and the seven green ears of corn). Leave whatever crops you harvest in their ears, except what you require for eating (use only what is necessary and store the rest). Thereafter seven difficult years (of drought) will follow (symbolized by the seven thin cows and the seven dry ears of corn) that you will consume (which the people will eat) all you would have stored for them (for the years of drought) except (besides) the little that you leave (the leftovers, except a little of what you had stored away as seeds to sow in the future). Thereafter a year will follow in which abundant rains will fall for the people and they will distill (squeeze) juices (because there will be abundant produce).'" (Yūsuf 12:47-49)

The phrase:

﴿تَزْرَعُونَ﴾

"You will farm."

Reflects working, earning, and diligently pursuing permissible means. People find results when they strive, and they will reap what they sow.

The phrase:

﴿فَمَا حَصَدتُّمْ فَذَرُوهُ فِي سُنۢبُلِهِۦٓ إِلَّا قَلِيلًا مِّمَّا تَأْكُلُونَ ۝٤٧﴾ [يوسف الآية ٤٧]

"Leave whatever crops you harvest in their ears, except what you require for eating (use only what is necessary and store the rest)."

Shows how to handle current expenditures - which relates to what is earned at present; as well as the need to plan for subsequent expenditures - which relates to saving for a future that is uncertain and may hold various difficulties.

Not everything that is earned should be spent immediately. It is careless and reckless to immediately spend everything that is acquired, and doing so reflects shortsightedness, inattentiveness, and a lack of caution. In contrast, taking the necessary precautions reflects sensibility and farsightedness which no individual or society can do without when planning for unforeseen circumstances and sudden crises.

This manner of saving which Allāh (ﷻ) has prescribed for people guarantees *Inshā' Allāh* that earnings will not be lost, nor diminished by debts which can force people to turn to others for help. This prescribed manner of saving will also eliminate extravagance, wastefulness, and likewise will remove greed - all of which are prohibited.

There is no doubt that when people save in the correct manner, and when doing so becomes prevalent, they will have a reserve from which they can seek assistance when hardships strike – after first and foremost seeking the succor from Allāh (ﷻ). Human beings will be able to benefit from this and fill the gaps in their finances, and be safe from having to ask others for help.

Allāh (ﷻ) says in the Qur'ān:

﴿وَلْيَخْشَ ٱلَّذِينَ لَوْ تَرَكُوا۟ مِنْ خَلْفِهِمْ ذُرِّيَّةً ضِعَـٰفًا خَافُوا۟ عَلَيْهِمْ فَلْيَتَّقُوا۟ ٱللَّهَ وَلْيَقُولُوا۟ قَوْلًا سَدِيدًا ۝٩﴾ [النِّسَاء الآية ٩]

> "And let those (who are distributing the estate i.e. guardian, trustee, executor) fear (for the welfare of the dependents heirs as) if they (themselves were to) leave behind them weak offspring about whom (whose welfare) they are concerned. They should fear Allāh (in their behaviour) and speak justly." (Nisā' 4:9)

This verse deals with those people who formulate a will on their deathbeds in which they deprive their dependents, and instead give preference to others.

When Saʿd ibn Abī Waqqāṣ (رضي الله عنه) wanted to bequest two-thirds of his property to other than his family members, the Prophet (ﷺ) told him:

«إِنَّكَ أَنْ تَذَرَ وَرَثَتَكَ أَغْنِيَاءَ، خَيْرٌ مِنْ أَنْ تَذَرَهُمْ عَالَةً يَتَكَفَّفُونَ النَّاسَ».

(رواه البخاري)

> "For you to leave your inheritors well-off is certainly better than for you to leave them poor and having to beg from other people." (Bukhārī)

Similarly, when Kaʿb ibn Mālik (رضي الله عنه) said:

«يَا رَسُولَ اللَّهِ، إِنَّ مِنْ تَوْبَتِي أَنْ أَنْخَلِعَ مِنْ مَالِي صَدَقَةً إِلَى اللَّهِ وَإِلَى رَسُولِهِ ﷺ».

> "O Messenger of Allāh, as part of my repentance, I want to give all of my property as charity to Allāh and His Messenger (ﷺ)."

The Prophet (ﷺ) expressed to him:

«أَمْسِكْ عَلَيْكَ بَعْضَ مَالِكَ، فَهُوَ خَيْرٌ لَكَ».

(رواه البخاري)

"Retain some of your property, for that is better for you." (Bukhārī)

CONCLUSION

- Start early. Today is the day to start our savings program.
- Save a definite amount.
- Save regularly and systematically.
- Employ our savings productively.
- Plan our spending.
- Save for the future.
- Be content with what we already have.
- Give back at least something to Allāh (ﷻ).

SIX KEYS TO SUCCESSFUL SAVING

1. Give to Allāh (ﷻ) first. As Muslims, our first financial priority, just as in every other area of life, should be Allāh (ﷻ) and His cause. Figuring out how much to give as a minimum is fairly easy. The Qur'ān instructs us to give something back to Allāh (ﷻ), but not everything. If you get this priority right, then each step afterwards is easier. Allāh (ﷻ) should receive the first fruits of our earnings, not the leftovers. The key to honouring the Almighty with our finances is remembering that our money is not our money. In reality, Allāh (ﷻ) owns it all and gives it to us as and when He wishes. If we wait until all of our needs and desires are met before we start to give, then it will never happen.

2. Set aside funds for regular savings. An important second step is to establish the discipline of setting aside money for inevitable expenses. Do not plan your savings after you plan your spending, because experience shows that those who try this rarely succeed. The issue of savings is one that requires a balanced perspective. The Qur'ān makes it clear that we are supposed to save, but it never tells us how much is too much or too little. The purpose of saving is to provide for legitimate future needs, and for some, it will allow them to fund the important needs of the community as well.

3. **Spend only on what you need.** The key to good money management is expense management. We need to learn to live below our means, and be content with whatever Allāh (ﷻ) has given us. This may be hard for some of us, but it is a vital life lesson. The key is to develop a good budget, which is basically a spending plan. Prioritize your expenditures between essentials and non-essentials.

4. **If you are married, always discuss finances as a couple.** One spouse likely has more financial skills than the other and will naturally take the lead, but this is no excuse for the other spouse not to be involved in the family financial situation. Both couples need to understand the issues that they are facing and make the decisions as a team. Financial problems are listed as a major cause of strife in some marriage relationships, and it often starts when one partner is being kept in the dark. Finances can even be a dividing factor for certain couples.

5. **Make a commitment to follow the budgeting plan.** A budget is a roadmap that guides you and tells you when you are on course. Budgeting will not ensure prosperity, but it will keep you from overspending your resources and help you to avoid the debt trap. Make a plan and stick to it.

6. **Ask Allāh (ﷻ) for self-sustainability and self-sufficiency.** If we take note of some of the supplications of the Prophet (ﷺ), then we notice that he often supplicated for self-sustainability and self-sufficiency.

The Prophet (ﷺ) would pray the following:

«اللَّهُمَّ اكْفِني بِحَلاَلِكَ عَنْ حَرَامِكَ، وَأَغْنِنِي بِفَضْلِكَ عَمَّنْ سِواكَ».

(رواه الترمذي)

"O Allāh, suffice me with Your lawful against Your prohibited, and make me independent of all of those besides You." (Tirmidhī)

«اللَّهُمَّ إِنِّي أَعُوذُ بِكَ مِنَ الْهَمِّ وَالْحَزَنِ، وَأَعُوذُ بِكَ مِنَ الْعَجْزِ وَالْكَسَلِ، وَأَعُوذُ بِكَ مِنَ الْجُبْنِ وَالْبُخْلِ، وَأَعُوذُ بِكَ مِنْ غَلَبَةِ الدَّيْنِ، وَقَهْرِ الرِّجَالِ».

(رواه أبو داود)

"O Allāh, I seek refuge in You from grief and sadness, and I seek refuge in You from weakness and laziness, and I seek refuge in You from miserliness and cowardice, and I seek refuge in You from being overcome by debt, and being put in subjection by men." (Abu Dāwūd)

«اللَّهُمَّ إِنِّي أَسْأَلُكَ الْهُدَى، وَالتُّقَى، وَالْعَفَافَ، وَالْغِنَى».

(رواه الترمذي)

"O Allāh! I ask You for guidance, piety, chastity, and self-sufficiency." (Tirmidhī)

The Prophet (ﷺ) also stated:

«مَنْ يَسْتَعْفِفْ يُعِفَّهُ اللهُ، وَمَنْ يَسْتَغْنِ يُغْنِهِ اللهُ».

(رواه البخاري)

"Whoever abstains from asking others, Allāh will make him contented, and whoever tries to make himself self-sufficient, Allāh will make him self-sufficient." (Bukhārī)

لا تحسبَنَّ الرِّزقَ يأتِي طَفرةً ۞ أو عُنوةً مِن دونِ سعيٍ، كلَّا

فاكسِبْ، وكُلْ، وابذُلْ لغيرِكَ، وادَّخِرْ ۞ واحذَرْ تكُنْ بينَ الخلائِقِ كلَّا

Do not ever think that provision comes suddenly or as a coincidence,
Without taking the steps necessary to attain it.
Things do not work that way,
Rather, you must earn, and consume, and give to others, and save some,
And protect yourself from being a burden upon others.

KHUṬBAH 59

Keys to a Lasting Marriage

There is no doubt that happiness in a marriage is an invaluable quality sought by both spouses, and it is the hope of all newlyweds. It is something that enables their lives to be set in order, and it allows their children to grow up in an atmosphere of love and harmony. This cannot come about without spouses treating each other with kindness, mercy, gentleness, and fulfilling the rights of one another.

Marriage is a solemn promise that is made between partners. It is a bond that begins in this world and even extends to the hereafter out of Allāh's (ﷻ) favour, mercy, and kindness.

Allāh (ﷻ) says in the Qur'ān:

﴿جَنَّٰتُ عَدۡنٍ يَدۡخُلُونَهَا وَمَن صَلَحَ مِنۡ ءَابَآئِهِمۡ وَأَزۡوَٰجِهِمۡ وَذُرِّيَّٰتِهِمۡۖ وَٱلۡمَلَٰٓئِكَةُ يَدۡخُلُونَ عَلَيۡهِم مِّن كُلِّ بَابٖ ٢٣ سَلَٰمٌ عَلَيۡكُم بِمَا صَبَرۡتُمۡۚ فَنِعۡمَ عُقۡبَى ٱلدَّارِ ٢٤﴾

[الرَّعْد من الآية ٢٣ الى الآية ٢٤]

> "They will be admitted to everlasting gardens in Paradise along with those who were righteous among their forefathers, spouses, and descendants. Furthermore, angels will enter their presence from every door saying: 'Peace be upon you for the patience (which) you observed. How excellent is the ultimate abode!'" (Raʿd 13:23-24)

Islām also stipulates that the spouses treat each other kindly, take good care of those under their guardianship, and fulfill each other's rights and obligations. This should be done in compliance with the directives of Allāh (ﷻ).

Allāh (ﷻ) says:

﴿وَعَاشِرُوهُنَّ بِٱلْمَعْرُوفِ ۚ﴾ [النِّسَاء الآية ١٩]

"And (you must ensure that you) live with them (your spouse) kindly (and fulfill their rights)." (Nisā' 4:19)

Living kindly with your spouse entails all of the interactions which Islām's teachings consider kind and praiseworthy, to the best of one's ability. It requires speaking well, having a pleasant appearance, and acting properly.

Living together with kindness and the fulfillment of rights includes assisting each other in accomplishing what is required as it relates to both religious and mundane matters.

A narration in the *Musnad* of Imām Aḥmad mentions that when 'Ā'ishah (رضي الله عنها) was asked if the Messenger of Allāh (ﷺ) did any tasks while at home, she replied:

«نَعَمْ، كَانَ رَسُولُ اللهِ ﷺ يَخْصِفُ نَعْلَهُ، وَيَخِيطُ ثَوْبَهُ، وَيَعْمَلُ فِي بَيْتِهِ كَمَا يَعْمَلُ أَحَدُكُمْ فِي بَيْتِهِ».

(مسند أحمد)

"Yes! The Messenger of Allāh (ﷺ) used to mend his footwear, stitch his garments, and do chores at home just like anyone of you does chores at his own home." (Musnad Aḥmad)

Neither spouse should see themselves as being above their partner, or think themselves free of any responsibility, or deem themselves worthy of reminding the other about the good which they did for the other partner.

The Prophet (ﷺ) has said:

«خَيْرُكُمْ خَيْرُكُمْ لأَهْلِهِ، وَأَنَا خَيْرُكُمْ لأَهْلِي».

(رواه الترمذي)

"The best of you are those who are best to their families, and I am the best among you to my family." (Tirmidhī)

Among the manifestations of living well with one another is for each spouse to be considerate of the other's circumstances, strive to remove the causes of distress, and take initiative to foster happiness.

A *ḥadīth* which has been recorded by both Imām al-Bukhārī and Imām Muslim (ﷺ) mentions that when the first revelation descended to the Prophet (ﷺ) telling him to:

﴿ٱقْرَأْ بِٱسْمِ رَبِّكَ ٱلَّذِى خَلَقَ ۝١﴾ [العَلَق الآية ١]

"Read in the name of your Lord who created all things" (ʿAlaq 96:1)

The Prophet (ﷺ) returned home with that revelation while his heart was racing. He went to his wife Khadījah (ﷺ) and said:

«زَمِّلُونِي زَمِّلُونِي».

"Cover me, cover me."

Abū Isḥāq (ﷺ) says (quoting the Prophet):

« لَقَدْ خَشِيتُ عَلَى نَفْسِي».

"I most certainly feared for myself."

Khadījah (ﷺ) consoled him and replied:

« كَلاَّ وَاللَّهِ مَا يُخْزِيكَ اللَّهُ أَبَدًا، إِنَّكَ لَتَصِلُ الرَّحِمَ، وَتَحْمِلُ الْكَلَّ، وَتَكْسِبُ الْمَعْدُومَ، وَتَقْرِي الضَّيْفَ، وَتُعِينُ عَلَى نَوَائِبِ الْحَقِّ».

"On the contrary, you should rest assured that it is a good indication. I swear that Allāh would never put you to disgrace. You undoubtedly uphold ties of kinship, help others who cannot make do on their own, give to the destitute, honour the guests, and help the deserving who are stricken with adversities."

Khadījah (ﷺ) then took him to Waraqah ibn Nawfal who eventually told him:

«هَذَا النَّامُوسُ الَّذِي أَنْزَلَ اللَّهُ عَلَى مُوسَى».

"That was the same angel who Allāh sent down to Prophet Mūsā."

Another manifestation of living together well is for a husband not to be miserly in supporting his wife so long as he has the means, and for him to place her on an equal standing with him regarding accommodation and standard of living.

Allāh (ﷻ) says:

﴿أَسْكِنُوهُنَّ مِنْ حَيْثُ سَكَنتُم مِّن وُجْدِكُمْ وَلَا تُضَآرُّوهُنَّ لِتُضَيِّقُواْ عَلَيْهِنَّ ۚ ٦﴾

[الطَّلَاق الآية ٦]

"House them where you dwell, according to your means, and do not harm (or harass) them in any way so as to make things difficult for them." (Ṭalāq 65:6)

The people most entitled for you to support them financially are your own family and dependents. Moreover, do not think of financial support as merely wasted money; on the contrary, it is a form of charity whose rewards will remain. The Prophet (ﷺ) stressed its importance as well as its manifold recompense.

A *ḥadīth* in *Ṣaḥīḥ Muslim* mentions that the Messenger of Allāh (ﷺ) said:

«دِينَارٌ أَنْفَقْتَهُ فِي سَبِيلِ اللهِ، وَدِينار أَنْفَقْتَهُ فِي رَقَبَةٍ، وَدِينارٌ تَصَدَّقْتَ بِهِ عَلَى مِسْكِينٍ، وَدِينَارٌ أَنْفَقْتَهُ عَلَى أَهْلِكَ، أَعْظَمُهَا أَجْرًا الَّذِي أَنْفَقْتَهُ عَلَى أَهْلِكَ».

(رواه مسلم)

"Between a *dīnār* which you give in Allāh's path, a *dīnār* that you give to free a slave, a *dīnār* which you give in charity to the needy, and a *dīnār* that you give to support your family - the one greatest in reward is the one which you give to support your family." (Muslim)

The Prophet (ﷺ) also said:

«إِنَّ الْمُسْلِمَ إِذَا أَنْفَقَ عَلَى أَهْلِهِ نَفَقَةً، وَهُوَ يَحْتَسِبُهَا، كَانَتْ لَهُ صَدَقَةً».

(رواه مسلم)

"Surely when a Muslim spends anything on his family, hoping for its reward (from Allāh), it will be a form of charity on his part." (Muslim)

Additionally, it is not permissible for a wife to demand from her husband support or expenditures that are beyond his ability to give, especially when the demands are for non-essential things. The teachings of Islām state that financial support is to be given in proportion to one's ability.

Allāh (ﷻ) says in the Qur'ān:

﴿لِيُنفِقْ ذُو سَعَةٍ مِّن سَعَتِهِۦ ۖ وَمَن قُدِرَ عَلَيْهِ رِزْقُهُۥ فَلْيُنفِقْ مِمَّآ ءَاتَىٰهُ ٱللَّهُ ۚ لَا يُكَلِّفُ ٱللَّهُ نَفْسًا إِلَّا مَآ ءَاتَىٰهَا ۚ سَيَجْعَلُ ٱللَّهُ بَعْدَ عُسْرٍ يُسْرًا ۝٧﴾ [الطَّلَاق الآية ٧]

"The man who is well-off must provide support according to his wealth (which Allāh has given him), and the man whose resources are restricted must provide support according to whatever means Allāh has given him. Allāh does not make any person responsible for what is beyond his ability. Allāh will cause a person's time of difficulty to be followed by one of ease." (Ṭalāq 65:7)

Wives must do their utmost to remain kind and gentle. Beware of excessive requests and demands, since this will produce problems and disputes. Avoid looking at those who have more material things than you, as this will lead you to feel that you have a miserable life. It will also lead you to become ungrateful to your husband, and ultimately, to your Lord.

The Prophet (ﷺ) sates:

«انْظُرُوا إِلَى مَنْ هُوَ أَسْفَلَ مِنْكُمْ، وَلَا تَنْظُرُوا إِلَى مَنْ هُوَ فَوْقَكُمْ، فَهُوَ أَجْدَرُ أَنْ لَا تَزْدَرُوا نِعْمَةَ اللَّهِ عَلَيْكُمْ».

(رواه مسلم)

> "Look at those who have less than you, and do not look at those who have more than you. (Do this) so that you will not belittle or scorn the blessings which Allāh has given you." (Muslim)

Part of a husband's dignity and honour is for him to not take any of his wife's property unless she gives it willingly. Her wealth is her own property. However, if a man is needy and Allāh (ﷻ) has blessed his wife with a surplus of money, then living well together entails that she assists her husband using what Allāh (ﷻ) has blessed her with.

Once on the day of *ʿĪd*, the Messenger of Allāh (ﷺ) addressed the people and said:

«أَيُّهَا النَّاسُ، تَصَدَّقُوا، فَمَرَّ عَلَى النِّسَاءِ، فَقَالَ: يَا مَعْشَرَ النِّسَاءِ، تَصَدَّقْنَ، فَإِنِّي رَأَيْتُكُنَّ أَكْثَرَ أَهْلِ النَّارِ».

> "O people! Give charity." Then he went towards the women and said: "O gathering of women! Give charity. I have seen that you constitute the majority of the hellfire's inhabitants."

He was approached afterwards when he reached his home by Zaynab (﵂), the wife of ʿAbdullāh ibn Masʿūd (﵁) who said:

«يَا نَبِيَّ اللَّهِ إِنَّكَ أَمَرْتَ الْيَوْمَ بِالصَّدَقَةِ، وَكَانَ عِنْدِي حُلِيٌّ لِي، فَأَرَدْتُ أَنْ أَتَصَدَّقَ بِهِ، فَزَعَمَ ابْنُ مَسْعُودٍ أَنَّهُ وَوَلَدَهُ أَحَقُّ مَنْ تَصَدَّقْتُ بِهِ عَلَيْهِمْ».

"O Prophet of Allāh, you instructed us to give charity today and I had some jewelry of mine with me which I wanted to give as charity. However, Ibn Masʿūd said that he and his children are the ones most entitled to the charity that I give."

Upon this the Prophet (ﷺ) said:

«صَدَقَ ابْنُ مَسْعُودٍ، زَوْجُكِ وَوَلَدُكِ أَحَقُّ مَنْ تَصَدَّقْتِ بِهِ عَلَيْهِمْ».

"What Ibn Masʿūd said is correct. Your husband and children are the ones most entitled to the charity that you give."

Another narration mentions that the Messenger of Allāh (ﷺ) said:

«نَعَمْ، لَهَا أَجْرَانِ، أَجْرُ الْقَرَابَةِ، وَأَجْرُ الصَّدَقَةِ».

(رواه البخاري)

"Yes (that is correct). In such a case, a woman will receive two rewards: one for supporting relatives, and another for giving charity." (Bukhārī)

A further element of living well together is having trust in one another. There is nothing blameworthy about feeling displeased when something wrong is done, so long as the displeasure remains within the bounds of Islām's teachings of moderation. Such feelings are part of a person's dignity and they emanate from the love of one for their spouse.

In fact, an authentic *ḥadīth* states:

«إِنَّ اللَّهَ يَغَارُ، وَإِنَّ الْمُؤْمِنَ يَغَارُ».

(رواه مسلم)

"Allāh is certainly displeased (when wrong is done), and a believer is (also) certainly displeased (when wrong is done)." (Muslim)

However, it is incorrect for a person to let the displeasure become excessive, such that it leads to suspicion. When that happens, any innocent word or inadvertent action will get interpreted in a harmful way. Life together will then become continually tainted, and the home that brings people together will end up being destroyed.

'Alī (؆) said:

»لَا تُكْثِرِ الْغَيْرَةَ عَلَى أَهْلِكَ، وَلَمْ تَرَ مِنْهَا سُوءًا فَتُرْمَى بِالشَّرِّ مِنْ أَجْلِكَ«

(حلية الأولياء وطبقات الأصفياء)

"Do not become excessive towards your spouse in your displeasure over wrong which you think may have been done, and then cause her to be accused of bad things because of you." (Ḥilyat al-Awliyā' wa Ṭabaqāt al-Aṣfiyā')

A further element of living together kindly is not divulging what is confidential between couples.

Allāh (؆) says:

﴿هُنَّ لِبَاسٌ لَّكُمْ وَأَنتُمْ لِبَاسٌ لَّهُنَّ﴾ [البَقَرَة الآية ١٨٧]

"They are a garment for you, and you are a garment for them." (Baqarah 2:187)

NOTE: The author of *Rūḥul Ma'ānī* writes that this verse means that each spouse is a source of contentment and courage for the other.[13]

Islām teaches that matters of privacy between spouses should remain confidential. Divulging them is a major form of betrayal and doing that will lead to a person being condemned to the lowest depths on the Day of Resurrection.

---

[13] The *ayah* of the Qur'ān of this is as follows:

﴿هُنَّ لِبَاسٌ لَّكُمْ وَأَنتُمْ لِبَاسٌ لَّهُنَّ﴾ [البقرة: 187]

In the *Ṣaḥīḥ* of Imām Muslim (ﷺ), there is a *ḥadīth* which mentions that the Messenger of Allāh (ﷺ) said:

«إِنَّ مِنْ أَشَرِّ النَّاسِ عِنْدَ اللهِ مَنْزِلَةً يَوْمَ الْقِيَامَةِ، الرَّجُلَ يُفْضِي إِلَى امْرَأَتِهِ، وَتُفْضِي إِلَيْهِ، ثُمَّ يَنْشُرُ سِرَّهَا».

(رواه مسلم)

"Among the people who will have the most deplorable of ranks to Allāh on the Day of Resurrection is a man who was intimate with his spouse, and she was intimate with him, but then he divulges private things about her." (Muslim)

Another element of living kindly together is enjoying some form of recreation that makes one's wife happy. When we examine the life of our Prophet (ﷺ), we find that even amidst the enormous responsibility of Prophethood which he bore, there were many manifestations of such recreation between him and his wives.

In the *Musnad* of Imām Aḥmad (ﷺ), there is a *ḥadīth* in which ʿĀ'ishah (ﷺ) relates:

«خَرَجْتُ مَعَ النَّبِيِّ ﷺ فِي بَعْضِ أَسْفَارِهِ وَأَنَا جَارِيَةٌ لَمْ أَحْمِلِ اللَّحْمَ وَلَمْ أَبْدُنْ، فَقَالَ لِلنَّاسِ: تَقَدَّمُوا فَتَقَدَّمُوا، ثُمَّ قَالَ لِي: تَعَالَيْ حَتَّى أُسَابِقَكِ فَسَابَقْتُهُ فَسَبَقْتُهُ، فَسَكَتَ عَنِّي، حَتَّى إِذَا حَمَلْتُ اللَّحْمَ وَبَدُنْتُ وَنَسِيتُ، خَرَجْتُ مَعَهُ فِي بَعْضِ أَسْفَارِهِ، فَقَالَ لِلنَّاسِ: تَقَدَّمُوا فَتَقَدَّمُوا، ثُمَّ قَالَ: تَعَالَيْ حَتَّى أُسَابِقَكِ فَسَابَقْتُهُ، فَسَبَقَنِي، فَجَعَلَ يَضْحَكُ، وَهُوَ يَقُولُ: هَذِهِ بِتِلْكَ».

(رواه أحمد)

"I once set out with the Prophet (ﷺ) on a journey of his while I was still young, and my body had yet not grown large or put on weight. He told the people: 'Proceed ahead,' and so they did. Then he said to me and said: 'Come so I can race you,' so I raced

> him, and I beat him. He then remained quiet about what I did until later on when my body had grown larger, and I had put on some weight, and I had forgotten about what had happened. In those circumstances, I again set out with him on a journey of his, and he told the people: 'Proceed ahead,' and so they did. Then he said to me and said: 'Come so I can race you,' so I raced him, and (this time) he beat me. He then started laughing and said: 'This one is payback for that one.'" (Aḥmad)

We must realize that if a person commends his wife about things like her appearance, food, and clothing - these things are a key to her heart and a path to attaining her love. Always keep in mind that when a person has true integrity, his heart will stay soft. Be towards your wife as you would like her to be towards you. She loves from you what you love from her.

'Abdullāh ibn 'Abbās (ﷺ) states:

«إِنِّي لَأُحِبُّ أَنْ أَتَزَيَّنَ لِلْمَرْأَةِ كَمَا أُحِبُّ أَنْ تَزَّيَّنَ لِي؛ لِأَنَّ اللهَ عَزَّ وَجَلَّ يَقُولُ: ﴿وَلَهُنَّ مِثْلُ ٱلَّذِى عَلَيْهِنَّ بِٱلْمَعْرُوفِۚ ﴿٢٢٨﴾﴾ [البَقَرَة الآية ٢٢٨]».

(السنن الكبرى للبيهقي)

> "I like to adorn myself for my spouse just as I like when she adorns herself for me. That is because Allāh has said, 'Wives have rights that their husbands must fulfill in an acceptable manner, just as husbands have rights which their wives must fulfill in an acceptable manner.'" (Baqarah 2:228) (Al-Sunan al-Kubrā of al-Bayhaqī)

Among the praiseworthy words that are part of living together kindly is for each spouse to tell the other one that they love them; and deeds of affection should also accompany one's words.

When the Prophet (ﷺ) was asked:

«أَيُّ النَّاسِ أَحَبُّ إِلَيْكَ؟ قَالَ: عَائِشَةُ».

(رواه مسلم)

"Which person is the most beloved to you?" He said: "ʿĀ'ishah." (Muslim)

In addition, ʿĀ'ishah (ﷺ) states:

«كُنْتُ أَشْرَبُ وَأَنَا حَائِضٌ، ثُمَّ أُنَاوِلُهُ النَّبِيَّ ﷺ فَيَضَعُ فَاهُ عَلَى مَوْضِعِ فِيَّ فَيَشْرَبُ، وَأَتَعَرَّقُ الْعَرْقَ وَأَنَا حَائِضٌ، ثُمَّ أُنَاوِلُهُ النَّبِيَّ ﷺ فَيَضَعُ فَاهُ عَلَى مَوْضِعِ فِيَّ».

(رواه مسلم)

"During my menses, I would drink from a cup and pass it to the Prophet (ﷺ) who would put his mouth on the same part of the cup and then drink from it. During my menses, I would bite meat off from a bone and while I was eating it, pass it to the Prophet (ﷺ) who would put his mouth on the same part of the bone." (Muslim)

She also said:

«كَانَ رَسُولُ اللهِ ﷺ يَتَّكِئُ فِي حِجْرِي وَأَنَا حَائِضٌ، فَيَقْرَأُ الْقُرْآنَ».

(رواه مسلم)

"During my menses, the Messenger of Allāh (ﷺ) would lie in my lap and recite the Qur'ān." (Muslim)

It must also be kept in mind that no matter how hard couples try to live together compassionately and fulfill each other's rights, there will be shortcomings, mistakes will happen, and differences will occur. In such scenarios, each spouse should pardon the other. Each one should make it their practice to overlook the faults of the other.

When a person is picked on for every little detail, they will end up being unable to do anything. When it comes to family life, both spouses must remember the noble values of cooperation, fostering affection and mercy, exercising care and self-control when dealing with each other, and creating a safe and loving atmosphere within the home.

Allāh (ﷻ) says in the Qur'ān:

﴿وَلَا تَنسَوُا۟ ٱلْفَضْلَ بَيْنَكُمْ ﴿٢٣٧﴾﴾ [البَقَرَة الآية ٢٣٧]

"And do not neglect magnanimity between yourselves (by giving more than what may be obligatory for you and also by foregoing some of your rights when dealing with others)." (Baqarah 2:237)

Neither spouse should keep pestering the other one at times of anger, nor should either keep thinking about the bad things which they may see in the other. Rather, it is a must for them to remember what is good about the other, not ignore their integrity, not to forget the praiseworthy qualities, and always remember the earlier kindness from them.

A *ḥadīth* in the *Ṣaḥīḥ* of Imām Muslim (رحمه الله) mentions that the Messenger of Allāh (ﷺ) said:

«لَا يَفْرَكْ مُؤْمِنٌ مُؤْمِنَةً، إِنْ كَرِهَ مِنْهَا خُلُقًا رَضِيَ مِنْهَا آخَرَ، أَوْ قَالَ: غَيْرَهُ».

(رواه مسلم)

"A believing man must not hate a believing woman. If he is displeased about some quality of hers, then there are others that please him." (Muslim)

As part of the elevated conduct personified by the Prophet (ﷺ), he would persevere in bearing any harshness that may have emanated from his wives.

A narration in *Ṣaḥīḥ al-Bukhārī* mentions that there were times when:

«وَإِنَّ إِحْدَاهُنَّ لَتَهْجُرُهُ الْيَوْمَ حَتَّى اللَّيْلِ».

(رواه البخاري)

> "One of them would avoid him for an entire day, all of the way until the night." (Bukhārī)

It must also be kept in mind that it is crucial to maintain the relationship between ourselves and Allāh (ﷻ). When we maintain our relationship with Allāh (ﷻ), then He will protect the relationship between us and our spouses.

There are many times when sins break apart families that were once very happy; and often times misdeeds can change a cheerful life to a miserable one.

Allāh (ﷻ) says:

﴿وَمَآ أَصَٰبَكُم مِّن مُّصِيبَةٍ فَبِمَا كَسَبَتْ أَيْدِيكُمْ وَيَعْفُوا۟ عَن كَثِيرٍ ۝٣٠﴾ [الشورى الآية ٣٠]

> "And whatever misfortune befalls you, it is because of what your own hands have committed, yet He overlooks many (of your faults)." (Shūrā 42:30)

CONCLUSION

Having tranquility in one's marriage is an immense blessing. No one knows its true value besides those who have been deprived of it.

The Qur'ān alludes to the significance of this blessing in a statement by Allāh (ﷻ) where He says:

﴿وَٱللَّهُ جَعَلَ لَكُم مِّنۢ بُيُوتِكُمْ سَكَنًا ۝٨٠﴾ [النحل الآية ٨٠]

> "And Allāh made your homes a source of tranquility for you." (Naḥl 16:80)

This tranquility also refers to stability, harmony, and companionship based on love and mercy. As a result, the soul finds peace, and the body finds rest; and this happens with someone whom the heart loves, is at ease with, and finds comfort in speaking with.

Life is certainly not a continuous series of lovely events and rosy dreams. Perfection is something which is very rare. There may be times when spouses disagree about something; and this is normal in life and is part of human nature.

Unity of the hearts and fostering love between spouses does not come about from furnishings and clothing, or from mere words and statements. Although it is true that these are things which may lead to harmony, but it must always be borne in mind that true harmony only comes from Allāh (ﷻ), and love is a blessing from Him.

Allāh (ﷻ) says in Qur'ān:

﴿وَأَلَّفَ بَيْنَ قُلُوبِهِمْ لَوْ أَنفَقْتَ مَا فِي ٱلْأَرْضِ جَمِيعًا مَّآ أَلَّفْتَ بَيْنَ قُلُوبِهِمْ وَلَـٰكِنَّ ٱللَّهَ أَلَّفَ بَيْنَهُمْ إِنَّهُۥ عَزِيزٌ حَكِيمٌ ۝٦٣﴾ [الأنفال الآية ٦٣]

> "And He created the bond of love (harmony) between their hearts. If you had spent whatever (wealth and resources) is in the earth, you will not have been able to create that bond of love between their hearts, but Allāh created that bond between them. Verily He is Mighty (can do whatever He wants), and Wise (in creating the bond of love between people). (Anfāl 8:63)

Mutual respect is one of the signs of a stable family, and it is an essential pillar which supports it. A woman must recognize the role, virtue, and status of her husband in the home: and a man must also bear in mind the condition and status of his wife, and deal with her as a life partner rather than a servant.

Overlooking slips and ignoring errors are the key elements to family stability. There are times when the various pressures of life may cause one to behave at home in an unanticipated or forthright manner. Thus, it is necessary to be considerate, understanding, and accepting.

Spouses need to avoid conflicts and disputes, be kind to each other in words and deeds, and communicate with one another gently without arguments. Discord gives rise to hatred within the hearts, and frequent disputes eradicate love and happiness.

To this effect, there is a proverb which says:

«طُولُ المُرافقة من كثرةِ المُوافقة».

"Long-lasting company is a result of frequent agreement."

Abū al-Dardā' (ﷺ) would say to his wife:

»إذا رأيتني غَضِبت، فَرَضِّني، وإذا رأيتُكِ غَضبتي رَضيتِكِ، فإذا لم نكن هكذا ما أسْرَعَ مَا نَفْتَرِقُ«.

(روضة العقلاء ونزهة الفضلاء)

"If you see me angry, then calm me down, and if I see you angry, then I will calm you down, otherwise it will be too difficult to live together." (Rawḍat al-'Uqalā' wa Nazhat al-Fuḍalā')

We must also realize that marriage is not based on love alone. Although it is obviously best when love exists, but marriage is also based on mercy.

In fact, love forms and grows as time passes, and more so when it is accompanied by living well with each other. In this way, Allāh (ﷻ) will place between the spouses - warmth, affection, happiness, and enjoyment. Living kindly and fulfilling the rights of one another are two elements which will foster love and mercy between spouses.

There is a narration in *Tārīkh al-Kabīr* by Imām al-Bukhārī (ﷺ), and *Sharḥ al-Sunnah* by Imām al-Baghawī (ﷺ) which mentions that during the reign of 'Umar (ﷺ), a man said to his wife:

»نَشَدْتُكِ بِاللَّهِ هَلْ تُحِبِّينِي؟ فَقَالَتْ أَمَّا إِذَا نَشَدْتَنِي بِاللَّهِ فَلَا، فَخَرَجَ الرَّجُلُ حَتَّى أَتَى عُمَرَ رضي الله عنه ، فَأَرْسَلَ إِلَيْهَا فَقَالَ أَنْتِ الَّتِي تَقُولِينَ لِزَوْجِكِ لَا أُحِبُّكَ، فَقَالَتْ يَا أَمِيرَ الْمُؤْمِنِينَ نَشَدَنِي بِاللَّهِ أَفَأَكْذِبُهُ؟ قَالَ نَعَمْ فَأَكْذِبِيهِ، لَيْسَ كُلُّ الْبُيُوتِ تُبْنَى عَلَى الْحُبِّ. وَلَكِنَّ النَّاسَ يَتَعَاشَرُونَ بِالْإِسْلَامِ وَالْإِحْسَانِ«.

(التأريخ الكبير للإمام البخاري، وشرح السنة للإمام البغوي)

"I ask you by Allāh, do you truly love me?" She replied: "If you have asked me by Allāh, then no, I do not." The man then left and went to ʿUmar who later sent for that man's wife. ʿUmar asked her: "Are you the woman who told your husband - 'I do not love you'?" She replied: "O leader of the believers, he asked me by Allāh. Am I supposed to say something untrue to him?" ʿUmar replied: "Yes, say something untrue in that situation. Not all homes are built upon just love alone. Rather, people live together based on Islām and kindness." (Tārīkh al-Kabīr of Imām al-Bukhārī, Sharḥ al-Sunnah of Imām al-Baghawī)

How precise is the saying of Allāh (ﷻ) where He says in the Qur'ān:

﴿وَمِنْ آيَاتِهِ أَنْ خَلَقَ لَكُم مِّنْ أَنفُسِكُمْ أَزْوَاجًا لِّتَسْكُنُوا إِلَيْهَا وَجَعَلَ بَيْنَكُم مَّوَدَّةً وَرَحْمَةً إِنَّ فِي ذَٰلِكَ لَآيَاتٍ لِّقَوْمٍ يَتَفَكَّرُونَ ﴿٢١﴾﴾ [الروم الآية 21]

"And among His signs is that He created for you spouses from your own kind so that your souls may find tranquility with them, and He placed love and mercy between you. Surely in that contains clear signs for a people who contemplate." (Rūm 30:21)

"MARRIAGE IS NOT A WORD WHICH YOU SPELL,
RATHER IT IS A LIFELONG SENTENCE!"

KHUṬBAH 60

Behold Your Elders: The Forgotten Ones

Man's life passes through successive stages: as an infant in the cradle, he is totally helpless; then, as he grows into adulthood, he acquires full-fledged strength; and finally, in a few years, he reverts to weakness once again.

Allāh (ﷻ) says in the Qur'ān:

﴿۞ ٱللَّهُ ٱلَّذِى خَلَقَكُم مِّن ضَعْفٍ ثُمَّ جَعَلَ مِنۢ بَعْدِ ضَعْفٍ قُوَّةً ثُمَّ جَعَلَ مِنۢ بَعْدِ قُوَّةٍ ضَعْفًا وَشَيْبَةً ۚ يَخْلُقُ مَا يَشَآءُ ۖ وَهُوَ ٱلْعَلِيمُ ٱلْقَدِيرُ ﴿٥٤﴾﴾ [الرُّوم الآية ٥٤]

> It is Allāh Who created you in a state of weakness (as a helpless infant), then substituted strength after the weakness (as you grew into an adult) and after the strength, will again give weakness (as you age) and (eventually) old age. Allāh creates whatever He wills, and He is the All-Knowing, the All-Powerful. (Rūm 30:54)

Our Prophet (ﷺ) would exhort Muslims to show mercy to the feeble, be they young or old, children or elderly, and he set an example for them in his words and deeds.

Imām Tirmidhī (رحمه الله) in his famous work on *ḥadīth, Sunan al-Tirmidhī* has recorded a Prophetic narration wherein Abū al-Dardā (رضي الله عنه) says:

«سَمِعْتُ النَّبِيَّ ﷺ يَقُولُ: ابْغُونِي ضُعَفَاءَكُمْ، فَإِنَّمَا تُرْزَقُونَ وَتُنْصَرُونَ بِضُعَفَائِكُمْ».

(رواه الترمذي)

> "I heard the Prophet (ﷺ) say: 'Seek my love, proximity, and satisfaction with the feeble among you - they cause sustenance and aid to be brought to you.'" (Tirmidhī)

In other words, when the Prophet (ﷺ) said seek my love, proximity, and satisfaction with the feeble among you, he meant that check in on their conditions, be kind to them, give them their rights, comfort them, and be kind to them in your words and deeds.

Examples of the Prophet's (ﷺ) compassion towards the feeble included his kindness towards youngsters.

Anas ibn Mālik (رضي الله عنه) reports:

«مَا رَأَيْتُ أَحَدًا كَانَ أَرْحَمَ بِالْعِيَالِ مِنْ رَسُولِ اللهِ ﷺ، قَالَ: كَانَ إِبْرَاهِيمُ مُسْتَرْضِعًا لَهُ فِي عَوَالِي الْمَدِينَةِ، فَكَانَ يَنْطَلِقُ وَنَحْنُ مَعَهُ فَيَدْخُلُ الْبَيْتَ وَإِنَّهُ لَيُدَّخَنُ، وَكَانَ ظِئْرُهُ قَيْنًا، فَيَأْخُذُهُ فَيُقَبِّلُهُ، ثُمَّ يَرْجِعُ».

(رواه مسلم)

> "I have not seen anyone more merciful to children than Allāh's Messenger (ﷺ). When Ibrāhīm (the Prophet's son) was entrusted to a wet nurse in one of Madīnah's suburbs, we used to go with the Prophet (ﷺ) to see him. He would enter the house, and it would be filled with smoke as his foster-father was a brick smith. He would take the boy, kiss him and then come back." (Muslim)

Imām al-Bukhārī (رحمه الله) in his *Ṣaḥīḥ* has reported that the Prophet (ﷺ) said to a man who would not kiss his children:

«أَوَ أَمْلِكُ لَكَ أَنْ نَزَعَ اللَّهُ مِنْ قَلْبِكَ الرَّحْمَةَ؟».

(رواه البخاري)

> "Is there anything that I can do for you if Allāh has stripped mercy off of your heart?" (Bukhārī)

The Prophet (ﷺ) used to take care of little children, mingle with them, joke with them, ask how they were doing, and pay attention to their feelings.

Anas ibn Mālik (رضي الله عنه) narrates:

«كَانَ النَّبِيُّ ﷺ أَحْسَنَ النَّاسِ خُلُقًا، وَكَانَ لِي أَخٌ يُقَالُ لَهُ أَبُو عُمَيْرٍ - قَالَ: أَحْسِبُهُ - فَطِيمًا، وَكَانَ إِذَا جَاءَ قَالَ: يَا أَبَا عُمَيْرٍ، مَا فَعَلَ النُّغَيْرُ؟ نُغَرٌ كَانَ يَلْعَبُ بِهِ، فَرُبَّمَا حَضَرَ الصَّلَاةَ وَهُوَ فِي بَيْتِنَا، فَيَأْمُرُ بِالْبِسَاطِ الَّذِي تَحْتَهُ فَيُكْنَسُ وَيُنْضَحُ، ثُمَّ يَقُومُ وَنَقُومُ خَلْفَهُ فَيُصَلِّي بِنَا».

(رواه البخاري)

> "The Prophet (ﷺ) was the best of all people in character. I had a brother called Abū ʿUmair who I think, had been newly weaned. Whenever he was brought [to the Prophet (ﷺ)] he used to say: 'O Abū ʿUmair! What did *al-nughayr* (nightingale bird) do?' It was a nightingale with which he used to play with. Sometimes the time of the prayer would set in while the Prophet (ﷺ) was in our house. He would order that the carpet underneath him be swept and sprayed with water, then he would stand up for the prayer, and we would line up behind him, and he would lead us in prayer." (Bukhārī)

The Prophet (ﷺ) was very kind to children. He understood them and their need to play. Therefore, he would educate them rather than scold them, and remind them rather than reproach them.

Anas ibn Mālik (رضي الله عنه) narrates:

«كَانَ رَسُولُ اللهِ ﷺ مِنْ أَحْسَنِ النَّاسِ خُلُقًا، فَأَرْسَلَنِي يَوْمًا لِحَاجَةٍ، فَقُلْتُ: وَاللهِ لَا أَذْهَبُ، وَفِي نَفْسِي أَنْ أَذْهَبَ لِمَا أَمَرَنِي بِهِ نَبِيُّ اللهِ ﷺ، فَخَرَجْتُ حَتَّى أَمُرَّ عَلَى صِبْيَانٍ وَهُمْ يَلْعَبُونَ فِي السُّوقِ، فَإِذَا رَسُولُ اللهِ ﷺ قَدْ قَبَضَ بِقَفَايَ مِنْ وَرَائِي، قَالَ: فَنَظَرْتُ إِلَيْهِ وَهُوَ يَضْحَكُ، فَقَالَ: يَا أُنَيْسُ أَذَهَبْتَ حَيْثُ أَمَرْتُكَ؟ قَالَ قُلْتُ: نَعَمْ، أَنَا أَذْهَبُ، يَا رَسُولَ اللهِ».

(رواه مسلم)

> "The Prophet (ﷺ) had the most sublime morals. One day, he sent me for an errand, and I said: 'By Allāh, I will not go,' though I intended to go and do what he had told me to do. When I went out, I happened to come across some children who had been playing in the street. In the meanwhile, the Prophet (ﷺ) came there and he caught me by the back of my neck from behind me. As I looked towards him, I found him smiling and he said: 'O Onais! Did you go where I told you?' 'Yes!' I answered. 'I am on my way, O Messenger of Allāh!'" (Muslim)

As the Prophet (ﷺ) ordered us to show mercy and compassion to children, he also ordered us to show respect to the elderly, treat them with reverence, give them due care, and hold them in high esteem.

Anas ibn Mālik (رضي الله عنه) narrates:

«جَاءَ شَيْخٌ يُرِيدُ النَّبِيَّ ﷺ فَأَبْطَأَ الْقَوْمُ عَنْهُ أَنْ يُوَسِّعُوا لَهُ، فَقَالَ النَّبِيُّ ﷺ: لَيْسَ مِنَّا مَنْ لَمْ يَرْحَمْ صَغِيرَنَا وَيُوَقِّرْ كَبِيرَنَا».

(رواه الترمذي)

> "An elderly man came to see the Prophet (ﷺ) and the people were slow in making room for him, so the Prophet (ﷺ) said, 'He is not from one of us who does not have mercy on our young, and does not respect our elders.'" (Tirmidhī)

In other words, a person who does not show kindness or compassion towards children, or has no respect or consideration for the elderly because they are old aged and frail - is not in line with the guidance and moral code of Islām.

Imām al-Bayhaqī (رحمه الله) in his work *Shuʿab al-Īmān* has recorded a narration in which the Prophet (ﷺ) promised that those who show mercy to the youngsters, and have reverence for the elderly will be in his company in Paradise.

Anas ibn Mālik (ﷺ) narrates that the Prophet (ﷺ) said:

«يَا أَنَسُ، وَقِّرِ الْكَبِيرَ، وَارْحَمِ الصَّغِيرَ، تُرَافِقْنِي فِي الْجَنَّةِ».

(شعب الإيمان للبيهقي)

"O Anas! Show respect for the elderly and have mercy on children, and you will be in my company in Paradise." (Shuʿab al-Īmān of al-Bayhaqī)

How can we not hold our elders in high esteem while the Messenger of Allāh (ﷺ) said:

«إِنَّ مِنْ إِجْلَالِ اللَّهِ إِكْرَامَ ذِي الشَّيْبَةِ الْمُسْلِمِ».

(سنن أبي داود)

"Part of the respect for Allāh is honouring the grey-haired (elderly) Muslim." (Sunan Abū Dāwūd)

How can we not show respect to our elders while the Messenger of Allāh (ﷺ) said:

«الْبَرَكَةُ مَعَ أَكَابِرِكُمْ».

(صحيح ابن حبان)

"Blessing lies with your elders." (Ṣaḥīḥ Ibn Ḥibbān)

There is a nice saying which says: "To earn respect you must show respect." A person who honours the elderly, Allāh (ﷻ) will grant him longevity and will facilitate for him someone to take care of him during his old age.

Anas ibn Mālik (ﷺ) narrates that the Prophet (ﷺ) said:

«مَا أَكْرَمَ شَابٌّ شَيْخًا لِسِنِّهِ إِلاَّ قَيَّضَ اللَّهُ لَهُ مَنْ يُكْرِمُهُ عِنْدَ سِنِّهِ».

(رواه الترمذي)

"If a young man honours an elderly person because of his old age, then Allāh will facilitate for him someone to honour him when he gets old." (Tirmidhī)

Our elders have the right to be honoured and revered. We should offer them the best places in any gathering so that they may embellish the event. We should call them by their desired names, and receive them with a joyful appearance.

In addition, we should forgive their shortcomings and faults, and mention their merits and traits, because at that age, they like and prefer to talk about their past life and their achievements. Our Messenger of Allāh (ﷺ) notwithstanding his great status and rank, taught us practically how to show an elderly person reverence, respect, kind-heartedness, and affection.

In the *Ṭabaqāt* of Ibn Saʿd (ؓ) it is mentioned that:

»لَمَّا فُتِحَتْ مَكَّةُ جَاءَ أَبُو بَكْرٍ بِأَبِيهِ حَتَّى بَايَعَ رَسُولَ اللهِ ﷺ، فَقَالَ رَسُولُ اللهِ ﷺ: أَلَا كُنْتَ تَرَكْتَ الشَّيْخَ فِي مَنْزِلِهِ حَتَّى نَكُونَ نَحْنُ الَّذِي نَأْتِيهِ؟ وَكَأَنَّ رَأْسَهُ ثَغَامَةٌ، فَقَالَ: غَيِّرْ هَذَا الْبَيَاضَ وَجَنِّبْهُ السَّوَادَ، فَأَجْلَسَهُ بَيْنَ يَدَيْهِ، ثُمَّ مَسَحَ صَدْرَهُ، ثُمَّ قَالَ لَهُ: أَسْلِمْ، فَأَسْلَمَ«.

(الطبقات الكبير لابن سعد)

Abū Bakr (ؓ) brought his father Abū Quḥāfah to the Prophet (ﷺ) on the Day of the Conquest of Makkah. He carried his father and put him down before the Prophet (ﷺ). Upon seeing him, the Prophet (ﷺ) said to Abū Bakr (ؓ): "If you had left him home, I would have gone to him." Then the Prophet (ﷺ) invited Abū Quḥāfah to Islām, and he embraced Islām. (Ṭabaqāt Kabīr of Ibn Saʿd)

Old age is generally a phase of infirmities, dullness, boredom, fatigue, weakness, and frailty, which in turn leads to impatience and discourteous language. However, the Prophet (ﷺ) would still be courteous, generous and humorous with them.

Ḥasan al-Baṣrī (ﷺ) narrates that:

«أَتَتْ عَجُوزٌ إِلَى النَّبِيِّ ﷺ، فَقَالَتْ: يَا رَسُولَ اللَّهِ، ادْعُ اللَّهَ أَنْ يُدْخِلَنِي الْجَنَّةَ، فَقَالَ: يَا أُمَّ فُلَانٍ، إِنَّ الْجَنَّةَ لَا تَدْخُلُهَا عَجُوزٌ، قَالَ: فَوَلَّتْ تَبْكِي فَقَالَ: أَخْبِرُوهَا أَنَّهَا لَا تَدْخُلُهَا وَهِيَ عَجُوزٌ، إِنَّ اللَّهَ تَعَالَى يَقُولُ: ﴿إِنَّآ أَنشَأْنَٰهُنَّ إِنشَآءً ﴿٣٥﴾ فَجَعَلْنَٰهُنَّ أَبْكَارًا ﴿٣٦﴾ عُرُبًا أَتْرَابًا ﴿٣٧﴾﴾ [الوَاقِعَة من الآية ٣٥ الى الآية ٣٧]».

(رواه الترمذي)

"An old woman came to the Prophet (ﷺ) and made a request: 'O Messenger of Allāh make *duʿā* that Allāh grants me entrance into Paradise.' The Prophet (ﷺ) replied: 'O Mother of so and so, an old woman cannot enter Paradise.' The woman started crying and began to leave. The Prophet (ﷺ) said: 'Say to the woman that one will not enter in a state of old age, but Allāh will make all of the women of Paradise young virgins. For surely Allāh, the Most High has said: 'Indeed We have created these damsels (whom the 'people of the right' shall marry) pure (without any impurities in their bodies or their behaviour). And We have made them all (pure) virgins. Most beloved (every facet of their appearance and behaviour will be pleasing to their husbands) and of equal (the same) age. (Wāqiʿah 56:35-37)'" (Tirmidhī)

Miswar ibn Makhramah (رضي الله عنه) narrates that:

«قَدِمَتْ عَلَى النَّبِيِّ ﷺ أَقْبِيَةٌ فَقَالَ لِي أَبِي، مَخْرَمَةُ انْطَلِقْ بِنَا إِلَيْهِ عَسَى أَنْ يُعْطِينَا مِنْهَا شَيْئًا، قَالَ: فَقَامَ أَبِي عَلَى الْبَابِ فَتَكَلَّمَ، فَعَرَفَ النَّبِيُّ ﷺ صَوْتَهُ فَخَرَجَ وَمَعَهُ قَبَاءٌ وَهُوَ يُرِيهِ مَحَاسِنَهُ، وَهُوَ يَقُولُ: خَبَأْتُ هَذَا لَكَ خَبَأْتُ هَذَا لَكَ، قَالَ أَيُّوبُ: بِثَوْبِهِ أَنَّهُ يُرِيهِ إِيَّاهُ، وَكَانَ فِي خُلُقِهِ شَيْءٌ».

(رواه البخاري)

> "The Prophet (ﷺ) received some *aqbīyah* (plural of *qabā*, outer garments with full-length sleeves). So my father, Makhramah, said to me: 'Let us go to him so that he may give us some of these garments.' My father stood at the door of the Prophet (ﷺ) and spoke. The Prophet (ﷺ) recognized his voice, so he came out holding a *qabā*, showing Makhramah its beauty, and said: 'I have set this aside for you; I have set this aside for you.' Ayyūb, the sub-narrator held his garment to show how the Prophet (ﷺ) showed the cloak to Makhramah who had something unfavourable about his temper, (i.e. was a bit harsh)." (Bukhārī)

Taking care of the elderly and watching over their interests and affairs is one of the greatest deeds that can bring a person closer to Allāh (ﷻ), and a superb means which will relieve people in times of ordeals and ease every difficult situation, especially if the elderly is a father or a mother.

An example of this is found in the incident of the three people who took shelter in a cave to spend the night. While they were inside, a rock fell down and blocked the cave's entrance. All of them began to supplicate to Allāh (ﷻ) to ease their hardship by mentioning a good deed of theirs. One of them supplicated to Allāh (ﷻ) and recalled his taking care of his very old parents. His supplication was thus accepted and his hardship was relieved.

The Prophet (ﷺ) once relayed to the companions (رضي الله عنهم) that:

«انْطَلَقَ ثَلاَثَةُ رَهْطٍ مِمَّنْ كَانَ قَبْلَكُمْ حَتَّى أَوَوُا المَبِيتَ إِلَى غَارٍ، فَدَخَلُوهُ فَانْحَدَرَتْ صَخْرَةٌ مِنَ الجَبَلِ، فَسَدَّتْ عَلَيْهِمُ الغَارَ، فَقَالُوا: إِنَّهُ لاَ يُنْجِيكُمْ مِنْ هَذِهِ الصَّخْرَةِ إِلَّا أَنْ تَدْعُوا اللَّهَ بِصَالِحِ أَعْمَالِكُمْ، فَقَالَ رَجُلٌ مِنْهُمْ: اللَّهُمَّ كَانَ لِي أَبَوَانِ شَيْخَانِ كَبِيرَانِ، وَكُنْتُ لاَ أَغْبِقُ قَبْلَهُمَا أَهْلاً، وَلاَ مَالاً فَنَأَى بِي فِي طَلَبِ شَيْءٍ يَوْمًا، فَلَمْ أُرِحْ عَلَيْهِمَا حَتَّى نَامَا، فَحَلَبْتُ لَهُمَا غَبُوقَهُمَا، فَوَجَدْتُهُمَا نَائِمَيْنِ وَكَرِهْتُ أَنْ أَغْبِقَ قَبْلَهُمَا أَهْلاً أَوْ مَالاً، فَلَبِثْتُ وَالقَدَحُ عَلَى يَدَيَّ، أَنْتَظِرُ

اسْتِيقَاظَهُمَا حَتَّى بَرَقَ الفَجْرُ، فَاسْتَيْقَظَا، فَشَرِبَا غَبُوقَهُمَا، اللَّهُمَّ إِنْ كُنْتُ فَعَلْتُ ذَلِكَ ابْتِغَاءَ وَجْهِكَ، فَفَرِّجْ عَنَّا مَا نَحْنُ فِيهِ مِنْ هَذِهِ الصَّخْرَةِ، فَانْفَرَجَتْ شَيْئًا».

(رواه البخاري)

"Three men from among those who were before you, set out together until they reached a cave at night and entered into it. A big rock rolled down the mountain and closed the mouth of the cave. They said (to each other): 'Nothing can save you from this rock but to invoke Allāh and give a reference to a righteous deed which you have done (only for the sake of Allāh and nothing else).' So, one of them said: 'O Allāh! I had old parents and I never provided my family (wife, children, etc.) with milk before them. One day, by chance I was delayed, and I came back late (at night) and they had already fallen asleep. I milked a sheep for them and took the milk to them, but I found them sleeping. I disliked providing my family with milk before them, so I waited for them to wake up and the bowl of milk was in my hand, and I kept on waiting for them to get up until the day dawned. Then they woke up and drank the milk. O Allāh! If I did that for Your sake only, then please relieve us from our critical situation caused by this rock.' So the rock shifted a little bit." (Bukhārī)

Taking care of one's old parents is equated to *jihād* in the cause of Allāh (ﷻ).

Kaʿb ibn ʿUjrah (رضي الله عنه) reports:

«مَرَّ عَلَى النَّبِيِّ ﷺ رَجُلٌ، فَرَأَى أَصْحَابُ رَسُولِ اللهِ ﷺ مِنْ جِلْدِهِ وَنَشَاطِهِ، فَقَالُوا: يَا رَسُولَ اللهِ: لَوْ كَانَ هَذَا فِي سَبِيلِ اللهِ؟، فَقَالَ رَسُولُ اللهِ ﷺ: إِنْ كَانَ خَرَجَ يَسْعَى عَلَى وَلَدِهِ صِغَارًا فَهُوَ فِي سَبِيلِ اللهِ، وَإِنْ كَانَ خَرَجَ يَسْعَى عَلَى أَبَوَيْنِ شَيْخَيْنِ كَبِيرَيْنِ فَهُوَ فِي سَبِيلِ اللهِ، وَإِنْ كَانَ

يَسْعَى عَلَى نَفْسِهِ يُعِفُّهَا فَهُوَ فِي سَبِيلِ اللهِ، وَإِنْ كَانَ خَرَجَ رِيَاءً وَمُفَاخَرَةً فَهُوَ فِي سَبِيلِ الشَّيْطَانِ».

(المعجم الصغير للطبراني)

"A man once passed by the Prophet (ﷺ) and the Prophet's companions (رضي الله عنهم) were impressed by his vigour and strength. They said: 'O Messenger of Allāh! How wonderful this would be if it was in the cause of Allāh! (Meaning that if this vigour and strength was invested in Allāh's cause, it would have been better).' The Prophet (ﷺ) replied: 'If he has gone out to work to provide for his little children, then it is in the cause of Allāh. If he has gone out to work in order to cater to his old parent's needs, then it is in the cause of Allāh. If he has gone out to work in order to earn his own livelihood and preserve his honour (by not then having to beg from others), then it is in the cause of Allāh. However, if he has gone out for hypocrisy and pride, then it is in for cause of Shayṭān.'" (Al-Muʿjam al-Ṣaghīr of al-Ṭabarānī)

Allāh (ﷻ) says:

﴿ ۞ وَقَضَىٰ رَبُّكَ أَلَّا تَعْبُدُوٓا۟ إِلَّآ إِيَّاهُ وَبِٱلْوَٰلِدَيْنِ إِحْسَٰنًا ۚ إِمَّا يَبْلُغَنَّ عِندَكَ ٱلْكِبَرَ أَحَدُهُمَآ أَوْ كِلَاهُمَا فَلَا تَقُل لَّهُمَآ أُفٍّ وَلَا تَنْهَرْهُمَا وَقُل لَّهُمَا قَوْلًا كَرِيمًا ۝٢٣ وَٱخْفِضْ لَهُمَا جَنَاحَ ٱلذُّلِّ مِنَ ٱلرَّحْمَةِ وَقُل رَّبِّ ٱرْحَمْهُمَا كَمَا رَبَّيَانِى صَغِيرًا ۝٢٤ ﴾

[الإسراء من الآية ٢٣ الى الآية ٢٤]

"And your Lord has commanded that you worship only Him and that you treat your parents kindly. If any one of the two (of your parents), or both of them reaches old age with you, then do not even tell them 'ugh!' (or anything else that may cause them hurt, in Arabic '*oof*' is the smallest thing you can say) and do not rebuke them (even though they may be at fault). (Always)

Speak gently to them. (Never raise your voice when speaking to them, speak with respect, and never speak to them harshly). Lower for them the wings of humility (always be humble and soft-hearted towards them). Out of compassion (and kindness) and say: 'O my Lord! Show mercy to them (my parents) as they had (been merciful towards me when they) raised me when I was young.' (Just as parents are merciful towards their children when their children are little and depend on them, the children should also show mercy towards their parents when their parents grow old and depend on them)." (Isrā' 17:23-24)

CONCLUSION

- Long life is a great blessing granted by Allāh (ﷻ) to whomever He wills among His servants. Therefore, let us use this blessing in what pleases our Lord and raises our status in the hereafter.
- We should endeavour to try and make up for the time that has passed by getting ready for what is coming - since what has remained of one's lifetime may not be longer than what has elapsed, since no one really knows when we will have to leave this temporary abode.
- Let us make obedience to Allāh (ﷻ) the concluding mark of our lifespan; for deeds are judged by their conclusions.
- Whoever lives constantly practicing something will die practicing it, and whoever dies practicing something will be resurrected in that condition.
- Indeed, a long life that is coupled with good deeds, may enable a person to gain a greater rank than that of a *mujāhid* in the cause of Allāh (ﷻ).

Ṭalḥa ibn ʿUbaidullāh (رضي الله عنه) reports that:

«أَنَّ رَجُلَيْنِ قَدِمَا عَلَى رَسُولِ اللَّهِ ﷺ وَكَانَ إِسْلامُهُمَا جَمِيعًا، وَكَانَ أَحَدُهُمَا أَشَدَّ اجْتِهَادًا مِنْ صَاحِبِهِ، فَغَزَا الْمُجْتَهِدُ مِنْهُمَا فَاسْتُشْهِدَ، ثُمَّ مَكَثَ الْآخَرُ بَعْدَهُ سَنَةً ثُمَّ تُوُفِّيَ، قَالَ طَلْحَةُ: فَرَأَيْتُ فِيمَا يَرَى النَّائِمُ كَأَنِّي عِنْدَ بَابِ الْجَنَّةِ، إِذَا أَنَا بِهِمَا وَقَدْ خَرَجَ خَارِجٌ مِنَ الْجَنَّةِ، فَأَذِنَ لِلَّذِي تُوُفِّيَ الْآخِرَ مِنْهُمَا، ثُمَّ خَرَجَ فَأَذِنَ لِلَّذِي اسْتُشْهِدَ، ثُمَّ رَجَعَا إِلَيَّ فَقَالا لِي: ارْجِعْ فَإِنَّهُ لَمْ يَأْنِ لَكَ بَعْدُ، فَأَصْبَحَ طَلْحَةُ يُحَدِّثُ بِهِ النَّاسَ فَعَجِبُوا لِذَلِكَ، فَبَلَغَ ذَلِكَ رَسُولَ اللَّهِ ﷺ فَقَالَ: مِنْ أَيِّ ذَلِكَ تَعْجَبُونَ؟ قَالُوا: يَا رَسُولَ اللَّهِ، هَذَا كَانَ أَشَدَّ اجْتِهَادًا ثُمَّ اسْتُشْهِدَ فِي سَبِيلِ اللَّهِ، وَدَخَلَ هَذَا الْجَنَّةَ قَبْلَهُ، فَقَالَ: أَلَيْسَ قَدْ مَكَثَ هَذَا بَعْدَهُ سَنَةً؟ قَالُوا: بَلَى. قَالَ: وَأَدْرَكَ رَمَضَانَ فَصَامَهُ؟ قَالُوا: بَلَى قَالَ: وَصَلَّى كَذَا وَكَذَا سَجْدَةً فِي السَّنَةِ؟ قَالُوا : بَلَى، قَالَ رَسُولُ اللَّهِ ﷺ: فَلَمَا بَيْنَهُمَا أَبْعَدُ مَا بَيْنَ السَّمَاءِ وَالْأَرْضِ».

(مسند أحمد)

Two men came to Prophet (ﷺ). They both embraced Islām, but one of them was more hard-working than the other. The hard-working one took part in a campaign and got martyred. The other one stayed behind for a year and then died in bed. Ṭalḥa ibn ʿUbaidullāh says: "I had a dream and felt as if I was standing at the gate of Paradise and saw both of these men. Then, somebody came out and allowed the one who died later on to go in (to Paradise); then he came out and gave permission to the other one who died as a martyr. Later, both of them came back to me and said: 'Go back - it is not your turn yet.'" In the morning, Ṭalḥa ibn ʿUbaidullāh started telling people about his dream, and they were impressed. The Prophet (ﷺ) heard about it and said: "What makes you feel amazed?" They replied: "O Messenger of Allāh! One was more hard-working and became a martyr in the cause of Allāh, but this (second) one entered Paradise before him." The Prophet (ﷺ) answered: "Didn't this man stay alive for one year after the other one?" They replied: "Yes." The Prophet (ﷺ) said: "He witnessed Ramaḍān and fasted in it?" They answered: "Yes." He continued: "And he performed prayers and made such and such number of prostrations during the year?" They said: "Yes." The Prophet (ﷺ) then said: "The difference between them is bigger than that (what is) between the heaven and the earth." (Musnad Aḥmad)

10 REASONS WHY WE SHOULD CARE FOR OUR ELDERLY

1. **They are our parents.** They raised us and made sacrifices for us in order to make sure that we grow up to be the person we are today. We need to provide them with the best care because they deserve it. They tended to us when we needed it, and now they are the ones who need us.
2. **They love us.** As we have grown, our elderly parents were there every step of the way. Through our fumbles and triumphs, they loved us unconditionally. We owe it to them and to ourselves that they are in good hands, and that we show our love to them in return by caring for them, and providing the same care that they showed to us.
3. **They made sacrifices for us.** From the moment that our mothers carried us in their wombs until we grew up to be who or what we are today, our parents have definitely made sacrifices. We need to do the same for them by providing them with quality care.
4. **Show you appreciate them.** Caring for them and attending to their needs is one of the many ways which we can show that we love and appreciate them.
5. **Learn from them.** They have probably been through things which we cannot even imagine. Throughout the years, they have weathered many storms of life, and from here we can learn precious life lessons. Therefore, take the time to heed what they say and gain insight from their lives.
6. **They need a sense of belonging.** Provide them with good elderly care from ourselves, or through the help of professionals will stop them from feeling isolated and

depressed. Our help should give them a sense of community, and social life that will empower and energize them.

7. **Gain insight into their values.** They lived through a time when the value system was quite different from ours. By spending time to talk with them and getting to know their history, we can gain insight into how they lived, how life was in their times, and learn values that we can also apply to our generation.
8. **They need to feel a sense of purpose.** Part of properly caring for our elderly and loved ones is to provide them with a sense of purpose so that they will always look forward to the days ahead of them instead of being filled with dread or uncertainty.
9. **They are nearing the end of their lives.** In reality, sooner or later due to their age, the future becomes more and more uncertain. This can take a toll on their physical and mental health. Make them live out the rest of their lives feeling happiness and at peace, as well as feeling loved and cared for.
10. **It is simply the right thing to do.** As a human being, it is just appropriate that we care for our elders. After all, we are soon going to become one as well. By caring for our elders, we show our own humanity and simply do what is desirable.

KHUṬBAH 61

Be Thankful in All Things

Part of Allāh's (ﷻ) wisdom is that He bestows different people with different amounts of provision. He gives to some but withholds from others. People's provisions and livelihoods in this world lie solely in the hands of Allāh (ﷻ). He is the only One who apportions them for His servants.

Allāh (ﷻ) mentions in the Qur'ān:

﴿ٱللَّهُ يَبْسُطُ ٱلرِّزْقَ لِمَن يَشَآءُ وَيَقْدِرُ ۚ ٢٦﴾ [الرَّعْد الآية ٢٦]

> Allāh increases sustenance for whoever He pleases and reduces (sustenance for whomsoever He pleases). (Ra'd 13:26)

Ḥāfiẓ ibn Kathīr (رحمه الله) explains that this means:

«أَيْ: يُوَسِّعُ عَلَى مَنْ يَشَاءُ، وَيُضَيِّقُ عَلَى مَنْ يَشَاءُ، وَلَهُ الْحِكْمَةُ وَالْعَدْلُ التَّامُّ».

(تفسير ابن كثير)

> "Allāh grants much to whomsoever He wills, and He grants little to whomsoever He wills; and He has complete wisdom and justice in all of that." (Tafsīr Ibn Kathīr)

However, many times people do not always recognize the blessings which Allāh (ﷻ) has given them, and this can lead a person to being unappreciative, complacent, taking blessings for granted, or wanting circumstances to change.

In this regard, there are several important lessons that we should learn from those nations who preceded us. The people of Banī Isrā'īl (i.e. the descendants from the children of Prophet Yaʿqūb ﷺ) had requested Prophet Mūsā (ﷺ) to let them have food which was different from the *manna* and *salwā* that they had been given but became bored of and could no longer tolerate.

Allāh (ﷻ) explains in the Qur'ān

﴿وَإِذْ قُلْتُمْ يَٰمُوسَىٰ لَن نَّصْبِرَ عَلَىٰ طَعَامٍ وَٰحِدٍ فَٱدْعُ لَنَا رَبَّكَ يُخْرِجْ لَنَا مِمَّا تُنۢبِتُ ٱلْأَرْضُ مِنۢ بَقْلِهَا وَقِثَّآئِهَا وَفُومِهَا وَعَدَسِهَا وَبَصَلِهَا ۖ قَالَ أَتَسْتَبْدِلُونَ ٱلَّذِى هُوَ أَدْنَىٰ بِٱلَّذِى هُوَ خَيْرٌ ٦١﴾ [البَقَرَة الآية ٦١]

"And (recall) when you (the Banī Isrā'īl) said: 'O Mūsā! We cannot tolerate (patiently bear to eat only) one type of food (*manna* (truffles) and *salwā* (quails)), so pray to your Lord on our behalf (ask Him) to bring forth for us what the earth produces, from its greens, cucumbers, wheat, lentils, and onions.' Mūsā said: 'Do you wish to receive what is inferior in exchange for that which is superior?'" (Baqarah 2:61)

Qatādah (ﷺ) mentions:

«كَانَ الْمَنُّ يَنْزِلُ عَلَيْهِمْ فِي مَحَلَّتِهِمْ سُقُوطَ الثَّلْجِ، أَشَدَّ بَيَاضًا مِنَ اللَّبَنِ، وَأَحْلَى مِنَ الْعَسَلِ، يَسْقُطُ عَلَيْهِمْ مِنْ طُلُوعِ الْفَجْرِ إِلَى طُلُوعِ الشَّمْسِ، يَأْخُذُ الرَّجُلُ مِنْهُمْ قَدْرَ مَا يَكْفِيهِ يَوْمَهُ ذَلِكَ؛ فَإِذَا تَعَدَّى ذَلِكَ فَسَدَ وَلَمْ يَبْقَ، حَتَّى إِذَا كَانَ يَوْمُ سَادِسِهِ، لِيَوْمِ جُمُعَتِهِ، أَخَذَ مَا يَكْفِيهِ لِيَوْمِ سَادِسِهِ وَيَوْمِ سَابِعِهِ؛ لِأَنَّهُ كَانَ يَوْمَ عِيدٍ لَا يَشْخَصُ فِيهِ لِأَمْرِ مَعِيشَتِهِ وَلَا يَطْلُبُهُ لِشَيْءٍ، وَهَذَا كُلُّهُ فِي الْبَرِّيَّةِ».

(تفسير ابن كثير)

"That *manna* would descend like snow, which was whiter than milk and sweeter than honey. It would come to them from the break of dawn until sunset. Each person was allowed to take as much as one required for a day. Whatever extra they took would spoil. However, on Fridays, they could collect all that they needed for the Friday and Saturday which followed. (Tafsīr Ibn Kathīr)

ʿAlī ibn Abī Ṭalḥa (ﷺ) reports that Ibn ʿAbbās (ﷺ) commented and said:

«كَانَ الْمَنُّ يَنْزِلُ عَلَيْهِمْ عَلَى الْأَشْجَارِ، فَيَغْدُونَ إِلَيْهِ فَيَأْكُلُونَ منه ما شاؤوا».

(تفسير ابن كثير)

"This *manna* used to descend upon them onto the trees, and they would harvest (collect) and eat whatever they wished of it." (Tafsīr Ibn Kathīr)

Qatādah (ﷺ) also states:

«السَّلْوَى مِنْ طَيْرٍ إِلَى الْحُمْرَةِ، تحشرها عَلَيْهِمُ الريحُ الجنوبُ. وَكَانَ الرَّجُلُ يَذْبَحُ مِنْهَا قَدْرَ مَا يَكْفِيهِ يَوْمَهُ ذَلِكَ».

(تفسير ابن كثير)

"*Salwā* was a type of bird that resembled the partridge. Allāh caused an abundance of it to come with the winds to the Bani Isrāʾīl. They would catch them easily, slaughter them, and prepare meals from them. (Tafsīr Ibn Kathīr)

With this request, they wanted to replace what they had with other things that were inferior in comparison, such as: herbs, vegetables, garlic, grains, legumes, and onions, etc. They desired those instead of the foods that they already had which were much better.

There were also the people of Sabāʾ whom Allāh (ﷻ) endowed with many blessings, protected from adversities, and granted them two immense fertile gardens. He made their land a land that had clean air, abundant water, fertile soil, and was free from disease, pests, and insects.

Allāh (ﷻ) makes mention of this in the Qurʾān:

﴿لَقَدْ كَانَ لِسَبَإٍ فِي مَسْكَنِهِمْ ءَايَةٌ جَنَّتَانِ عَن يَمِينٍ وَشِمَالٍ كُلُواْ مِن رِّزْقِ رَبِّكُمْ وَٱشْكُرُواْ لَهُۥ بَلْدَةٌ طَيِّبَةٌ وَرَبٌّ غَفُورٌ ۝١٥﴾ [سبإ الآية ١٥]

"There was certainly a sign for the people of Sabā' (a place in Yemen) in their (picturesque) settlements, (which consisted of) two (fertile) orchards, lying on the right and the left. (It was said to them): 'Eat from the provision of your Lord and be grateful to Him (for all that He has given you). (You should be grateful for having) Beautiful land and a forgiving Lord." (Sabā' 34:15)

They used to travel with ease between various towns. These towns were all situated on the roadside, and the people of Sabā' could easily enter them without being disrupted or having to prolong their journeys. Each town could be seen from the previous town, and because of this their journeys were never monotonous, and they could stay over in another town during any stage of their trip.

Allāh (ﷻ) divided their travels into easy stages, meaning that if one of them left his town in the morning, he would reach the next town by midday, and if he had to leave there after lunch, he would reach the next town by the evening. In this way, they never needed to carry food with them.

They also had no enemies to worry about. Some commentators have mentioned that each village was merely a mile away from the next. They had nothing to fear on their journeys during the days and even at night.

Allāh (ﷻ) expounds on the favours which He endowed them with in the Qur'ān:

﴿وَجَعَلْنَا بَيْنَهُمْ وَبَيْنَ ٱلْقُرَى ٱلَّتِي بَٰرَكْنَا فِيهَا قُرًى ظَٰهِرَةً وَقَدَّرْنَا فِيهَا ٱلسَّيْرَ سِيرُواْ فِيهَا لَيَالِيَ وَأَيَّامًا ءَامِنِينَ ۝١٨﴾ [سبإ الآية ١٨]

"And between them and the towns that We blessed (the towns of Shām to which they travelled for trade), We made several conspicuous (accessible) villages (where they could easily stop to trade and fulfill their needs), and made their journey in easy stages (so that they could reach a village whenever they needed to eat or rest). (It was said to them) 'Travel peacefully in security by them (by these stages) by night and by day (without any fear).'" (Sabā' 34:18)

However, instead of being grateful to Allāh (ﷻ), they took His blessings for granted and were ungrateful to Him. They asked Allāh (ﷻ) to make the legs of their journeys longer, and they even became tired of the safety and security which they had.

They unappreciatively said:

﴿فَقَالُواْ رَبَّنَا بَٰعِدۡ بَيۡنَ أَسۡفَارِنَا ١٩﴾ [سَبَإ الآية ١٩]

"However, (instead of appreciating these favours) they (greedily) said: 'O our Lord! Make our journeys (make the distance) longer (so that we can trod more and get more profits).'" (Sabā' 34:19)

As a result, Allāh (ﷻ) punished them by sending an unrelenting torrent which broke the dam that held the water back from them. It destroyed their fine fertile gardens which subsequently became trees that yielded no benefit.

Allāh (ﷻ) says:

﴿فَأَعۡرَضُواْ فَأَرۡسَلۡنَا عَلَيۡهِمۡ سَيۡلَ ٱلۡعَرِمِ وَبَدَّلۡنَٰهُم بِجَنَّتَيۡهِمۡ جَنَّتَيۡنِ ذَوَاتَيۡ أُكُلٍ خَمۡطٍ وَأَثۡلٍ وَشَيۡءٖ مِّن سِدۡرٖ قَلِيلٖ ١٦ ذَٰلِكَ جَزَيۡنَٰهُم بِمَا كَفَرُواْۖ وَهَلۡ نُجَٰزِيٓ إِلَّا ٱلۡكَفُورَ ١٧﴾ [سَبَإ من الآية ١٦ الى الآية ١٧]

"(However, instead of being grateful to Allāh) They turned away (from the advice and committed *kufr*), So We sent (to their city) the flood (water) of the (ruptured) dam (which destroyed everything in its path), and We replaced their two (flourishing) orchards with two orchards of foul-smelling (bitter) fruit, invasive shrubs and a few sparse lotus trees (these were the only things that grew there after their orchards were destroyed). This was the punishment We gave them for their ingratitude. We punish only the extremely ungrateful ones." (Sabā' 34:16-17)

Taking Allāh's (ﷻ) blessings for granted is a serious disease; and because of it, a person could lose all of the good that surrounds him, and then end up wishing that they had only remained pleased with what they previously had.

Imām Ibn al-Qayyim (رحمه الله) states:

«من الآفات الخفيَّة العامَّة: أن يكونَ العبدُ في نعمةٍ أنعم اللهُ بها عليه، واختارها له، فيملها العبدُ ويطلبَ الانتِقال منها إلى ما يزعُم لجهلِهِ أنَّه خيرٌ له منها، وربُّه برحمتِه لا يُخرجُه من تلك النِّعمة، ويَعذُره بجهلِهِ وسوءِ اختيارِهِ لنفسه، حتى إذا ضاق ذرعًا بتلك النِّعمةِ، وسخِطها، وتبرَّم بها، واستحكَم ملَلُهُ لها؛ سلبَه اللهُ إيَّاها، فإذا انتقل إلى ما طلبَه ورأى التَّفاوتَ بين ما كان فيه وما صار إليه؛ اشتدَّ قلقُه وندمُه، وطلب العودةَ إلى ما كان فيه، فإذا أراد اللهُ بعبدِه خيرًا ورشدًا؛ أشهدَه أن ما هو فيه نعمة من نعمِه عليه ورضاه به، وأوزعه شكرَه عليه».

(كتاب الفوائد)

"One of the inconspicuous ailments which affect people is for them to be surrounded by certain blessings that Allāh has chosen for them and granted them, yet the people then become fatigued with having those blessings and they seek something different which they claim – out of their own ignorance – (which they think) would be better for them. However, their Lord – out of His mercy – does not remove those blessings, and He excuses the people due to their ignorance and their choice of detrimental things for themselves. Then, when the people eventually take those blessings for granted, so much so that they become fed up with them, Allāh takes away the blessings from them. Afterwards, when the people have realized the stark contrast between what once surrounded them versus the

> circumstances which they ended up in after having what they wanted for themselves, they become even more unsettled and remorseful. They also seek to return to what they once had. Thus, when Allāh wants goodness and guidance for His servants, He allows them to recognize the blessings that they have, makes them content with those blessings, and enables them to be grateful to Him." (Kitāb al-Fawā'id)

There are people who do not realize the magnitude of the blessings which they have. As a result, they regularly complain and become dissatisfied.

ʿAbdullāh ibn Abī Nūḥ (ﷺ) recounts:

«قَالَ لِي رَجُلٌ عَلَى بَعْضِ السَّوَاحِلِ: كَمْ عَامَلْتَهُ تَبَارَكَ اسْمُهُ بِمَا يَكْرَهُ فَعَامَلَكَ بِمَا تُحِبُّ، قُلْتُ: مَا لَا أُحْصِي ذَلِكَ كَثْرَةً، قَالَ: فَهَلْ قَصَدْتَ إِلَيْهِ فِي أَمْرٍ كَرَبِكَ فَخَذَلَكَ؟ قُلْتُ: لَا وَاللَّهِ، وَلَكِنَّهُ أَحْسَنَ إِلَيَّ فَأَعَانَنِي، قَالَ: فَهَلْ سَأَلْتَهُ شَيْئًا قَطُّ فَأَعْطَاكَ؟ قُلْتُ: وَهَلْ مَنَعَنِي شَيْئًا سَأَلْتُهُ، مَا سَأَلْتُهُ شَيْئًا قَطُّ إِلَّا أَعْطَانِي، وَلَا اسْتَعَنْتُ بِهِ إِلَّا أَعَانَنِي قَالَ: أَرَأَيْتَ لَوْ أَنَّ ابْنَ آدَمَ فَعَلَ بِكَ بَعْضَ هَذِهِ الْخِلَالِ مَا كَانَ جَزَاؤُهُ عِنْدَكَ؟ قُلْتُ: مَا كُنْتُ أَقْدِرُ لَهُ عَلَى مُكَافَأَةٍ وَلَا جَزَاءٍ، قَالَ: فَرَبُّكَ أَحَقُّ وَأَحْرَى أَنْ بَذَلْتَ نَفْسَكَ لَهُ فِي أَدَاءِ شُكْرِ نِعَمِهِ عَلَيْكَ، وَهُوَ الْمُحْسِنُ قَدِيمًا وَحَدِيثًا إِلَيْكَ، وَاللَّهِ لِشُكْرِهِ أَيْسَرُ مِنْ مُكَافَأَةِ عِبَادِهِ، أَنَّهُ تَبَارَكَ وَتَعَالَى رَضِيَ بِالْحَمْدِ مِنَ الْعِبَادِ شُكْرًا».

(كتاب الشكر لابن أبي الدنيا)

> "A man once said to me while we were on a shoreline: 'How often have you been bad towards Allāh, yet He was good towards you?' I replied: 'So many that I cannot even enumerate them all.' The man said: 'Has He ever forsaken you when you resorted to Him in difficulty?' I replied: 'No. I swear by Allāh. On the contrary, He was kind to me and assisted me.' The man asked: 'Has Allāh ever not given you something when you asked Him?' I answered: 'Would Allāh deprive me of something

that I request of Him? Never did I ask of Him without being given it, and never did I seek relief from Him without being granted relief.' The man said: 'For argument's sake, if a person did those things for you, what would you give him in return?' I replied: 'I would be unable to repay him.' The man said: 'Your Lord is even more entitled to you humbling yourself in order to thank Him for His blessings. He is the One who has extended kindness to you, both in the past and present. I swear by Allāh that being grateful to Him is even easier than repaying His servants. Allāh is pleased with praise from His servants as gratitude.'" (Kitāb al-Shukr by Ibn Abī Dunyā)

Therefore, it is necessary for us to praise Allāh (ﷻ) continuously, throughout all circumstances, so as to acknowledge His blessings and be duly grateful to Him.

Imām al-Ṭabarānī (ﷺ) has recorded a *ḥadīth* from ʿAbdullāh ibn ʿAmr (ﷺ) who narrated that the Messenger of Allāh (ﷺ) once asked a man:

«كَيْفَ أَصْبَحْتَ يَا فُلَانُ؟ قَالَ: أَحْمَدُ اللهَ إِلَيْكَ يَا رَسُولَ اللهِ، فَقَالَ رَسُولُ اللهِ ﷺ: هَذَا الَّذِي أَرَدْتُ مِنْكَ».

(المعجم الأوسط للطبراني)

"In what state did you reach the morning?" The man replied: "O Messenger of Allāh, I inform you that I offer praise to Allāh." The Prophet (ﷺ) said: "That is what I wanted to hear from you," (referring to affirming the praise, gratitude, and glorification of Allāh.) (Al-Muʿjam al-Awsaṭ of al-Ṭabarānī)

Similarly, when Mughīrah ibn Muḥammad (ﷺ) was once asked:

«كَيْفَ أَصْبَحْتَ يَا أَبَا مُحَمَّدٍ؟ قَالَ: أَصْبَحْنَا مُغْرَقِينَ فِي النِّعَمِ، مُوقَّرِينَ مِنَ الشُّكْرِ، يَتَحَبَّبُ إِلَيْنَا رَبُّنَا وَهُوَ عَنَّا غَنِيٌّ، وَنَتَمَقَّتُ إِلَيْهِ وَنَحْنُ إِلَيْهِ مُحْتَاجُونَ».

(كتاب الشكر لإبن أبي الدنيا)

"O Abū Muḥammad, in what state did you reach the morning?" He replied: "We are immersed in the Lord's generosity and incapable of being sufficiently grateful. He is most loving towards us, even though He does not need us, and we are disrespectful towards Him, even though we are utterly dependant on Him." (Kitāb al-Shukr by Ibn Abī Dunyā)

ʿAmr ibn al-ʿĀṣ (ﷺ) would say:

«لاَ أَمَلُّ ثَوْبِي مَا وَسِعَنِي، وَلاَ أَمَلُّ زَوْجَتِي مَا أَحْسَنَتْ عِشْرَتِي، وَلاَ أَمَلُّ دَابَّتِي مَا حَمَلَتْنِي، إِنَّ المَلاَلَ مِنْ سَيِّئِ الأَخْلاَقِ».

(سير أعلام النبلاء)

"I do not grow fatigued (fed up, bored) with my garments so long as they continue to contain me; and I do not grow fatigued (fed up, bored) with my wife so long as she continues to live well with me; and I do not grow fatigued (fed up, bored) with my mount so long as it continues to carry me. Indeed, becoming fatigued is a bad characteristic." (Siyar Aʿlām al-Nubalā')

Becoming fatigued with the blessings which Allāh (ﷻ) has given us is indeed among the worst of traits because it can lead a servant of Allāh (ﷻ) to detest Allāh's (ﷻ) favours and become displeased with the provision that He has decreed for us.

It is a truly terrible thing for people to be amidst Allāh's (ﷻ) favours and blessings, yet take them for granted and become tired or fed up with them.

Imām Ibn al-Qayyim (ﷺ) states

«وليس على العبدِ أضر من مَلَلِه لنعم الله؛ فإنّه لا يراها نعمةً، ولا يشكرهُ عليها، ولا يفرح بها؛ بل يسخطها، ويعدها مصيبةً؛ هذا وهي من أعظم نِعم الله عليه! فأكثر النّاس أعداء نِعم الله

عليهم، ولا يشعرون بفتحِ الله عليهم نِعمَه، وهم مجتهِدون في دفعِها وردِّها -جهلًا وظُلمًا، فكم سعتْ إلى أحدِهم من نعمةٍ وهو ساعٍ في ردِّها بجهده! وكم وصلتْ إليه وهو ساعٍ في دفعِها وزوالِها بظلمه وجهله! قال تعالى: ﴿ذَٰلِكَ بِأَنَّ ٱللَّهَ لَمْ يَكُ مُغَيِّرًا نِّعْمَةً أَنْعَمَهَا عَلَىٰ قَوْمٍ حَتَّىٰ يُغَيِّرُوا۟ مَا بِأَنفُسِهِمْ ﴿٥٣﴾﴾ [الأنفال الآية ٥٣]».

(كتاب الفوائد)

"And nothing is more harmful to a person than becoming exhausted with Allāh's blessings. When that happens, he no longer sees them to be blessings, no longer thanks Allāh for them, and he is not happy to even have them. Rather, he becomes upset and complains about them, and sees them to be an affliction. He sees them this way even though they might be among the greatest of blessings that Allāh has granted him with. Most people are hostile towards the blessings which they receive from Allāh. They do not realize the favours that Allāh bestows upon them. In fact, they even strive to avert those from themselves out of their own ignorance and injustice. There are many times when a blessing comes to them in quickly, yet they hasten to exert themselves in driving it away. There are many times when a blessing reaches them yet they strive to remove it due to their own injustice and ignorance! The Most High says: 'This (punishment) is because Allāh will not change (will not take away) any favour that He gave to a nation until they change what is within themselves (until they corrupt their beliefs and actions, thereby inviting Allāh's chastisement, which will cause them to lose all of their bounties). (Anfāl 8:53)'" (Kitāb al-Fawā'id)

Abū Hurairah (ﷺ) reports that the Prophet (ﷺ) said:

«انْظُرُوا إِلَى مَنْ هُوَ أَسْفَلَ مِنْكُمْ، وَلَا تَنْظُرُوا إِلَى مَنْ هُوَ فَوْقَكُمْ، فَإِنَّهُ أَجْدَرُ أَنْ لَا تَزْدَرُوا نِعْمَةَ اللَّهِ عَلَيْكُمْ».

(رواه الترمذي)

> "Look at a person who is lower than you (in material things), and do not look at the person who is above you. For indeed that is more conducive (so that you will) not belittle Allāh's favours upon you." (Tirmidhī)

Having this type of perspective and outlook is most conducive for a person in order for them to be grateful for Allāh's (ﷻ) blessings, because then one will be content with what Allāh (ﷻ) has given them and their eyes will not be fixated on the things of this world which others have.

There are people who have many possessions in this world, but are in fact very deprived. They never feel pleased or content with what they have. On the contrary, they are always trying to attain more. There are also others who have been granted abundant provisions and many blessings but they transgress Allāh's (ﷻ) bounds and remain ungrateful to Him. As a result, the blessings which they have been given end up being detrimental for them.

Even more remarkable is the state of someone who desires to have things which are not decreed for him, or to have an abundance of blessings in order to attain luxury, copious provisions, and a high material standard of living; however, throughout it all, that poor individual remains oblivious to the fact that there is nothing which equals self-contentment.

The Prophet (ﷺ) states:

«لَيْسَ الغِنَى عَنْ كَثْرَةِ العَرَضِ، وَلَكِنَّ الغِنَى غِنَى النَّفْسِ».

(رواه مسلم)

> "Richness does not lie in the abundance of (worldly) goods, but true richness is the richness of the soul (self-contentment)." (Muslim)

A few well-known Arabic proverbs state:

«اَلقانِعُ غَنِيٌّ، وإنْ جاعَ وعَرى».

(غُرَرُ الحِكم و دُرَرُ الكَلِم)

"A content person is rich, even if he is hungry and unclothed." (Ghurar al-Ḥikam wa Durur al-Kalim)

«مَنِ اكْتَفى بِاليَسيرِ اِسْتَغْنى عَنِ الكَثيرِ».

(غُرَرُ الحِكم و دُرَرُ الكَلِم)

"A person who suffices with little becomes needless of plenty." (Ghurar al-Ḥikam wa Durur al-Kalim)

«ما أَحْسَنَ بِالإِنْسانِ أَنْ يَقْنَعَ بِالقَليلِ ويَجُودَ بِالجَزيلِ».

(غُرَرُ الحِكم و دُرَرُ الكَلِم)

"How good it is for a person to be content with little, and generous with much!" (Ghurar al-Ḥikam wa Durur al-Kalim)

CONCLUSION

The reality that we live in today is one in which there are various manifestations of people taking Allāh's (ﷻ) blessings for granted, and even finding them as causes for boredom or being fed up with them. This stems from lack of a strong connection with Allāh (ﷻ).

It is necessary for us to remain steadfast on our journey to the Almighty Creator, beware of deviating from the path of salvation, and be cautious of becoming disdainful towards acts of obedience to Allāh (ﷻ), or the blessings which He grants us. Remaining safe from such evils comes about from various methods which treat the illnesses of taking Allāh's (ﷻ) blessings for granted, and becoming fed up with them.

One of those methods is strengthening a person's connection with Allāh (ﷻ), and constantly making *duʿā* to Him asking for the ability and consistency to perform righteous deeds.

The *duʿā* most often made by the Prophet (ﷺ) was:

«يَا مُقَلِّبَ الْقُلُوبِ، ثَبِّتْ قَلْبِي عَلَى دِينِكَ».

(رواه الترمذي)

> "O Controller of the hearts, make my heart steadfast in Your religion." (Tirmidhī)

In addition, the Prophet (ﷺ) advised Muʿādh ibn Jabal (ﷺ) by saying:

«أُوصِيكَ يَا مُعَاذُ لاَ تَدَعَنَّ فِي دُبُرِ كُلِّ صَلاَةٍ تَقُولُ: اللَّهُمَّ أَعِنِّي عَلَى ذِكْرِكَ، وَشُكْرِكَ، وَحُسْنِ عِبَادَتِكَ».

(رواه أبو داود)

> "I advise you O Muʿādh, not to neglect to say at the end of each prayer: 'O Allāh, assist me in remembering You, being grateful to You, and worshipping You in the best way.'" (Abū Dāwūd)

Whenever the Prophet (ﷺ) would lift the tablecloth after having his meals, he would supplicate:

«الْحَمْدُ لِلَّهِ رَبِّنَا، غَيْرَ مَكْفِيٍّ وَلاَ مُوَدَّعٍ وَلاَ مُسْتَغْنًى، رَبَّنَا».

(رواه البخاري)

> "Praise be to Allāh, our Lord! We are not lifting this food regarding it to be sufficient, or biding it farewell (forever), or expressing no need for it. O our Lord." (Bukhārī)

Another method is to remain true to Allāh (ﷻ) and accept His directives with diligence, in order to rise above the pitfalls of laziness and complacency. This outlook is exactly what prompted ʿAlī ibn Abi Ṭālib

(ﷺ) to consistently say the words of *dhikr* which the Prophet (ﷺ) taught him and Fāṭimah (ﷺ) to say when they would go to bed. ʿAlī ibn Abi Ṭālib (ﷺ) did not even neglect to say them on the night of Ṣiffīn which was a time of great strife and conflict.

ʿAlī ibn Abi Ṭālib (ﷺ) recounts and says:

«مَا تَرَكْتُهُ مُنْذُ سَمِعْتُهُ مِنَ النَّبِيِّ ﷺ، قِيلَ لَهُ: وَلَا لَيْلَةَ صِفِّينَ؟ قَالَ: وَلَا لَيْلَةَ صِفِّينَ».

(رواه مسلم)

> "Ever since I heard this (supplication) from the Messenger of Allāh (ﷺ) I never abandoned it." It was asked of him: "Not even during the night of Ṣiffīn (encounter of Ṣiffīn)?" He replied: 'Not even on the night of Ṣiffīn.'" (Muslim)

Another method is to remember the hereafter and not be eager to live for a long time in this world. Doing that is one of the most effective ways of being devoted to Allāh (ﷻ) and initiating diligence within oneself.

We must all realize that this world is where the seeds of the hereafter are sown, and it is our only opportunity to acquire the righteous deeds that we need for the eternal abode. We require a strong motivation that will drive us to worship Allāh (ﷻ).

When a person is consistent in performing virtuous deeds, but perhaps sometimes he feels a sense of boredom, he should call to mind the true value of the acts that he wants to perform, as well as the rewards which they merit.

«كَانَ مَسْلَمَةُ بْنُ عَبْدِ الْمَلِكِ إِذَا كَثُرَ عَلَيْهِ أَصْحَابُ الْحَوَائِجِ وَخَافَ أَنْ يَضْجَرَ قَالَ لِآذِنِهِ ائْذَنْ لِجُلَسَائِي فَيَأْذَنُ لَهُمْ فَيَفْتَنُّ وَيَفْتَنُّونَ فِي مَحَاسِنِ النَّاسِ ومروءاتهم فَيَطْرَبُ لَهَا وَيَهْتَاجُ عَلَيْهَا وَيُصِيبُهُ مَا يُصِيبُ صَاحِبَ الشَّرَابِ فَيَقُولُ لِحَاجِبِهِ ائْذَنْ لِأَصْحَابِ الْحَوَائِجِ فَلَا يَبْقَى أَحَدٌ إِلَّا قُضِيَتْ حَاجَتُهُ».

(التذكرة الحمدونية)

> When Maslamah ibn ʿAbd al-Malik (ﷺ), the son of Malik ibn Marwān (ﷺ), had many people come to him requesting assistance in fulfilling their needs, he feared that he would become tired of them, so he would summon his companions who were well-versed in matters pertaining to sound conduct and they would discuss the fine morals, conduct, and ethics that people should personify. Once he would attain the right frame of mind, he would say: "Allow those with needs to enter," then he would subsequently fulfill the needs of all of those who came to him. (Al-Tadhkira al-Ḥamdunīyyah)

Similarly, when a person performs acts of worship with an alert heart, and keeps in mind the magnitude of what one is engaged in, they will feel pleased obeying Allāh (ﷻ), will be able to taste the sweetness of *īmān*, and their willpower will be fortified. Consequently, the individual will be able to continue carrying out virtuous deeds, and will not become fatigued.

ʿAwn ibn ʿAbdullāh ibn ʿUtbah reports:

«لَقَدْ أَتَيْنَا أُمَّ الدَّرْدَاءِ فَتَحَدَّثْنَا عِنْدَهَا فَقُلْنَا: أَمْلَلْنَاكِ يَا أُمَّ الدَّرْدَاءِ، فَقَالَتْ: مَا أَمْلَلْتُمُونِي لَقَدْ طَلَبْتُ الْعِبَادَةَ فِي كُلِّ شَيْءٍ فَمَا وَجَدْتُ شَيْئًا أَشْفَى لِنَفْسِي مِنْ مُذَاكَرَةِ الْعِلْمِ أَوْ قَالَ: مُذَاكَرَةُ الْفِقْهِ».

(جامع بيان العلم وفضله لابن عبد البر)

> "We went to Umm al-Dardā' and engaged in discussion while there. We eventually said: 'O Umm al-Dardā', we have fatigued you.' She replied: 'You have not fatigued me. I seek to worship Allāh in all matters, and I have not found anything which satisfies my soul more than discussing and reviewing the knowledge (of *dīn*),' or she said: 'discussing and reviewing the *fiqh*.'" (Jāmiʿ Bayān al-ʿIlm wa Faḍhluhu of Ibn ʿAbd al-Barr)

In addition, a servant of Allāh (ﷻ) must never feel total despair, and should not grow weary, tired, fatigued or fed up of repeatedly repenting to Allāh (ﷻ) whenever one errs.

Ḥasan al-Baṣrī (رحمه الله) was once asked:

«كَيْفَ لَا يَشْتَهِي أَحَدُنَا أَنَّهُ لَا يَزَالُ مُتَبَرِّكًا إِلَى رَبِّهِ يَسْتَغْفِرُ مِنْ ذَنْبٍ، ثُمَّ يَعُودُ ثُمَّ يَسْتَغْفِرُ ثُمَّ يَعُودُ، قَالَ: قَدْ ذُكِرَ لِلْحَسَنِ، فَقَالَ: وَدَّ الشَّيْطَانُ لَوْ ظَفِرَ مِنْكُمْ بِهَذِهِ فَلَا تَمَلُّوا مِنَ الِاسْتِغْفَارِ».

(التوبة لابن أبي الدنيا)

> "Should one of us not be ashamed of asking his Lord's forgiveness, but then returning to (the same) sins, and asking forgiveness again, and then returning to sins once more?" He replied: "Shayṭān loves to hear that from you. Do not grow weary of asking for (Allāh's) forgiveness." (Kitāb al-Tawbah by Ibn Abī al-Dunyā)

A person who deserves to feel fatigue and weary is the one who is open about the sins which he commits. He is the type of person who should become fed up with continuing to perpetrate what Allāh (ﷻ) has forbidden. He needs to stop doing what leads to his ruin, and beware of facing a miserable end. He needs to devote himself to the One who accepts repentance from His servants and pardons their sins.

As we continue along our path to the Almighty Allāh (ﷻ), we must always keep our focus on the guidance of our role model, which is Prophet Muḥammad (ﷺ). Although Allāh (ﷻ) forgave all of his prior and future sins, he never ceased worshipping Him. On the contrary, the Prophet constantly preserved his connection with his Lord, remained devoted to Him, and diligently strove to obey Him without ever becoming weary or exhausted.

KHUṬBAH 62

The Hazards of Haste

Allāh (ﷻ) has created human beings in a remarkable way. He placed within them various qualities. Allāh (ﷻ) also preordained that there are certain qualities in humans which, if left untreated and unrefined, will cause them great loss. Examples of such qualities are ignorance, pride, jealousy, greed, anger, animosity, impatience, and ungratefulness, etc.

Among those qualities, there is also the quality of haste, which is a basis of all failures and regret. It is a quality which has major effects on the personality of a person, and can lead to very detrimental consequences unless one rids oneself of it.

Allāh (ﷻ) says in the Qur'ān:

﴿خُلِقَ ٱلْإِنسَـٰنُ مِنْ عَجَلٍ سَأُو۟رِيكُمْ ءَايَـٰتِى فَلَا تَسْتَعْجِلُونِ ۝٣٧﴾ [الأنبياء الآية ٣٧]

> "Man has been created from haste (with a hasty nature, because of which he is always in a hurry to do things and expects to see results right away). I will shortly show you My signs (the punishment), so do not hurry Me (have patience)." (Anbiyā' 21:37)

A few definitions of haste are:

- Exhibiting a lack of careful thought or consideration.
- Something done very quickly, generally with little thought or attention.
- The quality of doing something quickly, sometimes so quickly such that you are careless and make mistakes.

Haste essentially means wanting to have something before its prerequisites are in place, or doing something before its time, without thinking things through carefully. Haste also includes rushing to do things clumsily, recklessly and thoughtlessly in such a way that makes the task at hand unproductive and ineffective.

A hasty approach can cause things to happen in a haphazard manner, and end up lacking the real fruits which they should bear. It produces failure instead of success, and loss instead of benefit.

Allāh (ﷻ) says:

﴿وَيَدْعُ ٱلْإِنسَٰنُ بِٱلشَّرِّ دُعَآءَهُۥ بِٱلْخَيْرِ ۖ وَكَانَ ٱلْإِنسَٰنُ عَجُولًا ۝١١﴾ [الإسراء الآية ١١]

"And (when experiencing hardship) man prays for evil (death) just as (fervently as) he prays for good (when he wants something good). Man (in general) was always hasty (he is prone to do things without thinking about the consequences)." (Isrā' 17:11)

Hastiness is almost always mentioned in the Qur'ān and *ḥadīth* in the context of being something blameworthy and prohibited. However, there are a few instances where hurriedness is mentioned as being praiseworthy, and that is only in the context of rushing to perform righteous deeds while the opportunity is still available.

Allāh (ﷻ) says:

﴿فَٱسْتَبِقُوا۟ ٱلْخَيْرَٰتِ ۚ إِلَى ٱللَّهِ مَرْجِعُكُمْ جَمِيعًا فَيُنَبِّئُكُم بِمَا كُنتُمْ فِيهِ تَخْتَلِفُونَ ۝٤٨﴾ [المائدة الآية ٤٨]

"So, hasten (you must all strive your utmost) to (do) good works! To Allāh shall you all return (on the Day of Judgement) and then He will inform you about that in which you used to differ (then each one will receive the rewards or punishment for what they did)." (Mā'idah 5:48)

﴿۞ وَسَارِعُوٓاْ إِلَىٰ مَغۡفِرَةٖ مِّن رَّبِّكُمۡ وَجَنَّةٍ عَرۡضُهَا ٱلسَّمَٰوَٰتُ وَٱلۡأَرۡضُ ١٣٣﴾ [آل عِمۡرَان الآية ١٣٣]

"And seize every opportunity that you can to attain your Lord's forgiveness, and to be admitted to a Garden whose expanse is that of the heavens and the earth." (Āle ʿImrān 3:133)

﴿سَابِقُوٓاْ إِلَىٰ مَغۡفِرَةٖ مِّن رَّبِّكُمۡ وَجَنَّةٍ عَرۡضُهَا كَعَرۡضِ ٱلسَّمَآءِ وَٱلۡأَرۡضِ ٢١﴾ [الحَدِيد الآية ٢١]

(Instead of chasing after the things of this world) Race towards (do all that you can to be foremost in attaining) the forgiveness of your Lord and a Garden, the width of which is like that of the sky and the earth. (The length is unimaginable). (Ḥadīd 57:21)

﴿أُوْلَٰٓئِكَ يُسَٰرِعُونَ فِي ٱلۡخَيۡرَٰتِ وَهُمۡ لَهَا سَٰبِقُونَ ٦١﴾ [المُؤۡمِنُون الآية ٦١]

"These people hasten to perform good acts and are the foremost in it (in the race to do good)." (Mu'minūn 23:61)

The texts of Islām warn us against being hasty and reckless, because in most cases, acting in that manner comes about from not thinking matters through, not considering consequences, and not being adequately prepared for things.

In order to truly grasp the real harms of haste, it is enough for us to bear in mind that when hastiness becomes rooted in people, they behave in a reckless, careless, and even foolish manner - following their own inclinations, being stubborn, and treating others lightly. Therefore, haste can be rightfully considered the root of many problems.

Allāh (ﷻ) forbade the Prophet (ﷺ) from being hasty regarding what was being sent down to him of the Qur'ān before its revelation was completed. Allāh (ﷻ) said to him:

﴿فَتَعَٰلَى ٱللَّهُ ٱلْمَلِكُ ٱلْحَقُّ ۗ وَلَا تَعْجَلْ بِٱلْقُرْءَانِ مِن قَبْلِ أَن يُقْضَىٰٓ إِلَيْكَ وَحْيُهُۥ ۖ
﴿١١٤﴾﴾ [طه الآية ١١٤]

"Exalted is Allāh, the True King. (O Prophet) Do not hasten with the Qur'ān (do not try to repeat the verses of the Qur'ān) before its revelation is completed to you [wait for Jibrā'īl (عليه السلام)] to recite the complete verses to you before attempting to repeat them)." (Ṭāhā 20:114)

Allāh (ﷻ) also condemned Prophet Mūsā (عليه السلام) for going ahead alone and leaving his people behind in order to reach the place which Allāh (ﷻ) had designated for them. Allāh (ﷻ) said:

﴿۞ وَمَآ أَعْجَلَكَ عَن قَوْمِكَ يَٰمُوسَىٰ ﴿٨٣﴾﴾ [طه الآية ٨٣]

(In his eagerness to receive the Torah from Allāh at Mount Ṭūr, Mūsā (عليه السلام) hurried ahead of some people who were supposed to accompany him there, causing them to remain behind with the rest of the people who eventually were involved in worshipping the calf. It was with reference to this that Allāh asked him:) "What has made you hasten ahead of your people, O Mūsā?" (Ṭāhā 20:83)

In addition, had Prophet Mūsā (عليه السلام) remained patient in accompanying Khiḍhr (عليه السلام) and not been hasty, he would have witnessed remarkable matters which Allāh (ﷻ) had decreed.

Allāh (ﷻ) also forbade our Prophet (ﷺ) from being like Prophet Yūnus (عليه السلام) who became frustrated with his people and left them, seeking to hasten Allāh's (ﷻ) chastisement. Allāh (ﷻ) told the Prophet (ﷺ):

﴿وَلَا تَكُن كَصَاحِبِ ٱلْحُوتِ إِذْ نَادَىٰ وَهُوَ مَكْظُومٌ ﴿٤٨﴾﴾ [القلم الآية ٤٨]

"And do not be (hasty for the chastisement to come to them immediately) like the person of the fish [Yūnus (عليه السلام)] who called (to Allāh for help) as he was suppressing (choking with) his grief (while in the stomach of the fish)." (Qalam 68:48)

NOTE: This verse is referring to the time when the community of Prophet Yūnus (عليه السلام) constantly demanded punishment, he became irate and prayed for the punishment to be sent down. The signs of punishment started appearing. Prophet Yūnus (عليه السلام) left the area and transferred himself elsewhere. In the meantime, the entire community wept, wailed, sincerely repented and begged for refuge from the Divine punishment. Allāh (ﷻ) pardoned them and removed the punishment. Prophet Yūnus (عليه السلام) felt embarrassed and thought that if he goes back to his people, they might think that he was a liar. As a result, without the clear permission of Allāh (ﷻ), he acted purely on his own *ijtihād* [independent judgement] that he would not go back to his people. In order to caution him, Allāh (ﷻ) created a situation where he had to undertake a sea voyage, and was then lowered into the sea where he was swallowed up by a fish.

Similarly, when two men climbed over a wall and came into the prayer chamber of Prophet Dāwūd (عليه السلام), one of them presented his case and Prophet Dāwūd (عليه السلام) judged in his favour before even listening to the other person. Prophet Dāwūd (عليه السلام) then realized that he had been hasty in doing so, and that Allāh (ﷻ) had tested him, so he asked for Allāh's (ﷻ) forgiveness, prostrated to Him, and repented.

Allāh (ﷻ) says:

﴿وَظَنَّ دَاوُۥدُ أَنَّمَا فَتَنَّـٰهُ فَٱسْتَغْفَرَ رَبَّهُۥ وَخَرَّ رَاكِعًا وَأَنَابَ ۩ ﴿٢٤﴾﴾ [ص الآية ٢٤]

"(When later reviewing the case) It occurred to Dāwūd (عليه السلام) that We had tested him (by presenting to him a case that appeared to be straightforward causing him to neglect to listen to both sides), so he sought forgiveness from his Lord, fell down bowing, and turned (to Him) in repentance." (Ṣād 38:24)

Another example of haste can be found in the fact that some of the companions (﷠) thought that promising results were taking a long time to come when they saw the circumstances and apparent longevity of those who were hostile to them, and their rejection of the truth. However, the Prophet (ﷺ) gave them glad tidings that Allāh (ﷻ) would see this matter through, but he told them that they were being hasty and needed to be patient.

Khabbāb ibn al-Arat (﷠) reports:

»شَكَوْنَا إِلَى رَسُولِ اللَّهِ ﷺ وَهُوَ مُتَوَسِّدٌ بُرْدَةً لَهُ فِي ظِلِّ الكَعْبَةِ فَقُلْنَا: أَلاَ تَسْتَنْصِرُ لَنَا أَلاَ تَدْعُو لَنَا؟«.

"We complained to the Messenger of Allāh (ﷺ) while he was leaning against his cloak in the shade of the Ka'bah. We said: 'Will you ask Allāh to help us? Will you supplicate to Allāh for us?'"

The Prophet (ﷺ) replied:

»قَدْ كَانَ مَنْ قَبْلَكُمْ، يُؤْخَذُ الرَّجُلُ فَيُحْفَرُ لَهُ فِي الأَرْضِ، فَيُجْعَلُ فِيهَا، فَيُجَاءُ بِالْمِنْشَارِ فَيُوضَعُ عَلَى رَأْسِهِ فَيُجْعَلُ نِصْفَيْنِ، وَيُمْشَطُ بِأَمْشَاطِ الحَدِيدِ، مَا دُونَ لَحْمِهِ وَعَظْمِهِ، فَمَا يَصُدُّهُ ذَلِكَ عَنْ دِينِهِ، وَاللَّهِ لَيُتِمَّنَّ هَذَا الأَمْرُ، حَتَّى يَسِيرَ الرَّاكِبُ مِنْ صَنْعَاءَ إِلَى حَضْرَمَوْتَ، لاَ يَخَافُ إِلَّا اللَّهَ، وَالذِّئْبَ عَلَى غَنَمِهِ، وَلَكِنَّكُمْ تَسْتَعْجِلُونَ«.

(رواه البخاري)

"Among those before you, a believer would be seized and a ditch would be dug for him and he would be thrown into it. Then, they would bring a saw which would be put on his head so that he is split into two halves. His flesh would be torn away from the bone with iron combs. Yet, all of this did not cause him to abandon his religion. By Allāh, this religion will be completed only when a rider travels from Yemen to Ḥaḍramaut fearing no one but Allāh, and the wolf lest it troubles his sheep. But you are impatient (hasty)." (Bukhārī)

During the Expedition of ʿUhud, some of the archers were hasty in presuming that their side had been victorious, and they did not fulfill the instructions of the Prophet (ﷺ) to remain firm at their post. As a result, it led to the reversal of victory for the Muslims in the conflict, and the ultimate demise of sixty-five *Anṣār* and four *Muhājirūn* companions (رضي الله عنهم), including Hamzah - the beloved uncle of the Prophet (ﷺ).

Blameworthy hastiness is a major problem for any person as they navigate their way through life. It is a major obstacle to success, which can lead to a person suffering, and even bring about their downfall. There are many times when haste ruins well-organized plans, spoils large projects, wastes irreplaceable opportunities, brings about deep regrets, and prevents people from achieving the best of results which are within their reach that they could have attained - if only they had remained patient.

An irresponsible word, a hasty decision, an impulsive action, a fit of anger, an instance of arrogance, or any action in general which is not restrained by patience, care, and sound thinking can create animosity, transform a friend into a foe, and destroy family ties.

ʿAmr ibn al-ʿĀṣ says:

«لَا يَزَالُ الْمَرْءُ يَجْتَنِي مِنْ ثَمَرَةِ الْعَجَلَةِ النَّدَامَةَ».

(تحفة الأحوذي)

"One will reap nothing but remorse as a result of haste." (Tuḥfat al-Aḥwadhī)

Haste can also deprive a person from having their supplications answered. Rushing to have one's *duʿās* answered is one of the reasons that it may not be answered. A person may make *duʿā* to Allāh (ﷻ), and the answer may be delayed for a reason that is known only to Allāh

(ﷻ). Shayṭān can then seize the chance and whisper to the one supplicating to abandon *du'ā* altogether.

The Prophet (ﷺ) states:

«يُسْتَجَابُ لِأَحَدِكُمْ مَا لَمْ يَعْجَلْ، يَقُولُ: دَعَوْتُ فَلَمْ يُسْتَجَبْ لِي».

(رواه البخاري)

> "Every one of you will have their supplications answered as long as he is not impatient and says: 'I have supplicated but I was not answered.'" (Bukhārī)

Imām Dāwādī (رحمه الله) states:

«قَالَ الدَّاوُدِيُّ يُخْشَى عَلَى مَنْ خَالَفَ وَقَالَ قَدْ دَعَوْتُ فَلَمْ يُسْتَجَبْ لِي أَنْ يُحْرَمَ الْإِجَابَةَ وَمَا قَامَ مَقَامَهَا مِنَ الِادِّخَارِ وَالتَّكْفِيرِ».

(فتح الباري)

> "I am afraid that the one who disobeys (the Prophet's advice) and says: 'I have supplicated to Allāh but my supplication has not been granted' - may be deprived of the answer and all that can substitute it, such as saving it for the Day of Judgement and expiating one's sins by virtue of it." (Fatḥ al-Bārī)

Another form of rushing in supplication is to supplicate to Allāh (ﷻ) before praising and glorifying Him, and before asking Him to bestow His peace and salutations on His Messenger (ﷺ).

Faḍālah ibn 'Ubaid (رضي الله عنه) narrates:

«سَمِعَ رَسُولُ اللَّهِ ﷺ رَجُلًا يَدْعُو فِي صَلَاتِهِ لَمْ يُمَجِّدِ اللَّهَ، وَلَمْ يُصَلِّ عَلَى النَّبِيِّ ﷺ فَقَالَ رَسُولُ اللَّهِ ﷺ: عَجِلْتَ أَيُّهَا الْمُصَلِّي، ثُمَّ عَلَّمَهُمْ رَسُولُ اللَّهِ ﷺ، وَسَمِعَ رَسُولُ اللَّهِ ﷺ رَجُلًا يُصَلِّي، فَمَجَّدَ اللَّهَ وَحَمِدَهُ، وَصَلَّى عَلَى النَّبِيِّ صَلَّى اللهُ عَلَيْهِ وَسَلَّمَ، فَقَالَ رَسُولُ اللَّهِ ﷺ: ادْعُ تُجَبْ، وَسَلْ تُعْطَ».

(رواه الترمذي)

> The Prophet of Allāh (ﷺ) heard a man supplicating during the prayer without glorifying Allāh, or asking Him to bestow His peace and salutations upon the Prophet (ﷺ). The Messenger of Allāh (ﷺ) said to him: "You are in a hurry, O worshipper!" Then the Messenger of Allāh (ﷺ) taught him the proper way of supplication. Thereafter the Messenger of Allāh (ﷺ) heard another man praying - he glorified and praised Allāh, and asked Him to bestow His peace and salutations upon the Prophet (ﷺ). The Messenger of Allāh (ﷺ) said to him: "Supplicate, and your supplication will be answered; ask from Allāh and your request will be granted." (Tirmidhī)

Haste can also nullify a person's daily prayers (*ṣalat*), as indicated by the narration referred to as '*ḥadīth al-musī' ṣalātuhū* - *ḥadīth* of the person who prayed badly':

«أَنَّ النَّبِيَّ ﷺ دَخَلَ المَسْجِدَ، فَدَخَلَ رَجُلٌ، فَصَلَّى، ثُمَّ جَاءَ، فَسَلَّمَ عَلَى النَّبِيِّ ﷺ فَرَدَّ النَّبِيُّ ﷺ، فَقَالَ: ارْجِعْ فَصَلِّ فَإِنَّكَ لَمْ تُصَلِّ، فَصَلَّى، ثُمَّ جَاءَ، فَسَلَّمَ عَلَى النَّبِيِّ ﷺ فَقَالَ: ارْجِعْ فَصَلِّ، فَإِنَّكَ لَمْ تُصَلِّ ثَلاَثًا، فَقَالَ: وَالَّذِي بَعَثَكَ بِالحَقِّ، فَمَا أُحْسِنُ غَيْرَهُ، فَعَلِّمْنِي، قَالَ: إِذَا قُمْتَ إِلَى الصَّلاَةِ، فَكَبِّرْ، ثُمَّ اقْرَأْ مَا تَيَسَّرَ مَعَكَ مِنَ القُرْآنِ، ثُمَّ ارْكَعْ حَتَّى تَطْمَئِنَّ رَاكِعًا، ثُمَّ ارْفَعْ حَتَّى تَعْتَدِلَ قَائِمًا، ثُمَّ اسْجُدْ حَتَّى تَطْمَئِنَّ سَاجِدًا، ثُمَّ ارْفَعْ حَتَّى تَطْمَئِنَّ جَالِسًا، ثُمَّ اسْجُدْ حَتَّى تَطْمَئِنَّ سَاجِدًا، ثُمَّ افْعَلْ ذَلِكَ فِي صَلاَتِكَ كُلِّهَا».

(رواه البخاري)

> Once the Prophet (ﷺ) entered the *masjid* and a man came in, offered the prayer and greeted the Prophet. The Prophet (ﷺ) returned his greeting and said to him: "Go back and pray again for you have not prayed." The man then offered the

> prayer again, came back and greeted the Prophet (ﷺ). He said to him three times: "Go back and pray again for you have not prayed." The man replied: "By Him Who has sent you with the truth! I do not know a better way of praying. Kindly teach me how to pray." The Prophet (ﷺ) told him: "When you stand for the prayer, say *takbīr* and then recite from the Qur'ān what you know, and then bow with calmness until you feel at ease, then rise from bowing until you stand up straight. Afterwards prostrate calmly until you feel at ease, then raise (your head) and sit with calmness until you feel at ease, then prostrate again with calmness until you feel at ease in prostration, and do the same in the whole of your prayer." (Bukhārī)

A person whose hastiness leads him to precede the *imām* in the movements of the prayer may even find themselves turned into the likeness of a donkey, as mentioned in an authentic *ḥadīth.*

«أَمَا يَخْشَى أَحَدُكُمْ - أَوْ: لاَ يَخْشَى أَحَدُكُمْ - إِذَا رَفَعَ رَأْسَهُ قَبْلَ الإِمَامِ، أَنْ يَجْعَلَ اللَّهُ رَأْسَهُ رَأْسَ حِمَارٍ، أَوْ يَجْعَلَ اللَّهُ صُورَتَهُ صُورَةَ حِمَارٍ».

(رواه البخاري)

> The Prophet (ﷺ) states: "Isn't he who raises his head before the *imām* afraid that Allāh may transform his head into that of a donkey, or his figure (face) into that of a donkey?" (Bukhārī)

NOTE: Opinions differ regarding the warning issued in this *ḥadīth.* The *ḥadīth* carries the possibility of physical distortion, or the figurative sense can apply. Some scholars state that the warning is figurative. A donkey often denotes stupidity, stubbornness, and idiocy. Some are of the opinion that this distortion of the face will occur on the Day of Judgement because on that day, all of the deeds and actions will be given a physical body and they will testify for or against those who performed them.

People might be hasty in considering someone to be righteous, knowledgeable, impious, involved in wrong beliefs and practices, or even outside of the religion of Islām altogether.

People may also be quick in belittling a person's efforts or finding fault with them. This happens due to people being blinded by their own arrogance, inclinations, making presumptions out of ignorance, being unjust in their thinking, not giving others the rights to which they are entitled, being haste in hating others or blaming them, and also rushing to love others and praise them as well.

ʿAlī (ﷺ) states:

«أَحْبِبْ حَبِيبَكَ هَوْنًا مَا، عَسَى أَنْ يَكُونَ بَغِيضَكَ يَوْمًا مَا، وَأَبْغِضْ بَغِيضَكَ هَوْنًا مَا، عَسَى أَنْ يَكُونَ حَبِيبَكَ يَوْمًا مَا».

(رواه الترمذي)

> "Be moderate in loving a person you love because you may one day end up hating them, and be moderate in hating a person you hate because one day you may end up loving them." (Tirmidhī)

We should not be swift in casting blame upon others around us either. They might have a legitimate excuse for doing something that we may have perceived to be blameworthy.

تأَنَّ وَلَا تُعْجِلْ بِلَوْمِكَ صَاحِبًا ۞ لَعَلَّ لَهُ عُذْرًا وَأَنْتَ تَلُومُ

Do not be too haste in reproaching your friend,
For, he may have an excuse which you are unaware of.

Hastiness is detrimental and it is a quality which blinds a person's insight and can lead to recklessness, erroneous decisions, rushed conclusions, and failure to put things in their right place.

Usāmah ibn Zayd (ﷺ) relates:

«بَعَثَنَا رَسُولُ اللَّهِ ﷺ إِلَى الحُرَقَةِ مِنْ جُهَيْنَةَ، قَالَ: فَصَبَّحْنَا القَوْمَ فَهَزَمْنَاهُمْ، قَالَ: وَلَحِقْتُ أَنَا وَرَجُلٌ مِنَ الأَنْصَارِ رَجُلًا مِنْهُمْ، قَالَ: فَلَمَّا غَشِينَاهُ قَالَ: لاَ إِلَهَ إِلَّا اللَّهُ، قَالَ: فَكَفَّ عَنْهُ الأَنْصَارِيُّ، فَطَعَنْتُهُ بِرُمْحِي حَتَّى قَتَلْتُهُ، قَالَ: فَلَمَّا قَدِمْنَا بَلَغَ ذَلِكَ النَّبِيَّ ﷺ، قَالَ: فَقَالَ لِي: يَا أُسَامَةُ، أَقَتَلْتَهُ بَعْدَ مَا قَالَ لاَ إِلَهَ إِلَّا اللَّهُ؟! قَالَ: قُلْتُ: يَا رَسُولَ اللَّهِ، إِنَّمَا كَانَ مُتَعَوِّذًا، قَالَ: أَقَتَلْتَهُ بَعْدَ مَا قَالَ لاَ إِلَهَ إِلَّا اللَّهُ؟! قَالَ: فَمَا زَالَ يُكَرِّرُهَا عَلَيَّ، حَتَّى تَمَنَّيْتُ أَنِّي لَمْ أَكُنْ أَسْلَمْتُ قَبْلَ ذَلِكَ اليَوْمِ».

(رواه البخاري)

"The Messenger of Allāh (ﷺ) sent us to Ḥurqah, a tribe of Juhaynah. We launched an offensive attack early in the morning and defeated them. A man from the *Anṣār* and I caught hold of a man from the defeated tribe. When we overcame him, he said: 'There is no god but Allāh.' Upon that, the man from the *Anṣār* spared him, but I killed him by stabbing him with my spear. By the time we went back to Madīnah, the news had already reached the Messenger of Allāh (ﷺ). He said to me: 'O Usāmah! Did you kill him after he said: 'There is no god but Allāh?'' I replied: 'He professed it only to save his life.' The Messenger of Allāh (ﷺ) kept repeating his reproach until I wished that I had not embraced Islām before that day (to avoid having committed such a grave sin)." (Bukhārī)

A person may even rush in acquiring the knowledge of the *dīn* and as a result, skip some necessary steps, and think they have completed learning. Consequently, they may become deprived of the inner dimensions and full grasp of knowledge, and this can lead them to issue inaccurate verdicts, understand the texts of Islām incorrectly, and make erroneous interpretations.

Imām Mālik (رحمه الله) in his *Muwaṭṭā* relates:

«أَنَّهُ بَلَغَهُ أَنَّ عَبْدَ اللَّهِ بْنَ عُمَرَ، مَكَثَ عَلَى سُورَةِ الْبَقَرَةِ، ثَمَانِيَ سِنِينَ يَتَعَلَّمُهَا».

(موطا الامام مالك)

> "It took ʿAbdullāh ibn ʿUmar (ﷺ) eight years to learn Sūrah al-Baqarah." (Muwaṭṭā of Imām Mālik)

It is reported that Ibn ʿAbdullāh ibn ʿUmar (ﷺ) said:

«إِنَّا كُنَّا صُدُورَ هَذِهِ الْأُمَّةِ، وَكَانَ الرَّجُلُ مِنْ خِيَارِ أَصْحَابِ رَسُولِ اللَّهِ وَصَالِحِيهِمْ مَا يُقِيمُ إِلَّا سُورَةً مِنَ الْقُرْآنِ أَوْ شِبْهَ ذَلِكَ، وَكَانَ الْقُرْآنُ ثَقِيلًا عَلَيْهِمْ وَرُزِقُوا عِلْمًا بِهِ وَعَمَلًا، وَإِنَّ آخِرَ هَذِهِ الْأُمَّةِ يَخِفُّ عَلَيْهِمُ الْقُرْآنُ حَتَّى يَقْرَأَهُ الصَّبِيُّ وَالْعَجَمِيُّ لَا يَعْلَمُونَ مِنْهُ شَيْئًا، وَلَا يُرْزَقُونَ الْعَمَلَ بِهِ».

(تفسير القرطبي)

> "We were the beginning [the heads] of this nation, and perhaps a man from the best of the companions of Allāh's Messenger (ﷺ), and the most righteous among them could maintain only one chapter of the Qur'ān or thereabouts. The Qur'ān was weighty upon them, and they were given knowledge of it, and the gift of acting by the Qur'ān. But the last of this nation will find the Qur'ān light [and easy] – a child, and a blind person will (be able to) recite it, without possessing any knowledge about it, but will not be given the gift of acting by it." (Tafsīr al-Qurṭubī)

Haste comes from Shayṭān. This is because Shayṭān was created from fire, and among the properties of fire are that it flares recklessly, it can move lightly and quickly, and it incinerates things. These are properties which all have a clear and direct relation to the detrimental consequences of hastiness.

The Prophet (ﷺ) has said:

«الْأَنَاةُ مِنَ اللَّهِ، وَالْعَجَلَةُ مِنَ الشَّيْطَانِ».

(رواه الترمذي)

"Thoughtfulness (caution) is from Allāh, and haste is from Shayṭān." (Tirmidhī)

CONCLUSION

- The affairs of a person overcome by haste will end up ruined.
- Haste is a quality which is part of human beings. No one can be protected from its harmful effects, unless they refine that haste by channeling it in a way which it should be used for, and what will bring about benefit.
- We should try to make ourselves accustomed to exercising caution and thinking matters through carefully before making any statement, carrying out any action, or forming any opinion.
- Exercising care is an incomparable virtue. It is one which Allāh (ﷻ) loves, and He grants insight to those who embody it.

The Prophet (ﷺ) once praised Ashaj ʿAbd al-Qays (رضي الله عنه) by saying:

«إِنَّ فِيكَ لَخَصْلَتَيْنِ يُحِبُّهُمَا اللَّهُ: الْحِلْمَ وَالْأَنَاةَ».

(رواه الترمذي)

"You certainly have two qualities which Allāh loves: forbearance and deliberateness." (Tirmidhī)

Imām Abū ʿUthmān al-Ḥaddād (رحمه الله) says:

«وَمَنْ تَأَنَّى وَتَثَبَّتَ تَهَيَّأَ لَهُ مِنَ الصَّوَابِ مَا لَا يَتَهَيَّأُ لِصَاحِبِ الْبَدِيهَةِ».

(إعلام الموقعين عن رب العالمين)

"Those who act cautiously and carefully will be guided to right actions which even the intelligent and quick-witted people will not be guided to." (ʿI'lām al-Muwaqiʿīn ʿan Rabb al-ʿĀlamīn)

The texts of Islām teach us that when it comes to righteous actions, and deeds for our hereafter, to be haste is praiseworthy. There is no need to put off or delay such deeds.

Saʿd ibn Abī Waqqāṣ narrates the Prophet (ﷺ) as having said:

«التُّؤَدَةُ فِي كُلِّ شَيْءٍ إِلَّا فِي عَمَلِ الْآخِرَةِ».

(سنن أبي داود)

> "Exercising caution in all matters is good except when it comes to deeds of the hereafter." (Sunan Abū Dāwūd)

Hastening to perform any righteous deeds in general, is something which Allāh (ﷻ) has prescribed for all of His servants. We should feel delighted in exhausting ourselves when it comes to seeking nearness to Allāh (ﷻ).

Our motto should be like what Prophet Mūsā (ﷺ) said to Allāh (ﷻ):

﴿وَعَجِلْتُ إِلَيْكَ رَبِّ لِتَرْضَىٰ ﴿٨٤﴾﴾ [طه الآية ٨٤]

> "And I have hastened to You, (O) my Lord, so that You may be pleased (with my promptness and eagerness)." (Ṭāhā 20:84)

In the teachings of Islām, we find the instruction to hasten in righteous actions because it relates to giving people the rights to which they are entitled, and asking others for forgiveness before death. This applies to things including: giving people their wages or merchandise, paying off our debts, dispersing of inheritance, fulfilling trusts, and returning loaned items. It is not permissible for a Muslim to hold onto what others are entitled to since doing so will amount to injustice and transgression.

Among the deeds which one must hasten to perform – and which must not be put off or neglected – are repentance and constantly asking for Allāh's (ﷻ) forgiveness for all of the sins which we have committed. Allāh (ﷻ) accepts repentance from His servants as long as one has not yet reached the brink of death.

Righteous deeds can only emanate from clean and sound hearts. The Prophet (ﷺ) has said:

«إِنَّ اللَّهَ عَزَّ وَجَلَّ لَيَقْبَلُ تَوْبَةَ الْعَبْدِ، مَا لَمْ يُغَرْغِرْ».

(رواه الترمذي)

"Indeed, Allāh accepts the repentance of a slave as long as (the soul does not reach the throat)." (Tirmidhī)

No one knows when death will come for them, leaving everyone with no further chance to repent.

لاَ تَعْجَلَنَّ لأَمْرٍ أَنْتَ طَالِبُهُ ۞ فَقَلَّمَا يُدْرِكُ الْمَطْلُوبَ ذُوْ الْعَجَلِ

فَذُوْ التَّأَنِّي مُصِيبٌ فِي مَقَاصِدِهِ ۞ وَذُوْ التَّعَجُّلِ لاَ يَخْلُوْ عَنِ الزَّلَلِ

Do not hasten to get something you are seeking,
For a hasty person rarely gets what he seeks.
A prudent person achieves his goals successfully,
A hasty one however, inevitably make mistakes.

KHUṬBAH 63

The Qur'ānic Narrative of Prophet Yūnus (عليه السلام)

The lives of the different Prophets (عليهم السلام) contain profound admonition and multitudes upon multitudes of enlightening teachings. Their stories certainly contain lessons for people of understanding. The Qur'ān is not a fabricated speech. On the contrary, it attests to the truth of the previous scriptures which Allāh (عز وجل) revealed. It explains all of the things that people need, and it is mercy and guidance for the people of faith.

Narratives of the Qur'ān were revealed to the Messenger of Allāh (ﷺ) in Makkah, at a time when the few Muslims who resided there were facing many challenging circumstances. The road ahead of them was long and rough, and there was almost no end to it in sight. These narratives and stories allowed them to see the end of the path, and to recognize the landmarks along it, guiding their steps and taking them by the hand. They also strengthened the heart of the Prophet (ﷺ).

Allāh (عز وجل) says:

﴿وَكُلًّا نَّقُصُّ عَلَيْكَ مِنْ أَنۢبَآءِ ٱلرُّسُلِ مَا نُثَبِّتُ بِهِۦ فُؤَادَكَ ۚ وَجَآءَكَ فِى هَٰذِهِ ٱلْحَقُّ وَمَوْعِظَةٌ وَذِكْرَىٰ لِلْمُؤْمِنِينَ ﴿١٢٠﴾﴾ [هود الآية ١٢٠]

"And all of the narratives of the previous Prophets which We reveal to you serve to strengthen your heart, and establish it firmly upon the truth. This revelation has come to you with the truth, and it has come as an admonition, as well as a reminder to the people of faith (*īmān*)." (Hūd 11:120)

Allāh (ﷻ) tells the Messenger (ﷺ) that he is not alone on this path; and that he should patiently persevere as the Messengers (عليهم السلام) before him did who also had strong determination and perseverance.

We shall examine the story of a Prophet, which explained to our Prophet (ﷺ) not to abandon the responsibility of Prophethood and inviting other people to Allāh (ﷻ). The Qur'ān says to him:

﴿فَٱصۡبِرۡ لِحُكۡمِ رَبِّكَ وَلَا تَكُن كَصَاحِبِ ٱلۡحُوتِ إِذۡ نَادَىٰ وَهُوَ مَكۡظُومٞ ٤٨﴾

[القلم الآية ٤٨]

"Patiently bear the decree of your Lord, and do not be like the one who called out in distress from the belly of the whale." (Qalam 68:48)

This is the story of Prophet Yūnus (عليه السلام) (Jonah) whom Allāh (ﷻ) sent to the people of Naynawā [Nineveh] in the land of Mawṣil [Mosul]. He invited them to worship Allāh (ﷻ) alone, but they rejected him and remained stubbornly rigid. When that went on for a long time, he left them in anger and warned them about an impending punishment which will take place after three days. When he left in fury, he did not think that Allāh (ﷻ) would restrict the earth around him despite its vast expanse, numerous towns, and many people.

He presumed that Allāh (ﷻ) would direct him to other people since his own people had denied him.

This is the meaning of:

﴿فَظَنَّ أَن لَّن نَّقۡدِرَ عَلَيۡهِ ٨٧﴾ [الأنبياء الآية ٨٧]

"He presumed that We would not put him through difficulty (as a result of what he did)." (Anbiyā' 21:87)

When Prophet Yūnus (عليه السلام) left his people, and they became certain about an imminent punishment, Allāh (ﷻ) placed within their hearts a desire to repent, and they felt deep remorse about how they had dealt with their Prophet.

It was an extraordinary moment in which they all humbled themselves to Allāh (ﷻ) and invoked Him earnestly. As a result, the punishment which was going to come down upon them was averted by the might, power, mercy, and kindness of Allāh (ﷻ).

This situation was unique only to the people of Yūnus (عليه السلام). No other people denied their Prophet, saw the approaching punishment, then accepted the message of their Prophet, and had their faith accepted from them.

In Sūrah Yūnus, Allāh (ﷻ) mentions:

﴿فَلَوْلَا كَانَتْ قَرْيَةٌ ءَامَنَتْ فَنَفَعَهَآ إِيمَـٰنُهَآ إِلَّا قَوْمَ يُونُسَ لَمَّآ ءَامَنُوا۟ كَشَفْنَا عَنْهُمْ
عَذَابَ ٱلْخِزْىِ فِى ٱلْحَيَوٰةِ ٱلدُّنْيَا وَمَتَّعْنَـٰهُمْ إِلَىٰ حِينٍ ﴿٩٨﴾﴾ [يُونُس الآية ٩٨]

"There are no people who declared their faith upon seeing the punishment, and their *īmān* availed them, except the people of Yūnus. When they declared their faith and repented, We saved them from the torment of disgrace in this world, and We allowed them to live until the ends of their appointed lifespans." (Yūnus 10:98)

Commenting on this verse, Ḥāfiẓ ibn Kathīr (رحمه الله) quoting Imām Qatādah (رحمه الله) mentions:

«لَمَّا فَقَدُوا نَبِيَّهُمْ وَظَنُّوا أَنَّ الْعَذَابَ قَدْ دَنَا مِنْهُمْ، قَذَفَ اللَّهُ فِي قُلُوبِهِمُ التَّوْبَةَ، وَلَبِسُوا الْمُسُوحَ، وفَرّقوا بَيْنَ كُلِّ بَهِيمَةٍ وَوَلَدِهَا ثُمَّ عَجّوا إِلَى اللَّهِ أَرْبَعِينَ لَيْلَةً. فَلَمَّا عَرَفَ اللَّهُ مِنْهُمُ الصِّدْقَ مِنْ قُلُوبِهِمْ، وَالتَّوْبَةَ وَالنَّدَامَةَ عَلَى مَا مَضَى مِنْهُمْ كَشَفَ اللَّهُ عَنْهُمُ الْعَذَابَ بَعْدَ أَنْ تَدَلَّى عَلَيْهِمْ».

(تفسير ابن كثير)

"When they lost their Prophet and thought that the punishment was close approaching them, Allāh placed in their hearts the desire to repent. So they wore their woolen fabrics, and separated each animal from its offspring. They then cried out to Allāh for forty nights. When Allāh saw the truth in their hearts and that they were sincere in their repentance and remorse, He removed the punishment from them." (Tafsīr Ibn Kathīr)

The anger of Prophet Yūnus (ﷺ) led him to the seashore where he boarded a ship filled with passengers and luggage. When the ship sailed to deep waters, it was battered by winds and waves. For those on board, this may have been a sign that one of the passengers had committed a sin and incurred the wrath of Allāh (ﷻ), and they had to throw him overboard to save the ship from sinking; or they may have simply wanted to reduce the load in order to prevent the ship from sinking. When they drew lots to determine who to throw overboard, the lot of Prophet Yūnus (ﷺ) was drawn, but they were not at ease to throw him into the water.

However, his lot was drawn repeatedly, and his name came coming up.

Ḥāfiẓ ibn Kathīr (ﷺ) writes:

«وَذَلِكَ أَنَّ السَّفِينَةَ تَلَعَّبَت بِهَا الْأَمْوَاجُ مِنْ كُلِّ جَانِبٍ، وَأَشْرَفُوا عَلَى الْغَرَقِ، فَسَاهَمُوا عَلَى مَنْ تَقَعُ عَلَيْهِ الْقُرْعَةُ يُلْقَى فِي الْبَحْرِ، لِتَخِفَّ بِهِمُ السَّفِينَةُ، فَوَقَعَتِ الْقُرْعَةُ عَلَى نَبِيِّ اللَّهِ يُونُسَ، عَلَيْهِ الصَّلَاةُ وَالسَّلَامُ ثَلَاثَ مَرَّاتٍ، وَهُمْ يَضِنُّونَ بِهِ أَنْ يُلْقَى مِنْ بَيْنِهِمْ، فَتَجَرَّدَ مِنْ ثِيَابِهِ لِيُلْقِيَ نَفْسَهُ وَهُمْ يَأْبَوْنَ عَلَيْهِ ذَلِكَ».

(تفسير ابن كثير)

"This was because the ship was being pounded by the waves on all sides, and they were at a risk of drowning, so they drew lots, and whoever lost would be thrown overboard to lighten the load. The Prophet of Allāh Yūnus (ﷺ) lost the draw all three times, but they did not want to throw him overboard. He took off his garment so that he could throw himself into the sea, and they tried to stop him." (Tafsīr Ibn Kathīr)

Allāh (ﷻ) describes the way that Prophet Yūnus (ﷺ) left his people as escaping - just like a slave escapes from his master because Prophet Yūnus (ﷺ) departed without the permission of Allāh (ﷻ).

Allāh (ﷻ) states:

﴿وَإِنَّ يُونُسَ لَمِنَ ٱلْمُرْسَلِينَ ۝١٣٩ إِذْ أَبَقَ إِلَى ٱلْفُلْكِ ٱلْمَشْحُونِ ۝١٤٠﴾ [الصّافّات من الآية ١٣٩ الى الآية ١٤٠]

"And surely, Yūnus was from among the messengers. (Remember) when he ran away towards the boat that was already loaded." (Ṣāffāt 37:139-140)

The word: أَبَقَ (*abaqa*) in the above verse:

إِذْ أَبَقَ إِلَى ٱلْفُلْكِ ٱلْمَشْحُونِ

"When he ran towards the boat that was already loaded," has been derived from: إِبَاقٌ (*ibāq*) which means 'the escaping of a slave from his master.' Allāh (ﷻ) used this word for Prophet Yūnus (ﷺ) because he started off and left his community without waiting for the revelation from his Lord. The noble Prophets are the close ones among the servants of Allāh, and the slightest slip from them will cause the swiftest grip. Hence comes this strong expression of '*abaqa*': 'he ran.' (Maʿārif al-Qur'ān)

ʿAbdullāh ibn ʿAbbās (ﷺ) says:

«هُوَ الْمُوَقَّرُ، أَيِ: الْمَمْلُوءُ بِالْأَمْتِعَةِ».

(تفسير ابن كثير)

"It (the ship) was filled with cargo." (Tafsīr Ibn Kathīr)

When the ship was in danger of sinking, lots were drawn, and this Prophet was thrown into the sea. There, a whale swallowed him while he was in a blameworthy state for having abandoned the mission which Allāh (ﷻ) had sent him with, and for angrily leaving his people before Allāh (ﷻ) had permitted him to do so. A whale devoured him whole, but did not eat any of his flesh or crush any of his bones.

Ḥāfiẓ ibn Kathīr (رحمه الله) writes:

«وَأَمَرَ اللَّهُ تَعَالَى حُوتًا مِنَ الْبَحْرِ الْأَخْضَرِ أَنْ يَشُقَّ الْبِحَارَ، وَأَنْ يَلْتَقِمَ، يُونُسَ عَلَيْهِ السَّلَامُ، فَلَا يَهْشِمُ لَهُ لَحْمًا، وَلَا يَكْسِرَ لَهُ عَظْمًا . فَجَاءَ ذَلِكَ الْحُوتُ وَأَلْقَى يُونُسُ، عَلَيْهِ السَّلَامُ، نَفْسَهُ فَالْتَقَمَهُ الْحُوتُ وَذَهَبَ بِهِ فَطَافَ بِهِ الْبِحَارَ كُلَّهَا. وَلَمَّا اسْتَقَرَّ يُونُسُ فِي بَطْنِ الْحُوتِ، حَسَبَ أَنَّهُ قَدْ مَاتَ ثُمَّ حَرَّكَ رَأْسَهُ وَرَجْلَيْهِ وَأَطْرَافَهُ فَإِذَا هُوَ حَيٌّ، فَقَامَ يُصَلِّي فِي بَطْنِ الْحُوتِ، وَكَانَ مِنْ جُمْلَةِ دُعَائِهِ: يَا رَبِّ، اتخذتُ لَكَ مَسْجِدًا فِي مَوْضِعٍ لَمْ يَبْلُغْهُ أَحَدٌ مِنَ النَّاسِ».

(تفسير ابن كثير)

"Then Allāh, the Most-High, commanded a large fish from the Green Sea (i.e., Mediterranean Sea) to cleave the oceans and come and swallow Yūnus (ﷺ), without cutting his flesh or breaking his bones. The fish came and Yūnus (ﷺ) threw himself overboard, and the fish swallowed him and took him away, traveling through the sea with him. When Yūnus (ﷺ) had stayed for some time in the fish's belly, he thought that he had died; then he moved his head, legs and arms, and realized that he was still alive. He stood up and prayed in the belly of the fish, and one of the things that he said in his main prayer was: 'O my Lord, I have taken as a place of worship to You a place which no other person has reached.'" (Tafsīr Ibn Kathīr)

Prophet Yūnus (ﷺ) remained in the whale's belly for as long as Allāh (ﷻ) willed. Commentators of the Qur'ān have differed as to how long Prophet Yūnus (ﷺ) spent in the belly of the fish.

«فقِيلَ: ثَلَاثَةَ أَيَّامٍ، قَالَهُ قَتَادَةُ. وَقِيلَ جُمْعَة قَالَهُ جَعْفَرُ الصَّادِقُ. وَقِيلَ: أَرْبَعِينَ يَوْمًا، قَالَهُ أَبُو مالك، وَقَالَ مُجَالد، عَنِ الشَّعْبِيِّ: الْتَقَمَهُ ضُحًى، وَقَذَفَهُ عَشِيَّةً، وَاللَّهُ أَعْلَمُ بِمِقْدَارِ ذَلِكَ».

(تفسير ابن كثير)

> "Some said three days - this was the view of Qatādah. Some said seven days - this was the view of Jaʿfar al-Ṣādiq. Some said forty days - this was the view of Abū Mālik. Mujāhid says, narrating from al-Shaʿbī that: 'It swallowed him in the morning and cast him forth in the evening.' But (only) Allāh knows best how long the duration period exactly was." (Tafsīr Ibn Kathīr)

However, Allāh (ﷻ) says:

﴿فَلَوْلَآ أَنَّهُۥ كَانَ مِنَ ٱلْمُسَبِّحِينَ ١٤٣ لَلَبِثَ فِى بَطْنِهِۦٓ إِلَىٰ يَوْمِ يُبْعَثُونَ ١٤٤﴾ [الصَّافَّات من الآية ١٤٣ الى الآية ١٤٤]

> "Had he not been of them who glorify Allāh, He would have indeed remained inside of its belly (the fish) until the Day of Resurrection." (Ṣāffāt 37:143-144)

Then from the depths of the many layers of darkness – the whale's belly, the sea, and the night – Prophet Yūnus (ﷺ) called out to Allāh (ﷻ) in all sincerity saying:

﴿لَّآ إِلَٰهَ إِلَّآ أَنتَ سُبْحَٰنَكَ إِنِّى كُنتُ مِنَ ٱلظَّٰلِمِينَ ٨٧﴾ [الأَنبِيَاء الآية ٨٧]

> "There is none worthy of worship except You. You are perfect in every way. I was indeed among those who perpetrated tremendous wrongdoing." (Anbiyā' 21:87)

Ḥāfiẓ ibn Kathīr (رحمه الله) writes:

«أَنَّ يُونُسَ النَّبِيَّ، عَلَيْهِ السَّلَامُ، حِينَ بَدَا لَهُ أَنْ يَدْعُوَ بِهَذِهِ الْكَلِمَاتِ وَهُوَ فِي بَطْنِ الْحُوتِ، قَالَ: اللَّهُمَّ، لَا إِلَهَ إِلَّا أَنْتَ، سُبْحَانَكَ، إِنِّي كُنْتُ مِنَ الظَّالِمِينَ. فَأَقْبَلَتْ هَذِهِ الدَّعْوَةُ تَحُفُّ

بِالْعَرْشِ، فَقَالَتِ الْمَلَائِكَةُ: يَا رَبِّ، صَوْتٌ ضَعِيفٌ مَعْرُوفٌ مِنْ بِلَادٍ غَرِيبَةٍ؟ فَقَالَ: أَمَا تَعْرِفُونَ ذَاكَ؟ قَالُوا: لَا يَا رَبِّ، وَمَنْ هُوَ؟ قَالَ: عَبْدِي يُونُسُ. قَالُوا: عَبْدُكَ يُونُسُ الَّذِي لَمْ يَزَلْ يُرْفَعُ لَهُ عَمَلٌ مُتَقَبَّلٌ، وَدَعْوَةٌ مُجَابَةٌ؟. قَالُوا: يَا رَبِّ، أَوَلَا تَرْحَمُ مَا كَانَ يَصْنَعُ فِي الرَّخَاءِ فَتُنَجِّيَهُ مِنَ الْبَلَاءِ؟ قَالَ: بَلَى. فَأَمَرَ الْحُوتَ فَطَرَحَهُ فِي الْعَرَاءِ».

(تفسير ابن كثير)

"When it occurred to Prophet Yūnus (ﷺ) to call (upon Allāh ﷻ) in these words when he was in the belly of the whale, he said: '*Lā ilāha illā anta subḥānaka innī kuntu minaẓ ẓālimīn.*' This call went and hovered around the (mighty) Throne, and the angels said: 'O Lord, this is the voice of one who is weak but known, in a faraway strange land.' Allāh said: 'How do you know this?' They said: 'O Lord, who is he?' Allāh replied: '(It is) My servant Yūnus.' The angels asked: 'Your servant Yūnus, from whom there kept coming acceptable deeds and supplications which were answered?' They continued: 'O Lord, will You not have mercy on him for what he did during his time of ease, and save him from this trial and tribulation?' He answered: 'Of course.' So, He commanded the whale, and it cast him forth on a barren shore." (Tafsīr Ibn Kathīr)

Had Prophet Yūnus (ﷺ) not been obedient to Allāh (ﷻ) in times of ease prior to the whale swallowing him – by praying and frequently remembering Allāh (ﷻ) – then he would have remained in the whale's belly until the Day of Judgement.

This concurs to the Prophetic statements wherein the Prophet (ﷺ) said:

«احْفَظِ اللَّهَ يَحْفَظْكَ، احْفَظِ اللَّهَ تَجِدْهُ تُجَاهَكَ».

(رواه الترمذي)

"Be dutiful to Allāh and He will protect you. Be dutiful to Allāh and you will find Him in front of you." (Tirmidhī)

«تَعَرَّفْ إِلَى اللهِ فِي الرَّخَاءِ، يَعْرِفْكَ فِي الشِّدَّةِ».

(رواه الترمذي)

"Remember Allāh during times of ease, and He will remember you during times of difficulty." (Tirmidhī)

Prophet Yūnus (ﷺ) glorified Allāh (ﷻ) and prayed to Him even in the belly of the whale, just like he used to do in times of comfort before that.

The whale then cast Prophet Yūnus (ﷺ) onto the seashore. He was in a very weak physical state, and in a place with no trees or anything else to shade him. Allāh (ﷻ) caused a *yaqṭīn* plant to grow over him; a plant which bears gourd vegetables. It shaded him with its broad leaves and warded off flies which are said to be repelled by this plant.

Allāh (ﷻ) says:

﴿۞ فَنَبَذْنَٰهُ بِٱلْعَرَآءِ وَهُوَ سَقِيمٌ ﴿١٤٥﴾ وَأَنۢبَتْنَا عَلَيْهِ شَجَرَةً مِّن يَقْطِينٍ ﴿١٤٦﴾﴾ [الصّافّات من الآية ١٤٥ الى الآية ١٤٦]

"(However, We rescued him from the fish and) We cast him onto a barren (forsaken) shore, and he was ill (after spending time in the fish). And then We caused a gourd vine to grow over him (to shade him as he regained his strength)." (Ṣāffāt 37:145-146)

ʿAbdullāh ibn Masʿūd (ﷺ) states:

«كَهَيْئَةِ الْفَرْخِ لَيْسَ عَلَيْهِ رِيشٌ».

(تفسير ابن كثير)

"Due to his stay in the hot belly of the fish, the body of Prophet Yūnus (ﷺ) had become extremely soft and tender, like the young one of a fowl which does not even have feathers on its body." (Tafsīr Ibn Kathīr)

Ḥāfiẓ ibn Kathīr (ﷺ) writes:

«قَالَ ابْنِ مَسْعُودٍ، وَابْنِ عَبَّاسٍ، وَمُجَاهِدٍ، وَعِكْرِمَةَ، وَسَعِيدِ بْنُ جُبَيْرٍ، وَوَهْبُ بْنُ مُنَبِّهٍ، وَهِلَالُ بْنُ يَسَافٍ وَعَبْدُ اللَّهِ بْنُ طَاوُسٍ، وَالسُّدِّيُّ، وَقَتَادَةُ، وَالضَّحَّاكُ، وَعَطَاءُ الْخُرَاسَانِيُّ وَغَيْرُ وَاحِدٍ قَالُوا كُلُّهُمْ: الْيَقْطِينُ هُوَ الْقَرْعُ، وَذَكَرَ بَعْضُهُمْ فِي الْقَرْعِ فَوَائِدَ، مِنْهَا: سُرْعَةُ نَبَاتِهِ، وتظليلُ وَرَقِهِ لِكِبَرِهِ، وَنُعُومَتِهِ، وَأَنَّهُ لَا يَقْرَبُهَا الذُّبَابُ، وَجَوْدَةُ أَغْذِيَةِ ثَمَرِهِ، وَأَنَّهُ يُؤْكَلُ نَيِّئًا وَمَطْبُوخًا بِلُبِّهِ وَقِشْرِهِ أَيْضًا. وَقَدْ ثَبَتَ أَنَّ رَسُولَ اللَّهِ ﷺ كَانَ يُحِبُّ الدُّبَّاءَ، وَيَتَتَبَّعُهُ مِنْ حَوَاشِي الصَّحْفَةِ».

(تفسير ابن كثير)

"ʿAbdullāh ibn Masʿūd and ʿAbdullāh ibn ʿAbbās (ﷺ) and several others, all said that gourd meant squash. Some of them mentioned that the squash has a number of benefits: it grows quickly, its leaves offer shade because of their large size and smooth texture, flies do not come near it, and its fruit provides good nourishment; they may be eaten raw or cooked, and both the pulp and the peel may be eaten. It is established that the Messenger of Allāh (ﷺ) used to like squash and would look for it wherever it was on a serving dish." (Tafsīr Ibn Kathīr)

Yaqṭīn in Arabic signifies every such tree which does not have a trunk.

Anas ibn Mālik (ﷺ) reports:

«إِنَّ خَيَّاطًا دَعَا رَسُولَ اللَّهِ ﷺ لِطَعَامٍ صَنَعَهُ، قَالَ أَنَسُ بْنُ مَالِكٍ فَذَهَبْتُ مَعَ رَسُولِ اللَّهِ ﷺ إِلَى ذَلِكَ الطَّعَامِ، فَقَرَّبَ إِلَى رَسُولِ اللَّهِ ﷺ خُبْزًا وَمَرَقًا فِيهِ دُبَّاءٌ وَقَدِيدٌ، فَرَأَيْتُ النَّبِيَّ ﷺ يَتَتَبَّعُ الدُّبَّاءَ مِنْ حَوَالَيِ الْقَصْعَةِ. قَالَ. فَلَمْ أَزَلْ أُحِبُّ الدُّبَّاءَ مِنْ يَوْمِئِذٍ».

(رواه البخاري)

"A tailor invited the Messenger of Allāh (ﷺ) to a meal which he had prepared." Anas ibn Mālik says: "I accompanied the Messenger of Allāh (ﷺ) to that meal. He (the tailor) served the Prophet (ﷺ) with bread and gravy made with gourd and meat. I saw the Prophet (ﷺ) picking the pieces of gourd from around the dish." Anas (رضي الله عنه) added: "Ever since that day I also began liking gourd." (Bukhārī)

Allāh (ﷻ) then commanded Prophet Yūnus (عليه السلام) to return to his people. They all accepted his message, and there were no less than one hundred thousand in number.

Allāh (ﷻ) says:

﴿وَأَرْسَلْنَٰهُ إِلَىٰ مِاْئَةِ أَلْفٍ أَوْ يَزِيدُونَ ﴿١٤٧﴾ فَـَٔامَنُواْ فَمَتَّعْنَٰهُمْ إِلَىٰ حِينٍ ﴿١٤٨﴾﴾ [الصَّافَّات من الآية ١٤٧ الى الآية ١٤٨]

"Then We sent him (to preach) to a nation of a hundred thousand or more. They (the people of his town) accepted *īmān* and We allowed them to enjoy themselves (to live) for a while (rather than suffer the punishment as Yūnus had assumed)." (Ṣāffāt 37:147-148)

This is the story of the noble Prophet Yūnus (عليه السلام).

Both Imām al-Bukhārī and Imām Muslim (رحمهما الله) have documented a *ḥadīth* wherein the Prophet (ﷺ) said:

«لاَ يَنْبَغِي لِعَبْدٍ أَنْ يَقُولَ: أَنَا خَيْرٌ مِنْ يُونُسَ بْنِ مَتَّى».

(رواه البخاري)

"No one should say that I am better than Yūnus, the son of Mattā." (Bukhārī)

He is one of several noble Prophets whom Allāh (ﷻ) specifically mentioned by name in Sūrah al-Nisā' and Sūrah al-Anʿām of the Qur'ān.

Allāh (ﷻ) instructed the Messenger (ﷺ) by saying:

﴿أُوْلَـٰٓئِكَ ٱلَّذِينَ هَدَى ٱللَّهُۖ فَبِهُدَىٰهُمُ ٱقْتَدِهْۗ ۝٩٠﴾ [الأنعام الآية ٩٠]

"Those (Prophets) are the people whom Allāh has guided, so follow their guidance (teachings)." (Anʿām 6:90)

The guidance to be followed from this story is what Allāh (ﷻ) said to His Prophet Muḥammad (ﷺ):

﴿فَٱصْبِرْ لِحُكْمِ رَبِّكَ وَلَا تَكُن كَصَاحِبِ ٱلْحُوتِ إِذْ نَادَىٰ وَهُوَ مَكْظُومٌ ۝٤٨﴾

[القلم الآية ٤٨]

"Patiently bear the decree of your Lord, and do not be like the companion of the whale when he called out while he was in distress." (Qalam 68:48)

CONCLUSION

When we are experiencing difficulties and distress, the prayers of the Prophets are an example for us to follow.

Both Imām Aḥmad and Imām Tirmidhī (رحمهما الله) have collected a *ṣaḥīḥ* narration from Saʿd ibn Abī Waqqāṣ (رضي الله عنه), where the Messenger of Allāh (ﷺ) said:

«دَعْوَةُ ذِي النُّونِ إِذْ دَعَا وَهُوَ فِي بَطْنِ الحُوتِ: لاَ إِلَهَ إِلاَّ أَنْتَ سُبْحَانَكَ إِنِّي كُنْتُ مِنَ الظَّالِمِينَ، فَإِنَّهُ لَمْ يَدْعُ بِهَا رَجُلٌ مُسْلِمٌ فِي شَيْءٍ قَطُّ إِلاَّ اسْتَجَابَ اللَّهُ لَهُ».

(رواه الإمام أحمد والترمذي)

"The supplication of Yūnus, while he was in the belly of the whale was: 'There is none worthy of worship except You. You are perfect in every way. I was indeed among those who perpetrated tremendous wrongdoing (*Lā ilāha illā anta subḥānaka innī kuntu minaẓ-ẓālimīn*).' No Muslim supplicates for anything using this prayer except that Allāh will respond to him." (Aḥmad and Tirmidhī)

Ḥāfiẓ ibn Kathīr (ﷺ) writes quoting Saʿd ibn Abī Waqqāṣ (ﷺ):

«مَرَرْتُ بِعُثْمَانَ بْنِ عَفَّانَ فِي الْمَسْجِدِ فَسَلَّمْتُ عَلَيْهِ، فَمَلأَ عَيْنَيْهِ مِنِّي ثُمَّ لَمْ يَرُدَّ عَلَيَّ السَّلَامَ، فَأَتَيْتُ أَمِيرَ الْمُؤْمِنِينَ عُمَرَ بْنَ الْخَطَّابِ، فَقُلْتُ: يَا أَمِيرَ الْمُؤْمِنِينَ، هَلْ حَدَثَ فِي الْإِسْلَامِ شَيْءٌ؟ مَرَّتَيْنِ قَالَ: لَا. وَمَا ذَاكَ؟ قَالَ: قُلْتُ: لَا. إِلا أَنِّي مَرَرْتُ بِعُثْمَانَ آنِفًا فِي الْمَسْجِدِ، فَسَلَّمْتُ عَلَيْهِ فَمَلأَ عَيْنَيْهِ مِنِّي، ثُمَّ لَمْ يَرُدَّ عَلَيَّ السَّلَامَ. قَالَ: فَأَرْسَلَ عُمَرُ إِلَى عُثْمَانَ فَدَعَاهُ، فَقَالَ: مَا مَنَعَكَ أَنْ لَا تَكُونَ رَدَدْتَ عَلَى أَخِيكَ السَّلَامَ؟ قَالَ عُثْمَانُ: مَا فَعَلْتُ قَالَ سَعْدٌ: قُلْتُ: بَلَى. قَالَ: حَتَّى حَلَفَ وَحَلَفْتُ، قَالَ: ثُمَّ إِنَّ عُثْمَانَ ذَكَرَ، فَقَالَ: بَلَى، وَأَسْتَغْفِرُ اللهَ وَأَتُوبُ إِلَيْهِ إِنَّكَ مَرَرْتَ بِي آنِفًا، وَأَنَا أُحَدِّثُ نَفْسِي بِكَلِمَةٍ سَمِعْتُهَا مِنْ رَسُولِ اللهِ ﷺ، لَا وَاللهِ مَا ذَكَرْتُهَا قَطُّ إِلا تَغَشَّى بَصَرِي وَقَلْبِي غِشَاوَةٌ، قَالَ: قَالَ سَعْدٌ: فَأَنَا أُنَبِّئُكَ بِهَا: إِنَّ رَسُولَ اللهِ ﷺ ذَكَرَ لَنَا أَوَّلَ دَعْوَةٍ، ثُمَّ جَاءَ أَعْرَابِيٌّ فَشَغَلَهُ حَتَّى قَامَ رَسُولُ اللهِ ﷺ، فَاتَّبَعْتُهُ فَلَمَّا أَشْفَقْتُ أَنْ يَسْبِقَنِي إِلَى مَنْزِلِهِ، ضَرَبْتُ بِقَدَمِي الْأَرْضَ، فَالْتَفَتَ إِلَيَّ رَسُولُ اللهِ ﷺ:. فَقَالَ: مَنْ هَذَا أَبُو إِسْحَاقَ؟ قَالَ: قُلْتُ: نَعَمْ يَا رَسُولَ اللهِ. قَالَ: فَمَهْ. قَالَ: قُلْتُ: لَا وَاللهِ، إِلا أَنَّكَ ذَكَرْتَ لَنَا أَوَّلَ دَعْوَةٍ ثُمَّ جَاءَ هَذَا الْأَعْرَابِيُّ فَشَغَلَكَ، قَالَ: نَعَمْ دَعْوَةُ ذِي النُّونِ إِذْ هُوَ فِي بَطْنِ الْحُوتِ: ﴿لَّآ إِلَٰهَ إِلَّآ أَنتَ سُبۡحَٰنَكَ إِنِّي كُنتُ مِنَ ٱلظَّٰلِمِينَ ٨٧﴾ [الأنبياء الآية ٨٧] فَإِنَّهُ لَمْ يَدْعُ بِهَا مُسْلِمٌ رَبَّهُ فِي شَيْءٍ قَطُّ إِلا اسْتَجَابَ لَهُ».

(تفسير ابن كثير)

"I passed by ʿUthmān ibn ʿAffān (ﷺ) in the *masjid* and greeted him. He stared at me but did not return my *salām*. I went to ʿUmar ibn al-Khaṭṭāb (ﷺ) and said: 'O Commander of the faithful, has something happened in Islām?' I said that twice. He said: 'No, why do you ask?' I questioned: 'I passed by

> ʿUthmān (ﷺ) a short while ago in the *masjid* and greeted him, and he stared at me, but he did not return my *salām*.' ʿUmar (ﷺ) sent for ʿUthmān (ﷺ) and asked him: 'Why did you not return your brother's *salām*?' He replied: 'That is not true.' Saʿd (ﷺ) said: 'Yes it is.' It reached the point where they both swore oaths. Then ʿUthmān remembered and said: 'Yes, you are right. I seek the forgiveness of Allāh and I repent to Him. You passed by me a short while ago, but I was preoccupied with thoughts about something that I had heard from the Messenger of Allāh (ﷺ) which I never think about, and a veil came down over my eyes and my heart.' Saʿd (ﷺ) said: 'I will tell you what it was. The Messenger of Allāh (ﷺ) told us the first part of a supplication, then a Bedouin came and kept him busy, then the Messenger of Allāh (ﷺ) got up and I followed him. When I felt worried that he would enter his house, I stamped my feet. I turned to the Messenger of Allāh (ﷺ) who asked: 'Who is this? Abū Isḥāq?' I replied: 'Yes, O Messenger of Allāh.' He questioned: 'What is the matter?' I replied: 'Nothing, by Allāh, except that you told us the first part of the supplication, but then this Bedouin came and kept you busy.' He said: 'Yes, the supplication of Dhū al-Nūn when he was in the belly of the fish: 'There is none worthy of worship except You. You are perfect in every way. I was indeed among those who perpetrated tremendous wrongdoing.' No Muslim ever prays to his Lord with these words for anything, but He will answer his prayer.'" (Tafsīr Ibn Kathīr)

This incredible supplication is so profound because it contains:

1. The attestation of the Oneness of Allāh (ﷻ):

﴿لَّآ إِلَٰهَ إِلَّآ أَنتَ﴾

"There is none worthy of worship except You."

2. It absolves Allāh (ﷻ) of any imperfection:

﴿سُبۡحَـٰنَكَ﴾

"You are perfect in every way."

3. It also contains a confession from those who recite it:

﴿إِنِّي كُنتُ مِنَ ٱلظَّـٰلِمِينَ﴾

"I was indeed among those who perpetrated tremendous wrongdoing."

Imām Aḥmad (رحمه الله) reports on the authority of ʿAbdullāh ibn Masʿūd (رضي الله عنه) that the Prophet (ﷺ) said:

«مَا قَالَ عَبْدٌ قَطُّ إِذَا أَصَابَهُ هَمٌّ وَحَزَنٌ: اللهُمَّ إِنِّي عَبْدُكَ، وَابْنُ عَبْدِكَ، ابْنُ أَمَتِكَ، نَاصِيَتِي بِيَدِكَ، مَاضٍ فِيَّ حُكْمُكَ، عَدْلٌ فِيَّ قَضَاؤُكَ، أَسْأَلُكَ بِكُلِّ اسْمٍ هُوَ لَكَ، سَمَّيْتَ بِهِ نَفْسَكَ، أَوْ أَنْزَلْتَهُ فِي كِتَابِكَ، أَوْ عَلَّمْتَهُ أَحَدًا مِنْ خَلْقِكَ، أَوِ اسْتَأْثَرْتَ بِهِ فِي عِلْمِ الْغَيْبِ عِنْدَكَ، أَنْ تَجْعَلَ الْقُرْآنَ رَبِيعَ قَلْبِي، وَنُورَ صَدْرِي، وَجِلَاءَ حُزْنِي، وَذَهَابَ هَمِّي، إِلَّا أَذْهَبَ اللهُ عَزَّ وَجَلَّ هَمَّهُ، وَأَبْدَلَهُ مَكَانَ حُزْنِهِ فَرَحًا، قَالُوا: يَا رَسُولَ اللهِ يَنْبَغِي لَنَا أَنْ نَتَعَلَّمَ هَؤُلَاءِ الْكَلِمَاتِ؟ قَالَ: أَجَلْ، يَنْبَغِي لِمَنْ سَمِعَهُنَّ أَنْ يَتَعَلَّمَهُنَّ».

(رواه أحمد)

"If a servant experiences sadness or distress, then Allāh will remove that distress and replace one's sadness with happiness or relief if they recite: 'O Allāh, I am Your servant, the son of Your male servant, the son of Your female servant. My forelock is in Your hand, I am subject to Your judgement, and all that You decree for me is just. O Allāh, by every name that You have – whether You named Yourself with it, taught it to any of Your creatures, revealed it in Your scriptures, or kept it as knowledge which only You have – I ask You to make the Qur'ān a solace and light for my heart, and the removal of my sorrow, worry, and distress.'" The companions asked: "O Messenger of Allāh, should we not learn these words?" He replied: "Yes. Whoever hears them should learn them." (Aḥmad)

Learning them includes: memorizing, understanding, and supplicating with them.

Imām al-Bukhārī (🕮) has mentioned that the Prophet (ﷺ) used to supplicate with the following words at times of adversity:

«لاَ إِلَهَ إِلاَّ اللَّهُ الْعَظِيمُ الْحَلِيمُ، لاَ إِلَهَ إِلاَّ اللَّهُ رَبُّ الْعَرْشِ الْعَظِيمِ، لاَ إِلَهَ إِلاَّ اللَّهُ رَبُّ السَّمَوَاتِ، وَرَبُّ الأَرْضِ، وَرَبُّ الْعَرْشِ الْكَرِيمِ».

(رواه البخاري)

"None has the right to be worshipped except Allāh, the Most Knowledgeable and the Most Forbearing. None has the right to be worshipped except Allāh, Lord of the magnificent throne. None has the right to be worshipped except Allāh, Lord of the heavens, Lord of the earth, and Lord of the noble throne." (Bukhārī)

These prayers are Prophetic cures for sadness and distress, and Allāh (🕮) will surely grant relief to anyone who uses them with full certainty.

وَسَلْ مِنْ رَبِّكَ التَّوْفِيقَ فِيهَا ۞ وَأَخْلِصْ فِي السُّؤَالِ إِذَا سَأَلْتَا
وَنَادِ إِذَا سَجَدْتَ لَهُ اعْتِرَافاً ۞ بِمَا نَادَاهُ ذُو النُّونِ ابْنُ مَتَّى
وَلَازِمْ بَابَهُ قَرْعاً عَسَاهُ ۞ سَيَفْتَحُ بَابَهُ لَكَ إِنْ قَرَعْتَا
وَأَكْثِرْ ذِكْرَهُ فِي الأَرْضِ دَأْباً ۞ لِتُذْكَرَ فِي السَّمَاءِ إِذَا ذَكَرْتَا

Ask your Lord in them for guidance and success,
And make your request sincere whenever you ask.
When you prostrate, call out to Him in full acknowledgment,
With the words used by Dhū al-Nūn, the son of Mattā.
Persist in knocking at His door,
Perhaps He may open it for you so long as you remain knocking.

Make constant mention of Him a regular practice while on this earth,
So that you will be mentioned in the heavens whenever you mention Him.

KHUṬBAH 64

On the Road to Righteousness of One's Words and Inner Thoughts

An individual's true success and salvation lies in their ability to control themselves, bring themselves to account for their actions, and closely watch whatever words one utters and deeds one performs, be they small or big.

Those who bring themselves to account for their actions, and control their words, deeds, and inner thoughts, ensuring that they are all pleasing to Allāh (ﷻ), will certainly attain great success.

Allāh (ﷻ) says:

﴿وَأَمَّا مَنْ خَافَ مَقَامَ رَبِّهِۦ وَنَهَى ٱلنَّفْسَ عَنِ ٱلْهَوَىٰ ۝٤٠ فَإِنَّ ٱلْجَنَّةَ هِيَ ٱلْمَأْوَىٰ ۝٤١﴾ [النّازِعَات من الآية ٤٠ الى الآية ٤١]

"But as for him who fears standing before his Lord (to account for his actions), and restrained himself from impure evil desires and lusts, then definitely, Paradise will be his abode." (Nāziʿāt 79:40-41)

﴿وَلِمَنْ خَافَ مَقَامَ رَبِّهِۦ جَنَّتَانِ ۝٤٦﴾ [الرَّحْمَٰن الآية ٤٦]

"And for the one who is fearful of having to stand before his Lord, there are two gardens." (Raḥmān 55:46)

﴿إِنَّ ٱلَّذِينَ ٱتَّقَوْاْ إِذَا مَسَّهُمْ طَٰٓئِفٌ مِّنَ ٱلشَّيْطَٰنِ تَذَكَّرُواْ فَإِذَا هُم مُّبْصِرُونَ ۝٢٠١﴾ [الأَعْرَاف الآية ٢٠١]

"Indeed, when the temptation (to do evil) from Shayṭān reaches those who fear Allāh, they remember (Allāh and engage in *dhikr*, thinking about His punishment and recalling the rewards for abstaining from sin) and their eyes instantly open (they realize Shayṭān's plot and ignore the temptation)." (Aʿrāf 7:201)

﴿وَلَآ أُقۡسِمُ بِٱلنَّفۡسِ ٱللَّوَّامَةِ ۝٢﴾ [القِيَامَة الآية ٢]

"And I swear by the rebuking *nafs* (the inner voice that reprimands a person when he does wrong or when his good deeds are deficient)!" (Qiyāmah 75:2)

Commentators on the Qur'ān say that: "Allāh (ﷻ) swears by the self-reproaching person, who reprimands himself often for neglecting duties and committing prohibited acts, so that he may follow the straight path."

The word *nafs* means 'soul' or 'life,' and the word *lawwāmah* is derived from *lawm* signifying 'to reproach or reprimand.' The phrase refers to the human conscience that rebukes a person for doing bad deeds. It reprimands one not only for doing bad deeds, but also for doing good deeds, in the sense of – 'why did you not do better, and attain higher stages (of development)?'

In short, a perfect believer reproaches and reprimands himself all of the time whether doing good or bad. His admonishing himself for bad deeds is quite understandable, but why should he blame or criticize himself for good deeds? He should try to reach for higher goals in life by doing better deeds, and thus he reprimands himself for missing out on that score.

This interpretation is reported from Ibn ʿAbbās (رضي الله عنهما) and other leading authorities on *Tafsīr*. (Maʿārif al-Qurʿān)

Abū Hurairah (رضي الله عنه) narrates that the Prophet (ﷺ) said:

«مَنْ كَانَ يُؤْمِنُ بِاللهِ وَالْيَوْمِ الْآخِرِ، فَلْيَقُلْ خَيْرًا أَوْ لِيَصْمُتْ».

(رواه البخاري)

"A person who believes in Allāh and the Last Day, must speak (that which is) good or remain silent." (Bukhārī)

This characteristic can only be achieved when a person takes account of oneself.

Shaddād ibn Aws (ﷺ) narrates that the Prophet (ﷺ) said:

«الكَيِّسُ مَنْ دَانَ نَفْسَهُ، وَعَمِلَ لِمَا بعدَ المَوتِ، والعَاجِزُ مَنْ أَتْبَعَ نَفْسَهُ هَواهَا وَتَمَنَّى عَلَى اللهِ».

(رواه الترمذي)

"A wise person is one who takes account of oneself and strives for that which is after death; and a helpless person is one who follows one's own whims then indulges in wishful thinking about Allāh." (Tirmidhī)

ʿUmar ibn al-Khaṭṭāb (ﷺ) would say:

«حَاسِبُوا أَنْفُسَكُمْ قَبْلَ أَنْ تُحَاسَبُوا، وَزِنُوا أَنْفُسَكُمْ قَبْلَ أَنْ تُوزَنُوا، فَإِنَّهُ أَهْوَنُ عَلَيْكُمْ فِي الْحِسَابِ غَدًا أَنْ تُحَاسِبُوا أَنْفُسَكُمُ الْيَوْمَ، وَتَزَيَّنُوا لِلْعَرْضِ الأَكْبَرِ».

(تفسير ابن كثير)

"Bring yourselves to account (for your deeds) before you are brought to account for, weigh your deeds before they are weighed for you, and prepare yourselves for the great exposure (on the Day of Judgement)." (Tafsīr Ibn Kathīr)

Maymūn ibn Mahrān (ﷺ) says:

«الْمُتَّقِي أَشَدُّ مُحَاسَبَةً لِنَفْسِهِ مِنَ الشَّرِيكِ الشَّحِيحِ لِشَرِيكِهِ».

(جامع العلوم والحكم)

"A pious person brings himself to account more thoroughly than a miserly associate checking accounts with his partners." (Jāmiʿ al-ʿUlūm wa al-Ḥikm)

Ḥārith ibn Suwayd (ﷺ) said:

«حَدَّثَنَا عَبْدُ اللَّهِ بْنُ مَسْعُودٍ، حَدِيثَيْنِ: أَحَدُهُمَا عَنِ النَّبِيِّ ﷺ، وَالآخَرُ عَنْ نَفْسِهِ، قَالَ: إِنَّ الْمُؤْمِنَ يَرَى ذُنُوبَهُ كَأَنَّهُ قَاعِدٌ تَحْتَ جَبَلٍ يَخَافُ أَنْ يَقَعَ عَلَيْهِ، وَإِنَّ الفَاجِرَ يَرَى ذُنُوبَهُ كَذُبَابٍ مَرَّ عَلَى أَنْفِهِ، فَقَالَ بِهِ هَكَذَا، قَالَ أَبُو شِهَابٍ: بِيَدِهِ فَوْقَ أَنْفِهِ».

(رواه البخاري)

"ʿAbdullāh ibn Masʿūd (ﷺ) related to us two narrations: One from the Prophet (ﷺ), and another one from himself, saying: 'A believer sees his sins as if he was sitting under a mountain, which he is afraid may fall on him; whereas a wicked person considers his sins as flies passing over his nose and he just drives them away like this.'" Abū Shihāb (the sub-narrator) moved his hand over his nose in illustration. (Bukhārī)

A true believer brings himself to account, watches over his own deeds, seeks to keep himself upright, and remain in the best possible condition. He calls himself to balance all of his deeds, and strive hard to perform all of the acts of worship and obedience to Allāh (ﷻ) in all sincerity, making certain that they are free from anything that may blemish them, such as showing off, pride, ego, etc.; and seeks nothing other than Allāh's (ﷻ) good pleasure and Paradise in the hereafter. He also brings himself to analyze his actions so that he may do more righteous deeds that confirm with the *sunnah* of the Prophet (ﷺ), and commit himself to doing righteous deeds continuously and perpetually.

Allāh (ﷻ) says in the Qur'ān:

﴿وَمَن جَٰهَدَ فَإِنَّمَا يُجَٰهِدُ لِنَفۡسِهِۦٓۚ إِنَّ ٱللَّهَ لَغَنِيٌّ عَنِ ٱلۡعَٰلَمِينَ ٦﴾ [العنكبوت الآية ٦]

"And whoever strives, strives only for himself (for his own benefit because he will attain the benefits and rewards). Surely Allāh is independent of the entire universe (and is not dependent on their worship or obedience). (He created us to confer blessings upon us)." (Ankabūt 29:6)

Sufyān al-Thawrī (ﷺ) says:

«مَا عَالَجْتُ شَيْئًا أَشَدَّ عَلَيَّ مِنْ نِيَّتِي، إِنَّهَا تَقَلَّبُ عَلَيَّ».

(جامع العلوم والحكم)

"I have never struggled with anything harder than my intentions - they keep shifting all of the time." (Jāmiʿ al-ʿUlūm wa al-Ḥikm)

Faḍl ibn Ziyād (ﷺ) says:

«سَأَلْتُ أَبَا عَبْدِ اللَّهِ - يَعْنِي أَحْمَدَ - عَنِ النِّيَّةِ فِي الْعَمَلِ، قُلْتُ كَيْفَ النِّيَّةُ؟ قَالَ: يُعَالِجُ نَفْسَهُ، إِذَا أَرَادَ عَمَلًا لَا يُرِيدُ بِهِ النَّاسَ».

(جامع العلوم والحكم)

"I asked Abā ʿAbdillāh, meaning (Imām) Aḥmad - about one's intentions regarding deeds, and so I said: 'What should one's intentions be like?' He replied: 'When a person intends to do something, he must struggle hard to ensure that this is done for the sake of Allāh, and not for the sake of people.'" (Jāmiʿ al-ʿUlūm wa al-Ḥikm)

Shaddād ibn Aws (ﷺ) narrates that the Prophet (ﷺ) said:

«مَنْ صَلَّى يُرَائِي فَقَدْ أَشْرَكَ، وَمَنْ صَامَ يُرَائِي فَقَدْ أَشْرَكَ، وَمَنْ تَصَدَّقَ يُرَائِي فَقَدْ أَشْرَكَ».

(رواه أحمد)

"Whoever prays with the intention of showing off has associated partners with Allāh, and whoever fasts with the intention of showing off has associated partners with Allāh, and whoever gives charity with the intention of showing off has associated partners with Allāh." (Aḥmad)

A Muslim should question oneself regarding every word that he utters, thus trying to prevent his tongue from uttering any false statements or prohibited words. He must remember that there are two angels delegated to write down each and every word which he utters, and every deed that he performs, and that he will be rewarded or punished accordingly for everything.

Allāh (ﷻ) says:

﴿وَإِنَّ عَلَيْكُمْ لَحَافِظِينَ ۝١٠ كِرَامًا كَاتِبِينَ ۝١١ يَعْلَمُونَ مَا تَفْعَلُونَ ۝١٢﴾

[الانفطار من الآية ١٠ الى الآية ١٢]

"And verily there are guardians (angels) upon you (with every person). Who are noble (honourable) and are (continuously) recording (everything you do and say). They know what you do (and record it so that you cannot deny it on the Day of Judgement)." (Infiṭār 82:10-12)

Allāh (ﷻ) also says:

﴿مَّا يَلْفِظُ مِن قَوْلٍ إِلَّا لَدَيْهِ رَقِيبٌ عَتِيدٌ ۝١٨﴾ [ق الآية ١٨]

"Whenever a word escapes (from a person's mouth), there is a guard ready by him. (An angel immediately records the good or bad speech)." (Qāf 50:18)

Commenting on this verse ʿAbdullāh ibn ʿAbbās (رضي الله عنهما) says:

«يُكْتَبُ كُلُّ مَا تَكَلَّمَ بِهِ مِنْ خَيْرٍ أَوْ شَرٍّ، حَتَّى إِنَّهُ لَيُكْتَبُ قَوْلُهُ أَكَلْتُ، شَرِبْتُ، ذَهَبْتُ جِئْتُ، رَأَيْتُ».

(تفسير ابن كثير)

"He (the angel) writes down every good or evil word that a person says, to such an extent that he even records words like: I ate, I drank, I went, I came, and I saw." (Tafsīr Ibn Kathīr)

Abū Hurairah (ﷺ) reports that the Prophet (ﷺ) said:

«إِنَّ الْعَبْدَ لَيَتَكَلَّمُ بِالْكَلِمَةِ مِنْ رِضْوَانِ اللَّهِ لا يُلْقِي لَهَا بَالاً، يَرْفَعُهُ اللَّهُ بِهَا دَرَجَاتٍ، وَإِنَّ الْعَبْدَ لَيَتَكَلَّمُ بِالْكَلِمَةِ مِنْ سَخَطِ اللَّهِ لا يُلْقِي لَهَا بَالاً، يَهْوِي بِهَا فِي جَهَنَّمَ».

(رواه البخاري)

"A slave (of Allāh) may utter a word which pleases Allāh without giving it much importance, and because of that Allāh will raise him degrees (of reward); and a slave (of Allāh) may utter a word (carelessly) which displeases Allāh without thinking about its gravity and because of that he will be thrown into the hell-fire." (Bukhārī)

ʿAbdullāh ibn Masʿūd (ﷺ) would say:

«وَاللَّهِ الَّذِي لَا إِلَهَ إِلَّا هُوَ، مَا عَلَى ظَهْرِ الْأَرْضِ شَيْءٌ أَحْوَجَ إِلَى طُولِ سِجْنٍ مِنْ لِسَانٍ».

(حلية الأولياء)

"By Allāh, the One other than Whom there is no god, nothing on the earth is more deserving of long imprisonment than one's tongue." (Ḥilyat al-Awliyāʾ)

Abū Bakr (ﷺ) would take hold of his tongue and say:

«إِنَّ هَذَا الَّذِي أَوْرَدَنِي الْمَوَارِدَ».

(حلية الأولياء)

"It is this that has led me to dangerous places." (Ḥilyat al-Awliyā')

A Muslim should also bring oneself to account and strive hard against oneself regarding the thoughts that come into his mind, and the whispers that creep into his heart; for the source of all good and all evil lies in the inner thoughts that come into one's mind. A Muslim should control such thoughts; and if a person welcomes the good ones, feels pleased by them and puts them into practice, then one will be successful and blessed.

Similarly, if a person keeps away Shayṭān's whispers and seeks refuge in Allāh (ﷻ) from them, then he will be saved from perpetrating sins and acts of disobedience to Allāh (ﷻ). On the other hand, if he accepts and obeys Shayṭān's whispers, then Shayṭān will only lead him to sins and prohibited acts.

Allāh (ﷻ) says:

﴿وَإِمَّا يَنزَغَنَّكَ مِنَ ٱلشَّيْطَٰنِ نَزْغٌ فَٱسْتَعِذْ بِٱللَّهِ ۖ إِنَّهُۥ هُوَ ٱلسَّمِيعُ ٱلْعَلِيمُ ﴿٣٦﴾﴾

[فُصِّلَت الآية ٣٦]

"And if any whisper (temptation to do evil) from Shayṭān has to reach you, then seek Allāh's protection. Undoubtedly, He is the All-Hearing (will hear your plea), the All-Knowing (knows exactly how to repel Shayṭān's influence)." (Fuṣṣilat 41:36)

It is for this reason that Allāh (ﷻ) commands us in Sūrah an-Nās to seek refuge in Him from this open enemy.

ʿAbdullāh ibn ʿAbbās (رضي الله عنهما) says:

«إِذَا ذَكَرَ اللَّهَ الْعَبْدُ خَنَسَ مِنْ قَلْبِهِ فَذَهَبَ، وَإِذَا غَفَلَ الْتَقَمَ قَلْبَهُ فَحَدَّثَهُ وَمَنَّاهُ».

(تفسير القرطبي)

"Shayṭān is lying over a man's heart all of the time; if he remembers Allāh, then Shayṭān will withdraw, and if he becomes heedless, then Shayṭān will whisper evil into his heart." (Tafsīr al-Qurṭubī)

Anas ibn Mālik (ﷺ) reports that the Prophet (ﷺ) said:

«إِنَّ الشَّيْطَانَ وَاضِعٌ خَطْمَهُ عَلَى قَلْبِ ابْنِ آدَمَ، فَإِنْ ذَكَرَ اللَّهَ خَنَسَ، وَإِنْ نَسِيَ الْتَقَمَ قَلْبَهُ فَذَلِكَ الْوَسْوَاسُ الْخَنَّاسُ».

(مسند أبي يعلى الموصلي)

"Shayṭān places his snout over the heart of a child of Ādam; if he remembers Allāh, then Shayṭān will withdraw, but if he forgets (Allāh), then he will start to whisper into his heart. This is the meaning of 'the whisperer' and 'the withdrawer.'" (Musnad of Abū Yāʿlā al-Mawṣulī)

In order to guard himself against sins, a Muslim should first pay attention to Shayṭān's whispers and be wary of his attempts to turn him away from the right path. At the same time a Muslim should also monitor his heart.

A live heart is one that is pleased with good deeds and bothered with wrongdoings; and a dead heart is one that does not suffer the pain of sin or does not feel it at all, and it is the heart that does not rejoice over good deeds or acts of obedience to Allāh (ﷻ) and does not give heed to the consequences of one's sins.

The Prophet (ﷺ) has stated:

«تُعْرَضُ الْفِتَنُ عَلَى الْقُلُوبِ كَالْحَصِيرِ عُودًا عُودًا، فَأَيُّ قَلْبٍ أُشْرِبَهَا، نُكِتَ فِيهِ نُكْتَةٌ سَوْدَاءُ، وَأَيُّ قَلْبٍ أَنْكَرَهَا، نُكِتَ فِيهِ نُكْتَةٌ بَيْضَاءُ، حَتَّى تَصِيرَ عَلَى قَلْبَيْنِ، عَلَى أَبْيَضَ مِثْلِ الصَّفَا فَلَا تَضُرُّهُ فِتْنَةٌ مَا دَامَتِ السَّمَاوَاتُ وَالْأَرْضُ، وَالْآخَرُ أَسْوَدُ مُرْبَادًّا كَالْكُوزِ، مُجَخِّيًا لَا يَعْرِفُ مَعْرُوفًا، وَلَا يُنْكِرُ مُنْكَرًا، إِلَّا مَا أُشْرِبَ مِنْ هَوَاهُ».

(رواه مسلم)

> "Trials and temptations will be presented to mens' hearts as a reed mat is woven stick by stick. Any heart which rejects them will be branded by a white mark, while any heart which is impregnated by them will be branded by a black mark. The result is that there will be two types of hearts: a white heart, like a pure stone, which will not be harmed by any trial or temptation so long as the heavens and the earth remain; and a black heart, like a vessel which is turned upside down, not recognizing any good, nor rejecting any evil, but being impregnated with its own desires." (Muslim)

Diseases of the heart weaken it and may even cause its death if a person does not bring oneself to account for their actions. It is better and very important for a person to bring oneself to account for their deeds every day and night, every week, every month, and every year, so that one can learn about and monitor their shortcomings, turn to Allāh (ﷻ) in repentance, and make up for whatever good deeds one may have neglected in the hope that one's endeavours will be accepted, and that they will be granted a good ending.

A believer should have a live heart and deep insight. He shows gratitude for what Allāh (ﷻ) gives him, turns to Him in repentance if he commits a sin, and demonstrates fortitude when he undergoes afflictions. A believer has an admonisher in his heart that wakes him up from his heedlessness and warns him against hazards.

Nawwās ibn Samʿān (رضي الله عنه) narrates that the Prophet (ﷺ) said:

«ضَرَبَ اللَّهُ مَثَلًا صِرَاطًا مُسْتَقِيمًا، وَعَلَى جَنْبَتَيِ الصِّرَاطِ سُورَانِ فِيهِمَا أَبْوَابٌ مُفَتَّحَةٌ، وَعَلَى الْأَبْوَابِ سُتُورٌ مُرْخَاةٌ، وَعَلَى بَابِ الصِّرَاطِ دَاعٍ يَقُولُ: يَا أَيُّهَا النَّاسُ، ادْخُلُوا الصِّرَاطَ جَمِيعًا وَلَا تُعَوِّجُوا، وَدَاعٍ يَدْعُو مِنْ فَوْقِ الصِّرَاطِ، فَإِذَا أَرَادَ الْإِنْسَانُ أَنْ يَفْتَحَ شَيْئًا مِنْ تِلْكَ الْأَبْوَابِ، قَالَ: وَيْحَكَ، لَا تَفْتَحْهُ؛ فَإِنَّكَ إِنْ تَفْتَحْهُ تَلِجْهُ. فَالصِّرَاطُ الْإِسْلَامُ، وَالسُّورَانِ

حُدُودُ اللَّهِ، وَالْأَبْوَابُ الْمُفَتَّحَةُ مَحَارِمُ اللَّهِ، وَذَلِكَ الدَّاعِي عَلَى رَأْسِ الصِّرَاطِ كِتَابُ اللَّهِ، وَالدَّاعِي مِنْ فَوْقِ الصِّرَاطِ وَاعِظُ اللَّهِ فِي قَلْبِ كُلِّ مُسْلِمٍ».

(تفسير ابن كثير)

"Allāh has given a parable about the straight path, and on either side of this path, there are two walls containing doorways. On these doorways, there are curtains that are lowered down, and on the gate of this path there is a caller heralding; 'O people! Come and enter the straight path all together and do not divide.' There is also another caller that heralds from above the path who says (the following) when a person wants to remove the curtain on any of these doors: 'Woe to you! Do not open this door, for if you open it, then you will enter into it.' The (straight) path is Islām, the two walls are Allāh's set limits, the open doors lead to Allāh's prohibitions, the caller on the gate of the path is Allāh's Book (the Qur'ān), and the caller from above the path is Allāh's admonisher which is the heart of every Muslim." (Tafsīr Ibn Kathīr)

Imām Ibn al-Qayyim (رحمه الله) writes

«وَأعلم أَن الخاطرات والوساوس تُؤَدِّي متعلقاتها إِلَى الْفِكر فيأخذها الْفِكر فيؤديها إِلَى التَّذَكُّر فيأخذها الذّكر فيؤديها إِلَى الْإِرَادَة فتأخذها الْإِرَادَة فتؤديها إِلَى الْجُوَارِح وَالْعَمَل فتستحكم فَتَصِير عَادَة فردّها من مبادئها أسهل من قطعهَا بعد قوتها وتمامها».

(كتاب الفوائد)

"You should repulse a (bad) thought. If you do not do so, then it will develop into a desire, therefore you should wage war against it. If you do not do this, then it will become a resolution and firm intention. If you do not repulse it, then it will develop into a deed. If you do not make up for it by doing the opposite thereof [the opposite of that evil deed], it will become a habit, and then it will then be very difficult for you to give it up" (Kitāb al-Fawā'id)

«مبدأ كل علم نَظَرِي وَعمل اخْتِيَارِي هُوَ الخواطر والأفكار فَإِنَّهَا توجب التصورات والتصورات تَدْعُو إِلَى الإرادات والإرادات تَقْتَضِي وُقُوع الْفِعْل وَكَثْرَة تكراره تُعْطِي الْعدة فصلح هَذِه الْمَرَاتِب بصلاح الخواطر والأفكار وفسادها بفسادها».

(كتاب الفوائد)

"You should know that the initial stage of every knowledge that is within your choice is your thoughts and notions. These thoughts and notions lead you into fantasies, and these fantasies lead you towards the will and desire to carry out (those fantasies). These wills and desires demand that the act should be committed, and repeatedly committing these acts will cause them to become a habit. So, the goodness of these stages lies in the goodness of thoughts and notions; and the wickedness of these thoughts lies in the wickedness of thoughts and notions." (Kitāb al-Fawā'id)

CONCLUSION

- Pay attention to your thoughts and do not let them just go by unnoticed. A strong Muslim is one who can control one's inner self as well as one's limbs.
- When a bad thought comes, try and fight it! When a good thought comes, act upon it!
- Be constantly watchful of your mind - like a predator, always ready to pounce on any unwanted thoughts, and attempt to cut off evil from its roots.
- Live consciously with the thought that there is a purpose to life.

- Know that we have been placed in this world to fulfill specific tasks, and we must remain mindful of this mission, and continually strive to fulfill our quest.

اَصْلِحُوْا الْخَلَلْ وَاَخْلِصُوْا النِّيَّةَ

وَقَوِّمُوْا الزَّلَلْ فَإِنَكُمْ مَسْؤُوْلُوْنَ غَدًا عَنِ الْقَوْلِ وَالْعَمَلْ

فَأَمَّا مَنْ ثَقُلَتْ مَوَازِينُهُ فَهُوَ فِي عِيشَةٍ رَاضِيَةٍ

وَأَمَّا مَنْ خَفَّتْ مَوَازِينُهُ فَأُمُّهُ هَاوِيَةٌ

Rectify errors and purify intentions,
Repair wrongdoings for the reason that tomorrow you will be questioned,
About your words and deeds.
So, one whose scales of deeds in the balance will be heavy,
Will be in luxury and delight;
But as for one whose scales of deeds in the balance will be light,
Their abode will be Hāwīyah (a pit in Hell)!

KHUṬBAH 65

Understanding Ikhtilāf in Islāmic Scholastic Traditions

One of the primary reasons for Allāh (ﷻ) sending Prophets (عليهم السلام) was to establish His religion, promote harmony and unity, and to eradicate divisions and differences.

Allāh (ﷻ) says in the Qur'ān:

﴿ شَرَعَ لَكُم مِّنَ ٱلدِّينِ مَا وَصَّىٰ بِهِۦ نُوحًا وَٱلَّذِيٓ أَوۡحَيۡنَآ إِلَيۡكَ وَمَا وَصَّيۡنَا بِهِۦٓ
إِبۡرَٰهِيمَ وَمُوسَىٰ وَعِيسَىٰٓۖ أَنۡ أَقِيمُواْ ٱلدِّينَ وَلَا تَتَفَرَّقُواْ فِيهِۚ ﴿١٣﴾ ﴾ [الشورى الآية ١٣]

"He (Allāh) has ordained (determined) for you the same religion that He ordained for Nūḥ (عليه السلام) as well as what He ordained (prescribed) for Ibrāhīm, Mūsā and 'Īsā (عليهم السلام). (We commanded these Prophets and their followers saying:) 'Establish the religion and do not be divided.'" (Shūrā' 42:13)

When the final Prophet (ﷺ) first set foot in Madīnah, a top priority of his mission was to build a *masjid* and establish fraternity among the *Muhājirīn* and the *Anṣār*. People consequently shifted from the hostility of pre-Islāmic state of *Jāhilīyyah* to the bond and friendship of Islām. As a result, strangers became brothers and friends of one another, and they even began sharing their homes and wealth.

Allāh (ﷻ) says about them in the Qur'ān:

﴿وَٱلَّذِينَ تَبَوَّءُو ٱلدَّارَ وَٱلْإِيمَٰنَ مِن قَبْلِهِمْ يُحِبُّونَ مَنْ هَاجَرَ إِلَيْهِمْ وَلَا يَجِدُونَ فِي صُدُورِهِمْ حَاجَةً مِّمَّآ أُوتُوا۟ وَيُؤْثِرُونَ عَلَىٰٓ أَنفُسِهِمْ وَلَوْ كَانَ بِهِمْ خَصَاصَةٌ ۚ وَمَن يُوقَ شُحَّ نَفْسِهِۦ فَأُو۟لَٰٓئِكَ هُمُ ٱلْمُفْلِحُونَ ۝٩﴾ [الحشر الآية ٩]

"And those (the *Anṣār*) who (had) adopted the place (Madīnah) as their home before them (before the *Muhājirīn*) and (had adopted) *īmān*. They (the *Anṣār*) love those who migrate to them (the *Muhājirīn*), and find no want (jealousy or envy) in their hearts for what they (the *Muhājirīn*) are given. They (the *Anṣār*) prefer (others) above themselves (they prefer to give to others) even though they are themselves in need (of the things which they give). (Like the *Anṣār*) Those who are saved (protected) from the miserliness (and greed) of the soul are really the successful ones (those who will attain salvation)." (Ḥashr 59:9)

Unfortunately, our era is one in which the trials of materialism have grown. It is also a time where many people have allowed their egos to go astray, and they see the wrong things which they do to be good and correct. There are even instances in which this type of mindset has resulted in some remaining stuck on error ridden opinions that contradict reasoning and logic. In addition, a certain scholar might hold a legitimate difference of opinion regarding matters in which individual scholarly interpretation and reasoning can be exercised. In such instances of contention and disagreement, each person involved says that only he is unquestionably right, allegiances are then formed because of views, and disavowals are made because of such perspectives.

In dealing with such situations, the brilliance of this religion shines through, and its remarkable distinguishing features are manifested. Islām's directives and rulings are infused with care and kindness. They seek to nurture harmony, unity, brotherhood, and compassion. These are crucial ethical bonds between individuals which need to be fostered. Islām's teachings of moderation encourage them, and its rulings and objectives emphasize them. That holds true even in cases that differ, and in fact Islām's teachings seek to limit channels leading to contention and disunity.

Allāh (ﷻ) says in the Qur'ān:

﴿وَٱعْتَصِمُوا۟ بِحَبْلِ ٱللَّهِ جَمِيعًا وَلَا تَفَرَّقُوا۟ ۚ ﴿١٠٣﴾﴾ [آل عِمْرَان الآية ١٠٣]

"Hold fast onto the rope of Allāh (Islām and particularly the Qur'ān as understood by the sayings of the Prophet (ﷺ) and the pious predecessors) all of you together, and do not separate (because Allāh's mercy lies in unity)." (Āle ʿImrān 3:103)

There are times when differing may be praiseworthy, and that is because it is part of the universal laws which Allāh (ﷻ) decrees.

Allāh (ﷻ) says in the Qur'ān.

﴿وَلَوْ شَآءَ رَبُّكَ لَجَعَلَ ٱلنَّاسَ أُمَّةً وَٰحِدَةً ۖ وَلَا يَزَالُونَ مُخْتَلِفِينَ ﴿١١٨﴾ إِلَّا مَن رَّحِمَ رَبُّكَ ۚ
وَلِذَٰلِكَ خَلَقَهُمْ ۗ ﴿١١٩﴾﴾ [هُود من الآية ١١٨ الى الآية ١١٩]

"And had your Lord willed, He would have made all of the people a single community. But they will continue in their differences, except those whom your Lord has blessed with mercy, and for that, He has created them (humans are meant to differ in this world)." (Hūd 11:118-119)

Ḥasan al-Baṣrī (رحمه الله) commenting on this verse says:

«﴿وَلِذَٰلِكَ خَلَقَهُمْ ۗ ﴿١١٩﴾﴾ [هُود الآية ١١٩] قَالَ: لِلْاخْتِلَافِ».

(تفسير ابن كثير)

"'And for that, He has created them' (Quran 11:119) means that Allāh created people with the tendency to differ." (Tafsīr Ibn Kathīr)

However, differing at times can also be unproductive because it can lead to contention, disputes, and unrest.

Scholars have pointed out that:

«مِنَ الْفَسَادِ مَا يُسَبِّبُهُ: التَّفَرُّقُ وَالِاخْتِلَافُ الْمُخَالِفُ لِلِاجْتِمَاعِ والائتلاف حَتَّى يَصِيرَ بَعْضُهُمْ يُبْغِضُ بَعْضًا وَيُعَادِيهِ وَيُحِبُّ بَعْضًا وَيُوَالِيهِ عَلَى غَيْرِ ذَاتِ اللَّهِ وَحَتَّى يُفْضِيَ الْأَمْرُ بِبَعْضِهِمْ إلَى الطَّعْنِ وَاللَّعْنِ وَالْهَمْزِ وَاللَّمْزِ. وَبِبَعْضِهِمْ إلَى الِاقْتِتَالِ بِالْأَيْدِي وَالسِّلَاحِ وَبِبَعْضِهِمْ إلَى الْمُهَاجَرَةِ وَالْمُقَاطَعَةِ حَتَّى لَا يُصَلِّيَ بَعْضُهُمْ خَلْفَ بَعْضٍ وَهَذَا كُلُّهُ مِنْ أَعْظَمِ الْأُمُورِ الَّتِي حَرَّمَهَا اللَّهُ وَرَسُولُهُ ﷺ».

(مجموع الفتاوى)

One facet of unrest which appears is what emanates from differences and divisions which oppose consensus and unity. This can lead to people renouncing one another and forming allegiances for reasons other than obeying Allāh. That may even escalate to some people belittling others, reviling them, and mocking them; some may even attack and fight against others, while some may boycott others to the extent that they will not pray behind them. All of these are among the gravest of matters which are prohibited by Allāh and His Messenger (ﷺ). (Majmūʿ al-Fatāwā)

Imām Ibn al-Qayyim (رحمه الله) has stated:

«وقوع الاختلاف بين الناس أمر ضروري لا بد منه؛ لتفاوت إرادتهم وأفهامهم وقدرات إدراكهم، ولكن المذموم بغي بعضهم على بعض وعدوانه، وإلا إذا كان الاختلاف على وجه لا يؤدي إلى التباين والتحزب، وكل من المختلفين قصده طاعة الله ورسوله، لم يضر ذلك الاختلاف».

(الصواعق المرسلة)

"Differences between people are inevitable due to the variations in their motives, understandings, and strength of comprehension. What is blameworthy though is when people transgress against others as a result of that and become hostile. However, when differences occur but do not produce divisions and bigotry, and each party involved aims to obey Allāh and His Messenger (ﷺ), then there is no harm in such differences." (Al-Ṣawāʿiq al-Mursalah)

It should also be kept in mind that when a person examines the differences which occur among scholars of a Muslim community, he must not disregard to distinguish between justifiable differences in matters which are open to individual reasoning, versus unjustifiable differences in foundational matters which no Muslim should oppose or be ignorant of.

The texts of Islām can be classified into four categories:

ما هو قطعيُّ الثبوتِ قطعيُّ الدلالةِ

1. Those texts whose authenticity and meanings are unequivocally established.

This category is not open to differences, interpretation, or independent reasoning.

ما هو قطعيُّ الثبوتِ ظنيُّ الدلالةِ

2. Those texts whose authenticity is established, but their meanings require analysis.

ما هو ظنيُّ الثبوتِ ظنيُّ الدلالةِ

3. Those texts whose authenticity and meanings require analysis.

ما هو ظنيُّ الثبوتِ قطعيُّ الدلالةِ

4. Those texts whose authenticity require analysis, but their meanings are established.

These three categories are open to legitimate independent scholarly interpretations and reasoning. They are the realm in which variances and differences can occur, but within the framework of Islāmic principles.

Keeping this in mind the aforementioned principles can become a means to unite rather than divide, and bring together rather than separate, *Inshā' Allāh.*

7 POINTS TO CONSIDER FOR UNDERSTANDING SCHOLARLY DIFFERENCES

[1] Maintaining a sound intention comes at the head of these principles. Anyone who examines differences between the scholars must ensure that he intends to arrive at the truth, as well as amend any mistakes while clarifying what is correct; not ridicule divergent opinions or make himself prominent. If someone is unable to maintain the foregoing intention, then he should restrain himself from going further, which will contribute to the well-being of himself and the community in general, and so as to not be restrictive concerning matters in which differences are acceptable.

[2] The second principle is training oneself to return to the truth. Returning to the truth is always better than persisting in falsehood.

A man once came to ʿAbdullah ibn Masʿūd (ﷺ) and said:

«عَلِّمْنِي كَلِمَاتٍ جَوَامِعَ نَوَافِعَ».

"Give me some comprehensive words of advice."

Among the things that ʿAbdullah ibn Masʿūd (ﷺ) told him were:

«مَنْ جَاءَكَ بِالْحَقِّ فَاقْبَلْ مِنْهُ، وَإِنْ كَانَ بَعِيدًا بَغِيضًا، وَمَنْ جَاءَكَ بِالْبَاطِلِ فَارْدُدْ عَلَيْهِ وَإِنْ كَانَ حَبِيبًا قَرِيبًا».

(حلية الأولياء)

"Whenever a person brings the truth to you, accept it from him even if he is someone distant, or someone who you dislike; and whenever someone brings falsehood to you, do not accept it even if he is someone close, or a person who you love." (Ḥilyat al-Awliyāʾ")

Imām Ibn al-Qayyim (ﷺ) has stated:

«فَعَلَى الْمُسْلِمِ أَنْ يَتَّبِعَ هَدْيَ النَّبِيِّ ﷺ فِي قَبُولِ الْحَقِّ مِمَّنْ جَاءَ بِهِ مِنْ وَلِيٍّ وَعَدُوٍّ وَحَبِيبٍ وَبَغِيضٍ وَبَرٍّ وَفَاجِرٍ، وَيَرُدُّ الْبَاطِلَ عَلَى مَنْ قَالَهُ كَائِنًا مَنْ كَانَ».

(إعلام الموقعين عن رب العالمين)

"It is necessary for a Muslim to follow the guidance of the Prophet (ﷺ) as it relates to accepting the truth regardless of who it comes from – whether friend or foe, loved or despised, righteous or impious; and also to reject falsehood regardless of who it comes from." (Iʿlām al-Muwaqqiʿīn ʿan Rabb al-ʿĀlamīn)

[3] The third principle is that differences should be dealt with while bearing in mind that their occurrences are something to be expected from the very nature of human beings.

Imām Shāṭbī (ﷺ) has commented that:

«فإن الله جَلَّ جَلَالُهُ حكَمَ بحكمته أن تكون فروعُ هذه الملة قابلةً للأنظار، ومجالاً للظنون، والخطأُ في الاجتهاد واردٌ، والأخذُ بالعذر معتَبَرٌ بشرطه عند أهل السُّنَّةِ والجماعةِ، وأهل الحِجَى تضطغن في الرأي عقولهم ولا تضطغن صدورهم».

(كتاب الاعتصام)

"Based on the wisdom of Allāh, the Most Exalted, He decreed that the subsidiary matters of this religion be open to different perspectives and be a realm that accepts interpretation and reasoning. It is possible for mistakes to happen when scholars exercise independent analysis and reasoning, and the Ahl al-Sunnah wa al-Jamāʿah holds that legitimate reasonings are to be accepted in such cases. The minds of intellectuals may be inclining strongly towards certain viewpoints; however, their hearts must not be." (Kitāb al-Iʿtiṣām)

Scholars have added that:

«وَكَانُوا يَتَنَاظَرُونَ فِي الْمَسْأَلَةِ مُنَاظَرَةَ مُشَاوَرَةٍ وَمُنَاصَحَةٍ وَرُبَّمَا اخْتَلَفَ قَوْلُهُمْ فِي الْمَسْأَلَةِ الْعِلْمِيَّةِ وَالْعَمَلِيَّةِ مَعَ بَقَاءِ الْأُلْفَةِ وَالْعِصْمَةِ وَأُخُوَّةِ الدِّينِ، وَلَوْ كَانَ كُلَّمَا اخْتَلَفَ مُسْلِمَانِ فِي شَيْءٍ تَهَاجَرَا لَمْ يَبْقَ بَيْنَ الْمُسْلِمِينَ عِصْمَةٌ وَلَا أُخُوَّةٌ».

(مجموع الفتاوى)

"Scholars of the past would examine and discuss both theoretical and practical issues among themselves while maintaining harmony, unity, and brotherhood taught by the religion. If every two Muslims were to boycott each other whenever any differences arise, then there would not remain any unity or brotherhood among Muslims as a whole." (Majmūʿ al-Fatāwā)

[4] The fourth principle is giving due consideration to pertinent circumstances considering how far the Islāmic community has extended, and how diverse its peoples have become; differences will surely arise in how issues are examined and how rulings are deduced. This will definitely lead to differences in the way that many of Islām's texts are interpreted and understood, as well as differences in determining the rulings pertaining to significant matters.

Imām Ibn al-Qayyim (ﷺ) has stated:

«فَإِنَّ الْفَتْوَى تَتَغَيَّرُ بِتَغَيُّرِ الزَّمَانِ وَالْمَكَانِ وَالْعَوَائِدِ وَالْأَحْوَالِ».

(إعلام الموقعين عن رب العالمين)

"*Fatwā* (the response given to questions about religious matters) can vary based on variations in times, places, situations, environments, and circumstances." (Iʿlām al-Muwaqqiʿīn ʿan Rabb al-ʿĀlamīn)

[5] The fifth principle is dealing fairly with those who hold an opposing view.

Allāh (ﷻ), who is perfect in every way, states:

﴿يَـٰٓأَيُّهَا ٱلَّذِينَ ءَامَنُوا۟ كُونُوا۟ قَوَّٰمِينَ لِلَّهِ شُهَدَآءَ بِٱلْقِسْطِ ۖ وَلَا يَجْرِمَنَّكُمْ شَنَـَٔانُ قَوْمٍ عَلَىٰٓ أَلَّا تَعْدِلُوا۟ ۚ ٱعْدِلُوا۟ هُوَ أَقْرَبُ لِلتَّقْوَىٰ ۖ وَٱتَّقُوا۟ ٱللَّهَ ۚ إِنَّ ٱللَّهَ خَبِيرٌۢ بِمَا تَعْمَلُونَ ٨﴾

[المائدة الآية ٨]

"O you who believe, always uphold the truth, sincerely seeking to please Allāh, and remain fair when giving testimony. Do not let your dislike for a people cause you to be unfair to them. Rather, you must deal with them fairly. That is nearest to observing *taqwā* (God consciousness); and you must continue to observe *taqwā* of Allāh. Indeed, Allāh is completely acquainted with everything that you do." (Mā'idah 5:8)

A poet says:

وَلَمْ تَزَلْ قِلَّةُ الإِنْصَافِ قَاطِعَةً ۞ بَيْنَ الرِّجَالِ وَلَوْ كَانُوا ذَوِي رَحِمِ

وَتَعَرَّ مِنْ ثَوبَيْنِ مَنْ يَلْبَسْهُمَا ۞ يَلْقَى الرَّدَى بِمَذَمَّةٍ وَهَوانِ

ثَوبٍ مِنَ الْجَهْلِ الْمُرَكَّبِ فَوقَهُ ۞ ثَوْبُ التَّعَصُّبِ بِئْسَتِ الثَّوبَانِ

وَتَحَلَّ بِالإِنْصَافِ أَفْخَرَ حُلَّةٍ ۞ زِينَتْ بِهَا الأَعْطَافُ وَالْكَتِفَانِ

"Lacking fairness is a trait that will continue to separate between people,
even when they share the bond of kinship.
There are two garments that you must remove from yourself, since
anyone dressed in them will end up blameworthy and disgraced.
One is that of compounded ignorance, and the other is that of prejudice.
Those two are awful garments to wear.
Instead, you must adorn yourself with fairness.
That is the finest of garments which a person can clothe oneself with."

Imām al-Dhahabī (رحمه الله) has mentioned that Yūnus al-Ṣadafī (رحمه الله) said:

«مَا رَأَيْتُ أَعْقَلَ مِنَ الشَّافِعِيِّ، نَاظَرْتُهُ يَوْماً فِي مَسْأَلَةٍ، ثُمَّ افْتَرَقْنَا، وَلَقِيَنِي، فَأَخَذَ بِيَدِي، ثُمَّ قَالَ: يَا أَبَا مُوْسَى، أَلاَ يَسْتَقِيمُ أَنْ نَكُوْنَ إِخْوَاناً وَإِنْ لَمْ نَتَّفِقْ فِي مَسْأَلَةٍ ؟!».

(سير أعلام النبلاء)

"I never encountered anyone more intelligent than al-Shāfi'ī. I debated with him one day about a certain matter and then we parted. He later met me and said: 'O Abā Mūsā, is it not alright for us to still remain brothers, even if we do not agree about a certain issue?'" (Siyar A'lām al-Nubalā')

This is the conduct to be observed when differences occur, as it fosters love and harmony. This is the way that the people of *īmān* maintain their conduct when dealing with such matters.

[6] The sixth principle is that no condemnation can be made concerning issues open to independent scholarly interpretation and reasoning - except when an authentic text of Islām proves otherwise.

Scholars have mentioned that:

«مَسَائِلُ الاِجْتِهَادِ مَنْ عَمِلَ فِيهَا بِقَوْلِ بَعْضِ الْعُلَمَاءِ لَمْ يُنْكَرْ عَلَيْهِ وَلَمْ يُهْجَرْ وَمَنْ عَمِلَ بِأَحَدِ الْقَوْلَيْنِ لَمْ يُنْكَرْ عَلَيْهِ وَإِذَا كَانَ فِي الْمَسْأَلَةِ قَوْلَانِ: فَإِنْ كَانَ الْإِنْسَانُ يَظْهَرُ لَهُ رُجْحَانُ أَحَدِ الْقَوْلَيْنِ عَمِلَ بِهِ وَإِلَّا قَلَّدَ بَعْضَ الْعُلَمَاءِ الَّذِينَ يُعْتَمَدُ عَلَيْهِمْ فِي بَيَانِ أَرْجَحِ الْقَوْلَيْنِ».

(مجموع الفتاوى)

"When it comes to such issues, if someone acts according to a view held by some of the scholars, then he should not be censored or boycotted. If someone acts according to one of two legitimate views about a certain issue, then he should not be censured. When there are two scholarly views about a given issue and one of them appears to an individual to be more accurate, then he should act according to that. Otherwise, he should follow what is held by the scholars who are relied upon for clarifying which of the two views is more accurate." (Majmūʿ al-Fatāwā)

They have further added:

«وَأَمَّا إِذَا لَمْ يَكُنْ فِي الْمَسْأَلَةِ سُنَّةٌ وَلَا إِجْمَاعٌ وَلِلِاجْتِهَادِ فِيهَا مَسَاغٌ لَمْ تُنْكَرْ عَلَى مَنْ عَمِلَ بِهَا مُجْتَهِدًا أَوْ مُقَلِّدًا».

(الفتاوى الكبرى)

"When there is nothing established by the *sunnah* or scholarly consensus about a given issue, and there is room for independent scholarly interpretation and reasoning, then a person should not be censured for acting in compliance with the view which he holds as correct, or if he follows a view held by reliable scholars." (Al-Fatāwā al-Kubrā)

[7] The seventh principle is to beware of praising oneself. When differing views takes place regarding any given matter, one should not have the belief that what he does is unmistakably correct, and that anyone with a different view is completely wrong. Who is there that has never been wrong, and who is there that will always be right?

Allāh (ﷻ) says:

﴿فَلَا تُزَكُّوٓاْ أَنفُسَكُمۡۖ هُوَ أَعۡلَمُ بِمَنِ ٱتَّقَىٰٓ ۝٣٢﴾ [النّجم الآية ٣٢]

"So do not ascribe purity (piety) to yourselves. He (meaning Allāh) knows best who is the most pious (whose level of *taqwā* is the highest)." (Najm 53:32)

After Muslims have been affected by so much division, splitting, and disputation, has the time not come for them to take heed of Islām's pristine teachings?

Differences about subsidiary issues must not be allowed to turn into a cause for disputes, divisions, accusations, or aspersions about the motives of others.

Today, we are in dire need of uniting the communities, bringing people's hearts closer, maintaining togetherness, and referring all of our issues back to the Book of Allāh (ﷻ), to the *sunnah* of His Prophet (ﷺ), and to the scholars who try to do what is most suitable and best for the Muslim community.

Allāh (ﷻ) says:

﴿وَإِذَا جَآءَهُمۡ أَمۡرٞ مِّنَ ٱلۡأَمۡنِ أَوِ ٱلۡخَوۡفِ أَذَاعُواْ بِهِۦۖ وَلَوۡ رَدُّوهُ إِلَى ٱلرَّسُولِ وَإِلَىٰٓ أُوْلِي ٱلۡأَمۡرِ مِنۡهُمۡ لَعَلِمَهُ ٱلَّذِينَ يَسۡتَنۢبِطُونَهُۥ مِنۡهُمۡۗ وَلَوۡلَا فَضۡلُ ٱللَّهِ عَلَيۡكُمۡ وَرَحۡمَتُهُۥ لَٱتَّبَعۡتُمُ ٱلشَّيۡطَٰنَ إِلَّا قَلِيلٗا ﴿٨٣﴾﴾ [النِّسَاء الآية ٨٣]

"And when any matter of safety or fear comes to them, they broadcast it. If they had referred the matter to the Messenger and those of them who have understanding, then it would surely be known to those of them who have insight. And had it not been for Allāh granting you His favour and mercy, you would have followed Shayṭān, except for a very few (of the people among you)." (Nisā' 4:83)

NOTE: In this verse, Allāh (ﷻ) advises the Muslims to refer information to the people of understanding. They will delve into the depths of the matter.

The word *'Yastambiṭūna'* (translated above as 'those who have insight') literally refers to extracting water from the depths of the earth. In this context, it refers to those people who possess that extra special ability to delve into matters and extract the truth.

Allāmah Baghawī (رحمه الله) writes in *Ma'ālimut Tanzīl* (vol 1, pg. 456) that this verse alludes to the permissibility of analogical deduction (*qiyās*).[14]

Certain laws and injunctions may be derived directly from a verse or a narration. However, others need to be extracted by delving into the

---

[14] The Arabic text of this is as follows:

وَفِي الْآيَةِ دَلِيلٌ عَلَى جَوَازِ الْقِيَاسِ، فَإِنَّ مِنَ الْعِلْمِ مَا يُدْرَكُ بِالتِّلَاوَةِ وَالرِّوَايَةِ وَهُوَ النَّصُّ، وَمِنْهُ مَا يُدْرَكُ بِالِاسْتِنْبَاطِ وَهُوَ الْقِيَاسُ عَلَى الْمَعَانِي الْمُودَعَةِ فِي النُّصُوصِ.

texts and extracting a law based on one's knowledge of the religion. This is what is meant by *'qiyās.'* This will of course, not be permissible when a law is directly obtainable from the religious texts.

When a ruling is required on an issue that is not discussed specifically in the Qur'ān and *sunnah*, then it will then be necessary to resort to *qiyās*. This was practised by the *'A'immah Mujtahidīn'* and is still practicable today by those who have in-depth knowledge about the necessary sciences.

If it is practised in today's times, then reference must also be made to the rulings of the previous scholars (*ʿulemā*) in similar situations.

CONCLUSION

- The unity of hearts and continuity of bonds cannot be obtained without yearning for it, resilience, humbleness and condescendence, i.e., voluntary descent from one's rank or dignity in dealings with an inferior.
- Unity and uniformity among Muslims are essential at all times; but we are in dire need of it now more than ever before.
- Nothing is more detrimental to uniformity and harmony than disunity and division of the hearts.
- The Prophet (ﷺ) was very keen on preserving the unity of the community, its uniformity, the keeping of its social build-up, and getting-together until his last breath.
- Compassionate and kind as he was, the Prophet (ﷺ) was harsh on anyone who wanted to undermine the unity of the community, or revive the slogans of *Jāhilīyyah* because the Prophet (ﷺ) knew that once the fire of discord, dissent, division, and disunity is ignited, it would be very difficult to put it out.
- No one has the right to make disagreements a cause for division and hatred. The Prophet (ﷺ) warned us against this.
- The unity of opinion demands us to forsake our personal and worldly gains.

- If we would really like to be united, then we need to recognize the multiplicity and diversity of opinions, and accommodate and tolerate them within the bounds of our blessed *Sharīʿah.*

إن التعاوُن قوَّةٌ علويَّةٌ ۞ تبنِي الرجالَ وتُبدِعُ الأشياءَ

بذلَ الجهودَ الصالِحاتِ صحابةٌ ۞ لا يسألون عن الجهودِ جزاءً

صحِبُوا رسولَ الله لا يألُونَه ۞ حبًّا وصِدقَ مودَّةٍ ووفاءً

Collaboration is a strong force,
Which builds men and produces ground-breaking developments.
The companions selflessly expended much effort,
And did not ask for anything in return.
They accompanied the Messenger of Allāh,
And did not withhold any of their love, honesty, or loyalty.

KHUṬBAH 66

When Opportunity Knocks

Allāh (ﷻ) is the One who has created humans and encouraged them to make beneficial use of the earth and develop it.

Allāh (ﷻ) says in the Qur'ān:

﴿هُوَ أَنشَأَكُم مِّنَ ٱلْأَرْضِ وَٱسْتَعْمَرَكُمْ فِيهَا ٦١﴾ [هود الآية ٦١]

> "He is the One who created you from the earth and enabled you to settle (prosper) upon it (and populate it)." (Hūd 11:61)

The populating and prospering referred to in this verse, encompasses all of that which is beneficial for Allāh's (ﷻ) creations and their lands, including agriculture, manufacturing, construction, and having means of safety.

Allāh (ﷻ) gave His servants everything that they need to develop His earth, and He granted them countless apparent and inconspicuous blessings, and He provided them with opportunities to attain success.

Thus, an individual who is truly successful is the one who is keen to take advantage of these blessings and opportunities in order to benefit oneself, and develop and uplift one's society and community.

A few definitions of opportunity are:

- A set of circumstances that makes it possible to do something;
- An occasion or situation that makes it possible to do something that you want to do or have to do, or the possibility of doing something;
- A chance for advancement, progress or profit;
- A situation or condition favourable for the attainment of a goal;

- A good position, chance, or prospect, for advancement or success;
- A chance to do something, or an occasion when it is easy for you to perform an action.

Opportunities may come in various forms, such as drawing nearer to Allāh (ﷻ) by performing certain prescribed acts of worship, performing acts of benevolence whose benefit extends to others, participating in developing one's nation, or using one's influence or position to benefit one's community or society.

A person of high aspirations makes opportunities from what one has been granted. He does not wait for opportunities to come knocking at his door, rather he takes the initiative to seize them, and this applies to whether they are related to this world or the hereafter.

Abū Nuʿaym al-Aṣbahānī (ﷺ) in his *Ḥilyat al-Awliyā'* has documented a narration from ʿAbdullāh ibn Masʿūd (ﷺ) in which he said:

«إِنِّي لَأَمْقُتُ الرَّجُلَ أَنْ أَرَاهُ، فَارِغًا، لَيْسَ فِي شَيْءٍ مِنْ عَمَلِ الدُّنْيَا، وَلَا عَمَلِ الْآخِرَةِ».

(حلية الأولياء)

"I detest seeing a person sitting idle without being engaged in a task of this world or the hereafter." (Ḥilyat al-Awliyā')

Furthermore, Allāh (ﷻ) praises the Prophets and Messengers (ﷺ) in the Qur'ān by saying:

﴿إِنَّهُمْ كَانُوا۟ يُسَـٰرِعُونَ فِى ٱلْخَيْرَٰتِ وَيَدْعُونَنَا رَغَبًا وَرَهَبًا ۖ وَكَانُوا۟ لَنَا خَـٰشِعِينَ ۝٩٠﴾

[الأنبياء الآية ٩٠]

"Indeed, they hastened to perform righteous deeds, they supplicated to Us in hope and fear, and they were humble to Us." (Anbiyā' 21:90)

This means that they took the initiatives to do good things, and did not neglect any opportunity to pursue whatever virtue they could attain.

One instance of this was when the heart of Prophet Mūsā (عليه السلام) became tranquil after Allāh (ﷻ) spoke to him, and knowing that Allāh (ﷻ) is the Originator of all causes, Prophet Mūsā (عليه السلام) seized the opportunity to supplicate.

قَالَ رَبِّ ٱشْرَحْ لِى صَدْرِى ﴿٢٥﴾ وَيَسِّرْ لِىٓ أَمْرِى ﴿٢٦﴾ وَٱحْلُلْ عُقْدَةً مِّن لِّسَانِى ﴿٢٧﴾ يَفْقَهُوا۟ قَوْلِى ﴿٢٨﴾ وَٱجْعَل لِّى وَزِيرًا مِّنْ أَهْلِى ﴿٢٩﴾ هَٰرُونَ أَخِى ﴿٣٠﴾ ٱشْدُدْ بِهِۦٓ أَزْرِى ﴿٣١﴾ وَأَشْرِكْهُ فِىٓ أَمْرِى ﴿٣٢﴾ كَىْ نُسَبِّحَكَ كَثِيرًا ﴿٣٣﴾ وَنَذْكُرَكَ كَثِيرًا ﴿٣٤﴾ إِنَّكَ كُنتَ بِنَا بَصِيرًا ﴿٣٥﴾﴾ [طه من الآية ٢٤ الى الآية ٣٥]

"He (Mūsā) said: 'O my Lord! Expand (broaden) my chest (to be able to bear Your message and to have the courage to propagate it). Make my task (of propagation) easy, and untie the knot (any unclear speech that may come) on my tongue (during the heat of the moment) so that they (the people I speak to) may understand my speech. Appoint for me an assistant (helper) from my family. (Namely) my brother Hārūn. Strengthen me with him (by my side); and make him a partner to my task (of propagation) so that we may (together) glorify You abundantly and remember You in abundance (because it is easier to achieve something when the responsibility is shared). Undoubtedly You are Ever-Watchful over us (over our external and internal conditions).'" (Ṭāhā 20:25–35)

Then came the response from Allāh (ﷻ):

﴿قَالَ قَدْ أُوتِيتَ سُؤْلَكَ يَٰمُوسَىٰ ﴿٣٦﴾﴾ [طه الآية ٣٦]

"He (Allāh) said: 'You have been granted all that you request, O Mūsā.'" (Ṭāhā 20:36)

A second instance was when Prophet Zakarīyya (ﷺ) entered the chamber where Maryam (ﷺ) used to worship Allāh (ﷻ). She was secluded, not engaged in any sort of trade or work, and had no source of earnings.

However, every time Prophet Zakarīyya (ﷺ) entered her place of worship, he found food by her, including fruit that was not in season and so he asked her:

﴿قَالَ يَٰمَرۡيَمُ أَنَّىٰ لَكِ هَٰذَاۖ قَالَتۡ هُوَ مِنۡ عِندِ ٱللَّهِۖ إِنَّ ٱللَّهَ يَرۡزُقُ مَن يَشَآءُ بِغَيۡرِ حِسَابٍ ٣٧﴾ [آل عِمْرَان الآية ٣٧]

"He said: 'O Maryam, from where did you get this from?' She replied: 'It is from Allāh. Allāh provides for whomsoever He pleases without count' (without any limit, in a manner that is beyond one's comprehension and imagination)." (Āle 'Imrān 3:37)

After witnessing such manifestations of Allāh's (ﷻ) mercy and bounty, Zakarīyya (ﷺ) implored Allāh (ﷻ) to grant him a righteous offspring. That was because he recognized that the One who provided for Maryam (ﷺ) without any material means was completely able to grant an elderly man an offspring. The Qur'ān continues:

﴿هُنَالِكَ دَعَا زَكَرِيَّا رَبَّهُۥۖ قَالَ رَبِّ هَبۡ لِي مِن لَّدُنكَ ذُرِّيَّةٗ طَيِّبَةًۖ إِنَّكَ سَمِيعُ ٱلدُّعَآءِ ٣٨ فَنَادَتۡهُ ٱلۡمَلَٰٓئِكَةُ وَهُوَ قَآئِمٞ يُصَلِّي فِي ٱلۡمِحۡرَابِ أَنَّ ٱللَّهَ يُبَشِّرُكَ بِيَحۡيَىٰ مُصَدِّقَۢا بِكَلِمَةٖ مِّنَ ٱللَّهِ وَسَيِّدٗا وَحَصُورٗا وَنَبِيّٗا مِّنَ ٱلصَّٰلِحِينَ ٣٩﴾ [آل عِمْرَان من الآية ٣٨ الى الآية ٣٩]

"At this point (when it occurred to him that just as Allāh can provide Maryam with fruit, even those that are out of season, He can grant a child to Zakarīyya and his wife even though they had passed the age of bearing children), Zakarīyya prayed to his Lord saying: 'My Lord, grant me pure (pious) children

> from Yourself (by Your grace). Without a doubt, You hear all prayers (and accept them).' So the angels (Jibrāʾīl (ﷺ)) called to him while he stood praying in the chamber (the place where he worshipped Allāh): 'Allāh gives you the good news of Yaḥyā who shall confirm the word from Allāh [will confirm the Prophethood of ʿIsā (ﷺ) and (who shall be) a guide, chaste (completely without carnal passions)], and a Prophet from among the righteous.'" (Āle ʿImrān 3:38-39)

A remarkable third instance was when Prophet Sulaymān (ﷺ) felt remorse about letting some well-trained horses of the highest breed preoccupy him from remembering his Lord, and from performing the evening prayer. He sought nearness to Allāh (ﷻ) by way of the very things that had preoccupied him.[15]

Prophet Sulaymān (ﷺ) instructed that they all be sacrificed, and then he gave their meat to the needy; and he seized the opportunity to repent, ask for Allāh's (ﷻ) forgiveness, and seek His mercy.[16]

﴿قَالَ رَبِّ ٱغْفِرْ لِى وَهَبْ لِى مُلْكًا لَّا يَنۢبَغِى لِأَحَدٍ مِّنۢ بَعْدِىٓ ۖ إِنَّكَ أَنتَ ٱلْوَهَّابُ ۝٣٥﴾

[ص الآية ٣٥]

> "He said: 'My Lord, forgive me, and bestow upon me a kingdom that will not belong to anyone else after me. Indeed, You (alone) are the Bestower.'" (Ṣād 38:35)

Allāh (ﷻ) then responded and granted him something even better than what he chose to forego.

---

[15] The Arabic text of this is as follows:

كَانَتِ الْخَيْلُ الَّتِي شَغَلَتْ سُلَيْمَانَ، عَلَيْهِ الصَّلَاةُ وَالسَّلَامُ عِشْرِينَ أَلْفَ فَرَسٍ، فَعَقَرَهَا وَهَذَا أَشْبَهُ وَاللَّهُ أَعْلَمُ.

(تفسير ابن كثير)

[16] The Arabic text of this is as follows:

قَالَ الْحَسَنُ الْبَصْرِيُّ. قَالَ: لَا وَاللَّهِ لَا تَشْغَلِينِي عَنْ عِبَادَةِ رَبِّي آخِرَ مَا عَلَيْكِ. ثُمَّ أَمَرَ بِهَا فَعُقِرَتْ.

(تفسير ابن كثير)

Allāh (ﷻ) says:

﴿فَسَخَّرْنَا لَهُ ٱلرِّيحَ تَجْرِى بِأَمْرِهِۦ رُخَآءً حَيْثُ أَصَابَ ۝٣٦ وَٱلشَّيَـٰطِينَ كُلَّ بَنَّآءٍ وَغَوَّاصٍ ۝٣٧ وَءَاخَرِينَ مُقَرَّنِينَ فِى ٱلْأَصْفَادِ ۝٣٨ هَـٰذَا عَطَآؤُنَا فَٱمْنُنْ أَوْ أَمْسِكْ بِغَيْرِ حِسَابٍ ۝٣٩﴾ [ص من الآية ٣٦ الى الآية ٣٩]

"So (in response to his supplication) We placed (subjected) the wind at his service, which would blow gently by his command (transporting him) wherever he wished to go; and (We also placed) the Shayāṭīn (at his service), who were builders and divers. (They dived for pearls and constructed large buildings for him). And (besides these -the Shayāṭīn who were builders and divers), there were others who were shackled (bound) in chains (for disobeying Sulaymān (ﷺ) and for committing other crimes). (After giving Sulaymān (ﷺ) all of these favours, Allāh (ﷻ) addressed him saying): 'This is Our gift, so spend (it as you wish) or withhold (as you wish) without any accountability (for you have complete control over your wealth with no one to answer to).'" (Ṣād 38:36-39)

Furthermore, our Prophet (ﷺ) also exemplified seizing the opportunities that he was granted. After migrating to Madīnah and being granted various blessings by Allāh (ﷻ), the Prophet (ﷺ) delegated duties, and also assigned certain tasks to those who were most fit for them.

For instance, Bilāl (رضي الله عنه) was entrusted with calling out the *adhān*, Khālid ibn Walīd (رضي الله عنه) was assigned with providing military planning, and Hasān ibn Thābit (رضي الله عنه) was delegated with providing poetic and verbal defense. May Allāh (ﷻ) be pleased with all of the companions (رضي الله عنهم) and grant them the highest of rewards.

One time the Prophet (ﷺ) passed by a marketplace in Madīnah while people were occupied with their trade. He wanted to remind them about what this world is worth, so that seeking its gains would not divert them from pursing the gains of the hereafter.

In order to seize the opportunity:

«فَمَرَّ بِجَدْيٍ أَسَكَّ مَيِّتٍ، فَتَنَاوَلَهُ فَأَخَذَ بِأُذُنِهِ، ثُمَّ قَالَ: أَيُّكُمْ يُحِبُّ أَنَّ هَذَا لَهُ بِدِرْهَمٍ؟ فَقَالُوا: مَا نُحِبُّ أَنَّهُ لَنَا بِشَيْءٍ، وَمَا نَصْنَعُ بِهِ؟ قَالَ: أَتُحِبُّونَ أَنَّهُ لَكُمْ؟ قَالُوا: وَاللهِ لَوْ كَانَ حَيًّا، كَانَ عَيْبًا فِيهِ، لِأَنَّهُ أَسَكُّ، فَكَيْفَ وَهُوَ مَيِّتٌ؟ فَقَالَ: فَوَاللهِ لَلدُّنْيَا أَهْوَنُ عَلَى اللهِ، مِنْ هَذَا عَلَيْكُمْ».[17]

(رواه مسلم)

He passed by the carcass of a lamb that had small ears. He picked it up by its ear and then made an offer in a raised voice. He said: "Which one of you would like to have this for a *dirham* (one silver coin)?" The people replied: "We would not like to have it for any price. What would we do with it anyway?" He then asked them: "Would you like to own it at all?" They answered: "We swear by Allāh that even if it was alive, it would still be considered defective due to its small ears. Why would we want it when it is dead?" He then told them: "I swear by Allāh that this world is even more worthless to Allāh than this carcass is to you." (Muslim)

A *ḥadīth* that is documented in the *Musnad* of Imām Aḥmad (رحمه الله) mentions that:

«أَنَّهُ كَانَ يَجْتَنِي سِوَاكًا مِنَ الْأَرَاكِ، وَكَانَ دَقِيقَ السَّاقَيْنِ، فَجَعَلَتِ الرِّيحُ تَكْفَؤُهُ، فَضَحِكَ الْقَوْمُ مِنْهُ، فَقَالَ رَسُولُ اللَّهِ ﷺ: مِمَّ تَضْحَكُونَ؟ قَالُوا: يَا نَبِيَّ اللَّهِ، مِنْ دِقَّةِ سَاقَيْهِ، فَقَالَ: وَالَّذِي نَفْسِي بِيَدِهِ، لَهُمَا أَثْقَلُ فِي الْمِيزَانِ مِنْ أُحُدٍ».

[17] The Arabic text of this is as follows:

قَوْلُهُ: (جَدْيٍ أَسَكَّ) أَيْ صَغِيرُ الْأُذُنَيْنِ.

(مسند أحمد)

> Once he (ʿAbdullāh ibn Masʿūd) climbed a tree to pick a siwāk [for the Messenger of Allāh (ﷺ)]. The shins (of ʿAbdullāh ibn Masʿūd) were quite thin and while he was up in the tree, the wind that was blowing caused him to lean. The people laughed at him so the Messenger of Allāh (ﷺ) asked: "What are you laughing about?" They replied: "O Prophet of Allāh, we are laughing about how thin his two shins are." Upon this, the Prophet (ﷺ) said: "I swear by the One in whose hand my soul lies, that the two of them will be heavier in the balance than (the mountain of) Uḥud." (Musnad Aḥmad)

Here, the Prophet (ﷺ) seized the opportunity to inform his companions that people will not have more virtue than others on the Day of Resurrection as a result of their stature or appearance.

On the contrary, they will only have more virtue due to the righteousness of their hearts and deeds. Allāh (ﷻ) does not look at people's appearance, colour, or stature. Rather, He looks at their hearts and deeds.

In the two *Ṣaḥīḥs* of Imām al-Bukhārī and Imām Muslim (رحمهما الله) it is mentioned that the Prophet (ﷺ) said:

«إِنَّهُ لَيَأْتِي الرَّجُلُ العَظِيمُ السَّمِينُ يَوْمَ القِيَامَةِ، لاَ يَزِنُ عِنْدَ اللَّهِ جَنَاحَ بَعُوضَةٍ، وَقَالَ: اقْرَءُوا، ﴿فَلَا نُقِيمُ لَهُمْ يَوْمَ ٱلْقِيَـٰمَةِ وَزْنًا ۝١٠٥﴾ [الكهف الآية ١٠٥]».

(متفق عليه)

> "A large, heavy man will be brought forth on the Day of Resurrection, but to Allāh he will not have weight even as little as the wing of a mosquito." Then [the Prophet (ﷺ)] added: "Read Allāh's statement: 'Therefore, on the Day of Resurrection, We will not give them any weight.' (Kahf 18:105)" (Agreed Upon)

A further instance that demonstrates seizing opportunities can be found in the *aḥādīth.*

ʿAbdullāh ibn ʿAbbās (ﷺ) narrates that once the Prophet (ﷺ) mentioned:

«يَدْخُلُ مِنْ أُمَّتِي الْجَنَّةَ سَبْعُونَ أَلْفًا بِغَيْرِ حِسَابٍ، فَقَالَ رَجُلٌ: يَا رَسُولَ اللهِ، ادْعُ اللهَ أَنْ يَجْعَلَنِي مِنْهُمْ، قَالَ: اللَّهُمَّ اجْعَلْهُ مِنْهُمْ، ثُمَّ قَامَ آخَرُ، فَقَالَ: يَا رَسُولَ اللهِ، ادْعُ اللهَ أَنْ يَجْعَلَنِي مِنْهُمْ قَالَ: سَبَقَكَ بِهَا عُكَّاشَةُ».

(رواه مسلم)

> "Seventy thousand people will enter Paradise without being held to account for, or being punished." As a result, ʿUkkāshah ibn Miḥsan (ﷺ) stood up and said: "O Messenger of Allāh, ask Allāh to make me one of them." The Prophet said: "O Allāh, make him one of them." Then, a man from among the *Anṣār* also stood up and said: "O Messenger of Allāh, ask Allāh to make me one of them." He replied: "ʿUkkāshah has preceded you in this matter." (Muslim)

Look at the initiative taken by ʿUkkāshah ibn Miḥsan (ﷺ) to seize that opportunity. In just a slight instant, he became among those who would be admitted to Paradise without being held to account for, or being punished.

Every chance to do something good – no matter how small it may seem – is a profitable opportunity. Therefore, we should endeavour to protect ourselves from Hell even if it is with only half-a-date. If we cannot find something that little, then with a kind word. We should never look down on any righteous deed, even something as simple as greeting others with a pleasant face.

In *Ṣaḥīḥ Muslim* there is a *ḥadīth* in which the Prophet (ﷺ) says:

«لَقَدْ رَأَيْتُ رَجُلًا يَتَقَلَّبُ فِي الْجَنَّةِ، فِي شَجَرَةٍ قَطَعَهَا مِنْ ظَهْرِ الطَّرِيقِ، كَانَتْ تُؤْذِي النَّاسَ».

(رواه مسلم)

> "I saw a person enjoying himself in Paradise because of a tree that he cut from the pathway which was a source of inconvenience to the people." (Muslim)

We must also realize that there are certain opportunities which have no other substitute. An example of such an opportunity comes in the form of having one or both of our parents still alive. They are the most virtuous gate to Paradise. A person can choose to do as one wishes regarding that gate, but will then have to bear the consequences accordingly.

Regarding this unique opportunity, the Prophet (ﷺ) states:

«رَغِمَ أَنْفُ، ثُمَّ رَغِمَ أَنْفُ، ثُمَّ رَغِمَ أَنْفُ، قِيلَ: مَنْ؟ يَا رَسُولَ اللهِ قَالَ: مَنْ أَدْرَكَ أَبَوَيْهِ عِنْدَ الْكِبَرِ، أَحَدَهُمَا أَوْ كِلَيْهِمَا فَلَمْ يَدْخُلِ الْجَنَّةَ».

(رواه مسلم)

> "May he be disgraced, may he be disgraced, may he be disgraced." The companions who were present asked: "O Messenger of Allāh, who are you referring to?" He replied: "A person who finds one or both of his parents in old age, yet still is not admitted to Paradise (by being dutiful to them)." (Muslim)

It is certainly a tragedy if both of a person's parents have passed away without him having seized the opportunity to treat them well.

The Prophet (ﷺ) states:

«رِضَا الرَّبِّ فِي رِضَا الوَالِدِ، وَسُخْطُ الرَّبِّ فِي سُخْطِ الوَالِدِ».

(رواه الترمذي)

> "Pleasing Allāh lies in pleasing (both of) one's parents, whereas incurring the wrath of Allāh lies in incurring the wrath of (both of) one's parents." (Tirmidhī)

Therefore, grab the opportunity while you can before it is too late!

Allāh (ﷻ) says in the Qur'ān:

﴿ ۞ وَسَارِعُوٓاْ إِلَىٰ مَغۡفِرَةٖ مِّن رَّبِّكُمۡ وَجَنَّةٍ عَرۡضُهَا ٱلسَّمَٰوَٰتُ وَٱلۡأَرۡضُ أُعِدَّتۡ لِلۡمُتَّقِينَ ١٣٣ ٱلَّذِينَ يُنفِقُونَ فِي ٱلسَّرَّآءِ وَٱلضَّرَّآءِ وَٱلۡكَٰظِمِينَ ٱلۡغَيۡظَ وَٱلۡعَافِينَ عَنِ ٱلنَّاسِۗ وَٱللَّهُ يُحِبُّ ٱلۡمُحۡسِنِينَ ١٣٤ ﴾ [آل عِمْرَان من الآية ١٣٣ الى الآية ١٣٤]

"And hasten (to seize every opportunity you can) to attain your Lord's forgiveness, and (to be admitted to) a garden whose expanse is that of the heavens and the earth (to give us humans an idea of the size), and which has been prepared for the people of *taqwā*. (Among their qualities is that) they give during both prosperity and hardship, they suppress their anger, and they pardon others (forgive those who wrong them, and even act pleasantly towards them); and Allāh loves those who do good." (Āle ʿImrān 3:133-134)

The fact of just being alive in this world provides us with the greatest of opportunities. If a person's deeds are righteous, then one should continue to perform more of them; but if a person's deeds are otherwise, then one should try their hardest to refrain from doing them and return back to Allāh (ﷻ).

Imām Nasā'ī in his *Al-Sunan al-Kubrā* has documented a Prophetic narration wherein the Prophet (ﷺ) states:

«اغْتَنِمْ خَمْسًا قَبْلَ خَمْسٍ: شَبَابَكَ قَبْلَ هَرَمِكَ، وَصِحَّتَكَ قَبْلَ سَقَمِكَ، وَغِنَاكَ قَبْلَ فَقْرِكَ، وَفَرَاغَكَ قَبْلَ شُغْلِكَ، وَحَيَاتَكَ قَبْلَ مَوْتِكَ».

(السنن الكبرى للنسائي)

"Take advantage of five (things) before another five (things happen): your youth before your old age, your health before your illness, your prosperity before your poverty, your free

> time before you become preoccupied, and your life before your death." (Al-Sunan al-Kubrā of al-Nasā'ī)

The more a person tries to be serious about life, and to avoid one's own rebellious inclinations, the more one will effectively seize opportunities, and outdo others in performing righteous deeds.

Part of Allāh's (ﷻ) favours upon us is that He has made it possible with the opportunities that we have, to continue until our very last moment.

Anas (ؓ) narrates that the Prophet (ﷺ) said:

«إِنْ قَامَتْ عَلَى أَحَدِكُمُ الْقِيَامَةُ، وَفِي يَدِهِ فَسِيلَةٌ فَلْيَغْرِسْهَا».

(مسند أحمد)

> "If one of you has a sapling in his hand when the Final Hour is imminent, and he is able to plant it before the Hour begins, then he should do so." (Musnad Aḥmad)

Therefore, we should all seize opportunities before it is too late. Always remember that opportunities are blessings, and blessings may not return once they depart.

Imām Ibn al-Qayyim (رحمه الله) writes:

«وَاللَّهُ سُبْحَانَهُ يُعَاقِبُ مَنْ فَتَحَ لَهُ بَابًا مِنَ الْخَيْرِ فَلَمْ يَنْتَهِزْهُ، بِأَنْ يَحُولَ بَيْنَ قَلْبِهِ وَإِرَادَتِهِ،

فَلَا يُمَكِّنُهُ بَعْدُ مِنْ إِرَادَتِهِ عُقُوبَةً لَهُ».

(زاد المعاد)

> "When Allāh – who is perfect in every way – opens a door to goodness for a person, but the person does not seize that opportunity, Allāh may come between that person and his heart, and prevent him from what he may hope for and want to do, and that will be a form of punishment for him." (Zād al-Maʿād)

Allāh (ﷻ) mentions in the Qur'ān:

﴿وَٱعۡلَمُوٓاْ أَنَّ ٱللَّهَ يَحُولُ بَيۡنَ ٱلۡمَرۡءِ وَقَلۡبِهِۦ وَأَنَّهُۥٓ إِلَيۡهِ تُحۡشَرُونَ ﴿٢٤﴾﴾ [الأنفال الآية

"And know that Allāh intervenes between a man and his heart (i.e. when He wills to keep a servant of His protected from evils, then He will put a barrier between his heart and sins; and when misfortune is decreed for someone, a barrier will be placed between his heart and any possible good deeds that he may be wanting to perform). And verily to Him, you shall (all) be gathered." (Anfāl 8:24)

When a person favours laziness and misses opportunities, he will regret it at a time when it is too late to make amends. Allāh (ﷻ) says:

﴿يَوۡمَئِذٖ يَتَذَكَّرُ ٱلۡإِنسَٰنُ وَأَنَّىٰ لَهُ ٱلذِّكۡرَىٰ ﴿٢٣﴾ يَقُولُ يَٰلَيۡتَنِي قَدَّمۡتُ لِحَيَاتِي ﴿٢٤﴾﴾

[الفجر من الآية ٢٣ الى الآية ٢٤]

"On that day, a person will remorsefully remember what passed, but what good will remorse do at that time? He will say: 'Oh dear! If only I had sent (good deeds) ahead (to earn rewards) for my life (here in the *ākhirah*)!'" (Fajr 89:23-24)

بَادِرِ الْفُرْصَةَ وَاحْذَرْ فَوْتَهَا ۞ فَبُلُوغُ الْعِزِّ فِي نَيْلِ الْفُرَصْ

وَاغْتَنِمْ عُمْرَكَ إِبَّانَ الصِّبَا ۞ فَهُوَ إِنْ زَادَ مَعَ الشَّيْبِ نَقَصْ

Hasten to seize opportunities and do not miss them.
Attaining true honour lies in seizing opportunities.
Make the most effective use of your life while you are still young.
Although life continues to be extended even as you become elderly,
The reality is that it still remains in decline.

KHUṬBAH 67

Recounting the Prophet's (ﷺ) Children

The entire life of the Prophet (ﷺ) was a brilliant light that still shines in all facets: education, calling to Allāh (ﷻ), mediation, conflict, worship, and personal conduct. We will find guidance in whichever part of it we draw from. Together, we wish to take a glimpse at the life of the final Prophet (ﷺ) with his daughters, sons, and grandchildren. May Allāh (ﷻ) send abundant *ṣalāt* (prayers) and *salām* (salutations) upon him and upon all of his family. We also aspire to clearly recognize his human and fatherly side, and get to know the compassionate person that he truly was.

His life also provides consolation to every parent who has ever lost a child, as they can relate to someone even better than themselves who went through the same trial.

The Messenger of Allāh (ﷺ) was a noteworthy young man among the tribe of Quraysh, who stood out from the others because of his honesty and integrity, to the extent that they actually called him *'al-Ṣādiq'* which means 'the truthful one;' and *'al-Amīn'* which means 'the trustworthy one.' His illustrious reputation spread among the people, just like the sun and moon rise and set over all of creation, without any exception.

As a result of his impeccable character, Khadījah binte Khuwaylid (رضي الله عنها) selected him to take charge of her business, and the trade caravan which she regularly sent to Shām. She sent along with him a young man, Maysarah, who was one of her attendants. That was how it all began. Khadījah (رضي الله عنها) became greatly impressed by the Messenger of Allāh (ﷺ), and he eventually married Khadījah (رضي الله عنها) when he was twenty-five years old, although she was older than him.

That was his first household, and it was one which was infused with happiness and faith. The Prophet (ﷺ) loved Khadījah (رضي الله عنها) very much, so much that the wives which he later married after Khadījah's (رضي الله عنها) death, were jealous of her.

He (ﷺ) used to say:

«إِنِّي قَدْ رُزِقْتُ حُبَّهَا».

(رواه مسلم)

> "Love for her was placed within me (meaning that her love had been nurtured in his heart by Allāh Himself)." (Muslim)

They remained together for twenty-five years until she passed away, and the Prophet (ﷺ) did not marry anyone else until after her death. She bore for him six children. Two sons: Qāsim and ʿAbdullāh; and four daughters: Zaynab, Ruqayyah, Umm Kulthūm, and Fāṭimah (رضي الله عنهن). Qāsim was the Prophet's (ﷺ) first child, and the *kunyah* (title or epitome) by which the Prophet (ﷺ) was known, Abū al-Qāsim, was because of this child.

This is the reason why the Prophet (ﷺ) has stated:

«تَسَمَّوْا بِاسْمِي، وَلَا تَكَنَّوْا بِكُنْيَتِي».

(رواه البخاري)

> "You may give yourselves the same name as me, but do not give yourselves the same *kunyah* as me." (Bukhārī)

Many scholars hold that this prohibition applied during his life, but was later abrogated.[18] This is based on a *ḥadīth* which has been recorded by Imām Muslim (رحمه الله) wherein Anas (رضي الله عنه) narrates:

«نَادَى رَجُلٌ رَجُلًا بِالْبَقِيعِ يَا أَبَا الْقَاسِمِ فَالْتَفَتَ إِلَيْهِ رَسُولُ اللهِ فَقَالَ يَا رَسُولَ اللهِ، إِنِّي لَمْ أَعْنِكَ إِنَّمَا دَعَوْتُ فُلَانًا، فَقَالَ رَسُولُ اللهِ ﷺ: تَسَمَّوْا بِاسْمِي وَلَا تَكَنَّوْا بِكُنْيَتِي».

(رواه مسلم)

> A man was in the area of Madīnah called al-Baqīʿ and he called out to another man by saying: "O Abū al-Qāsim!" The Prophet (ﷺ) was present, and as a result, he turned to the man who had called out. The man said: "O Messenger of Allāh, it was not you whom I intended. I was calling out to another person." The Messenger of Allāh (ﷺ) then said: "You may give yourselves the same name as me, but do not give yourselves the same *kunyah* as me." (Muslim)

Qāsim passed away while he was still a child, prior to his father being appointed by Allāh (ﷻ) as a Prophet and Messenger. After Qāsim, the Prophet was blessed with a daughter and he named her Zaynab.

One of the things that happened in her life was that the Prophet (ﷺ) gave her in marriage to Abu al-ʿĀṣ ibn al-Rabīʿ.[19] Later on, after the mission of the Prophet (ﷺ) began, she accepted Islām and migrated to Madīnah. Her husband did not accept Islām until just prior to the conquest of Makkah, and that was when the Prophet (ﷺ) allowed them to be reunited as a couple.

---

[18] The Arabic text of this is as follows:

أَنَّ هَذَا النَّهْيَ مَنْسُوخٌ؛ فَإِنَّ هَذَا الْحُكْمَ كَانَ فِي أَوَّلِ الْأَمْرِ لِهَذَا الْمَعْنَى الْمَذْكُورِ فِي الْحَدِيثِ، ثُمَّ نُسِخَ. قَالُوا: فَيُبَاحُ التَّكَنِّي الْيَوْمَ بِأَبِي الْقَاسِمِ لِكُلِّ أَحَدٍ، سَوَاءٌ مَنِ اسْمُهُ مُحَمَّدٌ وَأَحْمَدُ وَغَيْرُهُ، وَهَذَا مَذْهَبُ مَالِكٍ. قَالَ الْقَاضِي: وَبِهِ قَالَ جُمْهُورُ السَّلَفِ، وَفُقَهَاءُ الْأَمْصَارِ، وَجُمْهُورُ الْعُلَمَاءِ.

(شرح النووى على مسلم)

[19] His mother was Hālah binte Khuwaylid, Khadījah's (رضي الله عنها) sister. (Al-Iṣābah)

During the expedition of Badr, Abu al-ʿĀṣ ibn al-Rabīʿ was one of the people who was captured as a prisoner. The people of Makkah sent ransom for their relatives who had been taken as prisoners during the war. Zaynab (رضي الله عنها) sent some money and a necklace as a ransom for her husband. Khadījah (رضي الله عنها) had given that necklace as a gift to Zaynab (رضي الله عنها) on the day she got married.

When the Prophet (ﷺ) saw it, he felt great sympathy and remembered his earlier days. With his heart filled with compassion, he said to the companions (رضي الله عنهم):

«إِنْ رَأَيْتُمْ أَنْ تُطْلِقُوا لَهَا أَسِيرَهَا، وَتَرُدُّوا عَلَيْهَا الَّذِي لَهَا، فَافْعَلُوا فقَالُوا: نَعَمْ يَا رَسُولَ اللَّهِ».

(مسند أحمد)

> "If you deem it acceptable to free her prisoner and return what belongs to her, you may do so." The companions replied: "O Messenger of Allāh, we will." (Musnad Aḥmad)

Zaynab (رضي الله عنها) bore a daughter named Umāmah. The Prophet (ﷺ) was so compassionate and humble that he had carried Umāmah even while he was praying. He would carry her while he stood, and he would rest her down when he bowed in prostration.[20] From this, scholars have deduced that minor movement during the prayer is permissible when there is a need for it.[21]

---

[20] The Arabic text of this is as follows:

عَنْ أَبِي قَتَادَةَ الأَنْصَارِيِّ، أَنَّ رَسُولَ اللَّهِ صَلَّى اللَّهُ عَلَيْهِ وَسَلَّمَ كَانَ يُصَلِّي وَهُوَ حَامِلٌ أُمَامَةَ بِنْتَ زَيْنَبَ بِنْتِ رَسُولِ اللَّهِ صَلَّى اللَّهُ عَلَيْهِ وَسَلَّمَ، وَلِأَبِي العَاصِ بْنِ رَبِيعَةَ بْنِ عَبْدِ شَمْسٍ فَإِذَا سَجَدَ وَضَعَهَا، وَإِذَا قَامَ حَمَلَهَا.

(رواه البخاري)

[21] The Arabic text of this is as follows:

ذكر مَا يُسْتَفَاد مِنْهُ: تكلم النَّاس فِي حكم هَذَا الحَدِيث، فَقَالَ النَّوَوِيّ: هَذَا يدل لمَذْهَب الشَّافِعِي وَمن وَافقه أَنه يجوز حمل الصَّبِي والصبية وَغَيرهمَا من الْحَيَوَان فِي صَلَاة النَّفْل، وَيجوز للْإِمَام وَالْمُنْفَرد وَالْمَأْمُوم قلت: أما مَذْهَب أبي حنيفَة فِي هَذَا مَا ذكر صَاحب (الْبَدَائِع) وَفِي

ʿAlī (رضي الله عنه) married this same Umāmah after Fāṭimah (رضي الله عنها) passed away. Umāmah's mother, Zaynab (رضي الله عنها), passed away in the eighth year after the Hijrah.[22]

Women among the companions (رضي الله عنهن) prepared her body for burial, and one of her shrouds was the *izār* (a garment used to cover the lower half of the body) of the Prophet (ﷺ).[23]

There is a narration collected by Imām Aḥmad (رحمه الله) wherein ʿĀ'ishah (رضي الله عنها) mentions that:

«أَنَّ رَسُولَ اللهِ ﷺ أُهْدِيَتْ لَهُ هَدِيَّةٌ فِيهَا قِلَادَةٌ مِنْ جَزْعٍ، فَقَالَ: لَأَدْفَعَنَّهَا إِلَى أَحَبِّ أَهْلِي إِلَيَّ، فَقَالَتِ النِّسَاءُ: ذَهَبَتْ بِهَا ابْنَةُ أَبِي قُحَافَةَ، فَدَعَا النَّبِيُّ ﷺ أُمَامَةَ بِنْتَ زَيْنَبَ، فَعَلَّقَهَا فِي عُنُقِهَا».

(مسند أحمد)

The Messenger of Allāh (ﷺ) received a gift which contained a necklace made of beads. He said: "I will give it to the person in my family whom I love the most." The women guessed what would happen and said: "It will go to the daughter of Abū Quḥāfah." However, the Prophet (ﷺ) called for Umāmah,

---

بَيَان الْعَمَل الْكثير الَّذِي يفْسد الصَّلَاة والقليل الَّذِي لَا يُفْسِدهَا: فالكثير مَا يحْتَاج فِيهِ إِلَى اسْتِعْمَال الْيَدَيْنِ، والقليل مَا لَا يحْتَاج فِيهِ إِلَى ذَلِك.

(عمدة القاري)

[22] The Arabic text of this is as follows:

أنّ زينب تُوفيت في أول سنة ثمان من الهجرة.

(الإصابة في تميز الصحابة)

[23] The Arabic text of this is as follows:

فَلَمَّا فَرَغْنَا آذَنَّاهُ، فَأَعْطَانَا حِقْوَهُ، فَقَالَ: أَشْعِرْنَهَا إِيَّاهُ تَعْنِي إِزَارَهُ.

(رواه البخاري)

Zaynab's (رضي الله عنها) daughter, and he placed it around her neck. (Musnad Aḥmad)

After Zaynab (رضي الله عنها), the Prophet (ﷺ) was blessed with a daughter whom he named Ruqayyah (رضي الله عنها), and he gave her in marriage to ʿUthmān ibn ʿAffān (رضي الله عنه).

When the expedition of Badr was taking place, Ruqayyah (رضي الله عنها) became extremely ill, and as a result of this, ʿUthmān (رضي الله عنه) was not present in the expedition. Rather, he remained behind in order to tend to his wife during her illness, and she later passed away. The Prophet (ﷺ) still set aside a portion of the spoils for ʿUthmān (رضي الله عنه), just as he did for those who participated in the expedition.[24]

After Ruqayyah (رضي الله عنها) passed away, the Prophet (ﷺ) gave another daughter of his, Umm Kulthūm (رضي الله عنها), in marriage to ʿUthmān (رضي الله عنه) and that is why he was given the title of *Dhū al-Nūrayn*, (the possessor of two lights).[25]

Abū Hurairah (رضي الله عنه) reports:

---

[24] The Arabic text of this is as follows:

أَمَّا تَغَيُّبُهُ عَنْ بَدْرٍ فَإِنَّهُ كَانَتْ تَحْتَهُ بِنْتُ رَسُولِ اللَّهِ صَلَّى اللَّهُ عَلَيْهِ وَسَلَّمَ، وَكَانَتْ مَرِيضَةً، فَقَالَ لَهُ رَسُولُ اللَّهِ صَلَّى اللَّهُ عَلَيْهِ وَسَلَّمَ: إِنَّ لَكَ أَجْرَ رَجُلٍ مِمَّنْ شَهِدَ بَدْرًا.

(رواه البخاري)

وَأَمَّا تَغَيُّبُهُ عَنْ بَدْرٍ فَإِنَّهُ كَانَ تَحْتَهُ بِنْتُ رَسُولِ اللَّهِ صَلَّى اللَّهُ عَلَيْهِ وَسَلَّمَ هِيَ رُقَيَّةُ فَرَوَى الْحَاكِمُ فِي الْمُسْتَدْرَكِ مِنْ طَرِيقِ حَمَّادِ بْنِ سَلَمَةَ عَنْ هِشَامِ بْنِ عُرْوَةَ عَنْ أَبِيهِ قَالَ خَلَّفَ النَّبِيُّ صَلَّى اللَّهُ عَلَيْهِ وَسَلَّمَ عُثْمَانَ وَأُسَامَةَ بْنَ زَيْدٍ عَلَى رُقَيَّةَ فِي مَرَضِهَ.

(فتح الباري)

[25] The Arabic text of this is as follows:

(أخبرنا) أبو عبد الله الحافظ ، قال سمعت أبا نصر أحمد بن سهل يقول: سمعت صالح بن محمد يقول: سمعت عبد الله بن عمر بن أبان الجعفي يقول : قال لي خالي حسين الجعفي : يا بني ، تدري لم سمي عثمان ذو النورين ؟ قلت: لا أدري ، قال: لم يجمع بين ابنتي نبي منذ خلق الله آدم إلى أن تقوم الساعة غير عثمان بن عفان - رضي الله عنه - ؛ فلذلك سمي ذو النورين .

(السنن الكبرى)

«أَنَّ النَّبِيَّ ﷺ لَقِيَ عُثْمَانَ عِنْدَ بَابِ الْمَسْجِدِ، فَقَالَ: يَا عُثْمَانُ، هَذَا جِبْرِيلُ أَخْبَرَنِي أَنَّ اللَّهَ قَدْ زَوَّجَكَ أُمَّ كُلْثُومٍ بِمِثْلِ صَدَاقِ رُقَيَّةَ، عَلَى مِثْلِ صُحْبَتِهَا».

(رواه ابن ماجه)

The Prophet (ﷺ) met ʿUthmān (رضي الله عنه) at the entrance of the *masjid* and said: "ʿUthmān, Jibrāʾīl just came and told me that Allāh has given Umm Kulthūm to you in marriage for the same dowry as Ruqayyah, provided that you treat her with the same kindness." (Ibn Mājah)

The youngest daughter of the Prophet (ﷺ) was Fāṭimah (رضي الله عنها).

She was the daughter of the Prophet (ﷺ), wife of ʿAlī ibn Abī Ṭālib (رضي الله عنه), and mother of Ḥasan and Ḥusayn (رضي الله عنهما)! Who could ever come close to the virtues that she had?

Imām Muslim (رحمه الله) has recorded a *ḥadīth* on the authority of ʿAbdullāh ibn Masʿūd (رضي الله عنه) who states:

«بَيْنَمَا رَسُولُ اللهِ ﷺ يُصَلِّي عِنْدَ الْبَيْتِ، وَأَبُو جَهْلٍ وَأَصْحَابٌ لَهُ جُلُوسٌ، وَقَدْ نُحِرَتْ جَزُورٌ بِالْأَمْسِ، فَقَالَ أَبُو جَهْلٍ: أَيُّكُمْ يَقُومُ إِلَى سَلَا جَزُورِ بَنِي فُلَانٍ، فَيَأْخُذُهُ فَيَضَعُهُ فِي كَتِفَيْ مُحَمَّدٍ إِذَا سَجَدَ؟ فَانْبَعَثَ أَشْقَى الْقَوْمِ فَأَخَذَهُ، فَلَمَّا سَجَدَ النَّبِيُّ ﷺ وَضَعَهُ بَيْنَ كَتِفَيْهِ، قَالَ: فَاسْتَضْحَكُوا، وَجَعَلَ بَعْضُهُمْ يَمِيلُ عَلَى بَعْضٍ وَأَنَا قَائِمٌ أَنْظُرُ، لَوْ كَانَتْ لِي مَنَعَةٌ طَرَحْتُهُ عَنْ ظَهْرِ رَسُولِ اللهِ ﷺ، وَالنَّبِيُّ ﷺ سَاجِدٌ مَا يَرْفَعُ رَأْسَهُ حَتَّى انْطَلَقَ إِنْسَانٌ فَأَخْبَرَ فَاطِمَةَ، فَجَاءَتْ وَهِيَ جُوَيْرِيَةٌ، فَطَرَحَتْهُ عَنْهُ، ثُمَّ أَقْبَلَتْ عَلَيْهِمْ تَشْتِمُهُمْ، فَلَمَّا قَضَى النَّبِيُّ ﷺ صَلَاتَهُ، رَفَعَ صَوْتَهُ، ثُمَّ دَعَا عَلَيْهِمْ، وَكَانَ إِذَا دَعَا دَعَا ثَلَاثًا، وَإِذَا سَأَلَ سَأَلَ ثَلَاثًا، ثُمَّ قَالَ: اللَّهُمَّ، عَلَيْكَ بِقُرَيْشٍ، ثَلَاثَ مَرَّاتٍ، فَلَمَّا سَمِعُوا صَوْتَهُ ذَهَبَ عَنْهُمُ الضِّحْكُ، وَخَافُوا دَعْوَتَهُ».

(رواه مسلم)

> The Messenger of Allāh (ﷺ) was once praying near the Kaʿbah while Abū Jahl and some of his associates were sitting close by. A camel had been slaughtered the previous day, so Abū Jahl said: "Which one of you will get the placenta from the remains of the camel that the people slaughtered, and then put it on Muḥammad's two shoulders when he bows down to prostrate?" The worst person among them went and got it. When the Prophet (ﷺ) went down to prostrate, that person put it right in between his two shoulders. The others who were watching laughed, and even doubled-over towards each other because of how hard they were laughing. Ibn Masʿūd (رضي الله عنه) further said: "I stood there watching helplessly. I wished I had some sort of protection so I could have gone and removed it from the back of the Prophet (ﷺ)." The Prophet (ﷺ) remained in prostration and did not raise his head. Someone went to Fāṭimah and informed her about what had happened. She came, and although she was still a little girl, she removed it. She then turned to those people and rebuked them. When the Prophet (ﷺ) finished his prayer, he raised his voice and supplicated against them. When supplicating, he would do so three times; and when asking from Allāh, he would do so three times. He said: "O Allāh, punish the Quraysh," (and said this) three times. When they heard his voice, their laughter disappeared and they were stricken with fear because of his supplication. (Muslim)

The Prophet (ﷺ) gave Fāṭimah (رضي الله عنها) in marriage to ʿAlī ibn Abī Ṭālib (رضي الله عنه), who was the son of his paternal uncle Abū Ṭālib (رضي الله عنه). This marriage took place in the second year after the *hijrah*. She bore Ḥasan and Ḥusayn (رضي الله عنهما), the leaders of the youth who will be admitted to Paradise. The Prophet (ﷺ) had a very strong love for his two grandsons.

He would say:

«هُمَا رَيْحَانَتَايَ مِنَ الدُّنْيَا».

(رواه البخاري)

> "They are my two *Raiḥānah's* (fragrant flowers) in the life of this world." (Bukhārī)

Once when the Prophet (ﷺ) was delivering a sermon, al-Ḥasan and al-Ḥusayn (رضي الله عنهما) approached. Each one of them was wearing a red garment. They would trip, fall, and then get up again. The Prophet (ﷺ) descended from the *mimbar*, picked them up, ascended once more while carrying them, and said:

«صَدَقَ اللَّهُ: ﴿إِنَّمَآ أَمْوَٰلُكُمْ وَأَوْلَٰدُكُمْ فِتْنَةٌ ۚ ﴿١٥﴾﴾ [التَّغَابُن الآية ١٥]، رَأَيْتُ هَذَيْنِ فَلَمْ أَصْبِرْ، ثُمَّ أَخَذَ فِي الْخُطْبَةِ».

(رواه أبو داود)

> "Allāh has spoken the truth - 'Your wealth and your children are merely a test (to ascertain whether you will allow them to distract you from worshipping Allāh). (Taghābun 64:15)' I saw the two of them (stumbling over their shirts) and I could not bear it." He then continued his sermon. (Abū Dāwūd)

Once the Prophet (ﷺ) was leading the companions (رضي الله عنهم) in prayer and he prostrated for a long time. Afterward, they asked him about it:

« يَا رَسُولَ اللَّهِ، إِنَّكَ سَجَدْتَ بَيْنَ ظَهْرَانَيْ صَلَاتِكَ سَجْدَةً أَطَلْتَهَا حَتَّى ظَنَنَّا أَنَّهُ قَدْ حَدَثَ أَمْرٌ أَوْ أَنَّهُ يُوحَى إِلَيْكَ، قَالَ: كُلُّ ذَلِكَ لَمْ يَكُنْ وَلَكِنَّ ابْنِي ارْتَحَلَنِي فَكَرِهْتُ أَنْ أُعَجِّلَهُ حَتَّى يَقْضِيَ حَاجَتَهُ».

(رواه النسائي)

> "O Messenger of Allāh (ﷺ), you prostrated during the prayer for so long that we thought that something had happened, or that you were receiving a revelation." He replied: "No such

> thing happened. However, my son was sitting on top of me and I did want not to force him off (or disturb him) until he had enough." (Nasā'ī)

This was the heart of the Prophet (ﷺ), and this was how compassionate he was towards children. He did not chastise, beat, or shout at the toddler who climbed onto his back while he was praying. Rather, he lengthened his prostration, waited for him to come off, and then said:

«وَلَكِنَّ ابْنِي ارْتَحَلَنِي فَكَرِهْتُ أَنْ أُعَجِّلَهُ حَتَّى يَقْضِيَ حَاجَتَهُ».

> "My son was sitting on top of me and I did want not to force him off (or disturb him) until he had enough." (Nasā'ī)

The companion, Aqraʿ ibn Ḥābis (رضي الله عنه), once came to the Prophet (ﷺ) and saw him give Ḥasan (رضي الله عنه) a kiss, so he said:

«إِنَّ لِي عَشَرَةً مِنَ الوَلَدِ مَا قَبَّلْتُ مِنْهُمْ أَحَدًا، فَنَظَرَ إِلَيْهِ رَسُولُ اللَّهِ ﷺ ثُمَّ قَالَ: مَنْ لاَ يَرْحَمُ لاَ يُرْحَمُ».

(رواه البخاري)

> "I have ten children and I have never kissed a single one of them." The Messenger of Allāh (ﷺ) cast a look at him and replied: "If someone does not show mercy (to others), then he will not be shown mercy." (Bukhārī)

This is how the Prophet's (ﷺ) heart was. This is how he was compassionate towards young ones.

﴿لَّقَدْ كَانَ لَكُمْ فِي رَسُولِ ٱللَّهِ أُسْوَةٌ حَسَنَةٌ ٢١﴾ [الأحزاب الآية ٢١]

> "There is definitely an excellent example in the Messenger of Allāh" (Aḥzāb 33:21)

As for their mother, Fāṭimah (رضي الله عنها), she was a part of the Prophet (ﷺ). He (ﷺ) would say:

»إِنَّمَا فَاطِمَةُ بِضْعَةٌ مِنِّي يُؤْذِينِي مَا آذَاهَا وَيُنْصِبُنِي مَا أَنْصَبَهَا«.

(رواه الترمذي)

"Surely (my daughter) Fāṭimah is a part of me. Whatever distresses her distresses me; and whatever makes her uncomfortable makes me uncomfortable" (Tirmidhī)

She once came looking for the Prophet (ﷺ) to complain about her hands aching from the hand-mill that she used to grind the flour with, and to ask him (ﷺ) for a servant who could help her out. However, she did not find the Prophet (ﷺ) when she came, so she mentioned her situation to 'Ā'ishah (ؓ). When the Prophet (ﷺ) returned, 'Ā'ishah (ؓ) informed him about what had transpired.

'Alī (ؓ) states:

»فَجَاءَنَا وَقَدْ أَخَذْنَا مَضَاجِعَنَا، فَذَهَبْتُ أَقُومُ، فَقَالَ: مَكَانَكِ، فَجَلَسَ بَيْنَنَا حَتَّى وَجَدْتُ بَرْدَ قَدَمَيْهِ عَلَى صَدْرِي، فَقَالَ: أَلاَ أَدُلُّكُمَا عَلَى مَا هُوَ خَيْرٌ لَكُمَا مِنْ خَادِمٍ؟ إِذَا أَوَيْتُمَا إِلَى فِرَاشِكُمَا، أَوْ أَخَذْتُمَا مَضَاجِعَكُمَا، فَكَبِّرَا ثَلَاثًا وَثَلَاثِينَ، وَسَبِّحَا ثَلَاثًا وَثَلَاثِينَ، وَاحْمَدَا ثَلَاثًا وَثَلَاثِينَ، فَهَذَا خَيْرٌ لَكُمَا مِنْ خَادِمٍ«.

(رواه البخاري)

"He (the Prophet (ﷺ)) came to us at night after we had gone to bed. I was about to get up when he came, but he said: 'Stay where you are.' He then sat between us and I could feel the coolness of his feet on my chest. He said: 'Should I not tell the two of you what would be better for you both than a servant? When you go to bed recite: *Allāhu Akbar* thirty-four times, *Subḥān Allāh* thirty-three times, and *Alḥamduillāh* thirty-three times. That will be better for both of you than a servant.'" (Bukhārī)

Ḥāfiẓ ibn al-Ḥajr (ؓ) comments:

«أَنَّ الَّذِي يُلَازِمُ ذِكْرَ اللَّهِ يُعْطَى قُوَّةً أَعْظَمَ مِنَ الْقُوَّةِ الَّتِي يَعْمَلُهَا لَهُ الْخَادِمُ».

(فتح الباري)

"This shows that when someone is steadfast in making the *dhikr* of Allāh, that person will be granted more strength than could even be obtained from a servant working for them." (Fatḥ al-Bārī)

Both Imām al-Bukhārī and Imām Muslim (ﷺ) have recorded a narration wherein ʿĀ'ishah (ﷺ) reports:

«أَقْبَلَتْ فَاطِمَةُ تَمْشِي كَأَنَّ مِشْيَتَهَا مَشْيُ النَّبِيِّ ﷺ، فَقَالَ النَّبِيُّ ﷺ: مَرْحَبًا بِابْنَتِي، ثُمَّ أَجْلَسَهَا عَنْ يَمِينِهِ، أَوْ عَنْ شِمَالِهِ، ثُمَّ أَسَرَّ إِلَيْهَا حَدِيثًا فَبَكَتْ، فَقُلْتُ لَهَا: لِمَ تَبْكِينَ؟ ثُمَّ أَسَرَّ إِلَيْهَا حَدِيثًا فَضَحِكَتْ، فَقُلْتُ: مَا رَأَيْتُ كَالْيَوْمِ فَرَحًا أَقْرَبَ مِنْ حُزْنٍ، فَسَأَلْتُهَا عَمَّا قَالَ: فَقَالَتْ: مَا كُنْتُ لِأُفْشِيَ سِرَّ رَسُولِ اللَّهِ ﷺ، حَتَّى قُبِضَ النَّبِيُّ ﷺ، فَسَأَلْتُهَا، فَقَالَتْ: أَسَرَّ إِلَيَّ: إِنَّ جِبْرِيلَ كَانَ يُعَارِضُنِي الْقُرْآنَ كُلَّ سَنَةٍ مَرَّةً، وَإِنَّهُ عَارَضَنِي الْعَامَ مَرَّتَيْنِ، وَلَا أُرَاهُ إِلَّا حَضَرَ أَجَلِي، وَإِنَّكِ أَوَّلُ أَهْلِ بَيْتِي لَحَاقًا بِي. فَبَكَيْتُ، فَقَالَ: أَمَا تَرْضَيْنَ أَنْ تَكُونِي سَيِّدَةَ نِسَاءِ أَهْلِ الْجَنَّةِ، أَوْ نِسَاءِ الْمُؤْمِنِينَ، فَضَحِكْتُ لِذَلِكَ».

(رواه البخاري)

Fāṭimah once came walking, and it was as though she walked exactly the way the Prophet (ﷺ) walked. The Prophet (ﷺ) said: "Welcome, my daughter," and he had her sit beside him, at his right or his left. He then whispered something to her and she wept. ʿĀ'ishah (ﷺ) wondered why she had wept. After that, the Prophet (ﷺ) whispered something else to Fāṭimah (ﷺ) and she laughed. ʿĀ'ishah (ﷺ) commented that she had never seen any instance of happiness coming so soon after sadness as she had on that day. ʿĀ'ishah (ﷺ) then asked Fāṭimah (ﷺ) what the

Prophet (ﷺ) had told her, but she replied: "I will not divulge what the Prophet (ﷺ) confided in me." After the Prophet (ﷺ) passed away, 'Ā'ishah (◉) asked again, and Fāṭimah (◉) replied that he whispered to her saying: "Jibrā'īl used to review the Qur'ān with me once each year. This year, he reviewed it with me twice, and I do not think that it is for any other reason than that my death is near. Furthermore, you will be the first member of my family to join me." Fāṭimah (◉) said she wept when he said that, but he then whispered to her saying: "Would it not please you to be the leader of the women who reside in Paradise, or the leader of the women who have faith?" Fāṭimah (◉) states: "I laughed at that." (Bukhārī)

Fāṭimah (◉) passed away six months after the death of the Prophet (ﷺ).[26]

The youngest of the Prophet's (ﷺ) children from Khadījah (◉) was 'Abdullāh. He was also called Ṭayyib or Ṭāhir.[27] He was born after his father's (ﷺ) mission as a Prophet had begun, and he died while still a young child.

When he died, al-'Āṣ ibn Wā'il said about the Prophet (ﷺ):

«دَعُوهُ فَإِنَّهُ رَجُلٌ أَبْتَرُ لَا عَقِبَ لَهُ، فَإِذَا هَلَكَ انْقَطَعَ ذِكْرُهُ».

(تفسير ابن كثير)

---

[26] The Arabic text of this is as follows:

وقال الزهري عن عروة، عن عائشة، أن فاطمة عاشت بعد رسول الله ﷺ ستة أشهر، ودفنت ليلا.

(سير أعلام النبلاء)

[27] The Arabic text of this is as follows:

وَقَالَ الزُّبَيْرِ: ولد لِرَسُولِ اللَّهِ ﷺ: القاسم، وَهُوَ أكبر ولده، ثم زينب، ثم عَبْد اللَّهِ، وَكَانَ يقال له: الطيب، ويقال له: الطاهر ولد بعد النبوة، ثم أم كلثوم، ثم فاطمة، ثم رقية، هكذا الأول فالأول، ثم مات القاسم بمكة، وَهُوَ أول ميت مات من ولده، ثم مات عَبْد اللَّهِ أَيْضًا بمكة.

(الاستيعاب في معرفة الأصحاب)

> "Leave him alone. His lineage has been truncated. He will not be mentioned after he dies because he has no sons." (Tafsīr Ibn Kathīr)

It is on this occasion that Allāh (ﷻ) revealed Sūrah al-Kawthar.

﴿إِنَّآ أَعۡطَيۡنَٰكَ ٱلۡكَوۡثَرَ ۝١ فَصَلِّ لِرَبِّكَ وَٱنۡحَرۡ ۝٢ إِنَّ شَانِئَكَ هُوَ ٱلۡأَبۡتَرُ ۝٣﴾

[الكَوْثَر من الآية ١ الى الآية ٣]

> Verily We have granted you abundant good. (Allāh (ﷻ) granted the Messenger Prophethood, the honour of being the best of all of the *Ambiyā'*, the Qur'ān, the largest *ummah*, a *dīn* that has spread throughout the world and the high position of *Maqām al-Maḥmūd* in the *Ākhirah*. The spiritual fountain of *Kawthar*, apart from these things, there are numerous other bounties that Allāh (ﷻ) gave exclusively to the Prophet). So (as a token of gratitude, you should) offer *ṣalāt* (prayer) to your Lord and sacrifice. Surely it is the one who detests you, whose traces will be cut off. (Kawthar 108:1-3)

As for the Prophet (ﷺ), Allāh (ﷻ) says:

﴿وَرَفَعۡنَا لَكَ ذِكۡرَكَ ۝٤﴾ [الشَّرْح الآية ٤]

> "And We have elevated your mention (the esteem with which people hold you)." (Inshirāh 94:4)

NOTE: The Prophet's (ﷺ) name is mentioned together with Allāh's (ﷻ) name in the *kalimah*, the *adhān*, the *iqāmah*, in the sermons (given by scholars), and in the introductions of all Islāmic talks and books. When the Prophet (ﷺ) was taken on *Mi'rāj*, Jibrā'īl knocked on the doors of the heavens, and it was asked: "Who is there?" When Jibrā'īl identified himself, he was asked who was with him. He replied: "Muḥammad (ﷺ)." This occurred at each of the seven heavens. Therefore, the Prophet's (ﷺ) name was resounding in the heavens as well. All of the previous scriptures contain some mention about the Prophet (ﷺ), and all of the

Prophets (ﷺ) were commanded to inform their people about the coming of Prophet Muḥammad (ﷺ). In the next life, Prophet Muḥammad (ﷺ) will enjoy the highest position among all of the creations of Allāh (ﷻ) when he attains the high position of *Maqām al-Maḥmūd.*

Imām al-Qurṭubī (رحمه الله) has stated that all of the previous scriptures mention the Messenger of Allāh (ﷺ), and each of the Prophets (ﷺ) were commanded to inform their people about the coming of the final Messenger, Prophet Muḥammad (ﷺ).[28]

One morning the Prophet (ﷺ) came out and said to his companions (رضي الله عنهم):

«إِنَّهُ وُلِدَ لِي اللَّيْلَةَ غُلَامٌ، وَإِنِّي سَمَّيْتُهُ بِاسْمِ أَبِي إِبْرَاهِيمَ».

(الطبقات الكبرى لابن سعد)

"I was blessed with a son last night, and I gave him the name of my forefather, Ibrāhīm." (Ṭabaqāt al-Kubrā of Ibn al-Saʿd)

From this incident, the scholars have deduced that it is part of the *Sunnah* to name children on the day that they are born.

Imām al-Bayhaqī (رحمه الله) elucidates:

«تَسْمِيَةُ الْمَوْلُودِ حِينَ يُولَدُ أَصَحُّ مِنَ الْأَحَادِيثِ فِي تَسْمِيَتِهِ يَوْمَ السَّابِعِ».

(فتح الباري)

"Naming children on the day that they are born is more correct than the narrations regarding naming them on the seventh day after birth." (Fatḥ al-Bārī)

---

[28] The Arabic text of this is as follows:

أَيْ أَعْلَيْنَا ذِكْرَك، فَذَكَرْنَاك فِي الْكُتُب الْمُنَزَّلَة عَلَى الْأَنْبِيَاء قَبْلَك، وَأَمَرْنَاهُمْ بِالْبِشَارَة بِك.

(تفسير القرطبي)

This was Ibrāhīm. His mother was Māriyah whose lineage can be traced back to the Coptic people of Egypt. Muqawqis had given her as a gift to the Prophet (ﷺ), and she was the one who bore Ibrāhīm. She passed away during the time of ʿUmar ibn al-Khaṭṭāb (رضي الله عنه), and is buried in the cemetery of Baqīʿ.[29]

Anas ibn Mālik (رضي الله عنه) narrates:

«مَا رَأَيْتُ أَحَدًا كَانَ أَرْحَمَ بِالْعِيَالِ مِنْ رَسُولِ اللهِ ﷺ، قَالَ: كَانَ إِبْرَاهِيمُ مُسْتَرْضِعًا لَهُ فِي عَوَالِي الْمَدِينَةِ، فَكَانَ يَنْطَلِقُ وَنَحْنُ مَعَهُ فَيَدْخُلُ الْبَيْتَ وَإِنَّهُ لَيُدَّخَنُ، وَكَانَ ظِئْرُهُ قَيْنًا، فَيَأْخُذُهُ فَيُقَبِّلُهُ، ثُمَّ يَرْجِعُ».

(رواه مسلم)

> "I never saw anyone more compassionate towards his family than the Messenger of Allāh (ﷺ). Ibrāhīm was sent to be nursed in the outskirts of Madīnah; thus, the Prophet (ﷺ) would go all of the way there, and we would accompany him. He would then enter the house – which had smoke coming out of it since the husband of Ibrāhīm's foster mother was a blacksmith – and the Prophet (ﷺ) would pick up Ibrāhīm, kiss him, and then return." (Muslim)

Ibrāhīm passed away in the tenth year after *Hijrah*, when he was only eighteen months old,[30] and a solar eclipse occurred on the day that he

---

[29] The Arabic text of this is as follows:

مارية القبطية مولاة رسول الله صَلَّى الله عليه وسلم وأُم ولده إبراهيم، وهي مارية بنت شمعون، أهداها له المقوقس القبطي صاحب الإسكندرية ومصر، وتُوفيت مارية في خلافة عمر بن الخطَّاب، وذلك في المحرم من سنة ست عشرة، وكان عمر يحشر النّاس بنفسه لشهود جنازتها، وصلَّى عليها عمر، ودُفِنت بالبَقِيع.

(سير أعلام النبلاء)

[30] The Arabic text of this is as follows:

died. Consequently, some people thought that the eclipse happened because of his death.

Anas ibn Mālik (ﷺ) narrates:

«دَخَلْنَا مَعَ رَسُولِ اللَّهِ صَلَّى اللَّهُ عَلَيْهِ وَسَلَّمَ عَلَى أَبِي سَيْفٍ القَيْنِ، وَكَانَ ظِئْرًا لِإِبْرَاهِيمَ عَلَيْهِ السَّلاَمُ، فَأَخَذَ رَسُولُ اللَّهِ ﷺ إِبْرَاهِيمَ، فَقَبَّلَهُ، وَشَمَّهُ، ثُمَّ دَخَلْنَا عَلَيْهِ بَعْدَ ذَلِكَ وَإِبْرَاهِيمُ يَجُودُ بِنَفْسِهِ، فَجَعَلَتْ عَيْنَا رَسُولِ اللَّهِ ﷺ تَذْرِفَانِ، فَقَالَ لَهُ عَبْدُ الرَّحْمَنِ بْنُ عَوْفٍ رَضِيَ اللَّهُ عَنْهُ: وَأَنْتَ يَا رَسُولَ اللَّهِ؟ فَقَالَ: يَا ابْنَ عَوْفٍ إِنَّهَا رَحْمَةٌ، ثُمَّ أَتْبَعَهَا بِأُخْرَى، فَقَالَ صَلَّى اللَّهُ عَلَيْهِ وَسَلَّمَ: إِنَّ العَيْنَ تَدْمَعُ، وَالقَلْبَ يَحْزَنُ، وَلاَ نَقُولُ إِلَّا مَا يَرْضَى رَبُّنَا، وَإِنَّا بِفِرَاقِكَ يَا إِبْرَاهِيمُ لَمَحْزُونُونَ».

(رواه البخاري)

"We went with Allāh's Messenger (ﷺ) to the blacksmith Abū Sayf, and he was the husband of the foster mother of Ibrāhīm. Allāh's Messenger (ﷺ) took Ibrahim and kissed him and smelled him; and later we entered (Abū Say's house) and at that time Ibrāhīm was in his last breaths, and the eyes of Allāh's Messenger (ﷺ) started shedding tears." ʿAbd al-Raḥmān ibn ʿAwf (ﷺ) said: "And you, O Messenger of Allāh (you are weeping?)" He (the Prophet (ﷺ)) replied: "O Ibn ʿAwf, this is mercy." Then he (ﷺ) wept more and said: "The eyes shed tears and the heart grieves, but we do not say anything besides what pleases our Lord. O Ibrāhīm, indeed we are grieved by your separation." (Bukhārī)

The Prophet (ﷺ) also said that:

وأرفعُ ما فيه ما ذكره محمد بن إسحاق؛ قال: حدّثنا عبد الله بن أَبي بكر عن عمرة بنت عبد الرّحمن عن عائشة قالت: تُوفِّي إبراهيم ابن النّبيّ ﷺ وهو ابنُ ثمانية عشر شهرًا.

(الاستيعاب في معرفة الأصحاب)

«إِنَّ إِبْرَاهِيمَ ابْنِي، وَإِنَّهُ مَاتَ فِي الثَّدْيِ، وَإِنَّ لَهُ لَظِئْرَيْنِ تُكَمِّلَانِ رَضَاعَهُ فِي الْجَنَّةِ».

(رواه مسلم)

> "Surely Ibrāhīm is my son and he died as a suckling baby. He now has two foster-mothers in Paradise who will continue to nurse him." (Bukhārī)

In conclusion, these were the seven children of the Prophet (ﷺ): Qāsim, ʿAbdullāh, Ibrāhīm, Zaynab, Ruqayyah, Umm Kulthūm, and Fāṭimah. May Allāh (ﷻ) bless all of them.

«فَابْذُلْ مَا لَكَ فِي زَوْرَةِ مَسْجِدِهِ الَّذِي بَنَى فِيْهِ بِيَدِهِ وَالسَّلَامِ عَلَيْهِ عِنْدَ حُجْرَتِهِ فِي بَلَدِهِ، وَالْتَذَّ بِالنَّظَرِ إِلَى أُحُدِهِ وَأَحِبَّهُ، فَقَدْ كَانَ نَبِيُّكَ ﷺ يُحِبُّه، وَتَمَلَّأْ بِالحُلُوْلِ فِي رَوْضَتِهِ وَمَقْعَدِهِ، فَلَنْ تَكُوْنَ مُؤْمِناً حَتَّى يَكُوْنَ هَذَا السَّيِّدُ أَحَبَّ إِلَيْكَ مِنْ نَفْسِكَ وَوَلَدِكَ وَأَمْوَالِكَ وَالنَّاسِ كُلِّهِم».

(سير أعلام النبلاء)

> "So, spend what you have in visiting his *Masjid* which he built with his own hands; and send salutations upon him at his Chamber in his City; and cherish the sight of Uhud, and love it as your Prophet (ﷺ) loved it; and revive yourself by spending time in his Garden where he sat. For you shall not be a true believer until this master becomes more beloved to you than even yourself, your children, your wealth, and the whole of humanity." (Siyar ʿAlām al-Nubalā')

May Allāh (ﷻ) bless us to drink from the *Ḥawḍ of Kawthar* of the Prophet (ﷺ), grant us his intercession, bless us with his company on the Day of Resurrection, and guide us to adhere to his *sunnah* while we are in this world. *Āmīn*

KHUṬBAH 68

The Prophet (ﷺ) was Faithful in All Ways

The Messenger of Allāh, Muḥammad (ﷺ), was the only person who possessed greatness in every way humanly possible.

Normally, people have some parts of their lives which they make sure remain concealed (secret), and they do not want or allow anyone else to know about it. However, our final Messenger, Muḥammad (ﷺ) uncovered all of his life for everyone to see. It was like an open book without any pages hidden or lines erased. Anyone can read any part of it that they wish.

The Prophet (ﷺ) was the only person who permitted his companions (رضي الله عنهم) to publicize and convey everything which emanated from him. As a result, they narrated all of the things that they witnessed him say or do.

One of the splendid and graceful characteristics of the Messenger of Allāh (ﷺ) which the companions (رضي الله عنهم) conveyed to us was that of being faithful.

Some of the definitions of faithful are:

- The concept of unfailingly remaining loyal to someone or something, and putting that loyalty into consistent practice regardless of the extenuating circumstances.
- Loyal, full of faith or trust; firmly and resolutely staying with a person, group, cause, belief, or idea, without wavering, despite the circumstances.

In a broader sense, faithfulness means giving others their rights, reciprocating their kindness, maintaining love between people, and keeping promises.

Allāh (ﷻ) has instructed the people of faith to uphold their promises and remain faithful.

Allāh (ﷻ) says in the Qur'ān:

﴿يَٰٓأَيُّهَا ٱلَّذِينَ ءَامَنُوٓاْ أَوۡفُواْ بِٱلۡعُقُودِۚ ١﴾ [المَائـِدَة الآية ١]

> "O you who believe (people of *īmān*) fulfill your pledges (agreements, promises, and contracts that you make with Allāh, as well as those that you make with people)." (Mā'idah 5:1)

Therefore, faithfulness is a noble trait and a quality of people who observe *taqwā*. Faithfulness entails fulfilling trusts, preserving relationships, and protecting the rights of everyone. It cannot come about without people cooperating, or without agreements being fulfilled. It is something which each servant of Allāh (ﷻ) will be questioned about on the Day of Resurrection.

Allāh (ﷻ) states:

﴿وَأَوۡفُواْ بِٱلۡعَهۡدِۖ إِنَّ ٱلۡعَهۡدَ كَانَ مَسۡـُٔولٗا ٣٤﴾ [الإِسْرَاء الآية ٣٤]

> "And fulfill promises (agreements made with people, as well as pledges made with Allāh (ﷻ)). Certainly, questioning will take place (on the Day of Qiyāmah) with regard to the promises (and people will be taken to task for breaking their promises)." (Isrā' 17:34)

The Messenger of Allāh (ﷺ) reached the insurmountable pinnacle of these qualities, and is unmatched by anyone else.

The Prophet (ﷺ) was faithful in all ways. He was committed to his Lord, and was the most devoted from all of mankind to Him.

He accomplished what it meant to be a true worshipping servant, just like Prophet Ibrāhīm (ﷺ) about whom Allāh (ﷻ) said:

﴿وَإِبْرَٰهِيمَ ٱلَّذِى وَفَّىٰٓ ۝٣٧﴾ [النَّجم الآية ٣٧]

"And of Ibrāhīm, who was true to his trust." (Najm 53:37)

The Prophet (ﷺ) would say:

«أَمَا وَاللهِ، إِنِّي لَأَتْقَاكُمْ لِلَّهِ، وَأَخْشَاكُمْ لَهُ».

(رواه مسلم)

"By Allāh, from among all of you, I observe the most *taqwā* of Allāh, and I have the most reverential fear of Him." (Muslim)

The Messenger of Allāh (ﷺ) stood up and prayed for so long that his feet became swollen.

So ʿĀ'ishah (رضي الله عنها) asked him:

«يَا رَسُولَ اللهِ أَتَصْنَعُ هَذَا، وَقَدْ غُفِرَ لَكَ مَا تَقَدَّمَ مِنْ ذَنْبِكَ وَمَا تَأَخَّرَ».

"O Messenger of Allāh, you exert yourself this much even though your past and future sins have been forgiven?"

Upon this the Prophet (ﷺ) replied:

«يَا عَائِشَةُ، أَفَلَا أَكُونُ عَبْدًا شَكُورًا».

(رواه مسلم)

"O ʿĀ'ishah, should I not be a thankful, worshipping servant?" (Muslim)

The Prophet (ﷺ) would also seek Allāh's (ﷻ) forgiveness, and repent to Him more than one hundred times in a single day. [31]

[31] The Arabic text of this is as follows:

عَنْ أَبِي هُرَيْرَةَ قَالَ: قَالَ رَسُولُ اللهِ ﷺ. «إِنِّي لَأَسْتَغْفِرُ اللَّهَ وَأَتُوبُ إِلَيْهِ فِي الْيَوْمِ مِائَةَ مَرَّةٍ».

(رواه مسلم)

The people who are truly faithful to their promises are those who abide by their vow to Allāh (ﷻ). They fulfill His commandments, avoid His prohibitions, and do not transgress the limits set by Him.

ʿAbdullāh ibn ʿAbbās (رضي الله عنهما) states about His command that "O you who believe, fulfill your pledges" that:

«يَعْنِي بِالْعُهُودِ: يَعْنِي مَا أَحَلَّ اللَّهُ وَمَا حَرَّمَ، وَمَا فَرَضَ وَمَا حَدَّ فِي الْقُرْآنِ كُلِّهِ، فَلَا تَغْدِرُوا وَلَا تَنْكُثُوا».

(تفسير ابن كثير)

"Meaning the promises – meaning that everything which Allāh permitted, prohibited, and obligated in the Qur'ān constitutes the terms of a promise. Therefore, do not commit treachery or break the covenants." (Tafsīr Ibn Kathīr)

Consequently, establishing the prayers, giving charity, and kindness – whether by word or deed – are all parts of our promise to Allāh (ﷻ) which we must fulfill.

Allāh (ﷻ) says in the Qur'ān:

﴿وَإِذْ أَخَذْنَا مِيثَٰقَ بَنِيٓ إِسْرَٰٓءِيلَ لَا تَعْبُدُونَ إِلَّا ٱللَّهَ وَبِٱلْوَٰلِدَيْنِ إِحْسَانًا وَذِى ٱلْقُرْبَىٰ وَٱلْيَتَٰمَىٰ وَٱلْمَسَٰكِينِ وَقُولُوا۟ لِلنَّاسِ حُسْنًا وَأَقِيمُوا۟ ٱلصَّلَوٰةَ وَءَاتُوا۟ ٱلزَّكَوٰةَ ﴿٨٣﴾﴾

[البَقَرَة الآية ٨٣]

"And remember when We took a sworn promise from the *Banī Isrā'īl*, saying to them: Do not worship anyone besides Allāh; and always extend good treatment to parents, relatives, orphans, and the needy; and you must speak the best of words to people, and you must establish *ṣalāh* properly and give *zakāh*." (Baqarah 2:83)

Faithfulness is most due upon those who have the greatest of rights upon us, such as our children, siblings, spouses, and close friends. The

Prophet (ﷺ) was the most devoted of people in caring for his relatives, wives, and companions (رضي الله عنهم).

Furthermore, one of the greatest forms of being faithful is to fulfill the rights of one's parents. Keeping ties with parents is a means of drawing nearness to Allāh (ﷻ), speaking with them is obedience to Him, and their supplications contain much goodness. They are the ones who are the most entitled to your kindness, faithfulness, and company. This is especially so when they become elderly. That is a time when they are usually weak and in need of assistance.

When you were still young, you were the coolness of their eyes and you brought much joy to their lives. They wanted everything good for you. They felt joy over whatever made you happy, they wept over whatever hurt you, and they were never too tired to pray for you. Therefore, treating them well is even more virtuous than *hijrah* (migrating) and *jihād* (striving) in Allāh's (ﷻ) path.

There is a *ḥadīth* in *Ṣaḥīḥ Muslim* which mentions that a man approached the Messenger of Allāh (ﷺ) and said:

«أُبَايِعُكَ عَلَى الْهِجْرَةِ وَالْجِهَادِ، أَبْتَغِي الْأَجْرَ مِنَ اللهِ، قَالَ: فَهَلْ مِنْ وَالِدَيْكَ أَحَدٌ حَيٌّ؟ قَالَ: نَعَمْ، بَلْ كِلَاهُمَا، قَالَ: فَتَبْتَغِي الْأَجْرَ مِنَ اللهِ؟ قَالَ: نَعَمْ، قَالَ: فَارْجِعْ إِلَى وَالِدَيْكَ فَأَحْسِنْ صُحْبَتَهُمَا».

(رواه مسلم)

> "I pledge allegiance to you and promise that I will migrate and strive in Allāh's path, seeking Allāh's reward for doing so." The Prophet (ﷺ) asked him: "Are either of your parents still alive?" The man replied: "Yes, both of them are alive." The Prophet (ﷺ) asked him: "Do you seek Allāh's reward?" He replied: "Yes." The Prophet (ﷺ) told him: "Return to your two parents and be their best companion (look after them and treat them well)." (Muslim)

Many of the *Salaf al-Ṣāliḥīn* (righteous predecessors) (ﷺ) preferred treating their parents well over supererogatory acts of worship.

Muḥammad ibn al-Munkadir (ﷺ) recounts and says:

«بِتُّ أَغْمِزُ رِجْلَ أُمِّي، وَبَاتَ عُمَرُ يُصَلِّي، وَمَا يَسُرُّنِي أَنَّ لَيْلَتِي بِلَيْلَتِهِ».

(حلية الأولياء وطبقات الأصفياء)

> "I spent a night rubbing my mother's feet, while my brother ʿUmar spent the night praying, and it would not please me to have his night in exchange for mine." (Ḥilyat al-Awliyā' wa Ṭabaqāt al-Aṣfiyā')

There is a narration in *Al-Adab al-Mufrad* with a *ṣaḥīḥ* chain of transmission from ʿAbdullāh ibn ʿUmar (ﷺ) who asked a man:

«أَتَفْرَقُ النَّارَ، وَتُحِبُّ أَنْ تَدْخُلَ الْجَنَّةَ؟ قُلْتُ: إِي وَاللَّهِ، قَالَ: أَحَيٌّ وَالِدُكَ؟ قُلْتُ: عِنْدِي أُمِّي، قَالَ: فَوَاللَّهِ، لَوْ أَلَنْتَ لَهَا الْكَلَامَ، وَأَطْعَمْتَهَا الطَّعَامَ، لَتَدْخُلَنَّ الْجَنَّةَ مَا اجْتَنَبْتَ الْكَبَائِرَ».

(الأدب المفرد للبخاري)

> "Do you fear the hellfire, and would love to be admitted into Paradise?" The man replied: "I swear by Allāh that I most certainly would." Ibn ʿUmar asked him: "Are both of your parents still alive?" He replied: "My mother is." Ibn ʿUmar told him: "I swear by Allāh that if you continue to speak to her softly and provide her with food, then you will be admitted to Paradise provided that you avoid the major sins." (Al-Adab al-Mufrad of al-Bukhārī)

Remaining faithful to one's parents does not stop when their lives end.

A devoted child does not forget to pray for his parents and beseeches Allāh (ﷻ) to forgive them; and does not forget them in his charity, *duʿās*, and acts of benevolence.

There is a *ḥadīth* in *Ṣaḥīḥ al-Bukhārī* which mentions that Saʿd ibn ʿUbādah (ﷺ) gave an entire grove of date-palms in charity on his mother's behalf, out of his faithfulness towards her.

ʿAbdullāh ibn ʿAbbās (ﷺ) states that the mother of Saʿd ibn ʿUbādah (ﷺ) died in his absence, so he came to the Prophet (ﷺ) and said:

«إِنَّ أُمِّي تُوُفِّيَتْ وَأَنَا غَائِبٌ عَنْهَا، أَفَيَنْفَعُهَا إِنْ تَصَدَّقْتُ عَنْهَا؟ قَالَ: نَعَمْ ، قَالَ: فَإِنِّي أُشْهِدُكَ أَنَّ حَائِطِيَ الْمِخْرَافَ صَدَقَةٌ عَنْهَا».

(رواه البخاري)

"O Messenger of Allāh, my mother passed away in my absence. Would it benefit her if I gave charity on her behalf?" The Messenger (ﷺ) replied: "Yes, it would." Saʿd said: "With you as my witness, I give my garden called *al-Mikhrāf* in charity on her behalf." (Bukhārī)

In another narration, it is mentioned that Saʿd ibn ʿUbādah (ﷺ) dug a well and said: "This is on behalf of Saʿd's mother."[32]

ʿĀmir ibn ʿAbdullāh ibn al-Zubayr (ﷺ) states:

«مَاتَ أَبِي، فَمَا سَأَلْتُ اللهَ عَزَّ وَجَلَّ حَوْلًا كَامِلًا، إلا الْعَفْوَ عَنْهُ».

(المجالسة وجواهر العلم للدينوري)

"For an entire year after my father passed away, I did not ask Allāh, Grand and Majestic, for anything except that He pardons my father." (Al-Mujālasah wa-Jawāhir al-ʿIlm)

The Prophet (ﷺ) was faithful in all ways. Imām Muslim has collected a *ḥadīth* in which Abu Hurairah (ﷺ) narrates that:

---

[32] The Arabic text of this is as follows:

عَنْ سَعْدِ بْنِ عُبَادَةَ، أَنَّهُ قَالَ يَا رَسُولَ اللَّهِ إِنَّ أُمَّ سَعْدٍ مَاتَتْ فَأَيُّ الصَّدَقَةِ أَفْضَلُ قَالَ «الْمَاءُ» . قَالَ: «فَحَفَرَ بِئْرًا وَقَالَ هَذِهِ لأُمِّ سَعْدٍ».

(الأدب المفرد للبخاري)

«زَارَ النَّبِيُّ ﷺ قَبْرَ أُمِّهِ، فَبَكَى وَأَبْكَى مَنْ حَوْلَهُ، فَقَالَ: اسْتَأْذَنْتُ رَبِّي فِي أَنْ أَسْتَغْفِرَ لَهَا فَلَمْ يُؤْذَنْ لِي، وَاسْتَأْذَنْتُهُ فِي أَنْ أَزُورَ قَبْرَهَا فَأُذِنَ لِي، فَزُورُوا الْقُبُورَ فَإِنَّهَا تُذَكِّرُ الْمَوْتَ».

(رواه مسلم)

The Prophet (ﷺ) visited the grave of his mother. The Prophet (ﷺ) wept and that caused the people around him to weep as well. He said: "I asked my Lord for permission to seek His forgiveness for her, but I was not allowed. However, I asked for His permission to visit her grave and He allowed me. Thus, visit the graves because they will remind you of death." (Muslim)

The Prophet (ﷺ) was faithful in all ways. Once the uncle of the Prophet (ﷺ), ʿAbbās ibn al-Muṭṭalib (رضي الله عنه) asked:

«يَا رَسُولَ اللَّهِ، هَلْ نَفَعْتَ أَبَا طَالِبٍ بِشَيْءٍ، فَإِنَّهُ كَانَ يَحُوطُكَ وَيَغْضَبُ لَكَ؟ قَالَ: نَعَمْ، هُوَ فِي ضَحْضَاحٍ مِنْ نَارٍ، لَوْلاَ أَنَا لَكَانَ فِي الدَّرَكِ الأَسْفَلِ مِنَ النَّارِ».

(رواه البخاري)

"O Messenger of Allāh, have you benefitted Abū Ṭālib in any way? He used to protect you, and became angry if you experienced harm from anyone." He replied: "Yes I have. He is in a shallow part of the hellfire. If it was not for me, he would have been in its lowest depths." (Bukhārī)

The Prophet (ﷺ) was faithful in all ways. He was the most faithful and caring of people towards his wives.

«خَيْرُكُمْ خَيْرُكُمْ لأَهْلِهِ».

(رواه الترمذي)

"The best of you are those of you who are best to their families." (Tirmidhī)

Out of all of the people, Khadījah (﷠) provided the best of assistance to Allāh's (ﷻ) Messenger (ﷺ). She helped him bear the initial heavy phase of calling people to Allāh (ﷻ). She consoled him with herself and her property. She was the best wife towards her husband.

It is mentioned both in *Ṣaḥīḥ Muslim* and *Ṣaḥīḥ al-Bukhārī* that:

«أَتَى جِبْرِيلُ النَّبِيَّ ﷺ، فَقَالَ: يَا رَسُولَ اللَّهِ: هَذِهِ خَدِيجَةُ قَدْ أَتَتْ مَعَهَا إِنَاءٌ فِيهِ إِدَامٌ، أَوْ طَعَامٌ أَوْ شَرَابٌ، فَإِذَا هِيَ أَتَتْكَ فَاقْرَأْ عَلَيْهَا السَّلَامَ مِنْ رَبِّهَا وَمِنِّي وَبَشِّرْهَا بِبَيْتٍ فِي الْجَنَّةِ مِنْ قَصَبٍ لاَ صَخَبَ فِيهِ، وَلاَ نَصَبَ».

Jibrā'īl (﷠) came to the Prophet (ﷺ) and said: "O Messenger of Allāh, Khadījah is approaching and bringing a vessel that contains some broth, food, or drink. When she reaches you, convey to her the *salām* from her Lord and from myself, and convey to her the glad tidings of an abode in Paradise made of gems, containing no raucousness or fatigue."

Ḥāfiẓ ibn al-Ḥajr (﷫) quotes Imām al-Suhaylī (﷫) as follows:

«وهذا مناسب لما كانت عليه خديجة ﵂ من حُسْن الاستجابة والطاعة، فلم تُحوج زوجها إلى رفع صوت ولا منازعة ولا تعَب؛ بل أزالت عنه كل نَصَب، وآنسته من كل وحشة، وهوَّنَت عليه كل عصيب، وكانت حريصة على رضاه بكل ممكن، ولم يصدر منها ما يُغضبه قط؛ فناسَب أن يكون منزلها الذي بُشرت به من ربها بالصفة المقابلة لفعلها؛ فهي لم تصخب عليه، ولم تتعبه يومًا من الدهر».

(فتح الباري)

"This is quite fitting when taking into account all that Khadījah (﷠) did. She obediently accepted the call of her husband, the Prophet (ﷺ). She did not exhaust him, or provoke him to raise his voice or argue. Rather, she relieved him of his fatigue, consoled him, and eased his hardships. She did everything that

> she could to please him and never did anything to upset him. As a result, it is only appropriate that the abode which she received glad tidings about from her Lord, be one that matches her conduct. At no time did she upset her husband or behave harshly towards him." (Fatḥ al-Bārī)

Moreover, the Messenger of Allāh (ﷺ) reciprocated her faithfulness with even more than hers. He recognized her status and fulfilled her rights - both during her lifetime, and even after she passed away. He often mentioned her virtues and would send gifts to her close acquaintances.

When someone is beloved to a person, then one will also love what is beloved to them.

ʿĀ'ishah (رضي الله عنها) narrates:

«مَا غِرْتُ عَلَى أَحَدٍ مِنْ نِسَاءِ النَّبِيِّ ﷺ مَا غِرْتُ عَلَى خَدِيجَةَ، وَمَا رَأَيْتُهَا، وَلَكِنْ كَانَ النَّبِيُّ ﷺ يُكْثِرُ ذِكْرَهَا، وَرُبَّمَا ذَبَحَ الشَّاةَ، ثُمَّ يُقَطِّعُهَا أَعْضَاءً، ثُمَّ يَبْعَثُهَا فِي صَدَائِقِ خَدِيجَةَ، فَرُبَّمَا قُلْتُ لَهُ كَأَنَّهُ لَمْ يَكُنْ فِي الدُّنْيَا امْرَأَةٌ إِلاَّ خَدِيجَةُ. فَيَقُولُ إِنَّهَا كَانَتْ وَكَانَتْ، وَكَانَ لِي مِنْهَا وَلَدٌ».

(رواه البخاري)

> "I did not feel jealousy towards any of the wives of the Prophet (ﷺ) as much as I did towards Khadījah, although I never saw her. The Prophet (ﷺ) would mention her very often. There were times when he would sacrifice a sheep, cut it into sections, and send them to Khadījah's acquaintances. I even said to him that it was as though there were no other women in the world besides Khadījah. He replied by mentioning her virtuous qualities, and he also added: 'I had children from her.'" (Bukhārī)

Furthermore, he used to say:

«إِنِّي قَدْ رُزِقْتُ حُبَّهَا».

(رواه مسلم)

"Love for her was placed inside of me (i.e. her love had been nurtured in my heart by Allāh (ﷻ) Himself)." (Muslim)

The Prophet's (ﷺ) immense faithfulness towards her was also demonstrated by the fact that there was once a woman who came to him, and she was someone who had come when Khadījah (ؓ) was alive.

As a result, he became overjoyed and was kind towards her and he told his family:

«أَكْرِمُوهَا فَقَدْ كَانَتْ خَدِيجَةُ تُحِبُّهَا».

(شرح النووي على مسلم)

"Treat her well, for Khadījah was very fond of her." (Imām al-Nawawī's commentary on Muslim)

ʿĀ'ishah (ؓ) narrates:

«جَاءَتْ عَجُوزٌ إِلَى النَّبِيِّ ﷺ وَهُوَ عِنْدِي، فَقَالَ: لَهَا رَسُولُ اللهِ ﷺ: مَنْ أَنْتِ؟ قَالَتْ: أَنَا جَثَّامَةُ الْمُزَنِيَّةُ، فَقَالَ: بَلْ أَنْتِ حَسَّانَةُ الْمُزَنِيَّةُ، كَيْفَ أَنْتُمْ؟ كَيْفَ حَالُكُمْ؟ كَيْفَ كُنْتُمْ بَعْدَنَا؟ قَالَتْ: بِخَيْرٍ بِأَبِي أَنْتَ وَأُمِّي يَا رَسُولَ اللهِ، فَلَمَّا خَرَجَتْ قُلْتُ: يَا رَسُولَ اللهِ، تُقْبِلُ عَلَى هَذِهِ الْعَجُوزِ هَذَا الْإِقْبَالَ؟ فَقَالَ: إِنَّهَا كَانَتْ تَأْتِينَا زَمَنَ خَدِيجَةَ، وَإِنَّ حُسْنَ الْعَهْدِ مِنَ الْإِيمَانِ».

(مستدرك الحاكم)

"An elderly woman once came to the Prophet (ﷺ) while he was with me. The Messenger of Allāh (ﷺ) said to her: 'How are things with you, and how have you been after us?' She replied: 'O Messenger of Allāh, I have been well. May my own parents be sacrificed for you.' When she departed, I inquired: 'O Messenger of Allāh, how come you were so welcoming towards that elderly woman?' He replied: 'She used to come to us during

> Khadījah's days, and remaining faithful to one's trusts is a part of faith (*īmān*).'" (Mustadrak al-Ḥākim)

In addition, whenever the Prophet (ﷺ) heard the voice of Hālah, who was Khadījah's (رضي الله عنها) sister, it reminded him of the way that Khadījah (رضي الله عنها) used to ask permission. As a result, his spirits would change and he would feel happy. [33]

Imām al-Nawawī (رحمه الله) comments and says:

«وَفِي هَذَا كُلِّهِ دَلِيلٌ لِحُسْنِ الْعَهْدِ، وَحِفْظِ الْوُدِّ، وَرِعَايَةِ حُرْمَةِ الصَّاحِبِ وَالْعَشِيرِ فِي حَيَاتِهِ وَوَفَاتِهِ، وَإِكْرَامِ أَهْلِ ذَلِكَ الصَّاحِبِ».

(شرح النووى على مسلم)

> "All of this demonstrates that he remained faithful to his trusts and loved ones. He took care of those who were close to him – during their lives and even after they passed away – and he also extended kindness to the families of those who were close to him." (Imām al-Nawawī's commentary on Muslim)

The Prophet (ﷺ) was faithful in all ways. He was faithful towards relatives and in-laws. The Prophet (ﷺ) commanded that good care and treatment be extended to the people of Egypt.

Abū Dharr (رضي الله عنه) narrates that the Prophet (ﷺ) said:

«إِنَّكُمْ سَتَفْتَحُونَ مِصْرَ، وَهِيَ أَرْضٌ يُسَمَّى فِيهَا الْقِيرَاطُ، فَإِذَا فَتَحْتُمُوهَا، فَأَحْسِنُوا إِلَى أَهْلِهَا، فَإِنَّ لَهُمْ ذِمَّةً وَرَحِمًا، أَوْ قَالَ: ذِمَّةً وَصِهْرًا».

(رواه مسلم)

[33] The Arabic text of this is as follows:
عَنْ عَائِشَةَ، قَالَتِ: اسْتَأْذَنَتْ هَالَةُ بِنْتُ خُوَيْلِدٍ أُخْتُ خَدِيجَةَ عَلَى رَسُولِ اللَّهِ ﷺ فَعَرَفَ اسْتِئْذَانَ خَدِيجَةَ فَارْتَاحَ لِذَلِكَ.
(رواه مسلم)

> "You will conquer Egypt, and when that happens, take good care of its people because they are entitled to protection and they are our kin," or he said: "they are our in-laws." (Muslim)

NOTE: 'Kin' is in reference to Hājar (ﷺ) being from Egypt. She was the mother of Prophet Ismāʿīl (ﷺ), and the wife of Prophet Ibrāhīm (ﷺ). The Prophet (ﷺ) was one of their descendants. 'In-laws' is in reference to Māriyah being from Egypt. She was the mother of Ibrāhīm, one of the sons of the Prophet (ﷺ). [34]

The Prophet (ﷺ) was faithful in all ways. During the encounter against the tribe of *Hawāzin*, some of their women were captured. However, the Messenger of Allāh (ﷺ) had been nursed by people of that tribe when he was an infant.

A delegation from *Hawāzin* came to him and said:

«يَا رَسُولَ اللَّهِ، إِنَّ مَا فِي الْحَظَائِرِ مِنَ السَّبَايَا خَالَاتُكَ وَعَمَّاتُكَ وَحَوَاضِنُكَ اللَّاتِي كُنَّ يَكْفُلْنَكَ، فَامْنُنْ عَلَيْنَا مَنَّ اللَّهُ عَلَيْكَ».

(البداية والنهاية)

> "O Messenger of Allāh, women who nursed you and women who are your own aunts are among the captives, so be kind to us." (Al-Bidāyah wa al-Nihāyah)

«وَسَيَأْتِي أَنَّهُ عَلَيْهِ الصَّلَاةُ وَالسَّلَامُ أَطْلَقَ لَهُمُ الذُّرِّيَّةَ، وَكَانَتْ سِتَّةَ آلَافٍ مَا بَيْنَ صَبِيٍّ وَامْرَأَةٍ، وَأَعْطَاهُمْ أَنْعَامًا وَأَنَاسِيَّ كَثِيرًا حَتَّى قَالَ أَبُو الْحُسَيْنِ بْنُ فَارِسَ: فَكَانَ قِيمَةَ مَا أَطْلَقَ لَهُمْ يَوْمَئِذٍ خَمْسَمِائَةِ أَلْفِ أَلْفِ دِرْهَمٍ».

(البداية والنهاية)

---

[34] The Arabic text of this is as follows:

وَأَمَّا الرَّحِمُ فَلِكَوْنِ هَاجَرَ أُمِّ إِسْمَاعِيلَ مِنْهُمْ، وَأَمَّا الصِّهْرُ فَلِكَوْنِ مَارِيَةَ أُمِّ إِبْرَاهِيمَ مِنْهُمْ.

(شرح النووى على مسلم)

As a result, he freed 6,000 of the children and women, and in addition to that he gave them nearly half a million dirhams in goods as well. (Al-Bidāyah wa al-Nihāyah)

«لَمَّا كَانَ يَوْمُ فَتْحِ هَوَازِنَ جَاءَتْ جَارِيَةٌ إِلَى رَسُولِ اللَّهِ ﷺ فَقَالَتْ: يَا رَسُولَ اللَّهِ أَنَا أُخْتُكَ، أَنَا شَيْمَاءُ بِنْتُ الْحَارِثِ. فَقَالَ لَهَا: إِنْ تَكُونِي صَادِقَةً، فَإِنَّ بِكِ مِنِّي أَثَرٌ لَا يَبْلَى. قَالَ: فَكَشَفَتْ عَنْ عَضُدِهَا، فَقَالَتْ: نَعَمْ يَا رَسُولَ اللَّهِ، وَأَنْتَ صَغِيرٌ، فَعَضِضْتَنِي هَذِهِ الْعَضَّةَ. قَالَ: فَبَسَطَ لَهَا رَسُولُ اللَّهِ ﷺ رِدَاءَهُ، ثُمَّ قَالَ: سَلِي تُعْطَيْ، وَاشْفَعِي تُشَفَّعِي».

(البداية والنهاية)

In addition, when his foster sister, Shaymā', came to him, he spread his own garment for her to sit beside him, and he was also very kind and generous to her. (Al-Bidāyah wa al-Nihāyah)

The Prophet (ﷺ) was faithful in all ways. He was faithful, caring and loving to his companions (رضي الله عنهم). He highlighted their virtues, spoke highly about them, and prohibited others from insulting them. He gave special precedence to Abū Bakr (رضي الله عنه) who was with him while they hid in a cave during their migration from Makkah to Madīnah.

Abū al-Dardā' (رضي الله عنه) narrates:

«كُنْتُ جَالِسًا عِنْدَ النَّبِيِّ ﷺ، إِذْ أَقْبَلَ أَبُو بَكْرٍ آخِذًا بِطَرَفِ ثَوْبِهِ حَتَّى أَبْدَى عَنْ رُكْبَتِهِ، فَقَالَ النَّبِيُّ ﷺ: أَمَّا صَاحِبُكُمْ فَقَدْ غَامَرَ، فَسَلَّمَ وَقَالَ: إِنِّي كَانَ بَيْنِي وَبَيْنَ ابْنِ الْخَطَّابِ شَيْءٌ، فَأَسْرَعْتُ إِلَيْهِ ثُمَّ نَدِمْتُ، فَسَأَلْتُهُ أَنْ يَغْفِرَ لِي فَأَبَى عَلَيَّ، فَأَقْبَلْتُ إِلَيْكَ، فَقَالَ: يَغْفِرُ اللَّهُ لَكَ يَا أَبَا بَكْرٍ ثَلَاثًا، ثُمَّ إِنَّ عُمَرَ نَدِمَ، فَأَتَى مَنْزِلَ أَبِي بَكْرٍ، فَسَأَلَ: أَثَمَّ أَبُو بَكْرٍ؟ فَقَالُوا: لَا، فَأَتَى إِلَى النَّبِيِّ ﷺ فَسَلَّمَ، فَجَعَلَ وَجْهُ النَّبِيِّ ﷺ يَتَمَعَّرُ، حَتَّى أَشْفَقَ أَبُو بَكْرٍ، فَجَثَا عَلَى رُكْبَتَيْهِ، فَقَالَ: يَا رَسُولَ اللَّهِ، وَاللَّهِ أَنَا كُنْتُ أَظْلَمَ، مَرَّتَيْنِ، فَقَالَ النَّبِيُّ ﷺ: إِنَّ اللَّهَ بَعَثَنِي إِلَيْكُمْ فَقُلْتُمْ كَذَبْتَ، وَقَالَ أَبُو بَكْرٍ صَدَقَ، وَوَاسَانِي بِنَفْسِهِ وَمَالِهِ، فَهَلْ أَنْتُمْ تَارِكُوا لِي صَاحِبِي مَرَّتَيْنِ، فَمَا أُوذِيَ بَعْدَهَا».

(رواه البخاري)

Once he was sitting with the Prophet (ﷺ) when he saw Abū Bakr (رضي الله عنه) approaching from a distance. Abū Bakr (رضي الله عنه) was holding up the edge of his garment and rushing, so much so that his knee became uncovered. The Prophet (ﷺ) said: "Your companion has had an argument." When Abū Bakr (رضي الله عنه) arrived, he extended the *salām* and said: "An exchange took place between me and Ibn al-Khaṭṭāb. I upset him and I regret that. I asked him to forgive me but he refused, so I came to you." The Prophet (ﷺ) repeated three times: "Abū Bakr (رضي الله عنه), may Allāh forgive you." Meanwhile, ʿUmar (رضي الله عنه) also regretted his refusal so he went to Abū Bakr's (رضي الله عنه) home and asked if he was there. They replied in the negative so ʿUmar (رضي الله عنه) went to the Prophet (ﷺ) and extended his *salām* when he arrived there. However, anger was clearly visible on the face of the Prophet (ﷺ), and Abū Bakr (رضي الله عنه) feared that something bad might be said to ʿUmar (رضي الله عنه). Thus, Abū Bakr (رضي الله عنه) fell to his knees and said two times: "O Messenger of Allāh, I swear by Allāh that I was more at fault." The Prophet (ﷺ) said: "Indeed, Allāh sent me to you people. You belied me, but Abū Bakr (رضي الله عنه) said I was truthful, and he shared his life and wealth with me. Will you not then leave my companion alone?" He said this two times. Abū al-Dardā' (رضي الله عنه) also added that Abū Bakr (رضي الله عنه) was never harmed after that. (Bukhārī)

When the expedition of Ḥunayn took place, the Messenger of Allāh (ﷺ) distributed the spoils, but did not give the *Anṣār* anything, and they were somewhat unsettled on account of that.

So, the Messenger of Allāh (ﷺ) comforted and reassured them, and said to them:

«أَوَجَدْتُمْ فِي أَنْفُسِكُمْ يَا مَعْشَرَ الْأَنْصَارِ فِي لُعَاعَةٍ مِنَ الدُّنْيَا، تَأَلَّفْتُ بِهَا قَوْمًا لِيُسْلِمُوا، وَوَكَلْتُكُمْ إِلَى إِسْلَامِكُمْ؟ أَفَلَا تَرْضَوْنَ يَا مَعْشَرَ الْأَنْصَارِ أَنْ يَذْهَبَ النَّاسُ بِالشَّاةِ وَالْبَعِيرِ، وَتَرْجِعُونَ بِرَسُولِ اللهِ فِي رِحَالِكُمْ؟ فَوَالَّذِي نَفْسُ مُحَمَّدٍ بِيَدِهِ لَوْلَا الْهِجْرَةُ لَكُنْتُ امْرَأً مِنَ الْأَنْصَارِ، وَلَوْ سَلَكَ النَّاسُ شِعْبًا، وَسَلَكَتِ الْأَنْصَارُ شِعْبًا لَسَلَكْتُ شِعْبَ الْأَنْصَارِ، اللهُمَّ ارْحَمِ الْأَنْصَارَ، وَأَبْنَاءَ الْأَنْصَارِ، وَأَبْنَاءَ أَبْنَاءِ الْأَنْصَارِ قَالَ: فَبَكَى الْقَوْمُ، حَتَّى أَخْضَلُوا لِحَاهُمْ، وَقَالُوا: رَضِينَا بِرَسُولِ اللهِ قِسْمًا وَحَظًّا».

(رواه أحمد)

"O people of *Anṣār*, are you upset with me because I gave a few trifling things of this world to some people in order for them to accept Islām, while I entrusted you to the Islām which you already have? O people of *Anṣār*, would it not please you for the people to leave with a sheep and a camel, while you take the Messenger of Allāh (ﷺ) back with you? I swear by the One in whose hand the soul of Muḥammad lies, if it was not for the *hijrah*, I would be one of the *Anṣār*. If people tread on one path and the *Anṣār* tread another, I would tread the path of the *Anṣār*. O Allāh, have mercy upon the *Anṣār*, their children, and their children's children." When he said that, the people wept until their beards were soaked with their tears, and then they said: "We are content to take the Messenger of Allāh as our portion." (Aḥmad)

The Prophet (ﷺ) was faithful in all ways. He was faithful to his *ummah* by articulately conveying Allāh's (ﷻ) message, guiding them, and leaving them on a clear path.

Allāh (ﷻ) says in the Qur'ān:

﴿لَقَدْ جَآءَكُمْ رَسُولٌ مِّنْ أَنفُسِكُمْ عَزِيزٌ عَلَيْهِ مَا عَنِتُّمْ حَرِيصٌ عَلَيْكُم بِٱلْمُؤْمِنِينَ رَءُوفٌ رَّحِيمٌ ۝١٢٨﴾ [التَّوْبَة الآية ١٢٨]

> "There has indeed come to you a Messenger from among yourselves (someone whose lineage, morals, manners and integrity you know well). It grieves him that you should suffer. He is concerned about you (he is anxious for good to come to you) and extremely forgiving and merciful (gentle and kind) towards the believers." (Tawbah 9:128)

There were many actions which he left off in order to not cause people hardship. He would say that if it was not for the fear of putting his *ummah* through difficulty, he would have done certain things, or commanded them to do certain things. He would often say:

«لَوْلَا أَنْ أَشُقَّ عَلَى أُمَّتِي لَأَمَرْتُهُمْ أَنْ ....».

> "Had I not thought it difficult for my *ummah*, I would have commanded them to……"

ʿAbdullāh ibn ʿAmr ibn al-ʿĀṣ (ﷻ) narrates that onetime the final Messenger (ﷺ) recited what Prophet ʿĪsā (ﷺ) said to Allāh (ﷻ):

« وَقَالَ عِيسَى عَلَيْهِ السَّلَامُ: ﴿إِن تُعَذِّبْهُمْ فَإِنَّهُمْ عِبَادُكَ ۖ وَإِن تَغْفِرْ لَهُمْ فَإِنَّكَ أَنتَ ٱلْعَزِيزُ ٱلْحَكِيمُ ﴿١١٨﴾﴾ [المَائِـدَة الآية ١١٨] ، فَرَفَعَ يَدَيْهِ وَقَالَ: اللهُمَّ أُمَّتِي أُمَّتِي، وَبَكَى، فَقَالَ اللهُ عَزَّ وَجَلَّ: يَا جِبْرِيلُ اذْهَبْ إِلَى مُحَمَّدٍ، وَرَبُّكَ أَعْلَمُ، فَسَلْهُ مَا يُبْكِيكَ؟ فَأَتَاهُ جِبْرِيلُ عَلَيْهِ الصَّلَاةُ وَالسَّلَامُ، فَسَأَلَهُ فَأَخْبَرَهُ رَسُولُ اللهِ ﷺ بِمَا قَالَ، وَهُوَ أَعْلَمُ، فَقَالَ اللهُ: يَا جِبْرِيلُ، اذْهَبْ إِلَى مُحَمَّدٍ، فَقُلْ: إِنَّا سَنُرْضِيكَ فِي أُمَّتِكَ، وَلَا نَسُوءُكَ».

(رواه مسلم)

> "If You punish them, then verily they are Your slaves (and You are at liberty to treat them as You please), and if You forgive them, then surely You are the Mighty, the Wise (and Your reason for doing so is filled with wisdom)." After he recited these verses, the Prophet (ﷺ) raised his hands and said: "O Allāh, my *ummah*, my *ummah*," and he wept. Allāh then said:

"Jibrā'īl, go to Muḥammad (though your Lord knows it fully well) and ask him: "What makes you weep?" So Jibrā'īl (ﷺ) came to him and asked him (the reason for his weeping), and the Messenger of Allāh informed him what he had said (though Allāh knew it well). Upon this Allāh said: "O Jibrā'īl, go to Muḥammad (ﷺ) and say: 'We will surely please you regarding your *ummah* and We will not cause you to grieve over them.'" (Muslim)

CONCLUSION

- Faithfulness is a splendid quality which every person must strive to adorn themselves with.
- It represents sincerity without betrayal or deception.
- It represents an attitude of unlimited giving and selflessness.
- It would be beautiful for us to personify this quality sincerely with all of our body parts and limbs, without any faking or pretending.
- True relationships are those in which people maintain faithfulness, keep promises, and show kindness towards each other.
- Being faithful is a mark of one's religion and integrity.
- It is a quality of righteous people, and an element inherent to all virtuous characteristics.
- *Taqwā*, faithfulness, honesty, generosity, and integrity are inseparable traits. They brighten a person's face, earn one an honourable mention, increase one's rewards, and please Allāh (ﷻ).
- True loyalty only comes from a pure heart that is driven by sincere intentions.
- Faithfulness is a quality of the Prophets.

Allāh (ﷻ) says in the Qur'ān:

﴿وَإِبْرَٰهِيمَ ٱلَّذِى وَفَّىٰٓ ﴿٣٧﴾﴾ [النَّجم الآية ٣٧]

"And of Ibrāhīm, who was true (to his trusts)." (Najm 53:37)

﴿وَٱذْكُرْ فِى ٱلْكِتَٰبِ إِسْمَٰعِيلَ ۚ إِنَّهُۥ كَانَ صَادِقَ ٱلْوَعْدِ وَكَانَ رَسُولًا نَّبِيًّا ﴿٥٤﴾﴾ [مَرْيَم الآية ٥٤]

"And mention in the Book (Qur'ān), Ismāʿīl. He was indeed faithful to his promises, and he was a Messenger and a Prophet." (Maryam 19:54)

Faithfulness is a sign of one's faith, and among the qualities of people who have faith is being faithful.

Allāh (ﷻ) mentions:

﴿وَٱلْمُوفُونَ بِعَهْدِهِمْ إِذَا عَٰهَدُوا۟ ۖ ﴿١٧٧﴾﴾ [البَقَرَة الآية ١٧٧]

"And (those who) are faithful to their promises when they make them." (Baqarah 2:177)

Faithfulness allows one to attain the highest of ranks.

Allāh (ﷻ) says:

﴿وَمَنْ أَوْفَىٰ بِمَا عَٰهَدَ عَلَيْهُ ٱللَّهَ فَسَيُؤْتِيهِ أَجْرًا عَظِيمًا ﴿١٠﴾﴾ [الفَتْح الآية ١٠]

"And if someone remains faithful in fulfilling his promise to Allāh, then He shall grant that person a tremendous (great) reward." (Fatḥ 48:10)

Allāh (ﷻ) also commended the people of faith by describing them as:

﴿ٱلَّذِينَ يُوفُونَ بِعَهْدِ ٱللَّهِ وَلَا يَنقُضُونَ ٱلْمِيثَٰقَ ﴿٢٠﴾﴾ [الرَّعْد الآية ٢٠]

(The people of intelligence are) Those who are faithful in fulfilling (their promise) taken with Allāh, and do not betray their contracts." (Raʿd 13:20)

There are more than twenty verses in the Qur'ān that discuss being faithful. All of the verses which mention promises or agreements are also either implicitly or explicitly related to being faithful.

The greatest manifestation of faithfulness is to fulfill the rights of Allāh (ﷻ). He (ﷻ) says in the Qur'ān:

﴿وَأَوْفُوا۟ بِعَهْدِىٓ أُوفِ بِعَهْدِكُمْ وَإِيَّـٰىَ فَٱرْهَبُونِ ۝٤٠﴾ [البَقَرَة الآية ٤٠]

"Fulfill (your obligations to) My Covenant (which is upon you) so that I fulfill (My obligations to) your covenant (with Me), and fear none except Me." (Baqarah 2:40)

﴿وَبِعَهْدِ ٱللَّهِ أَوْفُوا۟ ۚ ۝١٥٢﴾ [الأَنْعَام الآية ١٥٢]

"And the covenant of Allāh fulfill." (An'ām 6:152)

The renowned commentator of the Qur'ān, Ḥāfiẓ ibn Jarīr al-Ṭabarī (رحمه الله) comments and says that:

«وَعَهْده إِيَّاهُمْ: أَنَّهُمْ إِذَا فَعَلُوا ذَلِكَ أَدْخَلَهُمُ الْجَنَّةَ».

(تفسير الطبري)

"Allāh promised them that if they fulfill their covenants, then they will be admitted to Paradise..." (Tafsīr al-Ṭabarī)

Additionally, being trustworthy and devoted is a necessary component of family life at all times. The greatest promise that there is between two people is the covenant of marriage.

The Prophet (ﷺ) has stated:

«أَحَقُّ مَا أَوْفَيْتُمْ مِنَ الشُّرُوطِ أَنْ تُوفُوا بِهِ مَا اسْتَحْلَلْتُمْ بِهِ الْفُرُوجَ».

(رواه البخاري)

"The conditions most deserving of being fulfilled are those which have made intimacy lawful for you (through the marriage contract)." (Bukhārī)

Allāh (ﷻ) further says:

﴿وَلَا تَنسَوُا۟ ٱلْفَضْلَ بَيْنَكُمْ ۚ ﴿٢٣٧﴾﴾ [البَقَرَة الآية ٢٣٧]

"And do not neglect (forget) kindness between yourselves." (Baqarah 2:237)

Since faithfulness is a quality which stems from faith (*īmān*) and God consciousness (*taqwā*), it is clear that treachery and betrayal are qualities which stem from hypocrisy (*nifāq*)[35] and disobedience to Allāh (ﷻ).

ʿAbdullāh ibn ʿAmr ibn al-ʿĀṣ (رضي الله عنهما) narrates that the Prophet (ﷺ) said:

«أَرْبَعٌ مَنْ كُنَّ فِيهِ كَانَ مُنَافِقًا خَالِصًا، وَمَنْ كَانَتْ فِيهِ خَصْلَةٌ مِنْهُنَّ كَانَتْ فِيهِ خَصْلَةٌ مِنَ النِّفَاقِ حَتَّى يَدَعَهَا إِذَا اؤْتُمِنَ خَانَ وَإِذَا حَدَّثَ كَذَبَ وَإِذَا عَاهَدَ غَدَرَ، وَإِذَا خَاصَمَ فَجَرَ».

(رواه البخاري)

"Whoever has the following four (characteristics) will be a pure hypocrite, and whoever has even one of the following four characteristics will have one characteristic of hypocrisy - unless the person gives it up:
1. Whenever he is entrusted, he betrays.
2. Whenever he speaks, he tells a lie.
3. Whenever he makes a covenant, he proves treacherous.
4. Whenever he quarrels, he behaves in a very imprudent, evil and insulting manner." (Bukhārī)

Therefore, let us continue to observe the *taqwā* of Allāh (ﷻ), and personify the beautiful conduct and noble qualities that our religion teaches us to embody.

إِذَا اجْتَمَعَ الآفَاتُ فَالبُخْلُ شَرُّهَا ۞ وَشَرٌّ مِنَ البُخْلِ المَوَاعِيدُ وَالمَطَلُ

وَلَا خَيْرَ فِي وَعْدٍ إِذَا كَانَ كَاذِبًا ۞ وَلَا خَيْرَ فِي قَوْلٍ إِذَا لَمْ يَكُنْ فِعَلُ

---

[35] In this context, *nifāq* refers to outwardly exhibiting a trait while harbouring the opposite within.

When there are a multitude of miseries, miserliness is the worst of them,
And worse than miserliness is false promises and tardiness.
There is no good in a promise when it is dishonest,
And there is no good in that which you say but do not do.

We seek refuge with Allāh (ﷻ) from being forsaken, and we seek His protection from the paths of Shayṭān.

الصُّبْحُ بَدَا مِنْ طَلْعَتِهِ ۞ وَاللَّيْلُ دَجَا مِنْ وَفْرَتِهِ

فَاقَ الرُّسْلاَ فَضْلاً وَعُلاَ ۞ أَهْدَى السُّبْلاَ لِدَلاَلَتِهِ

كَنْزُ الْكَرِيمِ مُوْلِي النِّعَمِ ۞ هَادِي الأُمَمِ لِشَرِيعَتِهِ

أَذْكَى النَّسَبِ أَعْلَى الْحَسَبِ ۞ كُلُّ الْعَرَبِ فِي خِدْمَتِهِ

سَعَتِ الشَّجَرُ نَطَقَ الْحَجَرُ ۞ شُقَّ الْقَمَرُ بِإِشَارَتِهِ

جِبْرِيلُ أَتَى لَيْلَةَ أَسْرَى ۞ وَالرَّبُّ دَعَاهُ لِحَضْرَتِهِ

نَالَ الشَّرَفَا وَاللهُ عَفَا ۞ عَمَّا سَلَفَا مِنْ أُمَّتِهِ

فَمُحَمَّدُنَا هُوَ سَيِّدُنَا ۞ فَالعِزُّ لَنَا لِإِجَابَتِهِ

The light of dawn is from the radiance of his face,
The sparkle of the night is from the glimmer of his hair.
He exceeded all of the Messengers in merit and rank,
He guided people to the paths with his signs and proofs.
Trees walked towards him; stones spoke to greet him,
The moon was split upon a signal of his hand.
[Archangel] Jibrā'īl came to him (with glad tidings from Allāh) on the Night of Ascension,
And the Lord invited him [to the heavens] and bestowed upon him honour.
He attained the highest honour, and Allāh pardoned,
All of his nation's past sins.
For Muḥammad is our master and leader,
Honour and pride are ours for accepting his call.

KHUṬBAH 69

He is Al-Fattāḥ, the All-Knowing

Understanding Allāh's (ﷻ) sublime names is an important area of knowledge. In fact, it is the most important type of understanding which we need to have. Cognizance of Allāh (ﷻ) leads to having love for Him, having reverence of Him, recognizing His majesty, fearing Him, keeping our hope in Him, and sincerely devoting one's deeds to Allāh (ﷻ) alone. As that knowledge becomes stronger within a person, it leads one to grow in devotion to Allāh (ﷻ), submit to His directives, fulfill Allāh's (ﷻ) commands, and avoid the prohibitions set by Him.

One of Allāh's (ﷻ) sublime names mentioned in the Qur'ān is *al-Fattāḥ*.

It is mentioned in two passages of the Qur'ān. One is:

﴿قُلْ يَجْمَعُ بَيْنَنَا رَبُّنَا ثُمَّ يَفْتَحُ بَيْنَنَا بِٱلْحَقِّ وَهُوَ ٱلْفَتَّاحُ ٱلْعَلِيمُ ﴿٢٦﴾﴾ [سبإ الآية ٢٦]

"Say: 'Our Lord will gather us (on the Day of Qiyāmah) and then decide between us with the truth (with justice). He is certainly the Best Judge, the All-Knowing.' (No information is hidden from Him)." (Sabā' 34:26)

The other verse is:

﴿وَسِعَ رَبُّنَا كُلَّ شَىْءٍ عِلْمًا ۚ عَلَى ٱللَّهِ تَوَكَّلْنَا ۚ رَبَّنَا ٱفْتَحْ بَيْنَنَا وَبَيْنَ قَوْمِنَا بِٱلْحَقِّ وَأَنتَ خَيْرُ ٱلْفَٰتِحِينَ ﴿٨٩﴾﴾ [الأعراف الآية ٨٩]

"The knowledge of our Lord surrounds (covers) everything and in Him alone do we trust (we trust that Allāh will keep us steadfast on His true religion and not cause us to deviate).

(However, when Prophet Shuʿayb realized that his people would not listen to him, he prayed) O our Lord! Decide between us and our people with the truth, for You are the best of deciders (let it be known who is on the right and who is not)." (Aʿrāf 7:89)

The scholars of Islām have elaborated on the meanings of Allāh's (ﷻ) name *al-Fattāḥ.*

Ibn al-Qayyim (رحمه الله) states that *al-Fattāḥ* conveys two meanings:

«الأول: يرجع إلى معنى الحُكْم الذي يفتح بين عباده، ويحكم بينَهم بشرعه، ويحكم بينَهم بإثابة الطائعينَ وعقوبة العاصينَ في الدنيا والآخرة، المعنى الثاني: فَتْحُه لعبادِه جميعَ أبواب الخيرات».

(فتح الرحيم الملك العلام للشيخ عبدالرحمن السعدي)

"One meaning has to do with giving judgement, and settling matters between His servants in this world and the hereafter by rewarding those who obey Him, and punishing those who disobey Him. The other meaning has to do with opening the gates to all forms of goodness for His servants." (Fatḥ al-Raḥīm al-Malik al-ʿAlām of Shaykh ʿAbd al-Raḥmān al-Saʿdī)

Allāh (ﷻ) says in the Qur'ān:

﴿مَّا يَفْتَحِ ٱللَّهُ لِلنَّاسِ مِن رَّحْمَةٍ فَلَا مُمْسِكَ لَهَا ۖ وَمَا يُمْسِكْ فَلَا مُرْسِلَ لَهُۥ مِنۢ بَعْدِهِۦ ۚ وَهُوَ ٱلْعَزِيزُ ٱلْحَكِيمُ ۝٢﴾ [فاطر الآية ٢]

"There is none to withhold the mercy which Allāh opens up to His people (such as rain, sustenance, spiritual upliftment), and there is none to release the mercy that He withholds. He is the Mighty (able to do as He pleases without anyone to challenge Him), the Wise (He knows exactly when and on whom to shower His mercy)." (Fāṭir 35:2)

Thus, Allāh (ﷻ) opens up for His servants various realms of benefit for them in this world and the hereafter. By His special favour and care, He also opens the locks upon people's hearts. He blesses them with an abundance of knowledge that comes from Him, and He strengthens their beliefs in such a way that matters are set right for them and they are guided to follow His straight path. He also unveils various facets of knowledge, thorough understanding, and light for the souls of His servants who are beloved to Him.

He also unlocks the gates of provision and the means to attain it for His chosen servants. He grants unanticipated means and provisions to those who observe *taqwā* by fulfilling His commands and avoiding His prohibitions. He also grants those who genuinely place their reliance upon Him more than they ask or hope for, and He makes difficulties easy for them to deal with, along with opening up doors for them that were previously closed.

Having correct beliefs about Allāh (ﷻ) being *al-Fattāḥ* will lead an individual to devote himself to Allāh (ﷻ) alone, and in turn He will would open up for that person the gates to guidance, provision, mercy, and also expand one's heart so that it accepts whatever is good and correct.

Allāh (ﷻ) says:

﴿أَفَمَن شَرَحَ ٱللَّهُ صَدْرَهُۥ لِلْإِسْلَٰمِ فَهُوَ عَلَىٰ نُورٍ مِّن رَّبِّهِۦ ۚ ﴿٢٢﴾﴾ [الزُّمَر الآية ٢٢]

> "Could someone whose heart Allāh has opened and guided to accept Islām, and he then proceeds directed by light from his Lord, ever be considered the same as someone else who is not like that?" (Zumar 39:22)

The opening referred to in this verse has no limit. Each person of *īmān* has a share in it, and Allāh (ﷻ) does not bar anyone from it except those who willfully reject Him.

It is indeed crucial for us to know about Allāh's (ﷻ) name *al-Fattāḥ*, contemplate on its meanings, and call upon Him using it since He is the One who responds to our prayers and actualizes our hopes. We must unwaveringly believe that Allāh (ﷻ) being *al-Fattāḥ* entails that He is the supreme judge of all matters, the One who raises and lowers, the One who uncovers realities, and the One who removes obscurities. With that belief, we should not feel disturbed about anything which we encounter. If anyone is ever insolent or wrongful towards us, then we should not feel fear or sorrow because Allāh (ﷻ) – *al-Fattāḥ* – is the One who will grant us the support which we require to overcome any obstacle.

When it is firmly established within our souls that Allāh (ﷻ), being *al-Fattāḥ* is the One who opens for us doors that are closed, and facilitates matters that may seem insurmountable, we should not feel anxiety about anything.

If we ever feel that people's doors are closed to us and we have been obstructed from what we seek, then we should not become irritated or impatient. Rather, we must take recourse to *al-Fattāḥ* since He is the One who is ultimately in control of all things.

Do we really understand who *al-Fattāḥ* is? He is the One who opens up for His servants all of the mundane and religious matters that are in their best interests. He unlocks for them the gates to all goodness. He opens for His servants the doors that may have been closed to them as a result of various problems and difficulties.

When these meanings are firm within our hearts, and we worship Allāh (ﷻ) according to them, then our inner power will be very strong compared to that of others, and we will find tranquility in knowing that we are with *al-Fattāḥ*.

When we worship the Almighty Creator, we must humble ourselves before His presence and beseech Him for our needs by invoking with words such as:

«يا فتّاحُ افتح لي أبوابَ رحمتك، يا فتاح افتح لي أبواب رزقِكَ».

> "O *Fattāḥ*, open for me the gates to Your mercy; and *O Fattāḥ*, open for me the gates of Your provision."

«ربِّ يسِّر ولا تُعَسِّر، وتَمِّمْ بالخَيرِ، وبِكَ نَستَعِينُ يا فَتَّاحُ».

> "My Lord, make things easy and do not make them difficult! My Lord, let [my affairs] end well! And from You alone do we seek assistance O *Fattāḥ*."

We can also invoke Him with these words:

«لا يملك تدبيرَ أمري ولا يفرّج همي إلا أنتَ يا فتاحُ، فافتح لي ما أُغلِقَ، ويسِّر لي ما عَسُرَ، وسهّل عليَّ ما صَعُبَ».

> "(O Allāh) No one controls all of my affairs and no one can dispel my sorrows except for You, O *Fattāḥ*. Thus, I beseech You to open for me what appears closed, and facilitate for me what appears difficult."

We must remember that Allāh (ﷻ) is the only One who can open for us the gates to guidance, sustenance, knowledge, and facilitation. We must call upon Him alone with sincerity, certainty, and trust in the fact that only He can provide for us from channels which we do not even anticipate. Therefore, we must resort to no one except for Him, call upon no one besides Him, and place our hope in the mercy and favour of only Him. All of our desires and wishes should be directed to Allāh (ﷻ) alone, who is perfect in every way.

The doors that Allāh (ﷻ) opens for His servants are many. Thus, we must be among those who seek their opening from the One who has full control of those doors.

Among them is the door to repentance. The Prophet (ﷺ) said:

«إِنَّ اللهَ تَعَالَى يَبْسُطُ يَدَهُ بِاللَّيْلِ لِيَتُوبَ مُسِيءُ النَّهَارِ، وَيَبْسُطُ يَدَهُ بِالنَّهَارِ لِيَتُوبَ مُسِيءُ اللَّيْلِ حَتَّى تَطْلُعَ الشَّمْسُ مِنْ مَغْرِبِهَا».

(رواه مسلم)

> "Indeed Allāh, the Almighty and Most Majestic, extends His hand in the night so that those who sinned during the day can repent, and He extends His hand in the day so that those who

sinned during the night can repent. This will continue until the sun rises from its point of setting." (Muslim)

Imām Ibn al-Qayyim (ﷺ) states:

«إذا أراد اللهُ بعبدِه خيرًا فتح له أبوابَ التوبة والندم والانكسار، والذل والافتقار، والاستعانة به، وصِدْق اللُّجأ إليه، ودوام التضرع والدعاء، والتقرب إليه بما أمكنه من الحسنات، ورؤية عيوب نفسه، ومشاهَدة فضل ربه وإحسانه ورحمته وجوده وبِرِّه».

(الوابل الصيب من الكلام الطيب)

"If Allāh wants good for His servant, He will open for that person the door to repentance, remorse, humility, recognizing his need for Allāh, seeking His assistance, genuinely taking recourse to Him; constantly being humble towards Him, invoking Him, and seeking nearness to Him by whatever righteous deeds are feasible; and recognizing his own faults as well as his Lord's favour, kindness, mercy, and generosity." (Al-Wābil al-Ṣayyib min al-Kalām al-Ṭayyib

Allāh (ﷻ), who is perfect in every way, also opens up the gates of the heavens so that the blessings descend, and supplications can be answered.

Allāh (ﷻ) says:

﴿وَلَوْ أَنَّ أَهْلَ ٱلْقُرَىٰٓ ءَامَنُوا۟ وَٱتَّقَوْا۟ لَفَتَحْنَا عَلَيْهِم بَرَكَـٰتٍ مِّنَ ٱلسَّمَآءِ وَٱلْأَرْضِ وَلَـٰكِن كَذَّبُوا۟ فَأَخَذْنَـٰهُم بِمَا كَانُوا۟ يَكْسِبُونَ ﴿٩٦﴾﴾ [الأعراف الآية ٩٦]

"And if only the inhabitants of the (various) towns had believed and adopted God consciousness (*taqwā*), We would have opened to them multitudes of blessings from the heavens (such as rain), and the earth (such as abundant crops and minerals). However, they denied (the messengers), so We seized (punished) them on account of what (evil actions) they earned." (Aʿrāf 7:96)

Allāh (ﷻ) also opens for His obedient servants the doors to performing righteous deeds before they pass away.

The Messenger of Allāh (ﷺ) states:

«إِذَا أَرَادَ اللَّهُ بِعَبْدٍ خَيْرًا، عَسَلَهُ، قِيلَ: وَمَا عَسَلُهُ؟ قَالَ: يَفْتَحُ اللَّهُ لَهُ عَمَلًا صَالِحًا قَبْلَ مَوْتِهِ، ثُمَّ يَقْبِضُهُ عَلَيْهِ».

(رواه أحمد)

> "If Allāh wants good for a servant of His, then He grants that person a certain sweetness." The companions present asked him: "What sweetness is that?" He replied: "Allāh opens for that person the gates to righteous deeds before his death, and then causes him to pass away while he is engaged in them." (Aḥmad)

On a similar note, Maʿrūf al-Karkhī (رحمه الله) said:

«إِذَا أَرَادَ اللهُ بِعَبْدٍ خَيْرًا فَتَحَ عَلَيْهِ بَابَ الْعَمَلِ وَأَغْلَقَ عَلَيْهِ بَابَ الْجَدَلِ، وَإِذَا أَرَادَ بِعَبْدٍ شَرًّا أَغْلَقَ عَلَيْهِ بَابَ الْعَمَلِ وَفَتَحَ عَلَيْهِ بَابَ الْجَدَلِ».

(حلية الأولياء)

> "If Allāh wants good for a servant of His, then He opens for him the gates to performing deeds and closes for him the gates to argumentation; and if Allāh wants evil for a servant of His, then He closes for him the gates to performing deeds and opens for him the gates to argumentation." (Ḥilyat al-Awliyā')

It is imperative for us to have the necessary reverence for Allāh (ﷻ) in our souls; and for us to know that no one can withhold anything that Allāh (ﷻ) opens up for His servants, and no one can open up anything that Allāh (ﷻ) withholds for anyone.

﴿مَّا يَفْتَحِ ٱللَّهُ لِلنَّاسِ مِن رَّحْمَةٍ فَلَا مُمْسِكَ لَهَا ۖ وَمَا يُمْسِكْ فَلَا مُرْسِلَ لَهُۥ مِنۢ بَعْدِهِۦ ۚ ﴿٢﴾﴾ [فاطر الآية ٢]

"Whatever mercy Allāh opens to people cannot be withheld by anyone, and whatever Allāh withholds from people cannot be granted by anyone besides Him." (Fāṭir 35:2)

He is the only One who opens the doors to all forms of mercy and sustenance. Out of His generosity, He opens for people the gates of riches and resources that only He controls.

When a person's heart grasps these meanings, his ideas and feelings will be entirely transformed throughout his life. This will lead a person to always be attached to Allāh (ﷻ), recognize one's need for Allāh (ﷻ) from all perspectives, not call upon anyone besides the Almighty Creator, and not direct fear or hope to anyone except for Allāh (ﷻ).

CONCLUSION

We need to contemplate the statement of Allāh (ﷻ) wherein He says:

﴿مَّا يَفْتَحِ ٱللَّهُ لِلنَّاسِ مِن رَّحْمَةٍ فَلَا مُمْسِكَ لَهَا ۖ ﴿٢﴾﴾ [فاطر الآية ٢]

"No one can withhold whatever mercy Allāh opens to people." (Fāṭir 35:2)

We have to remember that absolutely no one can withhold any of the mercy that Allāh (ﷻ) grants us. When we invoke Allāh (ﷻ) using His sublime names – including *al-Fattāḥ* – then by His permission, no door ahead of us will remain closed.

We need to place our trust in what lies with Allāh (ﷻ), and not be concerned about how people may gauge matters. If a severe illness falls upon a person, then some people may tell him: "This illness will kill you and there is no hope for successful treatment." If a person has certain channels of provision closed off from him, then certain people may say to him: "Do not even try anything, because you will not succeed, so there is no need to tire yourself out."

However, we must ask ourselves a serious question: Who can ever possibly come between a person and his Lord's mercy? Cure lies in the hands of Allāh (ﷻ) alone. There are many instances when a person may be on the brink of perishing, and relief comes to him from Allāh (ﷻ) and he is cured of what befell him, as though he had not even been ill to begin with.

There are many instances when a person strives to attain provision by taking all of the necessary means, and Allāh (ﷻ) then grants the person a lot of sustenance and blessings after he was previously poor. Nobody can obstruct any goodness that Allāh (ﷻ) wills to reach an individual.

Thus, we have to keep our hearts attached to Allāh (ﷻ), *al-Fattāḥ*. He is the One who can facilitate all matters for us, fulfill our needs, take care of everything that concerns us, and provide us with goodness and relief from where we never anticipated. His control of all things is above that of everyone besides Him, and His ability is limitless. All He has to say is "Be" and whatever He desires will come into being. The resources that belong to Him cannot be depleted, all provisions lie in His hands, and He is the Bestower of indescribably abundant blessings.

We have to remind ourselves about the counsel that was given by the Prophet (ﷺ) to a man who he told to keep his heart attached to Allāh (ﷻ), and not to what anyone else has.

Abū Ayyūb al-Anṣārī (رضي الله عنه) reports:

«أَتَى النَّبِيَّ ﷺ رَجُلٌ، فَقَالَ: عِظْنِي وَأَوْجِزْ قَالَ: إِذَا قُمْتَ فِي صَلَاتِكَ فَصَلِّ صَلَاةَ مُوَدِّعٍ، وَلَا تَكَلَّمَنَّ بِكَلَامٍ تَعْتَذِرُ مِنْهُ غَدًا، وَأَجْمِعِ الْيَأْسَ مِمَّا فِي أَيْدِي النَّاسِ».

(المعجم الكبير للطبراني)

"A man came to the Prophet (ﷺ) and said: 'O Messenger of Allāh, teach me but keep it concise.' The Prophet (ﷺ) said: 'When you stand for your prayer, pray as if you are bidding farewell. Do not say anything for which you will have to

> apologize tomorrow; and give up any desire to acquire what people have (remove from your heart any hope of attaining what lies in the hands of other people).'" (Al-Muʿjam al-Kabīr of al-Ṭabarānī)

This means that we must not hope to attain anything from people themselves, or by way of them. Rather, we must only put our complete trust and hope in Allāh (ﷻ) alone.

People who will end up forsaken in the worst way are those who remain attached to other than Allāh (ﷻ). We must never be heedless of these meanings. Additionally, we must also bear these in mind when we enter and exit the *masjid.*

The Prophet (ﷺ) has said:

«إِذَا دَخَلَ أَحَدُكُمُ الْمَسْجِدَ فَلْيَقُلْ: اللَّهُمَّ افْتَحْ لِي أَبْوَابَ رَحْمَتِكَ، وَإِذَا خَرَجَ فَلْيَقُلْ: اللَّهُمَّ إِنِّي أَسْأَلُكَ مِنْ فَضْلِكَ».

(رواه مسلم)

> "When any of you enters a *masjid,* one should say: 'O Allāh, I implore You to open for me the gates of Your mercy;' and when a person is exiting (a *masjid*) one should say: 'O Allāh, I beseech You for Your bounty.'" (Muslim)

From this, we understand that all mercy, bounty, and goodness lies in the hands of Allāh (ﷻ), and He is the only One who can open their gates for whomsoever He wills. All of the preceding are effects and manifestations of Allāh's (ﷻ) name *al-Fattāḥ.*

Allāh (ﷻ), who is perfect in every way, supports the truth and those who support the truth. He also defeats falsehood and those who perpetrate it, and eventually punishes them.

Another noteworthy detail about Allāh's (ﷻ) name *al-Fattāḥ* is that He opens to whomsoever He wills among His servants the gates to all forms of obedience and drawing nearness to Him. For some people, that comes in the form of reading and contemplating the Qur'ān; for others, it means performing many prayers; for others, supplicating much; or fasting; upholding the ties of kinship; assisting the needy and those in adverse conditions; encouraging people to do right and forbidding them from wrong; reconciling matters between people or speaking on their behalf; and for others, knowledge and understanding; and so on.

Therefore, O servants of Allāh (ﷻ), if you find that certain gates have been opened for you, then find within yourselves the inclination to seize those opportunities, and take advantage of them as much as you can.

Ḥakīm ibn ʿUmayr states:

«مَنْ فُتِحَ لَهُ بَابُ خَيْرٍ فَلْيَنْتَهِزْهُ، فَإِنَّهُ لَا يَدْرِي مَتَى يُغْلَقُ عَنْهُ».

(كتاب الزهد لأحمد بن حنبل)

"If the gate to perform any form of goodness is opened for a person, then he must seize that opportunity because he does not know when it will be closed on him." (Kitāb al-Zuhd of Aḥmad ibn Ḥanbal)

ازْرَعْ جَمِيلًا وَلَوْ فِي غَيْرِ مَوْضِعِهِ ۞ فَلَا يَضِيعُ جَمِيلٌ أَيْنَمَا زُرِعَا

إنَّ الجميلَ وإنْ طالَ الزمانُ بهِ ۞ فليسَ يَحصدُهُ إلا الذي زَرَعا

Cultivate graciousness, even at occasions not deserving it,
For graciousness is never wasted, no matter where it is cultivated.
Even after the passage of a long period of time following a gracious act,
It is certain that only the one who sows it will harvest it.

KHUṬBAH 70

Water in the Qur'ān

Allāh (ﷻ) has bestowed countless blessings upon His servants. Among the blessings that He has bestowed upon us is a favour that no human being, nor any other creation can do without under any circumstance; and it is from Allāh's (ﷻ) wisdom that He uncovers these blessings for us right before our eyes so that we can be grateful.

As a result, Allāh (ﷻ) commands His angles to move the clouds, to blow the winds, and to release the drops of rain from the sky so that His servants can get a taste of that favour.

Allāh (ﷻ) says in the Qur'ān:

﴿أَلَمْ تَرَ أَنَّ ٱللَّهَ يُزْجِى سَحَابًا ثُمَّ يُؤَلِّفُ بَيْنَهُۥ ثُمَّ يَجْعَلُهُۥ رُكَامًا فَتَرَى ٱلْوَدْقَ يَخْرُجُ مِنْ خِلَٰلِهِۦ ﴿٤٣﴾﴾ [النّور الآية ٤٣]

> "Do you not see that Allāh wafts (gently drives) the clouds (towards the place where He intends the rain to fall), then condenses (gathers) them (which causes the water vapour to form into water droplets) and stacks them in layers, after which (when Allāh decides) you will see rain falling from between them?" (Nūr 24:43)

Allāh (ﷻ) sends this rain down from the skies so that people see it with their own eyes in order that their hearts can turn towards Allāh (ﷻ) in gratitude and appreciation. Allāh (ﷻ) has made the rain a sign and proof of His Lordship and Majesty.

Allāh (ﷻ) says:

﴿أَوَلَمْ يَرَوْا۟ أَنَّا نَسُوقُ ٱلْمَآءَ إِلَى ٱلْأَرْضِ ٱلْجُرُزِ فَنُخْرِجُ بِهِۦ زَرْعًا تَأْكُلُ مِنْهُ أَنْعَٰمُهُمْ وَأَنفُسُهُمْ ۖ أَفَلَا يُبْصِرُونَ ﴿٢٧﴾﴾ [السَّجْدَة الآية ٢٧]

"Do they (the people) not see that We draw water (rain) to arid (dry and bare) land, using it to extract (bring forth) plants from which your animals and you eat? Do they not then see (that just as We revive dead land, We can easily revive dead bodies on the Day of Judgement)?" (Sajdah 32:27)

In the Qur'ān, Allāh (ﷻ) challenges the creation to bring down the rain other than what He sends down.

Allāh (ﷻ) says:

﴿أَفَرَءَيْتُمُ ٱلْمَآءَ ٱلَّذِى تَشْرَبُونَ ﴿٦٨﴾ ءَأَنتُمْ أَنزَلْتُمُوهُ مِنَ ٱلْمُزْنِ أَمْ نَحْنُ ٱلْمُنزِلُونَ ﴿٦٩﴾﴾

[الوَاقِعَة من الآية ٦٨ الى الآية ٦٩]

"Tell me about the water that you drink. Do you cause it to rain from the clouds or is it We who cause it to rain?" (Wāqi'ah 56:68-69)

In addition, no one knows when the rain is going to come down, or what benefits it contains other than Allāh (ﷻ). It is only Allāh (ﷻ) who sends down the rain from the sky.

Allāh (ﷻ) says:

﴿إِنَّ ٱللَّهَ عِندَهُۥ عِلْمُ ٱلسَّاعَةِ وَيُنَزِّلُ ٱلْغَيْثَ وَيَعْلَمُ مَا فِى ٱلْأَرْحَامِ ﴿٣٤﴾﴾ [لُقْمَان الآية ٣٤]

"Verily the knowledge of (when) the Hour (Qiyāmah will come) is only with Allāh. He sends the rains and knows (the details of) what is in the wombs (such as the character and future of the child)." (Luqmān 31:34)

The sending of the rain from the sky is one of the proofs of Allāh's (ﷻ) Oneness and His right to be worshipped alone with no other partners.

Allāh (ﷻ) says:

﴿ٱلَّذِى جَعَلَ لَكُمُ ٱلْأَرْضَ فِرَٰشًا وَٱلسَّمَآءَ بِنَآءً وَأَنزَلَ مِنَ ٱلسَّمَآءِ مَآءً فَأَخْرَجَ بِهِۦ مِنَ ٱلثَّمَرَٰتِ رِزْقًا لَّكُمْ ۖ فَلَا تَجْعَلُوا۟ لِلَّهِ أَندَادًا وَأَنتُمْ تَعْلَمُونَ ﴿٢٢﴾﴾ [البقرة الآية ٢٢]

"(Worship Allāh) Who made the earth a bedding for you (which is neither too hard, nor too soft), the sky a roof, and has sent water for you from the sky, using it (the water) to bring forth fruits (all types of foods) for your sustenance. So never make others equal (partners) to Allāh (in worship) when you know (that they cannot create as Allāh creates, and therefore do not deserve to be worshipped)." (Baqarah 2:22)

Rain is also from the evidences of Resurrection, and the coming back to life after death.

Allāh (ﷻ) says regarding one of his signs:

﴿وَمِنْ ءَايَٰتِهِۦٓ أَنَّكَ تَرَى ٱلْأَرْضَ خَٰشِعَةً فَإِذَآ أَنزَلْنَا عَلَيْهَا ٱلْمَآءَ ٱهْتَزَّتْ وَرَبَتْ ۚ إِنَّ ٱلَّذِىٓ أَحْيَاهَا لَمُحْىِ ٱلْمَوْتَىٰٓ ۚ إِنَّهُۥ عَلَىٰ كُلِّ شَىْءٍ قَدِيرٌ ﴿٣٩﴾﴾ [فصلت الآية ٣٩]

"And from His signs (demonstrating His great powers) is that you see the earth bare (dead). Then, when We send rain upon it, it begins to stir (with life) and flourish (with vegetation). Verily, the One who gives life to it (to the dead earth) is the One who gives life to the dead (who will resurrect people on the Day of Qiyāmah). Indeed, He has power over all things (can do anything). (Fuṣṣilat 41:39)

Sometimes Allāh (ﷻ) uses water as a mercy, and other times He can send it as a punishment.

In the Qur'ān, Allāh (ﷻ) says:

﴿وَأَلَّوِ ٱسْتَقَٰمُوا۟ عَلَى ٱلطَّرِيقَةِ لَأَسْقَيْنَٰهُم مَّآءً غَدَقًا ﴿١٦﴾﴾ [الجن الآية ١٦]

"(O Prophet, say that revelation has also come to me to inform me that) If they (the Mushrikīn of Makkah) remain steadfast upon the path (Islām), (then instead of punishing them with droughts,) We shall definitely bless them with abundant showers (rains)." (Jinn 72:16)

Water is a sign of glory, grandeur and power because the throne of Allāh (ﷻ) was upon the water before the creation of the heavens and the earth.

Allāh (ﷻ) says:

﴿وَكَانَ عَرۡشُهُۥ عَلَى ٱلۡمَآءِ ۝٧﴾ [هُود الآية ٧]

"And His throne was upon water." (Hūd 11:7)

Before Allāh (ﷻ) created the heavens and the earth, He created water which was to become the initial matter of life for all things.

Allāh (ﷻ) says:

﴿وَجَعَلۡنَا مِنَ ٱلۡمَآءِ كُلَّ شَيۡءٍ حَيٍّۚ أَفَلَا يُؤۡمِنُونَ ۝٣٠﴾ [الأنبياء الآية ٣٠]

"And We created every living thing from water. Will they not then believe?" (Anbiyā' 21:30)

﴿وَٱللَّهُ خَلَقَ كُلَّ دَآبَّةٖ مِّن مَّآءٖۖ ۝٤٥﴾ [النُّور الآية ٤٥]

"Allāh has created every (moving) creature from water." (Nūr 24:45)

From the above-mentioned verses, it becomes evident that every living thing originated from the rains - either directly or indirectly.

At that time in the beginning, Allāh's (ﷻ) throne was on the water as it is above the skies at this moment in time. In other words, water was the original matter of the universe and the source of life which is in the absolute control and power of Allāh (ﷻ), the Lord of the Throne; and it is subservient to the Absolute Sustentation (management) of Allāh (ﷻ).

Water is from among the many favours that Allāh (ﷻ) has blessed all of His creations with.

Whoever among the past generations was grateful to Allāh (ﷻ), He increased them in blessings, but those who were ungrateful were punished.

Allāh (ﷻ) says:

﴿أَلَمْ يَرَوْا۟ كَمْ أَهْلَكْنَا مِن قَبْلِهِم مِّن قَرْنٍ مَّكَّنَّـٰهُمْ فِى ٱلْأَرْضِ مَا لَمْ نُمَكِّن لَّكُمْ
وَأَرْسَلْنَا ٱلسَّمَآءَ عَلَيْهِم مِّدْرَارًا وَجَعَلْنَا ٱلْأَنْهَـٰرَ تَجْرِى مِن تَحْتِهِمْ فَأَهْلَكْنَـٰهُم
بِذُنُوبِهِمْ وَأَنشَأْنَا مِنۢ بَعْدِهِمْ قَرْنًا ءَاخَرِينَ ۝٦﴾ [الأنعام الآية ٦]

"Have they (people) not seen (as they passed the ruins of past nations on their journeys) how many nations We have destroyed before them, whom We had established on the earth as We have not established you? (We had given them more might and resources than We have given you). (Although) We sent to them abundant rains and made rivers flow beneath them (because of which they were very prosperous), then We destroyed them (the offenders) because of their sins and created other nations after them." (Anʿām 6:6)

Since rain is such a great blessing, Allāh (ﷻ) sends the winds before it which is a giver of good news.

Allāh (ﷻ) says:

﴿وَهُوَ ٱلَّذِى يُرْسِلُ ٱلرِّيَـٰحَ بُشْرًۢا بَيْنَ يَدَىْ رَحْمَتِهِۦ ۝٥٧﴾ [الأعراف الآية ٥٧]

"And it is He (Allāh) who sends the winds ahead of His mercy (before the rains) as a carrier of good news (indicating to the people that rain is about to fall)." (Aʿrāf 7:57)

The earth itself is delighted when the rain comes and as a result it stirs, quivers (to life), flourishes, and exhumes all of its wonderful beauty.

Allāh (ﷻ) also says:

﴿فَإِذَآ أَنزَلْنَا عَلَيْهَا ٱلْمَآءَ ٱهْتَزَّتْ وَرَبَتْ وَأَنۢبَتَتْ مِن كُلِّ زَوْجٍۭ بَهِيجٍ ۝٥﴾ [الحج الآية ٥]

> "And (another sign to prove the resurrection is that) you see the earth barren (without vegetation and foliage, seemingly dead), then We send down rain upon it, causing it to stir, flourish and grow every kind of beautiful species (of plant life)." (Ḥajj 22:5)

It is with water that Allāh (ﷻ) brings life to the earth after its death (how it becomes dormant in winter).

Allāh (ﷻ) says:

﴿وَيُنَزِّلُ مِنَ ٱلسَّمَآءِ مَآءً فَيُحۡيِۦ بِهِ ٱلۡأَرۡضَ بَعۡدَ مَوۡتِهَآ ۚ ﴿٢٤﴾﴾ [الرُّوم الآية ٢٤]

> "And He sends down rain from the sky, thereby reviving the earth after its death." (Rūm 30:24)

In addition, people also inform one another, rejoice with each other and express joy when rain is on its way.

Allāh (ﷻ) says:

﴿فَإِذَآ أَصَابَ بِهِۦ مَن يَشَآءُ مِنۡ عِبَادِهِۦٓ إِذَا هُمۡ يَسۡتَبۡشِرُونَ ﴿٤٨﴾﴾ [الرُّوم الآية ٤٨]

> "When Allāh sends it (the rain) to those bondsmen whom He wills, they become happy (rejoice)." (Rūm 30:48)

Water is a means of gaining Allāh's (ﷻ) pleasure, but this is conditional to if a person shows gratitude to Allāh (ﷻ) for it.

The Prophet (ﷺ) states:

«إِنَّ اللَّه لَيَرضي عَنِ الْعَبْدِ أَنْ يَأْكُلَ الأَكلَةَ، فَيَحْمَدُهُ عَلَيْهَا، أَوْ يَشْرِبَ الشَّرْبَةَ، فَيَحْمَدُهُ عَلَيْهَا».

(رواه مسلم)

> "Surely Allāh is pleased with His slave who eats a meal and praises Him for it, or takes a drink and praises Him for it." (Muslim)

Allāh (ﷻ) created water colourless and tasteless, and sent it down odorless. It is sent down to some lands whereby it produces crops, fruits, and lush vegetation. As well, Allāh (ﷻ) provides water in plentiful quantities to some areas, but He does not provide it to others.

Some water is fresh (sweet) and other is salty. Some of it may cause diseases, while others are actually a cure. It is a creation that is gentle enough to be internalized by the human body, yet also strong enough to overtake valleys and reach mountain tops. It is indeed a magnificent creation of Allāh (ﷻ).

If Allāh (ﷻ) sends it down as a punishment, then **only** He can remove and eliminate it. Allāh (ﷻ) says about the son of Prophet Nūḥ (عليه السلام):

﴿قَالَ سَـَٔاوِىٓ إِلَىٰ جَبَلٍ يَعۡصِمُنِي مِنَ ٱلۡمَآءِۚ قَالَ لَا عَاصِمَ ٱلۡيَوۡمَ مِنۡ أَمۡرِ ٱللَّهِ إِلَّا مَن رَّحِمَۚ ٤٣﴾ [هود الآية ٤٣]

> "He said: 'I shall shortly take refuge (shelter) on a mountain that will rescue (save) me from the water.' Nūḥ (عليه السلام) said: 'Today none can rescue (another) from the command (punishment) of Allāh except him on whom Allāh has (special) mercy.'" (Hūd 11:43)

The benefits of water are many and innumerable. It is pure, fresh, sweet and flowing which brings huge benefits to the body and the soul.

Allāh (ﷻ) says:

﴿وَأَسۡقَيۡنَـٰكُم مَّآءً فُرَاتًا ٢٧﴾ [المرسلات الآية ٢٧]

> "And We have given you (to drink) sweet water." (Mursalāt 77:27)

Water purifies the body and the soul.

Allāh (ﷻ) says:

﴿إِذۡ يُغَشِّيكُمُ ٱلنُّعَاسَ أَمَنَةً مِّنۡهُ وَيُنَزِّلُ عَلَيۡكُم مِّنَ ٱلسَّمَآءِ مَآءً لِّيُطَهِّرَكُم بِهِۦ وَيُذۡهِبَ عَنكُمۡ رِجۡزَ ٱلشَّيۡطَٰنِ ١١﴾ [الأنفال الآية ١١]

(When the two armies met at Badr, the polytheists camped at a place where there was enough water and where the ground was firm. On the other hand, the camp of the Muslims had no water and was covered with loose sand which made it difficult for them to move. To give courage to the believers, Allāh again called them to remember the time): "When (in the thick of battle) slumber was made to envelop you as a means of serenity from Him [so that you do not panic) and He sent down rain to you from the skies to purify you (so that you could perform your *wuḍū* for ṣalāt), to dispel the evil thoughts cast by Shayṭān (who told the believers that if they were on the right, then they would not have been in a position where there was no water for them to drink or clean themselves with)." (Anfāl 8:11)

Allāh (ﷻ) has created water incredibly blessed. Just a few drops can bring life to the earth and everything that is upon it. The streams, rivers, and valleys begin flowing from it.

Allāh (ﷻ) says:

﴿وَنَزَّلْنَا مِنَ ٱلسَّمَآءِ مَآءً مُّبَٰرَكًا ۝٩﴾ [ق الآية ٩]

"And We have sent down blessed rains from the sky." (Qāf 50:9)

It is through water that Allāh (ﷻ) causes the crops, plants and vegetation to grow.

Allāh (ﷻ) says:

﴿فَأَنزَلْنَا بِهِ ٱلْمَآءَ فَأَخْرَجْنَا بِهِۦ مِن كُلِّ ٱلثَّمَرَٰتِ ۝٥٧﴾ [الأعراف الآية ٥٧]

"We send down rains on it, bringing forth by it (by the rain) all kinds of fruit." (Aʿrāf 7:57)

Allāh (ﷻ) has made water a means of the expiation for our sins and shortcomings - like in the case of *wuḍū*.

The Prophet (ﷺ) states:

«إِذَا تَوَضَّأَ العَبْدُ المُسْلِمُ، أَو المُؤْمِنُ فَغَسَلَ وَجْهَهُ خَرَجَ مِنْ وَجْهِهِ كُلُّ خَطِيئَةٍ نَظَرَ إِلَيْهَا بِعَيْنِيهِ مَعَ المَاءِ، أَوْ مَعَ آخِرِ قَطْرِ المَاءِ، فَإِذا غَسَلَ يَدَيْهِ خَرَجَ مِنْ يَدَيهِ كُلُّ خَطِيئَةٍ كَانَ بَطَشَتْهَا يَدَاهُ مَعَ المَاءِ، أَوْ مَعَ آخِرِ قَطْرِ المَاءِ، فَإِذَا غَسَلَ رِجْلَيهِ خَرَجَتْ كُلُّ خَطِيئَةٍ مشتها رِجْلاَهُ مَعَ المَاءِ أَوْ مَعَ آخِرِ قَطْرِ المَاءِ حَتَّى يَخْرُجَ نَقِيًّا مِنَ الذُّنُوبِ».

(رواه مسلم)

> "When a Muslim or a believer washes his face in ablution, every sin that he committed with his eyes will be washed away with the last drop of water. When he washes his hands, every sin that he committed with his hands will be washed away with the last drop of water. When he washes his feet, every sin that he committed with his feet will be washed away with the last drop of water, until he emerges purified from sins." (Muslim)

Allāh (ﷻ) sends down each drop of water measured, calculated and its amount determined. This is from Allāh's (ﷻ) infinite wisdom and knowledge.

﴿وَأَنزَلْنَا مِنَ ٱلسَّمَآءِ مَآءًۢ بِقَدَرٍ فَأَسْكَنَّـٰهُ فِى ٱلْأَرْضِ ﴿١٨﴾﴾ [المُؤْمِنُون الآية ١٨]

> "And We send stipulated quantities of water from the skies, embedding it into the earth (irrigating the roots of plants and storing underground water)." (Mu'minūn 23:18)

In this verse Allāh (ﷻ) mentions His innumerable blessings to His servants, whereby He sends down rain in due measure, meaning according to what is needed, not so much that it damages the lands and buildings, and not so little that it is insufficient for crops and fruits, but whatever is needed for irrigation, drinking and other benefits.

Ḥāfiẓ ibn Kathīr (رحمه الله) says that the meaning of this verse is:

«أَيْ بِحَسَبِ الْكِفَايَةِ لِزُرُوعِكُمْ وَثِمَارِكُمْ وَشُرْبِكُمْ لِأَنْفُسِكُمْ وَلِأَنْعَامِكُمْ».

(تفسير ابن كثير)

"Allāh sends the rain down according to what is sufficient for your crops, fruits and drinking water for yourselves and your livestock." (Tafsīr Ibn Kathīr)

Water is an amazing sign from Allāh (ﷻ). The gorges and valleys flow by Allāh's (ﷻ) permission. Only Allāh (ﷻ) knows how this rain, or how the water descends to the earth, and how it is stored underground.

Allāh (ﷻ) says:

﴿أَلَمْ تَرَ أَنَّ ٱللَّهَ أَنزَلَ مِنَ ٱلسَّمَآءِ مَآءً فَسَلَكَهُۥ يَنَـٰبِيعَ فِى ٱلْأَرْضِ ﴿٢١﴾﴾ [الزُّمَر الآية ٢١]

"Do you not see that Allāh sends down rain from the sky, and then channels (directs) it (to people) in springs within the earth?" (Zumar 39:21)

There is some water that gushes forth from boulders and rocks.

Allāh (ﷻ) says:

﴿وَإِنَّ مِنَ ٱلْحِجَارَةِ لَمَا يَتَفَجَّرُ مِنْهُ ٱلْأَنْهَـٰرُ ۚ وَإِنَّ مِنْهَا لَمَا يَشَّقَّقُ فَيَخْرُجُ مِنْهُ ٱلْمَآءُ ۚ ﴿٧٤﴾﴾ [البَقَرَة الآية ٧٤]

"And there are those rocks from which rivers gush forth, while some of them split open causing water to flow from them." (Baqarah 2:74)

Water is a miraculous creation. When it is sent to a barren land it turns its colour into a spectacular sight.

Allāh (ﷻ) says:

﴿أَلَمْ تَرَ أَنَّ ٱللَّهَ أَنزَلَ مِنَ ٱلسَّمَآءِ مَآءً فَتُصْبِحُ ٱلْأَرْضُ مُخْضَرَّةً ۗ إِنَّ ٱللَّهَ لَطِيفٌ خَبِيرٌ ﴿٦٣﴾﴾ [الحَج الآية ٦٣]

"Do you not see that (it is) Allāh (and no one else who) sends down the rains from the skies, causing the earth to flourish with (much) greenery? Indeed, Allāh is Subtle and Aware." (Ḥajj 22:63)

Water is one of Allāh's (ﷻ) incredible creations and one of His remarkable favours. He sends it upon us and then stores it in the earth after sending it down for our usage.

Allāh (ﷻ) says:

﴿وَأَرْسَلْنَا ٱلرِّيَٰحَ لَوَٰقِحَ فَأَنزَلْنَا مِنَ ٱلسَّمَآءِ مَآءً فَأَسْقَيْنَٰكُمُوهُ وَمَآ أَنتُمْ لَهُۥ بِخَٰزِنِينَ ﴿٢٢﴾﴾ [الحِجر الآية ٢٢]

"And We send the winds that fill the clouds with water, then send water down from the sky which We give you to drink. And you do not have the ability to store it (man cannot store rainwater in as large a quantity as Allāh does when He stores water in lakes, dams, rivers and in underground reservoirs of groundwater where massive quantities of water are stored for people to use whenever they need to)." (Ḥijr 15:22)

Allāh (ﷻ) brings it out from the middle of the rocks, pure, clean, fresh, sweet and flowing. Easily accessible, simply palatable and effortlessly drinkable.

Allāh (ﷻ) says:

﴿قُلْ أَرَءَيْتُمْ إِنْ أَصْبَحَ مَآؤُكُمْ غَوْرًا فَمَن يَأْتِيكُم بِمَآءٍ مَّعِينٍ ﴿٣٠﴾﴾ [المُلك الآية ٣٠]

"Say: If your water sinks to the depths of the earth (beyond your reach), who (other than Allāh) can provide you with pure water?" (Mulk 67:30)

Even though water is a blessing, these tiny raindrops that people enjoy can turn into a form of punishment by Allāh's (ﷻ) command.

In fact, Allāh (ﷻ) has used this very water to drown people who turned away from him. Water was the first thing that was used to punish many of the previous nations.

﴿كَذَّبَتْ قَبْلَهُمْ قَوْمُ نُوحٍ فَكَذَّبُوا۟ عَبْدَنَا وَقَالُوا۟ مَجْنُونٌ وَٱزْدُجِرَ ۝٩ فَدَعَا رَبَّهُۥٓ أَنِّى مَغْلُوبٌ فَٱنتَصِرْ ۝١٠ فَفَتَحْنَآ أَبْوَٰبَ ٱلسَّمَآءِ بِمَآءٍ مُّنْهَمِرٍ ۝١١ وَفَجَّرْنَا ٱلْأَرْضَ عُيُونًا فَٱلْتَقَى ٱلْمَآءُ عَلَىٰٓ أَمْرٍ قَدْ قُدِرَ ۝١٢﴾ [القمر من الآية ٩ الى الآية ١٢]

"The nation of Nūḥ (ﷺ) rejected (*īmān*) before them (the polytheists of Makkah). They rejected Our servant [Nūḥ (ﷺ)] and said that he was a madman and he was rebuked (threatened, insulted and shunned by them). So, he made *du'ā* to his Lord (saying): 'Indeed I am overpowered, so assist me.' So (in reply to his *du'ā*) We opened the doors of the sky too (with) torrential rains. And (in addition to the waters from the sky) We opened springs in the earth (from which more water gushed forth), So that the waters (raining from the sky and gushing from the earth) met for a matter preordained (resulting in a flood as punishment for them)." (Qamar 54:9-12)

Fir'awn thought and believed himself to be higher than Prophet Mūsā (ﷺ). He boasted about his power even over the water.

Allāh (ﷻ) describes what Fir'awn arrogantly said:

﴿وَنَادَىٰ فِرْعَوْنُ فِى قَوْمِهِۦ قَالَ يَٰقَوْمِ أَلَيْسَ لِى مُلْكُ مِصْرَ وَهَٰذِهِ ٱلْأَنْهَٰرُ تَجْرِى مِن تَحْتِىٓ ۖ أَفَلَا تُبْصِرُونَ ۝٥١﴾ [الزُّخْرُف الآية ٥١]

"And Fir'awn called his people saying: 'Does not the land (kingdom) of Egypt and these rivers flowing beneath belong to me? Do you not see [that you should rather be listening to me instead of Mūsā (ﷺ)]?'" (Zukhruf 43:51)

So Allāh (ﷻ) destroyed Fir'awn with the same thing that he boasted to have control over, i.e. the water, and then He made him a lesson for all people.

Allāh (ﷻ) says:

﴿حَتَّىٰٓ إِذَآ أَدْرَكَهُ ٱلْغَرَقُ قَالَ ءَامَنتُ أَنَّهُۥ لَآ إِلَٰهَ إِلَّا ٱلَّذِىٓ ءَامَنَتْ بِهِۦ بَنُوٓا۟ إِسْرَٰٓءِيلَ وَأَنَا۠ مِنَ ٱلْمُسْلِمِينَ ۝﴾ [يُونُس الآية ٩٠]

"Until (the time came when the pathways in the sea closed and) he (Fir'awn) began to drown (then) he said: 'I believe that there is no deity (Ilāh) but Him in Whom the Banī Isrā'īl believe, and I am from those who surrender.'" (Yūnus 10:90)

Likewise, Allāh (ﷻ) made the water into a raging flood upon the people of Sabā' when they denied Allāh's (ﷻ) blessings and took them for granted. So Allāh (ﷻ) shattered them into fragments without any traces to be found.

Allāh (ﷻ) says:

﴿فَأَعْرَضُوا۟ فَأَرْسَلْنَا عَلَيْهِمْ سَيْلَ ٱلْعَرِمِ وَبَدَّلْنَٰهُم بِجَنَّتَيْهِمْ جَنَّتَيْنِ ذَوَاتَىْ أُكُلٍ خَمْطٍ وَأَثْلٍ وَشَىْءٍ مِّن سِدْرٍ قَلِيلٍ ۝﴾ [سَبَإٍ الآية ١٦]

"(However, instead of being grateful to Allāh) They turned away (from the advice and committed kufr), so We sent (to their city) the flood (water) of the (ruptured) dam (which destroyed everything in its path), and We replaced their two (flourishing) orchards with two orchards of foul-smelling (bitter) fruit, invasive shrubs (tamarisks), and a few sparse Lote trees (these were the only things that grew after their orchards were destroyed)." (Sabā' 34:16)

Allāh (ﷻ) made water a means of triumph and success for the Muslims during the battle of Badr.

Allāh (ﷻ) says:

﴿إِذْ يُغَشِّيكُمُ ٱلنُّعَاسَ أَمَنَةً مِّنْهُ وَيُنَزِّلُ عَلَيْكُم مِّنَ ٱلسَّمَآءِ مَآءً لِّيُطَهِّرَكُم بِهِۦ وَيُذْهِبَ عَنكُمْ رِجْزَ ٱلشَّيْطَٰنِ وَلِيَرْبِطَ عَلَىٰ قُلُوبِكُمْ وَيُثَبِّتَ بِهِ ٱلْأَقْدَامَ ۝﴾ [الأَنْفَال الآية ١١]

"(When the two armies met at Badr, the polytheists camped at a place where there was enough water and where the ground was firm. On the other hand, the camp of the Muslims had no water and was covered with loose sand which made it difficult for them to move. To give courage to the believers, Allāh again calls them to remember the time) When (in the thick of the battle) slumber was made to envelop you as a means of serenity from Him (so that you do not panic) and He sent rain to you from the skies to purify you (so that you could perform *wuḍū* for your *ṣalāt*), to dispel the evil thoughts cast by Shayṭān (who told the believers that if they were on the right, then they would not have been in a position where there was no water for them to drink or clean themselves with), to strengthen your hearts and to make your feet firm (with the rain, the ground in the Muslim camp became firm, while the ground in the polytheist camp became muddy and unstable)."(Anfāl 8:11)

Water is also one of the blessings that people will enjoy in Paradise.

Allāh (ﷻ) says:

﴿فِيهَآ أَنۡهَٰرٞ مِّن مَّآءٍ غَيۡرِ ءَاسِنٖ ١٥﴾ [محمد الآية ١٥]

"It has rivers of water that will never putrefy (and will never be contaminated, nor deteriorate in quality)." (Muḥammad 47:15)

Furthermore, the inhabitants of the hellfire will not request anything specific except for water.

Allāh (ﷻ) says:

﴿وَنَادَىٰٓ أَصۡحَٰبُ ٱلنَّارِ أَصۡحَٰبَ ٱلۡجَنَّةِ أَنۡ أَفِيضُواْ عَلَيۡنَا مِنَ ٱلۡمَآءِ أَوۡ مِمَّا رَزَقَكُمُ ٱللَّهُۚ ٥٠﴾ [الأعراف الآية ٥٠]

"And the people of the Fire will call to the people of Paradise saying: 'Pour some water on us or (give us) something (some food or drink) that Allāh has provided you with.'" (Aʿrāf 7:50)

Water is also from the signs of Allāh (ﷻ) that causes one's faith to increase.

Allāh (ﷻ) says:

﴿وَجَعَلْنَا مِنَ ٱلْمَآءِ كُلَّ شَىْءٍ حَىٍّ ۖ أَفَلَا يُؤْمِنُونَ ﴿٣٠﴾﴾ [الأنبياء الآية ٣٠]

"And We created every living thing from water. Will they not then believe?" (Anbiyā' 21:30)

CONCLUSION

Water is such a magnificent sign, and no one can deny that it is not from Allāh (ﷻ). Moreover, it proves that Allāh (ﷻ) is the only Originator and Creator of all things.

Allāh (ﷻ) says:

﴿وَلَئِن سَأَلْتَهُم مَّن نَّزَّلَ مِنَ ٱلسَّمَآءِ مَآءً فَأَحْيَا بِهِ ٱلْأَرْضَ مِنۢ بَعْدِ مَوْتِهَا لَيَقُولُنَّ ٱللَّهُ ۚ ﴿٦٣﴾﴾ [العنكبوت الآية ٦٣]

"And if you ask them (the polytheists) who sends down rain from the sky, thereby reviving the earth (by producing vegetation) after its death (after it had been unable to bear anything), they will certainly reply: 'Allāh!'" ('Ankabūt 29:63)

Water is a huge blessing from Allāh (ﷻ) that accompanies us in every point in time and place, so we must be very grateful for this blessing. We need to ponder over its significance and obey the Creator who gave it to us. We must not take this vital blessing for granted, waste it, nor be careless about it, but instead we must use it as an aid to prepare for our next life (*ākhirah*).

Allāh (ﷻ) has taken the responsibility of providing for His creations - both the righteous and the wicked. Whether the creature is large or small, an insect or anything else, Allāh (ﷻ) sustains it. Allāh (ﷻ) does not owe anything to anyone at all, but He provides for everyone and everything out of His never-ending mercy.

Allāh (ﷻ) says:

﴿وَمَا مِن دَآبَّةٖ فِي ٱلۡأَرۡضِ إِلَّا عَلَى ٱللَّهِ رِزۡقُهَا ۝٦﴾ [هُود الآية ٦]

"And the responsibility of sustaining every creature on the earth rests with Allāh." (Hūd 11:6)

The blessings of Allāh (ﷻ) from the sky and the earth are showered upon us by way of obedience and repentance *(taqwā and tawbah).* Through *taqwā* and *tawbah* we become deserving, worthy and eligible of Allāh's (ﷻ) bounties.

Allāh (ﷻ) says:

﴿وَلَوۡ أَنَّ أَهۡلَ ٱلۡقُرَىٰٓ ءَامَنُواْ وَٱتَّقَوۡاْ لَفَتَحۡنَا عَلَيۡهِم بَرَكَٰتٖ مِّنَ ٱلسَّمَآءِ وَٱلۡأَرۡضِ ۝٩٦﴾ [الأَعْرَاف الآية ٩٦]

"And if the inhabitants of the (various) towns believe and adopt *taqwā*, We will open to them multitudes of blessings from the heavens (such as rain) and the earth (such as abundant crops and minerals)." (Aʿrāf 7:96)

This verse outlines an overall rule that applies for all times.

When people are obedient to Allāh (ﷻ), then He will grant them abundance in provisions and good fortune. On the other hand, when they disregard His commandments, they will be overtaken with adversities and unfavourable conditions. As well, it is through gratitude, thankfulness and appreciation, that Allāh's (ﷻ) blessings will be preserved, increased and enlarged.

Allāh (ﷻ) says:

﴿وَإِذۡ تَأَذَّنَ رَبُّكُمۡ لَئِن شَكَرۡتُمۡ لَأَزِيدَنَّكُمۡۖ 7﴾ [إِبْرَاهِيم الآية ٧]

"And (remember also) when your Lord announced: 'If you show gratitude (for the favours I grant you), then I will definitely grant you (many) more (physical, spiritual and worldly favours).'" (Ibrāhīm 14:7)

سَلاماً أَيُّها الماء　فَمِنكَ الكُلُّ أَحياء

بِأَمْرِ مِنْ إِلَهِ الكَوْنِ   حَيَاةٌ فِيكَ يَا مَاء

فَكُلُّ الشُّكْرِ والحُبِّ   لِمَا أَنْزَلْتَ يَا رَبِّي

تَرْوِيتَا مَدَى الدَّهْر   بِمَاءِ بَاسِم الثّغرِ

وفِي عُسْر وفِي يُسْر   يَجُود المَاء بالخَير

وكُلُّ الفضلِ والاحسَانْ   بمَا أكْرمتَ يَا مَنّانْ

بمَاء غَنّت الاطيَارْ   ومَالَت أغْصن الاشجَار

بِهِ اهتزَّت أرَاضِينَا   وطَابَت أجْمَلُ الأثمَار

وكُلُّ الشُّكر والحَمدِ   لمَولاَنَا بلاَ حَدِّ

وسِرُّ الخَيرِ فِي الأكوَانْ   بِهَذَا المَاءِ يَا إِنسَان

فصُنه ومِنهُ لا تَهدِرْ   لِيَبقَى العَيشُ باطْمِئنَان

وطِيب العَيشِ يَا إخوَانْ   بطَاعَة رَبّنَا الرَّحْمَان

Peace be upon you, O water - everything is thriving as a result of you,
By the order of the universe's Lord, there is life in you, O water.
This is why, [I must express] every thanks and love for what you send [my way], O my Lord,
You quench our thirst repeatedly with water which we term as [a beautiful] natural spring water.
In times of difficulties and in times of ease, there is ample fresh water,
All benevolence and grace is for you, O Giver, for all that you have honoured (us with).
With water the birds chirp, and the tree branches beautifully curve,
With it our lands stir to life, and the beautiful fruits become delightful.
All praise and gratitude are for our Lord without any limits,
O mankind the secret of goodness in the universe is hidden in this water.

Safeguard water and never waste it, so that life can remain pleasant,
And O my brothers - for a pleasant life, adorn yourself with the obedience of our Lord, the Most Merciful.

KHUṬBAH 71

Indeed, the Religion of Allāh is of Ease

When we carefully examine Islām's texts, directives, and objectives, it becomes undoubtedly clear that they have been put in place so as to bring about the greatest good for Allāh's (ﷻ) servants, and to remove any difficulties from them in all religious and mundane matters.

Allāh (ﷻ) prescribed the directives of Islām as a means of kindness and mercy for all of humanity. Its directives are not beyond the ability of Allāh's (ﷻ) servants.

Rather, its directives accommodate people's abilities, provide them with encouragement, and relieve them of hardship.

Allāh (ﷻ) says in the Qur'ān:

﴿وَمَا جَعَلَ عَلَيْكُمْ فِي ٱلدِّينِ مِنْ حَرَجٍ ۚ ٧٨﴾ [الحج الآية ٧٨]

"And He has not placed any hardship (difficulty) upon you in the religion *(dīn)*." (Ḥajj 22:78)

Ḥāfiz ibn Kathīr (رحمه الله) commenting on this verse writes:

«أَيْ: مَا كَلَّفَكُمْ مَا لَا تُطِيقُونَ، وَمَا أَلْزَمَكُمْ بِشَيْءٍ فَشَقَّ عَلَيْكُمْ إِلَّا جَعَلَ اللهُ لَكُمْ فَرَجًا وَمَخْرَجًا، فَالصَّلَاةُ الَّتِي هِيَ أَكْبَرُ أَرْكَانِ الْإِسْلَامِ بَعْدَ الشَّهَادَتَيْنِ-تَجِبُ فِي الْحَضَرِ أَرْبَعًا وَفِي السَّفَرِ تُقْصَرُ إِلَى ثِنْتَيْنِ، وَفِي الْخَوْفِ يُصَلِّيهَا بَعْضُ الْأَئِمَّةِ رَكْعَةً، كَمَا وَرَدَ بِهِ الْحَدِيثُ، وَتُصَلَّى رِجَالًا وَرُكْبَانًا، مُسْتَقْبِلِي الْقِبْلَةِ وَغَيْرَ مُسْتَقْبِلِيهَا. وَكَذَا فِي النَّافِلَةِ فِي السَّفَرِ إِلَى الْقِبْلَةِ وَغَيْرِهَا، وَالْقِيَامُ فِيهَا يَسْقُطُ بِعُذْرِ الْمَرَضِ، فَيُصَلِّيهَا الْمَرِيضُ جَالِسًا، فَإِنْ لَمْ يَسْتَطِعْ فَعَلَى جَنْبِهِ، إِلَى غَيْرِ ذَلِكَ مِنَ الرُّخَصِ وَالتَّخْفِيفَاتِ، فِي سَائِرِ الْفَرَائِضِ وَالْوَاجِبَاتِ».

(تفسير ابن كثير)

> "He has not obliged you to do anything that will cause you difficulty except that He created for you a way out. So the *ṣalāt*, which is the most important pillar of Islām after the two testimonies of faith, is obligatory; and it is four *rakʿah* when one is settled, but are shortened to two *rakʿah* when one is traveling. According to some imāms, only one *rakʿah* is obligatory at times of fear, as was recorded in the *ḥadīth*. A person may pray while walking or riding, facing the *qiblah* or otherwise. When praying optional prayers while traveling, one may face the *qiblah* or not. A person is not obliged to stand during the prayer if one is sick; the sick person may pray sitting down, and if he is not able to do that then he may pray lying on his side. There are several other exemptions and concessions which may apply to the obligatory prayers and even other duties." (Tafsīr Ibn Kathīr)

The Prophet (ﷺ) said:

«بُعِثْتُ بِالْحَنِيفِيَّةِ السَّمْحَةِ».

(رواه أحمد)

> "I have been sent with the easy and *ḥanafī* way (devoting all worship to Allāh alone)." (Aḥmad)

Thus, Islām is a religion characterized by ease, facilitation, and moderation.

The basic foundations of Islām's directives do not dictate that all matters be treated the same. In fact, some of those foundations carry directives that are very simple to fulfill. This results from giving consideration to circumstances, consequences, and times.

Allāh (ﷻ) prescribed certain rulings as exceptions to the default in order to make matters easy for His servants, and the scholars refer to these exceptional rulings as concessions (الرُّخَصُ). Moreover, Allāh (ﷻ)

encouraged His servants to make use of those concessions whenever the circumstances require that.

Imām Aḥmad (ﷺ) has documented a *ḥadīth* in his *Musnad* on the authority of Ibn ʿUmar (ﷺ) who narrated that the Messenger of Allāh (ﷺ) said:

«إِنَّ اللهَ يُحِبُّ أَنْ تُؤْتَى رُخَصُهُ، كَمَا يَكْرَهُ أَنْ تُؤْتَى مَعْصِيَتُهُ».

(رواه أحمد)

"Allāh certainly loves for His concessions to be accepted, just as He detests for His prohibitions to be perpetrated." (Aḥmad)

Consequently, in any instance where there is no definitive text of Islām concerning a particular matter, the rulings of Islām accommodate varying circumstances, customs, and norms. This clearly displays that Islām's directives are ones that promote ease and avert difficulty.

Instances of ease in Islām's directives include the permissibility of wiping over one's socks when performing *wuḍū.*

Gaining the proper understanding of the religion is a requirement for every Muslim. Whoever has little or no understanding of the *dīn* will have incorrect actions, and as a result, their ignorance will lead them down the wrong path. Every Muslim should strive to learn so that they can worship Allāh (ﷻ) correctly with proper understanding.

When winter arrives and the temperatures get colder, people start wearing socks and cover their feet to gain warmth. Wiping over leather socks when performing *wuḍū* is permissible and a confirmed *sunnah.* The Messenger of Allāh (ﷺ) would wipe over his leather socks. Wiping over leather socks is also authentically attributed to numerous companions (ﷺ).

Ḥasan al-Baṣrī (ﷺ) states the following:

«حَدَّثَنِي سَبْعُونَ مِنَ الصَّحَابَةِ بِالْمَسْحِ عَلَى الْخُفَّيْنِ».

(فتح الباري لابن حجر)

"Seventy among the companions (ﷺ) narrated to me that they used to wipe over their leather socks." (Fatḥ al-Bārī of Ibn Ḥajr)

Ḥāfiẓ ibn al-Ḥajr (ﷺ) states:

«وَقَدْ صَرَّحَ جَمْعٌ مِنَ الْحُفَّاظِ بِأَنَّ الْمَسْحَ عَلَى الْخُفَّيْنِ مُتَوَاتِرٌ وَجَمَعَ بَعْضُهُمْ رُوَاتَهُ فَجَاوَزُوا الثَّمَانِينَ مِنْهُمُ الْعَشَرَةُ».

(نيل الأوطار)

"An overwhelming group of the *Ḥuffāz* (experts in *ḥadīth*) have declared that wiping over leather socks is established by *tawātur* (an overwhelming number of authentic narrations), and some of them have mentioned that they collected and enumerated the narrations from the companions of the Prophet (ﷺ), and found them to be more than eighty in number, from which ten of them are narrated by the ten companions (ﷺ) that were given glad tidings of Paradise from the Prophet (ﷺ)." (Nayl al-Awtār)

Imām Abū Ḥanīfah (ﷺ) states:

«مَا قُلْتُ بِالْمَسْحِ حَتَّى جَاءَنِي فِيهِ مِثْلُ ضَوْءِ النَّهَارِ».

(فتح القدير)

"I did not declare the validity of performing *masḥ* on leather socks until its evidence was clear to me as daylight." (Fatḥ al-Qadīr)

Permission to wipe over the socks is one of the ways that Islāmic law brings ease and comfort to the believers. This is because there is a need to wear socks, and at times it is difficult to take them off, such as in workplaces, public washrooms, etc.

It is crucial that whoever wishes to wipe over their socks must know the regulations, time limit, characteristics of the socks, conditions for being allowed to wipe, what nullifies this type of purification, what happens if it gets nullified, etc. and other related issues.

REGULATIONS RELATING TO WIPING OVER ONE'S SOCKS

- A *khuf* is a sock made out of leather.[36]
- It is called a *khuf* which comes from the word *khaffa* which means to be light because the *khuf* is light upon the feet.[37]
- Some scholars say that the ruling is lightened because washing the feet is obligatory, and wiping over the *khuf* becomes permissible which is easier than washing.[38]
- As for the *jawrab* which is a non-leather sock, it is anything that covers the feet and is made of cotton, wool, animal hair, fabric, etc., and this is called *jawrab* or socks.[39]

---

[36] The Arabic text of this is as follows:

الْخُفُّ مَا يُلْبَسُ فِي الرِّجْل مِنْ جِلْدٍ رَقِيقٍ وَجَمْعُهُ أَخْفَافٌ. وَالْمُرَادُ بِهِ فِي بَابِ الطَّهَارَةِ: هُوَ السَّاتِرُ لِلْكَعْبَيْنِ فَأَكْثَرُ مِنْ جِلْدٍ وَنَحْوِهِ.

(الموسوعة الفقهية الكويتية)

[37] The Arabic text of this is as follows:

وَسُمِّيَ الْخُفُّ خُفًّا مِنْ الْخِفَّةِ؛ لِأَنَّ الْحُكْمَ خَفَّ بِهِ مِنْ الْغَسْلِ إلَى الْمَسْحِ.

(كتاب البحر الرائق)

[38] The Arabic text of this is as follows:

إنَّمَا سُمِّيَ خُفًّا لِخِفَّةِ الْحُكْمِ بِهِ مِنْ الْغُسْلِ إلَى الْمَسْحِ.

(الدر المختار وحاشية ابن عابدين)

[39] The Arabic text of this is as follows:

قال شمس الأئمة: هذا في شرح كتاب الصلاة الجورب أنواع: منها ما يكون من غزل وصوف، ومنها ما يكون من غزل، ومنها ما يكون من شعر.

والأول: أن لا يجوز عليه المسح عندهم جميعاً.

وأما الثاني: فإن كان رقيقاً: لا يجوز المسح عليه بلا خلاف، وإن كان ثخيناً مستمسكاً ويستر الكعب ستراً لا يراه الناظر كما هو جوارب أهل مرو، فعلى قول أبي حنيفة رحمه الله: لا يجوز المسح عليه، إلا إذا كان منعلاً أو مبطناً، وعلى قولهما: يجوز.

(المحيط البرهاني في الفقه النعماني)

- It is required for the socks to be made of pure material, and that they cover the feet including the ankles.[40]
- They must be thick enough such that they do not show what is underneath them.[41]
- If they are see-through or thin socks, and the wetness of the hands due to the wiping can reach the skin of the feet, and if the skin can be seen through the socks, then it is not allowed to wipe over them.
- They must prevent the amount of water present on the hand to reach the skin at the time of wiping.
- They do not need to be waterproof, but they must prevent the amount of water from reaching the skin.[42]
- If the socks however, are not see-through and their thickness prevents the water to reach the feet, then it is allowed to wipe on them according to the stronger scholarly opinion.[43]

---

40 The Arabic text of this is as follows:

أَنْ يَكُونَ الْخُفُّ سَاتِرًا لِلْمَحَل الْمَفْرُوضِ غَسْلُهُ فِي الْوُضُوءِ فَلاَ يَجُوزُ الْمَسْحُ عَلَى خُفٍّ غَيْرِ سَاتِرٍ لِلْكَعْبَيْنِ مَعَ الْقَدَمِ.

(حواشي على ملتقى الأبحر)

41 The Arabic text of this is as follows:

وَالثَّخِينِ الَّذِي لَيْسَ مُجَلَّدًا وَلَا مُنَعَّلًا بِشَرْطِ أَنْ يَسْتَمْسِكَ عَلَى السَّاقِ بِلَا رَبْطٍ وَلَا يُرَى مَا تَحْتَهُ وَعَلَيْهِ الْفَتْوَى. كَذَا فِي النَّهْرِ الْفَائِقِ.

(الفتاوى الهندية)

42 The Arabic text of this is as follows:

و الشرط السادس منعهما وصول الماء إلى الجسد فلا يشفان الماء.

(مراقي الفلاح شرح نور الإيضاح)

43 The Arabic text of this is as follows:

اتفق الأئمة على جواز المسح على الجوربين المجلدين والمنعلين وكذلك اتفقوا على عدم جوازه على الرقيقين يشفان واختلفوا في الثخينين فالجمهور جوزوه ومنعه أبو حنيفة، وروي عنه الرجوع إلى قول صاحبيه قبل وفاته بأيام وذلك. أنه مسح على جوربيه في مرضه ثم قال لعواده فعلت ما كنت أمنع الناس عنه، فاستدلوا به على رجوعه، قال صاحب الهداية: وعليه الفتوى.

(إعلاء السنن)

- It is required that a person wears the socks after a complete act of purification with water alone.[44] Whether it is with *wuḍū* or *ghusl.*[45]
- If a person wipes over the socks that he wore before completing his purification with water, then his *wuḍū* and prayer will be invalid.
- If a person washes one of his feet then wears its sock, then washes the other foot then wears its sock, then it is not allowed to wipe over that sock according to the strong scholarly opinion.

This is because it is stated in a *ḥadīth* of Abū Bakrah (ﷺ):

«أَنَّهُ رَخَّصَ لِلْمُسَافِرِ ثَلَاثَةَ أَيَّامٍ وَلَيَالِيَهُنَّ، وَلِلْمُقِيمِ يَوْمًا وَلَيْلَةً، إِذَا تَطَهَّرَ فَلَبِسَ خُفَّيْهِ: أَنْ يَمْسَحَ عَلَيْهِمَا».

(رواه ابن خزيمة)

"He (the Prophet (ﷺ)) gave permission for a traveler to perform *masḥ* (wiping) over his leather socks for three days and nights, and for a non-traveler for a day and night when he purified himself then wore his two socks." (Ibn Khuzaymah)

- In this narration, the letter *"fā"* implies sequence and order (التعقيب والترتيب). Hence the *"fā"* means "then" which indicates that wearing the socks should come after the entire process of purification. Therefore, one must complete the purification

---

[44] The Arabic text of this is as follows:

(قَوْلُهُ: إِنْ لَبِسَهُمَا عَلَى وُضُوءٍ تَامٍّ وَقْتَ الْحَدَثِ) يَعْنِي الْمَسْحَ جَائِزٌ بِشَرْطِ أَنْ يَكُونَ اللُّبْسُ عَلَى طَهَارَةٍ كَامِلَةٍ.

(كتاب البحر الرائق)

[45] The Arabic text of this is as follows:

فَالْجُمْهُورُ غَيْرُ الشَّافِعِيَّةِ يَشْتَرِطُونَ أَنْ تَكُونَ الطَّهَارَةُ بِالْمَاءِ مِنْ وُضُوءٍ أَوْ غُسْلٍ.

(حواشي على ملتقى الأبحر)

process, finish his *wuḍū*, and wash both of his feet, then they can wear their socks that they wish to wipe over.
- The one residing (in his home) can wipe for a total of one day and one night, meaning 24 hours; while the traveler can wipe for a total of three days and nights, meaning for 72 hours.[46]
- The time starts ticking when a person first wipes over his socks after breaking his *wuḍū*, according to the stronger opinion.[47]
- Thus, from the time a person first wipes over his socks after breaking his *wuḍū*, he can continue wiping for a period of 24 hours if he is a resident, and 72 hours if he is a traveler.

'Umar (؈) states regarding a non-traveler:

«يَمْسَحُ عَلَيْهِمَا إِلَى مِثْلِ سَاعَتِهِ مِنْ يَوْمِهِ وَلَيْلَتِهِ».

(مصنف عبد الرزاق)

"He will wipe over them (his socks) until the same time the following day." (Muṣnaf ʿAbd al-Razzāq)

- Once the time expires, his purification is nullified according to some scholars.[48]
- Others have said that his *wuḍū* is still intact and thus if he was praying when the time expired, he should continue his prayer[49]

---

[46] The Arabic text of this is as follows:

وَيَجُوزُ لِلْمُقِيمِ يَوْمًا وَلَيْلَةً وَلِلْمُسَافِرِ ثَلَاثَةَ أَيَّامٍ وَلَيَالِيهَا.

(فتح القدير)

[47] The Arabic text of this is as follows:

وَابْتِدَاؤُهَا عَقِيبَ الْحَدَثِ.

(فتح القدير)

[48] The Arabic text of this is as follows:

(قَوْلُهُ: وَمُضِيُّ الْمُدَّةِ) أَيْ وَيَنْقُضُهُ أَيْضًا مُضِيُّ الْمُدَّةِ لِلْأَحَادِيثِ الدَّالَّةِ عَلَى التَّأْقِيتِ.

(البحر الرائق)

[49] The Arabic text of this is as follows:

because the expiration of the time is not considered one of the nullifications of *wuḍū*.[50]

- The first opinion is definitely safer for the correctness of the prayer.
- Avoiding anything that will not fulfill the conditions of the prayer is always better.
- If a person breaks one's *wuḍū* after the time has expired, then they cannot wipe over their socks until they take them off and perform a complete new *wuḍū*, washing both feet.
- A person can wipe in the specified time period as long one does not become sexually impure.
- If that occurs due to intercourse, a wet dream, or for any other reason (ejaculation) - then one can no longer wipe over their socks. They must perform a *ghusl* by taking a complete bath, washing their entire body and feet.

Ṣafwān ibn ʿAssāl (ﷺ) states:

«كَانَ رَسُولُ اللهِ ﷺ يَأْمُرُنَا إِذَا كُنَّا سَفَرًا أَنْ لاَ نَنْزِعَ خِفَافَنَا ثَلاَثَةَ أَيَّامٍ وَلَيَالِيهِنَّ، إِلاَّ مِنْ جَنَابَةٍ، وَلَكِنْ مِنْ غَائِطٍ وَبَوْلٍ وَنَوْمٍ».

(سنن الترمذي)

"When we were traveling, the Messenger of Allāh (ﷺ) would order us not to remove our leather socks for three days and nights, except in the case of *janābah* (ejaculation or sexual

الرَّابِعُ لَا شئ عَلَيْهِ لَا غَسْلَ الْقَدَمَيْنِ وَلَا غَيْرَهُ بَلْ طَهَارَتُهُ صَحِيحَةٌ يُصَلِّي بِهَا مَا لَمْ يُحْدِثْ كَمَا لَوْ لَمْ يَخْلَعْ: وَهَذَا الْمَذْهَبُ حَكَاهُ ابْنُ الْمُنْذِرِ عَنْ الْحَسَنِ الْبَصْرِيِّ وَقَتَادَةَ وَسُلَيْمَانَ بْنِ حَرْبٍ وَاخْتَارَهُ ابْنُ الْمُنْذِرِ وَهُوَ الْمُخْتَارُ الْأَقْوَى وَحَكَاهُ أَصْحَابُنَا عَنْ دَاوُد.

(كتاب المجموع)

[50] The Arabic text of this is as follows:

وَالطَّهَارَةُ لَا يَنْقُضُهَا إِلَّا الْأَحْدَاثُ، أَوْ نَصٌّ وَارِدٌ بِانْتِقَاضِهَا وَأَنَّهُ لَمْ يَكُنْ حَدَثٌ وَلَا نَصٌّ هَهُنَا عَلَى انْتِقَاضِ طَهَارَتِهِ وَلَا عَلَى انْتِقَاضِ بَعْضِهَا فَبَطَلَ هَذَا الْقَوْلُ، وَصَحَّ الْقَوْلُ بِأَنَّهُ عَلَى طَهَارَتِهِ، وَأَنَّهُ يُصَلِّي مَا لَمْ يُحْدِثْ.

(المحلى بالآثار)

impurity), but not for attending the call of nature, urinating, or sleeping." (Sunan of al-Tirmidhī)

- If a person is in doubt whether the time has expired or not, then they cannot wipe as long as this doubt remains, because they are not certain that the condition of wiping has been fulfilled.[51]
- If a person takes off one or both of their socks at any given time, then the purification that they gained after wiping would be nullified and their *wuḍū* would be invalid.[52]
- It is not enough in this case, to just wash the two feet then wear the socks again. If they want to wipe over the socks, then they must perform a complete new *wuḍū* with water, according to the stronger opinion, then they can wear the socks and wipe over them. This is safer for one's prayer.
- If a sock has holes or tears in it which show part of the foot which must normally be washed, and there are a lot of holes or they are very large, then one cannot wipe on such socks; however if there is only a little amount or they are small in size, then this is excused.[53]
- If the hole of the sock is above the ankles, then there is no harm in it.[54]

---

[51] The Arabic text of this is as follows:

ولا مسح لشاكّ في بقاء المدة، انقضت أو لا، أو شك المسافر، هل ابتدأ في السفر أو في الحضر؛ لأن المسح رخصة بشروط، منها المدة، فإذا شك فيها رجع إلى الأصل وهو الغسل.

(الفقه الإسلامي)

[52] The Arabic text of this is as follows:

وَيَنْقُضُهُ أَيْضًا نَزْعُ الْخُفِّ لِسِرَايَةِ الْحَدَثِ إلَى الْقَدَمِ حَيْثُ زَالَ الْمَانِعُ، وَكَذَا نَزْعُ أَحَدِهِمَا.

(فتح القدير)

[53] The Arabic text of this is as follows:

وَلَا يَجُوزُ الْمَسْحُ عَلَى خُفٍّ فِيهِ خَرْقٌ كَبِيرٌ يُبَيِّنُ مِنْهُ قَدْرَ ثَلَاثِ أَصَابِعَ مِنْ أَصَابِعِ الرِّجْلِ، فَإِنْ كَانَ أَقَلَّ مِنْ ذَلِكَ جَازَ.

(فتح القدير)

[54] The Arabic text of this is as follows:

- It is obligatory to wipe the upper part of the sock and not the lower part, the back or the ankles.[55]
- The way to wipe the socks is to place both wet hands with fingers spread out on the toes of the two feet than to pass them over the upper part of the foot until one reaches the ankles.[56]
- It is not recommended to wipe over the bottom of the foot, the back of the foot or the ankles according to the most accurate opinion.

This is because ʿAlī ibn Abī Ṭālib (ؓ) states:

»لَوْ كَانَ الدِّينُ بِالرَّأْيِ لَكَانَ أَسْفَلُ الْخُفِّ أَوْلَى بِالْمَسْحِ مِنْ أَعْلَاهُ، وَقَدْ رَأَيْتُ رَسُولَ اللَّهِ ﷺ يَمْسَحُ عَلَى ظَاهِرِ خُفَّيْهِ«.

(أبو داود)

"If the religion was based on opinion, then it would be more important to wipe over the underparts of the leather socks than the upper, but I have seen the Messenger of Allāh (ﷺ) wiping over the upper parts of his leather socks." (Abū Dāwūd)

وَلَوْ كَانَ فِي الْكَعْبِ لَمْ يَمْنَعْ وَإِنْ كَثُرَ كَذَا فِي الِاخْتِيَارِ.
(فتح القدير)

[55] The Arabic text of this is as follows:
ثُمَّ الْمَسْحُ عَلَى الظَّاهِرِ حَتْمٌ حَتَّى لَا يَجُوزَ عَلَى بَاطِنِ الْخُفِّ وَعَقِبِهِ وَسَاقِهِ.
(فتح القدير)

[56] The Arabic text of this is as follows:
صُورَتُهُ أَنْ يَضَعَ أَصَابِعَ الْيُمْنَى عَلَى مُقَدَّمِ خُفِّهِ الْأَيْمَنِ وَأَصَابِعَ الْيُسْرَى عَلَى مُقَدَّمِ الْأَيْسَرِ وَيَمُدَّهُمَا إِلَى السَّاقِ فَوْقَ الْكَعْبَيْنِ وَيُفَرِّجُ أَصَابِعَهُ، هَذَا هُوَ الْوَجْهُ الْمَسْنُونُ.
(فتح القدير)

- If a person does not wipe the upper part of their socks, then their *wuḍū* is invalid by scholarly consensus;[57] and their prayers would be invalid if they were to pray in that way.

A poet says:

وتارك المسح للأعلى أبطل ۞ ويمسحهما جميعا۞ اليمنى باليمنى واليسرى باليسرى

"The one who leaves wiping the top will nullify their wuḍū and prayer.
He should wipe both socks at the same time.
The right foot with his right hand, and the left foot with his left hand."

- Some scholars say that it is recommended to wipe the right foot before the left one.[58]

Imām Aḥmad (ﷺ) states:

«كَيفَما فَعَلْتَ فهو جائِزٌ؛ باليَدِ الواحِدَةِ، أو باليَدَين».

(شرح الزركشي على مختصر الخرقي)

"Whichever way you do it is permissible, whether it is with one hand or both hands." (Sharḥ al-Zarakshī ʿala Mukhtaṣar al-Kharqī)

- It is not recommended to wipe more than one time because this has not been reported.[59]

---

[57] The Arabic text of this is as follows:

فإن مسح باطن الخف دون ظاهره لم يجز، فإن موضع المسح ظهر القدم.

(البناية في شرح الهداية)

[58] The Arabic text of this is as follows:

وزاد: قال في البلغة: ويسن تقديم اليمين.

(شرح الزركشي على مختصر الخرقي)

[59] The Arabic text of this is as follows:

- One cannot wipe over an impure sock.[60]
- Whoever is traveling and the time for wiping starts while he is traveling, and he wipes for less than a day and night then he returns to his hometown can continue wiping until the 24 hours expire.
- However, if he has wiped while traveling for 24 hours or more, then he returns to his hometown, he must remove his socks and refresh his *wuḍū* because the time expired as soon as he arrived in his hometown.[61]
- If he wipes while he is in his hometown, and he travels before the 24 hours expires, then he can wipe up to 72 hours from the time that he started wiping - meaning he gets a time extension.[62]
- If a person makes complete *wuḍū* with water, then wears his socks and does not break his *wuḍū* until after he wears another set of socks on top of them, then he is permitted to wipe over the second layer of socks.

(قَوْلُهُ لِحَدِيثِ الْمُغِيرَةِ - رَضِيَ اللَّهُ عَنْهُ - أَنَّ النَّبِيَّ - ﷺ - وَضَعَ يَدَيْهِ عَلَى خُفَّيْهِ وَمَدَّهُمَا مِنْ الْأَصَابِعِ إلَى أَعْلَاهُمَا مَسْحَةً وَاحِدَةً، وَكَأَنِّي أَنْظُرُ إلَى أَثَرِ الْمَسْحِ عَلَى خُفِّ رَسُولِ اللَّهِ - ﷺ - خُطُوطًا بِالْأَصَابِعِ) وَفِيهِ مَسْحَةٌ وَاحِدَةٌ فَأَخَذُوا مِنْهُ أَنَّ تَكْرَارَ الْمَسْحِ عَلَى الْخُفَّيْنِ غَيْرُ مَشْرُوعٍ.

(فتح القدير)

60 The Arabic text of this is as follows:

أَنْ يَكُونَ الْخُفُّ طَاهِرًا، فَلاَ يَجُوزُ الْمَسْحُ عَلَى خُفٍّ نَجِسٍ كَجِلْدِ الْمَيْتَةِ قَبْل الدَّبْغِ.

(الموسوعة الفقهية)

61 The Arabic text of this is as follows:

وَلَوْ أَقَامَ الْمُسَافِرُ بَعْدَ يَوْمٍ وَلَيْلَةٍ نَزَعَ، وَإِلَّا يُتِمَّ يَوْمًا وَلَيْلَةً.

(البحر الرائق)

62 The Arabic text of this is as follows:

وَلَوْ مَسَحَ مُقِيمٌ فَسَافَرَ قَبْلَ تَمَامِ يَوْمٍ وَلَيْلَةٍ مَسَحَ ثَلَاثًا.

(البحر الرائق)

- If he wipes over the second layer of socks, then takes them off, his *wuḍū* becomes invalid.[63]
- If he makes a complete *wuḍū* with water alone, then wears his socks, but breaks his *wuḍū* before wearing the second layer of socks, then it is not permitted for him to wipe over that second layer of socks because he did not wear them in a state of purity.[64]
- If he wears socks after a complete *wuḍū* with water then breaks his *wuḍū* and wipes over those socks, then he wears another layer of socks, he is not allowed to wipe over that top layer because he wore them in a state of purity which involved wiping over socks, and it was not a *wuḍū* performed with water alone.[65]

It is also obligatory upon the one wearing socks to take care of their socks because they quickly start to smell bad. When they do start to smell bad one must remove them to avoid bothering and inconveniencing others, especially those praying next to him in the *masjid.*

In the past, the Arabs would equate rotten and smelly things to smelly socks in their expressions. They would say:

---

[63] The Arabic text of this is as follows:

وَإِنْ لَبِسَ خُفًّا عَلَى آخَرَ قَبْلَ الْحَدَثِ وَمَسَحَ الأَعْلَى، ثُمَّ نَزَعَ الْمَمْسُوحَ الأَعْلَى لَزِمَهُ نَزْعُ التَّحْتَانِيِّ وَإِعَادَةُ الْوُضُوءِ، لِأَنَّهُ مَحَلُّ الْمَسْحِ، وَنَزْعُهُ كَنَزْعِهِمَا، وَالرُّخْصَةُ تَعَلَّقَتْ بِهِمَا، فَصَارَ كَانْكِشَافِ الْقَدَمِ.

(حواشي على ملتقى الأبحر)

[64] The Arabic text of this is as follows:

وَإِنْ تَوَضَّأَ وَلَبِسَ خُفًّا ثُمَّ أَحْدَثَ ثُمَّ لَبِسَ الْخُفَّ الآخَرَ لَمْ يَجُزِ الْمَسْحُ عَلَيْهِ، لِأَنَّهُ لَبِسَهُ عَلَى غَيْرِ طَهَارَةٍ.

(حواشي على ملتقى الأبحر)

[65] The Arabic text of this is as follows:

أَوْ مَسَحَ الْخُفَّ الأَوَّل بَعْدَ حَدَثِهِ ثُمَّ لَبِسَ الْخُفَّ الثَّانِيَ وَلَوْ عَلَى طَهَارَةٍ لَمْ يَجُزِ الْمَسْحُ عَلَى الثَّانِي، لِأَنَّ الْخُفَّ الْمَمْسُوحَ بَدَلٌ عَنْ غَسْل مَا تَحْتَهُ، وَالْبَدَل لاَ يَجُوزُ لَهُ بَدَلٌ آخَرُ.

(حواشي على ملتقى الأبحر)

«وهُوَ أَنْتَنُ مِنْ رِيحِ الجَوْرَبِ».

(تاج العروس)

"It is smellier than the smell of socks!" (Tāj al-ʿUrūs)

Sometimes the poet would dispraise a person by saying:

غزا ابن عمير غزوةً تركت له ۞ ثناءً كريح الجورب المتعرّق

(كتاب الحيوان)

> "Ibn ʿUmair went to a battle which gave him praise equivalent to the smell of sweaty socks." (Kitāb al-Ḥayawān)

أَثْنِي عَلَيَّ بِمَا عَلِمْتِ فَإِنَّنِي ۞ مُثْنٍ عَلَيْكَ بِمِثْلِ رِيحِ الجَوْرَبِ

(كتاب مجمع الأمثال)

> "Praise me with which you know for I will praise you with what is equivalent to the smell of socks." (Kitāb Majmaʿ al-Amthāl)

It is praiseworthy to adopt these safer opinions for the sake of the acceptance of one's prayers, and to exercise caution especially when it comes to issues of wiping over the socks.

It is also vital to make sure that the socks one is wiping over meet the requirements for wiping. Sealskinz and DexShell socks fit the above-mentioned principles and therefore can be worn for wiping during *wuḍū.*

When in doubt always ask the *'ulemā'* - the scholars of *fiqh*, who especially outline that avoiding points of contention and uncertainty in matters of *fiqh* is highly recommended. The Prophet (ﷺ) always used to take the safer route and ruled by it in many well-known instances.

Anas ibn Mālik (رضي الله عنه) reports the following:

«مَرَّ النَّبِيُّ ﷺ، بِتَمْرَةٍ مَسْقُوطَةٍ فقَالَ: لَوْلاَ أَنْ تَكُونَ مِنْ صَدَقَةٍ لَأَكَلْتُهَا».

(صحيح البخاري)

The Prophet (ﷺ) passed by a fallen date and said: "If it was not for my doubt that this might have been from charity, I would have eaten it." (Ṣaḥīḥ al-Bukhārī)

At the same time, we should have open hearts and tolerance when it comes to differences of opinions and varying *fiqh* rulings. We should not let it become a cause of discord, friction, bitterness, dispute, animosity and hostility towards one another.

Rather we should praise Allāh (ﷻ) and express gratitude to Him for the many wonderful blessings that He has bestowed upon us. We need to remind ourselves about how many people walk barefooted, and how many people do not have anything to warm themselves with. Some people sleep in the open without any covering over them, others live on the pavements and sleep on the bare ground.

Alḥamdulillāh we are blessed with a luxurious life, wealth and many other countless favours. Therefore, it is imperative to be grateful to Allāh (ﷻ) for showering His innumerable blessings and favours upon us. An appreciative, obedient servant will gain more virtue, honour and blessings; whereas an ungrateful and disobedient person will lead oneself to disgrace, deprivation and ruin.

لك الحمدُ تعظيمًا لوجهِكَ قائِمًا ۞ وأنتَ إلهِي ما أحَقَّ وما أحرَى

لك الحمدُ يا ذا الكِبرِيَاءِ ومَنْ يَكُنْ ۞ بحمدِكَ ذا شُكرٍ فقد أحرَزَ الشُّكرَا

My Lord, You deserve all praise as befits Your glorious face,
You are the Most Magnificent.
And anyone who thanks You by praising You,
Has indeed excelled in expressing gratitude.

KHUṬBAH 72

The Gift of Wealth

Wealth is something that life revolves around. Life's core, completion, happiness, and dignity are all tied to it in one way or another. Wealth is what allows a person to have food, drink, clothing, and dwelling. Wealth affords a person the means of being fed, clothed, sheltered, and protected. Wealth is required as it relates to health, knowledge, strength, development, and advancement. Allāh (ﷻ) has decreed that wealth be linked to livelihood and living; in fact, He made it a foundation of life.

Allāh (ﷻ) says in the Qur'ān:

﴿وَلَا تُؤْتُوا۟ ٱلسُّفَهَآءَ أَمْوَٰلَكُمُ ٱلَّتِى جَعَلَ ٱللَّهُ لَكُمْ قِيَـٰمًا ۝٥﴾ [النِّساء الآية ٥]

> "And do not give your wealth to those under your care if they are not competent to independently handle it. This wealth is what Allāh has made a foundation of people's livelihood and well-being." (Nisā' 4:5)

The foundation of something is what protects it and keeps it in order.

As a result, wealth is a foundation of livelihood, as well as all general and personal well-being. Consequently, the preservation of wealth is a major objective of Islām's teachings, and it is one of the necessities that Islām treats as indispensable.

Wealth has been mentioned in the Qur'ān more than eighty times. In some instances, Allāh (ﷻ) refers to wealth using the Arabic word *"khayr"* which refers to something that is good.

Allāh (ﷻ) says:

﴿وَإِنَّهُۥ لِحُبِّ ٱلْخَيْرِ لَشَدِيدٌ ۝٨﴾ [العَادِيَات الآية ٨]

"The human's love for wealth (*khayr*) is truly intense." (ʿĀdiyāt 100:8)

Allāh (ﷻ) has also referred to wealth with the same word (*khayr*) in the following verses:

﴿يَسْـَٔلُونَكَ مَاذَا يُنفِقُونَ ۖ قُلْ مَآ أَنفَقْتُم مِّنْ خَيْرٍ فَلِلْوَٰلِدَيْنِ وَٱلْأَقْرَبِينَ وَٱلْيَتَـٰمَىٰ وَٱلْمَسَـٰكِينِ وَٱبْنِ ٱلسَّبِيلِ ۗ وَمَا تَفْعَلُوا۟ مِنْ خَيْرٍ فَإِنَّ ٱللَّهَ بِهِۦ عَلِيمٌ ۝٢١٥﴾ [البَقَرَة الآية ٢١٥]

"They ask you (O Messenger of Allāh), what they should give (from their property as a deed that will bring them nearer to Allāh). Say (tell them): 'Give whatever is feasible for you from *khayr* (your lawfully earned wealth). Give that to parents, relatives, orphans, the needy, and stranded travelers. Whenever you do any amount of good, Allāh most certainly knows it.'" (Baqarah 2:215)

﴿كُتِبَ عَلَيْكُمْ إِذَا حَضَرَ أَحَدَكُمُ ٱلْمَوْتُ إِن تَرَكَ خَيْرًا ٱلْوَصِيَّةُ لِلْوَٰلِدَيْنِ وَٱلْأَقْرَبِينَ بِٱلْمَعْرُوفِ ۖ حَقًّا عَلَى ٱلْمُتَّقِينَ ۝١٨٠﴾ [البَقَرَة الآية ١٨٠]

"When any person among you begins to experience the initial stages of death, and he has a good deal of *khayr* (wealth) which he will leave behind, Allāh has obligated that the person fairly give (bequeath) some of his property to the parents, as well as the near relatives. That is an established duty which the people of *taqwā* are to fulfill." (Baqarah 2:180)

Wealth indeed has an unquestionable significance.

It has been mentioned in a *ḥadīth*:

«لَا يَحِلُّ مَالُ امْرِئٍ مُسْلِمٍ إِلَّا بِطِيبِ نَفْسٍ مِنْهُ، وَمَنْ حَلَفَ عَلَى يَمِينِ صَبْرٍ، يَقْتَطِعُ بِهَا مَالَ امْرِئٍ مُسْلِمٍ هُوَ فِيهَا فَاجِرٌ، لَقِيَ اللَّهَ وَهُوَ عَلَيْهِ غَضْبَانُ».

(متفق عليه)

"It is not permissible to take the wealth of a Muslim unless he gives it willingly. If someone deliberately lies when swearing an oath in order to unlawfully take any wealth that belongs to his Muslim brother, then that person will meet Allāh while Allāh is angry with him." (Agreed Upon)

Another *ḥadīth* mentions:

«مَنْ قُتِلَ دُونَ مَالِهِ فَهُوَ شَهِيدٌ».

(متفق عليه)

"If a person loses his life while defending his wealth, then he is considered a martyr." (Agreed Upon)

It is only out of Allāh's (ﷻ) kindness and favour upon His servants that He has blessed them with wealth.

Allāh (ﷻ) describes what Prophet Nūḥ (ﷺ) told his people:

﴿فَقُلْتُ ٱسْتَغْفِرُوا۟ رَبَّكُمْ إِنَّهُۥ كَانَ غَفَّارًا ﴿١٠﴾ يُرْسِلِ ٱلسَّمَآءَ عَلَيْكُم مِّدْرَارًا ﴿١١﴾ وَيُمْدِدْكُم بِأَمْوَٰلٍ وَبَنِينَ وَيَجْعَل لَّكُمْ جَنَّـٰتٍ وَيَجْعَل لَّكُمْ أَنْهَـٰرًا ﴿١٢﴾﴾ [نوح من الآية ١٠ الى الآية ١٢]

"So I told (the people): Seek forgiveness from your Lord, as He is certainly always forgiving. (If you do so) He will send down rain upon you in abundance, grant you an increase in wealth and children, and bestow upon you gardens, and bestow upon you rivers." (Nūḥ 71:10-12)

Allāh (ﷻ) also says:

﴿وَمَن يَتَّقِ ٱللَّهَ يَجْعَل لَّهُۥ مَخْرَجًا ﴿٢﴾ وَيَرْزُقْهُ مِنْ حَيْثُ لَا يَحْتَسِبُ ﴿٣﴾﴾ [الطّلاق من الآية ٢ الى الآية ٣]

"If a person observes God consciousness (*taqwā*), then Allāh will give him a way out of every difficulty, and provide for him from where he never anticipated." (Ṭalāq 65:2-3)

Furthermore, Allāh (ﷻ) tells us about the Messenger (ﷺ):

﴿وَوَجَدَكَ عَآئِلًا فَأَغۡنَىٰ ۝٨﴾ [الضُّحَى الآية ٨]

"And did Allāh not find you poor, then enrich you?" (Ḍuḥā 93:8)

In addition, the Prophet (ﷺ) once told ʿAmr ibn al-ʿĀṣ (رضي الله عنه):

«نِعْمَ المالُ الصَّالحُ للمَرءِ الصَّالحِ».

(رواه أحمد)

"Wholesome wealth is a remarkable blessing for a wholesome individual." (Aḥmad)

The Prophet (ﷺ) also said:

«مَا نَفَعَنِي مَالٌ قَطُّ، مَا نَفَعَنِي مَالُ أَبِي بَكْرٍ».

(رواه أحمد)

"No wealth benefitted me the way Abū Bakr's wealth did." (Aḥmad)

Another *ḥadīth* mentions that some of the companions (رضي الله عنهم) said:

«ذَهَبَ أَهْلُ الدُّثُورِ بِالأُجُورِ».

(متفق عليه)

"The wealthy have made it off with all of the rewards." (Agreed Upon)

A further *ḥadīth* states:

«الْيَدُ الْعُلْيَا خَيْرٌ مِنَ الْيَدِ السُّفْلَى».

(متفق عليه)

"The giving hand is more virtuous than the receiving one." (Agreed Upon)

The longest verse in the Qur'ān has to do with the organization, recording, and preservation of wealth.

Allāh (ﷻ) says:

﴿يَـٰٓأَيُّهَا ٱلَّذِينَ ءَامَنُوٓاْ إِذَا تَدَايَنتُم بِدَيْنٍ إِلَىٰٓ أَجَلٍ مُّسَمًّى فَٱكْتُبُوهُ ۚ ﴿٢٨٢﴾﴾ [البقرة الآية ٢٨٢]

"O you who believe, when you loan money to others for a defined period, put the terms of the loan in writing..." (Baqarah 2:282)

The respected scholars have made a profound comprehensive remark about wealth and its significance.

One of the things that they have said is:

«وأعلم اللهُ -سبحانه- أنه جَعل المالَ قِوامًا للأنفس، وأمَر بحفظه، ونهى أن يؤتَى السفهاءُ من الرجال والنساء والأولاد وغيرهم، ومدَحه النبي -ﷺ- بقوله: نِعْمَ المالُ الصالحُ للمرءِ الصالحِ».

(عدة الصابرين)

"That Allāh informed us that He made wealth a foundation of people's lives, He instructed them to preserve it, and He forbade them from giving it to anyone – whether man, woman, or child – who cannot handle it competently on their own, and that the Prophet (ﷺ) has praised wealth by saying: 'Wholesome wealth is a remarkable blessing for a wholesome individual.'" ('Uddat al-Ṣābirīn)

Saʿīd ibn al-Musayyib (رحمه الله) states:

«لا خيرَ فيمن لا يريد جمع المال مِنْ حِلِّهِ، يكفُّ به وجهَه عن الناس، ويصل رحمَه، ويعطي حقَّه».

(عدة الصابرين)

"There is no goodness in a person who does not want to acquire wealth by permissible means in order to preserve his own dignity, prevent him from asking of others, uphold his ties of kinship, and give wealth the right that it deserves." ('Uddat al-Ṣābirīn)

Abū Isḥāq al-Sabī'ī (ﷺ) states:

«كانوا يرون السعة عونا على الدين».

(عدة الصابرين)

"(The foremost generation of Islām) considered an abundance of wealth a means of support for the religion." ('Uddat al-Ṣābirīn)

Muḥammad ibn al-Munkadir (ﷺ) said:

«نِعْم الغنى عونٌ على التُّقَى».

(عدة الصابرين)

"Wealth is a remarkable support for observing *taqwā*." ('Uddat al-Ṣābirīn)

Sufyān al-Thawrī (ﷺ) said:

«المال في زماننا هذا سلاح المؤمن».

(عدة الصابرين)

> “Wealth in this time of ours is a weapon for a person who has faith.” (ʿUddat al-Ṣābirīn)

Yūsuf ibn Asbāṭ (ﷺ) states:

«ما كان المال في زمان منذ خُلِقت الدنيا أنفعَ منه في هذا الزمن، والخيرُ كالخيل، لرجل سِتْر، وعلى رجل وِزْر».

(عدة الصابرين)

> “Since the beginning of this world, there was no time when wealth provided as much benefit as it does in our time. The outcome of wealth is just like how a horse can be a source of protection for one person, yet sin for another.” (ʿUddat al-Ṣābirīn)

Among the benefits of wealth which are mentioned by the scholars is that it provides support for worshipping and obeying Allāh (ﷻ), facilitates *ḥajj*, as well as striving in the path of Allāh (ﷻ).

Wealth also allows for obligatory and optional acts of giving. It allows for the establishment of endowments, as well as the building of *masājid*, Islāmic institutions, youth support centers, shelters, medical clinics, etc.

It allows for people’s true dignity and generosity to be exhibited. It preserves integrity, and fosters ties between siblings and friends. It allows the righteous to attain the highest of ranks, and be in the company of those upon whom Allāh (ﷻ) bestows His favours. It is a ladder by which one can ascend to the highest levels of Paradise, but if misused – topple to the lowest depths of Hell. It even helps maintain the respect of certain individuals who use it appropriately.

Some of the Salaf al-Ṣāliḥīn would say:

«لَا مَجْدَ إِلَّا بِفِعَالٍ، وَلَا فِعَالَ إِلَّا بِمَالٍ».

(سير أعلام النبلاء)

"Respect does not come about without actions, and (some) actions do not come about without wealth." (Siyar al-A'lām al-Nubalā')

Some of them (the Salaf al-Ṣāliḥīn) would also supplicate:

«اللَّهُمَّ إِنِّي مِنْ عِبَادِكَ الْمُؤْمِنِينَ الَّذِينَ لَا يُصْلِحُهُمْ إِلَّا الْغِنَى، فَلَا تُفْقِرْنِي بِرَحْمَتِكَ».

(تفسير القرطبي)

"O Allāh, I am one of Your worshipping servants who is left in disorder when without wealth. Do not make be impoverished through Your mercy." (Tafsīr al-Qurṭubī)

Wealth can be a means of pleasing Allāh (ﷻ), or angering Him, depending on how we utilitize it.

Abū Bakr, 'Umar, 'Uthmān, Zubayr ibn al-'Awwām and 'Abd al-Raḥmān ibn 'Awf (رضي الله عنهم) were among the most virtuous of the companions although they were wealthy. The effects that they had in contributing to Islām were greater than those of the *Ahl al-Suffah* - the poor and homeless who lived in a portion of *Masjid al-Nabawī* (ﷺ).

The Messenger of Allāh (ﷺ) warned against wasting wealth, and he stated that a person leaving his heirs well-off is better than leaving them poor.

He also informed us that any time a person with wealth spends from it sincerely for the sake of Allāh (ﷻ), then that person will attain an additional rank in standing with the Almighty. The Prophet (ﷺ) said:

«إِنَّكَ أَنْ تَدَعَ وَرَثَتَكَ أَغْنِيَاءَ خَيْرٌ مِنْ أَنْ تَدَعَهُمْ عَالَةً يَتَكَفَّفُونَ النَّاسَ فِي أَيْدِيهِمْ، وَإِنَّكَ مَهْمَا أَنْفَقْتَ مِنْ نَفَقَةٍ فَإِنَّهَا صَدَقَةٌ، حَتَّى اللُّقْمَةُ الَّتِي تَرْفَعُهَا إِلَى فِي امْرَأَتِكَ».

(رواه البخاري)

"It is better for you to leave your inheritors wealthy than to leave them poor and having to beg from others, and whatever you spend for Allāh's sake will be considered as a charitable deed - even a handful of food that you put into your wife's mouth." (Bukhārī)

«إِنَّكَ لَنْ تُنْفِقَ نَفَقَةً تَبْتَغِي بِهَا وَجْهَ اللهِ إِلَّا ازْدَدْتَ بِهَا دَرَجَةً وَرِفْعَةً حَتَّى اللُّقْمَةَ تَضَعُهَا فِي فِيِّ امْرَأَتِكَ».

(رواه البخاري)

"You will attain an additional rank in standing with Allāh for whatever you spend in His way, even if it is a morsel which you put in your wife's mouth." (Bukhārī)

Not only that:

«وقد استعاذ رسول الله من الفقر وقرنه بالكفر فقال اللهم إني أعوذ بك من الكفر والفقر فإن الخير نوعان خير الآخرة والكفر مضاده وخير الدنيا والفقر مضاده فالفقر سبب عذاب الدنيا والكفر سبب عذاب الآخرة والله سبحانه وتعالى جعل إعطاء الزكاة وظيفة الأغنياء وأخذها وظيفة الفقراء وفرق بين اليدين شرعا وقدرا وجعل يد المعطى أعلى من الآخذ وجعل الزكاة أوساخ المال ولذلك حرمها على أطيب خلقه وعلى آله صيانة لهم وتشريفا ورفعا لأقدارهم».

(عدة الصابرين)

"The Messenger of Allāh sought refuge from poverty and he mentioned it along with *kufr* (ingratitude, or ultimately rejecting the truth from Allāh). There are two types of goodness: that of the hereafter and that of this world. *Kufr* is the opposite of the goodness of the hereafter, and poverty is the opposite of the goodness of this world. Poverty is a cause of punishment in this world, and *kufr* is a cause of punishment in the hereafter. Allāh made giving *zakāh* (obligatory charity) for the wealthy, and He made receiving it for the poor. He decreed that there be a distinction between the two hands: the hand that gives is more virtuous than the hand that receives. Allāh also made

> *zakāh* wealth soiled in a way, and therefore He prohibited it being taken by the purest individual among mankind, as well as an individual's family. That was done to preserve them, safeguard their nobility, and raise their status." ('Uddat al-Ṣābirīn)

Wealth has a major role in maintaining the order of life and producing progress and development. Without it, the world would not remain in order; giving would end and development would collapse. Although wealth itself is very important, every individual is accountable for how one acquires it and how one uses it.

Wealth is not an end in and of itself. Rather, it is a means to spending, fostering commerce, investing, bringing about benefit for people, and sincerely seeking to please Allāh (ﷻ) and attain His bounty through it.

Allāh (ﷻ) says:

﴿كَيۡ لَا يَكُونَ دُولَةَۢ بَيۡنَ ٱلۡأَغۡنِيَآءِ مِنكُمۡۚ ٧﴾ [الحشر الآية ٧]

> "A division has been prescribed so that wealth is not monopolized by the rich among you such that it only flows among them while the poor are left deprived." (Ḥashr 59:7)

All wealth ultimately belongs to Allāh (ﷻ).

Allāh (ﷻ) instructs us:

﴿وَءَاتُوهُم مِّن مَّالِ ٱللَّهِ ٱلَّذِيٓ ءَاتَىٰكُمۡۚ ٣٣﴾ [النور الآية ٣٣]

> "And give them from the wealth of Allāh which He has given you." (Nūr 24:33)

The wealth in a person's hand is merely for safekeeping - it is not actually his.

Allāh (ﷻ) says:

﴿وَأَنفِقُواْ مِمَّا جَعَلَكُم مُّسۡتَخۡلَفِينَ فِيهِۖ فَٱلَّذِينَ ءَامَنُواْ مِنكُمۡ وَأَنفَقُواْ لَهُمۡ أَجۡرٞ كَبِيرٞ ٧﴾ [الحديد الآية ٧]

> "And spend (in charity to please Allāh) from the wealth over which He has made you trustees (to use according to the directives which He has prescribed). There shall be a great reward for those of you who have faith and who spend (in charity for Allāh's pleasure)." (Ḥadīd 57:7)

When a person acquires wealth by permissible means that is when Allāh (ﷻ) places blessings in it for him. Wealth is a blessing from Allāh (ﷻ) that allows life to continue, and Allāh (ﷻ) has instructed us to acquire it in ways which He has permitted, and spend it in ways He has advised. It is not something to be entirely rejected in and of itself.

The Prophet (ﷺ) has said:

«لَا بَأْسَ بِالْغِنَى لِمَنِ اتَّقَى، وَالصِّحَّةُ لِمَنِ اتَّقَى خَيْرٌ مِنَ الْغِنَى».

(سنن ابن ماجه)

> "There is nothing wrong with being rich for one who has *taqwā* (piety), but good health for one who has *taqwā* (piety) is better than riches." (Sunan Ibn Mājah)

It can be a means to much goodness.

The Prophet (ﷺ) said:

«إِنَّمَا الدُّنْيَا لِأَرْبَعَةِ نَفَرٍ، عَبْدٍ رَزَقَهُ اللَّهُ مَالًا وَعِلْمًا فَهُوَ يَتَّقِي فِيهِ رَبَّهُ، وَيَصِلُ فِيهِ رَحِمَهُ، وَيَعْلَمُ لِلَّهِ فِيهِ حَقًّا، فَهَذَا بِأَفْضَلِ الْمَنَازِلِ، وَعَبْدٍ رَزَقَهُ اللَّهُ عِلْمًا وَلَمْ يَرْزُقْهُ مَالًا فَهُوَ صَادِقُ النِّيَّةِ يَقُولُ: لَوْ أَنَّ لِي مَالًا لَعَمِلْتُ بِعَمَلِ فُلَانٍ فَهُوَ بِنِيَّتِهِ فَأَجْرُهُمَا سَوَاءٌ، وَعَبْدٍ رَزَقَهُ اللَّهُ مَالًا وَلَمْ يَرْزُقْهُ عِلْمًا، فَهُوَ يَخْبِطُ فِي مَالِهِ بِغَيْرِ عِلْمٍ لَا يَتَّقِي فِيهِ رَبَّهُ، وَلَا يَصِلُ فِيهِ رَحِمَهُ، وَلَا يَعْلَمُ لِلَّهِ فِيهِ حَقًّا، فَهَذَا بِأَخْبَثِ الْمَنَازِلِ، وَعَبْدٍ لَمْ يَرْزُقْهُ اللَّهُ مَالًا وَلَا عِلْمًا فَهُوَ يَقُولُ: لَوْ أَنَّ لِي مَالًا لَعَمِلْتُ فِيهِ بِعَمَلِ فُلَانٍ فَهُوَ بِنِيَّتِهِ فَوِزْرُهُمَا سَوَاءٌ».

(رواه الترمذي)

> "The world is used by four kinds of people. (1) One upon whom Allāh has bestowed wealth and knowledge, so he fears his Lord in respect to them, joins the ties of blood relationship, and acknowledges the rights of Allāh upon him (and fulfills them); this group of people will have the best position (in Paradise). (2) Those upon whom Allāh has conferred knowledge, but no wealth, and he is sincere in his intention and says: 'Had I possessed wealth, I would have acted like so-and-so.' If that is his intention, then his reward will be the same as that of the other (the first group). (3) The third group are those whom Allāh has given wealth, but no knowledge and he wastes his wealth ignorantly, does not fear Allāh in respect to it, does not discharge the obligations of kinship, and does not acknowledge the rights of Allāh. Such a person will be in the worst position (in the hereafter). (4) The last group are those upon whom Allāh has bestowed neither wealth, nor knowledge and he says: 'Had I possessed wealth, I would have acted like so-and-so (implying that he would have wasted his wealth).' If this is his intention, then both will have an equal sin." (Tirmidhī)

Effort in this world is not confined to focusing on the hereafter while neglecting one's livelihood. In fact, livelihood itself can lead to a better hereafter and assist one in attaining the best of it. This world is where the seeds for the hereafter are sown.

Sulaymān al-Dārānī (ﷺ) said:

«لَيْسَ الْعِبَادَةُ عِنْدَنَا أَنْ تَصُفَّ قَدَمَيْكَ وَغَيْرُكَ يَقُتُّ لَكَ، وَلَكِنِ ابْدَأْ بِرَغِيفَيْكَ فَأَحْرِزْهُمَا ثُمَّ تَعَبَّدْ».

(حلية الأولياء لأبي نعيم)

> "To us, worship does not mean only lining up your feet while someone else provides for you. Rather, secure your two pieces of bread first and then devote yourself to worship." (Ḥilyat al-Awliyā' of Abū Nuʿaym)

The love humans have for wealth is part of their innate nature.

Allāh (ﷻ) says:

﴿وَتُحِبُّونَ ٱلْمَالَ حُبًّا جَمًّا ۝٢٠﴾ [الفجر الآية ٢٠]

"And your love to hoard wealth is truly intense." (Fajr 89:20)

﴿وَإِنَّهُۥ لِحُبِّ ٱلْخَيْرِ لَشَدِيدٌ ۝٨﴾ [العاديات الآية ٨]

"And indeed, his love for wealth is truly intense." (ʿĀdiyāt 100:8)

The desire to acquire and own things is among the strongest inclinations within a human being, and it urges him to have wealth, store it, increase it, and protect it.

Allāh (ﷻ) says:

﴿زُيِّنَ لِلنَّاسِ حُبُّ ٱلشَّهَوَٰتِ مِنَ ٱلنِّسَآءِ وَٱلْبَنِينَ وَٱلْقَنَٰطِيرِ ٱلْمُقَنطَرَةِ مِنَ ٱلذَّهَبِ وَٱلْفِضَّةِ وَٱلْخَيْلِ ٱلْمُسَوَّمَةِ وَٱلْأَنْعَٰمِ وَٱلْحَرْثِ ۗ ذَٰلِكَ مَتَٰعُ ٱلْحَيَوٰةِ ٱلدُّنْيَا ۖ وَٱللَّهُ عِندَهُۥ حُسْنُ ٱلْمَـَٔابِ ۝١٤﴾ [آل عمران الآية ١٤]

"Love for certain pleasures of life has been made attractive to people. Those include women, children, amassed wealth of gold and silver, fine horses, livestock, and farmland. Those are the temporary pleasures of this worldly life (which are not merely there for personal gratification. Rather, they are to be utilized in the ways that Allāh has prescribed so as to obey Him), and the best, final outcome lies with Allāh (meaning Paradise)." (Āle ʿImrān 3:14)

We must recognize that one way in which our wealth is protected is by using it to fulfill Allāh's (ﷻ) rights concerning it. That includes obligatory and optional charity, other acts of generosity, upholding the ties of kinship, caring for the needy, and being moderate in spending by doing so without extravagance or stinginess.

Allāh (ﷻ) says:

﴿وَٱلَّذِينَ إِذَآ أَنفَقُواْ لَمۡ يُسۡرِفُواْ وَلَمۡ يَقۡتُرُواْ وَكَانَ بَيۡنَ ذَٰلِكَ قَوَامٗا ٦٧﴾ [الفرقان الآية ٦٧]

"And they are neither extravagant nor miserly when they spend. Rather, they are moderate between those." (Furqān 25:67)

﴿وَءَاتِ ذَا ٱلۡقُرۡبَىٰ حَقَّهُۥ وَٱلۡمِسۡكِينَ وَٱبۡنَ ٱلسَّبِيلِ وَلَا تُبَذِّرۡ تَبۡذِيرًا ٢٦ إِنَّ ٱلۡمُبَذِّرِينَ كَانُوٓاْ إِخۡوَٰنَ ٱلشَّيَٰطِينِۖ وَكَانَ ٱلشَّيۡطَٰنُ لِرَبِّهِۦ كَفُورٗا ٢٧﴾ [الإسراء من الآية ٢٦ الى الآية ٢٧]

"And give the relative his right (maintain good relations with relatives), as well (give the rights to) the poor and the traveler (assist them in their need). And do not be extravagant (do not be wasteful). Without doubt, the extravagant ones (those who waste) are the brothers of the Shayāṭīn (because they behave just like the Shayāṭīn). And Shayṭān (Iblīs) was ever ungrateful to his Lord. (Whereas Allāh gave Iblīs the bounty of intelligence, he was ungrateful by using it to disobey Allāh's command. Muslims should avoid behaving in this manner. They should therefore, use the bounty of wealth in ways that will please Allāh and in ways that go against His commands.)" (Isrā' 17:26-27)

Something else that protects wealth is avoiding consuming the impermissible. This is done by staying away from things such as theft, unlawfully taking other people's property, bribery, deception in transactions, monopolizing goods to raise their prices, gambling, deliberately ruining people's property, and all forms of prohibited wealth.

It has been mentioned that:

«كُلُّ الْمُسْلِمِ عَلَى الْمُسْلِمِ حَرَامٌ مَالُهُ، وَعِرْضُهُ، وَدَمُهُ حَسْبُ امْرِئٍ مِنَ الشَّرِّ أَنْ يَحْقِرَ أَخَاهُ الْمُسْلِمَ».

(رواه مسلم)

"Everything of a Muslim is sacred to a Muslim: his property, his integrity, and his blood. It is enough evil for a man to despise his brother Muslim." (Muslim)

Wealth is a companion of life and dignity. We are also instructed to safeguard the wealth of orphans and those under our guardianship. If a person consumes that wealth, then he is consuming the hellfire into his belly.

Allāh (ﷻ) says:

﴿إِنَّ ٱلَّذِينَ يَأْكُلُونَ أَمْوَٰلَ ٱلْيَتَٰمَىٰ ظُلْمًا إِنَّمَا يَأْكُلُونَ فِى بُطُونِهِمْ نَارًا ۖ ﴿١٠﴾﴾

[النِّسَاء الآية ١٠]

"Indeed, those who unjustly eat (use) the wealth of the orphans, they eat only fire in their bellies (because the end result of this will be their entry into the hellfire)." (Nisā' 4:10)

CONCLUSION

- Allāh (ﷻ) made wealth a means of preserving the body.
- Preserving the body leads to preserving the soul.
- The soul is a place for the knowledge of Allāh (ﷻ), and correct beliefs about Him, accepting Allāh's (ﷻ) Messengers, loving Him, and repenting to the Almighty.
- Wealth is a means of developing this world and the hereafter.
- Wealth will become a detrimental thing when it is acquired in ways prohibited by Allāh (ﷻ), or when it is spent in impermissible ways, when it enslaves a person, when it takes control of his heart, or when it diverts one away from Allāh (ﷻ) and the hereafter.
- It is blameworthy when a person who has it uses it for corrupt objectives and allows it to take one away from praiseworthy objectives.

- The real source of blame is a person using the wealth in an appropriate manner, not the wealth in and of itself – and this is why wealth can be a source of trial and transgression.
- The Qur'ān explains this to us very clearly.

Allāh (ﷻ) says:

﴿كَلَّآ إِنَّ ٱلْإِنسَٰنَ لَيَطْغَىٰٓ ۝٦ أَن رَّءَاهُ ٱسْتَغْنَىٰٓ ۝٧﴾ [العَلَق من الآية ٦ الى الآية ٧]

"It is absolutely true that the defiantly disobedient human violates the limits set by Allāh. This is because he thinks that he has no need for Allāh." (ʿAlaq 96:6-7)

Furthermore, Allāh (ﷻ) tells us:

﴿إِنَّمَآ أَمْوَٰلُكُمْ وَأَوْلَٰدُكُمْ فِتْنَةٌ ۚ وَٱللَّهُ عِندَهُۥٓ أَجْرٌ عَظِيمٌ ۝١٥ فَٱتَّقُوا۟ ٱللَّهَ مَا ٱسْتَطَعْتُمْ وَٱسْمَعُوا۟ وَأَطِيعُوا۟ وَأَنفِقُوا۟ خَيْرًا لِّأَنفُسِكُمْ ۗ وَمَن يُوقَ شُحَّ نَفْسِهِۦ فَأُو۟لَٰٓئِكَ هُمُ ٱلْمُفْلِحُونَ ۝١٦ إِن تُقْرِضُوا۟ ٱللَّهَ قَرْضًا حَسَنًا يُضَٰعِفْهُ لَكُمْ وَيَغْفِرْ لَكُمْ ۚ وَٱللَّهُ شَكُورٌ حَلِيمٌ ۝١٧ عَٰلِمُ ٱلْغَيْبِ وَٱلشَّهَٰدَةِ ٱلْعَزِيزُ ٱلْحَكِيمُ ۝١٨﴾ [التَّغَابُن من الآية ١٥ الى الآية ١٨]

"Your properties and your offspring are nothing less than a trial for you in this world, whereas Allāh has a tremendous reward (in store for those who give obeying Him precedence over being preoccupied with obeying others besides Him). Therefore, (you must do everything that is within your ability to) observe God consciousness (*taqwā*) of Allāh. In addition, you must listen (to the Messenger), obey (his commands, avoid his prohibitions), and give from what Allāh has provided you with. Doing those things is best for you, and when people are saved from the greed of their own souls, they are the ones who will be truly successful. If you (generously and willingly) loan your wealth to Allāh (by sincerely giving in His path), He will multiply its reward for you, and He will forgive (your sins). And

Allāh is Most Appreciative (rewards His servants magnificently for their righteous deeds) and He is Most Forbearing. He has complete knowledge (of everything that humans cannot see), as well as everything that they can see. He is the Almighty, the Most Wise." (Taghābun 64:15-18)

أَيَا سَامِعاً لَيْسَ السَّمَاعُ بِنَافِعٍ ۞ إِذَا أَنْتَ لَمْ تَفْعَلْ فَمَا أَنْتَ سَامِعُ
إِذَا كُنْتَ فِي الدُّنْيَا مِنَ الْخَيْرِ عَاجِزاً ۞ فَمَا أَنْتَ فِي يَوْمِ الْقِيَامَةِ صَانِعُ

(تفسير روح البيان)

O listener mere listening is not beneficial,
If you don't do what you hear?
When you are helpless in this world from doing good,
Consequently what are you going to do the Day of Resurrection?

KHUṬBAH 73

Divorce: The Most Hated of Permissible Things

It is a well-established fact that marriage in Islām is a strong tie that binds a man and a woman together. It is a bond that brings about peace and happiness to the soul.

Allāh (ﷻ) says in the Qur'ān:

﴿وَمِنْ ءَايَـٰتِهِۦٓ أَنْ خَلَقَ لَكُم مِّنْ أَنفُسِكُمْ أَزْوَٰجًا لِّتَسْكُنُوٓا۟ إِلَيْهَا ﴿٢١﴾﴾ [الرّوم الآية ٢١]

> "And among His signs is that He created for you spouses from your own kind so that you (your souls) may find solace (tranquility, peace and rest) with them." (Rūm 30:21)

In addition, one of the supplications mentioned in the Qur'ān is:

﴿رَبَّنَا هَبْ لَنَا مِنْ أَزْوَٰجِنَا وَذُرِّيَّـٰتِنَا قُرَّةَ أَعْيُنٍ وَٱجْعَلْنَا لِلْمُتَّقِينَ إِمَامًا ﴿٧٤﴾﴾ [الفُرْقان الآية ٧٤]

> "O our Lord! Grant us the coolness (comfort) of our eyes (grant us pleasure and satisfaction) from our spouses and children (so that they never become a source of regret or distress for us in either world when they follow Islām properly), and make us guides (*imāms*) of the pious (make our progeny pious and make us pious enough to guide other people)." (Furqān 25:74)

Out of Allāh's (ﷻ) infinite wisdom, He prescribed directives that give great importance to preserving the togetherness of families, encourage upholding the bond of marriage, and encourage husbands to live with their wives in an acceptable manner, even if the husbands may dislike something about their wives for some mundane reason.

Allāh (ﷻ) says:

﴿وَعَاشِرُوهُنَّ بِٱلْمَعْرُوفِۚ فَإِن كَرِهْتُمُوهُنَّ فَعَسَىٰٓ أَن تَكْرَهُوا۟ شَيْـًٔا وَيَجْعَلَ ٱللَّهُ فِيهِ خَيْرًا كَثِيرًا ١٩﴾ [النِّسَاء الآية ١٩]

"And live with them in kindness (treat them well). If you dislike (anything in) them, then (be tolerant because) it may well be that you dislike something, when in fact, Allāh brings about much goodness by it." (Nisā' 4:19)

The Prophet (ﷺ) states:

«لَا يَفْرَكْ مُؤْمِنٌ مُؤْمِنَةً، إِنْ كَرِهَ مِنْهَا خُلُقًا رَضِيَ مِنْهَا آخَرَ، أَوْ قَالَ: غَيْرَهُ».

(رواه مسلم)

"A believing man should not hate a believing woman; even if he dislikes one of her characteristics, he will be pleased with another." (Muslim)

Allāh (ﷻ) also describes the bond of marriage as a strong pledge.

Allāh (ﷻ) says in the Qur'ān:

﴿وَأَخَذْنَ مِنكُم مِّيثَٰقًا غَلِيظًا ٢١﴾ [النِّسَاء الآية ٢١]

"And they (your wives) have taken a strong pledge from you (when you married them, you accepted Allāh's command to treat them well and to care for them)." (Nisā' 4:21)

The fact that marriage was characterized this way dictates that it is a bond of continuity, tranquility, and stability. Therefore, it is necessary for both spouses to avert everything that may pose to be a threat to those objectives. They must overlook whatever marital differences may arise that could possibly ruin the strong bond that should exist between them.

The default when requesting separation, or for marriage to be dissolved, is prohibition. Such a request must only be resorted to when remaining in the marriage becomes impossible after exhausting all of the methods for conflict resolution as prescribed by Islām.

The Prophet (ﷺ) states:

«أَبْغَضُ الْحَلَالِ إِلَى اللهِ تَعَالَى الطَّلَاقُ».

(سنن أبي داود)

"The most hateful of lawful matters to Allāh is divorce." (Sunan Abū Dāwūd)

Imām al-Sarakhsī (رحمه الله), a great *Ḥanafī* jurist writes:

«أنَّ الزَّواجَ نِعمةٌ، والأصلُ حِفظُها، وفي الطَّلاقِ بدونِ حاجةٍ كُفرانٌ للنِّعمةِ».

(المبسوط للسرخسي)

"Marriage is a blessing and the fundamental rule regarding it is preservation. Whereas to divorce without (an absolute) need is ingratitude for this blessing." (Al-Mabsūṭ of Sarakhsī)

«صنَّف كتاب المبسوط في الفقه في أربعة عشر مجلدا، أملاه من خاطره من غير مطالعة كتاب، ولا مراجعة تعليق؛ بل كان محبوسا في جب بسبب كلمةٍ نَصَحَ بها. وكان يملي عليهم من الجب وهم على أعلى الجب يكتبون ما يملي عليهم».

(تاج التراجم في طبقات الحنفية)

<u>NOTE</u>: It is worthwhile to mention that Imām al-Sarakhsī (رحمه الله) would dictate orally to his students from memory from the bottom of the well in which he was incarcerated. This is how his remarkable work titled *'Al-Mabsūṭ'* was produced. The astonishing thing is not just that it is a remarkable work in 30 volumes, rather the truly incredible thing is the fact that he wrote it while in prison in a well without paper or pen! He

would teach his students from the bottom of the well and they wrote it down for him outside of the prison. (Tāj al-Tarājim fī Ṭabaqāt al-Ḥanafīyya)

Other scholars write that:

«فَإِنَّ الْأَصْلَ فِي الطَّلَاقِ الْحَظْرُ، وَإِنَّمَا أُبِيحَ مِنْهُ قَدْرُ الْحَاجَةِ».

(مجموع فتاوى)

> "The default ruling which applies to divorce is prohibition. It is only permitted in circumstances which require it." (Majmūʿ Fatāwā)

There is an authentic *ḥadīth* narrated on the authority of Jābir (ﷺ) that the Prophet (ﷺ) said:

«إِنَّ إِبْلِيسَ يَضَعُ عَرْشَهُ عَلَى الْمَاءِ، ثُمَّ يَبْعَثُ سَرَايَاهُ، فَأَدْنَاهُمْ مِنْهُ مَنْزِلَةً أَعْظَمُهُمْ فِتْنَةً، يَجِيءُ أَحَدُهُمْ، فَيَقُولُ: فَعَلْتُ كَذَا وَكَذَا، فَيَقُولُ: مَا صَنَعْتَ شَيْئًا، قَالَ: وَيَجِيءُ أَحَدُهُمْ، فَيَقُولُ: مَا تَرَكْتُهُ حَتَّى فَرَّقْتُ بَيْنَهُ وَبَيْنَ أَهْلِهِ، قَالَ: فَيُدْنِيهِ مِنْهُ - أَوْ قَالَ: فَيَلْتَزِمُهُ - وَيَقُولُ: نِعْمَ أَنْتَ أَنْتَ!».

(رواه مسلم)

> "Iblīs sets his throne over water and then sends forth his troops. The ones among them who hold the highest status with him are the ones who cause the worst strife. One of them comes and says: 'I did such-and-such,' but Iblīs tells him: 'You did not accomplish anything.' Then another one comes and says: 'I did not leave the person I was assigned to until I managed to separate him from his wife,' and Iblīs calls him closer, embraces him and says to him: 'You have truly achieved something.'" (Muslim)

Al-Aʿmash (ﷺ), one of the narrators of *ḥadīth*, reports that he recalls the fact that Iblīs embraces the devil (Shayṭān) who splits up a couple.

«قَالَ الْأَعْمَشُ: أُرَاهُ قَالَ: فَيَلْتَزِمُهُ».

(رواه مسلم)

Al-Aʿmash said: "He then embraces him." (Muslim)

Furthermore, in the context of denouncing sorcery and black magic, Allāh (ﷻ) says:

﴿فَيَتَعَلَّمُونَ مِنْهُمَا مَا يُفَرِّقُونَ بِهِۦ بَيْنَ ٱلْمَرْءِ وَزَوْجِهِۦۚ ۝١٠٢﴾ [البَقَرَة الآية ١٠٢]

> "So, they learned from the two of them (*Hārūt* and *Mārūt*) such things whereby they could separate a man from his wife." (Baqarah 2:102)

Magic was extremely popular in Babylon. Impressed by the feats of the magicians, people considered them to be blessed and venerable men.

To expose the harm and evil of magic, Allāh (ﷻ) sent two angels named *Hārūt* and *Mārūt* to Babylon. They were to show people the clear distinction between magic and miracles. They were also a test for the people, in order to distinguish those who would want to pursue evil from those who abstained therefrom.

Whenever people would come to them to learn magic, they would first tell them:

﴿نَحْنُ فِتْنَةٌ فَلَا تَكْفُرْ ۝١٠٢﴾ [البَقَرَة الآية ١٠٢]

> "We are merely a test, so do not disbelieve." (Meaning do not forsake your religion by learning this evil science). (Baqarah 2:102)

They advised people to learn magic with good intentions, otherwise they should not even bother with it. They taught it only to those who pledged not to utilize the knowledge for evil aims. Of course, many did not conform to the conditions of their pledge.

One of the many ill effects of black magic is that it can be used to split up a loving couple. Only this effect is mentioned because it is one of the most detestable actions in the sight of Allāh (ﷻ).

Another *ḥadīth* mentions:

«الْمُنْتَزِعَاتُ، وَالْمُخْتَلِعَاتُ هُنَّ الْمُنَافِقَاتُ».

(سنن النسائي)

"Women who ask for divorce and seek separation without any valid reason are committing *nifāq* (meaning that they disobey Allāh inwardly, although they may outwardly display obedience to Him)." (Sunan al-Nasā'ī)

Shaykh Ibn Taymīyyah (ﷺ) and many other jurists have outlined that:

«وَلِهَذَا لَمْ يُبَحْ إِلَّا ثَلَاثَ مَرَّاتٍ، وَحُرِّمَتْ عَلَيْهِ الْمَرْأَةُ بَعْدَ الثَّالِثَةِ حَتَّى تَنْكِحَ زَوْجًا غَيْرَهُ، وَإِذَا كَانَ إِنَّمَا أُبِيحَ لِلْحَاجَةِ، فَالْحَاجَةُ تَنْدَفِعُ بِوَاحِدَةٍ، فَمَا زَادَ فَهُوَ بَاقٍ عَلَى الْحَظْرِ».

(مجموع فتاوى)

"Divorcing a wife is only permitted up to a maximum of three times. After the third time, it is not permissible for a husband to remarry the divorced wife unless she subsequently marries a different husband. Furthermore, since divorce is only permitted in a situation of necessity, a single divorce under these conditions suffices, and the default ruling of prohibition will apply to anything more than that." (Majmūʿ Fatāwā)

The foregoing is further emphasized by texts of the *sunnah* that warn against contravening Islām's directives in ways that may lead to divorce.

Abū Hurairah (ﷺ) narrates that the Prophet (ﷺ) said:

«لَيْسَ مِنَّا مَنْ خَبَّبَ امْرَأَةً عَلَى زَوْجِهَا أَوْ عَبْدًا عَلَى سَيِّدِهِ».

(رواه أبو داود)

"Anyone who incites a woman against her husband, or a slave against his master is not from among us." (Abū Dāwūd)

Thawbān (ﷺ) narrates that the Prophet (ﷺ) said:

«أَيُّمَا امْرَأَةٍ سَأَلَتْ زَوْجَهَا طَلاَقًا فِي غَيْرِ مَا بَأْسٍ فَحَرَامٌ عَلَيْهَا رَائِحَةُ الْجَنَّةِ».

(رواه أبو داود)

> "Any woman who requests a divorce from her husband without a strong reason (for a reason other than experiencing serious legitimate harm) will be barred from even smelling the fragrance of Paradise." (Abū Dāwūd)

With that being said, we must realize that divorce today within the Muslim communities has gone way beyond its proper understanding, and purpose according to Islām.

Divorce in Islām is prescribed as a solution for exceedingly difficult problems that arise between spouses, and as a last resort for treating them. However, we find that some people's usage of divorce has now become a problem in and of itself. It has become like a toy in the hands of those who manipulate others aimlessly, and a word easily uttered by the reckless who do not see any point to married life, and who do not give it any significance. Such individuals are people who get married one day and divorce the next, completely belittling the gravity of this bond that comes with duties and responsibilities as prescribed by Allāh (ﷻ).

It is very unfortunate to see that the rate of divorce has greatly increased, and has become a common phenomenon. Divorce cases have become widespread, and the frequency of cases in which couples seek separation has unmistakably grown. The percentages of those seeking divorce or annulment of marriages has reached alarming proportions, and this indicates significant dangers for Muslim communities.

Upon examination, we find that there is a vast array of domestic problems that may upset life between spouses, and ultimately lead to divorce. Some of the reasons include the following:

1) Spouses are not making the appropriate choices when getting married. One of them might embark upon marriage without

knowing anything about their partner's conduct or religious practice, and then be unpleasantly surprised after living with them.

2) Falling short in adhering to the teachings of Islām; being negligent in fulfilling Allāh's (ﷻ)rights, especially the obligatory prayers; not using the recitation of the Qur'ān and the prescribed words of *dhikr* to protect oneself; committing sins and finding that acceptable. All of this can lead to ills and disputes between spouses, and in the end can result to a divorce.
3) It is also no secret that there are accounts of men who consume intoxicants such as alcohol, or they are addicted to drugs, and then they physically harm their wives, verbally abuse them, kick them out of the home, or declare them to be divorced.
4) Another marital problem that can arise is failing to fulfill certain responsibilities that are obligatory upon a husband and a wife.

For instance, a husband may fail to take care of the running of the home, or providing the necessary things; and instead, occupy himself with social gatherings, spending nights out with friends, staying out of the home without need, and then end up neglecting the rights of those who are under his care, such as his wife and children.

Likewise, a wife might not take care of her home, and instead, occupy herself with her phone and social media for most of the time, and then end up neglecting the rights of her husband and family.

5) We should also point out here that some people overdo using social media, become addicted to it, or repeatedly visit harmful websites on the internet. These then lead to major ills that will affect an individual's beliefs, morals, and conduct. This can include instances where a man may be attracted to a woman other than his wife, let his heart become attached to her, and then engage in an illicit relationship with her. Consequently, the man may end up scorning his wife, avoiding her, and then eventually divorcing her.

6) Likewise, there are instances where spouses end up betraying each other by engaging in private conversations and relationships over social media, etc. with unrelated men/women; and as a result, end up entering into secret illicit, extra marital relationships. It only gets worse when those matters become exposed. We seek refuge with Allāh (ﷻ) from such things.
7) Another problem which exists is the lack of stability in life between spouses, or the absence of a proper understanding of what married life is supposed to be.

In such scenarios, the spouses fail to fulfill each other's rights, and they lose harmony between themselves. As a result of this, their life becomes permeated by an atmosphere of enmity, argumentation, and conflict. Further compounding of the situation is when either of the spouses start to treat matters of divorce lightly. The husband may start to threaten his wife with divorce, wielding that as a weapon against her; and the wife may repeatedly start asking for divorce, or perhaps even provoke her husband until he eventually divorces her.

Other similar contraventions of Islām's teachings may occur as well.

8) A further problem which can lead to divorce is for unbefitting and unwise things to be done as it relates to marital life.

This includes one spouse thinking ill about the other, overdoing having doubts about them, and going to excesses in matters of suspicions. It also includes one spouse insulting the other about their age, or something about their body. It includes a husband preventing his wife from keeping ties with her parents or visiting them when he has no justifiable reason in Islām to do so. It can further include a husband being miserly by not providing the financial support that he is obligated to give his wife such as shelter, food, drink, clothing, and medicine, etc.

In addition, there are wives who exhaust their husbands with requests that are beyond their husband's ability to provide, and there are also wives who look down upon their husbands because the wives may be better educated, have better jobs, or be from families of higher social status.

9) Another problem may be psychological and behavioural issues from which some spouses suffer, and this can lead to constant conflicts.

This may lead a husband to dislike his wife and avoid her, and he may be unwilling to seek treatment which could enable him to remain in a relationship of love, affection, and harmony with his wife.

A related issue is that some people's nature may be one of anger, and short-sightedness; and they may not be able to handle things well when it comes to situations that require wisdom. There are many times when disputes arise between spouses over minor things, like a husband requesting something from his wife, but she forgets or delays; or like a wife asking her husband to purchase something and he ends up occupied with something else or prolongs getting it. These and other similar matters are things which a person should not allow to incite them or make them lose their composure such that one then acts irrationally and aggravates disputes, which lead to blameworthy consequences.

10) A further problem is a man not considering a woman's nature – whether physically, psychologically, or intellectually – or the various changing circumstances which often women may experience.

For instance, after giving birth, a woman's appearance and body may somewhat change. However, there are husbands who mock their wives due to that, and even crush their emotions to a point that the wives would prefer to be divorced rather than remain with husbands who treat them in such an ill manner.

11) Another problem is when the family of either the husband or the wife interferes in the private matters between the spouses, or perhaps even instigates one of them against the other, which

ends up aggravating existing differences which they may already have, but then this ends up resulting in divorce.

12) Another problem is that some wives aspire to have a very high standard of living and remain discontent with whatever they have.

They look at those who have more than them, and perhaps even become influenced by irresponsible women who flaunt and brag about what they own. This may cause some wives to no longer consider the privacy of their homes and marital lives. They may spread images of their furnishings, attire, and food, etc. by way of Facebook, WhatsApp or other platforms, and as a result, initiate problems with their husbands. In some cases, this can ruin homes and contribute to family problems that may even end up in divorce.

These are some of the domestic problems that may lead to divorce. The point of mentioning them is to learn from the errors prevailing within our communities, take the necessary lessons, and avoid falling into the same mistakes.

CONCLUSION

It is normal for differences to occur between spouses in domestic matters and in day-to-day life. This is a reality that is consistent with the nature of life in this world which is not continually pleasant.

Even within the pure household of the Prophet (ﷺ), there were certain issues that caused strain, and there were instances of jealously that occurred between some of the women.

Spouses must not imagine that having a happy life together means a life which will always remain problem-free. Even the most virtuous generations of Islām did not have such things. Rather, it means being able to solve problems, limit the occurrence of conflicts, and not allow obstacles to affect relationships.

What is required from us is to recognize that a problem exists. The greatest threat to marital life is to treat the matter of divorce lightly, and not give any attention to the very negative consequences that it has. Divorces have led to the collapse of many homes, splitting of several families, severing the ties of kinship, and incurring sins. Divorce has a very negative effect on women especially, and after it many women feel sad, depressed and discouraged.

It is necessary for us to know the reasons behind the existence of this problem, and treat it properly. Our communities – at the organizational and individual levels – need to contribute to that treatment in their respective capacities. Individuals who are in 'leadership roles' must attempt to raise people's awareness about the extent to which this dangerous matter is belittled, and then work towards effective treatments for it.

One of the practical solutions for the phenomenon of the rising divorce rates is to offer educational and training seminars for those who will be embarking upon marriage. Preemptive prevention is better than subsequent treatment. Addressing problems before they arise by way of educating potential spouses properly, can reduce the occurrence of divorce.

When valuable information, sincere advice, proper counseling, and pertinent education are offered, they can bring about major benefits for people in their lives after they get married. This will contribute to forming families that are built upon solid foundations, and can hopefully guarantee successful marriages by Allāh's (ﷻ) permission.

Another treatment is striving to reconcile between spouses when differences occur. Doing this is in fact, a major means of acquiring immense reward from Allāh (ﷻ).

Allāh (ﷻ) says in the Qur'ān:

﴿لَّا خَيْرَ فِي كَثِيرٍ مِّن نَّجْوَىٰهُمْ إِلَّا مَنْ أَمَرَ بِصَدَقَةٍ أَوْ مَعْرُوفٍ أَوْ إِصْلَٰحٍ بَيْنَ ٱلنَّاسِ ۚ وَمَن يَفْعَلْ ذَٰلِكَ ٱبْتِغَآءَ مَرْضَاتِ ٱللَّهِ فَسَوْفَ نُؤْتِيهِ أَجْرًا عَظِيمًا ﴿١١٤﴾﴾ [النساء الآية ١١٤]

"There is no good in much of what individuals discuss privately unless it involves giving charity, commanding what is right, or reconciling between people. And if someone does those hoping to please Allāh, We will grant him a magnificent reward." (Nisā' 4:114)

The Prophet (ﷺ) once asked the companions (رضي الله عنهم):

«أَلَا أُخْبِرُكُمْ بِأَفْضَلَ مِنْ دَرَجَةِ الصِّيَامِ وَالصَّلَاةِ وَالصَّدَقَةِ، قَالُوا: بَلَى، قَالَ: صَلَاحُ ذَاتِ الْبَيْنِ، فَإِنَّ فَسَادَ ذَاتِ الْبَيْنِ هِيَ الْحَالِقَةُ، لَا أَقُولُ تَحْلِقُ الشَّعَرَ، وَلَكِنْ تَحْلِقُ الدِّينَ».

(رواه أحمد)

"Should I not inform you about something which is even more virtuous than the rank of fasting, prayer, and charity?" They replied: "Of course." He said: "Reconciling between people. As for making problems between people, that shaves things away. It does not shave away hairs - rather, it shaves away a person's religious practice." (Aḥmad)

May Allāh (ﷻ) guide us to the straight path and enable us to follow the examples set by the Prophet (ﷺ).

KHUṬBAH 74

Visiting Others: Manners and Etiquettes

Humans are social beings by their very nature, and Islām is a religion of togetherness and harmony. A person who mixes with the people while bearing their harms attains a reward greater than a person who does not mix with people or bear their harms.

The Prophet (ﷺ) said:

«الْمُؤْمِنُ الَّذِي يُخَالِطُ النَّاسَ، وَيَصْبِرُ عَلَى أَذَاهُمْ، أَعْظَمُ أَجْرًا مِنَ الْمُؤْمِنِ الَّذِي لَا يُخَالِطُ النَّاسَ، وَلَا يَصْبِرُ عَلَى أَذَاهُمْ».

(سنن ابن ماجه)

> "A believer who mixes with the people and endures their harm has a greater reward than one who does not mix the people nor endures their harm." (Sunan Ibn Mājah)

Love for the sake of Allāh (ﷻ) is one of the strongest bonds of faith and is one of the most important foundations on which Muslim society is based.

It is a basis by means of which the ties of friendship and harmony among the people are attained, so that they love one another, visit one another, are sincere towards one another, intermarry, enjoin what is right and forbid what is wrong, and consequently can attain true Islāmic bonds. Through their interactions, companionship, and friendship, people may also obtain the love of Allāh (ﷻ).

The Prophet (ﷺ) states:

«يَأْثِرُ عَنِ اللَّهِ عَزَّ وَجَلَّ: حَقَّتْ مَحَبَّتِي لِلْمُتَحَابِّينَ فِيَّ، وَحَقَّتْ مَحَبَّتِي لِلْمُتَوَاصِلِينَ فِيَّ، وَحَقَّتْ مَحَبَّتِي لِلْمُتَزَاوِرِينَ فِيَّ، وَحَقَّتْ مَحَبَّتِي لِلْمُتَبَاذِلِينَ فِيَّ».

(رواه احمد)

"Allāh says: 'My love is due for those who love one another for My sake; and My love is due for those who visit one another for My sake; and My love is due for those who help one another for My sake; and My love is due for those whose hearts are free of grudges, and who uphold ties with one another for My sake.'" (Aḥmad)

Four things that foster love are:

1) Visiting one another
2) Extending the *Salām*
3) Shaking hands (with people of the same gender)
4) Giving gifts to each other

Imām al-Nawawī (ﷺ) writes:

«يُسْتَحَبُّ اسْتِحْبَابًا مُتَأَكِّدًا زِيَارَةُ الصَّالِحِينَ وَالْإِخْوَانِ وَالْجِيرَانِ وَالْأَصْدِقَاءِ وَالْأَقَارِبِ وَإِكْرَامُهُمْ وَبِرُّهُمْ وَصِلَتُهُمْ، وَضَبْطُ ذَلِكَ يَخْتَلِفُ بِاخْتِلَافِ أَحْوَالِهِمْ وَمَرَاتِبِهِمْ وَفَرَاغِهِمْ، وَيَنْبَغِي أَنْ تَكُونَ زِيَارَتُهُ عَلَى وَجْهٍ يَرْتَضُونَهُ وَفِي وَقْتٍ لَا يَكْرَهُونَهُ».

(كتاب الأذكار للنووي)

"It is a source of much reward to visit righteous individuals, brothers, neighbours, acquaintances, and relatives; and to treat them kindly and maintain ties with them. He also commented that how those take place among the people is different based on the variations in their circumstances, responsibilities, and availability. Visiting others should take place in a manner which they do not dislike, and at a time that is suitable for them." (Kitāb al-Adhkār of al-Nawawī)

With that being said, we will now draw our attention to some of the things which scholars have mentioned regarding the manners related to visiting other people.

One should have the correct intention for visiting others, and the motive should be to maintain ties with them for the sake of Allāh (ﷻ) and in order to fulfill their rights.

The Prophet (ﷺ) said:

«مَنْ عَادَ مَرِيضًا أَوْ زَارَ أَخًا لَهُ فِي اللهِ عَزَّ وَجَلَّ، نَادَاهُ مُنَادٍ مِنَ السَّمَاءِ: طِبْتَ، وَطَابَ مَمْشَاكَ، وَتَبَوَّأْتَ مِنَ الْجَنَّةِ مَنْزِلًا».

(رواه الترمذي)

> "Whoever visits a sick person, or visits one's brother in faith, a caller calls out: 'May you be blessed, and may your steps be blessed, and may you have a place in Paradise.'" (Tirmidhī)

Allāh (ﷻ) also says:

« وَجَبَتْ مَحَبَّتِي لِلْمُتَحَابِّينَ فِيَّ وَالْمُتَجَالِسِينَ فِيَّ وَالْمُتَزَاوِرِينَ فِيَّ وَالْمُتَبَاذِلِينَ فِيَّ».

(موطأ مالك)

> "My love is for those who love one another for My sake, meet one another for My sake, visit one another for My sake, and spend in charity for My sake." (Muwaṭṭā Mālik)

An appropriate time should be chosen: one which is customarily expected to be a time in which visitors are to be received.

Arrangements for visiting should be made, and the manners of seeking permission should be observed. Unsettling surprise visits should be avoided.

Agree on a time in which your brother/sister will be prepared to receive and meet with you; and if he/she has to excuse himself/herself, you should be prepared to accept that with a clean conscience.

People's circumstances must be given consideration, as is mentioned in the exalted conduct outlined in the Qur'ān.

Allāh (ﷻ) says:

﴿فَإِن لَّمْ تَجِدُواْ فِيهَآ أَحَدًا فَلَا تَدْخُلُوهَا حَتَّىٰ يُؤْذَنَ لَكُمْۖ وَإِن قِيلَ لَكُمُ ٱرْجِعُواْ فَٱرْجِعُواْۖ هُوَ أَزْكَىٰ لَكُمْۚ وَٱللَّهُ بِمَا تَعْمَلُونَ عَلِيمٌ ﴿٢٨﴾﴾ [النُّور الآية ٢٨]

"If you do not find anyone there (if no one permits you to enter), then do not enter until you are permitted to enter (so leave the place and return at another time). (However) If you are told to return (not to enter), then return (from where you came and do not force your way in or remain standing there). This is purer for you (because you will not be disturbing others). Allāh is Aware of what you do (and will take you to task if you disturb people)." (Nūr 24:28)

The Prophet (ﷺ) said:

«إِذَا اسْتَأْذَنَ أَحَدُكُمْ ثَلاَثًا فَلَمْ يُؤْذَنْ لَهُ، فَلْيَرْجِعْ».

(رواه البخاري)

"When one of you asks for permission three times, but it is not granted to him, then he should go away." (Bukhārī)

Other points to be observed when seeking permission are clearly identifying oneself by name and asking permission politely.

Jābir (رضي الله عنه) narrates:

«أَتَيْتُ النَّبِيَّ ﷺ فِي دَيْنٍ كَانَ عَلَى أَبِي، فَدَقَقْتُ الْبَابَ، فَقَالَ: مَنْ ذَا؟ فَقُلْتُ: أَنَا، قَالَ: أَنَا، أَنَا؟، كَأَنَّهُ كَرِهَهُ».

(رواه الترمذي)

"I came to the Messenger of Allāh (ﷺ) about a debt that my father owed. I knocked on the door and he asked: 'Who is it?'

'Me,' I replied. He said: 'Me? Me?' As if he disliked that." (Tirmidhī)

Shaykh 'Abdul Fattāḥ Abū Ghuddah (﷭) writes:

»إذا طرقت باب أخيك أوصديقك أوبعض معارفك، أوأحد تقصده، فدق الباب دقا رفيقا يعرفه وجود طارق بالباب، ولا تدقه بعنف وشدة آدق الظلمة والزبانية فتروعه وتخل بالأدب، جاءت امرأة إلى الإمام أحمد بن حنبل ﵁، لتسأله عن شيء من أمور الدين، ودقت الباب دقا فيه بعض العنف، فخرج وهو يقول: هذا الشرط - جمع شرطي».

(من أدب الإسلام)

"Knock on the door or ring the doorbell in a pleasant way, not louder than is necessary to make your presence known. Do not knock loudly and violently, or ring the bell continuously. Remember that you are a visitor, and not a thug or an oppressor who is raiding the house and wanting to frighten its occupants. A woman came to Imām Aḥmad (﷭) seeking his opinion on a religious matter. She banged on his door loudly. He came out saying: 'This is the banging of policemen.'" (Islāmic Manners)

Imām al-Bukhārī (﷭) in his *Al-Adab al-Mufrad* has documented that:

»إِنَّ أَبْوَابَ النَّبِيِّ ﷺ كَانَتْ تُقْرَعُ بِالأَظَافِيرِ«.

(الأدب المفرد)

"The companions of the Prophet (ﷺ) used to knock on the door of the Prophet (ﷺ) with the tips of their nails." (Al-Adab al-Mufrad)

In addition, a person must be mindful regarding the length of one's visit. It should neither be so long that it induces disinterest, nor so short that it fails to fulfill the objectives of maintaining ties and fostering love.

How these manners are practically observed is governed by the relationship between the parties involved in any visit, as well as the degree of closeness that exists between them.

Shaykh ʿAbdul Fattāḥ Abū Ghuddah (ﷺ) writes:

«وينبغي أن تتخير الوقت الملائم للزيارة، وأن تجلس المدة المناسبة التي تتلاقى مع مقامك عند المزور، ومع الحال التي هو عليها، فلا تطل، ولا تثقل، ولا تأت في وقت غير ملائم لزيارته، كوقت الطعام أو النوم أو الراحة أو ا لسكون».

(من أدب الإسلام)

"Choose an appropriate time for your visit. Do not visit at inconvenient times such as mealtime, or when people are sleeping, resting, or relaxing. The length of the visit should be in accordance with how well you know the hosts, as well as their circumstances and conditions. Do not overstay your welcome by making your visit too long or burdensome." (Islāmic Manners)

The time specified by a host should also be observed.

Allāh (ﷻ) says:

﴿فَإِذَا طَعِمْتُمْ فَٱنتَشِرُوا۟ وَلَا مُسْتَـْٔنِسِينَ لِحَدِيثٍ ۚ إِنَّ ذَٰلِكُمْ كَانَ يُؤْذِى ٱلنَّبِىَّ فَيَسْتَحْىِۦ مِنكُمْ ۖ وَٱللَّهُ لَا يَسْتَحْىِۦ مِنَ ٱلْحَقِّ ۚ 53﴾ [الأحزاب الآية ٥٣]

"And disperse (depart) once you have eaten without (remaining behind and) engaging in a (lengthy) conversation. Indeed this (arriving too early and remaining behind afterwards) hurts the Prophet, but he is too shy for you (out of modesty he does not tell you lest you feel offended). (However) Allāh does not shy away (avoid) from the truth (and makes it clear to all without exception)." (Aḥzāb 33:53)

Something else to be given consideration during visits is using time for beneficial purposes, in addition to being lighthearted, making others happy, and being a good companion. Beneficial purposes for visits include things like maintaining ties, fostering love, learning from a scholar, and emulating the good conduct of those who personify it. These should be done while attentively listening to others, respecting them, benefitting from those who have specialized knowledge; and also presenting issues and problems respectfully and with a proper approach, not with argumentation since this will eliminate the potential of gaining benefit, and it can also incite animosity and malice. In addition, care should be taken not to raise one's voice unless there is a need for it.

Shaykh 'Abdul Fattāḥ Abū Ghuddah (؈) writes:

»ومن أدب المجالسة أنك إذا حادثت ضيفك أوأحدا من الناس، فليكن صوتك لطيفا خفيضا، وليكن جهرك بالكلام على قدر الحاجة، فإن الجهر الزائد عن الحاجة يخل بأدب المتحدث، ويدل على قلة الاحترام للمتحدث إليه. وهذا الأدب تنبغي مراعاته مع الصديق والمثيل، ومع من تعرفه ومن لا تعرفه، ومع الأصغرمنك والأكبر، وتزداد مراعاته تأكيدا مع الوالدين أومن في مقامهما، ومع من تعظمه من الناس الأفاضل والأكابر.«

(من أدب الإسلام)

"If you speak to a guest or any other person, whether in a gathering or alone, make sure that your voice is pleasant, with a low, audible tone. Raising your voice is contrary to proper manners and indicates a lack of respect for the person with whom you are talking. This manner should be maintained with friends, peers, acquaintances, strangers, the young and the old. It is more important even to adhere to this with one's parents or someone of their status, or with people for whom you have great respect." (Islāmic Manners)

Imām al-Dhahabī (؈) has written in his biography about Imām Ibn Sīrīn (؈) that:

«أَنَّ مُحَمَّدًا كَانَ إِذَا كَانَ عِنْدَ أُمِّهِ، لَوْ رَآهُ رَجُلٌ لاَ يَعْرِفُهُ ظَنَّ أَنَّ بِهِ مَرَضًا مِنْ خَفْضِهِ كَلاَمَهُ عِنْدَهَا».

(سير أعلام النبلاء)

> "Whenever Muhammad was in his mother's presence, he would talk in such a low voice that you would think that he was ill." (Siyar Aʿlām al-Nubalā')

«أَنَّهُ نَادَتْهُ أُمُّهُ فَأَجَابَهَا فَعَلَا صَوْتُهُ صَوْتَهَا فَأَعْتَقَ رَقَبَتَيْنِ».

(سير أعلام النبلاء)

> "One time his mother called him and because he responded with a voice louder than hers, he was fearful and repentant, so he freed two slaves." (Siyar Aʿlām al-Nubalā')

In the advice that Luqmān (ﷺ) gave to his son, he said:

﴿وَٱغْضُضْ مِن صَوْتِكَ ۚ إِنَّ أَنكَرَ ٱلْأَصْوَٰتِ لَصَوْتُ ٱلْحَمِيرِ ﴿١٩﴾﴾ [لُقْمَان الآية ١٩]

> "And lower your voice (speak gently to people). Indeed, the most hateful sound is the braying of a donkey (which ends in a high pitch that grates one's ears. People should therefore avoid speaking in this manner)." (Luqmān 31:19)

Also, among the manners to be observed when visiting someone are: avoid talking too much, moving about excessively, and do not interfere in the host's private matters.

In fact, it is obligatory for a person to avert one's glance from what is not permissible for one to look at, and to refrain from looking all over a host's house and examining its contents.

Furthermore, one should not converse about things that a host dislikes, such as asking intrusive questions or discussing things that a person would not want others to know about. You should not extend your eyes to certain things, just like you would not extend your hands to certain things.

Shaykh ʿAbdul Fattāh Abū Ghuddah (ﷺ) writes:

«إذا دخلت بيت أخيك أو صديقك ، وأقعدك فيه، أوأنامك فيه ، فلا تتفقده ببصرك تفقد الفاحص المحص، بل غض بصرك في أثناء قعودك أومنامك فيه، قاصرا نظرك على ما تحتاج إليه فحسب، ولا تفتح مغلقا من خزانة، أو صندوق، أو محفظة، أو صرة ملفوفة، أو شيء مستور، فإن هذا خلاف أدب الإسلام والأمانة التي خولك بها أخوك أو محبك دخول بيته والمقام عنده، فاعرف لزيارتك آدابها، واسلك لحسن المعاشرة أبوابها، تزداد عند مضيفك حبا وأدبا».

(من أدب الإسلام)

"When you enter a home, whether as a visitor or an overnight guest, do not closely examine its contents as an inspector would. Limit your observation to what you need to see. Do not open closed closets, or boxes. Do not inspect a wallet, a package, or a covered object. This is against Islāmic manners and an impolite betrayal of the trust which your host has accorded to you. Uphold these manners during your visit, and seek to cultivate your host's love and respect." (Islāmic Manners)

In addition, one should avoid belittling the actions that he may observe, or the food or drink with which he is presented. The only exception is if a person is offering sincere counsel about those things, provided that one offers it with wisdom in how and when it is done.

ʿAbdullāh ibn ʿUbaid ibn ʿUmair (ﷺ) said:

«دَخَلَ عَلَى جَابِرٍ نَفَرٌ مِنْ أَصْحَابِ النَّبِيِّ صَلَّى اللهُ عَلَيْهِ وَسَلَّمَ، فَقَدَّمَ إِلَيْهِمْ خُبْزًا وَخَلًّا، فَقَالَ: كُلُوا، فَإِنِّي سَمِعْتُ رَسُولَ اللَّهِ صَلَّى اللهُ عَلَيْهِ وَسَلَّمَ يَقُولُ: نِعْمَ الْإِدَامُ الْخَلُّ، إِنَّهُ هَلَاكٌ بِالرَّجُلِ

أَنْ يَدْخُلَ عَلَيْهِ النَّفَرُ مِنْ إِخْوَانِهِ، فَيَحْتَقِرَ مَا فِي بَيْتِهِ أَنْ يُقَدِّمَهُ إِلَيْهِمْ، وَهَلَاكٌ بِالْقَوْمِ أَنْ يَحْتَقِرُوا مَا قُدِّمَ إِلَيْهِمْ».

(رواه احمد)

"Jābir came to me with a group of the companions of the Prophet (ﷺ). He (Jābir) placed before them bread and vinegar and said: 'Eat, I have heard from the Prophet (ﷺ) that: 'Vinegar is the best curry. Verily a man is ruined, when some brothers come to his house and he considers it low to place before them things that he has in his house; and ruined are those people who consider low that what is being placed before them.''" (Aḥmad)

Another narration mentions:

«وَكَفَى بِالْمَرْءِ شَرًّا أَنْ يَتَسَخَّطَ مَا قُرِّبَ إِلَيْهِ».

(مسند أبي يعلى الموصلي)

"It is evil enough for a person to consider low what is presented to him." (Musnad Abū Yaʿlā al-Mawṣilī)

A guest should sit where he is allowed to by his host, since the host is the one most entitled to arrange the seating of his guests. The Prophet (ﷺ) drew attention to this in his statement:

«وَلاَ يُؤَمُّ الرَّجُلُ فِي سُلْطَانِهِ، وَلاَ يُجْلَسُ عَلَى تَكْرِمَتِهِ فِي بَيْتِهِ إِلاَّ بِإِذْنِهِ».

(رواه الترمذي)

"No man should lead another in prayer while in that man's home, or sit on his furnishings in his house except with his permission." (Tirmidhī)

Ibn Kathīr (ﷺ) has narrated in *Al-Bidāyah wa al-Nihāyah* that the honoured companion ʿAdī ibn Ḥātim al-Ṭāʾī (ﷺ) converted to Islām and came to Madīnah to see the Prophet (ﷺ). The Prophet (ﷺ) honoured Ḥātim al-Ṭāʾī (ﷺ) by seating him on a cushion, while he himself sat on the floor.

ʿAdī ibn Ḥātim al-Ṭāʾī (ﷺ) recounts:

«ثُمَّ مَضَى بِي رَسُولُ اللهِ ﷺ حَتَّى إِذَا دَخَلَ بِي بَيْتَهُ، تَنَاوَلَ وِسَادَةً مِنْ أَدَمٍ مَحْشُوَّةٍ لِيفًا، فَقَذَفَهَا إِلَيَّ، فَقَالَ: اجْلِسْ عَلَى هَذِهِ، قَالَ: قُلْتُ: بَلْ أَنْتَ فَاجْلِسْ عَلَيْهَا، فَقَالَ: بَلْ أَنْتَ، فَجَلَسْتُ عَلَيْهَا، وَجَلَسَ رَسُولُ اللهِ ﷺ بِالْأَرْضِ».

(البداية والنهاية)

"Then the Prophet (ﷺ) took me along and upon reaching his house, he took a leather cushion filled with palm fiber and threw it on the floor. 'Sit on this,' he said. 'No, you sit on it,' I answered. The Prophet insisted, 'No you.' So, I sat on it while the Prophet (ﷺ) sat on the floor." (Al-Bidāyah wa al-Nihāyah)

Once Khārijah ibn Zayd (ﷺ) visited Ibn Sīrīn (ﷺ):

«ودخل خارجة بن زيد على ابن سيرين زائرا له، فوجد ابن سيرين جالسا على الأرض إلى وسادة، فأراد أن يجلس معه وقال له: قد رضيت لنفسي مارضيت لنفسك، فقال ابن سيرين: إني لا أرضى لك في بيتي بما أرضى به لنفسي فاجلس حيث تؤمر. ولا تجلس في مكان صاحب المنزل إلا إذا دعاك الى الجلوس فيه».

(من أدب الإسلام)

He found Ibn Sīrīn sitting on a cushion on the floor and also wanted to sit on a cushion and said: "I am content as you are." Ibn Sīrīn replied: "In my home, I will not be content until I provide you with what I am usually comfortable with. Sit where you are asked to sit. Do not sit in the patron's seat unless he invites you to it." (Islāmic Manners)

One should not leave the house unless he requests the host's permission to do so. He should also extend the *salām* when leaving just like he did when entering, since the first is no more entitled to being extended than the latter.

Allāh (ﷻ) says:

﴿إِنَّمَا ٱلْمُؤْمِنُونَ ٱلَّذِينَ ءَامَنُوا۟ بِٱللَّهِ وَرَسُولِهِۦ وَإِذَا كَانُوا۟ مَعَهُۥ عَلَىٰٓ أَمْرٍ جَامِعٍ لَّمْ يَذْهَبُوا۟ حَتَّىٰ يَسْتَـْٔذِنُوهُ ﴿٦٢﴾﴾ [النور الآية ٦٢]

"The believers are only those who believe in Allāh and His Messenger, and when they are [meeting] with him for a matter of common interest, they do not depart until they have asked for his permission." (Nūr 24:62)

NOTE: This is another matter of etiquette in which Allāh (ﷻ) has guided His believing servants. Just like He commands them to seek permission when entering, He also commands them to seek permission when leaving.

The Prophet (ﷺ) has said:

«إِذَا انْتَهَى أَحَدُكُمْ إِلَى الْمَجْلِسِ، فَلْيُسَلِّمْ فَإِذَا أَرَادَ أَنْ يَقُومَ، فَلْيُسَلِّمْ فَلَيْسَتِ الْأُولَى بِأَحَقَّ مِنَ الْآخِرَةِ».

(سنن أبي داود)

"When any of you joins a gathering, then let him say *salām*, and when he wants to leave, then again let him say *salām*. The former is not more important than the latter." (Sunan Abū Dāwūd)

Other manners to be observed include receiving guests nicely, treating them kindly, and being cheerful around them.

Imām al-Awzāʿī (﷭) was asked about what honouring guests entails and he replied:

«كَرَامَةُ الضَّيْفِ طَلَاقَةُ الْوَجْهِ، وَطِيبُ الْكَلَامِ».

(إحياء علوم الدين)

"Honouring guests means a cheerful face, and pleasant words." (Iḥyā' al-ʿUlūm al-Dīn)

Al-Fuḍayl ibn ʿIyāḍ (﷭) remarked:

«لِأَنْ يلاطف الرجل أهل مجلسه ويحسن خلقه معهم خير له من قيام ليله وصيام نهاره».

(كتاب وفيات الأعيان)

"For a man to be pleasant towards those who accompany him, and observe sound conduct around them, is better for him than standing to pray in the night and fasting in the day." (Kitāb Wafayāt al-Āʿyān)

Al-Fuḍayl ibn ʿIyāḍ (﷭) most probably drew this conclusion from the *ḥadīth* of the Prophet (ﷺ) in which he stated:

«إِنَّ الْمُؤْمِنَ لَيُدْرِكُ بِحُسْنِ خُلُقِهِ دَرَجَةَ الصَّائِمِ الْقَائِمِ».

(سنن أبي داود)

"By one's good character, a believer will most certainly attain the rank of someone who prays (throughout the night), and fasts (throughout the day)." (Sunan Abū Dāwūd)

Another manner to be observed is to listen well and attentively. This entails waiting until one's companion finishes before one speaks himself, facing him when listening, and not interrupting him even if one knows what he will say.

ʿAṭā' ibn Abī Rabāḥ (﷭) says:

»إن الشاب ليحدثني بحديث فأستمع له كأني لم أسمعه ولقد سمعته قبل أن يولد«.

(من أدب الإسلام)

"A young person may narrate a *ḥadīth* to me and I will listen to him as if I had not previously heard it, even though in reality, I already heard that *ḥadīth* even before he was born." (Islāmic Manners)

Ibrāhīm ibn al-Junayd (🙵) said:

»تعلم حسن الاستماع، كما تتعلم حسن الكلام، فإن حسن الاستماع إمهالك للمتكلم حتى يفضي إليك بحديثه، وإقبالك بالوجه والنظر عليه، وترك المشاركة له في حديث أنت تعرفه«.

(من أدب الإسلام)

"Learn the art of listening like you learn the art of speaking! Listening well means maintaining eye contact, allowing the speaker to finish his discourse, and restraining yourself from interrupting his speech." (Islāmic Manners)

وَلَا تُشَارِكْ فِي الْحَدِيثِ أَهْلَهُ ❂ وَإِنْ عَرَفْتَ فَرْعَهُ وَأَصْلَهُ

A talk never interrupt,
Though you know it in and out.

A further etiquette to observe is keeping one's gatherings clear of anything that contradicts the teachings of Islām, such as impermissible forms of mixing, forbidden foods or drinks, slander, and backbiting.

People should be trustworthy companions, and what others confide in them should remain in their hearts and not be divulged.

Some of the most apparent signs of brotherhood as it relates to visiting others is to accept their excuses, make up for their shortcomings, and overlook their mistakes.

If a guest has young children, one should keep them under control and restrain them from behaving in any way that may disturb the host or others in attendance, whether by way of movements, words, or noise.

A host should see his/her visitors off and accompany them to the door. This is part of being a good host and completing respectable conduct.

Imām al-Shaʿbī (﷤) says:

»مِنْ تَمَامِ إِكْرَامِ الزَّائِرِ أَنْ تَمْشِيَ مَعَهُ إِلَى بَابِ الدَّارِ وَتَأْخُذَ بِرِكَابِهِ.«

(الآداب الشرعية)

"Part of completing a visit is for you (the host) to walk with your guest to the door and take hold of his mount." (Al-Adāb al-Sharʿīyah)

CONCLUSION

- Visit your brothers and relatives, acquire their love and supplications, find out about their circumstances, and do good to them which will foster affection.
- Do not wait for anyone to repay you for the good that you extend to them.

It is mentioned in a Prophetic narration that:

»أَنَّ رَجُلًا زَارَ أَخًا لَهُ فِي قَرْيَةٍ أُخْرَى، فَأَرْصَدَ اللهُ لَهُ، عَلَى مَدْرَجَتِهِ، مَلَكًا فَلَمَّا أَتَى عَلَيْهِ، قَالَ: أَيْنَ تُرِيدُ؟ قَالَ: أُرِيدُ أَخًا لِي فِي هَذِهِ الْقَرْيَةِ، قَالَ: هَلْ لَكَ عَلَيْهِ مِنْ نِعْمَةٍ تَرُبُّهَا؟ قَالَ: لَا، غَيْرَ أَنِّي أَحْبَبْتُهُ فِي اللهِ عَزَّ وَجَلَّ، قَالَ: فَإِنِّي رَسُولُ اللهِ إِلَيْكَ، بِأَنَّ اللهَ قَدْ أَحَبَّكَ كَمَا أَحْبَبْتَهُ فِيهِ.«

(رواه مسلم)

"There was a man who set out to visit a brother of his in another town. So, Allāh deputed an angel at a point along his path. When the man reached that point, the angel asked him: 'Where are you headed?' He replied: 'I am heading to a brother of mine in that town.' The angel asked: 'Is there something that one of you owes the other?' He replied: 'No. I am going because I love him for the sake of Allāh.' The angel then said: 'Allāh sent me as a messenger to inform you that Allāh loves you, and that is due to you loving your brother for Allāh's sake.'" (Muslim)

- Visiting one another draws the hearts of people together just like it draws people together physically.
- Going to see others will also enable people to foster love, find out about how others are doing, exchange expertise, consult with each other, solve problems together, support one another, remind the heedless, educate the ignorant, give the souls comfort, alleviate difficulties, spread happiness, and console the grieving ones.

It was said to Muḥammad ibn al-Munkadir (ﷺ):

«مَا بَقِيَ مِنْ لَذَّتِكَ؟ قَالَ: الْتِقَاءُ الإِخْوَانِ، وَإِدْخَالُ السُّرُورِ عَلَيْهِمْ».

(البداية والنهاية)

"What is left of your pleasure?" He said: "Meeting up with one's brothers and making them feel happy." (Al-Bidāyah wa al-Nihāyah)

We must also realize that overdoing things when it comes to visits can lead people to be distant and feel burdened. However, when hearts are clean, nothing needs to be overdone. When people overdo things, or importance is given to appearances, then priorities will be neglected, showing off will become an objective, minds and bodies will become preoccupied, and pockets will be emptied. These may bring about a feeling of being burdened and can they lead people to increase in distance from each other.

Having love for others is the closest of lineage, and this kind of love does not require sharing lineage with them.

Visiting each other while observing the foregoing manners is one of the most prominent features of a Muslim community, and it strengthens affinity and ties. Your immediate family and friends are the most deserving of your good conduct and manners.

In this regard, Imām al-Bukhārī and Imām Muslim (ﷺ) both have reported:

«قَالَ رَجُلٌ: يَا رَسُولَ اللهِ مَنْ أَحَقُّ النَّاسِ بِحُسْنِ الصُّحْبَةِ؟ قَالَ: أُمُّكَ، ثُمَّ أُمُّكَ، ثُمَّ أُمُّكَ، ثُمَّ أَبُوكَ، ثُمَّ أَدْنَاكَ أَدْنَاكَ».

(متفق عليه)

> "A man asked the Prophet (ﷺ): 'Who amongst the people is most deserving of my good treatment?' He replied: 'Your mother, again your mother, again your mother, then your father, then your nearest relatives according to the order (of nearness).'" (Agreed Upon)

Therefore, we should not overlook these matters when interacting with people, and we must act nicely and amicably with others. If we do not behave properly, then we will degrade ourselves, abuse the duty that we have been entrusted with, and abandon the guidance of the Messenger of Allāh (ﷺ).

May Allāh (ﷻ) protect us, our relatives and our beloved ones; and may He help us obey His orders, remain obedient to Him, and follow the example of His Prophet (ﷺ). May Allāh (ﷻ) grant us His love, grace and generosity. *Āmīn.*

KHUṬBAH 75

So, For This Let the Competitors Compete

One of the most beautiful and praiseworthy traits that a person can embody is to always to have high aspirations. A person's true status and worth is proportional to how high their objectives are.

A wise and sensible person of faith will always attempt to accomplish everything that will lead to one's betterment in this world and the next. They will try to scale the greatest of heights when it comes to doing what it is right, and will strive to be foremost in doing what Allāh (ﷻ) has instructed humankind to do.

If a person does not seek excellence, then one will remain deficient. If a person does not have a lofty objective, then one will fall short in one's efforts and actions.

Imām Ṭabarānī (ﷺ) in his *Muʿjam al-Kabīr* has recorded a *ḥadīth* reported by the grandson of the Prophet (ﷺ), Ḥusayn ibn ʿAlī (ﷺ), who narrates that the Messenger of Allāh (ﷺ) said:

«إِنَّ اللَّهَ يُحِبُّ مَعَالِيَ الْأُمُورِ وَأَشْرَافَهَا، وَيَكْرَهُ سَفْسَافَهَا».

(رواه الطبراني)

> "Indeed, Allāh loves those matters which are superior and highest in rank, and He despises those which are inferior." (Ṭabarānī)

Inferiority here refers to those things which are lowly in general, are of little value, and reflect a lack of integrity on the part of the person involved in them.

In the Qur'ān, Allāh (ﷻ) has informed us about a certain group of people who have faith and are people of abundant goodness. They are individuals who have a strong willpower and high ambitions. Allāh (ﷻ) commended them and made mention of them by saying:

﴿وَٱلسَّٰبِقُونَ ٱلسَّٰبِقُونَ ۝ أُوْلَٰٓئِكَ ٱلْمُقَرَّبُونَ ۝﴾ [الواقعة من الآية ١٠ الى الآية]

"And those foremost will be foremost (Al-Sābiqūn, Al-Sābiqūn). They are the ones who will be nearest to Allāh." (Wāqi'ah 56:10-11)

Commentators of *tafsīr* have explained that:

«وَالسَّابِقُونَ السَّابِقُونَ وَالتَّكْرِيرُ فِيهِ لِلتَّفْخِيمِ وَالتَّعْظِيمِ.»

(فتح القدير للشوكاني)

"The word السَّابِقُونَ being repeated in this verse indicates that these people are very honourable and privileged." (Fath al-Qadīr of al-Shawkānī)

Imām Ahmad has recorded a *hadīth* on the authority of 'Ā'ishah (ؓ) that once the Prophet (ﷺ) asked the companions (ؓ):

«أَتَدْرُونَ مَنِ السَّابِقُونَ إِلَى ظِلِّ اللهِ عَزَّ وَجَلَّ يَوْمَ الْقِيَامَةِ؟» قَالُوا: اللهُ وَرَسُولُهُ أَعْلَمُ، قَالَ: «الَّذِينَ إِذَا أُعْطُوا الْحَقَّ قَبِلُوهُ، وَإِذَا سُئِلُوهُ بَذَلُوهُ، وَحَكَمُوا لِلنَّاسِ كَحُكْمِهِمْ لِأَنْفُسِهِمْ».

(مسند أحمد)

"Do you know who will be the first (foremost) to be accommodated in the Divine Shade on the Day of Resurrection?" They replied: "Allāh and His Messenger know best." He (the Messenger) replied: "They are those who accept the truth when it is presented to them; when they are asked for the rights due from them, they fulfill them; and they judge about the matters of others as they would judge about themselves." (Musnad Aḥmad)

Commentators of the Qur'ān have provided various explanations on the word *Al-Sābiqūn*:

«وَقَالَ مُحَمَّدُ بْنُ كَعْبٍ وَأَبُو حَرْزَةَ يَعْقُوبُ بْنُ مُجَاهِدٍ: {وَالسَّابِقُونَ السَّابِقُونَ} : هُمُ الْأَنْبِيَاءُ، عَلَيْهِمُ السَّلَامُ. وَقَالَ السُّدِّيّ: هُمْ أَهْلُ عِلِّيِّينَ. وَقَالَ ابْنُ أَبِي حَاتِمٍ: وَذَكَرَ مُحَمَّدُ بْنُ أَبِي حَمَّادٍ، حَدَّثَنَا مِهْرَان، عَنْ خَارِجَةَ، عَنْ قُرَّةَ، عَنِ ابْنِ سِيرِين: {وَالسَّابِقُونَ السَّابِقُونَ} الَّذِينَ صَلَّوْا لِلْقِبْلَتَيْنِ. وَقَالَ الْحَسَنُ وقَتَادَةُ: {وَالسَّابِقُونَ السَّابِقُونَ} أَيْ: مِنْ كُلِّ أُمَّةٍ. وَقَالَ الْأَوْزَاعِيُّ، عَنْ عُثْمَانَ بْنِ أَبِي سَوْدَةَ أَنَّهُ قَرَأَ هَذِهِ الْآيَةَ: {وَالسَّابِقُونَ السَّابِقُونَ. أُولَئِكَ الْمُقَرَّبُونَ} ثُمَّ قَالَ: أَوَّلُهُمْ رَوَاحًا إِلَى الْمَسْجِدِ، وَأَوَّلُهُمْ خُرُوجًا فِي سَبِيلِ اللهِ. وَهَذِهِ الْأَقْوَالُ كُلُّهَا صَحِيحَةٌ، فَإِنَّ الْمُرَادَ بِالسَّابِقِينَ هُمُ الْمُبَادِرُونَ إِلَى فِعْلِ الْخَيْرَاتِ كَمَا أُمِرُوا».

(تفسير ابن كثير)

1) Abū Ḥarza Yaʿqūb ibn Mujāhid (ﷺ) says that *Al-Sābiqūn* (the Foremost) refers to 'the Prophets,' peace be upon them.
2) Ibn Sīrīn (ﷺ) says that it refers to the early Muslims who performed their prayers facing the two *qiblahs*, namely, Bayt al-Maqdis and the Ka'bah.
3) Suddī (ﷺ) says that it refers to the people of *ʿIllīyīn* (a place of bliss in the seventh heaven where the records of the sincere believers are placed).
4) Ḥasan and Qatādah (ﷺ) say that in every nation there will be *Al-Sābiqūn.*
5) Some of the commentators express the view that they are those people who are the first to go to the *masjid.*
6) Ibn Kathīr (ﷺ) cites all of these views and concludes that they are all correct and authentic in their own right, because the meaning of *Al-Sābiqūn* (the Foremost) is that they were

foremost in performing the acts of righteousness, just as Allāh (ﷻ) commanded them. (Tafsīr Ibn Kathīr)

Ibn ʿAṭīyah (ﷺ) in *Tafsīr al-Muḥarar al-Wajīz* says that this verse is even more comprehensive in meaning and explains that:

«فالسابِقُون هم الذين سبَقَت لهم السعادة، وكانت أعمالهم في الدنيا سَبقًا إلى التوبةِ، وأعمالِ البرِّ، وتركِ المعاصِي، وهم المُبادِرُون إلى فعلِ الخيرات».

(المحرر الوجيز)

"*Al-Sābiqūn* comprises all of those who will attain happiness in the hereafter, and whose deeds in this world amount to being foremost in repenting to Allāh, obeying Him, avoiding sins, and in performing righteous actions." (Tafsīr al-Muḥarar al-Wajīz)

In the Qur'ān, Allāh (ﷻ) tells us that the *Sābiqūn* are those who are foremost in performing righteous deeds.

Allāh (ﷻ) says:

﴿فَٱسْتَبِقُوا۟ ٱلْخَيْرَٰتِ ۚ إِلَى ٱللَّهِ مَرْجِعُكُمْ جَمِيعًا فَيُنَبِّئُكُم بِمَا كُنتُمْ فِيهِ تَخْتَلِفُونَ ﴿٤٨﴾﴾ [المَائـِدَة الآية ٤٨]

"So, hasten (you must all strive your utmost) to (do) good works! To Allāh shall you all return (on the Day of Judgement) and then He will inform you about that in which you used to differ (then everyone will receive the rewards or punishments for what they did)." (Mā'idah 5:48)

﴿۞ وَسَارِعُوٓا۟ إِلَىٰ مَغْفِرَةٍ مِّن رَّبِّكُمْ وَجَنَّةٍ عَرْضُهَا ٱلسَّمَٰوَٰتُ وَٱلْأَرْضُ أُعِدَّتْ لِلْمُتَّقِينَ ﴿١٣٣﴾﴾ [آل عِمْرَان الآية ١٣٣]

"And seize every opportunity that you can to attain your Lord's forgiveness, and to be admitted to a garden whose expanse is that of the heavens and the earth, prepared for the righteous." (Āle ʿImrān 3:133)

﴿سَابِقُوٓاْ إِلَىٰ مَغۡفِرَةٖ مِّن رَّبِّكُمۡ وَجَنَّةٍ عَرۡضُهَا كَعَرۡضِ ٱلسَّمَآءِ وَٱلۡأَرۡضِ ٢١﴾

[الحديد الآية ٢١]

(Instead of chasing after the things of this world) Race towards (do all that you can to be foremost in attaining) the forgiveness of your Lord and a garden, the width of which is like that of the sky and the earth. (The length is unimaginable)." (Ḥadīd 57:21)

NOTE: Although Paradise is much larger than the heavens and the earth that we know, the comparison is merely to give us an idea of its enormous size.

﴿أُوْلَٰٓئِكَ يُسَٰرِعُونَ فِي ٱلۡخَيۡرَٰتِ وَهُمۡ لَهَا سَٰبِقُونَ ٦١﴾ [المؤمنون الآية ٦١]

"These people hasten to perform good acts and are the foremost in it (in the race to do good)." (Mu'minūn 23:61)

The people who will be foremost in having Allāh (ﷻ) pleased with them in the hereafter and in being admitted to Paradise, are those who are the foremost to perform righteous deeds and obey Allāh (ﷻ) in this world. Being foremost there (in the hereafter) has a direct correlation to being foremost here (in this world).

It is worthwhile to note that when Allāh (ﷻ) referred to the *Sābiqūn* in the verse:

﴿وَٱلسَّٰبِقُونَ ٱلسَّٰبِقُونَ ١٠ أُوْلَٰٓئِكَ ٱلۡمُقَرَّبُونَ ١١﴾ [الواقعة من الآية ١٠ الى الآية

"And those foremost will be foremost (*Al-Sābiqūn, Al-Sābiqūn*). They are the ones who will be nearest to Allāh." (Wāqiʿah 56:10-11)

He did not specify any deeds in particular which they are foremost in performing. Some scholars have explained that this was done in order to make *Al-Sābiqūn* a title for all of those who are foremost in performing righteous deeds in all realms without any distinction.

It is also worthwhile to note that the majority of the *Sābiqūn* among this nation will come from its earlier generations.

Allāh (ﷻ) says:

﴿ثُلَّةٌ مِّنَ ٱلۡأَوَّلِينَ ١٣ وَقَلِيلٌ مِّنَ ٱلۡأٓخِرِينَ ١٤﴾ [الوَاقِعَة من الآية ١٣ الى الآية ١٤]

"Many from the earlier generations, and of a small number from the later ones." (Wāqiʿah 56:13-14)

«(الثُّلَّةُ) بِالضَّمِّ الْجَمَاعَةُ مِنَ النَّاسِ».

The word *thullatu,* means a party, group, company from the people.

«وَالثُّلَّةُ: جَمَاعَةٌ غَيْرُ مَحْصُورَةِ الْعَدَدِ».

(تفسير البغوي)

Imām Baghawī (ﷺ) says:

"And *thullatu* refers to a throng or a large number of people." (Tafsīr al-Baghawī)

According to many commentators of the Qur'an like Ḥāfiẓ ibn Kathīr, Imām al-Qurṭubī, ʿAllāmah Ālūsī (ﷺ) and others, 'the earlier generations' and 'the later generations' imply: the earlier and the later followers of the Prophet's (ﷺ) own nation. 'Earlier generations' in their view, are the companions of the Prophet (ﷺ) and their contemporaries, who are termed in the *ḥadīth* as *'khayr al-qurūn'* (the best generation), and the 'later generations' include all of those who came after them.

Accordingly ثُلَّةٌ مِنَ الْأَوَّلِينَ -'many from the earlier generations' refers to the earlier generation of this nation, and وَقَلِيلٌ مِنَ الْآخِرِينَ - 'a small number from the later generations' refers to the later generation of this nation from whom a small number will be included in the category of the *'Al-Sābiqūn'* - the Foremost.

ʿAllāmah Ālūsī (ﷺ) in *Rūḥ al-Maʿānī* puts forward the following Prophetic *ḥadīth* with a good chain of transmitters in support of this interpretation and transmits that:

«وَأَخْرَجَ مُسَدَّدٌ فِي مُسْنَدِهِ وَابْنُ الْمُنْذِرِ وَالطَّبَرَانِيُّ وَابْنُ مَرْدَوَيْهِ بِسَنَدٍ حَسَنٍ عَنْ أَبِي بَكْرَةَ عَنِ النَّبِيِّ ﷺ فِي قَوْلِهِ: ثُلَّةٌ مِنَ الْأَوَّلِينَ وَثُلَّةٌ مِنَ الْآخِرِينَ قَالَ: جَمِيعُهُمَا مِنْ هَذِهِ الْأُمَّةِ».

(روح المعاني)

> "Musaddad in his *Musnad*, Ibn al-Mundhir, Ṭabarānī and Ibn Marduwīyah report with a good chain on the authority of Abī Bakrah (ﷺ) that while interpreting the verses: 'Many from the earlier generations and a small number from the later ones,' the Prophet (ﷺ) said: 'They are both from this nation.'" (Rūḥ al-Maʿānī)

This indicates that the overall excellence will be possessed by the earlier generations of the nation since they will make up more of those who are nearest to Allāh (ﷻ) rather than from the later generations.

Consequently, it will only be right for us to acquaint ourselves with how we can reach the level of those esteemed people who will be nearest to Allāh (ﷻ) by performing the deeds which they performed, and following the path that they followed in beliefs, words, actions, and in having praiseworthy qualities overall.

Allāh (ﷻ) explains the merits of those who were foremost from the earlier generations, as well as those who follow their path.

﴿وَٱلسَّٰبِقُونَ ٱلْأَوَّلُونَ مِنَ ٱلْمُهَٰجِرِينَ وَٱلْأَنصَارِ وَٱلَّذِينَ ٱتَّبَعُوهُم بِإِحْسَٰنٍ رَّضِىَ ٱللَّهُ عَنْهُمْ وَرَضُوا۟ عَنْهُ وَأَعَدَّ لَهُمْ جَنَّٰتٍ تَجْرِى تَحْتَهَا ٱلْأَنْهَٰرُ خَٰلِدِينَ فِيهَآ أَبَدًا ۚ ذَٰلِكَ ٱلْفَوْزُ ٱلْعَظِيمُ ﴿١٠٠﴾﴾ [التَّوبَة الآية ١٠٠]

> "And the first to lead the way from the *Muhājirīn*, and the *Anṣār*, and those who followed them (in beliefs, words, and deeds) with sincerity, Allāh is pleased with them and they are pleased

with Him; and He has prepared for them such gardens beneath which rivers flow, in which they shall live forever. This is the ultimate success. (Tawbah 9:100)

In this verse, Allāh (ﷻ) has clearly stated that the *Muhājirīn* and the *Anṣār* were among the foremost. Allāh (ﷻ) also states that when people follow their path, it will allow them to be among those with whom Allāh (ﷻ) is pleased, and they are pleased with Him, whom He will allow to reside in Paradise endlessly, and will bless with the greatest success.

This verse also clearly illustrates the great status of the companions (رضي الله عنهم), and it is therefore wrong to insult, condemn and speak ill about them.

At another juncture in the Qur'ān, Allāh (ﷻ) mentions that a person who follows the path of those who were foremost from the earlier generations will also share in the goodness that they will receive.

Allāh (ﷻ) says:

﴿وَٱلَّذِينَ ءَامَنُواْ مِنۢ بَعۡدُ وَهَاجَرُواْ وَجَٰهَدُواْ مَعَكُمۡ فَأُوْلَٰٓئِكَ مِنكُمۡۚ ٧٥﴾ [الأنفال الآية ٧٥]

"And as for those who believed later on, (after the earliest *Muhājirīn* and *Anṣār*), and migrated and struggled alongside with you (and with the companions in Allāh's path), they are (considered as being) from among you." (Anfāl 8:75)

This means that the later generations are also considered to be among the foremost people of faith, i.e. the *Muhājirīn* and *Anṣār*, and they will have the same privileges and honour which those earlier people of faith had.

Commenting on this verse, Ḥāfiẓ ibn Kathīr (رحمه الله) says:

«ثُمَّ ذَكَرَ أَنَّ الْأَتْبَاعَ لَهُمْ فِي الدُّنْيَا عَلَى مَا كَانُوا عَلَيْهِ مِنَ الْإِيمَانِ وَالْعَمَلِ الصَّالِحِ فَهُمْ مَعَهُمْ فِي الْآخِرَةِ».

"Allāh then mentions that those who follow the path of the (early generations of) believers in faith, and perform good deeds, will be with them in the hereafter."

A *ḥadīth* which is in the two *Ṣaḥīḥs*, and is *Mutawātir* [66] and has several authentic chains of narrations, mentions that the Messenger of Allāh (ﷺ) said:

«الْمَرْءُ مَعَ مَنْ أَحَبَّ».

"A person will be in the company of those whom one loves."

Another *ḥadīth* mentions:

«مَنْ أَحَبَّ قَوْمًا فَهُوَ مِنْهُمْ».

"A person who loves a group (or kind) of people is one of them."

In another narration, the Prophet (ﷺ) said:

«حُشِرَ مَعَهُمْ».

(تفسير ابن كثير)

"(They) will be gathered with them (on the Day of Resurrection)" (Tafsīr Ibn Kathīr)

In a Prophetic narration, it has been highlighted that the Prophet (ﷺ) himself referred to those from among his nation, but who will be from the later generations as his brothers.

Anas ibn Mālik (ﷺ) narrates that the Prophet (ﷺ) said:

«وَدِدْتُ أَنِّي لَقِيتُ إِخْوَانِي، قَالَ: فَقَالَ أَصْحَابُ النَّبِيِّ ﷺ: أَوَلَيْسَ نَحْنُ إِخْوَانَكَ؟ قَالَ: أَنْتُمْ أَصْحَابِي، وَلَكِنْ إِخْوَانِي الَّذِينَ آمَنُوا بِي وَلَمْ يَرَوْنِي».

[66] A *Mutawātir ḥadīth* is one which is reported by such a large number of people that it cannot be expected that all of them together would have agreed upon a lie.

(مسند أحمد)

> "I wish I could meet my brothers." The Prophet's (ﷺ) companions said: "Are we not your brothers?" The Prophet replied: "You are my companions, but my brothers are those who (will) have faith in me – even though they never saw me." (Musnad Aḥmad)

Yet still, in another narration, we find the deep love of the Prophet (ﷺ) for those from among his *ummah* who will be from the later generations.

Abū Hurairah (رضي الله عنه) narrates that the Prophet (ﷺ) said:

«مِنْ أَشَدِّ أُمَّتِي لِي حُبًّا، نَاسٌ يَكُونُونَ بَعْدِي، يَوَدُّ أَحَدُهُمْ لَوْ رَآنِي بِأَهْلِهِ وَمَالِهِ».

(رواه مسلم)

> "The people most beloved to me from among my nation are those who will come after me, and everyone from among them will have the keenest desire to catch a glimpse of me - even at the cost of his family and wealth (they will be willing to forfeit their own family and property for that objective)." (Muslim)

A person who holds on to one's faith in times that require endurance will have a reward equal to that of fifty of the Prophet's (ﷺ) companions (رضي الله عنهم).

The Prophet (ﷺ) has been quoted as saying:

«إِنَّ مِنْ وَرَائِكُمْ أَيَّامَ الصَّبْرِ، الْمُتَمَسِّكُ فِيهِنَّ يَوْمَئِذٍ بِمِثْلِ مَا أَنْتُمْ عَلَيْهِ لَهُ كَأَجْرِ خَمْسِينَ مِنْكُمْ، قَالُوا: يَا نَبِيَّ اللهِ، أَوَمِنْهُمْ؟ قَالَ: بَلْ مِنْكُمْ، قَالُوا: يَا نَبِيَّ اللهِ، أَوَمِنْهُمْ؟ قَالَ: لَا، بَلْ مِنْكُمْ، ثَلَاثَ مَرَّاتٍ أَوْ أَرْبَعًا».

(رواه الترمذي)

> "Indeed, ahead of you are days of patience, wherein patience will be like grasping (pieces of) hot coals, and the one who does good deeds will have the reward of fifty men who do likewise." They asked: "O Messenger of Allāh, (the reward of fifty) from among them?" He replied: "Rather, (the reward of fifty) from among you. They again said: "O Messenger of Allāh, (the reward of fifty) from among them?" He replied: "Rather, (the reward of fifty) from among you." He repeated this, three or four times. (Tirmidhī)

Similarly, the reward of worship in challenging times is equal to the reward of migration to the Prophet's (ﷺ) city of Madīnah.

«الْعِبَادَةُ فِي الْهَرْجِ كَهِجْرَةٍ إِلَيَّ».

(رواه مسلم)

> "Worship during the time of tribulation and confusion is like migration to me." (Muslim)

It is truly momentous for a person to do what would make one part of Allāh's (ﷻ) statement:

﴿أُوْلَـٰٓئِكَ يُسَـٰرِعُونَ فِى ٱلْخَيْرَٰتِ وَهُمْ لَهَا سَـٰبِقُونَ ﴿٦١﴾﴾ [المُؤْمِنُون الآية ٦١]

> "It is those people who hasten to perform good acts, and are the foremost in it (in the race to do good)." (Mu'minūn 23:61)

Therefore, we must endeavour to aim high and strive our utmost to do all of that which will benefit us *Inshā' Allāh.*

It is for this very reason that Wuhayb ibn al-Ward (rahimahullah) said:

«إن استطعتَ أن لا يسبقَكَ إلى الله أحدٌ فافعلْ».

(لطائف المعارف)

> "If you can outdo others in reaching Allāh, then do so." (Laṭā'if al-Maʿārif)

Likewise, Ḥasan al-Baṣrī (ﷺ) said:

«من نافسَكَ في دينِك فنافِسْه، ومن نافسَكَ في دُنياه فألقِها في نَحرِه».

(لطائف المعارف)

> "If someone outdoes you in your religion, then try to be better than him; but if someone outdoes you in the matters of this world, then leave them to him." (Laṭā'if al-Maʿārif)

This is similar to what Allāh (ﷻ) tells us:

﴿وَفِي ذَٰلِكَ فَلْيَتَنَافَسِ ٱلْمُتَنَٰفِسُونَ ۝٢٦﴾ [المُطَفِّفِين الآية ٢٦]

> "It is for this that the competitors (those who strive) should compete (instead of competing for the inferior things of this world)." (Muṭaffifīn 83:26)

CONCLUSION

As we progress on this journey towards Allāh (ﷻ), the succeeding *ḥadīth* serves as an encouragement for us to aim high, strengthen our resolve, do all that is required of us in order to achieve the greatest of objectives, not let things get in our way, and not surrender to weakness or failure.

Ibn ʿUmar (ﷺ) narrates that the Prophet (ﷺ) said:

«لِكُلِّ قَرْنٍ مِنْ أُمَّتِي سَابِقُونَ».

(حلية الأولياء)

> "Every generation of my nation (*ummah*) will contain people who are foremost in performing righteous deeds." (Ḥilyat al-Awlīyā')

This *ḥadīth* states that every generation will have *Sābiqūn*. This means that no generation will be empty of them, *Alḥamdulillāh*.

In each generation, Allāh (ﷻ) reinforces conviction within the hearts of the people of this nation by the presence of individuals who strive to be foremost in performing righteous deeds, and in turn other people follow their lead and example.

Imām Ibn al-Qayyim (رحمه الله) states that:

«فَاعْلَمْ أَن العَبْد إِنَّمَا يقطع منَازِل السّير إِلَى الله بِقَلْبِه، وهمته، وَلَا بِبدنِهِ، وَالتَّقوى فِي الْحَقِيقَة تقوى الْقُلُوب، لَا تقوى الْجَوَارِح».

"You must realize that a person who is truly progressing through the legs of his journey towards Allāh – it will only happen by way of his heart and his resolve, and not merely physically. True piety is piety of the heart, not piety that exists only on the limbs."

«فالكيِّسُ يقطعُ من المسافة بصحَّة العزيمة، وعلُوِّ الهِمَّة، وتجريد القَصد وصحَّة النيَّة، مع العمل القليلِ أضعافَ أضعافِ ما يقطعُه الفارِغُ من ذلك مع التعبِ الكثير، والسفَر الشاقِّ؛ فإن العزيمةَ والمحبَّة تُذهِبُ المشقَّة، وتُطيِّبُ السَّيرَ والتقدُّم».

"Therefore, a truly wise person progresses along the legs of his journey by maintaining firm resolve, aiming high, and keeping his intention pure. Sound intention combined with even relatively few deeds will allow a person to cover far more distance than someone else who lacks proper intention and exhausts himself greatly while taking on a strenuous journey. Love and firm resolve will remove the difficulty, and will make moving forward easy."

«والسَّبقُ إلى الله سُبْحَانَهُ وَتَعَالَىٰ إنما هو بالهِمَم، وصِدق الرَّغبَة والعزيمة، فيتقدَّمُ صاحبُ الهِمَّة مع سُكُونه صاحبَ العمل الكثير بمراحِل؛ فالسَّيرُ سَيرُ القلوب، والسَّبْقُ سَبْقُ الهِمَم».

(كتاب الفوائد)

> "The essence of being foremost in reaching Allāh lies in having a genuine desire and firm resolve. A person of such resolve, even when stationary, will overtake and move far ahead of someone else who lacks those internal qualities, but performs many deeds. True movement and progress along the path is that of the heart, and being foremost has to do with how high a person aims." (Kitāb al-Fawā'id)

The true people of faith are those who seek to attain the highest of levels and aspire to be admitted to the loftiest ranks of Paradise, known as *Jannah al-Firdaws.*

This is what the Messenger of Allāh (ﷺ) advised us to seek when he said:

«فَإِذَا سَأَلْتُمُ اللهَ فَاسْأَلُوهُ الْفِرْدَوْسَ».

(رواه البخاري)

> "When you ask Allāh (for something), ask for *al-Firdaws.*" (Bukhārī)

People who tread the path of the *Sābiqūn* are dignified and unique individuals. They follow the course of Allāh's Messenger (ﷺ) and adhere to His religion. Their hearts are constantly attached to the hereafter. They do not live just for themselves in order to fulfill their own interests, or to satisfy their own desires. Rather, they live for their religion and for their *ummah.* They invest their time in what will benefit them and others, and they are careful to not squander any of it.

People of high aspirations give all that they have in order to achieve their aims. They bear the responsibilities of their religion and work to further its cause. They do not despair on account of the crises and disasters which the *ummah* is experiencing. Rather, they remain firm in their outlook and are optimistic about the fact that the best final outcome will be for the people of piety (*taqwā*) who are the close friends (*Awlīyā'*) of Allāh (ﷻ).

وَاحَسْرَتَاهْ تَقَضَّى الْعُمُرُ وَانْصَرَمَتْ ۞ سَاعَاتُهُ بَيْنَ ذُلِّ الْعَجْزِ وَالْكَسَلِ

وَالْقَوْمُ قَدْ أَخَذُوا دَرْبَ النَّجَاةِ وَقَدْ ۞ سَارُوا إِلَى الْمَطْلَبِ الْأَعْلَى عَلَى مَهْلِ

A person will have deep regrets when he realizes that life is over,
And it was spent in humiliation, inability, and laziness,
While others tread the path to salvation,
And consistently headed towards the highest objective.

KHUṬBAH 76

Magnanimity and Generosity during the Holy Month of Ramaḍān

In our religion, there are many comprehensive directives which have been prescribed in order for people to have harmony with one another and care for each other. These directives inculcate within people the desire to perform righteous deeds and extend kindness to others. There is a promise of immense reward for such deeds.

One of those deeds is magnanimity and generosity. When discussing the topic of generosity during the month of generosity, there is no shortage of remarkable points that can be mentioned. How can there be when the big-heartedness of our magnanimous Prophet (ﷺ) was like the fair wind which continually blew with mercy that extended far and wide, and the peak of his generosity was during the month of Ramaḍān!

Ibn ʿAbbas (رضي الله عنهما) states:

«كَانَ النَّبِيُّ ﷺ أَجْوَدَ النَّاسِ، وَأَجْوَدُ مَا يَكُونُ فِي رَمَضَانَ، حِينَ يَلْقَاهُ جِبْرِيلُ، وَكَانَ جِبْرِيلُ عَلَيْهِ السَّلَامُ. يَلْقَاهُ فِي كُلِّ لَيْلَةٍ مِنْ رَمَضَانَ، فَيُدَارِسُهُ الْقُرْآنَ فَلَرَسُولُ اللَّهِ ﷺ أَجْوَدُ بِالْخَيْرِ مِنَ الرِّيحِ الْمُرْسَلَةِ».

(رواه البخاري)

"The Messenger of Allāh (ﷺ) was the most generous of people, and he was more generous than ever in Ramaḍān when Jibrāʾīl (عليه السلام) used to meet him. Every night in Ramaḍān, Jibrāʾīl (عليه السلام) used to come to him and the Messenger of Allāh would read the

Qur'ān to him. When he (Jibrā'īl (ﷺ)) came to him, the Messenger of Allāh (ﷺ) was more generous in giving charity than the blowing (nourishing) wind." (Bukhārī)

Commenting on the above-mentioned narration, Imām al-Nawawī (ﷺ) states:

«قَالَ أَصْحَابُنَا وَالْجُودُ وَالْأَفْضَالُ مُسْتَحَبٌّ فِي شَهْرِ رَمَضَانَ وَفِي الْعَشْرِ الْأَوَاخِرِ أَفْضَلُ اقْتِدَاءً بِرَسُولِ اللَّهِ ﷺ وَبِالسَّلَفِ وَلِأَنَّهُ شَهْرٌ شَرِيفٌ فَالْحَسَنَةُ فِيهِ أَفْضَلُ مِنْ غَيْرِهِ».

(المجموع شرح المهذب)

"Our scholars say that being generous and performing favours are highly recommended during the month of Ramaḍān, specifically during the last ten nights. By doing so, we emulate the example of the Prophet (ﷺ) as well as our predecessors. This month is honoured, and good deeds performed in this month are more blessed than they are at any other time." (Al-Majmū' Sharḥ al-Muhaddhab)

Imām al-Baghawī (ﷺ) in his renowned work *Tafsīr al-Baghawī* has mentioned the following in highlighting the magnanimity and generosity of the Prophet (ﷺ):

«بَيْنَا رَسُولُ اللَّهِ ﷺ قَاعِدًا فِيمَا بَيْنَ أَصْحَابِهِ أَتَاهُ صَبِيٌّ فَقَالَ: يَا رَسُولَ اللَّهِ إِنَّ أُمِّي تَسْتَكْسِيكَ دِرْعًا وَلَمْ يَكُنْ عِنْدَ رَسُولِ اللَّهِ ﷺ إِلَّا قَمِيصُهُ، فَقَالَ لِلصَّبِيِّ: مِنْ سَاعَةٍ إِلَى سَاعَةٍ يَظْهَرُ كَذَا، فَعُدْ إِلَيْنَا وَقْتًا آخَرَ، فَعَادَ إِلَى أُمِّهِ، فَقَالَتْ قُلْ لَهُ: أُمِّي تَسْتَكْسِيكَ الْقَمِيصَ الَّذِي عَلَيْكَ، فَدَخَلَ رَسُولُ اللَّهِ ﷺ دَارَهُ وَنَزَعَ قَمِيصَهُ وَأَعْطَاهُ».

(تفسير البغوي)

"One time while the Prophet (ﷺ) was seated with his companions, a boy came to the Prophet (ﷺ) and said: 'O Messenger of Allāh, my mother asks of you a shirt.' At that time,

> the Prophet of Allāh (ﷺ) had no shirt except for the one that was on his blessed body. He told the boy: 'Come some other time when we have enough means to respond to what your mother is asking for.' The boy went back home, and returned and said: 'My mother says that you kindly give her the very shirt that you have on your blessed body.' Hearing this, the Prophet (ﷺ) took the shirt off and gave it to him." (Tafsīr al-Baghawī)

Some of the definitions of generosity are:

- The quality or fact of being plentiful or large.
- The quality of being noble and kind.
- The quality of being willing to share more than is usual or expected.
- The freedom from pettiness in character and mind.

From these definitions, we can conclude that generosity and magnanimity are not limited to giving money only. Rather, it is a much more comprehensive concept.

Generosity, kindness, and magnanimity all go together and complement one another. They are noble words which apply to all that is praiseworthy, and to every kind of goodness, giving, and honourable conduct.

It is for this very reason that some scholars have said:

«الكرمُ اسمٌ واقعٌ على كل أنواعِ الفضائل، ولفظٌ جامعٌ لمعاني السماحةِ والبذلِ والنوائِلِ».

(مكارم الأخلاق)

> "Magnanimity is a term that covers every type of virtuous conduct, and it is a comprehensive word which includes all meanings of tolerance and giving." (Makārim al-Akhlāq)

Nobility and magnanimity are comprehensive concepts. A person should be benevolent when dealing with one's Lord. That comes about by having the correct beliefs, worshipping Allāh (ﷻ) in the best way, and being sincerely devoted to Him.

A person should be magnanimous in dealing with Prophet Muḥammad (ﷺ). That comes about by emulating, loving, and respecting him.

A person should be considerate when dealing with oneself as well. That comes about by doing what preserves one's dignity and brings one honour, and by keeping away from all that which can lead a person to disgrace, humiliation and embarrassment.

Allāh (ﷻ) says about such people:

﴿وَإِذَا مَرُّوا۟ بِٱللَّغْوِ مَرُّوا۟ كِرَامًا ﴿٧٢﴾﴾ [الفُرْقَان الآية ٧٢]

> "And, when they pass by frivolous (useless) acts, they pass by gracefully (they walk away with dignity without unnecessarily arguing with the participants, and they do not partake in such things)." (Furqān 25:72)

A person should be magnanimous in dealing with his family, relatives, and people in general. That comes about by treating them with fairness, kindness, generosity, and tolerance.

When a person sacrifices one's own personal comforts and tires oneself in order to benefit others, that is the utmost form of nobility and magnanimity which anyone can offer.

Our honoured Messenger (ﷺ) set the best example of magnanimity and generosity - he gave all that he had, and all kinds of different things. He devoted himself and all that he had to other people.

Anas (رضي الله عنه) narrates:

«مَا سُئِلَ رَسُولُ اللهِ ﷺ شَيْئًا إِلَّا أَعْطَاهُ، قَالَ: فَجَاءَهُ رَجُلٌ فَأَعْطَاهُ غَنَمًا بَيْنَ جَبَلَيْنِ».

(رواه مسلم)

> "There was nothing that the Messenger (ﷺ) was asked for but he gave it away. A man once asked him for a herd of sheep that

were grazing between two mountains, and he gave it to him." (Muslim)

Those who experienced the kindness and generosity of the Prophet (ﷺ) first hand would say:

«فَإِنَّ مُحَمَّدًا يُعْطِي عَطَاءً لاَ يَخْشَى الْفَاقَةَ».

(رواه مسلم)

"Muḥammad gives so much as if he has no fear of poverty." (Muslim)

A truly noble and generous person spends his time to serve others. They also utilize the prominence that they have for good causes, such as interceding to help others, assisting the downtrodden, and helping the weak fulfill their needs. The Prophet's (ﷺ) companions (رضي الله عنهم) also followed his example in magnanimity and generosity until they reached the heights of benevolence.

ʿUmar ibn al-Khaṭṭāb (رضي الله عنه) used to go every night to the house of a blind and disabled old woman who had no one to help her, in order to attend to her needs and take the garbage out of her house.

Imām al-Awzāʿī reports:

«أَنَّ عُمَرَ بْنَ الْخَطَّابِ، رَضِيَ اللهُ عَنْهُ خَرَجَ فِي سَوَادِ اللَّيْلِ اللَّيْلِ فَرَآهُ طَلْحَةُ، فَذَهَبَ عُمَرُ فَدَخَلَ بَيْتًا ثُمَّ دَخَلَ بَيْتًا آخَرَ، فَلَمَّا أَصْبَحَ طَلْحَةُ ذَهَبَ إِلَى ذَلِكَ الْبَيْتِ فَإِذَا بِعَجُوزٍ عَمْيَاءَ مُقْعَدَةٍ، فَقَالَ لَهَا: مَا بَالُ هَذَا الرَّجُلِ يَأْتِيكِ؟ قَالَتْ: إِنَّهُ يَتَعَاهَدُنِي مُنْذُ كَذَا وَكَذَا، يَأْتِينِي بِمَا يُصْلِحُنِي، وَيُخْرِجُ عَنِّي الْأَذَى، فَقَالَ طَلْحَةُ: ثَكِلَتْكَ أُمُّكَ يَا طَلْحَةُ أَعَثَرَاتِ عُمَرَ تَتْبَعُ؟».

(حلية الأولياء لأبي نعيم)

"ʿUmar (رضي الله عنه) used to walk out of his house secretly at night. One night Ṭalḥa saw this and so he followed him. Ṭalḥa saw ʿUmar going to one house, and after some time he came out and proceeded to another house before he returned to his own

> home. In the morning, Ṭalḥa went to the house which he saw 'Umar entering at night. He knocked on the door to find a blind old woman who was handicapped and disabled. He asked her: 'Who is the man that visited you last night?' She replied: 'He has been taking care of me for such a long time now. He brings me whatever I need, and then he removes the garbage.' Ṭalḥa excused himself and left, then he admonished himself and said: 'May your mother mourn for you and be bereaved over you. O Ṭalḥa, you are spying on 'Umar and questioning his deeds?'" (Ḥilyat al-Awliyā' of Ibn Nuʿaym)

Therefore, there has to be big-heartedness in magnanimity and generosity by giving from one's own self through personifying distinguished conduct, smiling, remaining patient, being gentle, tolerating and overlooking the wrong which others might do, and staying far away from malice, jealousy, and hatred.

Both inwardly and outwardly, a person should love for others what one loves for oneself. An individual should feel happy when others are happy, sad when they are sad, and one should not seek to take away what others have.

Imām al-Nawawī (ﷺ) defining envy writes:

«وَهُوَ تمني زوالُ النعمة عن صاحبها: سواءٌ كَانَتْ نعمة دينٍ أَوْ دنيا».

(رياض الصالحين)

> "Envy is the desire for someone who has a blessing to be deprived of it, whether it is a religious or worldly blessing." (Riyāḍ al-Ṣāliḥīn)

People of magnanimity and generosity know no miserliness, stinginess, or hatred, because they know that if they give something, they will gain multiples of what they gave.

Allāh (ﷻ) says in the Qur'ān:

﴿مَن جَآءَ بِٱلۡحَسَنَةِ فَلَهُۥ عَشۡرُ أَمۡثَالِهَاۖ وَمَن جَآءَ بِٱلسَّيِّئَةِ فَلَا يُجۡزَىٰٓ إِلَّا مِثۡلَهَا ١٦٠﴾

[الأَنْعَام الآية ١٦٠]

"Whoever brings a good deed (carries out an accepted act) will receive ten times as much (in reward, and even more)." (Anʿām 6:160)

The door is open for plentiful forms of magnanimity and kindness, such as pardoning those who did wrong to you, overlooking those who offended you, visiting those who cut off ties with you, extending invitations to both Muslims and non-Muslims, accepting people's apologies, and forgiving their mistakes.

Nobility and generosity may also be realized by a useful idea that you offer to your workplace or to your society. It could include giving money, knowledge, and providing information and experience. You can help others by contributing your time and efforts as well.

Magnanimity and charity can be realized by removing harmful objects from the roads or sidewalks, and acting in the best interests of people.

Altruism and generosity should be ordained for all categories and classes of people, and it is not hard to achieve this: smiling at others, visiting relatives, uttering a good word, praying for someone else, spending some of your own money on others, etc. are all acts of magnanimity and selflessness.

Each one of us is capable of such etiquettes and we can serve Allāh's (ﷻ) creation with our deeds and words.

It has been narrated that:

«مَرَّ رَجُلٌ بِغُصْنِ شَجَرَةٍ عَلَى ظَهْرِ طَرِيقٍ، فَقَالَ : وَاللّٰهِ لَأُنَحِّيَنَّ هَذَا عَنِ الْمُسْلِمِينَ لَا يُؤْذِيهِمْ فَأُدْخِلَ الْجَنَّةَ».

(رواه مسلم)

"A man passed by a branch of a tree leaning over a road and decided to remove it, saying to himself: 'By Allāh! I will remove this from the path of the Muslims so that it would not harm them.' (On account of this) he was admitted to Paradise." (Muslim)

Another narration mentions:

«أَنَّ امْرَأَةً بَغِيًّا رَأَتْ كَلْبًا فِي يَوْمٍ حَارٍّ يُطِيفُ بِبِئْرٍ، قَدْ أَدْلَعَ لِسَانَهُ مِنَ الْعَطَشِ، فَنَزَعَتْ لَهُ بِمُوقِهَا فَغُفِرَ لَهَا».

(رواه مسلم)

"A prostitute saw a dog circling around a well on a hot day and hanging out its tongue because of thirst. She drew water for it in her shoe and as a result, she was pardoned (for this act of hers)." (Muslim)

It has also been mentioned that the Prophet (ﷺ) said:

«أَحَبُّ النَّاسِ إِلَى اللَّهِ أَنْفَعُهُمْ لِلنَّاسِ، وَأَحَبُّ الْأَعْمَالِ إِلَى اللَّهِ سُرُورٍ تُدْخِلُهُ عَلَى مُسْلِمٍ، أَوْ تَكْشِفُ عَنْهُ كُرْبَةً، أَوْ تَقْضِي عَنْهُ دِينًا، أَوْ تُطْرَدُ عَنْهُ جُوعًا، وَلِأَنْ أَمْشِيَ مَعَ أَخٍ لِي فِي حَاجَةٍ أَحَبُّ إِلَيَّ مِنْ أَنْ أَعْتَكِفَ فِي هَذَا الْمَسْجِدِ، يَعْنِي مَسْجِدَ الْمَدِينَةِ ، شَهْرًا، وَمَنْ مَشَى مَعَ أَخِيهِ فِي حَاجَةٍ حَتَّى أَثْبَتَهَا لَهُ أَثْبَتَ اللَّهُ عَزَّ وَجَلَّ قَدَمَهُ عَلَى الصِّرَاطِ يَوْمَ تَزِلُّ فِيهِ الْأَقْدَامُ».

(المعجم الأوسط للطبراني)

"The most beloved people to Allāh are those who are most beneficial to the people. The most beloved deed to Allāh is to make a Muslim happy, or to remove one of his troubles, or to forgive his debt, or to feed his hunger. If I walk with a brother regarding a need (go with him in order to try and fulfill his difficulty), it is more beloved to me than if I was to seclude myself in this *masjid* in Madīnah for a month. Whoever walks with his brother regarding a need until he secures it for him, Allāh will make his footing firm across the bridge on the day when the footings will shake." (Al-Muʿjam al-Awsaṭ of al-Ṭabarānī)

Generosity, nobility, and magnanimity are all qualities that prompt people to extend good to others without reminding them, taunting them, or making them feel as if they have done them a favour.

Allāh (ﷻ) says:

﴿يَـٰٓأَيُّهَا ٱلَّذِينَ ءَامَنُوا۟ لَا تُبْطِلُوا۟ صَدَقَـٰتِكُم بِٱلْمَنِّ وَٱلْأَذَىٰ﴾ [البَقَرَة الآية ٢٦٤]

"O you who believe! Do not make your charities fruitless (invalidated) by reproachfully reminding the recipient about your favour or making them feel insulted." (Baqarah 2:264)

Furthermore, the best form of nobility and munificence is to personify admirable conduct.

Jaʿfar ibn Muḥammad al-Ṣādiq (رحمه الله) states:

«إِنَّ للهِ مِنْ خَلْقِهِ وُجُوهًا خَلَقَهُمْ لِحَوَائِجِ النَّاسِ يَرْغَبُونَ فِي الأَجْرِ، وَيَعُدُّونَ الجُودَ مَجْدًا، وَاللهُ يُحِبُّ مَكَارِمَ الأَخْلاقِ».

(ربيع الأبرار ونصوص الأخيار للزمخشري)

"Indeed, Allāh has placed among people certain individuals who are prominent and influential. He created them in order to fulfill the needs of His servants. They see generosity as an honour, and they see extending goodness as a profit. Allāh truly loves noble conduct." (Rabīʿ al-Abrār wa Nuṣūṣ al-Akhyār of al-Zamakhsharī)

Part of being big-hearted is to pray for others.

Some righteous people have wisely stated:

«إنني أسأل الجنة لإخواني في صلاتي، أفأبخل عليهم في صِلاتي؟!».

(موسوعة نضرة النعيم)

> "When I pray, I certainly ask Allāh to grant my brothers Paradise. How can I be miserly towards them even in my prayer?" (Mawsūʿah Naḍrat al-Naʿīm)

Part of magnanimity is to do good to others.

ʿAbdullāh ibn Jaʿfar (ﷺ) states:

«أَمْطِرِ الْمَعْرُوفَ مَطَرًا فَإِنْ أَصَابَ الْكِرَامَ كَانُوا لَهُ أَهْلًا، وَإِنْ أَصَابَ اللِّئَامَ كُنْتَ لَهُ أَهْلًا».

(موسوعة نضرة النعيم)

> "Strive to do good to others as abundantly and inclusively as the rainfall. If it reaches noble people, then that will befit them because they deserve it. If it reaches ignoble people, then that will still befit your generosity." (Mawsūʿah Naḍrat al-Naʿīm)

Part of magnanimity and kindness is to honour and respect other people.

«من أكرمكَ فأكرِمه، ومن استخفَّ بك فأكرِم نفسَك بالكفِّ عنه».

(روضة العقلاء)

> "When someone honours you, then honour him in return. When someone belittles you, then honour yourself by leaving him alone." (Rawḍat al-ʿUqalāʾ)

Magnanimity and generosity have positive effects on the benefactor, community, and the whole society at large.

These noble etiquettes have no limits and are not subject to any conditions, and should be extended to those whom we love, and even to those whom we may not love.

ʿAlī ibn Abī Ṭālib (ﷺ) says:

«إِذَا أَقْبَلَتْ عَلَيْكَ الدُّنْيَا، فَأَنْفِقْ، فَإِنَّهَا لا تَفْنَى، وَإِذَا أَدْبَرَتْ عَنْكَ، فَأَنْفِقْ ، فَإِنَّهَا لا تَبْقَى».

(موسوعة نضرة النعيم)

"If you are blessed with affluence in this world, then give of what you have (to others) because it will not finish. If you are not blessed with affluence, then still give because the life of this world is temporary." (Mawsūʿah Naḍrat al-Naʿīm)

«وكرمُ الرجلِ يُحبِّبُه إلى عُبَّاده، وبُخلُه يُبغِّضُه إلى أولادِه، ومن جادَ سادَ، والجُودُ حارِسُ الأعراض».

(موسوعة نضرة النعيم)

"When a man is noble and generous, that will make him beloved even to his opponents, but when he is miserly, even his own children will despise him. When a person is generous, that is when he will have true prominence. Generosity will guard a person's integrity." (Mawsūʿah Naḍrat al-Naʿīm)

Ibn al-Sammāk (ﷺ) says:

«عجِبتُ لمن يشتري المماليكَ بمالِه، ولا يشتِري الأحرارَ بمعروفِه».

(موسوعة نضرة النعيم)

"I am astonished that someone will purchase slaves with his wealth, but will not purchase free people by winning them over with his kind treatment." (Mawsūʿah Naḍrat al-Naʿīm)

This is why the Prophet (ﷺ) has alluded to the fact that:

«إِنَّكُمْ لَنْ تَسَعُوا النَّاسَ بِأَمْوَالِكُمْ، وَلَكِنْ يَسَعُهُمْ مِنْكُمْ بَسْطُ الْوَجْهِ وَحُسْنُ الْخُلُقِ».

(مصنف ابن أبي شيبة)

"You can never gain people's love and admiration by your money, rather let your smiling faces and noble character gain their love and admiration." (Muṣannaf Ibn Abī Shaybah)

Therefore, the scholars say that in a comprehensive sense, magnanimity and generosity is:

«السخاءُ أن تكون بمالِك مُتبرِّعًا، وعما في يدِ غيرِك مُتورِّعًا».

(الوابل الصيب)

"To give from what you own, and refrain from taking what other people own." (Al-Wābil al-Ṣayyib)

At the same time, a noble and generous person must be aware of never letting fear of embarrassment be the factor that motivates one to give. Rather, a person must give voluntarily out of one's own benevolence, not reluctantly or out of fear.

A famous proverb says:

«لا تكُنْ مثلَ الصائدِ يُلقي الحَبَّ للطائرِ وهو لا يُريدُ نفعَه، بل يُريدُ نفعَ نفسِه».

(العقد الفريد)

"Do not be like a hunter who tosses seeds for birds, but he does not intend to do good for them. Rather, his goal is to achieve personal gain." (Al-ʿIqd al-Farīd)

This is why ʿAlī ibn Abī Ṭālib (؈) said:

«السَّخَاءُ مَا كَانَ ابْتِدَاءً فَأَمَّا مَا كَانَ عَنْ مَسْأَلَةٍ فَحَيَاءٌ وَتَذَمُّمٌ».

(ربيع الأبرار ونصوص الأخيار للزمخشري)

"True magnanimity is to give pre-emptively without being asked. As for giving after being asked, that is motivated by a person's shyness or his fear of being blamed if he does not give anything." (Rabīʿ al-Abrār wa Nuṣūṣ al-Akhyār of al-Zamakhsharī)

At the same time, we must remove all of the obstacles in order to attain magnanimity and generosity, the most important of which is helplessness, which is often the main cause of disregard.

The Prophet (ﷺ) would supplicate:

«اللَّهُمَّ إِنِّي أَعُوذُ بِكَ مِنَ الْعَجْزِ».

(رواه مسلم)

> "O Allāh! I seek refuge in You from helplessness (to do good)." (Muslim)

The Prophet (ﷺ) also encouraged us to seek the assistance of Allāh (ﷻ) and not feel helpless.

The Prophet (ﷺ) stated:

«وَاسْتَعِنْ بِاللَّهِ، وَلَا تَعْجَزْ».

(رواه مسلم)

> "Seek the help of Allāh, and do not give up (do not feel helpless)." (Muslim)

The feeling of helplessness will weaken determination, kill ambition, and make one lose the desire to be noble and generous, which is an important part of a human's personality and potential. A weak person will look for trivial reasons and excuses to justify one's helplessness and inability.

Scholars of *ḥadīth* explain that: "To seek the assistance of Allāh and not feel helpless" means:

«قُم وانهَض وبادِر وانطلِق، وقبل ذلك ومعه وبعده: استعِن بالله، وستجِدُ الخيرَ يتدفَّق، والعونَ يتزايَد، والتوفيقَ من ربِّك حادِيكَ وناصِرُك».

> "Rise, take the initiative, and move forward, but in all cases seek the help of Allāh, and you will find that good, flowing

assistance will increase, and your Lord will support you and grant you success."

Consequently, this noble month is one of benevolence, giving, and kindness. So, let us continue to be kind and considerate, however little it may be, because regular, small deeds are better than big, intermittent ones.

The Prophet (ﷺ) said:

«أَحَبُّ الأَعْمَالِ إِلَى اللَّهِ تَعَالَى أَدْوَمُهَا وَإِنْ قَلَّ».

(رواه مسلم)

"The acts most pleasing of actions to Allāh, the Most-High are those which are done regularly, even if they are small." (Muslim)

A continuous drop of water can one day become a large stream.

حَاوِلْ جَسِيمَاتِ الأُمُورِ وَلا تَقُلْ ۞ إِنَّ الْمَحَامِدَ وَالْعُلَى أَرْزَاقُ

وَارْغَبْ بِنَفْسِكَ أَنْ تَكُونَ مُقَصِّرًا ۞ عَنْ غَايَةٍ فِيهَا الطِّلابُ سِبَاقُ

(فيض القدير شرح الجامع الصغير)

Do not back out of important tasks. Rather, endeavour to accomplish them without saying that:
"Great achievements have already been decreed by Allāh for people other than me."
Do not allow yourself to fall short in any objective which deserves to be striven for.

(Fayḍ al-Qadīr Sharh al-Jāmiʿ al-Ṣaghīr)

KHUṬBAH 77

Not Losing One's Good Deeds in the Month of Ramaḍān

The month of Ramaḍān is a tremendously blessed month which has many virtues, provides numerous opportunities to obey Allāh (ﷻ), and perform various acts of worship. We are now in the final and best nights and days of this month, those being the last ten.

Our Prophet (ﷺ) would exert himself during these final ten days by performing additional acts of worship. He would pray during the nights, and also advise his family members to do the same.

ʿĀ'ishah (رضي الله عنها) states:

«إِذَا دَخَلَ الْعَشْرُ، أَحْيَا اللَّيْلَ، وَأَيْقَظَ أَهْلَهُ، وَجَدَّ وَشَدَّ الْمِئْزَرَ».

(متفق عليه)

> "When the last ten nights (of Ramaḍān) would begin, the Messenger of Allāh (ﷺ) would keep awake at night (for prayers and devotion), awaken his family, and prepare himself to be more diligent in worship." (Agreed Upon)

Accordingly, we must remain steadfast in performing righteous deeds, hope for Allāh's (ﷻ) reward, and take advantage of the opportunities which Allāh (ﷻ) offers us in order to earn His ultimate mercy and forgiveness. However, we must be cautious of not becoming proud, or thinking highly of the acts of worship that we carry out.

Since the month of Ramaḍān is the month of the Qur'ān, let us take this opportunity to reflect on a verse (*āyah*) from the Book of Allāh, as an encouragement to remain resolute and keep ourselves in check. It is an *āyah* which should soften the hearts that have become hard, and awaken the souls that are neglectful; an *āyah* which calls for deep contemplation and reflection; and it is an *āyah* which places reverential fear in the hearts of Allāh's (ﷻ) servants and causes their tears to flow.

The *Salaf al-Ṣāliḥīn* (رحمهم الله) contemplated on the meanings of the Qur'ān and had a deep understanding of it. As a result, the admonitions of the Qur'ān affected them profoundly, and they took heed of its warnings.

The *āyah* being referred to which we want to reflect upon is the statement of Allāh (ﷻ) where He says:

﴿وَبَدَا لَهُم مِّنَ ٱللَّهِ مَا لَمْ يَكُونُوا۟ يَحْتَسِبُونَ ﴿٤٧﴾﴾ [الزُّمَر الآية ٤٧]

> "And such things will (then) become apparent (appear) to them from Allāh, which they had never taken into account (they did not imagine or did not expect)." (Zumar 39:47)

The *Salaf al-Ṣāliḥīn* (رحمهم الله) would fear for themselves due to this *āyah*.

Sufyān ibn 'Uyaynah (رحمه الله) relates:

«لَمَّا حَضَرَتْ مُحَمَّدَ بنَ المنكدرِ الوفاةُ جَزِعَ فَدَعُوا له أبا حازمٍ ليُخفِّفَ عنه من جزَعِه، فقال له ابنُ المُنكَدِر: إن الله يقول: ﴿وَبَدَا لَهُم مِّنَ ٱللَّهِ مَا لَمْ يَكُونُوا۟ يَحْتَسِبُونَ ﴿٤٧﴾﴾ [الزُّمَر الآية ٤٧]، فأخافُ أن يبدُوَ لي من الله ما لم أكن أحتسِب. فجعل يبكِيَان. فقال أهلُ ابنِ المُنكَدِر: دعوناكَ لتُخفِّف عنه، فزِدتَّه جزَعًا».

(سير أعلام النبلاء)

> "When Muḥammad ibn al-Munkadir was on his deathbed, he became very frightened and anxious. They called Abū Ḥāzim to put him to ease. However, Muḥammad ibn al-Munkadir said to him: 'Allāh has indeed said: 'And that which they did not

expect from Allāh will become apparent to them,' and I am worried that what I did not expect from Allāh will become apparent to me.' Then both men started weeping, and the family of Muḥammad ibn al-Munkadir said to Abū Ḥāzim: 'We sought your help to put him to ease, but all you did was intensify his fear and anxiety.'" (Siyar Aʿlām al-Nubalā')

Once someone told Sulaymān al-Taymī (ﷺ):

«أنت أنت، ومن مثلُك؟! فقال: مَهْ! لا تقولوا هذا، لا أدري ما يبدُو لي من الله، سمعتُ الله يقول: ﴿وَبَدَا لَهُم مِّنَ ٱللَّهِ مَا لَمْ يَكُونُواْ يَحْتَسِبُونَ ﴿٤٧﴾﴾ [الزُّمَر الآية ٤٧]».

(سير أعلام النبلاء)

"You are one of a kind! There is no one like you." He responded by saying: "What do you mean? Do not say that! I do not know what Allāh will do to me. I have heard His statement: 'And that which they did not expect from Allāh will become apparent to them.'" (Siyar Aʿlām al-Nubalā')

It is reported that Sufyān al-Thawrī (ﷺ) read this *āyah* and said:

«وَيْلٌ لِأَهْلِ الرِّيَاءِ وَيْلٌ لِأَهْلِ الرِّيَاءِ هَذِهِ آيَتُهُمْ وَقِصَّتُهُمْ».

(تفسير القرطبي)

"Ruined are those who do good deeds only to pretend their piety before people, i.e. those who show off their deeds. (He repeated this sentence twice) This verse is in reference to them." (Tafsīr al-Qurṭubī)

Muqātil (ﷺ) says:

«ظَهَرَ لَهُمْ حِينَ بُعِثُوا مَا لَمْ يَحْتَسِبُوا فِي الدُّنْيَا أَنَّهُ نَازِلٌ بِهِمْ فِي الْآخِرَةِ».

(تفسير البغوي)

"While they were in this world, they never expected that certain things would happen to them in the hereafter. However, when they are brought back to life, they will have to face those things." (Tafsīr al-Baghawī)

Imām al-Suddī (ﷺ) states:

«ظَنُّوا أَنَّهَا حَسَنَاتٌ فَبَدَتْ لَهُمْ سَيِّئَاتٍ».

(تفسير البغوي)

"They thought that their deeds were righteous, only to find that they were all sins." (Tafsīr al-Baghawī)

Scholars have explained that:

«إن من الذين يبدُو لهم من الله ما لم يكونوا يحتسِبُون: قومٌ عمِلُوا أعمالًا صالِحةً، ولكن كانت عليهم مظالِم، فظنُّوا أن أعمالَهم الصالِحة ستُنجِيهم، فجاء الحسابُ، فبدَا لهم من الله ما لم يكونوا يحتسِبُون».

(تفسير البغوي)

"The people who will find what they did not expect from Allāh are the ones who performed righteous deeds, but they wronged others, and thought that their righteous deeds will save them. Consequently, at the time of reckoning, that which they did not expect from Allāh will become apparent to them." (Tafsīr al-Baghawī)

Ibn ʿAṭiyyah (ﷺ) says:

«كانت ظنونٌ في الدنيا مُتفرّقةً مُتنوّعة حسب ضلالاتهم وتخيُّلاتهم فيما يعتقِدون، فإذا عايَنوا العذابَ يوم القيامة، وقصَّرَت بهم حالاتُهم، ظهرَ لكل واحدٍ ما كان يظنُّ».

(المحرر الوجيز في تفسير الكتاب العزيز - تفسير ابن عطية)

> "While they were still in this world, they had various expectations based on their own imaginations and deviant beliefs. However, on the Day of Reckoning when they see the punishment with their very own eyes, and their deeds fall short, then they will realize the falsity of what they previously believed." (Al-Muḥarrar al-Wajīz fī Tafsīr al-Kitāb al-ʿAzīz – Tafsīr of ibn ʿAṭīyah)

This should bring to our minds the *ḥadīth* about someone who will end up bankrupt on the Day of Judgement - he will have mountains of good deeds, but because he physically harmed others, insulted them, and took their property unlawfully, they will have nothing.

Abū Hurairah (ﷺ) narrates that once the Prophet (ﷺ) asked:

«أَتَدْرُونَ مَا الْمُفْلِسُ؟ قَالُوا: الْمُفْلِسُ فِينَا مَنْ لَا دِرْهَمَ لَهُ وَلَا مَتَاعَ، فَقَالَ: إِنَّ الْمُفْلِسَ مِنْ أُمَّتِي يَأْتِي يَوْمَ الْقِيَامَةِ بِصَلَاةٍ، وَصِيَامٍ، وَزَكَاةٍ، وَيَأْتِي قَدْ شَتَمَ هَذَا، وَقَذَفَ هَذَا، وَأَكَلَ مَالَ هَذَا، وَسَفَكَ دَمَ هَذَا، وَضَرَبَ هَذَا، فَيُعْطَى هَذَا مِنْ حَسَنَاتِهِ، وَهَذَا مِنْ حَسَنَاتِهِ، فَإِنْ فَنِيَتْ حَسَنَاتُهُ قَبْلَ أَنْ يُقْضَى مَا عَلَيْهِ أُخِذَ مِنْ خَطَايَاهُمْ فَطُرِحَتْ عَلَيْهِ، ثُمَّ طُرِحَ فِي النَّارِ».

(رواه مسلم)

"Do you know who is poor?" The companions replied: "The poor among us is the one who has neither money, nor any property." The Prophet (ﷺ) explained: "The poor amongst my nation is the one who will come on the Day of Resurrection with (a lot) of *ṣalāt*, *ṣawm*, and *zakāt*, but who had abused somebody, slandered someone, usurped the goods of another person, shed blood or beaten another person. So this one and that one will be given a part of the aggressor's good deeds, and should his good deeds fall short before he clears what he owes (to other people), then the aggrieved person's sins and faults will be transferred over from them to him, and he will be thrown into the hellfire." (Muslim)

Some of the *Salaf al-Ṣāliḥīn* (﷢) state that:

«كم من موقفٍ خِزيٍ يوم القيامة لم يخطُر على بالِك قطُّ».

(مجموع رسائل ابن رجب الحنبلي)

"There are many situations which may disgrace you on the Day of Judgement, but they never crossed your mind." (Majmūʿ Rasāʾil of Ibn Rajab al-Ḥanbalī)

Allāh (ﷻ) says in the Qurʾān:

﴿لَّقَدْ كُنتَ فِى غَفْلَةٍ مِّنْ هَٰذَا فَكَشَفْنَا عَنكَ غِطَآءَكَ فَبَصَرُكَ ٱلْيَوْمَ حَدِيدٌ ۝﴾

[ق الآية ٢٢]

"You were certainly heedless (unmindful) about this (day). We have removed your veils from you (opened your eyes) and your vision (insight) is ever sharp today (you can now see what was unseen to you in the world)." (Qāf 50:22)

What will happen to a person who performed deeds which one thought were righteous, but forgot all about the sins, thought nothing of them, or had the wrong intentions, and then that which one did not expect from Allāh (ﷻ) will become apparent to them?

Allāh (ﷻ) says:

﴿ٱلَّذِينَ ضَلَّ سَعْيُهُمْ فِى ٱلْحَيَوٰةِ ٱلدُّنْيَا وَهُمْ يَحْسَبُونَ أَنَّهُمْ يُحْسِنُونَ صُنْعًا ۝﴾

[الكهف الآية ١٠٤]

"They are those whose efforts (good acts) are destroyed in this worldly life (not accepted by Allāh because their intentions are incorrect), while they think that they are (definitely) carrying out good acts (and that they will be rewarded)." (Kahf 18:104)

﴿وَقَدِمْنَآ إِلَىٰ مَا عَمِلُوا۟ مِنْ عَمَلٍ فَجَعَلْنَٰهُ هَبَآءً مَّنثُورًا ۝﴾ [الفرقان الآية ٢٣]

"And We will then turn (Our attention) to their (good) deeds and reduce them to scattered dust (render them worthless)."
(Furqān 25:23)

NOTE: The dust referred to in this verse are those microscopic particles of dust that are usually seen in rays of sunlight that filters through tiny holes like air vents. Although they are many in number, but they cannot serve any purpose. Similarly, the deeds of many people will be of no avail to them in the hereafter.[67]

Likewise, it is always important to remember that during this blessed month, just like during other times of the year, we must be cautious of not committing any sins, even while we are alone, and think that no one can see us.

Thawbān (ﷺ) narrates that the Prophet (ﷺ) said:

«لَأَعْلَمَنَّ أَقْوَامًا مِنْ أُمَّتِي يَأْتُونَ يَوْمَ الْقِيَامَةِ بِحَسَنَاتٍ أَمْثَالِ جِبَالِ تِهَامَةَ بِيضًا، فَيَجْعَلُهَا اللَّهُ عَزَّ وَجَلَّ هَبَاءً مَنْثُورًا، قَالَ ثَوْبَانُ: يَا رَسُولَ اللَّهِ صِفْهُمْ لَنَا، جَلِّهِمْ لَنَا أَنْ لَا نَكُونَ مِنْهُمْ، وَنَحْنُ لَا نَعْلَمُ، قَالَ: أَمَا إِنَّهُمْ إِخْوَانُكُمْ، وَمِنْ جِلْدَتِكُمْ، وَيَأْخُذُونَ مِنَ اللَّيْلِ كَمَا تَأْخُذُونَ، وَلَكِنَّهُمْ أَقْوَامٌ إِذَا خَلَوْا بِمَحَارِمِ اللَّهِ انْتَهَكُوهَا».

(سنن ابن ماجه)

"There will be people among my nation who will have deeds as large as the mountains of Tihāmah. However, Allāh will turn those deeds into dust." Thawbān asked: "O Messenger of Allāh, describe them to us clearly so that we will not be among them without realizing it." The Prophet (ﷺ) explained: "They are your brothers, and are people just like you. They pray at night

---

[67] The Arabic text of this is as follows:

وَالْهَبَاءُ: هُوَ الَّذِي يُرَى كَهَيْئَةِ الْغُبَارِ إِذَا دَخَلَ ضَوْءُ الشَّمْسِ مِنْ كُوَّةٍ يَحْسَبُهُ النَّاظِرُ غُبَارًا لَيْسَ بِشَيْءٍ تَقْبِضُ عَلَيْهِ الْأَيْدِي، وَلَا تَمَسَّهُ، وَلَا يُرَى ذَلِكَ فِي الظِّلِّ.

(تفسير الطبري)

just like you do, but when they are alone, they perpetrate what Allāh has prohibited." (Sunan Ibn Mājah)

Sālim, the freed slave of Abū Ḥudhayfah (ﷺ) says:

«خَشِيتُ أَنْ أَكُونَ مِنْهُمْ، فَقَالَ: أَمَا إِنَّهُمْ كَانُوا يَصُومُونَ، وَيُصَلُّونَ، وَيَقُومُونَ لَيْلَهُمْ، وَلَكِنَّهُمْ إِذَا شَرَعَ لَهُمْ شَيْءٌ مِنَ الْحَرَامِ وَثَبُوا عَلَيْهِ، فَأَحْبَطَ اللَّهُ عَزَّ وَجَلَّ أَعْمَالَهُمْ».

(حلية الأولياء وطبقات الأصفياء)

"I feared that I would be one of them," and then he added: "Perhaps if anything impermissible is presented to them, they engage in it, and then Allāh will render their deeds void as a result of this." (Ḥilyat al-Awliyā' wa Ṭabaqāt al-Aṣfiyā')

Allāh (ﷻ) says:

﴿وَتَحْسَبُونَهُۥ هَيِّنًا وَهُوَ عِندَ ٱللَّهِ عَظِيمٌ ﴿١٥﴾﴾ [النُّور الآية ١٥]

"And you think that it is very small, whereas it is tremendously grave with Allāh." (Nūr 24:15)

Therefore, we must be careful of self-admiration and false hopes, while indulging in sins. Beware of belittling misdeeds, and never think that any sin is too small.

Anas (ﷺ) would say:

«إِنَّكُمْ تَعْمَلُونَ أَعْمَالًا هِيَ أَدَقُّ فِي أَعْيُنِكُمْ مِنَ الشَّعْرِ، إِنْ كُنَّا لَنَعُدُّهَا عَلَى عَهْدِ النَّبِيِّ ﷺ مِنَ الْمُوبِقَاتِ».

(رواه البخاري)

"You perpetrate (evil) acts which you consider smaller than a hair, however during the time of the Messenger of Allāh (ﷺ) we used to consider them as major sins that could destroy someone." (Bukhārī)

There are some sins which nullify deeds and eat away their rewards such as: envy, wanting others to see and hear about what you do, backbiting, slander, arrogance, oppression, conceit, consuming impermissible things, severing ties of kinship, etc.

The most vital development and growth that must take place is to fill our souls and hearts with Allāh (ﷻ); and when someone thinks well of Allāh (ﷻ) and expects the best from Him, then that person will perform the best deeds that one can.

Ibn ʿAwn (رحمه الله) states:

«لَا تَثِقْ بِكَثْرَةِ الْعَمَلِ، فَإِنَّكَ لَا تَدْرِي تُقْبَلُ مِنْكَ أَمْ لَا، وَلَا تَأْمَنْ ذُنُوبَكَ، فَإِنَّكَ لَا تَدْرِي هَلْ كُفِّرَتْ عَنْكَ أَمْ لَا، إِنَّ عَمَلَكَ عَنْكَ مُغَيَّبٌ مَا تَدْرِي مَا اللهُ صَانِعٌ فِيهِ، أَيَجْعَلُهُ فِي سِجِّينَ، أَمْ يَجْعَلُهُ فِي عِلِّيِّينَ».

(شعب الإيمان للبيهقي)

"Do not feel secure about a great number of deeds (that you may have performed) because you do not know whether or not they were accepted; and do not feel immune about the consequences of your sins because you do not know whether or not they were forgiven. You do not know what Allāh will do with your deeds because their outcome is concealed from you." (Shuʿab al-Īmān of al-Bayhaqī)

When someone follows his own inclinations and hopes to be forgiven without repenting or taking the necessary steps, then he is truly incapable of attaining his objective.

The *Salaf al-Ṣāliḥīn* (رحمهم الله) worked diligently in perfecting their actions and making them faultless, then after that, they showed great concern for the acceptance of their actions. They did this because they feared that their actions would be rejected.

It is reported that ʿAlī ibn Abī Ṭālib (رضي الله عنه) said:

«كُونُوا لِقَبُولِ الْعَمَلِ أَشَدَّ هَمًّا مِنْكُمْ بِالْعَمَلِ، أَلَمْ تَسْمَعُوا اللّٰهَ يَقُولُ: ﴿إِنَّمَا يَتَقَبَّلُ ٱللَّهُ مِنَ ٱلْمُتَّقِينَ ۝٢٧﴾ [المَائِـدَة الآية ٢٧]».

(لطائف المعارف)

"Be more concerned that your actions are accepted instead of your concern about performing the action itself. Did you not hear the statement of Allāh: 'Verily Allāh only accepts from the pious ones (*muttaqīn*).' (Surah Māidah 5:27)" (Laṭā'if al-Maʿārif)

Faḍālah ibn ʿUbaid (ﷺ) states:

«لَأَنْ أَعْلَمَ أَنَّ اللّٰهَ تَقَبَّلَ مِنِّي مِثْقَالَ حَبَّةٍ مِنْ خَرْدَلٍ أَحَبُّ إِلَيَّ مِنَ الدُّنْيَا وَمَا فِيهَا لِأَنَّ اللّٰهَ تَعَالَى يَقُولُ: ﴿إِنَّمَا يَتَقَبَّلُ ٱللَّهُ مِنَ ٱلْمُتَّقِينَ ۝٢٧﴾ [المَائِـدَة الآية ٢٧]».

(لطائف المعارف)

"For me to know that Allāh has accepted from me an action the size of a mustard seed, is more beloved to me than this world and everything within it. This is because of the statement of Allāh: 'Verily Allāh only accepts from the pious ones (*muttaqīn*).' Surah Māidah 5:27)" (Laṭā'if al-Maʿārif)

Mālik ibn Dīnār (ﷺ) would say:

«الْخَوْفُ عَلَى الْعَمَلِ أَنْ لَا يُتَقَبَّلَ أَشَدُّ مِنَ الْعَمَلِ».

(لطائف المعارف)

"The fear that an action is not accepted is more difficult than performing the action itself." (Laṭā'if al-Maʿārif)

ʿAbdul ʿAzīz ibn Rawwād (ﷺ) states:

«أَدْرَكْتُهُمْ يَجْتَهِدُونَ فِي الْأَعْمَالِ فَإِذَا بَلَغُوهَا أُلْقِيَ عَلَيْهِمُ الْهَمُّ وَالْحَزَنُ لَا يَدْرُونَ قُبِلَتْ مِنْهُمْ أَوْ رُدَّتْ عَلَيْهِمْ؟».

(لطائف المعارف)

"I have met people who were very diligent in performing actions, and upon completion of those actions, they faced sadness and fear about the action being accepted or not." (Laṭā'if al-Ma'ārif)

Some of the *Salaf al-Ṣāliḥīn* (﷽) used to say:

«كَانُوا يَدْعُونَ اللَّهَ سِتَّةَ أَشْهُرٍ أَنْ يُبَلِّغَهُمْ شَهْرَ رَمَضَانَ، ثُمَّ يَدْعُونَ اللَّهَ سِتَّةَ أَشْهُرٍ أَنْ يَتَقَبَّلَهُ مِنْهُمْ».

(لطائف المعارف)

"The people of the past would supplicate to Allāh for six months to allow them to reach the month of Ramaḍān, and then upon completion of the month, they would again supplicate for six months (begging) for the acceptance of them (their fasts and actions)." (Laṭā'if al-Ma'ārif)

It is also mentioned that:

«كَانَ بَعْضُ السَّلَفِ يَظْهَرُ عَلَيْهِ الْحَزَنُ يَوْمَ عِيدِ الْفِطْرِ، فَيُقَالُ لَهُ: إِنَّهُ يَوْمُ فَرَحٍ وَسُرُورٍ، فَيَقُولُ: صَدَقْتُمْ، وَلَكِنِّي عَبْدٌ أَمَرَنِي مَوْلَايَ أَنْ أَعْمَلَ لَهُ عَمَلًا، فَلَا أَدْرِي أَيَقْبَلُهُ مِنِّي أَمْ لَا؟».

(لطائف المعارف)

"Some of the *Salaf al-Ṣāliḥīn* would display sadness on the day of 'Īd. It was said to them: 'This is a day of happiness and joy!' They would respond: 'You have spoken the truth, but I am a servant and my Lord has ordered me to perform an action, but

I am not sure if He will accept it from me or not.'" (Laṭā'if al-Maʿārif)

Wuhayb (ﷺ) noticed people laughing on the day of ʿĪd, upon seeing this he said:

«إِنْ كَانَ هَؤُلَاءِ تُقُبِّلَ عَنْهُمْ صِيَامُهُمْ فَمَا هَذَا فِعْلُ الشَّاكِرِينَ، وَإِنْ كَانَ هَؤُلَاءِ لَمْ يُتَقَبَّلْ مِنْهُمْ صِيَامُهُمْ فَمَا هَذَا فِعْلُ الْخَائِفِينَ».

(لطائف المعارف)

"If their fasts were accepted, then know that this is not the action of those who are grateful; and if they were not accepted, then this is not the action of those who are afraid." (Laṭā'if al-Maʿārif)

Ḥasan al-Baṣrī (ﷺ) states:

«إِنَّ الْمُؤْمِنَ جَمَعَ إِحْسَانًا وَشَفَقَةً، وَإِنَّ الْمُنَافِقَ جَمَعَ إِسَاءَةً وَأَمْنًا».

(الزهد والرقائق لابن المبارك)

"A believer combines striving for perfection with a sense of apprehension, whereas a hypocrite combines the performance of inferior deeds with complacency." (Al-Zuhd wa al-Raqā'iq of Ibn al-Mubārak)

﴿يَوْمَ تَجِدُ كُلُّ نَفْسٍ مَّا عَمِلَتْ مِنْ خَيْرٍ مُّحْضَرًا وَمَا عَمِلَتْ مِن سُوٓءٍ تَوَدُّ لَوْ أَنَّ بَيْنَهَا وَبَيْنَهُۥٓ أَمَدًا بَعِيدًا ۗ ﴿٣٠﴾﴾ [آل عِمْرَان الآية ٣٠]

"On the Day when every soul will be confronted with all of the good he has done, and all of the evil he has done, and it will wish that there was a great distance between itself and his evil." (Āle ʿImrān 3:30)

May Allāh (ﷻ) grant all of us His mercy. Let us make the best use of the remainder of this month. Let us be diligent in seeking *Laylat al-*

Qadr, a night which is better than one thousand months, when Allāh (ﷻ) opens doors, draws His beloved servants close to Him, and grants tremendous rewards.

It is not necessary to know which specific night it falls on in order to earn that reward, so let us strive during this time to seek good from Allāh (ﷻ) and be cautious of neglectfulness because that will lead to ruin and destruction.

On the other hand, when a person's deeds have been accepted by Allāh (ﷻ), virtuous times of the year only increase their diligence in striving to worship Allāh (ﷻ), and do more righteous deeds. When those times conclude, their effects will still remain in that person's life and conduct. They follow one righteous action with another. That is someone who will have the best outcome and abode in both this world and the next, *Inshā' Allāh*.

عليكَ بتقوىَ اللهِ سرًّا وجهرةً ۞ ففيها جميعُ الخيرِ حقًّا تأكَّدَا
لتُجْزَى من اللهِ الكريمِ بفضلِهِ ۞ مُبوَّأ صدقٍ في الجِنانِ مُخلَّدَا

You have to fear Allāh in public and in private,
For in fearing Allāh all good is certainly contained.
Thus, you may be rewarded by the Grace of Allāh, the Generous,
With a position of truth in the everlasting Paradise.

KHUṬBAH 78

Finding Inner Strength in the Month of Ramaḍān

The religion of Islām is indeed one of strength, honour, and nobility. A person of faith who is strong in their beliefs is more beloved to Allāh (ﷻ) than one who is weak.

Abū Hurairah (رضي الله عنه) narrates that the Prophet (ﷺ) said:

«الْمُؤْمِنُ الْقَوِيُّ، خَيْرٌ وَأَحَبُّ إِلَى اللهِ مِنَ الْمُؤْمِنِ الضَّعِيفِ، وَفِي كُلٍّ خَيْرٌ».

(رواه مسلم)

> "A strong believer is better and more beloved to Allāh than a weak believer, although there is goodness in both of them." (Muslim)

Strength in this *ḥadīth* refers to strength in faith (*īmān*), knowledge, soul, willpower, sound judgement, and obedience to Allāh (ﷻ).

Physical strength can also be included, provided that it assists a person in performing righteous deeds.

Imām al-Nawawī (رحمه الله) commenting on this *ḥadīth* writes:

«وَالْمُرَادُ بِالْقُوَّةِ هُنَا عَزِيمَةُ النَّفْسِ وَالْقَرِيحَةُ فِي أُمُورِ الْآخِرَةِ، فَيَكُونُ صَاحِبُ هَذَا الْوَصْفِ أَكْثَرَ إِقْدَامًا عَلَى الْعَدُوِّ فِي الْجِهَادِ، وَأَسْرَعَ خُرُوجًا إِلَيْهِ، وَذَهَابًا فِي طَلَبِهِ ، وَأَشَدَّ عَزِيمَةً فِي الْأَمْرِ بِالْمَعْرُوفِ وَالنَّهْيِ عَنِ الْمُنْكَرِ، وَالصَّبْرِ عَلَى الْأَذَى فِي كُلِّ ذَلِكَ، وَاحْتِمَالِ الْمَشَاقِّ فِي ذَاتِ اللهِ تَعَالَى ، وَأَرْغَبَ فِي الصَّلَاةِ وَالصَّوْمِ وَالْأَذْكَارِ وَسَائِرِ الْعِبَادَاتِ، وَأَنْشَطَ طَلَبًا لَهَا، وَمُحَافَظَةً عَلَيْهَا، وَنَحْوَ ذَلِكَ».

(شرح النووى على مسلم)

"Strength in the foregoing *ḥadīth* refers to having firm resolve as it relates to matters of the hereafter. Someone with that trait will have the greatest preparation and willingness to face opponents during combat as an example, and utmost keenness in pursuing them. Someone with the aforementioned resolve will also be more diligent in telling others to do what is right, forbidding them from wrong, persevering through the harm that one may face while doing that, and bearing hardships for the sake of Allāh. Such a person will also be more desirous of engaging in prayers, fasting, *dhikr*, and all other acts of worship. He will be most eager to perform them and maintain their consistency." (Imām al-Nawawī's commentary on Muslim)

There is also another narration which has been reported by Aswad ibn Yazīd on the authority of ʿĀ'ishah (ﷺ) who narrates that:

«ثُمَّ يَنَامُ، فَإِذَا كَانَ عِنْدَ النِّدَاءِ الْأَوَّلِ - قَالَتْ - وَثَبَ - وَلَا وَاللَّهِ مَا قَالَتْ قَامَ».

(رواه مسلم)

"The Prophet (ﷺ) would sleep, but when he would hear the first call for the *fajr* prayer, he would stand up quickly." (Muslim)

NOTE: Aswad ibn Yazīd, the narrator of this narration says: "By Allāh, she, i.e. ʿĀ'ishah (ﷺ), did not say that he stood up."

Imām al-Nawawī (ﷺ) commenting on this *ḥadīth* writes that:

«قَوْلُهُ وَثَبَ أَيْ قَامَ بِسُرْعَةٍ فَفِيهِ الِاهْتِمَامُ بِالْعِبَادَةِ وَالْإِقْبَالُ عَلَيْهَا بِنَشَاطٍ وَهُوَ بَعْضُ مَعْنَى الْحَدِيثِ الصَّحِيحِ الْمُؤْمِنُ الْقَوِيُّ خَيْرٌ وَأَحَبُّ إِلَى اللَّهِ مِنَ الْمُؤْمِنِ الضَّعِيفِ».

(شرح النووى على مسلم)

"This demonstrates the importance which the Prophet (ﷺ) gave to the acts of worship, and the fact that he embarked upon

> them with energy. This is part of the meaning included in the authentic *ḥadīth* which states: "A strong believer is better and more beloved to Allāh than a weak believer." (Imām al-Nawawī's commentary on Muslim)

Abū al-Ḥasan al-Sindī (ﷺ) explains that:

«(الْمُؤْمِنُ الْقَوِيُّ) أَيْ عَلَى أَعْمَالِ الْبِرِّ وَمَشَاقِّ الطَّاعَةِ وَالصَّبُورُ عَلَى تَحَمُّلِ مَا يُصِيبُهُ مِنَ الْبَلَاءِ وَالْمُتَيَقِّظِ فِي الْأُمُورِ الْمُهْتَدِي إِلَى التَّدْبِيرِ وَالْمَصْلَحَةِ بِالنَّظَرِ إِلَى الْأَسْبَابِ وَاسْتِعْمَالِ الْفِكْرِ فِي الْعَاقِبَةِ».

(حاشية السندي على سنن ابن ماجه)

> "(A strong believer is): One who is strong in performing righteous deeds, bearing difficulties when obeying Allāh, persevering through adversities, remaining alert, and carefully thinking matters through so as to facilitate sound planning and to identify what will lead to the best final outcome." (Ḥāshiyat al-Sindī ʿalā Sunan Ibn Mājah)

Therefore, if we keep this in mind, then we will realize that part of the wisdom behind fasting is that it strengthens people's souls.

A servant of Allāh (ﷻ) – by his own will and choosing – refrains during the daytime from food, drink, intimacy, and all of the other things which break one's fast - although those are things which are completely normal for a person to partake in during the remainder of the year. During the days of the month of Ramaḍān, one refrains from them in order to seek Allāh's (ﷻ) pleasure and in order to attain His rewards. When a Muslim succeeds in doing so, then he will triumph over his soul and its desires, and that will prepares the individual to shoulder immense and heavy tasks, such as struggling in making sacrifices to obey Allāh (ﷻ), and giving from oneself for the sake of Allāh (ﷻ).

It was for these very reasons that when Ṭālūt (ﷺ) set out to face his adversaries, Allāh (ﷻ) tested those with him at a river.

Allāh (ﷻ) mentions what Ṭālūt (ﷺ) told them:

﴿فَلَمَّا فَصَلَ طَالُوتُ بِٱلْجُنُودِ قَالَ إِنَّ ٱللَّهَ مُبْتَلِيكُم بِنَهَرٍ فَمَن شَرِبَ مِنْهُ فَلَيْسَ مِنِّي وَمَن لَّمْ يَطْعَمْهُ فَإِنَّهُۥ مِنِّيٓ إِلَّا مَنِ ٱغْتَرَفَ غُرْفَةًۢ بِيَدِهِۦۚ ﴿٢٤٩﴾﴾ [البَقَرَة الآية ٢٤٩]

When Ṭālūt set out with the army (with 80,000 from Bayt al-Maqdis in extreme heat), he said to them: 'Surely Allāh shall test you with a river (the Jordan River, to see who will obey their king and who will not). Whoever drinks from it (to his heart's content) is not of me (not my faithful followers), and whoever does not taste (the water) except for a handful that he takes (and no more) is from me.'" (Baqarah 2:249)[68]

Therefore, those who possessed strength and perseverance passed the test by overcoming their own inclinations. However, the others who fell back were the ones overcome by the wants and inclinations of their souls, imprisoned by their own desires.

Ibn ʿAbbās (ﷺ) says:

«مَنِ اغْتَرَفَ مِنْهُ بِيَدِهِ رَوِيَ، وَمَنْ شَرِبَ مِنْهُ لَمْ يُرْوَ».

(تفسير ابن كثير)

"Whoever took some of it (the river's water) in the hollow of his hand, quenched his thirst; and as for those who drank freely from it, their thirst was not quenched." (Tafsīr Ibn Kathīr)

Ibn ʿAbbās (ﷺ) further adds:

---

[68] The Arabic text of this is as follows:

وَكَانَ عَدَد الْجُنُود - فِي قَوْل السُّدِّيّ - ثَمَانِينَ أَلْفًا

(تفسير الطبري)

«أَنَّ الْأَكْثَرَ شَرِبُوا عَلَى قَدْرِ يَقِينِهِمْ، فَشَرِبَ الْكُفَّارُ شُرْبَ الْهِيمِ، وَشَرِبَ الْعَاصُونَ دُونَ ذَلِكَ، وَانْصَرَفَ مِنَ الْقَوْمِ سِتَّةٌ وَسَبْعُونَ أَلْفًا، وَبَقِيَ بَعْضُ الْمُؤْمِنِينَ لَمْ يَشْرَبْ شَيْئًا، وَأَخَذَ بَعْضُهُمُ الْغُرْفَةَ. فَأَمَّا مَنْ شَرِبَ فَلَمْ يُرْوَ، بَلْ بَرِحَ بِهِ الْعَطَشُ، وَأَمَّا مَنْ تَرَكَ الْمَاءَ فَحَسُنَتْ حَالُهُ، وَكَانَ أَجْدَرَ مِمَّنْ أَخَذَ الْغُرْفَةَ».

(تفسير القرطبي)

"They drank according to the degree of their certainty. The unbelievers drank eagerly, and those who were merely disobedient drank a bit less than that. 76,000 of the people failed the test and only the believers remained, some of whom did not drink at all and some of whom took only a handful. Those who drank (a lot) were not quenched, but remained intensely thirsty. As for those who did not drink at all, their condition improved and they were even more energetic than those who had taken a handful." (Tafsīr al-Qurṭubī)

Ibn ʿAbbās (رضي الله عنه) also adds:

«جَازَ مَعَهُ فِي النَّهَرِ أَرْبَعَةُ آلَافِ رَجُلٍ فِيهِمْ مَنْ شَرِبَ، فَلَمَّا نَظَرُوا إِلَى جَالُوتَ وَجُنُودِهِ وَكَانُوا مِائَةَ أَلْفٍ كُلُّهُمْ شَاكُونَ فِي السِّلَاحِ رَجَعَ مِنْهُمْ ثَلَاثَةُ آلَافٍ وَسِتُّمِائَةٍ وَبِضْعَةٌ وَثَمَانُونَ، فَعَلَى هَذَا الْقَوْلِ قَالَ الْمُؤْمِنُونَ الْمُوقِنُونَ بِالْبَعْثِ وَالرُّجُوعِ إِلَى اللهِ تَعَالَى عِنْدَ ذَلِكَ وَهُمْ عِدَّةُ أَهْلِ بَدْرٍ».

(تفسير القرطبي)

"4,000 men crossed the river with him, including those who drank from it. When they saw Jālūt and his armies, which numbered 100,000, all of them heavily armed - 3,680 of his army left. If this is so, then the believers who had certainty in the resurrection and the return to Allāh were the same number as the people of Badr." (Tafsīr al-Qurṭubī)

Consequently, having firm conviction (*yaqīn*) and correct beliefs provides a person with an inexhaustible source of energy, as well as the ability to face difficulties.

The very nature of faith is that when it takes firm root in one's soul, it provides an individual with strength that manifests itself in all areas of one's conduct. When he speaks, he does so with knowledge; when he acts, he does so with diligence; and when he undertakes any endeavour, he does so with a clear purpose.

A true believer (*mū'min)* must not involve oneself in matters that are not correct according to Allāh's (ﷻ) directives. As well, a true believer must not surrender to one's disobedient inclinations; otherwise one will be held captive by a person's soul's desires.

The month of Ramaḍān is a time of strength, will, sacrifice, bravery, and victory. We should reflect on what happened to the Muslims during the battle of Badr[69] when they displayed incredible examples of courage and selflessness. The Muslims were only about 300 when they faced 1,000 of the enemy, yet they attained the very first military triumph ever recorded in Islāmic history. They came to the battlegrounds with true and firm faith that was remarkably strong, and Allāh (ﷻ) helped them with angels to grant them success over their opponents.

Imām al-Qurṭubī (رحمه الله) commenting on the verse:

﴿إِذْ تَسْتَغِيثُونَ رَبَّكُمْ فَٱسْتَجَابَ لَكُمْ أَنِّي مُمِدُّكُم بِأَلْفٍ مِّنَ ٱلْمَلَٰٓئِكَةِ مُرْدِفِينَ ۝٩﴾ [الأنفال الآية ٩]

> "(Remember) When you were calling your Lord for help, so He responded to you (saying): 'I am going to support you with 1,000 of the angels, one following the other (in succession).'" (Anfāl 8:9)

Quotes Qatādah (رحمه الله):

---

[69] 17th of the month of Ramaḍān in the 2nd Hijrah.

«قَالَ قَتَادَةُ: كَانَ هَذَا يَوْمَ بَدْرٍ، أَمَدَّهُمُ اللَّهُ بِأَلْفٍ ثُمَّ صَارُوا ثَلَاثَةَ آلَافٍ، ثُمَّ صَارُوا خَمْسَةَ آلَافٍ، فَذَلِكَ قَوْلُهُ تَعَالَى: ﴿إِذْ تَسْتَغِيثُونَ رَبَّكُمْ فَاسْتَجَابَ لَكُمْ أَنِّي مُمِدُّكُم بِأَلْفٍ مِّنَ الْمَلَائِكَةِ مُرْدِفِينَ ﴾ [الأنفال الآية ٩]».

(تفسير القرطبي)

"Allāh aided the Muslims on the day of Badr with 1,000 (angels), then He increased them in help, so they were 3,000, then He increased them in help, so they were 5,000." (Tafsīr al-Qurṭubī)

We have to ask ourselves a question: What did the Muslims have when they faced their hostile opponents, and what was it that gave the Muslims distinction over their opponents? What the Muslims had was inner strength - strength in their beliefs, conduct, and spirit.

There were many subsequent expeditions in which the Muslims participated during the month of Ramaḍān, such as Fatḥ al-Makkah[70], al-Qādisīyah[71], Spain (al-Andalus)[72], Ḥaṭṭīn (Jerusalem)[73], and others as well.

Do we think that they would have ended with remarkable results if the Muslims had not adorned themselves with the conduct of those who fast – traits including being content, aiming high, making sacrifices, bearing hardships, being completely humble before Allāh (ﷻ)? Do we think that they would have remained so incredibly steadfast if they came to the frontlines with souls too feeble to overcome even their own desires, and so weak that impulses from Shayṭān would leave them incapable of even fending off mere hunger and thirst for just a number of hours? Absolutely not!

The fasting which Allāh (ﷻ) has prescribed combines two strengths for a Muslim.

---

70 20th day of Ramaḍān, in the 8th year of Hijrah.

71 15th year of Hijrah in Ramaḍān under the leadership of Saʿd ibn Abī Waqqās (رضي الله عنه).

72 In Ramaḍān of 92 Hijrah under the leadership of Ṭāriq bin Ziyād.

73 In Ramaḍān of 582 Hijrah under the leadership of Ṣalāḥ al-Dīn al-Ayyūbī.

1. One is strength in terms of health - since fasting protects the body from various ailments and cleanses it of numerous impurities.
2. The other is strength in terms of one's soul, and this is the more important one.

Therefore, fasting provides a person with inner strength in many ways, and this has a major effect on the happiness of people at both the individual and collective levels. Fasting gives one strength and perseverance during their lives, orderliness in different things, diligence in matters, increases one's faith, and assists in the true obedience of Allāh (ﷻ).

During Ramaḍān, a believer must strive to attain as many virtues and perform as many righteous deeds, as possible. A person must not let the self be distracted by diversions which only pollute the spiritual atmosphere of this holy month and extinguish its light.

No one would regress into such negligence except for those who waste themselves and are ensnared by Shayṭān's traps. Being in that state will lead people to violate the sanctity of this month due to the poisons with which they continue to inundate themselves. They do not break free from such influences even during times that are virtuous and sacred. As a result, they end up unable to make any progress or seize any opportunity.

What good can there be in a person's life when virtuous occasions come time after time, and one witnesses the greatest chances to earn rewards and draw closer to Allāh (ﷻ), yet one gives no mind to that and chooses to remain heedless?

Imām Ibn al-Qayyim (رحمه الله) states:

«لا شيء أقبح بالإنسان من أن يكون غافلا عن الفضائل الدينية والعلوم النافعة، والأعمال الصالحة، فمن كان كذلك فهو من الهمج الرعاع الذين يكدرون الماءَ ويُغلون الأسعارَ، إن عاش عاش غيرَ حميدٍ، وإن مات مات غيرَ فقيدٍ، فقدُهم راحةٌ للبلاد والعباد، ولا تبكي عليهم السماءُ ولا تستوحش لهم الغبراءُ».

(مفتاح دار السعادة)

> "It is certainly awful for someone to remain heedless of religious virtues, beneficial knowledge, and righteous deeds. When a person becomes that way, then he is like an imprudent individual who pollutes water and inflates its price. If he lives, he has no good to show for it; and if he dies, then he will not be missed. In fact, his absence is something good for people and their lands. Even the sky will not weep over them." (Miftāḥ Dār al-Saʿādah)

We must realize – especially in the month of Ramaḍān – that Allāh (ﷻ) wants us to be a certain way, but there will always be factors that will push us to be a different way.

Allāh (ﷻ) says:

﴿وَٱللَّهُ يُرِيدُ أَن يَتُوبَ عَلَيۡكُمۡ وَيُرِيدُ ٱلَّذِينَ يَتَّبِعُونَ ٱلشَّهَوَٰتِ أَن تَمِيلُواْ مَيۡلًا عَظِيمٗا ٢٧﴾ [النِّسَاء الآية ٢٧]

> "Allāh wants to accept your repentance, but those who allow themselves to be controlled by their disobedient desires want you to stray far away from the correct path." (Nisā' 4:27)

CONCLUSION

Ramaḍān teaches us to be strong, and keep our aspirations high. Therefore, we must not feel weak in the face of our desires.

There are signs which indicate that a believer is strong and has a complete personality. Among them are that he hastens to perform righteous deeds, strives diligently in his acts of worship, endeavours to earn Allāh's (ﷻ) reward, and seeks to take full advantage of the many opportunities that Allāh (ﷻ) gives all of humankind. Thus, the strength of such a person and the efforts which one expends should all be directed towards pleasing Allāh (ﷻ).

Other signs which indicate that a believer is strong include having lofty objectives, as well as strong willpower which does not falter.

These believers remain courageous throughout trials, and steadfast throughout adversities, without being shaken. No matter what circumstances they encounter, they face them with determination and fortitude. Even if they become ill, their perseverance and resolve remain like they were when they were healthy.

The signs which indicate that a believer is strong also include keenness to protect Islām when people attack it; and not being pleased when one sees the prohibitions of Allāh (ﷻ) being perpetrated. It is Allāh's (ﷻ) religion that one should seek to defend, not one's own personal interests. A person should follow the example set by Allāh's Messenger (ﷺ) who did not seek to avenge the wrong which was done to him personally. The Prophet (ﷺ) pardoned others when they did not fulfill his rights, but he ensured that Allāh's (ﷻ) rights were always obeyed.

Other signs which indicate the strength of a believer also include self-control and restraint when difficult circumstances may cause one's inner self to depart from its usual temperament.

The Prophet (ﷺ) said:

«لَيْسَ الشَّدِيدُ بِالصُّرَعَةِ، إِنَّمَا الشَّدِيدُ الَّذِي يَمْلِكُ نَفْسَهُ عِنْدَ الغَضَبِ».

(متفق عليه)

> "Strength does not just mean being able to physically overpower others. Rather, strength most certainly means restraining oneself when angry." (Agreed Upon)

Consequently, in reality, a strong person is not the one who can overpower an opponent before he himself is overcome by that opponent.

Rather, a truly courageous person is the one who can overpower his anger when it tries to overcome him. This is why the Prophet (ﷺ) said: "Rather, strength most certainly means restraining oneself when angry."

So, if a person is strong, then he will restrain himself when angry; but if he is weak, then his anger will overpower him, and perhaps even lead him to say or do things which he will regret later on.

Among the manners of conduct which a person should observe while fasting is avoiding things such as: arguing, insulting, or being angry. When a Muslim fasts, he should control himself, be forbearing, keep his emotions in check, guard his tongue, and avoid letting himself be provoked by negligible things. One must not depart from remaining composed due to annoyances, or because of disputes regarding mundane matters.

The Prophet (ﷺ) said:

«إِذَا كَانَ يَوْمُ صَوْمِ أَحَدِكُمْ فَلَا يَرْفُثْ وَلَا يَجْهَلْ، فَإِنِ امْرُؤٌ شَاتَمَهُ أَوْ قَاتَلَهُ فَلْيَقُلْ: إِنِّي صَائِمٌ، إِنِّي صَائِمٌ، إِنِّي صَائِمٌ».

(متفق عليه)

> "When one of you is fasting, one must not say foul things, dispute (with others), or raise one's voice. If anyone seeks to provoke him by insulting him or fighting against him, then he should just say: 'I am fasting, I am fasting, I am fasting.'" (Agreed Upon)

Therefore, it is extremely crucial for a servant of Allāh (ﷻ) to struggle against the disobedient desires of one's soul; and a person must do that in order to attain Allāh's (ﷻ) guidance.

As Allāh (ﷻ) says:

﴿وَٱلَّذِينَ جَٰهَدُواْ فِينَا لَنَهْدِيَنَّهُمْ سُبُلَنَاۚ ﴿٦٩﴾﴾ [العنكبوت الآية ٦٩]

> "And as for the people who strive for Us, We shall certainly guide them to Our paths (avenues of guidance and insight which will lead one to Paradise)." (ʿAnkabūt 29:69)

In addition, Faḍālah ibn ʿUbayd (رضي الله عنه) narrates that the Prophet (ﷺ) said:

> «الْمُجَاهِدُ مَنْ جَاهَدَ نَفْسَهُ فِي طَاعَةِ اللَّهِ، وَالْمُهَاجِرُ مَنْ هَجَرَ الْخَطَايَا وَالذُّنُوبَ».
>
> (رواه أحمد)

"A (true) *mujāhid* is the one who struggles with his soul to make it obey Allāh, and a (true) *muhājir* is the one who forsakes sins and misdeeds." (Aḥmad)

As we struggle with our souls, we also need to patiently persevere. Ḥāfiẓ ibn Rajab (﷭) comments and says:

> «فهذا الجهاد يحتاجُ أيضًا إلى صبر، فمن صبر على مجاهدة نفسه وهواه وشيطانه غلبه، وحصل له النصر والظفر، وملَكَ نفسه، فصار عزيزًا ملكًا، ومن جَزِعَ ولم يَصبر على مجاهدة ذلك، غُلِب وقُهر وأُسر، وصار عبدًا ذليلًا أسيرًا في يدي شيطانه وهواه».
>
> (جامع العلوم والحكم)

"This struggle requires perseverance. When someone perseveres in struggling against his soul, his disobedient inclinations, and the influences of Shayṭān, then that person will eventually overcome and be triumph, becoming like a prominent conqueror. On the other hand, if someone is impatient and does not persevere in the aforementioned struggle, then that person will lose, be overpowered, and be taken as a prisoner, becoming like a slave who is captivated and humiliated by his own disobedient inclinations and by Shayṭān." (Jāmʿi al-ʿUlūm wa al-Ḥikm)

Let us diligently strive to obey our Guardian – the Almighty Lord, seize the opportunities that He grants us with to obtain His endless bounty, and take full advantage of the time which we have left in our lives. Let us make the most of this holy month. Our lives are passing by very quickly. Therefore, it is absolutely necessary for us to seize what we have before our time in this world runs out, and no further chance remains for us.

يَا رِجَالَ اللَّيْلِ جِدُّوا ۞ رُبَّ صَوْتٍ لا يُرَدُّ
مَا يَقُومُ اللَّيْلُ إِلَّا ۞ مَنْ لَهُ عَزْمٌ وَجِدُّ

O those of you praying at night, continue your diligence.
You may well be among those whose prayers are answered.
No one sincerely stands to pray at night except,
Those who have determination and firm resolve.

KHUṬBAH 79

Angels: Allāh's Heavenly Messengers

Allāh (ﷻ) is the Most Majestic. Everything in His creation contains signs that lead us to Him. Those signs show us that Allāh (ﷻ) is Unique, Invincible, All-Powerful, and the Most-Great. Allāh (ﷻ) perfected all things which He created and fashioned them in a remarkable way. No minds can encompass His extraordinary ability or imagine the true magnitude of His greatness.

One of the most extraordinary components of Allāh's (ﷻ) creation which unmistakably describes to us Allāh's (ﷻ) infinite ability and magnificence is the world of His noble angels. They are creations which He has favoured, and they represent one of the manifestations of His glory and supremacy. That is why one of the pillars of faith is to have correct beliefs concerning the angels. This includes knowing about them, as well as believing in their existence and the duties which they perform. Those beliefs are an essential pillar of faith. A person who lacks sound beliefs concerning any of the pillars of Islām in fact, has wandered away from the truth.

Allāh (ﷻ) says in the Qur'ān:

﴿وَمَن يَكْفُرْ بِٱللَّهِ وَمَلَٰٓئِكَتِهِۦ وَكُتُبِهِۦ وَرُسُلِهِۦ وَٱلْيَوْمِ ٱلْءَاخِرِ فَقَدْ ضَلَّ ضَلَٰلًۢا بَعِيدًا ﴿١٣٦﴾﴾ [النِّسَاء الآية ١٣٦]

"And whoever disbelieves in Allāh, His angels, His scriptures, His Messengers, and the Last Day, then indeed he has strayed far away." (Nisā' 4:136)

Discussing some facts about the angels according to what we know from the many authentic religious texts can undoubtedly increase and strengthen our faith. It can firmly ingrain certainty within ourselves, and fill our hearts with reverence of Allāh (ﷻ). It can also make us realize how weak we are, and the fact that there are many creations who are greater and stronger than us. The world of the angels is a tremendous part of Allāh's (ﷻ) immensely expansive creation. It is a world of purity and fascination. Allāh (ﷻ) created the angels from light.

ʿĀ'ishah (رضي الله عنها) narrates that the Prophet (ﷺ) said:

«خُلِقَتِ الْمَلَائِكَةُ مِنْ نُورٍ، وَخُلِقَ الْجَانُّ مِنْ مَارِجٍ مِنْ نَارٍ، وَخُلِقَ آدَمُ مِمَّا وُصِفَ لَكُمْ».

(رواه مسلم)

> "The angels were created from light, and the *jinn* were created from smokeless fire, and humankind is created from what you have been told about (in the Qur'ān, i.e. he is fashioned out of clay)." (Muslim)

Angels are among the earliest and greatest of Allāh's (ﷻ) creations. He has endowed them with the ability to take on various forms.[74] He created some with two wings, some with three, some with four, and others with even more.

Allāh (ﷻ) mentions in the Qur'ān:

﴿ٱلْحَمْدُ لِلَّهِ فَاطِرِ ٱلسَّمَٰوَٰتِ وَٱلْأَرْضِ جَاعِلِ ٱلْمَلَٰٓئِكَةِ رُسُلًا أُو۟لِىٓ أَجْنِحَةٍ مَّثْنَىٰ وَثُلَٰثَ وَرُبَٰعَ ۚ يَزِيدُ فِى ٱلْخَلْقِ مَا يَشَآءُ ۚ ١﴾ [فاطر الآية ١]

> All praise be to Allāh, the Creator of the heavens and the earth. Who made (some of) the angels messengers (carrying His messages to the Prophets), possessing wings, two, three and

[74] The Arabic text of this is as follows:

قَالَ جُمْهُورُ أَهْلِ الْكَلَامِ مِنَ الْمُسْلِمِينَ الْمَلَائِكَةُ أَجْسَامٌ لَطِيفَةٌ أُعْطِيَتْ قُدْرَةً عَلَى التشكل بأشكال مُخْتَلِفَة ومسكنها السَّمَاوَات.

(فتح الباري)

> four. Allāh increases His creation as He pleases (making some larger and more powerful than others). (Fāṭir 35:1)

The angels do not eat, drink, or breed.[75] Allāh (ﷻ) granted them strength, ability, and remarkable speed with which they carry out His orders.[76] They do not disobey Allāh (ﷻ) in any way, and they always perform whatever they are commanded to do. Allāh (ﷻ) says:

﴿لَّا يَعْصُونَ ٱللَّهَ مَآ أَمَرَهُمْ وَيَفْعَلُونَ مَا يُؤْمَرُونَ ۝٦﴾ [التَّحْرِيم الآية ٦]

> "They (angels) who never disobey what Allāh commands them, and who carry out exactly what they are instructed (to do)." (Taḥrīm 66:6)

Allāh (ﷻ) made the angels unbelievably beautiful. This is a fact ingrained in people's inborn nature. One example which proves this is what the women said when they described the beauty of the Prophet Yūsuf (ﷺ).
Upon seeing his beauty, they said:

﴿حَٰشَ لِلَّهِ مَا هَٰذَا بَشَرًا إِنْ هَٰذَآ إِلَّا مَلَكٌ كَرِيمٌ ۝٣١﴾ [يُوسُف الآية ٣١]

> "By God! This cannot be a human (because no human can possibly be so handsome)! This is none but a noble angel!" (Yūsuf 12:31)

---

[75] The Arabic text of this is as follows:

عَنْ سَعِيدِ بْنِ الْمُسَيَّبِ قَالَ الْمَلاَئِكَةُ لَيْسُوا ذُكُورًا وَلاَ إِنَاثًا وَلاَ يَأْكُلُونَ وَلاَ يَشْرَبُونَ وَلاَ يَتَنَاكَحُونَ وَلاَ يَتَوَالَدُونَ .

(فتح الباري)

[76] The Arabic text of this is as follows:

تَعْرُجُ الْمَلاَئِكَةُ وَالرُّوحُ إِلَيْهِ فِي يَوْمٍ كَانَ مِقْدَارُهُ خَمْسِينَ أَلْفَ سَنَةٍ: أَيْ عُرُوج الْمَلاَئِكَة إِلَى الْمَكَان الَّذِي هُوَ مَحَلّهمْ فِي وَقْت كَانَ مِقْدَاره عَلَى غَيْرهمْ لَوْ صَعِدَ خَمْسِينَ أَلْف سَنَة.

(تفسير القرطبي)

The final Prophet (ﷺ) saw the angel Jibrāʾīl (ؑ) in his true form two times.[77] He saw Jibrāʾīl's (ؑ) form filling the entire horizon, and on one of those occasions, he saw Jibrāʾīl (ؑ) having 600 wings with multicoloured pearls and gems falling from them.

The Prophet (ﷺ) states:

«رَأَيْتُ جِبْرِيلَ وَلَهُ سِتُّ مِائَةِ جَنَاحٍ، يَنْتَثِرُ مِنْ رِيشِهِ التَّهَاوِيلُ: الدُّرُّ، وَالْيَاقُوتُ».

(مسند أحمد)

> "I saw Jibrāʾīl while he had 600 wings and a colourful array of pearls and rubies falling from the feathers of his wings." (Musnad Aḥmad)

Imām Aḥmad (رحمه الله) has documented a narration in his *Musnad* which states:

«رَأَى رَسُولُ اللَّهِ ﷺ جِبْرِيلَ فِي صُورَتِهِ، وَلَهُ سِتُّ مِائَةِ جَنَاحٍ، كُلُّ جَنَاحٍ مِنْهَا قَدْ سَدَّ الْأُفُقَ يَسْقُطُ مِنْ جَنَاحِهِ مِنَ التَّهَاوِيلِ وَالدُّرِّ وَالْيَاقُوتِ مَا اللَّهُ بِهِ عَلِيمٌ».

(مسند أحمد)

> "The Messenger of Allāh (ﷺ) saw Jibrāʾīl in his original form while Jibrāʾīl had 600 wings, each wing covering the side of the horizon. From his wings, precious stones were dropping of which only Allāh has knowledge." (Musnad Aḥmad)

Allāh (ﷻ) permitted the Prophet (ﷺ) to describe to the people one of the angels who bears Allāh's (ﷻ) throne.

He (ﷺ) described him by saying:

[77] Once soon after the revelation commenced, and the second time when he was taken up to the heavens during the Meʿrāj.

«أُذِنَ لِي أَنْ أُحَدِّثَ عَنْ مَلَكٍ مِنْ حَمَلَةِ الْعَرْشِ، رِجْلَاهُ فِي الْأَرْضِ السُّفْلَى، وَعَلَى قَرْنِهِ الْعَرْشُ، وَبَيْنَ شَحْمَةِ أُذُنِهِ وَعَاتِقِهِ خَفَقَانُ الطَّيْرِ سَبْعِمِائَةِ سَنَةٍ، يَقُولُ الْمَلَكُ: سُبْحَانَكَ حَيْثُ كُنْتَ»

(المعجم الأوسط للطبراني)

"That angel's two feet are in the lowest earth, the throne is above his head, the distance between his earlobe and his shoulder is the distance that a bird would cover by flying for 700 years, and that angel glorifies Allāh by saying: 'You are perfect in every way where You are.'" (Al-Muʿjam al-Awsaṭ of al-Ṭabarānī)

Angels are the honoured servants of Allāh (ﷻ).

Allāh (ﷻ) says:

﴿وَقَالُوا۟ ٱتَّخَذَ ٱلرَّحْمَـٰنُ وَلَدًا ۗ سُبْحَـٰنَهُۥ ۚ بَلْ عِبَادٌ مُّكْرَمُونَ ﴿٢٦﴾﴾ [الأنبياء الآية ٢٦]

"And they (the polytheists) say: 'The Most Merciful (Al-Raḥmān) has taken a child (for Himself).' He is Exalted (from needing children)! Rather, they (the angels whom they say are Allāh's children) are but honourable servants (of Allāh)." (Anbiyā' 21:26)

The angels are noble and obedient scribes and messengers.

The Prophet (ﷺ) states:

«الْمَاهِرُ بِالْقُرْآنِ مَعَ السَّفَرَةِ الْكِرَامِ الْبَرَرَةِ».

(رواه مسلم)

"The one who is proficient in the Qur'ān will be in the company of the angels who are scribes, honoured and righteous." (Muslim)

They are outstanding in their worship of Allāh (ﷻ). They never cease to glorify Him by day and by night, nor do they ever grow weary of doing so.

﴿يُسَبِّحُونَ ٱلَّيْلَ وَٱلنَّهَارَ لَا يَفْتُرُونَ ۝٢٠﴾ [الأنبياء الآية ٢٠]

"They glorify Him night and day without being lax (without growing weary)." (Anbiyā' 21:20)

﴿وَمَنْ عِندَهُۥ لَا يَسْتَكْبِرُونَ عَنْ عِبَادَتِهِۦ وَلَا يَسْتَحْسِرُونَ ۝١٩﴾ [الأنبياء الآية ١٩]

"And those (the angels) who are with Him are not ashamed (idle) to worship Him, nor do they tire (in worshipping Him)." (Anbiyā' 21:19)

They do not speak before Allāh (ﷻ) commands them. Meaning, they do not initiate any matter before Him, nor do they go against His commands; on the contrary, they hasten to do as He instructs:

﴿لَا يَسْبِقُونَهُۥ بِٱلْقَوْلِ وَهُم بِأَمْرِهِۦ يَعْمَلُونَ ۝٢٧﴾ [الأنبياء الآية ٢٧]

"They (the angels) do not speak before Him and duly carry out His orders (in complete submission)." (Anbiyā' 21:27)

They remain in fear of Allāh (ﷻ) out of their reverence for Him.

﴿وَهُم مِّنْ خَشْيَتِهِۦ مُشْفِقُونَ ۝٢٨﴾ [الأنبياء الآية ٢٨]

"And they tremble with fear for Him." (Anbiyā' 21:28)

The most honourable of them to Allāh (ﷻ) is Jibrā'īl (ﷺ), who is entrusted with the duty of conveying the revelation which provides life for people's hearts.

Another angel, Mīkā'īl, is entrusted with directing the rainfall which provides life for the earth, and for the bodies of Allāh's (ﷻ) creatures. The angel Isrāfīl is entrusted with blowing the horn to mark the time when people will be restored to life, and resurrected from their graves.

There is an authentic *ḥadīth* which mentions that Isrāfīl has the horn held to his mouth, and his head is tilted listening attentively and waiting for the command to blow the horn.

Abū Saʿīd al-Khudrī (ﷺ) reports that the Prophet (ﷺ) said:

«كَيْفَ أَنْعَمُ وَقَدِ الْتَقَمَ صَاحِبُ الْقَرْنِ الْقَرْنَ وَحَنَى جَبْهَتَهُ، وَأَصْغَى سَمْعَهُ يَنْتَظِرُ أَنْ يُؤْمَرَ أَنْ يَنْفُخَ فَيَنْفُخَ».

(رواه الترمذي)

> "How can I be relaxed when the one with the horn is holding it in his lips and his forehead is leaning forward, waiting to be given permission to blow?" (Tirmidhī)

The angels arrange themselves side-by-side in complete, well-organized rows in the heavens before their Lord.

﴿وَإِنَّا لَنَحْنُ ٱلصَّآفُّونَ ۝١٦٥﴾ [الصَّافَّات الآية ١٦٥]

> "And indeed, we are standing in rows (worshipping Allāh)." (Ṣāffāt 37:165)

There is no spot in the heavens which does not have an angel standing or prostrating there.

«مَا فِيهَا مَوْضِعُ أَرْبَعِ أَصَابِعَ إِلَّا وَمَلَكٌ وَاضِعٌ جَبْهَتَهُ سَاجِدًا لِلَّهِ».

(رواه الترمذي)

> "There is no spot, the size of four fingers in them, except that there is an angel placing his forehead in it, prostrating to Allāh." (Tirmidhī)

This shows that the angels are so many that no one can enumerate them besides Allāh (ﷻ).

﴿وَمَا يَعْلَمُ جُنُودَ رَبِّكَ إِلَّا هُوَ ۝٣١﴾ [المُدَّثِّر الآية ٣١]

> "And none knows the soldiers (regiment) of your Lord except Him (the number of angels or other forces that He uses)." (Muddathir 74:31)

There is a *ḥadīth* which states that every day, 70,000 angels enter *Bayt al-Maʿmūr* in the seventh heaven and those angels never return to it again.

The Prophet (ﷺ) said:

«فَرُفِعَ لِي الْبَيْتُ الْمَعْمُورُ، فَسَأَلْتُ جِبْرِيلَ فَقَالَ: هَذَا الْبَيْتُ الْمَعْمُورُ، يُصَلِّي فِيهِ كُلَّ يَوْمٍ
سَبْعُونَ أَلْفَ مَلَكٍ، إِذَا خَرَجُوا لَمْ يَعُودُوا إِلَيْهِ آخِرَ مَا عَلَيْهِمْ».

(رواه البخاري)

> "Then I was shown *Bayt al-Maʿmūr*. I asked Jibrāʾīl about it and he said: 'This is *Bayt al-Maʿmūr* where 70,000 angels perform prayers daily, and when they leave, they never return to it (but always a fresh batch of angels come into it daily).'" (Bukhārī)

In addition, on the Day of Resurrection, the hellfire will be brought forth. It will have 70,000 reins, each one of which will be pulled by 70,000 angels.

«يُؤْتَى بِجَهَنَّمَ يَوْمَئِذٍ لَهَا سَبْعُونَ أَلْفَ زِمَامٍ، مَعَ كُلِّ زِمَامٍ سَبْعُونَ أَلْفَ مَلَكٍ يَجُرُّونَهَا».

(رواه الترمذي)

> "Hellfire will be brought forth on the Day of Resurrection. It will have 70,000 reins, each one of which will be pulled by 70,000 angels." (Tirmidhī)

Allāh (ﷻ) has entrusted these noble angels with numerous duties throughout this vast universe.

There are angels who carry the throne of Allāh (ﷻ), and the throne is the largest of Allāh's (ﷻ) creation. There are angels who oversee the functioning of certain parts of this universe, including the paths followed by the stars.

There are angels who guard the heavens against any rebellious Shayāṭīn. There are angels who distribute whatever Allāh has commanded them to. There are angels who direct clouds, rain, and winds. There are angels of mercy, and also others of punishment.

Allāh (ﷻ) has informed us about the aforementioned angels at the beginning of certain chapters of the Qur'ān such as in Sūrahs Ṣāffāt, Dhāriyāt, Mursalāt, Nāziʿāt, and others.

Some angels are entrusted with duties that affect all people in general, while other angels have duties that affect the people of faith specifically.

When Prophet Ādam (عليه السلام) passed away, it was the angels who prepared him for burial by washing his body with water an odd number of times, shrouding him, and then burying him in order to teach his children what to do.

Imām Aḥmad (رحمه الله) has documented a narration in his *Musnad* on the authority of ʿUtay ibn Ḍamrah al-Tamīmī (رحمه الله) which mentions that when Prophet Ādam (عليه السلام) passed away the angels:

«فَقَبَضُوهُ، وَغَسَّلُوهُ وَكَفَّنُوهُ وَحَنَّطُوهُ، وَحفَرُوا لَهُ وَأَلْحَدُوا لَهُ، وَصَلَّوْا عَلَيْهِ، ثُمَّ دَخَلُوا قَبْرَهُ فَوَضَعُوهُ فِي قَبْرِهِ وَوَضَعُوا عَلَيْهِ اللَّبِنَ، ثُمَّ خَرَجُوا مِنَ الْقَبْرِ، ثُمَّ حَثَوْا عَلَيْهِ التُّرَابَ، ثُمَّ قَالُوا: يَا بَنِي آدَمَ هَذِهِ سُنَّتُكُمْ».

(مسند أحمد)

"Took his soul, washed his body, wrapped him in his shroud, perfumed his body, dug his grave, prayed upon him, buried him, covered the grave with mud-brick, and filled it with soil saying: 'O Children of Ādam, this is your tradition at the time of death.'" (Musnad Aḥmad)

Another narration which has been documented by Imām al-Ṭabarānī (رحمه الله) on the authority of Ubay ibn Kaʿb (رضي الله عنه) mentions that the Prophet (ﷺ) said:

«لَمَّا تُوُفِّيَ آدَمُ غَسَّلَتْهُ الْمَلَائِكَةُ بِالْمَاءِ وِتْرًا، وَلَحَدَ لَهُ، وَقَالَتْ: هَذِهِ سُنَّةُ آدَمَ وَوَلَدِهِ».

(المعجم الأوسط للطبراني)

> "When Ādam died, the angels washed his body with water an odd number of times, then they buried him in a grave with a niche (*lahd*), and said: 'This is the way of the sons of Ādam.'" (Al-Muʿjam al-Awsaṭ of al-Ṭabarānī)

During the fetal development of each human being, Allāh (ﷻ) sends an angel at an appointed time after the phases of being drops of fluid, a clot of blood, and a piece of flesh have elapsed. That angel is entrusted with giving the fetus its features, sight, and hearing as instructed by Allāh (ﷻ). That angel then asks Allāh (ﷻ) if the person will be a male or a female, fortunate or miserable, and asks about the person's provision and lifespan. The angel writes the response given, and then blows the soul of life into the fetus.

ʿAbdullāh ibn Masʿūd (رضي الله عنه) narrates that he heard the Messenger of Allāh (ﷺ) say:

«إِذَا مَرَّ بِالنُّطْفَةِ ثِنْتَانِ وَأَرْبَعُونَ لَيْلَةً، بَعَثَ اللهُ إِلَيْهَا مَلَكًا، فَصَوَّرَهَا وَخَلَقَ سَمْعَهَا وَبَصَرَهَا وَجِلْدَهَا وَلَحْمَهَا وَعِظَامَهَا، ثُمَّ قَالَ: يَا رَبِّ أَذَكَرٌ أَمْ أُنْثَى؟ فَيَقْضِي رَبُّكَ مَا شَاءَ، وَيَكْتُبُ الْمَلَكُ، ثُمَّ يَقُولُ: يَا رَبِّ أَجَلُهُ، فَيَقُولُ رَبُّكَ مَا شَاءَ، وَيَكْتُبُ الْمَلَكُ، ثُمَّ يَقُولُ: يَا رَبِّ رِزْقُهُ، فَيَقْضِي رَبُّكَ مَا شَاءَ، وَيَكْتُبُ الْمَلَكُ، ثُمَّ يَخْرُجُ الْمَلَكُ بِالصَّحِيفَةِ فِي يَدِهِ، فَلَا يَزِيدُ عَلَى مَا أُمِرَ وَلَا يَنْقُصُ».

(رواه مسلم)

"When forty-two nights pass after the semen goes into the womb, Allāh sends an angel to give him shape. Then he creates his sense of hearing, sense of sight, his skin, his flesh, his bones, and then says: 'My Lord, will it be male or female?' Then your Lord decides as He desires, and the angel then puts down that also and then says: 'My Lord, what about his/her age?' Your Lord decides as He likes it, and the angel puts it down. Then he says: 'My Lord, what about the livelihood?' Then the Lord decides as He likes, and the angel writes it down, and then the angel gets out with his scroll of destiny in his hand and nothing is added to it and nothing is subtracted from it." (Muslim)

Later on, angels are entrusted with recording the deeds that every person performs throughout one's life, and even the very words that one utters.

Allāh (ﷻ) says:

﴿مَّا يَلْفِظُ مِن قَوْلٍ إِلَّا لَدَيْهِ رَقِيبٌ عَتِيدٌ ۝١٨﴾ [ق الآية ١٨]

"Whenever a word escapes (from a person's mouth), there is a guard ready by him (an angel immediately records the good or bad speech)." (Qāf 50:18)

﴿وَإِنَّ عَلَيْكُمْ لَحَافِظِينَ ۝١٠ كِرَامًا كَاتِبِينَ ۝١١ يَعْلَمُونَ مَا تَفْعَلُونَ ۝١٢﴾

[الانفطار من الآية ١٠ الى الآية ١٢]

"And verily there are guardians (angels) upon you (with every person). Who are noble (honourable) and are (continuously) recording (everything that you do and say). They know what you do (and record it so that you cannot deny it on the Day of Judgement)." (Infiṭār 82:10-12)

There are also angels who guard a person, whether one is Muslim or not. They protect them from things that have not been decreed to affect them.

Allāh (ﷻ) says:

﴿لَهُۥ مُعَقِّبَٰتٌ مِّنۢ بَيۡنِ يَدَيۡهِ وَمِنۡ خَلۡفِهِۦ يَحۡفَظُونَهُۥ مِنۡ أَمۡرِ ٱللَّهِۗ ﴿١١﴾﴾ [الرَّعْد الآية ١١]

"For everyone there are followers (guardian angels) in front of him and behind him, protecting him (from harm) by Allāh's order." (Raʿd 13:11)

Commenting on this verse Mujāhid (ﷺ) states:

«مَا مِنْ عَبْدٍ إِلَّا لَهُ مَلَكٌ مُوَكَّلٌ يَحْفَظُهُ فِي نَوْمِهِ وَيَقَظَتِهِ مِنَ الْجِنِّ وَالْإِنْسِ وَالْهَوَامِّ».

(تفسير الطبري)

"Every single person has an angel who has been assigned to protect him – both while asleep and awake – from the *jinn*, the people, and the harmful creatures." (Tafsīr al-Ṭabarī)

The angels have a special bond with the people of faith to the exclusion of all other people; they intercede for the people of faith, continuously make *duʿā* for them, and invoke Allāh (ﷻ) to forgive them.

﴿ ٱلَّذِينَ يَحۡمِلُونَ ٱلۡعَرۡشَ وَمَنۡ حَوۡلَهُۥ يُسَبِّحُونَ بِحَمۡدِ رَبِّهِمۡ وَيُؤۡمِنُونَ بِهِۦ وَيَسۡتَغۡفِرُونَ لِلَّذِينَ ءَامَنُواْۖ رَبَّنَا وَسِعۡتَ كُلَّ شَيۡءٖ رَّحۡمَةٗ وَعِلۡمٗا فَٱغۡفِرۡ لِلَّذِينَ تَابُواْ وَٱتَّبَعُواْ سَبِيلَكَ وَقِهِمۡ عَذَابَ ٱلۡجَحِيمِ ﴿٧﴾ رَبَّنَا وَأَدۡخِلۡهُمۡ جَنَّٰتِ عَدۡنٍ ٱلَّتِي وَعَدتَّهُمۡ وَمَن صَلَحَ مِنۡ ءَابَآئِهِمۡ وَأَزۡوَٰجِهِمۡ وَذُرِّيَّٰتِهِمۡۚ إِنَّكَ أَنتَ ٱلۡعَزِيزُ ٱلۡحَكِيمُ ﴿٨﴾ وَقِهِمُ ٱلسَّيِّـَٔاتِۚ وَمَن تَقِ ٱلسَّيِّـَٔاتِ يَوۡمَئِذٖ فَقَدۡ رَحِمۡتَهُۥۚ وَذَٰلِكَ هُوَ ٱلۡفَوۡزُ ٱلۡعَظِيمُ ﴿٩﴾﴾ [غافر من الآية ٧ الى الآية ٩]

"The angels carrying the Throne, as well as those around them, glorify the praises of their Lord, believe in Him, and seek forgiveness for those who have faith. (They make *duʿā* for them by saying) 'O our Lord! Your mercy and knowledge encompass (embrace) all things. So forgive those who repent and who follow Your path; and save them from the punishment of the Blaze (hellfire). O our Lord! Admit them into the Paradise of eternity, which You have promised them, as well as the righteous ones from among their fathers, their spouses, and their progeny (allow them all to live together in Paradise as they did in the world). Undoubtedly, You are the Mighty, the Wise. And save them from the difficulties (evils). You have certainly showered Your mercy on the one whom You have saved from difficulties on that day (of Judgement). And that is indeed the greatest success.'" (Ghāfir 40:7-9)

The angels also ask Allāh (ﷻ) to forgive someone who seeks knowledge, and they lower their wings (for that person) because they are pleased with what he/she does.

«مَا مِنْ خَارِجٍ خَرَجَ مِنْ بَيْتِهِ فِي طَلَبِ الْعِلْمِ، إِلَّا وَضَعَتْ لَهُ الْمَلَائِكَةُ أَجْنِحَتَهَا رِضًا بِمَا يَصْنَعُ».

(سنن ابن ماجه)

"There is no one who goes out of his house in order to seek knowledge, but that the angels lower their wings in approval of his action." (Ibn Mājah)

The angels invoke Allāh (ﷻ) to honour and mention those people who teach others what is right, who perform the obligatory prayers in the front row, and also those who complete the rows.

«إِنَّ اللَّهَ وَمَلَائِكَتَهُ وَأَهْلَ السَّمَوَاتِ وَالأَرَضِينَ حَتَّى النَّمْلَةَ فِي جُحْرِهَا وَحَتَّى الحُوتَ لَيُصَلُّونَ عَلَى مُعَلِّمِ النَّاسِ الخَيْرَ».

(رواه الترمذي)

"Indeed Allāh, and His Angels, and the inhabitants of the heavens and the earth - even the ant in his hole and the fish – send *ṣalāt* (blessings, invoke mercy, grace, and honour) upon the one who teaches people goodness (*khayr*)." (Tirmidhī)

«إِنَّ اللَّهَ وَمَلاَئِكَتَهُ يُصَلُّونَ عَلَى الَّذِينَ يَصِلُونَ الصُّفُوفَ، وَمَنْ سَدَّ فُرْجَةً رَفَعَهُ اللَّهُ بِهَا دَرَجَةً».

(سنن ابن ماجه)

"Surely Allāh and His angels send blessings upon those who complete the rows, and whoever fills a gap; and Allāh will raise him one degree in status thereby." (Sunan Ibn Mājah)

«إِنَّ اللَّهَ وَمَلاَئِكَتَهُ يُصَلُّونَ عَلَى الصُّفُوفِ الْمُتَقَدِّمَةِ».

(سنن ابن ماجه)

"Surely Allāh and His angels invoke blessings upon the first rows." (Sunan Ibn Mājah)

When a person makes a *duʿā* for someone else, the angels ask Allāh (ﷻ) to accept his *duʿā*, and they say to the supplicant: "May you also receive the same."

«دَعْوَةُ الْمَرْءِ الْمُسْلِمِ لِأَخِيهِ بِظَهْرِ الْغَيْبِ مُسْتَجَابَةٌ، عِنْدَ رَأْسِهِ مَلَكٌ مُوَكَّلٌ كُلَّمَا دَعَا لِأَخِيهِ بِخَيْرٍ، قَالَ الْمَلَكُ الْمُوَكَّلُ بِهِ: آمِينَ وَلَكَ بِمِثْلٍ».

(رواه مسلم)

"The supplication of a Muslim for his (Muslim) brother in his absence will certainly be answered. Whenever a person makes a supplication for good for one's brother, the angel appointed for this particular task will say: '*Āmīn*! May the same be for you, too.'" (Muslim)

When Allāh (ﷻ) loves one of His servants, the angel Jibrāʾīl (ﷺ) and the rest of the angels also love that person. Love and acceptance of that person are placed in the hearts of people upon the earth as well.

«إِنَّ اللّٰهَ إِذَا أَحَبَّ عَبْدًا دَعَا جِبْرِيلَ فَقَالَ: إِنِّي أُحِبُّ فُلَانًا فَأَحِبَّهُ، قَالَ: فَيُحِبُّهُ جِبْرِيلُ، ثُمَّ يُنَادِي فِي السَّمَاءِ فَيَقُولُ: إِنَّ اللّٰهَ يُحِبُّ فُلَانًا فَأَحِبُّوهُ، فَيُحِبُّهُ أَهْلُ السَّمَاءِ، قَالَ ثُمَّ يُوضَعُ لَهُ الْقَبُولُ فِي الْأَرْضِ».

(رواه مسلم)

> "Verily when Allāh loves a servant, He calls on Jibrāʾīl and says: 'Verily, I love so and so, hence you should also love him;' and then Jibrāʾīl begins to love him too. Then he makes an announcement in the heavens saying: 'Allāh loves so and so, therefore you should also love him;' and then the inhabitants of the heavens (the angels) also begin to love him, and then the acceptance is placed in the earth for him (as well)." (Muslim)

Allāh (ﷻ) sends angels to the righteous people and they encourage them to perform more virtuous deeds. Those angels accompany them almost all of the time, protecting them, supporting them with the truth, assisting them to say and do what is right, placing wisdom in their hearts, inspiring them to perform good deeds, and to helping them to remain steadfast in doing so.

As for someone who is openly disobedient, Allāh (ﷻ) unleashes the Shayāṭīn upon that person. They urge him to disobey Allāh (ﷻ), they cast doubts and wrong beliefs into his heart, and they provoke him to be involved in evil and falsehood.

The Prophet (ﷺ) has informed us that angels have an influence on people's hearts, and so do the Shayāṭīn.

«إِنَّ لِلشَّيْطَانِ لَمَّةً مِنَ ابْنِ آدَمَ وَلِلْمَلَكِ لَمَّةً: فَأَمَّا لَمَّةُ الشَّيْطَانِ: فَإِيعَادٌ بِالشَّرِّ، وَتَكْذِيبٌ بِالْحَقِّ؛ وَأَمَّا لَمَّةُ الْمَلَكِ: فَإِيعَادٌ بِالْخَيْرِ، وَتَصْدِيقٌ بِالْحَقِّ، فَمَنْ وَجَدَ ذَلِكَ فَلْيَعْلَمْ أَنَّهُ مِنَ اللّٰهِ

وَلْيَحْمَدِ اللَّهَ، وَمَنْ وَجَدَ الْأُخْرَى فَلْيَتَعَوَّذْ بِاللَّهِ مِنَ الشَّيْطَانِ، ثُمَّ قَرَأَ: ﴿ٱلشَّيْطَٰنُ يَعِدُكُمُ ٱلْفَقْرَ وَيَأْمُرُكُم بِٱلْفَحْشَآءِ ۖ ﴿٢٦٨﴾﴾ [البَقَرَة الآية ٢٦٨]».

(رواه الترمذي)

> "Indeed, Shayṭān has an effect on the son of Ādam, and the angel also has an effect. As for Shayṭān, it is by threatening evil consequences and rejecting the truth. As for the effect of the angel, it is by his promise of a good end and believing in the truth. Whoever finds the latter, let him know that it is coming from Allāh and let him thank Allāh for it. Whoever finds the former, let him seek refuge in Allāh from Shayṭān, the outcast. The Prophet then recited (from the Qur'ān): 'Shayṭān promises (threatens) you with poverty (telling you that you will become poor if you spend in charity), and orders you to (do acts of) immodesty (Baqarah 2:268).'" (Tirmidhī)

The angels come to a believer at the time of death. They convey to him the glad tidings of Paradise and that Allāh (ﷻ) is pleased with him. They make his heart firm and remove his soul smoothly and mercifully. The angel of death takes his soul, and carries it to the heavens while emitting a pleasant scent, and the gates of the heavens are opened for it.

«إِنَّ الْعَبْدَ الْمُؤْمِنَ إِذَا كَانَ فِي انْقِطَاعٍ مِنَ الدُّنْيَا وَإِقْبَالٍ مِنَ الْآخِرَةِ، نَزَلَ إِلَيْهِ مَلَائِكَةٌ مِنَ السَّمَاءِ بِيضُ الْوُجُوهِ، كَأَنَّ وُجُوهَهُمُ الشَّمْسُ، مَعَهُمْ كَفَنٌ مِنْ أَكْفَانِ الْجَنَّةِ، وَحَنُوطٌ مِنْ حَنُوطِ الْجَنَّةِ، حَتَّى يَجْلِسُوا مِنْهُ مَدَّ الْبَصَرِ، ثُمَّ يَجِيءُ مَلَكُ الْمَوْتِ، عَلَيْهِ السَّلَامُ، حَتَّى يَجْلِسَ عِنْدَ رَأْسِهِ، فَيَقُولُ: أَيَّتُهَا النَّفْسُ الطَّيِّبَةُ، اخْرُجِي إِلَى مَغْفِرَةٍ مِنَ اللَّهِ وَرِضْوَانٍ. قَالَ: فَتَخْرُجُ تَسِيلُ كَمَا تَسِيلُ الْقَطْرَةُ مِنْ فِي السِّقَاءِ، فَيَأْخُذُهَا، فَإِذَا أَخَذَهَا لَمْ يَدَعُوهَا فِي يَدِهِ طَرْفَةَ عَيْنٍ حَتَّى يَأْخُذُوهَا، فَيَجْعَلُوهَا فِي ذَلِكَ الْكَفَنِ، وَفِي ذَلِكَ الْحَنُوطِ، وَيَخْرُجُ مِنْهَا كَأَطْيَبِ نَفْحَةِ مِسْكٍ وُجِدَتْ عَلَى وَجْهِ الْأَرْضِ، قَالَ: فَيَصْعَدُونَ بِهَا، فَلَا يَمُرُّونَ، يَعْنِي بِهَا، عَلَى مَلَإٍ مِنَ الْمَلَائِكَةِ،

إِلَّا قَالُوا: مَا هَذَا الرُّوحُ الطَّيِّبُ؟ فَيَقُولُونَ: فُلَانُ بْنُ فُلَانٍ، بِأَحْسَنِ أَسْمَائِهِ الَّتِي كَانُوا يُسَمُّونَهُ بِهَا فِي الدُّنْيَا، حَتَّى يَنْتَهُوا بِهَا إِلَى السَّمَاءِ الدُّنْيَا، فَيَسْتَفْتِحُونَ لَهُ، فَيُفْتَحُ لَهُمْ فَيُشَيِّعُهُ مِنْ كُلِّ سَمَاءٍ مُقَرَّبُوهَا إِلَى السَّمَاءِ الَّتِي تَلِيهَا، حَتَّى يُنْتَهَى بِهِ إِلَى السَّمَاءِ السَّابِعَةِ، فَيَقُولُ اللَّهُ عَزَّ وَجَلَّ: اكْتُبُوا كِتَابَ عَبْدِي فِي عِلِّيِّينَ، وَأَعِيدُوهُ إِلَى الْأَرْضِ، فَإِنِّي مِنْهَا خَلَقْتُهُمْ، وَفِيهَا أُعِيدُهُمْ، وَمِنْهَا أُخْرِجُهُمْ تَارَةً أُخْرَى. قَالَ: فَتُعَادُ رُوحُهُ فِي جَسَدِهِ، فَيَأْتِيهِ مَلَكَانِ، فَيُجْلِسَانِهِ، فَيَقُولَانِ لَهُ: مَنْ رَبُّكَ؟ فَيَقُولُ: رَبِّيَ اللَّهُ، فَيَقُولَانِ لَهُ: مَا دِينُكَ؟ فَيَقُولُ: دِينِيَ الْإِسْلَامُ، فَيَقُولَانِ لَهُ: مَا هَذَا الرَّجُلُ الَّذِي بُعِثَ فِيكُمْ؟ فَيَقُولُ: هُوَ رَسُولُ اللَّهِ ﷺ، فَيَقُولَانِ لَهُ: وَمَا عِلْمُكَ؟ فَيَقُولُ: قَرَأْتُ كِتَابَ اللَّهِ، فَآمَنْتُ بِهِ وَصَدَّقْتُ، فَيُنَادِي مُنَادٍ فِي السَّمَاءِ: أَنْ صَدَقَ عَبْدِي، فَأَفْرِشُوهُ مِنَ الْجَنَّةِ، وَأَلْبِسُوهُ مِنَ الْجَنَّةِ، وَافْتَحُوا لَهُ بَابًا إِلَى الْجَنَّةِ ". قَالَ: فَيَأْتِيهِ مِنْ رَوْحِهَا، وَطِيبِهَا، وَيُفْسَحُ لَهُ فِي قَبْرِهِ مَدَّ بَصَرِهِ. قَالَ: وَيَأْتِيهِ رَجُلٌ حَسَنُ الْوَجْهِ، حَسَنُ الثِّيَابِ، طَيِّبُ الرِّيحِ، فَيَقُولُ: أَبْشِرْ بِالَّذِي يَسُرُّكَ، هَذَا يَوْمُكَ الَّذِي كُنْتَ تُوعَدُ، فَيَقُولُ لَهُ: مَنْ أَنْتَ؟ فَوَجْهُكَ الْوَجْهُ يَجِيءُ بِالْخَيْرِ، فَيَقُولُ: أَنَا عَمَلُكَ الصَّالِحُ، فَيَقُولُ: رَبِّ أَقِمِ السَّاعَةَ حَتَّى أَرْجِعَ إِلَى أَهْلِي، وَمَالِي».

(مسند أحمد)

The Prophet (ﷺ) states:

"When a believing slave is about to depart from this world and enter the hereafter, there comes down to him from heaven angels with white faces like the sun, and they sit around him as far as the eye can see. They bring with them shrouds and perfumes from Paradise. Then the Angel of Death comes and sits by his head and says: 'O good soul, come forth to forgiveness from Allāh and His pleasure.' Then it comes out easily like a drop of water from the mouth of a water bag. When he seizes it, the other angels do not leave it in his hand for an instant, and they take it and put it in a shroud with perfume, and there comes from it a fragrance like the finest musk on the face of the earth. Then they ascend and they do not pass by any group of angels but that they say: 'Who is this good soul?' and they reply: 'It is so and so, the son of so and so,' calling him by the best names by which he was known in this world, until they reach the lowest heaven. They ask for it to be opened to them and it is opened, and (the soul) is welcomed and accompanied to the next heaven by those who are closest to Allāh, until they reach the seventh heaven. Then Allāh says: 'Record the book of My slave in the *ʿIllīyīn* (a place above the seven heavens where the souls of the deceased believers are kept), and return him to the earth, for from it I created them, to it I will return them, and from it I will bring them forth once again.' So his soul is returned to his body and there comes to him two angels who make him sit up, and they say to him: 'Who is your Lord?' He replies: 'Allāh.' Then they ask: 'What is your religion?' He answers: 'My religion is Islām.' They question: 'Who is this man who was sent among you?' He replies: 'He is the Messenger of Allāh (ﷺ).' Then they say: 'What did you do?' He answers: 'I read the Book of Allāh and I believed in it.' Then a voice calls out from heaven: 'My slave has spoken the truth, so prepare for him a bed from Paradise, and clothe him from Paradise, and open for him a gate to Paradise.' Then there comes to him some of its fragrance, and his grave is made wide, as far as he can see. Then there comes to him a man with a handsome face, handsome clothes, and a good fragrance, who says: 'Receive the glad tidings which will bring you joy this day.' He asks: 'Who are you? Your face is a face which brings glad tidings.' He replies: 'I am your righteous deeds.' Then he says: 'O Lord, hasten the Hour so that I may return to my family and my wealth.'" (Musnad Aḥmad)

The angels are present at the funerals of the righteous people. 70 000 angels were present at the funeral of Saʿd ibn Muʿādh (رضي الله عنه).

«هَذَا الَّذِي تَحَرَّكَ لَهُ الْعَرْشُ، وَفُتِحَتْ لَهُ أَبْوَابُ السَّمَاءِ، وَشَهِدَهُ سَبْعُونَ أَلْفًا مِنَ الْمَلَائِكَةِ، لَقَدْ ضُمَّ ضَمَّةً، ثُمَّ فُرِّجَ عَنْهُ».

(سنن النسائي)

"This is the one at whose death the Throne shook, the gates of the sky were opened for him, and 70,000 angels attended his funeral. It squeezed him once then released him." (Sunan al-Nasā'ī)

It is also narrated in authentic narrations that the angels washed Ḥanẓalah ibn Abū ʿĀmir (ﷺ) who was martyred in the battle of Uḥud. The Messenger of Allāh (ﷺ) said to the companions (ﷺ) after Ḥanẓalah (ﷺ) was killed:

«إِنَّ صَاحِبَكُمْ لَتُغَسِّلُهُ الْمَلَائِكَةُ، يَعْنِي حَنْظَلَةَ، فَسَلُوا أَهْلَهُ: مَا شَأْنُهُ؟ فَسُئِلَتْ صَاحِبَتُهُ فَقَالَتْ: خَرَجَ وَهُوَ جُنُبٌ حِينَ سَمِعَ الْهَائِعَةَ، فَقَالَ رَسُولُ اللهِ ﷺ: لِذَلِكَ غَسَّلَتْهُ الْمَلَائِكَةُ».

(السنن الكبير للبيهقي)

"The angels are washing your companion" - meaning Ḥanẓalah - and said: "Ask his wife." The companions inquired with his wife, and she said that he had gone out when he heard the call to *jihād*, but he was in a state of ritual impurity following marital relations. The Messenger of Allāh (ﷺ) said: "That is why the angels washed his body." (Al-Sunan al-Kabīr of al-Bayhaqī)

Consequently Ḥanẓalah (ﷺ) is known as *'Ghasīl al-Malā'ikah'* (i.e. one washed by the angels).

Allāh (ﷻ) also has angels who travel throughout the earth and are present in settings and gatherings where Allāh (ﷻ) is mentioned, and where knowledge is imparted, whether in the *masājid* or other locations, and the angels surround the people in attendance with their wings.

«إِنَّ لِلَّهِ مَلائكَةً يَطُوفُونَ فِي الطُّرُقِ يَلْتَمِسُونَ أَهْلَ الذِّكْرِ، فَإِذَا وَجَدُوا قَوْمًا يَذْكُرُونَ اللَّهَ تَنَادَوْا: هَلُمُّوا إِلَى حَاجَتِكُمْ، قَالَ: فَيَحُفُّونَهُمْ بِأَجْنِحَتِهِمْ إِلَى السَّمَاءِ الدُّنْيَا».

(رواه البخاري)

> "Surely Allāh has teams of angels who go about on the roads seeking those who are in remembrance (of Allāh). When they find some people remembering Allāh they call to one another and say: 'Come to what you are looking for,' and so they surround them with their wings until the space between them and the lowest sky is fully covered." (Bukhārī)

The angels invoke Allāh (ﷻ) to forgive an individual for as long as he is in the spot where he prays, provided that he remains in a state of *ṭahārah*.

«المَلاَئِكَةُ تُصَلِّي عَلَى أَحَدِكُمْ مَا دَامَ فِي مُصَلَّاهُ، مَا لَمْ يُحْدِثْ: اللَّهُمَّ اغْفِرْ لَهُ، اللَّهُمَّ ارْحَمْهُ».

(رواه البخاري)

> "The angels supplicate in favour of you, so long as he remains in the place where he performed *ṣalāt* (prayer) in a state of *wuḍū.'* They (the angels) say: 'O Allāh! Forgive him. O Allāh! Have mercy on him.'" (Bukhārī)

On Fridays, the angels stand at the entrances to the *masājid* and they record the names of all of those who enter, in the order of their arrival. Once the Imām comes out to the *mimbar*, they fold away their scrolls, and sit to listen to his sermon.

«إِذَا كَانَ يَوْمُ الجُمُعَةِ وَقَفَتِ المَلاَئِكَةُ عَلَى بَابِ المَسْجِدِ يَكْتُبُونَ الأَوَّلَ فَالأَوَّلَ، فَإِذَا خَرَجَ الإِمَامُ طَوَوْا صُحُفَهُمْ، وَيَسْتَمِعُونَ الذِّكْرَ».

(رواه البخاري)

"When it is Friday, the angels stand at the gate of the *masjid* and keep on writing the names of the people (coming to the *masjid*) in succession according to their arrivals. When the Imām comes out (for the *Jumuʿah* prayer), they (the angels) close the register and listen to the sermon (khuṭbah)." (Bukhārī)

The angels also love to listen to the Qur'ān when it is being recited. They may even descend to the earth when they hear someone reciting the Qur'ān beautifully, as happened when a companion, Usayd ibn Ḥuḍayr (رضي الله عنه), was reciting the Qur'ān.

Abū Saʿīd al-Khudrī (رضي الله عنه) narrates that:

«هُوَ لَيْلَةً يَقْرَأُ فِي مِرْبَدِهِ، إِذْ جَالَتْ فَرَسُهُ، فَقَرَأَ، ثُمَّ جَالَتْ أُخْرَى، فَقَرَأَ، ثُمَّ جَالَتْ أَيْضًا، قَالَ أُسَيْدٌ: فَخَشِيتُ أَنْ تَطَأَ يَحْيَى، فَقُمْتُ إِلَيْهَا، فَإِذَا مِثْلُ الظُّلَّةِ فَوْقَ رَأْسِي فِيهَا أَمْثَالُ السُّرُجِ، عَرَجَتْ فِي الْجَوِّ حَتَّى مَا أَرَاهَا، قَالَ: فَغَدَوْتُ عَلَى رَسُولِ اللهِ ﷺ، فَقُلْتُ: يَا رَسُولَ اللهِ بَيْنَمَا أَنَا الْبَارِحَةَ مِنْ جَوْفِ اللَّيْلِ أَقْرَأُ فِي مِرْبَدِي، إِذْ جَالَتْ فَرَسِي، فَقَالَ رَسُولُ اللهِ ﷺ: اقْرَأِ ابْنَ حُضَيْرٍ، قَالَ: فَقَرَأْتُ، ثُمَّ جَالَتْ أَيْضًا، فَقَالَ رَسُولُ اللهِ ﷺ: اقْرَأِ ابْنَ حُضَيْرٍ، قَالَ: فَقَرَأْتُ، ثُمَّ جَالَتْ أَيْضًا، فَقَالَ رَسُولُ اللهِ ﷺ: اقْرَأِ ابْنَ حُضَيْرٍ، قَالَ: فَانْصَرَفْتُ، وَكَانَ يَحْيَى قَرِيبًا مِنْهَا، خَشِيتُ أَنْ تَطَأَهُ، فَرَأَيْتُ مِثْلَ الظُّلَّةِ فِيهَا أَمْثَالُ السُّرُجِ، عَرَجَتْ فِي الْجَوِّ حَتَّى مَا أَرَاهَا، فَقَالَ رَسُولُ اللهِ ﷺ: تِلْكَ الْمَلَائِكَةُ كَانَتْ تَسْتَمِعُ لَكَ، وَلَوْ قَرَأْتَ لَأَصْبَحَتْ يَرَاهَا النَّاسُ مَا تَسْتَتِرُ مِنْهُمْ».

(رواه البخاري)

"One night Usayd ibn Ḥuḍayr (رضي الله عنه) was reciting the Qur'ān in his enclosure when a horse began to jump about. He again recited and (the horse) again jumped. He again recited and it jumped as before. Usayd said: 'I was afraid that it might trample (his son) Yaḥyā. I stood near it (the horse) and saw something like a canopy over my head with what seemed to be lamps in it, rising up in the sky until it disappeared.' He went to the Messenger of Allāh (ﷺ) the next day and said: 'O Messenger of Allāh, I was reciting the Qur'ān during the night in my enclosure and my horse began to jump.' Upon this, the Messenger of Allāh (ﷺ) said: 'You should have kept on reciting, Ibn Ḥuḍayr.' He (Ibn Ḥuḍayr) said: 'I recited and it jumped (as before).' Upon this, the Messenger of Allāh (ﷺ) again said: 'You should have kept on reciting, Ibn Ḥuḍayr.' He (Ibn Ḥuḍayr) said: 'I recited, and it again jumped (as before).' The Messenger of Allāh (ﷺ) again said: 'You should have kept on reciting, Ibn Ḥuḍayr.' He (Ibn Ḥuḍayr) said: '(Messenger of Allāh) I finished (the recitation) because Yaḥyā was near (the horse) and I was afraid that it might trample him. I saw something like a canopy with what seemed to be lamps in it rising up in the sky until it disappeared.' Upon hearing this, the Messenger of Allāh (ﷺ) explained: 'Those were the angels who listened to you, and if you had continued reciting, the people would have seen them in the morning, and they would not have concealed themselves from them.'" (Bukhārī)

Allāh (ﷻ) has assigned an angel to be by the head of the Prophet (ﷺ) at his grave. That angel conveys to him the *ṣalāt* and *salām* from the individuals of his nation, and mentions each person specifically by name.

ʿAmmār ibn Yāsir (رضي الله عنه) narrates that the Messenger of Allāh (ﷺ) said:

«إِنَّ اللَّهَ وَكَّلَ بِقَبْرِي مَلَكًا، أَعْطَاهُ أَسْمَاعَ الْخَلَائِقِ، فَلا يُصَلِّي عَلَيَّ أَحَدٌ إِلَى يَوْمِ الْقِيَامَةِ إِلا أَبْلَغَنِي بِاسْمِهِ وَاسْمِ أَبِيهِ، هَذَا فُلانُ بْنُ فُلانٍ قَدْ صَلَّى عَلَيْكَ».

(مسند البزار)

"Verily, Allāh has appointed an angel at my grave to whom He has granted the ability to hear the whole of creation. Thus, until

> the Day of Judgement, there is no person who confers blessings upon me except that this angel conveys to me the blessings of that person, along with his name and his father's name, saying: 'The son of so-and-so person has conferred blessings upon you.'" (Musnad al-Bazzār)

There are groups of angels that Allāh (ﷻ) has assigned to come and leave in succession at every *fajr* and *'aṣr* prayer. At those times, they take the deeds carried out by Allāh's (ﷻ) servants to Him.

«يَتَعَاقَبُونَ فِيكُمْ مَلاَئِكَةٌ بِاللَّيْلِ وَمَلاَئِكَةٌ بِالنَّهَارِ، وَيَجْتَمِعُونَ فِي صَلاَةِ الْفَجْرِ وَصَلاَةِ الْعَصْرِ، ثُمَّ يَعْرُجُ الَّذِينَ بَاتُوا فِيكُمْ، فَيَسْأَلُهُمْ وَهُوَ أَعْلَمُ بِهِمْ: كَيْفَ تَرَكْتُمْ عِبَادِي؟ فَيَقُولُونَ: تَرَكْنَاهُمْ وَهُمْ يُصَلُّونَ، وَأَتَيْنَاهُمْ وَهُمْ يُصَلُّونَ».

(رواه البخاري)

> "There are angels coming to you in succession at night, and others during the day, and they all gather at the time of *'aṣr* and *fajr* prayers. Those who have spent the night with you, ascend to the heaven. He (Allāh) asks them, although He perfectly knows their affairs: 'In what condition did you leave My slaves?' They reply: 'We left them while they were praying, and we came to them while they were praying.'" (Bukhārī)

There are other angels who guard Makkah and Madīnah from the plague, and from the *Dajjāl* who will appear near the end of this world. There are also angels who spread their wings over the region of Shām.

«الْمَدِينَةُ وَمَكَّةُ مَحْفُوفَتَانِ بِالْمَلاَئِكَةِ، عَلَى كُلِّ نَقْبٍ مِنْهَا مَلَكٌ لاَ يَدْخُلُهَا الدَّجَّالُ، وَلاَ الطَّاعُونُ».

(مسند أحمد)

"Makkah and Madīnah are surrounded by angels, each path leading to it having an angel (guarding it) - neither *Dajjāl*, nor any plague will ever enter it." (Musnad Aḥmad)

Zayd ibn Thābit (؇) narrates:

»كُنَّا عِنْدَ رَسُولِ اللهِ ﷺ نُؤَلِّفُ الْقُرْآنَ مِنَ الرِّقَاعِ فَقَالَ رَسُولُ اللهِ ﷺ: طُوبَى لِلشَّامِ، فَقُلْنَا: لِأَيِّ ذَلِكَ يَا رَسُولَ اللهِ؟ قَالَ: لِأَنَّ مَلَائِكَةَ الرَّحْمَنِ بَاسِطَةٌ أَجْنِحَتَهَا عَلَيْهَا«.

(رواه الترمذي)

"We were with the Messenger of Allāh (؇) collecting the Qur'ān on pieces of cloth, and the Messenger of Allāh (؇) said: 'Glad tidings for Shām.' So we said: 'What is the reason for this, O Messenger of Allāh?' He replied: 'Due to the fact that the angels of the All-Merciful have spread their wings upon there.'" (Tirmidhī)

Angels are also entrusted with bringing and inflicting Allāh's (؇) punishment upon those who reject the clear truth, as Jibrā'īl (؇) did to the people who rejected Prophet Lūṭ (؇). Jibrā'īl (؇) raised their entire town with his wing and then turned it over on top of them. That was followed by Allāh (؇) being angry with them, expelling them from His mercy, and pelting those people with stones of baked clay that were marked specifically for them.

Such a severe punishment from Allāh (؇) is never farfetched in the case of people who wrong themselves and others.

Allāh (؇) says in the Qur'ān:

﴿فَلَمَّا جَاءَ أَمْرُنَا جَعَلْنَا عَالِيَهَا سَافِلَهَا وَأَمْطَرْنَا عَلَيْهَا حِجَارَةً مِّن سِجِّيلٍ مَّنضُودٍ ۝ مُّسَوَّمَةً عِندَ رَبِّكَ ۖ وَمَا هِىَ مِنَ ٱلظَّٰلِمِينَ بِبَعِيدٍ ۝﴾ [هود من الآية ٨٢ الى الآية ٨٣]

> "So when Our order (punishment) came, We made the upper portion of the land the lower portion (the cities were lifted and then thrown upside down), and We rained down on the land continuously falling stones of pottery clay that were marked by your Lord (every stone bore the name of the person that it was meant to strike). And such a punishment is not from the wrongdoers far away." (Hūd 11:82-83)

CONCLUSION

Belief in the angels is one of the essential principles and foundations of Islām, and there are many texts which prove that. One of those texts is a *ḥadīth* which mentions that Jibrā'īl (ﷺ) once came to the Prophet (ﷺ) towards the end of his life to affirm the foundational beliefs of Islām, and to teach the people their religion. He informed them about the fact that sound beliefs in the angels are one of those foundations which people must learn. Those beliefs increase and strengthen a person's faith, and they contribute to him remaining steadfast in this life.

When someone believes in the angels and their functions, he will call to mind that they are with him, they support him, they defend him, and they help him remain firm. That is why it is an obligation for every believer to learn about this essential pillar of *īmān*. A person must ensure that one gives the noble angels of Allāh (ﷻ) due respect, and performs those actions which will lead to them being present around them. One must also ensure that he avoids anything that would harm them, or distance them from him so that he will not be deprived of the immense care, goodness, and blessings which come from their company.

There are authentic narrations which prove that the angels can be harmed by things which harm people, such as foul odors, filth, and impurities.

«مَنْ أَكَلَ الْبَصَلَ وَالثُّومَ وَالْكُرَّاثَ فَلَا يَقْرَبَنَّ مَسْجِدَنَا، فَإِنَّ الْمَلَائِكَةَ تَتَأَذَّى مِمَّا يَتَأَذَّى مِنْهُ بَنُو آدَمَ».

(رواه مسلم)

> "A person who has eaten onion, garlic, or leek should not approach our *masjid*, because the angels are also offended by the strong smells that offend the children of Ādam." (Muslim)

The angels also invoke Allāh (ﷻ) to expel from His mercy certain types of people which include: someone who raises a weapon, or a sharp object in the face of someone without any right to do so.

«مَنْ أَشَارَ إِلَى أَخِيهِ بِحَدِيدَةٍ، فَإِنَّ الْمَلَائِكَةَ تَلْعَنُهُ، حَتَّى يَدَعَهُ وَإِنْ كَانَ أَخَاهُ لِأَبِيهِ وَأُمِّهِ».

(رواه مسلم)

> "Whoever points a piece of iron (weapon, dagger, etc.) at his brother, angels will curse him even if the other person is his real brother." (Muslim)

A woman who refuses to respond to her husband's intimate request for no valid reason is also cursed.

«إِذَا بَاتَتِ الْمَرْأَةُ، هَاجِرَةً فِرَاشَ زَوْجِهَا، لَعَنَتْهَا الْمَلَائِكَةُ حَتَّى تُصْبِحَ».

(رواه مسلم)

> "When a woman spends the night away from the bed of her husband, the angels curse her until morning." (Muslim)

Anyone who insults the companions (رضي الله عنهم). The Prophet (ﷺ) has said:

«مَنْ سَبَّ أَصْحَابِي فَعَلَيْهِ لَعْنَةُ اللهِ وَالْمَلَائِكَةِ وَالنَّاسِ أَجْمَعِينَ، لَا يَقْبَلُ اللهُ مِنْهُ صَرْفًا وَلَا عَدْلًا».[78]

[78] The Arabic text of this is as follows:

(صَرْفًا وَلَا عَدْلًا) فِي النِّهَايَةِ الصَّرْفُ التَّوْبَةُ أَوِ الْمُنَافَلَةُ وَالْعَدْلُ الْفِدْيَةُ أَوِ الْفَرِيضَةُ

(المعجم الكبير للطبراني)

"Anyone who curses my companions has the curse of Allāh upon him, and of the angels, and of all people. Allāh will not accept any of his compulsory or optional good deeds." (Al-Muʿjam al-Kabīr al-Ṭabarānī)

As well, anyone who ascribes himself to other than his real lineage due to his dislike for it.

«وَمَنِ ادَّعَى إِلَى غَيْرِ أَبِيهِ، أَوِ انْتَمَى إِلَى غَيْرِ مَوَالِيهِ، فَعَلَيْهِ لَعْنَةُ اللهِ وَالْمَلَائِكَةِ وَالنَّاسِ أَجْمَعِينَ، لَا يَقْبَلُ اللهُ مِنْهُ يَوْمَ الْقِيَامَةِ صَرْفًا، وَلَا عَدْلًا».

(رواه مسلم)

"A person who claims anyone else as his father besides his own father, or attributes someone else as his master other than his (real) master, will incur the curse of Allāh, the angels and all of the people; and none of his compulsory or optional good deeds will be accepted on the Day of Resurrection." (Muslim)

The angels will not come near certain people, including a man who smothers himself with fragrances used specifically by women, or a person in the state of *janābah* until one performs *ghusl* or *wuḍū'*, and anyone who is drunk.

«ثَلاثَةٌ لا تَقْرَبُهُمُ الْمَلائِكَةُ، الْجُنُبُ، وَالسَّكْرَانُ، وَالْمُتَضَمِّخُ بِالْخَلُوقِ» .

(كشف الأستار عن زوائد البزار)

"There are three (groups of people) whom the angels do not go near: someone who is in the state of *janābah*, someone who is drunk, and someone who smears himself with *khalūq* (saffron)." (Kashf al-Astār ʿan Zawā'id al-Bazzār)

The angels do not come close to a home whose residents abandon the Qur'ān; and where instead of the *dhikr* of Allāh (ﷻ), the sounds are replaced with impermissible music or instruments of Shayṭān; and the people indulge in acts of disobedience to Allāh (ﷻ). They also do not enter a house that contains any dogs, or revered animate imageries, pictures or statues.

«لاَ تَدْخُلُ المَلاَئِكَةُ بَيْتًا فِيهِ كَلْبٌ وَلاَ صُورَةٌ، يُرِيدُ التَّمَاثِيلَ الَّتِي فِيهَا الأَرْوَاحُ».

(رواه البخاري)

> "The angels (of mercy) do not enter a house in which there exists a dog, or a picture (i.e. of animate objects). He meant the images of creatures that have souls." (Bukhārī)

The above-mentioned are examples of things which harm angels and keep them away from a person, or actions that could incur the curse of them upon humankind.

There are some people who complain about being affected by black magic, the spiteful envy of others, or by Shayṭān's influence. They complain of sensing negative changes in themselves, their families, and their homes.

However, the striking reality is that some of the people who complain about these things are themselves responsible for bringing such misfortunes upon themselves. They are the consequences of disobedience to Allāh (ﷻ) that is perpetrated by those same people concerning themselves, their homes, and their families. Their actions disturb the angels and drive them away.

When the angels avoid a person and his home, then life will become devoid of peace and tranquility. That void clears the atmosphere for the Shayāṭīn to attack him from every direction, control him, and afflict him with pain, sorrow, and mental anguish. It is well-known that the presence of the angels drives away the Shayāṭīn and humiliates them.

One such occasion was when Shayṭān fled upon seeing angels descend during the expedition of Badr.

Allāh (ﷻ) tells us in the Qur'ān that Shayṭān retreated in extreme fear and said to the polytheists:

﴿نَكَصَ عَلَىٰ عَقِبَيْهِ وَقَالَ إِنِّي بَرِيٓءٌ مِّنكُمْ إِنِّيٓ أَرَىٰ مَا لَا تَرَوْنَ ۝٤٨﴾ [الأنفال الآية ٤٨]

"He (*Iblīs*) turned on his heels (ran away) and said: 'I have nothing to do with you! Without a doubt I can see what you cannot see (I can see the angels coming down to assist the Muslims).'" (Anfāl 8:48)

Furthermore, Allāh (ﷻ) tells us that in the hellfire, Shayṭān will address the people there and tell them:

﴿وَمَا كَانَ لِيَ عَلَيْكُم مِّن سُلْطَٰنٍ إِلَّآ أَن دَعَوْتُكُمْ فَٱسْتَجَبْتُمْ لِي ۖ فَلَا تَلُومُونِي وَلُومُوٓا۟ أَنفُسَكُم ۖ ۝٢٢﴾ [إبراهيم الآية ٢٢]

"And I did not have the authority to force you to follow me. I merely called you, and you responded to me. Therefore, do not blame me; rather, blame your own selves." (Ibrāhīm 14:22)

We must realize that the angels are creatures who are obedient to Allāh (ﷻ) and have noble standing with Him.

Some of the most magnificent duties which they perform include: protecting the people of faith, supporting them, and reinforcing goodness in their hearts. The angels are bashful towards any righteous person who has faith, and that is because of their respect for him, as was the case with the companion, ʿUthmān (رضي الله عنه).

«إِنَّ عُثْمَانَ حَيِيٌّ سِتِيرٌ، تَسْتَحْيِي مِنْهُ الْمَلَائِكَةُ».

(المعجم الأوسط للطبراني)

"Surely, ʿUthmān was modest and concealing; so even the angels felt bashful in his presence." (Al-Muʿjam al-Awsaṭ of al-Ṭabarānī)

Therefore, in conclusion, we must not harm or disregard the angels, or do anything to drive them away from us or our homes. Rather, we must honour them by being considerate and respectful towards them. Observing such conduct will allow us to lead a happy and enjoyable life. Mercy will envelop us, tranquility will descend upon us, and Allāh (ﷻ) will protect us and our families in all situations *Inshā' Allāh.*

القول بالملائك الكرام ۞ فريضة لصحة الإسلام

وهم عباد الخالق القهار ۞ قد خلقوا من خالص الأنوار

حياتهم بالذكر والتسبيح ۞ وما لهم في الذكر من تبريح

قاموا صفوفا للعزيز الماجد ۞ يدعونه على مقام واحد

قد طهروا عن شهوة العصيان ۞ وعن شرور النفس والشيطان

وما لهم نسل ولا ولادة ۞ ولا لهم شغل سوى العبادة

فمنهم كاتب أعمال الورى ۞ ومنهم حافظ سكان الثرى

ومنهم موكل بالرزق ۞ يوصل أو يزوى بأمر الحق

فوصف حال القوم بالتفضيل ۞ في صحف الآثار والتنزيل

ونفيهم بالجحد والإنكار ۞ كفر صريح موجب للنار

ومن جرى لسانه بالطعن ۞ والنقص فيهم فهو أهل اللعن

(التعليق الصبيح على مشكاة المصابيح)

To testify in the (belief of the) honourable angels is binding for the validity of (one's) Islām,
They are servants of the Creator, the All-Dominant. Indeed, they have been created from pure light.
Their lives revolve around the remembrance and glorification of Allāh,
And there is no strain for them in making the dhikr of Allāh.

They stand in rows before the Glorified and All-Mighty One,
Calling upon Him in one place.
Indeed, they have been purified from the lust of disobedience, and the evils of the heart and Shayṭān,
They have no offspring and no birth, except for worship they have no other work.
From among them are the recorder of mankind's deeds,
And others are guardians of the Earth's inhabitants,
And some are entrusted with livelihood,
Reaching or receding by order of truth.
Their detailed account is in the ḥadīth and Qur'ān,
And refutation (of their existence) with rejection and denial,
Is outright disbelief deserving of the fire,
And whoever speaks in vilification and criticism regarding them are accursed.

KHUṬBAH 80

Your Grave: Either a Garden or a Pit. Decide Which You Want It to Be!

A human being's journey in this life goes through various stages. At one stage a person lives in the mother's womb; at another, one lives on the face of the earth; and yet at another stage, one rests underneath its surface until the final resurrection.

The 5 stages of humans until they finally reach the hereafter are the following:

1. The first stage is in the non-existence.
2. The second stage is when in the mother's womb.
3. The third stage is when one is born into this life.
4. The fourth stage is when one enters the grave.
5. The fifth stage is when everyone is raised up from the grave for the Day of Judgement.

This journey seems to be long, but in reality it is brief, and its end is imminent. Indeed, this present world is not an eternal abode for anyone. A sensible person always contemplates the changing conditions and the end of life terms, which should soften one's heart and make one take heed from the lessons contained in this. The abode that no one can escape from is the grave, and this is sufficient as a warning.

The Prophet (ﷺ) mentioning the severity of the grave once said:

«إِنَّ لِلْقَبْرِ ضَغْطَةً، وَلَوْ كَانَ أَحَدٌ نَاجِيًا مِنْهَا نَجَا مِنْهَا سَعْدُ بْنُ مُعَاذٍ».

(فضائل الصحابة لابن حنبل)

> "Surely the grave will squeeze the dead body; if anyone could be saved from its pressure, it would have been Saʿd ibn Muʿādh." (Faḍā'il al-Ṣaḥābah of Ibn Ḥanbal)

Whenever ʿUthmān ibn ʿAffān (ﷺ) stood by a grave, he would weep until his beard was soaked with tears. It was once said to him:

«تُذْكَرُ الجَنَّةُ وَالنَّارُ فَلاَ تَبْكِي وَتَبْكِي مِنْ هَذَا؟ فَقَالَ: إِنَّ رَسُولَ اللهِ ﷺ قَالَ: إِنَّ القَبْرَ أَوَّلُ مَنْزِلٍ مِنْ مَنَازِلِ الآخِرَةِ، فَإِنْ نَجَا مِنْهُ فَمَا بَعْدَهُ أَيْسَرُ مِنْهُ، وَإِنْ لَمْ يَنْجُ مِنْهُ فَمَا بَعْدَهُ أَشَدُّ مِنْهُ. قَالَ: وَقَالَ رَسُولُ اللهِ صَلَّى اللَّهُ عَلَيْهِ وَسَلَّمَ: مَا رَأَيْتُ مَنْظَرًا قَطُّ إِلاَّ وَالقَبْرُ أَفْظَعُ مِنْهُ».

(رواه الترمذي)

> "Why is it that you remember the Paradise and the Hellfire you do not weep, but you weep because of the grave?" He replied: "The Messenger of Allāh (ﷺ) said: 'The grave is the first stage of the hereafter. If one is saved from its torture, then what follows it will be easier; but if one is not saved from it, then what follows it will be even harder.'" ʿUthmān ibn ʿAffān (ﷺ) then added: "The Messenger of Allāh (ﷺ) said: 'By Allāh, the grave is more horrible than anything that I have ever seen.'" (Tirmidhī)

One of the pillars of belief in the hereafter is to believe in the true reality of bliss and torment in the grave, i.e. to believe that those who obey Allāh (ﷻ) will experience bliss in the grave, and that the sinful and the wicked will suffer torment in the grave if they deserve it.

The Prophet (ﷺ) has stated:

«لَوْلَا أَنْ لَا تَدَافَنُوا لَدَعَوْتُ اللهَ أَنْ يُسْمِعَكُمْ مِنْ عَذَابِ الْقَبْرِ».

(رواه مسلم)

> "If it was not (for the fact) that you bury one another, I would have indeed supplicated to Allāh to make you hear the torment of the grave as I can hear it." (Muslim)

Visiting the graves to take admonition and learn a lesson from death is a *sunnah* of the Prophet (ﷺ), and a means of drawing closer to Allāh (ﷻ). The one who visits the graves will remember the dead - those who were once in fact his acquaintances and associates. This will make a person realize that one will also inevitably die and be buried just like them, and that everyone will eventually be called to account in the grave for their actions.

The Prophet (ﷺ) said:

«زُورُوا الْقُبُورَ؛ فَإِنَّهَا تُذَكِّرُكُمُ الْآخِرَةَ».

(سنن ابن ماجة)

> "Visit the graves; for it will remind you of the hereafter." (Sunan Ibn Mājah)

When someone is buried, and is taken away from one's family and wealth, the first visitors in the grave will be two angels who will come to test the deceased.

The Prophet (ﷺ) states:

إِنَّ الْمَيِّتَ إِذَا وُضِعَ فِي قَبْرِهِ إِنَّهُ يَسْمَعُ خَفْقَ نِعَالِهِمْ حِينَ يُوَلُّونَ عَنْهُ، فَإِنْ كَانَ مُؤْمِنًا، كَانَتِ الصَّلَاةُ عِنْدَ رَأْسِهِ، وَكَانَ الصِّيَامُ عَنْ يَمِينِهِ، وَكَانَتِ الزَّكَاةُ عَنْ شِمَالِهِ، وَكَانَ فِعْلُ الْخَيْرَاتِ مِنَ الصَّدَقَةِ وَالصِّلَةِ وَالْمَعْرُوفِ وَالْإِحْسَانِ إِلَى النَّاسِ عِنْدَ رِجْلَيْهِ، فَيُؤْتَى مِنْ قِبَلِ رَأْسِهِ، فَتَقُولُ الصَّلَاةُ: مَا قِبَلِي مَدْخَلٌ، ثُمَّ يُؤْتَى عَنْ يَمِينِهِ، فَيَقُولُ الصِّيَامُ: مَا قِبَلِي مَدْخَلٌ، ثُمَّ يُؤْتَى عَنْ يَسَارِهِ، فَتَقُولُ الزَّكَاةُ: مَا قِبَلِي مَدْخَلٌ، ثُمَّ يُؤْتَى مِنْ قِبَلِ رِجْلَيْهِ، فَتَقُولُ فَعْلُ الْخَيْرَاتِ مِنَ الصَّدَقَةِ وَالصِّلَةِ وَالْمَعْرُوفِ وَالْإِحْسَانِ إِلَى النَّاسِ: مَا قِبَلِي مَدْخَلٌ، فَيُقَالُ لَهُ: اجْلِسْ فَيَجْلِسُ، وَقَدْ مُثِّلَتْ لَهُ الشَّمْسُ وَقَدْ أُدْنِيَتْ لِلْغُرُوبِ، فَيُقَالُ لَهُ: أَرَأَيْتَكَ هَذَا الرَّجُلَ الَّذِي

كَانَ فِيكُمْ مَا تَقُولُ فِيهِ، وَمَاذَا تَشْهَدُ بِهِ عَلَيْهِ؟ فَيَقُولُ: دَعُونِي حَتَّى أُصَلِّيَ، فَيَقُولُونَ: إِنَّكَ سَتَفْعَلُ، أَخْبِرْنِي عَمَّا نَسْأَلُكَ عَنْهُ، أَرَأَيْتَكَ هَذَا الرَّجُلَ الَّذِي كَانَ فِيكُمْ مَا تَقُولُ فِيهِ، وَمَاذَا تَشْهَدُ عَلَيْهِ؟ قَالَ: فَيَقُولُ: مُحَمَّدٌ أَشْهَدُ أَنَّهُ رَسُولُ اللَّهِ، وَأَنَّهُ جَاءَ بِالْحَقِّ مِنْ عِنْدِ اللَّهِ، فَيُقَالُ لَهُ: عَلَى ذَلِكَ حَيِيتَ وَعَلَى ذَلِكَ مِتَّ، وَعَلَى ذَلِكَ تُبْعَثُ إِنْ شَاءَ اللَّهُ، ثُمَّ يُفْتَحُ لَهُ بَابٌ مِنْ أَبْوَابِ الْجَنَّةِ، فَيُقَالُ لَهُ: هَذَا مَقْعَدُكَ مِنْهَا، وَمَا أَعَدَّ اللَّهُ لَكَ فِيهَا، فَيَزْدَادُ غِبْطَةً وَسُرُورًا، ثُمَّ يُفْتَحُ لَهُ بَابٌ مِنْ أَبْوَابِ النَّارِ، فَيُقَالُ لَهُ: هَذَا مَقْعَدُكَ مِنْهَا وَمَا أَعَدَّ اللَّهُ لَكَ فِيهَا لَوْ عَصَيْتَهُ، فَيَزْدَادُ غِبْطَةً وَسُرُورًا، ثُمَّ يُفْسَحُ لَهُ فِي قَبْرِهِ سَبْعُونَ ذِرَاعًا، وَيُنَوَّرُ لَهُ فِيهِ، وَيُعَادُ الْجَسَدُ لِمَا بَدَأَ مِنْهُ، فَتُجْعَلُ نَسَمَتُهُ فِي النَّسَمِ الطَّيِّبِ وَهِيَ طَيْرٌ يَعْلُقُ فِي شَجَرِ الْجَنَّةِ، قَالَ: فَذَلِكَ قَوْلُهُ تَعَالَى: ﴿يُثَبِّتُ ٱللَّهُ ٱلَّذِينَ ءَامَنُوا۟ بِٱلْقَوْلِ ٱلثَّابِتِ فِى ٱلْحَيَوٰةِ ٱلدُّنْيَا وَفِى ٱلْءَاخِرَةِ ۖ وَيُضِلُّ ٱللَّهُ ٱلظَّـٰلِمِينَ ۚ وَيَفْعَلُ ٱللَّهُ مَا يَشَآءُ ﴿٢٧﴾﴾ [إِبْرَاهِيم الآية ٢٧]».

«قَالَ: وَإِنَّ الْكَافِرَ إِذَا أُتِيَ مِنْ قِبَلِ رَأْسِهِ، لَمْ يُوجَدْ شَيْءٌ، ثُمَّ أُتِيَ عَنْ يَمِينِهِ، فَلَا يُوجَدُ شَيْءٌ، ثُمَّ أُتِيَ عَنْ شِمَالِهِ، فَلَا يُوجَدُ شَيْءٌ، ثُمَّ أُتِيَ مِنْ قِبَلِ رِجْلَيْهِ، فَلَا يُوجَدُ شَيْءٌ، فَيُقَالُ لَهُ: اجْلِسْ، فَيَجْلِسُ خَائِفًا مَرْعُوبًا، فَيُقَالُ لَهُ: أَرَأَيْتَكَ هَذَا الرَّجُلَ الَّذِي كَانَ فِيكُمْ مَاذَا تَقُولُ فِيهِ؟ وَمَاذَا تَشْهَدُ بِهِ عَلَيْهِ؟ فَيَقُولُ: أَيُّ رَجُلٍ؟ فَيُقَالُ: الَّذِي كَانَ فِيكُمْ، فَلَا يَهْتَدِي لِاسْمِهِ حَتَّى يُقَالَ لَهُ: مُحَمَّدٌ، فَيَقُولُ: مَا أَدْرِي، سَمِعْتُ النَّاسَ قَالُوا قَوْلًا، فَقُلْتُ كَمَا قَالَ النَّاسُ، فَيُقَالُ لَهُ: عَلَى ذَلِكَ حَيِيتَ، وَعَلَى ذَلِكَ مِتَّ، وَعَلَى ذَلِكَ تُبْعَثُ إِنْ شَاءَ اللَّهُ، ثُمَّ يُفْتَحُ لَهُ بَابٌ مِنْ أَبْوَابِ النَّارِ، فَيُقَالُ لَهُ: هَذَا مَقْعَدُكَ مِنَ النَّارِ، وَمَا أَعَدَّ اللَّهُ لَكَ فِيهَا، فَيَزْدَادُ حَسْرَةً وَثُبُورًا، ثُمَّ يُفْتَحُ لَهُ بَابٌ مِنْ أَبْوَابِ الْجَنَّةِ، فَيُقَالُ لَهُ: ذَلِكَ مَقْعَدُكَ مِنَ الْجَنَّةِ، وَمَا أَعَدَّ اللَّهُ لَكَ فِيهِ لَوْ أَطَعْتَهُ فَيَزْدَادُ حَسْرَةً وَثُبُورًا، ثُمَّ يُضَيَّقُ عَلَيْهِ قَبْرُهُ حَتَّى تَخْتَلِفَ فِيهِ أَضْلَاعُهُ، فَتِلْكَ الْمَعِيشَةُ الضَّنْكَةُ الَّتِي قَالَ اللَّهُ: ﴿وَمَنْ أَعْرَضَ عَن ذِكْرِى فَإِنَّ لَهُۥ مَعِيشَةً ضَنكًا وَنَحْشُرُهُۥ يَوْمَ ٱلْقِيَـٰمَةِ أَعْمَىٰ ﴿١٢٤﴾﴾ [طه الآية ١٢٤] ».

(مسند أحمد)

"When a dead person is laid in his grave, he can hear the sounds of the footsteps of the people as they leave him. If he is a believer, then the prayer will be at his head, fasting will be on his right, *zakāh* will be on his left, and good deeds such as charity, maintaining the ties of kinship, and kindness to people will be at his feet. He will be approached (by evil) from the direction of his head, but the prayer will say: 'There is no entrance from my side.' Then he will be approached from his right, but fasting will say: 'There is no entrance from my side.' Then he will be approached from his left, but *zakāh* will say: 'There is no entrance from my side.' Then he will be approached from the direction of his feet, but the good deeds of charity, maintaining the ties of kinship, kindness, and beneficence towards people will say: 'There is no entrance from my side.'

Then it will be said to him: 'Sit up.' So he will sit up and the sun will appear to him as if it is about to set. It will be said to him: 'Tell us, what do you say about that man who was sent to you, and what is your testimony about him?' He will say: 'Allow me to perform my prayers first.' It will be said to him: 'You will do that shortly, but first answer the questions which we ask you. Tell us, what do you say about that man who was sent to you, and what is your testimony about him?' He will reply: 'He is Muhammad. I testify that he is the Messenger of Allāh and that he came with the truth from Allāh.' It will be said to him: 'It was upon this that you lived, it was upon this that you died, and it will be upon this that you will be resurrected, by the will of Allāh.'

Then one of the gates of Paradise will be opened for him, and it will be said to him: 'This is your place, and this is what Allāh has prepared for you in it.' This will increase his joy and delight. Then one of the gates of the hellfire will be opened for him and it will be said to him: 'This would have been your place, as well as what Allāh has prepared for you in it if you had disobeyed Him.' This will further increase his joy and delight.

Then his grave will be widened for him by seventy cubits and it will be lit up, and his body will be returned to its origin (in the earth). Then his soul will be placed among the good souls, residing with birds attached to the trees in Paradise. This explains Allāh's statement: 'Allāh keeps those who have faith steadfast by a firm word (the *kalimah*) in this world, and in the next life (the *ākhirah* - especially in the grave when it will allow a person to correctly answer the questions asked there). And Allāh will cause to go astray those who are the wrongdoers (they will therefore be unable to reply to the questions in the grave and will suffer punishment in the grave and thereafter in Hell). Allāh does as He pleases (He has perfect knowledge of everything and none can question what He does).' (Ibrāhīm 14:27)."

"As for the unbeliever, when he is approached from the direction of his head, nothing will be found there. When he is approached from his right, nothing will be found there. When he is approached from his left, nothing will be found there. Finally, when he is approached from the direction of his feet, nothing will be found there. It will be said to him: 'Sit up.' He will sit up, scared and horrified, and it will be said to him: 'Tell us, what do you say about that man who was sent to you, and what is your testimony about him?' He will ask: 'What man?' It will be said to him: 'The one who was sent to you.' He will not be able to say his name until he is told that it was Muhammad. Then he will reply: 'I do not know. I heard people saying something and I said as they did.' It will be said to him: 'It was upon this that you lived, it was upon this you that died, and it will be upon this you will be resurrected, by the will of Allāh.'

Then one of the gates of the hellfire will be opened for him, and it will be said to him: 'This is your place in the hellfire and

> this is what Allāh has prepared for you in it.' This will increase his remorse and regret. Then one of the gates of Paradise will be opened for him and it will be said to him: 'This would have been your place in Paradise, as well as what Allāh has prepared for you in it if you had obeyed Him.' This will further increase his remorse and regret.
>
> Then his grave will be tightened for him, and he will be pressed so hard that his ribs will interlock. This is the life of hardship about which Allāh says: '(On the other hand) Whoever turns away from My remembrance (the Qur'ān and the *dhikr*) shall surely have a narrowed (difficult) life in this world), and We shall raise him blind on the Day of Judgement (after which his sight will be restored to see Hell).' (Ṭāhā 20:124)." (Musnad Aḥmad)

A sensible person prepares for death before it comes. He furnishes his grave with righteous deeds so that it will be one of the gardens of Paradise.

The Messenger of Allāh (ﷺ) said:

«إِنَّ مِمَّا يَلْحَقُ الْمُؤْمِنَ مِنْ عَمَلِهِ وَحَسَنَاتِهِ بَعْدَ مَوْتِهِ عِلْمًا عَلَّمَهُ وَنَشَرَهُ، وَوَلَدًا صَالِحًا تَرَكَهُ، وَمُصْحَفًا وَرَّثَهُ، أَوْ مَسْجِدًا بَنَاهُ، أَوْ بَيْتًا لِابْنِ السَّبِيلِ بَنَاهُ، أَوْ نَهْرًا أَجْرَاهُ، أَوْ صَدَقَةً أَخْرَجَهَا مِنْ مَالِهِ فِي صِحَّتِهِ وَحَيَاتِهِ، يَلْحَقُهُ مِنْ بَعْدِ مَوْتِهِ».

(سنن ابن ماجة)

> "There are certain good deeds whose rewards will continue to benefit a believer even after his death. These include: knowledge which he taught and spread, a righteous child that he left behind, a copy of the Qur'ān that he left as a legacy, a *masjid* that he built, a house that he built for wayfarers, a canal that he dug, and charity which he gave during his lifetime when he was in good health. These deeds will

continue to benefit him even after his death." (Sunan Ibn Mājah)

A person who frequently remembers death will fill his grave with righteous deeds before he is buried in it, for he believes beyond any doubt that if he lives until the morning, he should not expect to live until the evening; and that if he lives until the evening, he should not expect to live until the following morning. Therefore, he hastens to perform acts of worship before he becomes unable to do so.

It is reported about ʿAmr ibn al-ʿĀṣ (ﷺ) that:

«يرَى ميِّتًا يُقبَر، فأسرَعَ إلى المسجِدِ فصلَّى ركعتَين، فقِيل له: لِمَ فعَلتَ هذا؟ قال: المقبَرة! تذكَّرتُ قولَ الله عزَّ وجل: ﴿وَحِيلَ بَيْنَهُمْ وَبَيْنَ مَا يَشْتَهُونَ كَمَا فُعِلَ بِأَشْيَاعِهِم مِّن قَبْلُ ۚ إِنَّهُمْ كَانُوا۟ فِى شَكٍّ مُّرِيبٍۭ ﴿٥٤﴾﴾ [سَبَإ الآية ٥٤]، فاشتَهَيتُ الصلاةَ قبل أن يُحالَ بينِي وبينَها».

(الزهد والرقائق لابن المبارك)

"Once he saw a dead man being buried, so he hurried to the *masjid* and offered two *rakʿahs* of prayer. He was asked: 'What made you do that?' He replied: 'The grave! I remembered the statement of Allāh: 'And a barrier will fall (be set) between them and the desires that they hoped for, just as it occurred to the groups before them. (They will therefore not be given the opportunity to repent and accept faith. All of the expectations which they had about their gods saving them in the next life will also vanish into thin air). Indeed, they were ever in a confused doubt (and therefore they did not accept faith).' (Saba' 34:54). Therefore, I desired prayer before a barrier is set between it and me.'" (Al-Zuhd wa al-Raqā'iq of Ibn al-Mubārak)

Whoever wants a companion in the grave to keep him company, enlighten his grave, and take his loneliness away should adhere to the Qur'ān and its teachings.

One of the means of deliverance from the trials and torment of the grave is to frequently recite Sūrah al-Mulk and act upon its teachings. A Muslim can also be granted steadfastness in his grave by virtue of the believers' prayers and supplications to Allāh (ﷻ) to forgive him.

Whenever Allāh's Messenger (ﷺ) finished burying a dead man, he would stand by the grave and say to those around him:

«اسْتَغْفِرُوا لأَخِيكُمْ وَسَلُوا لَهُ التَّثْبِيتَ، فَإِنَّهُ الآنَ يُسأَلُ».

(رواه أبو داود)

> "Seek forgiveness for your brother and pray for him to be steadfast because he is now being questioned." (Abū Dāwūd)

If we want to protect ourselves from the torment of the grave, then we should constantly supplicate to Allāh (ﷻ) in each prayer, seek refuge in Him from the trials of the grave, just like the Messenger of Allāh (ﷺ) used to do. He would supplicate to Allāh (ﷻ) saying:

«اللَّهُمَّ إِنِّي أَعُوذُ بِكَ مِنْ عَذَابِ القَبْرِ، وَمِنْ عَذَابِ النَّارِ، وَمِنْ فِتْنَةِ المَحْيَا وَالمَمَاتِ، وَمِنْ فِتْنَةِ المَسِيحِ الدَّجَّالِ».

(رواه البخاري)

> "O Allāh! I seek refuge with you from the punishment in the grave, and from the punishment of the hellfire, and from the afflictions of life and death, and the afflictions of *al-Masīḥ ad-Dajjāl.*" (Bukhārī)

A sensible Muslim is constantly cautious about the causes of error and destruction that could corrupt his end and put him to hard trials in his grave. One such cause is to propagate and spread lies. In the *ḥadīth* of *Isrā'* and *Meʿrāj* (the Prophet's Night Journey and Ascension to the heavens), the angel Jibrā'īl (ﷺ) said to the Prophet (ﷺ):

«وأمَّا الرَّجُلُ الَّذِي أَتَيْتَ عَلَيْهِ يُشَرْشَرُ شِدْقُهُ إِلَى قَفَاهُ، وِمِنْخَرُهُ إِلَى قَفَاهُ، وَعَيْنُهُ إِلَى قَفَاهُ، فإِنَّهُ الرَّجُلُ يَغْدُو مِنْ بَيْتِهِ فَيَكْذِبُ الكِذْبَةَ تَبْلُغُ الآفاقَ».

(رواه البخاري)

"As for the man that you came upon whose mouth corners, nostrils, and eyes were being torn off from the front to back, he is the one who used to go out of his house in the morning and tell a lie that reached the horizons." (Bukhārī)

Another cause of trials in the grave is to consume *ribā* (usury) and consider it *ḥalāl* (permissible). In the *ḥadīth* of *Isrā'* and *Meʿrāj*, Jibrā'īl (ﷺ) said to the Prophet (ﷺ):

«وَأَمَّا الرَّجُلُ الَّذِي أَتَيْتَ عَلَيْهِ يَسْبَحُ فِي النَّهَرِ وَيُلْقَمُ الحَجَرَ، فَإِنَّهُ آكِلُ الرِّبَا».

(رواه البخاري)

"As for the man whom you came upon while he was swimming in the river and was given stones to swallow, he is the one who used to consume usury." (Bukhārī)

Another cause of trials in the grave is to sleep, rather than perform the prescribed prayers, and to abandon the Qur'ān. In the same *ḥadīth* of *Isrā'* and *Meʿrāj*, Jibrā'īl (ﷺ) said to the Prophet (ﷺ):

«أَمَّا الرَّجُلُ الأَوَّلُ الَّذِي أَتَيْتَ عَلَيْهِ يُثْلَغُ رَأْسُهُ بِالحَجَرِ، فَإِنَّهُ الرَّجُلُ يَأْخُذُ القُرْآنَ فَيَرْفُضُهُ وَيَنَامُ عَنِ الصَّلَاةِ المَكْتُوبَةِ».

(رواه البخاري)

"As for the first man that you came upon while his head was being smashed with a rock, he is the one who learned the Qur'ān but then abandoned it; and who slept while neglecting the prescribed prayers." (Bukhārī)

One of the causes of the torment of the grave is to go about spreading malicious gossip among people, and being neglectful in ritual purification. The Messenger of Allāh (ﷺ) once passed by two graves and said about those buried in them:

«إِنَّهُمَا لَيُعَذَّبَانِ، وَمَا يُعَذَّبَانِ فِي كَبِيرٍ، أَمَّا أَحَدُهُمَا فَكَانَ لَا يَسْتَنْزِهُ مِنْ بَوْلِهِ، وَأَمَّا الْآخَرُ فَكَانَ يَمْشِي بِالنَّمِيمَةِ».

(سنن ابن ماجة)

"They are being punished, but they are not being punished for anything major. One of them was heedless about preventing urine from getting on his clothes; and the other one used to walk about spreading malicious gossip." (Sunan Ibn Mājah)

CONCLUSION

- The life of a Muslim on this earth is a short one, but his deeds and actions are eternal, so he should channel them in the right directions.
- Although the lifespan of a Muslim is very short, and while the deeds and actions normally cease after death, a Muslim may continue to earn rewards for certain things even after his death.
- Life in this world is a temporary one; but the real life is the one in the hereafter.
- No one knows when and where a person will die, or even how.
- Without coming to this world, and without dying we cannot go to Paradise. We cannot dream to go to Paradise without tasting death. So, we have to die whether we like it or not.
- Death is the truth (*ḥaqq*); and it is the passage to Paradise. Therefore, every one of us must remember death and prepare ourselves for that day.
- We are here on a trial basis, we are here on a temporary basis, and we are here for a passage to heaven and Paradise. The real life of eternal rest is that of the hereafter.

- We do not know when our time of death will come. Young or old – we all have to go back to Allāh (ﷻ) one day.
- The only thing that will count is what we did with our time here on Earth.
- What you sow - good or bad - is what you will reap.

الْمَوْتُ بَابٌ وَكُلُّ النَّاسِ دَاخِلُهُ ۞ فَلَيْتَ شَعْرِي بَعْدَ الْبَابِ مَا الدَّارُ

الدَّارُ جَنَّاتُ عَدْنٍ إِنْ عَمِلْتَ بِمَا ۞ يُرْضِي الْإِلَهَ وَإِنْ خَالَفْتَ فَالنَّارُ

هُمَا مَحَلَّانِ مَا لِلنَّاسِ غَيْرُهُمَا ۞ فَانْظُرْ لِنَفْسِكَ مَاذَا أَنْتَ مُخْتَارُ

Death is a doorway through which all people have to enter,
I wonder which home I will have after entering it!
Your home will be the Garden of Eden,
If you act in a way that pleases Allāh.
But if you neglect your duty, then the hellfire will be your home;
There will only be two abodes for people,
So, see for yourself which one you want to choose.

DUʿĀ

We raise our hands in supplication before Allāh (ﷻ), the Almighty, asking Him to accept this work. May He make it a way of gaining the correct understanding of His religion, and make it a means of success and salvation for the readers and the writer equally. *Āmīn*

«اللَّهُمَّ انْفَعْنَا بِمَا عَلَّمْتَنَا، وَعَلِّمْنَا مَا يَنْفَعُنَا، وَزِدْنَا عِلْمًا».

"O Allāh, help us benefit from what You have enabled us to learn, and help us learn what is beneficial for us, and increase us in knowledge."

إِنِّي بِالْيَقِينِ أَشْهَدُ ۞ شَهَادَةَ الْإِخْلَاصِ أَنْ لَا يُعْبَدُ

بِالْحَقِّ مَأْلُوهٌ سِوَى الرَّحْمَنِ ۞ مَنْ جَلَّ عَنْ عَيْبٍ وَعَنْ نُقْصَانِ

وَأَنَّ خَيْرَ خَلْقِهِ مُحَمَّدَا ۞ مَنْ جَاءَنَا بِالْبَيِّنَاتِ وَالْهُدَى

صَلَّى عَلَيْهِ رَبُّنَا وَمَجَّدَا ۞ وَالْآلِ وَالصَّحْبِ دَوَامًا سَرْمَدَا

يَا رَبِّ فَاجْمَعْنَا مَعًا وَنَبِيِّنَا ۞ فِي جَنَّةٍ تَثْنِي عُيُونَ الْحُسَّدِ

فِي جَنَّةِ الْفِرْدَوْسِ فَاكْتُبْهَا لَنَا ۞ يَا ذَا الْجَلَالِ وَذَا الْعُلَا وَالسُّؤْدَدِ

With full certainty and in all sincerity, I bear witness that no one
Should truly be worshipped except the Most Gracious,
Who is free from all faults and deficiencies;
And that Muḥammad is the best of all of His creations,
Who came to us with clear proofs and guidance.
May our Lord bestow His peace and blessings upon him,
And upon his family and the companions forever.
O Lord! Bring us together with our Prophet,
In a garden that will keep us away from the enviers' evil eye.
Make us among the dwellers of the Gardens of Paradise,
O Owner of Majesty, Sublimity, and Sovereignty!

«الْحَمْدُ لِلَّهِ الَّذِي بِنِعْمَتِهِ تَتِمُّ الصَّالِحَاتُ».

Praise be to Allāh by whose grace, good deeds are completed.

Mohammed ibn Salim Badat
Ottawa, Canada
August 6th, 2020 – 17th Dhū al-Ḥijjah, 1441
Thursday after *'Ishā* - During the Global Coronavirus [COVID-19] pandemic

GLOSSARY OF ARABIC TERMS

Ablution: The Islāmic procedure for washing parts of the body using water, in preparation for daily ritual prayers, and also before handling the Qur'ān.

ʿĀd: The name of an ancient civilization living in southern Arabia.

Adhān: The Islāmic call to daily prayers.

Alḥamdulillāh: Means Praise be to Allāh (ﷻ).

Ākhirah: An Islāmic term denoting the afterlife or the hereafter.

Al-Firdaws: The highest level of Paradise.

Allāh: The One and Only God, the Divine Creator and Sustainer of the universe, and Master of everything.

Āmīn: The Arabic form of Amen. Which literally means 'may it be so' or 'it is so.'

Anṣār: Helpers; Muslims in Madīnah who hosted the emigrants who came from Makkah.

ʿArsh: The Divine Throne of Allāh (ﷻ).

ʿĀshūrā: The tenth day of the first month (Muḥarram) of the Islāmic calendar. ʿĀshūrā also marks the day that Prophet Mūsā (ﷺ) and the Israelites were saved from Pharaoh when Allāh (ﷻ) created a path for them in the sea.

Athar (pl. Āthār): Sayings, actions, and consensus of the companions of Prophet Muḥammad (ﷺ).

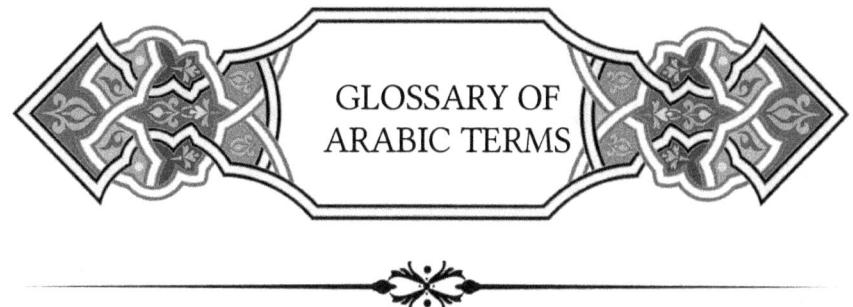

Badr: A city in Saudi Arabia.

Banū (Banī) Isrā'īl: The Israelites.

Bāṭin: Literally means inner, inward or hidden.

Bayt al-Mā'mūr: Literally means 'Frequented House.' It is a *masjid* which is situated outside of the human realm. It is located directly above the *Ka'bah* (the cube-shaped structure located near the centre of the Sacred *Masjid* in Makkah, Saudi Arabia) in the highest heaven; and just above it, is Allāh's (ﷻ) Throne. Every day 70,000 angels perform prayers in it, and when they leave, they never return to it again.

Ṣaḥiḥ al-Bukhārī: One of the six major *ḥadīth* collections in Sunnī Islām.

Dajjāl: Also known as the false Messiah, he is an evil figure in Islāmic tradition, who will appear at a time in the future, before the Day of Resurrection, the Judgement Day.

Dhikr: Denotes those devotional acts in Islām in which short phrases or prayers are repeatedly recited - silently within the mind, or out loud. Also refers to the remembrance of Allāh (ﷻ).

Dhū al-Ḥijjah: The twelfth and final month of the Islāmic calendar.

Dīn: Religion or a way of life in which righteous Muslims adapt to comply with the Divine law (Qur'ān and *Sunnah*).

Du'ā: Invocation; an act of supplication or prayer.

Ḍuḥā: A voluntary Islāmic (forenoon) prayer offered between the obligatory Islāmic prayers of dawn and afternoon.

Fajr: The dawn prayer.

Fir'awn: Pharaoh.

Ḥadīth (pl. aḥādīth): Narration; a report of something that Prophet Muḥammad (ﷺ) did, said or approved of.

Ḥāfiẓ: A term used by Muslims for people who have completely memorized the entire Qur'ān, or one who has mastered the science of Prophetic narrations.

Ḥajj: An annual Islāmic pilgrimage to Makkah, the holiest city for Muslims, and a mandatory religious duty for Muslims that must be carried out at least once in their lifetime by all adult Muslims who are physically and financially capable of undertaking the journey, and can support their families during their absence.

Hijrah: The migration or journey of Prophet Muḥammad (ﷺ) and his followers from Makkah to Madīnah in the year 622 AD. Marks the beginning of the Islāmic years.

Ḥirā: A cave about three kilometers from Makkah, on a mountain named *Jabal al-Nūr* in Saudi Arabia. It is notable for being the location where Prophet Muḥammad (ﷺ) received his first revelations, and where the Qur'ān was first revealed, from Allāh (ﷻ) through the angel Jibrāʾīl (ﷺ).

Hoopoe: Colourful birds found across Afro-Eurasia, notable for their distinctive 'crown' of feathers.

ʿIbādah: An Arabic word meaning service or servitude. In Islām, *ʿibādah* is usually translated as 'worship' and has the connotations of obedience, submission, and humility. The word linguistically means 'obedience with submission.'

Ijtihād: Effort, physical or mental, expended in a particular activity. It is an Islāmic legal term referring to independent reasoning, or the thorough exertion of a jurist's mental faculty in finding a solution to a legal question.

Ikhlāṣ: Sincerity.

Imām: Title of an Islāmic leadership position. It is most commonly used in the context of a worship leader in a *masjid* or Muslim community. The title Imām also is given to the specially trained Muslims who lead prayers in the *masājid.*

Istiʿādhah: Means seeking refuge or protection.

Istikhārah: Means to turn to Allāh (ﷻ) and seek goodness from Him.

Jahannum: Refers to an afterlife place of punishment for the evil doers. The punishments are carried out in accordance with the degree of evil that one committed during one's lifetime.

Janābah: Refers to a state of spiritual impurity that occurs due to sexual intercourse or the discharge of semen.

Jumuʿah: The day of Friday. *Salat al-Jumuʿah* is a congregational prayer that Muslims hold every Friday, just after noon instead of the *ḍhuhr* (afternoon) prayer.

Kaʿbah: The cube-shaped structure located near the center of the Sacred *Masjid* in Makkah, Saudi Arabia.

Kalimah: Refers to the declaration that signifies one's belief in the Oneness of Allāh (ﷻ), and Prophet Muḥammad (ﷺ) as the final Messenger of Allāh (ﷻ).

Khamīṣah: A fine garment of silk or wool.

Khaṭīb: A person who delivers the sermon.

Khusūf: A lunar eclipse.

Khuṭbah (pl. khuṭab): Sermon or sermons.

Kunnīyah: An honourific in place of, or a given name in the Arab world and the Islāmic world more generally.

Kusūf: A Solar eclipse.

Laylat al-Qadr: One of the nights in the last ten nights of the month of Ramaḍān.

Madīnah: A city in Saudi Arabia; the burial place of Prophet Muḥammad (ﷺ). The Prophet migrated to here after severe persecution by the disbelievers in Makkah.

Makkah: A city in Saudi Arabia which was the birthplace of Prophet Muḥammad (ﷺ).

Maqām al-Maḥmūd: 'The station of praise and glory' - a place or position where Prophet Muḥammad (ﷺ) will ask for forgiveness 'intercede' for his followers on the Day of Resurrection.

Miʿrāj: Prophet Muḥammad's (ﷺ) (night journey) ascent to heaven and return to the world.

Mubārak: Blessed.

Muḥarram: The first month of the Islāmic calendar.

Muḥrim: A person who is in a state of *iḥrām* which is a sacred state which a Muslim must enter in order to perform the major pilgrimage (*ḥajj*), or the minor pilgrimage (*ʿumrah*).

Mushrikīn: Polytheists.

Musnad: Type of *ḥadīth* collection which is arranged according to the name of the companion narrating each *ḥadīth.*

Naṣīḥah: To give advice.

Nūr: A special light.

Qadr: Refers to predestination which is the concept of Divine destiny in Islām.

Qiyāmah: The Day of Resurrection or the Day of Judgement.

Qur'ān: Literally means 'The Recital.' The Final scripture which was revealed to Prophet Muḥammad (ﷺ) for all of humanity, and the Holy Book of Islām.

Quraysh: The most powerful tribe of Makkah during the time of Prophet Muḥammad (ﷺ).

Raḥmatun lil ʿĀlamīn: A mercy to all of the worlds, referring to Prophet Muḥammad (ﷺ).

Raiḥānah: A type of flower whose scent is fragrant.

Rakʿah: Refers to a single unit of the Islāmic prayers which consists of the prescribed movements and words followed by Muslims while offering prayers to Allāh (ﷻ).

Sabā: Sheeba was a southwestern Arabian kingdom located in modern day Yemen. It was the home of the Queen of Sheeba.

Ṣaḥīḥ: An Arabic word that means genuine/authentic/sound. It is used in the classification of *aḥādīth,* and is the highest level of authenticity given to a narration.

Ṣalāt: A physical, mental, and spiritual act of worship that is observed five times every day at certain prescribed times. It is one of the five Pillars of the faith of Islām, and is an obligatory religious duty for all Muslims to perform.

Salām: An Arabic word which literally means 'peace,' but it is also used as a general greeting by Muslims.

Ṣalawāt: A special Arabic phrase meaning prayer, salutation, greeting and mercy. It contains wordings of salutations upon Prophet Muḥammad (ﷺ), which Muslims say in their prayers, and also when hearing or uttering the name of Prophet Muḥammad (ﷺ).

Shaʿbān: The eighth month of the Islāmic calendar.

Shahādah: The declaration that there is nothing worthy of worship except Allāh, and that Prophet Muḥammad (ﷺ) is the Messenger of Allāh (ﷻ).

Shamāʾil: An Arabic word that denotes the intricate details of Prophet Muḥammad's (ﷺ) appearance, belongings, manners, and life.

Sharīʿah: A code of law that governs the lives of Muslims.

Shaykh (pl. Shuyūkh): A title which carries the meaning of leader, elder, or noble.

Shayṭān (pl. Shayāṭīn): Satan.

Shirk: Polytheism.

Shūrā: An Arabic word for consultation.

Sujūd: An Arabic word meaning prostration to God.

Sunnah: A way of life prescribed for Muslims on the basis of the teachings and practices of Prophet Muḥammad (ﷺ).

Sūrah: A chapter of the Qur'ān. There are a total of 114 chapters in the Qur'ān.

Tābiʿī: The generation of Muslims who were born after the passing away of Prophet Muḥammad (ﷺ), but who were contemporaries of the companions of the Prophet (ﷺ).

Tafsīr (pl. Tafāsīr): The Arabic word for exegesis, usually refers to the exegesis or explanation of the Qur'ān.

Tahajjud: A special prayer which is recommended (but not compulsory) for all Muslims to perform. The *tahajjud* prayer can be recited anytime after *ʿishā* (the obligatory nightly prayer), and before *fajr* (the obligatory dawn prayer).

Tahlīl: To pronounce the formula by uttering the phrase: *Lā Ilāha Illā Allāh* – which means: There is no deity but Allāh.

Taḥmīd: The saying of the praise formula *Alḥamdulillāh* - which means: Praise be to Allāh.

Takbīr: To pronounce the formula *Allāhu Akbar* – which means: Allāh is the Greatest.

Talbīyah: Ritual formula recited repeatedly by Muslims during the major pilgrimage (*ḥajj*), or the minor pilgrimage (*ʿumrah*).

Tartīl: Slow and measured recitation of the Qur'ān.

Tawḥīd: The indivisible concept of monotheism in Islām, the Oneness of Allāh (ﷻ).

Uḥud: A mountain north of Madīnah, Saudi Arabia.

'Ulemā: A body of Muslim scholars recognized as having specialized knowledge of Islāmic sacred law and theology.

'Umrah: The minor pilgrimage, which can be performed at almost any time during the year.

Wasmah: A plant that is used for dyeing one's hair.

Wuḍū: Ablution, the Islāmic procedure for washing parts of the body using water, in preparation for the daily ritual prayers, and also before handling the Qur'ān.

Ẓāhir: The exterior, surface, outward appearance, or apparent meaning of things.

Zakāh: A form of obligatory charity or almsgiving.

Zamzam: A water well that is located within the Sacred *Masjid* in Makkah, Saudi Arabia.

www.ingramcontent.com/pod-product-compliance
Lightning Source LLC
Chambersburg PA
CBHW051531230426
43669CB00015B/2560
* 9 7 8 0 9 9 5 0 7 8 7 3 4 *